D0881416

BIOETHICS
IN CANADA

BIOETHICS
IN CANADA
A Philosophical Introduction

SECOND EDITION

by Carol Collier
and Rachel Haliburton

Canadian Scholars' Press Inc.

Toronto

CONTENTS

Preface

The authors of this book have both been teaching biomedical ethics to undergraduate students for almost two decades. We have, over the years, tried different textbooks, and have put together course packs of readings on our own. However, we have been unable to find the right combination of text, readings, and case studies to satisfy us. As professors of philosophy in a Canadian university, we have found that most textbooks lack Canadian content and reflect too much of the American situation (which, with respect to some issues, is considerably different from that of Canada). We have also not found enough philosophical content in most textbooks, and have worked to expand our own course material over the years to cover metaphysical and epistemological questions relating to life, death, body, soul, science and technology, and so forth, along with larger ethical and political questions relating to autonomy, community, and human flourishing. For this reason we decided to write our own book—from a Canadian perspective and with a more obvious philosophical slant.

As a result, our discussion of the bioethical issues in this book is, wherever possible, situated clearly within a philosophical framework. Our aim is to encourage students to identify and analyze the often hidden values, assumptions, and commitments underlying the issues. To this end, each chapter ends with a reflection that draws attention to deeper philosophical—often, metaphysical—concepts related to the chapter theme. The chapter on abortion, for example, ends with a philosophical reflection on life, soul, and body; the chapter on organ transplantation with a reflection on the body-machine. These reflections, while designed to lead the students into a deeper analysis of issues, remain accessible to the average undergraduate.

Our philosophical approach to some of the issues also leads us to question the usual analysis found in most biomedical ethics textbooks. For example, the practice of organ transplantation is often discussed as a simple question of distributive justice: how to allocate a scarce medical resource. We believe that seeing organs as a "resource," without ever asking what the status of the human body is, let alone a human organ outside a human body, begs the question. Thus we ask what understanding of the human body, and of death and dying, must be operative for us to be able to think of an organ as a resource for allocation in the first place. Likewise, while it is now so standard in the medical (and bioethical) context to accept the importance of autonomous choice that it has become very hard to ask questions about the value of what is chosen, the concept of autonomy—a concept drawn primarily from political and social philosophy—is one that we submit to philosophical and ethical analysis.

Our textbook is unique because of its inclusion of a chapter on medical paradigms and non-standard treatments. We ask questions about the scientific framework of medicine itself, broaching the issue of alternative medicine, for example, as a serious question of epistemology and metaphysics. In so doing, we challenge the discipline of biomedical ethics to examine the framework on which it has constructed its principles and its analyses and to question the framework itself.

While we attempt to situate our analysis of bioethics in a more philosophical framework, we also recognize that discussions of the ethics of any issue are most fruitful when they originate in an examination of concrete cases. Thus we have developed original and challenging case studies for each chapter, and included study questions to aid in analyzing the cases. We also open each chapter with a landmark case that helps frame the discussion and analysis of the issues in the chapter.

One of the realities of this discipline is that a teacher must frame ethical and philosophical discussions within an ever-shifting empirical reality. This is particularly relevant in such areas as reproductive and genetic technologies, where the technology is moving at such a rate that it is difficult to keep up with the practices and procedures that are being offered and discussed publicly. Not only the advances in technology, but also the advances in thinking about certain conditions, can radically change the picture in a matter of months. In the course of drafting the section on what was called "apotemnophilia," the obsessive desire to have a healthy limb amputated, we realized that the empirical situation was changing even at the moment of our writing; a new website had come into being along with a new name for the condition: Body Integrity Identity Disorder (BIID). Similarly, the diagnosis and treatment of intersex conditions has advanced considerably in the last five years, and much that we had analyzed and written only a few years ago was already out of date. On the one hand, this demonstrates the already recognized fact that it is difficult for our ethics to keep up with our technology; on the other hand, it challenges the writer to be forever on her toes in both her empirical and her philosophical analysis. In the end, however, it can be stated with confidence that even as the empirical situation changes, most of the philosophical analysis still applies.

While we have not avoided the popular articles found in most biomedical ethics textbooks (and most of them can be found among the suggested readings at the end of each chapter), we have chosen our excerpts from authors whose views might sometimes be seen as more challenging to the standard interpretation of the questions. This is intentional: we want students to think more broadly and deeply about the issues presented in the chapters. Further, most of the articles chosen for our suggested readings are readily available electronically from university libraries, and the standard articles can be found there.

The late R.M. Hare, a British philosopher of ethics, thought that the questions of bioethics were the biggest philosophical questions of our time and that if the philosopher could not contribute to sorting them out, then he might as well, in his words, shut up shop. We have attempted, in our approach in this book, to keep the door to the philosophical shop open.

In preparing a second edition of *Bioethics in Canada*, we have not veered from our initial goal of writing a book that is philosophical in approach and, as much as possible, Canadian in content. While we have made additions, deletions, and modifications based on comments by users and on our own experience of using the textbook in teaching (as well as bringing in recent developments on certain issues), the basic framework and goals of our project remain unchanged. In keeping with Canadians' growing awareness of multicultural issues, we have highlighted multicultural concerns in several chapters and added case studies that bring to light certain conflicts and dilemmas that arise in treating people from countries with different values and approaches to health and illness. We have changed several landmark cases to make them more relevant to the current Canadian context and expanded on issues that are emerging in certain areas (for example, transplant tourism). We have also added a section highlighting interesting legal cases from Canada and elsewhere to most chapters. Our recommended reading lists and relevant web resources have also been updated.

ACKNOWLEDGEMENTS

The collaboration of the authors began 10 years ago at the University of Sudbury with researching and preparing a correspondence course on bioethics. They wish to thank the University of Sudbury for the time granted to undertake the research for that project, as well as for permission to use the results of that research in the preparation of this textbook.

The authors gratefully acknowledge the contribution of Rebecca Vendetti, whose originality, enthusiasm, and dedicated hard work on the case studies were a boon to the final product. Thank you, Rebecca. The authors also gratefully acknowledge the contribution of Mason Morningstar for his research on, and excellent summary of, the many interesting legal cases found at the end of the relevant chapters.

Finally, Rachel would like to thank the "library ladies" for providing the comfortable and productive environment in which most of her research and writing was done.

Chapter 1

ETHICAL THEORY

THE ULTIMATE CASE STUDY

You are a technician at a cryogenics institute. A worldwide pandemic has broken out. The virus is untreatable and there is no vaccine, although scientists around the world are working on one. This virus has a high fatality rate and is spreading rapidly, and it is unlikely that a vaccine will be created quickly enough to halt the spread of the disease. You have received orders from the government: you are to select individuals, from a list provided to you, to be cryogenically frozen. This list includes those who have made significant contributions to society, as well as those who will be useful if it is necessary to restart civilization in the aftermath of the pandemic. You may make allowances for close family ties.

There are 10 cryogenic chambers at your facility. There are a few dozen other such facilities worldwide, at which technicians must make similar choices. Together, the labs must ensure that the right people are chosen to maintain the genetic diversity of the human species, as well as those possessing the necessary knowledge and skills to guarantee immediate and long-term survival. This means that at least five hundred people must be put into cryostasis—a condition in which they are preserved at very low temperatures—in order to sustain a genetically diverse population. There are six hundred chambers available in all the cryogenics labs worldwide. One hundred of these, however, are currently occupied. Your own lab has five chambers occupied.

In the occupied chambers are: a famous movie director, whose films are loved by millions of children for their cute cartoon characters; a rich playboy, notorious for his drinking, gambling, and drug addictions, who has no practical skills and who inherited enough money to live in luxury and buy himself a cryogenics chamber in which he was placed after falling into an irreversible coma after a drug overdose; a woman who became rich through the exploitation of third-world workers and who possesses skills useful within a capitalist economy; the founder of the cryogenics facility; and a world-famous physicist, whose work forms the basis for current research in space exploration. Each of these people was suffering from a terminal illness, and was put into cryostasis shortly before natural death. Each signed a contract with the company, which committed to keeping them in this state until medicine advanced enough to cure the disease that was killing them. If they remain in cryostasis, a cure may be found for their conditions. If they are removed, they will "die."

Despite the contracts, you have been given permission to remove any, or all, of these people from the chambers. You have also been told that it is up to you to decide who might be placed into them. Potential candidates have been moved to a nearby motel to await your decision. The cryogenics facility is set up to survive power outages and natural disasters. The chambers are also programmed to reanimate the individuals inside at a specified time in the future, in case there is no one left to perform this task manually. You have just set this time to 50 years to ensure that the virus has run its course before reanimation takes place.

Those whom you may freeze include two politicians. One is the president of a modern democracy, who was recently elected in a landslide as a result of his stunning oratorical skills. The second is the leader of a communist country, who, while not open to democratic reforms, has managed to substantially increase the standard of living her citizens enjoy. Each is of reproductive age, and both possess useful leadership skills. Also on the list is a doctor, who, in addition to his noted "bedside manner," possesses impressive surgical skills. Unfortunately, he was recently convicted of sexually exploiting a number of young female patients and would now be in jail were it not for the pandemic crisis. In addition, there is a famous elderly novelist who is at the height of his creative powers. If any living writer has the capacity to capture in literary form the tragedy unfolding for humanity, it is he. You must also consider including a water treatment specialist, who has extensive experience providing clean water in remote parts of Africa, and a young female environmental scientist currently working on wind energy technology. A great spiritual leader is also on the list; although elderly, he is loved for his profound spiritual insights, his gentleness, and his commitment to human rights. He would provide much-needed spiritual guidance in a new society. He has, however, offered to be taken off the list so that someone else can be preserved in his place. A young farmer, his wife, and daughter are also among the candidates, since farmers will be important to ensure food supplies. The daughter, an infant, is physically and mentally handicapped as a result of oxygen deprivation during birth. Since allowances have been made for family ties, you can choose to keep them together. Moreover, the farmer and his wife are ideal candidates to help ensure the continuance of the human species. The farmer has told you that he will refuse to be saved unless his wife and daughter are as well.

You and your young female co-worker, a fellow technician, are also on the list; while the facility can automatically reanimate people, those who are may experience problems that you have both been trained to deal with, so at least one of you should be preserved as well. While you are the senior technician, you know that your colleague is more proficient than you are. Also, one technician should stay outside the chambers to monitor the cryogenics process until it is complete. Finally, since the allowance for family ties also extends to you, you must also consider your own daughter and her beloved young dog. Just before your wife died last year, she bought this dog for your daughter, and it has now become her best friend. You fear that if you save your daughter, but not her dog, she will be distraught, and even suicidal: given the length of time that cryostasis will need to be maintained, the dog will long since have died a natural death before she is reanimated 50 years in the future.

Just as you are wondering whom to choose for preservation, a notorious gangster with underworld connections appears. He tells you that he will kill you and your colleague unless you preserve him, and, since he is unable to preserve himself without your help, he will then destroy the cryogenics facility: if he can't be saved, no one else should be! Although your facility was designed to cope with power outages and natural disasters, it was not designed to withstand deliberate sabotage. One possibility occurs to you: you could pretend to agree, begin the cryogenics process, stop it part way through, and then remove him from the chamber. This would cause his death and resolve the dilemma posed by his threats, but it would also involve lying to him and deliberately killing him.

You now have a number of decisions to make: Whom should you choose to preserve? Should you remove those who have already been placed in cryostasis? And how should you respond to the gangster?

INTRODUCTION

Humans inhabit a world constructed out of ideas. Our societies are organized on the basis of economic and political ideas. We successfully negotiate social space with other people because we have shared understandings about what side of the road to drive on and how to use money. And we participate in institutions such as schools and law courts that only exist because we believe that education is valuable, and a legal system, important. The pervasive role ideas play in our lives becomes even more evident when we consider that many of the physical elements that surround us began as ideas: cars, buildings, cereal boxes, computers, all existed in someone's head before they became tangible or visual objects. Ideas structure what we do, what we believe, and how we live. However, we seldom notice their presence: their very importance makes them invisible to us.

Philosophy examines ideas. It considers the nature of thought and belief, as well as what, in particular, is thought and believed. Philosophers make ideas visible in order to examine and evaluate them, and they do this through the presentation and analysis of arguments. Philosophy is a rational activity that identifies beliefs, clarifies concepts, and makes judgments about whether the beliefs should be held and whether the concepts make sense. The purpose of this activity is to get closer to the truth about the matters being considered. Pojman suggests that the philosopher and the scientist have much in common. The philosopher, like the scientist, constructs theories, tests hypotheses, and looks at the evidence that can be given in support of any particular position being advanced. However, in the case of philosophy, it is rational argumentation, rather than empirical verification, that counts: "The laboratory of the philosopher is the domain of ideas—the mind, where imaginative thought experiments take place; the study, where ideas are written down and examined; and wherever conversation or debate about the perennial questions takes place, where thesis and counterexample and counter thesis are considered."[1]

Ethics is a branch of philosophy that considers ideas about how humans should treat one another, and how societies should be organized. The subject matter of ethics is central to our lives; as Socrates puts it, "[W]hat we are talking about is how one should live."[2] **Theoretical ethics** asks questions about how we ought to act, what our responsibilities are to other people, what sort of persons we should try to become, and the arguments that can be given in support of any of the claims about these things being made. Bioethics (or biomedical ethics) is a branch of ethics that applies these theoretical considerations to specific issues that arise in connection with the body, with the practice of medicine, and with technological developments that have implications for human beings and how we live. The issues considered by bioethicists range from reproductive technologies to euthanasia, from the obligations health care professionals have to patients, to the responsibilities patients have for their own choices, and from the limitations of our bodies, to the possibility of overcoming these limitations with technology.

Because humans are complex, and because societies must balance diverse and competing interests, ethical dilemmas arise. An ethical dilemma occurs whenever we must make a decision and none of the possible courses of action open to us is entirely satisfactory because each violates a value we think important.[3] For example, we know that fetuses can suffer permanent damage if their mothers take certain drugs before they are born. Suppose we know a pregnant woman, suffering from drug addiction, who intends to continue the pregnancy and who refuses to accept help. Should she be compelled to accept treatment for her addictions against her will? On the one hand, by forcing her into treatment, we will prevent permanent harm to the future child. On the other, we believe that people should be free to make their own decisions about how they live their lives—and that this freedom does not disappear for a woman when she is pregnant. What is the right thing to do in a case like this?[4] The purpose of ethical theory is to help us think clearly about what is at issue and to make a rational decision—a decision that has the best arguments in its favour—about what should be done. Ethical theories help us to be conscientious moral agents by alerting us to our obligations, and by providing guidance for our choices. The guidance these theories provide also allows us to make consistent, not arbitrary, decisions and to justify them to others. As Martin puts it, "[E]thical theories aspire to present moral ideas and issues clearly, consistently, in comprehensive frameworks that provide balance and perspective on all moral issues, and in ways compatible with relevant facts. Above all, theories attempt to fit together and build upon what we most confidently and firmly believe about fundamental moral matters, and, thereafter, to extend our judgments into less certain areas."[5]

The Challenge of Relativism

Since the role of ethical theory is to provide guidelines for decision making, thinking in ethical terms requires us to make moral judgments. It has now become common, however, for many people to avoid making such judgments, particularly when it comes to evaluating the actions and choices of others. To make judgments about what other people do, particularly when their actions are rooted in their personal beliefs, desires, or cultural and religious traditions, is seen as disrespectful and intolerant.

There are two approaches to morality that attempt to capture this perspective: ethical relativism and subjectivism. Modern ethical relativism has its roots in the discoveries of anthropologists, who observed that different cultures have different beliefs about what is right and wrong, and manifest in their traditions, rituals, and laws a variety of approaches to moral issues. For example, many countries, including Canada, do not apply the death penalty to even the most serious crimes, because their governments and citizens came to believe that the death penalty was morally wrong. Other jurisdictions, however, retain the death penalty in their legal systems because this punishment is seen to be a morally suitable response to certain crimes. Likewise, standards of dress and sexual morality, and forms of marriage differ from culture to culture. This fact about human societies is often termed "cultural relativism."

Ethical Relativism

Ethical relativism—the belief that we cannot make moral judgments about what people do when their actions are rooted in cultural practices and beliefs—is a common response to cultural relativism. A famous argument in support of ethical relativism is provided by Benedict, who observed that a number of human behaviours that are considered normal and morally acceptable in some cultures are considered abnormal and morally wrong in others. She gives the example of homosexuality, which has been viewed very differently across cultures, from the positive approach taken in Ancient Greece, to the negative approach taken in many other societies. She also observes that individuals with a capacity for "ecstatic experiences" are seen as suffering from a mental illness in cultures that have no place for this trait, while individuals who possess it in other cultures can be seen as gifted, and even saintly. As she puts it, it "is hard for us, born and brought up in a culture that makes no use of the experience, to realize how important a role it may play and how many individuals are capable of it, once it has been given an honourable place in any society."[6] She concludes that our claims about what is morally good and bad are culturally determined. We therefore should not believe that a universal account of morality, one that is valid for all people, everywhere, can be given: "We recognize that morality differs in every society, and is a convenient term for socially approved habits. Mankind has always preferred to say 'It is morally good,' rather than 'It is habitual'. . . . [B]ut historically the two phrases are synonymous."[7]

Subjectivism

Some people take this approach a step further, and reduce morality to individual preferences. Ethical subjectivists assert that each individual creates his or her own morality. There are no universal ethical principles that apply to everyone even within a culture, let alone to all humans, everywhere. Ethical subjectivism treats moral judgments as essentially being like matters of taste, as things about which no real argument is possible. For example, if I say that coffee tastes better than tea, and you believe the opposite, we have nothing to argue about; we simply like different things. Likewise, according to ethical subjectivism, if I say that child abuse is wrong, or that we are morally required to give money to the poor, nothing obliges you to share my beliefs. In fact, you may believe the opposite, and we have no way—and no reason—to discuss the matter further. At best, all we can give are our opinions. As Pojman observes, "[O]n the basis of subjectivism, it could very easily turn out that Adolf Hitler is as moral as Gandhi, so long as each believes he is living by his chosen principles. Notions of moral good and bad, right and wrong, cease to have interpersonal evaluative meaning."[8]

Ethical relativism and subjectivism are inadequate approaches to morality. First, they can be used to justify the morally unjustifiable. For example, if we accept ethical relativism, then, as long as most members of a culture share such a hatred of a particular minority group that they decide to engage in acts of genocide, we must deem this morally acceptable. Likewise, if we are subjectivists, we cannot say that child molesters have done anything wrong as long as they sincerely believe that what they are doing is right.

Second, both approaches shut down the moral conversation. The task of the ethicist is to consider, not what some individuals actually believe or do, or what beliefs members of various cultures (including our own) share and what actions follow from those beliefs, but, rather, what people ought to believe and do. We cannot even pursue this question if we are relativists or subjectivists.

Third, far from providing support to the values of tolerance and respect, ethical relativists and subjectivists can give no arguments for these principles. In the former case, they are simply cultural values that have no claim to universal validity; in the latter, they are simply expressions of personal preference. In either case, nothing can be said to those who are intolerant or disrespectful to others, and we have no justification for interfering in their actions when they put these beliefs into effect. We cannot engage in the task of thinking and talking about ethics if we believe that ethical relativism or subjectivism is correct. What we do need to do, however, is determine when and how the cultural backgrounds of individuals need to be accommodated, and when their preferences and beliefs should prevail in medical decision making. We need to determine what respect and tolerance really demand of us. This requires that we engage in reasoned conversation with one another that makes reference to the moral theories that constitute the framework of bioethics.

ETHICAL THEORIES, ETHICAL DILEMMAS, AND THE CASE STUDY IN BIOETHICS

We will consider four ethical theories: utilitarianism, Kantianism, virtue ethics, and feminist ethics. Utilitarianism, Kantianism, and virtue ethics are the "Big Three"—the most satisfying and influential ethical theories yet articulated. Feminist approaches to ethics fall into two categories: feminist bioethics and the ethics of care. Each of these theories captures fundamental moral insights, gives reason a place, generates ethical consistency, provides relatively clear guidelines for moral decision making, and gives us a means of justifying such decisions.

However, each theory captures a different fundamental insight, and the consistency comes at a high cost: following the guidelines proposed by one theory in all cases may produce results that seem wrong. This difficulty results from the fact that the subject matter considered by ethics—how we should live—is so complex that no one theory seems capable of capturing the subject matter in its entirety. And yet, the subject matter is so important that it cannot be avoided. All of us are required to think about ethical questions, and to make moral decisions, whether we want to or not. These points are demonstrated in "The Ultimate Case Study" above, which presents in microcosm the ethical issues confronting any society. This case will be used to illustrate how each theory works and its strengths and weaknesses.

There are a multiplicity of ethical issues in this case study and no clear way of resolving them satisfactorily. Bioethics is structured around cases such as this: short, dramatic presentations of individuals facing moral dilemmas in a bioethical context, such as a hospital, a genetic counsellor's office—or in a pandemic situation, in which a choice must be made about who will live and who will die. As Murray observes, it "is impossible to do bioethics, at least any form of bioethics that involves talking about real issues or real cases, without using a particular kind of narrative—the case."[9] In bioethics, case narratives have a common form—they present us with what are essentially short stories about people struggling with a moral dilemma, and ask us to be the decision-maker. Consequently, they provide a way of making the issues real, of testing our ethical intuitions, theories, and principles, and of exercising our reason.

You will be exploring many case studies in this book. Some of them will be based on real events, while others will be works of the imagination. We present a method for working through case studies at the end of this book. For now, you should notice that the technician's dilemma reflects the complexities of human interactions, institutions, and societies, and illustrates both the difficulty of making moral decisions and the necessity of making them: doing nothing is not an option. In this case, the dilemma is stark: who lives, who dies, and how should this be decided? More specifically, should those already in cryostasis be removed from the chambers to die? Who on the list should be saved? What role, if any, should emotions play in the decision? What should be done about the gangster? Should you save the most powerful, the best loved, or the youngest? If your mandate is to save the most socially useful, how will you decide what this means in practice? How will you weigh political gifts against scientific knowledge, and both against reproductive potential?

Ethical theories help us work through these issues. Each theory directs us to a different aspect of the situation, and tells us to ask a different question about it.[10] Utilitarianism directs us to ask, "What happens if I perform this action?" That is to say, it directs us to consider the consequences of our actions. Kantianism requires us to ask, "Is this action right or wrong, morally speaking, regardless of the consequences?" This theory holds that some actions are simply wrong, in and of themselves, while others are simply right. Virtue ethics directs our attention away from actions and toward those who perform them: it suggests that we ask "What kind of person should I be?" Finally, feminist approaches to ethics pose the question: "What might a female perspective add to our ethical understanding?" Feminists ask whether women are treated as full moral agents in traditional ethical theory.

UTILITARIANISM: HAPPINESS, AND THE GREATEST GOOD FOR THE GREATEST NUMBER

Utilitarianism was developed in the 19th century. At the time, the Industrial Revolution was just beginning, and conditions for the working class were appalling. The modern nation-state was emerging out of the upheavals of the American and French revolutions, and old values were being challenged. People began to look for secular and scientific solutions to the problems facing them, rather than religious ones. These changes are reflected in the radical nature of utilitarianism. It makes no reference to God as the source of moral commands, it claims to be scientific, and it is egalitarian. It is, in its own way, as radical as two other theories that emerged at the same time, Marxism and Darwinism.[11]

This "auto-icon" of Jeremy Bentham can be viewed at University College, London. It is composed of his preserved body, along with a wax model of his head. It demonstrates Bentham's commitment to utilitarian principles, as he stipulated in his will that his body be dissected during a public lecture on anatomy and then displayed to further medical knowledge and to encourage others to donate their bodies for this purpose.

Two thinkers are credited with the most complete versions of utilitarianism, Jeremy Bentham (1748–1832) and John Stuart Mill (1806–1873). Bentham saw the theory as "a practical tool of social reform ... as a means of scientifically determining which action or policy is morally preferable."[12] Bentham proposed a guide—called the Hedonic Calculus—to moral decision making, a guide designed to be useful both to individuals in their daily lives, and to those who, like politicians, are in a position to make decisions affecting many people. What we are to do, when considering what action to perform, is imagine the likely consequences that our actions will have; we are then to "sum up all the values of all the *pleasures* on the one side, and those of all the pains on the other.... Take the balance; which, on the side of *pleasure*, will give the general *good tendency* of the act, with respect to the total number or community of individuals concerned; if on the side of pain, the general *evil tendency*, with respect to the same community."[13] We are to do the thing that will provide the greatest amount of pleasure and the least amount of pain to the greatest number of people.

In Bentham's version of utilitarianism, no distinction is made between sources of pleasure—"Pushpin is as good as poetry,"[14] as he put it (we might say something like "Hockey is as good as opera")—or whose pleasures they are: the pleasures of an important person, such as the prime minister, are no more heavily weighted than the pleasures of the least important citizen. His theory is radically egalitarian: everyone is to count equally, and everyone's pleasures and pains must be factored into the calculation. His theory is so egalitarian that it is radical even today—he also included animals, something that no ethical theory besides utilitarianism has done. It is not the ability to speak or reason that determines whose interests count, but merely the capacity to suffer. (In the pandemic situation, most ethical theories would simply assume that the dog is not a candidate for cryopreservation. On Bentham's account, however, this is not necessarily the case; the dog may be young and healthy, while at least two of the people—the spiritual leader and the novelist—are elderly and do not have long to live. In addition, the farmer's daughter has handicaps that may impede her capacity to live a happy life, and her survival will place a burden on her parents. Perhaps these people should be excluded instead. Finally, those already in cryostasis are terminally ill: perhaps they should be removed and allowed to die, so that space can be made for those who, including the dog, have a greater likelihood of surviving for a number of years.)

Bentham's utilitarianism was criticized on a number of fronts. First, because of his refusal to distinguish between sources of pleasure (and perhaps because of his inclusion of animals), Bentham was accused of advancing a "swinish" philosophy, one fit only for pigs. Second, the apparent simplicity provided by Bentham's willingness to count pleasures and pains from all sources comes at a high cost to our moral intuitions: aren't there some pleasures that we want to exclude from consideration? Why should we count the pleasure of the torturer, or the rapist, in our calculations? (Surely, we don't want to count the pleasure the doctor takes in his abuse of young girls when we consider the good things that might result if we were to save him?)

Third, is pleasure all that counts? For utilitarians, pleasure alone has intrinsic value, value in and of itself. Everything else is merely instrumentally valuable, valuable because it is a means for producing pleasure or avoiding pain. But this doesn't seem correct. There seem to be other things—love, perhaps, or justice—with intrinsic value, even if they don't always produce pleasure.

Finally, although Bentham claimed that he was offering a scientific way to approach ethical decisions, there seems to be something missing: What units are being used in our calculations, and how are they derived? Utilitarians sometimes call these units "hedons" or "utiles," but it is not clear what they are. How can I determine how many utiles I get from reading a book, compared to the number I get from watching television? How can I determine how many utiles I get from eating a sandwich when I am hungry to the number I get from drinking a glass of vintage port? How do we determine and compare the utiles of pleasure and pain the spiritual leader might get from giving up his spot with the pleasure felt by the person who takes his place? How do we compare the pleasure that might be experienced by the survivors if the novelist is saved and writes his masterpiece with the pleasure the farmer will feel if his daughter is saved? While we all know what it is to feel pleasure and pain, these feelings seem difficult to translate into numbers. It is for all these reasons that Mill made refinements to the theory. Mill hoped that he could preserve the insights of utilitarianism while eliminating the weaknesses of Bentham's version.

BOX 1.1

JOHN STUART MILL, *UTILITARIANISM*

The creed which accepts as the foundation of morals, Utility, or the Greatest Happiness Principle, holds that actions are right in proportion as they tend to promote happiness, wrong as they tend to promote the reverse of happiness. By happiness is intended pleasure, and the absence of pain; by unhappiness, pain, and the privation of pleasure.... [P]leasure, and freedom from pain, are the only things desirable as ends; and ... all desirable things ... are desirable either for the pleasure inherent in themselves, or as means to the promotion of pleasure and the prevention of pain....

It is quite compatible with the principle of utility to recognize the fact, that some *kinds* of pleasure are more desirable and more valuable than others. It would be absurd that while, in estimating all other things, quality is considered as well as quantity, the estima-tion of pleasures should be supposed to depend on quantity alone....

Of two pleasures, if there be one to which all or almost all who have experience of both give a decided preference ... that is the more desirable pleasure. If one of the two is, by those who are competently acquainted with both, placed so far above the other that they prefer it, even know-ing it to be attended with a greater amount of discontent, and would not resign it for any quantity of the other pleasure ... we are justified in ascribing to the preferred enjoyment a superiority in quality, so far outweighing quantity as to render it, in comparison, of small account....

It is indisputable that the being whose capacities of enjoyment are low, has the greatest chance of having them fully satisfied; and a highly endowed being will always feel that any happiness which he can look for ... is imperfect.... It is better to be a human being dissatisfied than a pig satisfied; better to be Socrates dissatisfied than a fool satisfied. And if the fool, or the pig, are of a different opinion, it is because they only know their own side of the question. The other party to the comparison knows both sides....

I must again repeat, what the assailants of Utilitarianism seldom have the justice to acknowl-edge, that the happiness which forms the Utilitarian standard of what is right in conduct, is not the agent's own happiness, but that of all concerned. As between his own happiness and that of others, Utilitarianism requires him to be as strictly impartial as a disinterested and benevolent spectator.... To do as you would be done by, and to love your neighbour as yourself, constitute the ideal perfection of Utilitarian morality. As the means of making the nearest approach of this ideal, utility would enjoin, first, that laws and social arrangements should place the happiness ... of every individual, as nearly as possible in harmony with the interest of the whole; and secondly, that education and opinion, which have so vast a power over human character, should so use that power as to establish in the mind of every individual an indissoluble association between his own happiness and the good of the whole.

Source: J.S. Mill, *Utilitarianism, On Liberty, and Considerations on Representative Government*, ed. H.B. Acton (London: Everyman's Library, 1972), 7–18.

MILL'S REFINEMENT OF UTILITARIAN THEORY

Mill provides two characterizations of the principle of utility, which he calls "The Greatest Happiness Principle." The first characterization states that "actions are right in proportion as they tend to promote happiness, wrong as they tend to promote the reverse of happiness."[15] Mill understands "happiness" and "unhappiness" to mean the following: "By happiness is intended pleasure and the absence of pain; by unhappiness, pain, and the absence of pleasure."[16] For Mill, only happiness has intrinsic value; everything else is only valuable because it promotes happiness: "pleasure, and the freedom from pain, are the only things desirable as ends; and ... all desirable things ... are desirable either for the pleasure inherent in themselves, or as a means to the promotion of pleasure and the absence of pain."[17]

A caricature of John Stuart Mill from *Vanity Fair*, 1873. Mill's version of utilitarianism is the one most often used today.

So far, Mill's theory sounds much like Bentham's. But Mill makes an important change; unlike Bentham, he argues that pleasures are qualitatively different, depending on their origin. Consequently, some pleasures should count more heavily in our calculations: "It is quite compatible with the principle of utility to recognize the fact that some *kinds* of pleasure are more desirable and more valuable than others.... Of two pleasures, if there be one to which all or almost all who have experience of both give a decided preference ... that is the more desirable pleasure."[18] Mill believes that the pleasures that are most desirable are those that employ the "higher faculties": the pleasures provided by the development and exercise of the intellect and of our aesthetic capacities, rather than the pleasures provided by entertainment, and the satisfaction of bodily needs and desires. For Mill, poetry is more valuable than pushpin, opera more valuable than hockey, and a gourmet meal, which satisfies aesthetic sensibilities as much as bodily needs, is more valuable than a Whopper and fries.

The distinction between higher and lower pleasures has provoked debate among philosophers. On the one hand, it allows Mill to avoid some of the problems generated by Bentham's more simple formulation. In Mill's version, utilitarians cannot easily be accused of promoting a "swinish" philosophy, and this distinction may allow the utilitarian to exclude the pleasures generated from dubious sources—or at least weigh them very lightly in the calculus. If the pleasure gained from stuffing oneself at an all-you-can-eat buffet counts for less than the pleasure achieved by reading a difficult philosophical text, surely the pleasures of the pedophile or the racist count for very little. On the other hand, if the comparison between pleasures necessary for the sorts of calculations utilitarianism requires was difficult with Bentham's formulation, Mill's distinction complicates matters significantly.

Further, it can be argued that this distinction requires appeal to a standard that is independent of the utilitarian framework, because it suggests that there are things other than pleasure that are intrinsically valuable. As Martin notes, "[H]ow can some pleasures be ranked as better or worse without assuming we already know what is right or wrong or morally desirable or undesirable, independently of the utilitarian standard?"[19] If someone gets more pleasure from pizza, beer, and *Hockey Night in Canada* than from a gourmet meal, fine wine, and *Twelfth Night*, how can a utilitarian consistently say that he is mistaken and should prefer the latter to the former? Mill suggests that he can make this distinction by consulting people who have had access to both sources of pleasure, and that they will unquestionably "give a most marked preference to the manner of existence that employs their higher faculties."[20] But, Rosenstand argues, Mill "rigs" his own test when he argues that "capacity for the nobler feelings is in most natures a very tender plant, easily killed, not only by hostile influences, but by mere want of substance; and in the majority of young persons it speedily dies away if the occupations to which their position in life has devoted them, and the society into which it has thrown them, are not favourable to keeping that higher capacity in exercise."[21] What this means is that if you prefer the "lower" pleasures to the "higher" ones, all Mill needs to say is that you have lost the capacity for enjoying the "higher" ones, and that your opinion can be disregarded![22] This distinction, then, while avoiding some of the problems generated by Bentham's assertion that all pleasures and pains, regardless of their source, must be counted, raises new concerns.

Mill's second characterization of the principle of utility holds that "the happiness which forms the Utilitarian standard of what is right in conduct, is not the agent's own happiness, but that of all concerned. As between his own happiness and that of others, Utilitarianism requires him to be as strictly impartial as a disinterested and benevolent spectator."[23] The conscientious utilitarian moral agent should not count her own happiness any more heavily than the happiness of anyone else who will be affected by her actions. All that should be considered is what action will produce the greatest amount of happiness for the greatest number of people. If we apply this rule to the pandemic situation, it seems clear that you should save your colleague rather than yourself, since she is both the better technician and a woman of reproductive age. You will have to consider whether your daughter's survival will be as beneficial to humanity as that of the farmer, the water treatment specialist, or the environmental scientist. And saving her dog is out of the question. Likewise, the farmer and his wife should let their daughter die, since she is more of a burden than a benefit, no matter how much they love her. On the other hand, you should perhaps save the spiritual leader. Despite the fact that he volunteered to give someone else his place, spiritual comfort will probably be in short supply. You should not hesitate to remove everyone already preserved in the chambers, since they cannot yet be cured. Likewise, you must take seriously the possibility of lying to, and then killing, the gangster to eliminate the threat he poses to everyone's survival.

Act Utilitarianism

This version of utilitarianism, which tells us that we should choose the action that will produce the greatest amount of happiness for the greatest number of people, is known as *act utilitarianism*. While it provides relatively clear guidance for moral decision making, it has been criticized on a number of grounds, including the fact that nothing is inherently forbidden and that obligations to particular people are unaccounted for.

Nothing Is Inherently Forbidden

According to act utilitarianism, we are to choose the action that will give the greatest amount of happiness to the greatest number of people, whatever that action may be. Suppose a large number of people derive a great deal of happiness from seeing a small number of people tortured, humiliated, and finally put to death on live television; act utilitarianism tells us that it is morally acceptable, even required, to sacrifice these people. Or, suppose we can only develop an effective vaccine for HIV by testing it on a small number of people, some of whom we know will die as a result of this testing. If we are act utilitarians, we should have no hesitation about undertaking this testing because of the large number of people who will eventually benefit. Likewise, in certain situations we can break promises and punish the innocent, so long as this makes more people happy than unhappy. But surely, critics say, this is wrong: there are some things that we shouldn't do, regardless of the good consequences that might result.

Act Utilitarianism and Particular Obligations

Act utilitarianism tells us that we are to weigh our own happiness no more heavily than the happiness of anyone else. In addition, we are to adopt the viewpoint of a disinterested spectator who can make a rational decision about which action will generate the most happiness. What this means is that utilitarianism may require us to sacrifice our own interests if by doing so we can provide greater benefits to others. Likewise, we cannot weigh the interests of people who are close to us—our friends, spouses, or children—any more heavily than the interests of strangers. We might, indeed, be required to sacrifice our own happiness, or the happiness of our children, if by so doing more people are made happy than unhappy. Suppose the water treatment specialist, who has saved the lives of thousands of Africans, had a wife and family that he deserted in order to help these suffering people. He feels badly about doing so, and about the fact that his wife committed suicide and his four children were traumatized by his actions, but takes comfort in the knowledge that he selflessly sacrificed his own happiness and theirs for the happiness of a greater number.

While his actions can be justified from a utilitarian perspective, they seem wrong. Our relationships with particular people generate special obligations toward them: our friends can expect more from us than mere acquaintances can; we should make sure that our children are taken care of before we worry about those down the street; and when we choose to get married, we are choosing to accept particular obligations to that person.

Rule Utilitarianism

For these reasons, philosophers committed to utilitarianism have suggested that the theory should be modified so that it is applied to rules or principles, rather than actions. Rule utilitarianism requires us to "follow a set of rules that, were they adopted by the society in which one lives, would produce the most good for the most people.... Individual acts are right, then, when they conform to the moral code that would produce more overall good than would alternative moral codes."[24] We might, for instance, have rules such as "Keep your promises, unless great harm will result from doing so," "Only punish those who are guilty," and "Meet the needs of your own children before meeting the needs of other people's." Rule utilitarians argue that this move is compatible with the insights of Mill and Bentham in that societies that respect rules like these will be happier than those that don't. Further, the move to rules allows us to account for obligations to particular people.

If we apply rule utilitarianism to the dilemma facing you, the technician, we get a different result than we did when we applied act utilitarianism. First, if we accept a rule that states that parents have an obligation to take care of their children, saving your daughter will no longer be a violation of your duties as a utilitarian. Likewise, the farmer's insistence that his daughter be saved follows this rule. Moreover, if a rule such as "Keep your promises" is accepted, then it will not be easy to remove those who have already been preserved from their chambers: you will have to consider whether the contracts they signed constitute a promise made by the company to them, which you must respect.

Problems with Act and Rule Utilitarianism

While rule utilitarianism avoids some of the difficulties that afflicted act utilitarianism, both versions share some weaknesses. First, the problem of measurement remains: since it is difficult to compare the utility of different actions, it seems equally difficult to calculate the utility produced by particular rules. How much utility is produced when everyone follows a rule such as "Keep your promises"? How can we compare this amount to what is produced when the rule is generally followed, but occasional exceptions are made? The problem here is one of incommensurability. Two items are said to be incommensurable when they have no common elements that can serve as a basis of comparison. Utilitarianism requires us to compare incommensurable things: how can we compare the value of health to the value of education, of freedom to security, or of jobs to an unspoiled environment? Some philosophers have tried to deal with this difficulty by assigning a monetary value to incommensurables; in this way, costs (for instance, pollution) can be compared to benefits (jobs), and a relatively straightforward calculation carried out. In short, they replace utiles with dollars. While we are sometimes comfortable with such comparisons (life insurance and compensation for workplace accidents can be seen as an application of this approach), the problem remains: money seems incommensurable with some of the things we value most. How much would you pay someone to be friends with you? How many dollars is a baby worth? How much would your employer have to pay to make your job worthwhile if it will destroy your health? These questions make little sense, because friendships, babies, and health are not things that can be bought and sold. Consequently, the turn to a monetary measure does not resolve the problem, it merely constructs it differently.

Second, because utilitarianism, in either form, requires us to make decisions and choices on the basis of what is likely to happen in the future, the rightness or wrongness of what we do now depends on things over which we have no control. That is to say, "in considering the consequences of a given action in determining whether it is right, one is required to have knowledge of all the possible consequences related to the act as well as all the consequences of every other action that is equally available at the moment. Compounding this is the fact that a comparison must be made between all the rightness and wrongness of all the possible consequences."[25]

Moreover, our actions have consequences that are unexpected and unpredictable. For instance, in the pandemic scenario, suppose you save the communist leader rather than the farmer's wife, because the leader possesses useful political skills and is a young woman who can contribute to the survival of the species. However, suppose it turns out that she is infertile: then your choice appears unjustified. Or suppose that you choose to save the water treatment specialist, and he does not survive the reanimation process because of an undiagnosed health condition. Again, your decision was the wrong one, and you should have chosen someone else instead. Or suppose you save the charismatic democratic leader, and, after the pandemic danger has passed and a new society is created, it turns out that he has tyrannical tendencies and uses his oratorical gifts to become a dictator. Many people suffer as a result, and most believe that they would have been much happier had he not been saved. Again, your decision was the wrong one, although you could not possibly have known this at the time you made it. The fact that choices are justified by what happens in the future is a peculiar requirement for a moral theory meant to guide our moral thinking when faced with dilemmas in the present! Utilitarians have responded to such criticisms by saying that we should follow our "best guess" of the consequences of our actions, but this seems a far cry from the hope that Bentham and Mill had of articulating a rational and scientific ethical theory.

Finally, justice and rights are a problem for both act and rule utilitarianism. Justice requires us to treat people fairly, and requires, among other things, that we not punish the innocent, or sacrifice some to benefit others. Rights, a concept that asserts that humans have an inherent worth and dignity, no matter who they are, places limits on what we may do to them, regardless of the good consequences that might be produced. Act utilitarians seem unable to account for justice and rights, given the claim that happiness is the only thing that has intrinsic value. Justice and rights are only instrumentally valuable, and will be respected only when doing so produces more happiness than is produced by ignoring them. Rule utilitarians have a different problem: while they can accommodate these concepts in particular rules, they don't seem to promote them in the right way. While violating justice and rights may produce less utility in a society in the long run than respecting them would, this doesn't seem to be the reason they are important. Imagine a society in which most people believe that convicted murderers should be executed and their organs sold to those who need them. The government gets revenues from this market in organs, and those who need them are happy that this market exists. Over time, however, the supply of convicted murderers dries up, and, in order to maintain the supply of organs, the government changes the law so that execution becomes the standard punishment for even the most minor offences, such as shoplifting and speeding. Furthermore, shortcuts in the legal procedures are encouraged, and a number of people who are innocent are executed. Eventually, most people realize that they could be accused of a crime they didn't commit, or executed for the most trivial offence, and so they become unhappy and demand that changes are made to the laws and that organ sales cease. At this point, the rule utilitarian can agree that these changes should be made. But surely the first executions of innocent people were as wrong as the final ones, regardless of how much happiness was produced.

Why Utilitarianism Remains an Important Moral Theory

Despite the problems discussed above, utilitarianism remains an indispensable tool in the ethicist's toolbox because it captures important ethical insights. The first of these insights is that, sometimes, consequences are important. The second is that sometimes it is appropriate to weigh the interests of the many over the interests of the few, and the third is the inclusion of animals. Constructing elaborate imaginary scenarios and then discrediting utilitarianism on that basis, is, utilitarians claim, unfair. What we should do instead is confine ourselves to real dilemmas, make our best judgments about the likely consequences of our actions, and then consider which of the likely consequences of our actions is likely to benefit the most people.

First, Gawande's account of surgeons learning how to perform a new kind of heart operation illustrates the insight that consequences can be important:

> Consider the experience reported by the pediatric-surgery unit of the renowned Great Ormond Street Hospital.... The doctors described their results in operating on three hundred and twenty-five consecutive babies with a severe heart defect ... over a period (from 1978 to 1998) when its surgeons changed from doing one operation [the Senning procedure] for the condition to another [the switch procedure]. With the new procedure, life expectancy improved from forty-seven years to sixty-three.... But the price of learning to do it was appalling. In their first seventy switch operations, the doctors had a 25 percent surgical death rate, compared with just 6 percent with the Senning procedure. (Eighteen babies died, more than twice the number of the entire Senning era.) Only with time did they master it: in their next hundred switch operations, just five babies died.[26]

In terms of the first insight, then, a defender of utilitarianism would say that we make utilitarian calculations frequently, and that we are justified in doing so when the good consequences of our actions outweigh the bad ones.

Second, utilitarianism is useful for those who must weigh interests against one another. Consider the situation when disasters occur and medical resources are limited. In such situations, decisions have to be made about who will be treated first, how resources will be distributed, and who can be saved and who is beyond hope. It is reasonable, in such situations, to consider what actions will produce the greatest good for the greatest number of people. Likewise, hospital administrators, Ministers of Health, and governmental policy-makers may find that utilitarian considerations provide guidance. Suppose that 10 long-term-care beds cost the same amount as one heart transplant does. When medical resources are scarce, it is not inappropriate for hospital administrators to decide that they will provide the additional beds rather than the transplant surgery, thereby benefiting 10 people rather than one.

Finally, some ethicists believe that one of the strengths of utilitarianism is that it provides a framework within which the interests of animals can be considered. While we might decide not to save the dog, it doesn't hurt to be reminded that we share this planet with other beings who can suffer, and that we should, at the very least, not cause them gratuitous and excessive pain.

KANTIANISM: IS MY ACTION RIGHT OR WRONG?

The second ethical theory we will consider was developed by Immanuel Kant (1724–1804). Kant's theory is powerful; like utilitarianism, it captures some indispensable insights and has been tremendously influential. The insights it captures, however, are very different from those articulated by utilitarians. Indeed, if we wanted to create an ethical theory that was the opposite of utilitarianism in almost every significant way, it would be difficult to come up with something better than Kant's theory. For utilitarians, only happiness has intrinsic value; for Kant, only a good will does. For utilitarians, the consequences of our actions are what count; for Kant, what is important is that we perform the right action for the right reasons. Because Kant's theory focuses on duty, or obligation, it is known as a **deontological theory**.

Immanuel Kant's ethical theory has been enormously influential. It has provided theoretical support for contemporary understandings of the important ethical concepts of autonomy and human rights.

Kant's theory is complex—so complex, indeed, that certain aspects of it are initially difficult to grasp since they seem so counterintuitive, so different from the way in which we normally view our actions and our relationships with others. It is useful, therefore, to begin with a scenario that illustrates important aspects of the theory.

Suppose you save the water treatment specialist and the environmental scientist, and both are successfully reanimated once the pandemic is over. It turns out that the worst-case scenarios were correct, and all humans who were not preserved have died. Therefore, only those who were placed in cryostasis in institutions around the world are left to recreate society and ensure the survival of the human race. So much time has passed, moreover, that the physical infrastructure has collapsed, and all water and electrical systems have disintegrated. The expertise provided by the water treatment specialist and the environmental scientist is much needed; both, however, have very different motivations and characters. The water treatment specialist is selfless and altruistic, cares nothing for money or power, and only wishes to help others. The environmental scientist, in contrast, worked for a multinational oil company that was branching out into "green technologies" because it wanted to control this market. The scientist approved of the company's ambitions and was well paid for her services.

The charismatic politician that you decided to save manages to set himself up as leader of the new society and gives in to his despotic tendencies. He creates a society that he rules through a combination of threats and bribes, aided and abetted by individuals who hope to benefit if they support him. He sees that both the water treatment specialist and the environmental scientist possess useful skills and suggests that they work with him to create a monopolistic market in clean water and solar-powered electrical generators. In return, he will ensure that they occupy privileged places in the new society and have the best of what meagre goods are available. The water treatment specialist refuses the offer, and states that he believes that water should be provided for free to everyone. Moreover, he asserts that he will try to set up water treatment systems on his own so that no one will have to be beholden to the dictator in order to get this necessary resource. He begins this work, but makes very slow progress since he is lacking resources, both mechanical and human: the dictator threatens to harm anyone who works with him.

The environmental scientist, in contrast, who also knows something about water treatment (one of the projects she worked on for the oil company was in this area, since water was expected to be "as valuable as oil" in the future) agrees to the dictator's proposal, and, with the help of the resources he can provide, quickly gets a treatment plant up and running, ensuring that those who want clean water must commit themselves to the regime of the dictator in order to get it. Consequently, despite his best efforts, the water treatment specialist never succeeds in making his dream a reality, and no one benefits from his efforts. Many people, however, are provided with this resource as a result of the actions of the environmental scientist, and live longer and healthier lives than they would have been able to had clean water not been made available to them. From a utilitarian perspective, even though the environmental scientist was acting from egotistical rather than utilitarian motives (her goal was to maximize her own well-being, not the well-being of all), her actions nonetheless seem justified by their results: they have made more people happy than unhappy, and that is what counts. For a Kantian, however, it is the water treatment specialist who should get credit for being a conscientious moral agent, even though, in the end, he did not save a single life. We will explain why through an examination of Kant's theory.

How Kant's Theory Works

The Good Will

For Kant, only a "good will" is intrinsically good: "Nothing in the world—indeed nothing even beyond the world—can possibly be conceived which could be called good without qualification except a *good will*."[27] All positive attributes—intelligence, courage, resolution, wit—are valuable only when they are accompanied by a good will. Without the presence of a good will, these traits make the possessor worse: the humour of a murderer, the intelligence of a child molester, and the courage of a bank robber add no moral worth to these people and give no "pleasure to a rational impartial observer."[28] And a good will remains good even if it accomplishes nothing: "The good will is not good because of what it effects or accomplishes ... [but simply] ... it is good of itself.... Even if it should happen that ... this will should be wholly lacking in power to accomplish its purpose, and if even the greatest effort should not avail it to achieve anything of its end, and if there remained only the good will ... it would sparkle like a jewel in its own right, as something that had its full worth in itself."[29] Kant is here describing one of his central moral insights. If we compare the two survivors, the water treatment specialist, with his good intentions and the ethical behaviour he demonstrates in his actions, seems more morally praiseworthy than the environmental scientist, even though he failed in his efforts. Given her greed and her disregard for others, no one would prefer to have the environmental scientist as a friend or a colleague, despite her intelligence and success.

Reason

Reason plays a central role in Kant's theory. What makes a good will good is its willingness to act in accordance with the rules, laws, or obligations dictated by reason. Reason tells us what we ought to do. For Kant, any moral rule (such as, for instance, "Do not cheat," "Do not lie," or "Do not break promises") is both discovered by reason and absolute, admitting of no exceptions. For Kant, moral reasoning involves "the same kind of logical reasoning that establishes such indisputable truths in mathematics and logic as 2 + 2 = 4, No circles are squares, and All triangles are three-sided."[30] It follows from this that moral truths are objective truths, truths that exist in the world regardless of whether we acknowledge them or not (just as triangles would still have three sides even if no humans existed to recognize them) and that everyone should come up with the same moral rules, since these are discovered (not made up) through the exercise of reason.

Duties

A good will acts in accordance with the moral laws established by reason. To this Kant adds that the act is morally good only when it is done for the sake of duty: "[T]he moral worth of an action does not lie in the effect which is expected from it or in any principle of action which has to borrow its motive from this expected effect. For all these effects ... could be brought about through other causes and would not require the will of a rational being, while the highest and unconditional good can be found only in such a will."[31] This means that two identical actions, performed in identical circumstances, can carry different moral weights; one will be truly moral, while the other will only have that appearance.

This is a puzzling claim, but understanding this point is key to understanding his theory. His claim is that it makes a difference whether we do things for the right reasons or the wrong ones. Consider, for example, the spiritual leader: we would view his human rights work very differently if we knew that, rather than being motivated by a deep belief in its value, he secretly revels in the good publicity he gets because it satisfies a deep narcissism in his character. Or take the political leaders: knowing whether they sought political office in order to do good things for their fellow citizens or simply because they desired power will affect how we view them. Kant suggests, however, that more is going on here than how we view them: an actual qualitative difference is involved.

Our motives affect how we will behave over time. If the spiritual leader is motivated by duty, he will, over time, treat people differently than he will if he is motivated by a desire for publicity. For instance, if the fickle media spotlight moves elsewhere, he will continue his work in the former case, but not in the latter. Likewise, in the case of the politicians, if they are motivated by duty, they will not care about power for its own sake. However, if it is power that motivates them, their actions will change as soon as they obtain it. As Kant observes, acting for the sake of duty will continue to produce the morally appropriate actions while acting for other reasons will not, since any conformity of these actions to what duty requires will be simply a result of inclination and contingency.

It follows that even actions performed from good motives (such as kindness, love, generosity, or sympathy) are not as morally sound as those performed for the sake of duty. They, too, even if in conformity with what duty requires, are merely contingent: if our inclinations had been otherwise, we would have behaved differently. Imagine a nurse who feels genuine affection for some of her patients and irritation and dislike for others. If she acts from duty, she will treat all of them with the care and attention she is morally obligated to provide. If she acts on the basis of her inclinations, however, she will treat those she likes very well while doing the bare minimum for the others, or perhaps even leaving their needs unmet.

In Kant's view, duty and inclination are distinct and often opposed: we usually desire to do other than what duty demands of us. Moreover, our inclinations are not based on our rationality, but on our personality traits, emotions, and whims. Consequently, only duty can be counted on to ensure that we follow moral rules.

The Categorical Imperative

The purpose of moral theory is to provide us with guidance when we need to make ethical decisions. Kant provides a simple test, called the Categorical Imperative (C.I.), which our actions must pass before we can be certain that we have done what is morally required. Kant gives a number of formulations of the C.I. that he seems to think equivalent to one another, although most commentators view them as distinct. We will consider the three most important formulations of the C.I.

Categorical and Hypothetical Imperatives

Before examining these formulations, we must distinguish categorical imperatives from hypothetical ones. Imperatives tell us to do something; categorical imperatives tell us to do something without regard to consequences, because the action is morally required: "The categorical imperative would be one which presented an action as of itself objectively necessary, without regard to any other end."[32] Categorical imperatives have the form "Do X!" ("Keep promises!" "Tell the truth!"), and duty requires us to act on them. They constitute the basis of the moral law and are, Kant believes, absolute—they admit of no exceptions: "Such imperatives are intuitive, immediate, absolute injunctions that all rational agents understand by virtue of their rationality."[33] Hypothetical imperatives, in contrast, have the form "If you want A, you should do B" ("If you want to do well in school, you should study for your exams"; "If you want to have a comfortable retirement, you should start saving your money early"). Hypothetical imperatives are dependent on desires and goals, and, because inclinations and duties are often opposed, should be overridden by the requirements of the C.I.

The Universalization Formulation

The first significant formulation of the C.I. states: "Act only according to that maxim by which you can at the same time will that it should become a universal law."[34] This formulation captures something essential to any satisfactory moral theory, namely, that we cannot make an exception of ourselves when doing what is morally required. (Utilitarianism captures the same insight when it tells us that it is not the happiness of the person making the decision that is to be maximized, but the happiness of all.) Kant's articulation of this insight is distinct and powerful. It provides moral decisions with consistency in two ways: it is a rational test, which is logically consistent; and it applies to all rational agents in the same way, without exception.

The C.I. is, first and foremost, a logical test. It requires that our actions not be "self-contradictory, such as the statement 'A circle is a square' would be."[35] When we make a moral decision, we must not generate a self-contradiction. Consider the example Kant gives of making a lying promise in the excerpt found in Box 1.2.

BOX 1.2

IMMANUEL KANT, *FOUNDATIONS OF THE METAPHYSICS OF MORALS*

There is ... only one categorical imperative. It is: act only according to that maxim by which you can will that it should become a universal law....

We shall now innumerate some duties....

A ... man finds himself forced by need to borrow money. He well knows that he will not be able to repay it, but he also sees that nothing will be loaned to him if he does not firmly promise to repay it at a certain time. He desires to make such a promise, but he has enough conscience to ask himself whether it is not improper and opposed to duty to relieve his distress in such a way. Now, assuming he does decide to do so, the maxim of his action would be as follows: When I believe myself to be in need of money, I will borrow money and promise to repay it, although I know I shall never do so.... He ... then puts the question: How would it be if my maxim became a universal law? He immediately sees that it could never hold as a universal law of nature and be consistent with itself; rather, it must necessarily contradict itself. For the universality of a law which says that anyone who believes himself to be in need could promise what he pleased with the intention of not fulfilling it would make the promise itself and the end to be accomplished by it impossible; no one would believe what was promised to him but would only laugh at any such assertion as vain pretence.

Source: Immanuel Kant, *Foundations of the Metaphysics of Morals*, ed. Robert Paul Wolff, trans. Lewis White Beck (Indianapolis, IN: Bobbs-Merrill Educational Publishing, 1969), 44–46.

Kant is telling us that, when we ask ourselves whether we should perform an action, we must be sure that it passes a logical test: that it not generate a self-contradiction if everyone were to perform it. We perform the test by first putting our proposed action into the form of a statement, called a maxim (such as "I will make a deceitful promise, when in distress, with the intention not to keep it"), and then by universalizing it—generalizing it so that it covers all moral agents ("Everyone may make a deceitful promise when in distress with the intention not to keep it"). If it contradicts itself when generalized—as it does in this case, because if everyone were to make promises with the intention of breaking them, the concept of making a promise would become meaningless—then it has failed the test, and should not be performed.

Kant believes that actions such as lying, stealing, killing, breaking promises, and cheating all contradict themselves in this way; if they are universalized, they will undermine the practices on which they are based. Take cheating, for example. While one student can get away with cheating on an exam, if all students were to cheat, then the whole purpose of examinations—to test students on what they know, and grade them accordingly—would break down. Exam results would be meaningless. In Kant's view, all moral actions must pass this test of consistency.

This test requires a different sort of consistency as well, consistency-across-moral-agents: what applies to one moral agent must apply, in the same way, to all other moral agents, without exception. If it is wrong for you to lie, cheat, or break promises, then it is wrong for me to do these things as well. Again, this is a logical claim, not an emotional one or a plea for fairness.

This gives us a means of articulating the moral difference between the water treatment specialist and the environmental scientist. The scientist has failed to meet both of these requirements of logical consistency. Consider her willingness to work for a dictator, and to make people pay for a resource like clean water through the services they are compelled to provide. If she were to apply Kant's test before she entered into this arrangement, her maxim might be "Whenever scientists want to gain power and wealth, they will use their scientific knowledge to achieve this end." This would be inconsistent with the role of the scientist, who is, ideally, meant to pursue knowledge in order to benefit other human beings. Consequently, making this kind of arrangement with the dictator fails the first test of logical consistency. If all scientists were to seek only their own self-interest, then science would not be located in the elevated social space it currently occupies. This location is predicated on the understanding that the practice of science is beneficial to all, and that scientists pursue knowledge for the sake of the greater good. Her actions fail to meet the requirements of the second form of consistency as well: the environmental scientist is trying to make an exception of herself, because she would not want to be treated in the way that she is treating others.

This first formulation of the C.I. puts us in the place of those who will be affected by our actions. We must think of ourselves not only as the ones making deceitful promises, cheating on exams, or charging people for clean water, but also as those who have promises made to them broken, as honest students who do worse on exams than those who cheat, and as people who must pay exorbitant prices for natural resources.

The Means-Ends Formulation

The second significant formulation of the C.I. is "Act so that you treat humanity, whether in your own person or in that of another, always as an end and never as a means only."[36] This formulation has been extremely influential, as it underpins claims about dignity and rights. It tells us that there are absolute limits on how we may treat other people: we are never to treat others merely as tools for our purposes, but must always remember that each rational creature has a worth and dignity equal to that of every other rational creature. This worth and dignity cannot be ignored, even for the sake of wonderful goals that will bring benefits to many. It is this formulation that most distinguishes Kantianism from utilitarianism, because it rules out the ethical calculations that utilitarians engage in. We cannot, for instance, justify deceiving research subjects, or sacrificing some people to benefit others; both of these activities would require us to ignore the fact that these people have a worth and dignity that should never be compromised. If this principle is applied to the pandemic situation, at the time when you, the technician, are deciding who to rule out, it tells you that you have one choice and that is to eliminate the dog. The real difficulty will lie in choosing who should be saved because, from the perspective articulated by this principle, there are no criteria you can use to determine who should live: all have an equal moral worth.

This inherent worth and dignity lies in our rationality; indeed, all rational beings possess it. This places limits not only on what we may do to others, but, also, on what we may do to ourselves. We must not waste our talents, destroy our bodies, or allow ourselves to become mere tools for the purposes of others. The rich young man currently in cryostasis in your clinic has failed to treat himself as an end: he has wasted his talents, and become a tool for drug dealers and casino owners. We might also ask whether the spiritual leader is treating himself as an end when he volunteers to be taken off the list of candidates for cryogenic preservation.

We should note that Kant is telling us that we should not treat others as a means only. Of course, in most, if not all, human relationships, we treat each other as means as well as ends. Teachers treat their students as a means to a paycheque, students use teachers as a means to gain knowledge, and shopkeepers and customers need one another; even husbands and wives, parents and children, benefit in various ways from their relationships. What this principle requires is that human relationships be characterized, at all times, by mutual respect: it rules out actions such as bullying, manipulation, deception, and exploitation. Each of these activities is only possible when we ignore the worth and dignity of others.

The Autonomy Formulation

The third important aspect of Kant's theory follows from the first two: we have a duty to respect others, we have a duty to respect ourselves, and our ability to recognize these duties, as well as the reason they exist, lies in our rationality. Rational creatures are ends in themselves because they are rational, and because they can understand that rationality allows them to discover what duty requires of them. This means that humans have the capacity to be autonomous beings: beings that discover for themselves what they ought to do and can determine their own ends and goals. Kant writes, "The only moral authority that can tell us to do something and not to do something else is our own reason."[37] It is because we are autonomous that we are ends in ourselves. Our autonomy—our rational capacity to follow the moral law for its own sake—is the source of human dignity, and this dignity underlies the requirement that rational creatures be treated with respect. This emphasis on autonomy, on recognizing that rational creatures have the capacity to be self-determining, and that we have a corresponding obligation to respect their decisions, has important implications for our self-understandings and our choices. This aspect of Kant's theory allows us to adjust the point made above concerning self-sacrifice. On one interpretation of the means-ends formulation of the C.I., self-sacrifice, such as that proposed by the spiritual leader, seems to be ruled out because he is treating himself as a means. What can be said now, however, is that what is important is that he voluntarily consented to serve others in this way. There is an important difference between using persons against their will and without their consent, and recognizing that self-determining moral agents can choose, for good reasons, to serve others in this way. This has implications for medical research: Kant's theory rules out deception, manipulation, and coercion in research, but it allows people to consent to participate in it. According to Beauchamp and Walters, "He argues only that we must not treat another *exclusively* as a means to our own ends. When adult human research subjects are asked to volunteer ... they are treated as a means to researcher's ends. However, they are not exclusively used for others' purposes, because they do not become mere servants or objects. Their consent justifies using them as a means to the end of research."[38]

STRENGTHS AND WEAKNESSES OF THE THEORY

The greatest strength of Kantianism is that it encompasses what utilitarianism cannot: justice and dignity. Kantianism asks us to recognize the moral worth of all rational creatures, which limits what we may do to others and requires that we take responsibility for our actions. Despite its strengths, however, Kantianism has a number of weaknesses; it, like utilitarianism, is unable to encompass everything that morality requires. The weaknesses fall into two general categories: those that are internal to it, and those that are external to it.

Internal Questions

Conflicts of Duties

According to Kantianism, we are to do what duty requires; however, there are times when duties come into conflict. Suppose that we promise a friend, recently diagnosed with a serious illness, that we will do whatever we can to make sure that she is never in pain. When we make this promise, we believe that we can keep it by ensuring that she has sufficient medication to keep her pain manageable. However, as her illness progresses, it becomes apparent that no amount of medication is adequate for this task. In agony, she begs us to euthanize her. What should we do? We have a duty to keep our promise, and we also have a duty not to kill.

Maxims

The first formulation of the C.I. tells us that we are to determine what duty requires of us by articulating a maxim that describes the intended action, and then universalizing it. If it can be universalized without generating a logical contradiction, then our intended action has passed the test; if it cannot be universalized without contradiction, then it has failed, and it should not be done. However, it can be difficult to determine what maxim is appropriate, and, depending on the maxim used, the same action, in the same circumstances, can pass or fail the test of universalization.

Consider any cryogenics technician in the situation set forth in the case study: should he save himself? He might come up with the following maxims: "I will preserve my own life at the expense of others"; "I will let people die when I can save them"; and "Whenever a male cryogenics technician who runs this particular cryogenics institute is faced with a global pandemic disease that requires him to choose who to cryogenically preserve, he will save his own life." If we universalize each of these maxims, we get, first, "Everyone will preserve his or her own life at the expense of the lives of others": this maxim fails the test of universalization, because no one could logically will that everyone act in accordance with this principle. Likewise, the second maxim, which becomes "Everyone will let others die when he or she could save them," also fails. But the last maxim, when universalized, generates no such contradictions: it is so specific that, even when generalized, it will not apply to anyone except the technician at that particular institute, and he can perfectly consistently will that it be a universal law. This problem is not only theoretical, but practical as well: we need to know which maxims to test if Kantian ethics is to provide us with clear guidance when we make moral decisions, and we need, therefore, to be able to identify the appropriate maxim with some degree of confidence—but this can be very difficult to do.

External Questions

Rigidity

Kant believes some moral rules to be absolute, including rules such as "Do not break promises," "Do not kill," and "Do not tell lies." We can, however, easily think of situations in which it is morally correct to ignore one of these duties. We should break a promise to meet a friend for lunch if we see someone lying injured by the side of the road as we drive to the restaurant and stop to take him to hospital; we should not kill lightly, but a right to self-defence is commonly recognized; and we should lie to the murderer who asks where his intended victim is. The reason Kant makes moral rules absolute is his desire for consistency-across-persons: what applies to you, as a moral requirement, applies to me as well, no exceptions. So, if I would not like you to lie to me, then I shouldn't lie to you either. However, we can preserve the ethical insight that Kant captures without the corresponding rigidity, simply by saying that "all that is required … is that when we violate a rule, we do so for a reason that we would be willing for everyone to accept, were they in our position."[39]

Rational Creatures

Kant's theory tells us that we must treat others as ends in themselves because rational creatures must be treated with dignity and respect. This is a powerful claim, but it raises questions about who counts in the moral scheme. Clearly, animals are not included. But consider the farmer's baby in the case study: she has serious mental and physical handicaps, and this is likely to mean that she will never become a fully autonomous agent who can understand what duty requires and act accordingly. But this surely does not mean that she has no inherent moral worth or that she should not be treated with respect. And we can think of other persons who are not rational but who still need to be treated with care and dignity: for example, very young children, people in comas, and those suffering from severe dementia. In fact, a case might be made that such persons are so vulnerable that the test of how ethical we really are is how well we treat them: they are entirely at our mercy. The irony here is that Kant is able to make the case that utilitarians cannot when it comes to putting absolute limits on what we may permissibly do to people; however, the basis on which this case is made arguably leaves out some of those persons who most need it to be made for them, since they are unable to make it for themselves. And what may compel us to treat such persons with dignity and respect are emotions and inclinations (such as sympathy, kindness, and pity), the very things that Kant wants to remove as motivating factors for ethical behaviour.

Duty

Kant believes duty to be the only adequate basis for ensuring that our moral decisions are correct. If we rely on inclination, we cannot be certain that the right choices will be made on every occasion. It is only when we act for the sake of duty that we can be sure that we are doing the right thing for the right reasons. This seems plausible when we are interacting with those with whom we do not have a close relationship, such as strangers, acquaintances, and people we work with. It seems oddly cold, however, when we consider relationships with those whom we are closer to, such as friends and family. This coldness is conveyed in Atkinson's description of a mother contemplating her four daughters, only one of whom she really loves:

> Jane emerged from beneath the hydrangeas looking querulous with heat. How was Rosemary ever going to turn them back into English schoolchildren when the new term began? Their open-air life had transformed them into gypsies, their skin brown and scratched, their sun-scorched hair thick and tangled, and they seemed to be permanently filthy, no matter how many baths they took. A drowsy Olivia stood at the opening of the tent, and Rosemary's heart gave a little twitch.... Olivia was her only beautiful child. Julia, with her dark curls and snub nose was pretty but her character wasn't, Sylvia—poor Sylvia, what could you say? And Amelia was somehow ... bland, but Olivia, Olivia was spun from light.... Olivia was the only one she loved, although God knows she tried her best with the others. Everything was done from duty, nothing from love. Duty killed you in the end.[40]

This passage illustrates that, while we can will ourselves to act from duty, we cannot will love, and that there is something deeply wrong in a family when things are done only for the sake of duty.[41]

While Kant is right to think that duty is important, and that even close and intimate relationships bring with them moral obligations that must be met (parents, for instance, have a duty to ensure that their children's needs are met and that they are provided with the tools that will allow them to become independent), healthy relationships need more than this. Utilitarianism seems similarly unsatisfactory on this point, although for different reasons, when it asks us to count the happiness of our family members and friends no more heavily in our moral decision making than the happiness of strangers.

Kantianism and the Medical Context

Despite these concerns, Kant's theory is important in medical contexts, as we can see when we consider things like human experimentation, the right of patients to make their own medical decisions, and the obligations of health care providers to respect these decisions and ensure that they are informed. If we take Kant's ethics seriously, we can see that it is a requirement (because we are autonomous, self-regulating creatures) that physicians provide patients with sufficient information to make informed decisions about their own medical choices, and that they respect the decision that is made. Kant's ethics rule out manipulation, coercion, lying, and even under-informing in doctor-patient relationships. In addition, Kant tells us that we have duties to ourselves and must take these into account when we make our decisions; we must be willing to inform ourselves and to take responsibility for our choices. This requirement, too, follows from our status as autonomous beings.

This detail from Raphael's *School of Athens* portrays Plato and Aristotle, two of the most important philosophers in the Western tradition. Their views shaped Western thought in ways that still affect us today.

VIRTUE ETHICS: WHAT SORT OF PERSON SHOULD I BE?

Dr. Nancy Morrison was charged with first-degree murder after an investigation into the death of one of her patients. The patient, Paul Mills, had been admitted to hospital for treatment of cancer of the esophagus. After six major operations, Mr. Mills was critically ill, and his family requested that he be given no medication except for painkillers and that his life supports be removed. He was given pain medication, including morphine, and was heavily sedated. The intensive care nurse said later that what she was witnessing was the "most torturous, agonizing death of her eight-year career."[42] The patient was in extreme pain, gasping for air, and the drugs being administered for sedation and pain were ineffective. The nurse called Dr. Morrison and asked her to do something; she remarked to the doctor that "Mr. Mills seemed to be indestructible, and [she] could not imagine what it would take to end his suffering, unless it was something like potassium chloride."[43] Dr. Morrison administered two drugs, first, what she said was nitroglycerine, and second, what she said was potassium chloride (which can stop the heart from beating). Seconds after the second injection was put into Mr. Mills' intravenous line, he died. The hospital suspended Dr. Morrison for three months, and police later laid the murder charges. (Dr. Morrison was subsequently cleared of the charge, because the judge "concluded there wasn't enough evidence for a jury to convict the doctor of any offence. He said Mr. Mills's death could have been caused by the administration of potassium chloride, or by massive amounts of dilaudid, a painkiller ... [that he was receiving]. A third possibility was that the intravenous line became detached from Mr. Mills, and that the drugs never entered his body."[44])

This case generated much debate. What was striking about the discussion was that much of it was focused, not on the rightness or wrongness of the act that Dr. Morrison was said to have performed, but on her character. What kind of person would do something like this? A good one, or a bad one? A compassionate one, trying to reduce suffering? One with poor judgment who took shortcuts? Or a killer, who violated not only appropriate standards of medical practice but also one of the most important of all human taboos, that we not commit murder? People also asked whether they would want to have, as their physician, someone who was willing to do what Dr. Morrison was accused of doing. Some felt that, if they were suffering as Mr. Mills apparently was, they would want a physician to display the courage that Dr. Morrison did, while others felt very differently, that they would absolutely not want someone who was willing to kill in charge of their medical care. In short, a large part of the discussion provoked by this case was focused on Dr. Morrison's character, rather than on her purported action.

The third theory we will consider takes character as its primary focus. This theory is known as virtue ethics, and the most influential account of an ethics of virtue is provided by Aristotle. Aristotle was born in 384 B.C.E., so his theory is the oldest we will examine. While virtue ethics surveys the same terrain as action-oriented theories (namely, how we should respond to the ethical challenges we encounter), its focus on character draws our attention to different features of the landscape. We are asked to focus not just on what we do but also on who we are, and, as a result, virtue ethics requires us to consider not merely discrete events (such as Dr. Morrison's injection of a fluid into Mr. Mills' intravenous line) but whole lives. (If Dr. Morrison did indeed inject potassium chloride, what brought her to this point, and how will this action shape her in the future?) Since the context in which virtue ethics asks us to consider ethical decision making is the context of a whole human life, it views such choices not merely as rational decisions, but as an activity that incorporates rationality, emotion, and settled dispositions. While virtue ethics was sidelined for many years by action-based theories, it has recently enjoyed a resurgence. This is because it seems to capture important elements that the other theories are unable to, including the role that emotions play in our relationships with others, and the way in which the things that we do both reveal who we are and shape who we will become.

BOX 1.3

ARISTOTLE, *THE NICOMACHEAN ETHICS*

We must ... not only describe virtue as a state of character, but also say what sort of state it is. We may remark, then, that every virtue or excellence both brings into good condition the thing of which it is the excellence and makes the work of that thing be done well; e.g. the excellence of the eye makes both the eye and its work good; for it is by the excellence of the eye that we see well. Similarly the excellence of the horse makes a horse both good in itself and good at running and at carrying its rider and at awaiting the attack of the enemy. Therefore, if this is true in every case, the virtue of man also will be the state of character which makes a man good and which makes him do his own work well....

If it is thus, then, that every art does its work well—by looking to the intermediate and judging its works by this standard (so that we often say of good works of art that it is not possible either to take away or to add anything, implying that excess and defect destroy the goodness of works of art, while the mean preserves it …), and if, further, virtue is more exact and better than any art, as nature also is, then virtue must have the quality of aiming at the intermediate. I mean moral virtue; for it is this that is concerned with passions and actions, and in these there is excess, defect, and the intermediate. For instance, both fear and confidence and appetite and anger and pity and in general pleasure and pain may be felt both too much and too little, and in both cases not well; but to feel them at the right times, with reference to the right objects, towards the right people, with the right motive, and in the right way, is what is both intermediate and best, and this is characteristic of virtue. Similarly with regard to actions also there is excess, defect, and the intermediate. Now virtue is concerned with passions and actions, in which excess is a form of failure, and so is defect, while the intermediate is praised and is a form of success; and being praised and being successful are both characteristics of virtue. Therefore, virtue is a kind of mean, since … it aims at what is intermediate.…

But not every action nor every passion admits of a mean; for some have names that already imply badness, e.g. spite, shamelessness, envy, and in the case of actions adultery, theft, murder; for all of these and suchlike things imply by their names that they are themselves bad, and not in the excesses or deficiencies of them. It is not possible, then, ever to be right with respect to them; one must always be wrong.…

[W]e must also consider the things towards which we ourselves are easily carried away; for some of us tend to one thing, some to another; and this will be recognizable from the pleasure and pain we feel. We must drag ourselves away to the contrary extreme; for we shall get into the intermediate state by drawing well away from error.…

Source: Aristotle, *The Nicomachean Ethics*, trans. David Ross (Oxford, UK: Oxford University Press, 1986), 36–46.

Teleology

Aristotle was a **teleologist**, who believed that everything that exists has a goal or purpose. This teleology is natural: the goals or purposes are built in by nature, not by something external or supernatural. What is true of natural objects is true of human actions as well: whenever we do something, we have some end in view. For instance, if you were to be asked "Why are you reading this book?" and you were to respond "Because I want to learn something about bioethics," you would have given a teleological explanation of your activity. Likewise, we exercise for the sake of our health, or to lose weight; we go to university because we seek knowledge, or because we hope that having a university degree will help us get a better job; and if we strive for money, we do so because we think that good things, such as wealth or security, will result. We consider every end that we strive for—education, wealth, or anything else—to be valuable (no one strives for something he considers bad). According to Aristotle, "Every art and every inquiry, and similarly every action and pursuit, is thought to aim at some good; and for this reason the good has rightly been declared to be that at which all things aim."[45]

While we do things for the sake of something else, there must be an ultimate goal, something valued for its own sake. We may exercise because we believe it will help us lose weight and that we will be healthier as a result; we may take a course in university because we want to get a degree, which will help us get a better job, and, in turn, allow us to earn more money so that we can retire at a young age and go fishing; or we, conversely, go to university because we want to gain knowledge. In the first case, the end that is sought is health; in the second, the freedom to go fishing; and, in the third, it is knowledge. It is obvious that there are many things each person pursues and that each of our particular activities has its own end: "the end of the medical art is health, that of shipbuilding a vessel, that of strategy victory, that of economics wealth."[46]

Happiness

Aristotle asks whether there is something beyond each of these particular ends, some highest good for the sake of which everything else is done. What is it that health, the freedom to go fishing, and knowledge have in common? If we can find out what they have in common, to what each serves as a means, then we will have discovered the "chief good,"[47] the purpose of all human activity.

Aristotle believes that there is only one thing that is ultimately desired for itself, and not as a means to anything else, and that is happiness. This may sound surprisingly like the claims made by utilitarians, but there is a very important difference between the utilitarian understanding of this term and Aristotle's understanding of it: for utilitarians, happiness is synonymous with pleasure, while for Aristotle, happiness means living well or doing well. Consequently, Aristotle's conception of happiness (also called *eudaimonia*) is much broader in scope than the concept considered by the utilitarians. It encompasses the notion of human flourishing along all its dimensions. In fact, Aristotle explicitly distinguishes the sort of happiness he considers the final end of human activities from both amusement and pleasure. *Eudaimonia* is not a feeling; rather, it is a way of being that requires us to live life fully and actively, in accordance with what reason tells us is the proper purpose of human beings.

Function and Excellence

In the search for a final purpose for human activities, we have seen one aspect of Aristotle's teleology. To understand his ethics, however, we need to understand another aspect as well. This is his claim that everything has a purpose or a function, and that it is good or excellent when it performs its function well. While we are comfortable with the idea that human activities have purposes (we go to the gym, engage in leisure activities, and study physics for a reason), and can easily accommodate the notion that man-made objects have a purpose (the purpose of a car is to get us where we want to go, the purpose of a chair is to sit on), Aristotle asks us to accept as well that human beings have a purpose (as do acorns, tadpoles, and rocks).

We do not know what something is until we have grasped its function or purpose. Acorns, for instance, have as their built-in purpose to become oak trees. In the words of Talisse, "Thus we may say that *what it is to be* an acorn is to be something that by nature strives to become an oak. In this way, the acorn is *defined* in terms of its purpose, its goal. Therefore, the oak is *prior* to the acorn in the order of explanation; that is, in order to understand what an acorn is, one must first understand what an oak is."[48]

Something is good when it performs its function well. Someone is a teacher by virtue of having a certain function to perform, namely, teaching. Someone is a good teacher when he performs his function well. A doctor is also defined by her function: her purpose is to make, and keep, her patients healthy, and if she does this well, then she is a good doctor. The function of an ear is to allow us to hear; a good ear allows us to hear well. And, if the function of a car is to take us where we want to go, then a good or excellent car is one that is reliable, that starts in the winter, and that meets certain safety standards.

What, however, is the function of a human being, and how might we discover this? Aristotle believes that we can discover the purpose of something by finding its essence, the thing that is essential to it and that distinguishes it from other things, even other similar things. What is it that distinguishes us from gorillas, chimpanzees, and other animals (as well as from trees, cars, and rocks)? Aristotle's answer is reminiscent of Kant's: it is our rationality. So, the function of human beings is to live in accordance with reason and to do this with excellence.

Living in accordance with our function, and doing this with excellence, will make us happy. We need, then, to work to be the best human beings we can be, which means that we must be virtuous because it is in this that our excellence consists: "[H]appiness is an activity of the soul in accordance with perfect virtue."[49] Aristotle makes it clear that his focus is an entire lifetime. Genuine happiness cannot be something fleeting or fragile, like fame or fortune; likewise, we are not virtuous if we only act as we should on occasion and inconsistently (just as a car is not excellent if it will only start on warm days): "One swallow does not make a summer, nor does one day; and so too one day, or a short time, does not make a man blessed and happy."[50]

The Mean

Human excellence, then, consists in living in accordance with reason and doing this well. This means that we must become virtuous, and that doing so will make us happy. In his account of learning to be a surgeon, Gawande describes a process that captures the central elements of virtue ethics. Gawande relates his difficulties in learning to insert a central line into the vena cava, the main blood vessel leading to the heart. The procedure involves sticking a needle into the chest, and then inserting a catheter with the help of a guidewire. If this procedure is done incorrectly, the patient can suffer from a collapsed lung, or even die. After watching experienced surgeons perform the procedure on a number of occasions, Gawande is given his chance to try it for himself. He makes a number of mistakes, including trying to push the line in at the wrong angle. The surgeon training him tells him that he will learn with practice. However, the next time he tries, he is also unsuccessful: the needle goes in too shallowly, and then too deeply; the patient begins bleeding; and someone else has to take over. Then he failed with a third patient, and "the doubts really set in."[51] Although he tries to avoid doing the procedure, eventually he must attempt it again—and this time, he succeeds easily. Gawande writes, "I still have no idea what I did differently that day. But from then on, my lines went in. Practice is funny that way. For days and days, you make out only fragments of what to do. And then one day you've got the thing whole. Conscious learning becomes unconscious knowledge. And you cannot say precisely how."[52] Studies have shown that what makes the difference between those who are excellent performers (whether they are surgeons, violinists, or chess players), Gawande notes, is not talent, but the amount of deliberative practice they have had and their willingness to keep on practising.

Aristotle's description of how we become excellent human beings shares many elements with this account of how surgical excellence is achieved: we learn to be virtuous through practice, through observing other people, and through developing the proper dispositions. The virtues are habits or dispositions— ways of doing, and of feeling. If we are temperate, we will be disposed toward moderation in the pursuit of pleasures, while courage requires us to do brave things. Being virtuous means having the right feelings "at the right times, with reference to the right objects, towards the right people, with the right motive, and in the right way"[53] and to act on those feelings—also in the right way and in the right amount. In both our emotions and our actions we should aim for the mean—the intermediate state between excess and deficiency. And, while we all have some natural capacity for acquiring the virtues, we learn to be virtuous with practice. We usually don't get it right the first few times we try—we do too much or too little, feel too strongly or not strongly enough—but, over time, we get it right. Learning to be virtuous, according to Aristotle's account, is like learning any other skill, whether it be surgery, chess playing, or cooking—the more we do it, the better at it we become. In the case of virtue, there is a kind of back-and-forth movement between our dispositions (how we feel) and our actions (what we do): we cannot become courageous unless we do courageous things, we cannot become temperate unless we practice moderation in the pursuit of pleasures, and we cannot become honest unless we habitually tell the truth. When we learn to be virtuous, we no longer have to think about what we are doing as we will do it naturally (just as most of us don't have to think about whether or not we will shoplift today, or murder a passing stranger—the idea of doing these things never even enters our mind).

The claim that virtue is achieved through practice has important implications: it means that virtue can be taught and that other people can serve as examples to emulate. Aristotle's theory, unlike many modern ethical theories, does not consider only the "adult moral agent" and what he should do, but also how children can be taught to be that moral agent: children can learn to be virtuous if their parents bring them up in the right way, by teaching them to take pleasure in the right things, guiding their choices, and providing an example to follow. Likewise, we can continue to learn how to be virtuous by emulating the virtuous behaviour we see demonstrated by others.

Aristotle believes that virtue lies in hitting the mean between excess and deficiency, both in what we feel and what we do. What is virtuous lies somewhere between what is excessive and what is deficient. Courage, for instance, lies somewhere between cowardice and rashness; patience lies somewhere between impatience and indifference; and honesty lies somewhere between deceit and rudeness. The mean between excess and deficiency doesn't necessarily lie right in the middle: one of the extremes is often closer to the virtue than the other. Courage is closer to rashness than to cowardice, patience is closer to indifference than to impatience, and honesty is closer to rudeness than to deceit. This helps guide us as we strive to hit the mean: "of the extremes one is more erroneous, one less so; therefore, since to hit the mean is hard in the extreme, we must ... take the least of the evils."[54] We should note that there is not a mean for everything: some things are just bad, and there is no good way to do them. There is no good way, for instance, to commit murder or adultery.

What Aristotle's ethics captures is the sense that the domain of ethics is a whole life, a life lived with other people and full of activities. We do not act as moral agents only when we are faced with a difficult moral dilemma, as though ethics were somehow cordoned off from other aspects of our lives, but remain such agents in everything we do. For Aristotle, the good and happy life is an active life (although he does give contemplation a special place), a life which includes "parents, children, wife, ... friends and fellow-citizens, for man is born for citizenship."[55] Today, we tend to think of a virtuous person as someone who is rather dull and boring—someone we might like to have as a priest or a doctor, but not someone we would like to spend time in a bar with; for Aristotle, however, being virtuous carries with it none of these connotations. The virtuous person is the one who knows how to do everything in the right way, at the right time, with the right feelings—including how to have fun with friends.

Rationality allows us to live a good and happy life because it is through rationality that we discover the mean. Discovering the mean is an objective activity, not a subjective one (the mean in any particular case is what it is, not what we believe, or wish, it to be), but it is one that allows us to be very sensitive to different circumstances. (In this sense, it is an ethical theory that captures both the flexibility of the utilitarian and the principled stance of the Kantian.) For example, consider the virtue of courage: different situations will require us to exhibit this virtue in different ways, but in each case what courage requires can be discovered through rationality. It takes courage to fight in battle, but it can also take courage to speak out against injustice, or—depending on our temperament, inclinations, and previous experience—to trust other people, face a serious illness, or drive during a severe snowstorm.

STRENGTHS OF THE THEORY

Virtue ethics has a number of strengths. First, the emphasis on a whole life provides actions with a context. Consider, for instance, the environmental scientist and the water treatment specialist, as the former accepts the dictator's offer, and the latter rejects it: these are not discrete actions that can be considered on their own. They are, rather, choices that are connected to the characters of the two agents and to the choices they made in the past that have shaped them. The water treatment specialist's character is revealed not only in this particular instance, but also in his earlier choice to go to Africa. Likewise, the environmental scientist's actions were motivated by greed in the past, and she has, in consequence, become a greedy person. However, according to virtue ethics, she should examine herself and her choices, since taking responsibility for one's actions is an integral part of this approach. Actions don't exist apart from persons and cannot be considered in isolation as though they did. The environmental scientist, in short, must ask what sort of person she is and what sort she should try to become, and act in a way that will narrow the gap between the two.

The emphasis on a whole life means that we must continuously work to be virtuous, although as we get closer to this goal, being virtuous becomes easier and easier. For example, take the spiritual leader and his willingness to sacrifice himself for others. This decision seems easy for him because it fits with the orientation of his whole life. In fact, if he were to demand—or perhaps even accept—a cryogenics chamber in this situation, this would undermine everything that he has worked to become. He can die, knowing that his life was virtuous, and, therefore, happy. Death takes nothing away from this achievement.

Second, virtue ethics connects actions to character. It is not merely the case that someone performed an action that is important, but that this action reveals something about his character and shapes how that character will develop. If we relate this insight to the pandemic situation, it is apparent that there is no one moral agent here, no one decision-maker: rather, each person must strive to be virtuous by determining what hitting the mean requires of them, and each has a responsibility to do the right thing. There may, for instance, be virtues that everyone should display, such as courage: faced with a dangerous situation, it does not help for anyone to behave in a cowardly way, to threaten others, or to demand special treatment. However, what this means for each of them, given their personal histories and their inclinations, may well be different.

Third, virtue ethics accounts for emotion in two ways. First, it gives us a reason to be virtuous: being virtuous means living well, and living well makes us happy. Far from inclination and moral obligation being opposed to one another, doing the right thing also means doing what we want to do. The virtue ethicist, then, has no problem providing a motivation for moral behaviour and moral living. Second, virtue ethics is rooted in our everyday lives; ethics is not something set apart from who we are and what we normally do—it is not something that only comes into play on special occasions. In addition, since these everyday lives include other people, it is only natural that we treat our children, parents, and friends differently from other people's children, parents, and friends: part of what it means to be a virtuous parent, child, or friend is that we acknowledge the special nature of those particular relationships. (We should note, however, that this does not mean that we can treat strangers and acquaintances in any way we please. We must behave virtuously toward them also—but what virtuous behaviour is required will be different in these cases.)

Finally, virtue ethics is particularly useful for grounding considerations of professional ethics, for getting at what is appropriate to expect of those with whom we have a special relationship—such as a doctor, lawyer, or therapist. Consider the Morrison case: in certain professions, it is appropriate to ask questions about the character of those who want to enter and practise them. We would not want a physician who was callous and enjoyed inflicting pain; we would not want a lawyer who was dishonest; we would not want a therapist who revealed our deepest secrets and fears to others. Notice that what is of concern here is not merely what we can legally expect of these people: a callous physician might lose his or her licence to practise, a dishonest lawyer can be disbarred, and a therapist with a big mouth would quickly get a bad reputation and be removed from the profession. What is at issue, rather, is that we expect professionals not merely to act in certain ways, but to display particular virtues, virtues that come along with the role and make it the kind of role that it is, rather than something else. (We should also note, however, that everyone, from the perspective of virtue ethics, should strive to develop a virtuous character. Patients and clients, too, should display virtues such as courage, honesty, and patience.)

WEAKNESSES OF THE THEORY

While virtue ethics has strengths, critics have argued that it has a big weakness: it does not tell us what to do. It's all very well for virtue ethics to tell us that we should strive to hit the mean, but we still need to know what to do on particular occasions, and virtue ethics does not help us here. If Dr. Morrison injected potassium chloride into Paul Mills' IV line, was this the right thing to do? If everyone on the cryogenics list should be courageous, what, precisely, does courage require of them in this situation? Who are we going to pick to live and who to die? Rachels states the objection in this way:

> [T]heories that emphasize right action seem incomplete because they neglect the question of character. Virtue theory remedies this problem by making the question of character its central concern. But as a result, virtue theory runs the risk of being incomplete in the opposite way. Moral problems are frequently problems about what we should *do*. It is not obvious how, according to virtue theory, we should go about deciding what to do. What can this theory tell us about the assessment, not of character, but of action?[56]

Moreover, critics assert, virtues change: what is seen as virtuous for one society, at one point in history, can seem a vice for another. Aristotle considered pride to be a virtue, while for Christians, pride is considered a vice. Given this, how do we know what we should aim for?

Arguably, neither of these objections is insurmountable. In the case of the second, more minor objection, while different sets of virtues may be articulated in different times and places, the advice to aim for the mean seems correct. Moreover, there seem to be some virtues—such as courage and justice—that will always hold an important place in any set. Finally, we can, through discussion, articulate a set of virtues that we can make a case for on rational grounds: the fact that they may differ to some extent from those that were articulated by people before us, and from those that may be articulated by people who come after us, does not mean that they are subjective or relative.

With regard to the objection that virtue ethics is incomplete, this suggests that we need to connect the insights of virtue theory to utilitarian and Kantian recommendations. Indeed, virtue ethics allows us to make a place for both: the virtuous person, who aims for the mean, will be able to ascertain in particular situations which kind of action is required. She will not have to decide whether to be consequentialist or deontological; rather, she will be able to say, on particular occasions, that the virtuous thing to do is what is best for the largest number of people, and, on other occasions, that moral rules should be followed. What it means to be a person of virtue is that one will be able to make a sound and defensible judgment about what the right approach is in particular situations, and will act accordingly.

FEMINIST APPROACHES TO ETHICS

The newest of the moral theories that will be considered are feminist approaches, which emerged in the mid-1960s. Feminist approaches are difficult to summarize, because there is no central person who articulates the position, as there is with the other theories. Instead, feminist approaches are articulated by a number of theorists who say similar, but not identical, things. The diffuse nature of this approach may also result from its newness: perhaps, in the future, it will become more clear and cohesive. However, it can be said that feminist approaches to ethics fall into two main categories: the ethics of care and feminist ethics.

While these approaches are distinct, they share a number of features. First, proponents of both take a critical stance toward "standard" or "dominant" ethical theories. Second, both approaches make a place for emotions in ethical judgment. Third, both approaches endorse a different model of personhood than that envisioned in Kantian and utilitarian thinking in particular, in which it is assumed that humans are individualistic, freely choosing moral agents who are primarily motivated by self-interest. Finally, proponents of both the ethics of care and of feminist ethics believe that the perspectives and experiences of women differ from the perspectives and experiences of men, and that the "dominant" ethical theories have taken men as their model and ignored women: to the extent that women's perspectives have been considered by these traditional ethical theorists, they have been designated as morally inferior.

While these assumptions are shared by the ethics of care and feminist ethics, these approaches differ from one another in two important ways. First, they differ in how critically they examine the sources and effects of women's emotions as these relate to moral thinking and action. Second, they are distinguished on the basis of how important they believe it is to challenge, on political and social grounds, the structural arrangements that are seen to be oppressive to women and other vulnerable groups. While proponents of the ethics of care argue that women's voices need to be heard when we think about ethical dilemmas, feminist ethicists believe that political institutions and social expectations need to be restructured so that they allow everyone to make choices that are fully free. Ironically, some of the social expectations facing women that feminist ethicists challenge are precisely those that are embodied in the ethics of care; consequently, some of the sharpest criticisms of the ethics of care approach have come from feminist ethicists.

THE ETHICS OF CARE: FROM PSYCHOLOGY TO PHILOSOPHY

The origins of the ethics of care are usually traced to the studies psychologist Carol Gilligan made in response to fellow psychologist Lawrence Kohlberg's claims about moral development. Kohlberg identified three main stages of moral development, from lower to higher, but did his research exclusively on men. When Gilligan focused her research on women, she found that women approached moral conflicts differently than men did: while men typically tried to find some universal and impartial principle to apply to the situation so that it could be resolved, women tended to focus on the relationships of the people involved in the conflict, and to try to find solutions that helped everyone. Gilligan termed the latter approach an "ethic of care" and the former approach an "ethic of justice." Because the ethics of care has its roots in the ethical responses of real women, some commentators believe that it has important insights to offer that are lacking in other ethical theories: Gilligan's account "marked the first time that a moral theory would be based on real life or 'doing morality,' as opposed to the traditional approach of using theoretical morality, 'thinking about morality' to guide conduct."[57]

While questions have been raised about Gilligan's data and the conclusions she drew from it, the correctness of the data is not necessarily crucial to the usefulness of the theory. As Munson observes, it "is enough for the care ethics theorist to demonstrate the importance of the values that belong to the ethic of care by showing how they can play a role in the moral life of individuals and society and how they can be employed as guides in resolving cases of moral doubt and conflict."[58] The ethics of care can be understood as an approach to ethics that has moved beyond its origins in psychology. Moreover, like feminist approaches to ethics more generally, it has advocates who believe that it can stand as an alternative to competing ethical theories.

Held claims that an ethics of care has the following features. First, an ethics of care has, as its central focus, "the compelling moral salience of attending to and meeting the needs of particular others for whom we take responsibility."[59] Consequently, it focuses on relationships and, in particular, on the relationships between those who are dependent and their caregivers. Second, rather than excluding emotions from our ethical deliberations (as Kantians and utilitarians, in particular, seek to do), the ethics of care values emotions and sees ethical approaches that depend "entirely on reason and rationalistic deductions or calculations"[60] as deficient.

Third, the ethics of care challenges the assumption, central to Kantianism and utilitarianism, that it is impartiality that the moral decision-maker should strive for; in these theories, we are asked to determine what would be best when the situation is viewed from the perspective of an impartial spectator or a rational moral agent moved by duty, which means that personal perspectives and feelings should play no role in our thinking. Rather than this abstract perspective, an ethics of care recommends that the decision-maker seek "to preserve or promote an actual human relation between themselves and *particular others*."[61]

Fourth, the ethics of care rejects the distinction between "public" and "private," between the sphere outside the family and the sphere of the home. Proponents of this approach believe that this distinction is harmful to women, because it makes it difficult to address the ways in which women and children may be disadvantaged within the domestic sphere. By envisioning morality as governing relations between self-sufficient, independent, and mutually indifferent individuals, Kantians and utilitarians miss the moral issues that arise within social groups, friendships, and families. As Held puts it, in "the context of the family, it is typical for relations to be between persons with highly unequal power who did not choose the ties and obligations in which they find themselves. For instance, no child can choose her parents yet she may well have obligations to care for them."[62]

Finally, the ethics of care has a particular conception of persons—of what human beings are—at its core. Unlike Kantianism and utilitarianism, which see persons as self-interested, rational, and autonomous or self-directed, the ethics of care sees humans as interdependent with one another and formed through relationships. As Held observes, "Every person starts out as a child dependent on those providing us care, and we remain interdependent with others in thoroughly fundamental ways throughout our lives."[63]

When we apply the ethics of care to the case study, it appears that you, the cryogenics technician, as the decision-maker, should focus on the relationships between yourself and those you have to choose among and should pay attention, in particular, to the needs of those who are dependent on you. This suggests that you should not hesitate to save your daughter: this is simply what is morally required of you since you are her father. You also need to take seriously the relationship that exists between the farmer, his wife, and their infant daughter: as members of a family, they have important connections to one another that should be respected and preserved. Moreover, their daughter's handicaps make her particularly vulnerable and dependent. From an ethics of care perspective, she is the person whose requirements most need to be considered, since she is completely unable to care for herself. Consequently, it would appear that an ethics of care approach to the dilemma of whom to choose would suggest, at the very least, that this family should be kept together. Moreover, an ethics of care also recommends that you should speak to everyone on the list to determine what they want and need, and how they feel about the situation they find themselves in. You should also make an attempt to talk to the gangster: he is clearly scared and deeply emotional, and his threats probably arise from the pain he feels. Indeed, perhaps he embarked on a life of crime in the first place because he was not properly nurtured as a child. This, too, is something that you might explore with him.

Strengths of the Theory

The great strength of the ethics of care is that it draws our attention to the importance of considering relationships in our ethical thinking. Because it focuses on the needs of those who are most dependent within relationships, it is seen by some to be particularly applicable to medical contexts, which are shaped as much by relationships as they are by medical practice. Relationships exist between doctors and nurses, between health care providers and patients, and between health care providers and the families of those they are treating. As Oberle and Bonchal observe, "A kind of vulnerability is built in to being a patient; patients require something from health care providers that could be withheld, which gives care providers power. The voice of the patient (or family) has seldom been heard in deliberations about care decisions, and the most vulnerable, such as the elderly or the mentally challenged, have been silenced the most."[64] Consequently, they place an ethics of care "at the centre in nursing ethics."[65]

Weaknesses of the Theory

Despite its positive features, the ethics of care has been criticized by a number of commentators. These criticisms fall into three general categories: theoretical, feminist, and practical.

First, on a theoretical level, some theorists see the ethics of care as simply an extension of virtue ethics.[66] Aristotle also places an emphasis on relationships. Indeed, his best-known work on ethics, *The Nicomachean Ethics*, is thought by many to be dedicated to his son, Nicomachus,[67] and can be understood, in part, as providing guidance to parents on how to bring up children. Aristotle also recognizes the importance of the emotions in ethical practice. In addition, an ethics of care, with its focus on the traits required for nurturing, seems to be emphasizing the importance of virtue and character. Consequently, many of the criticisms levelled by care ethicists at "traditional" approaches to ethics seem to apply more easily to Kantianism and utilitarianism than they do to Aristotle's theory. As some commentators have noted, even if many of the virtues mentioned by Aristotle are described in masculine terms, this does not mean that his theory cannot be modified to accommodate the insights of the ethics of care. As Cates and Lauritzen put it, an "Aristotelian approach takes moral selves to be construed in and through ongoing relationships with other selves, especially friends; hence, a critical reappraisal of Aristotle can provide a way past individualistic conceptions of the self,"[68] and can strengthen care ethics by providing a context for balancing justice and care, something which is arguably important.

Second, feminist ethicists have pointed out that, if society is patriarchal, focused on the needs and desires of men (which feminists believe it is), then we cannot be sure how many of the nurturing tendencies observed in women by proponents of the ethics of care are *genuinely* their own, as opposed to coping mechanisms developed in response to upbringing and societal expectations. As Sherwin forcefully observes, the fact that women are good at caring for others may indicate nothing more than that they have a subordinate social status: "Within dominance relations, those who are assigned to the subordinate position, that is, those with less power, have special reason to be sensitive to the emotional pulse of others, to see things in relational terms, and to be pleasing and compliant. Thus the nurturing and caring at which women excel are, among other things, the survival skills of an oppressed group that lives in close contact with its oppressors."[69] Consequently, some feminists have asked whether endorsing an ethics of care might not simply entrench and perpetuate the very power structures and social expectations that have made women subordinate in the first place.

The final objection to the ethics of care is a practical one: it provides limited guidance. Consider, again, what it suggests about how to approach the dilemma facing you, the cryogenics technician: even if it is clear that you should save your daughter, it does not tell you who else should be saved; even if it tells you that the farmer and his family should be kept intact, it does not tell you whether this means that you should save all three of them, or leave them to die together; and even if it tells you that you should talk to the gangster and try to understand how he feels, it does not tell you what you should do if he persists in his threats. Consequently, some critics have argued that, even if we accept some of the insights of an ethics of care, we need to balance them with the ethics of justice approach. (Indeed, this is what Gilligan herself proposed.[70]) They would advise us to talk to everyone in the manner recommended by the ethics of care, but employ Kantian or utilitarian reasoning to help us make our final decision.

FEMINIST ETHICS

Feminist ethics also takes a critical stance toward the assumptions built into "traditional" ethical theory. Like care ethics, feminist ethics emphasizes the importance of relationships, of making a place for the emotions in our ethical deliberations, and of listening to the voices of women in order to discern how they might differ from the voices of men. Unlike the ethics of care, however, feminist ethics asks critical questions about the ways in which women's expectations, emotions, and desires may have been constructed by the framework and institutions of a patriarchal society. Consequently, some feminist ethicists see the ethics of care as endorsing a feminine approach to ethics, one that, while it correctly recognizes the need to notice gender differences in ethical thought, is insufficiently critical about power differentials within relationships, and insufficiently aware of exploitative political and social structures that make some people vulnerable to the actions of others.

Sherwin suggests that what is most important about feminist ethics is its "commitment to the feminist agenda of eliminating the subordination of women—and of other oppressed persons—in all of its manifestations. The principal insight of feminist ethics is that oppression, however it is practiced, is morally wrong. Therefore, moral considerations demand that we uncover and examine the moral injustice of actual oppression in its many guises."[71] This focus on oppression, as it applies to both men and women, distinguishes feminist ethics not only from the ethics of care, but from other ethical theories as well, which tend to view ethical dilemmas in terms of conflicts between individuals, rather than focusing on the larger political, institutional, and social contexts within which these conflicts occur.

If we apply the feminist ethics approach to the case study, it recommends doing everything that the ethics of care approach recommended. However, in addition, it requires us to examine our assumptions as we choose who lives and who dies. Feminist ethicists, for example, might ask what the long-term social implications are of viewing women as valuable primarily because of their reproductive capacities, and might suggest, further, that the male technician's hesitation about saving his colleague, with her superior abilities, may be as much a manifestation of sexism as it is of anything else. In addition, feminists might explore the question of whether any of the candidates are members of vulnerable cultural or racial groups and, if so, would take care to ensure that past injustices toward these groups were not perpetuated by present choices.

Strengths of the Theory

Like the ethics of care, feminist ethics does a valuable service in making us pay attention to features of the moral landscape that we might otherwise overlook. The focus on exploitation, power, and discrimination may be particularly useful in medical situations in which some people (health care providers, particularly doctors) have more power than others (patients and their families). As a result, feminist ethics has paid attention to ethical issues such as abortion, genetic testing, and reproductive technologies, all of which have the potential to exploit individuals as well as to empower them.

Weaknesses of the Theory

There are, however, weaknesses in the feminist ethics approach, some of which parallel those already indicated with respect to the ethics of care. First, some theorists have argued that the competing ethical theories, either understood correctly, or with some modifications, are capable of accommodating the insights of feminist ethics. Not only can some of these concerns be met by virtue ethics, but utilitarians, for example, are also able to deal with exploitation and oppression, while Kantians, with their focus on respect and dignity, can consider institutional structures and political arrangements and whether or not they allow individuals to make genuinely free choices, the kinds of choices that are required for moral accountability.

Second, partly, perhaps, as a result of the newness of the approach advocated by feminist ethics, and partly as a result of the diversity of voices now participating in the conversation about what feminist ethics is and what it requires, there is substantial disagreement about what constitutes "the feminist position" on a number of issues. Consider the case of abortion. All feminists agree that women need to achieve genuine equality in society and that oppressive power structures should be dismantled. Is free and easy access to abortion, however, the way to achieve equality, or is it not? Sherwin, representing the most common feminist position, believes that women must have access to reliable abortion services "if patriarchal dominance over women is to come to an end."[72] Callahan, in contrast, makes a case for what she calls "pro-life feminism" and asserts that "women can never achieve the fulfilment of feminist goals in a society permissive toward abortion,"[73] in part because this absolves both men and the larger community from taking responsibility for children and the women who bear them: if the decision to abort is seen as the woman's alone, then the decision to have a child, and the responsibility for raising it, can be seen as hers alone as well.

Finally, the guidance offered by feminist ethics may be unclear in particular cases. Who should we save, and who should we let die? Like the ethics of care, it, too, seems to need to be supplemented by other ethical approaches. Even Sherwin states, "I do not envision feminist ethics to be a comprehensive, universal, single-principle theory that can be expected to resolve every moral question with which it is confronted. It is a theoretical perspective that must be combined with other considerations to address the magnitude of moral dilemmas that confront human beings."[74]

CONCLUSION

Ethical theories provide the theoretical framework for a consideration of moral issues, but since these theories do not provide a coherent or consistent approach to ethical questions, bioethicists have turned to principles in order to find a mechanism by which to approach and resolve particular moral problems about which proponents of different ethical perspectives can agree. What these principles do is allow those working in bioethics to share a common approach.

In their discussion of the principles of bioethics, Beauchamp and Childress note that

> [C]ontemporary biomedical ethics incorporates theoretical conflicts of considerable complexity.... Competition exists among the various normative theories, and in addition we find a body of competing conceptions as to how such theories should be related to biomedical practice. Thus, persons who agree on a particular type of ethical theory may still find themselves in sharp disagreement regard-

ing how to relate their theory to the treatment of particular moral problems. Nonetheless, we stand to learn from all these theories. Where one theory is weak in accounting for some part of the moral life, another is often strong. Although each type of theory clashes at some point with deep moral convictions, each also articulates norms that we are reluctant to relinquish.[75]

The adoption of principles allows bioethicists to make use of particular aspects of each moral theory while not requiring that a particular ethical theory be accepted and the others excluded. The most important principles used in bioethics are drawn primarily from utilitarianism and Kantianism. The utilitarian principles are non-malfeasance (also called non-maleficence) and beneficence. Non-malfeasance tells us that we should not do things which are harmful to others, while beneficence tells us that we ought to do good, and promote well-being. Since they are drawn from utilitarianism, these principles are **consequentialist**: they draw our attention to the results of our actions. Despite their utilitarian origins, however, in their focus on directly benefiting others, we can also see in these principles some of the insights of the ethics of care and feminist ethics. The Kantian principles are autonomy and justice. Autonomy requires that we respect the choices of others, even when we don't agree with them and would prefer that they choose differently. Justice requires us to be fair in our treatment of others and to treat equivalent cases in the same way, without expressing personal biases or prejudices. Since these are Kantian principles, they reflect the Kantian value of respect for the dignity of persons. You will see these principles referred to, and discussed in more detail and depth, in many of the issues that will be considered. A discussion of all the principles and values of bioethics, along with a method for resolving case studies, is provided in the appendix at the end of this book.

PHILOSOPHICAL REFLECTION ON RELIGION AND ETHICS

People in different times, places, and cultures have believed that there is a close connection between religion and ethics, since both are concerned with how people ought to behave and how we ought to treat one another. Furthermore, many religious leaders make pronouncements on ethical issues: some religious leaders have denounced abortion and euthanasia and have told their followers how to behave in matters ranging from sexual practices, to divorce, to whether they should accept blood transfusions. So: does morality depend on religion? Should we be turning to religious texts, doctrines, or authorities when we are faced with the need to make an ethical decision?

These questions were discussed by Plato in a dialogue called *Euthyphro*. In this dialogue, Plato (through the person of Socrates) asks whether something is holy (and therefore morally good) because the gods love it, or whether they love it because it is holy. As the discussion progresses, it becomes clear that the response that something is morally right because the gods love it makes no sense. The gods must either be completely arbitrary—in which case they can change their minds, and what they love today they can hate tomorrow (so that if murder is immoral today, because today the gods hate it, if they change their minds tomorrow and switch to loving it, murder will become morally required)—or they must have a reason to approve of some actions and disapprove of others. The first option makes no sense, so we must accept the second. And, if the gods must have a reason for their likes and dislikes, then that is what we should be looking for and what should guide us in our own choices—in which case, we don't have to make any appeal to the gods at all.

Ethics, then, is a rational activity, not a matter of religious faith: from an ethical perspective, what is important is that we do what reason tells us is the best thing to do. Religion and ethics are distinct domains, so ethics does not rely on religious principles, and even those who have no religious beliefs can determine what is ethically required and act accordingly.

This point is reinforced when we consider that we live in a pluralistic and multicultural society in which fellow citizens may not share world views or religious beliefs. In such a society, it is clear that there are multiple perspectives, and the task of ethics is to determine what is required of everyone, despite these differences. It is reason and argument that must be our guide, not particular religious claims.

In short, while some individuals may be guided by their religious beliefs when they make ethical choices, there is no need for those who do not share those beliefs to be guided by these religious principles. And, while reason tells us that we ought to respect the deeply held beliefs that others have, not all of these beliefs can be defended on rational grounds: religious beliefs are ultimately grounded in faith, not in reason.

CASE STUDIES[76]

Scenario One

You are a manager at a branch of a large automotive company. You have three employees. Due to a downturn in the economy, your bosses at head office tell you that you must lay off one of the employees (if you refuse, they tell you that they will let you go and send in someone from the corporate office to make the decision). One of your employees is a single mother with three children, one of whom is handicapped; you know that she depends on the benefits provided by the company to deal with his particular needs. One is a good friend who is taking care of a sick wife who is unable to work because of her illness; when he was hired, you promised him that you would do everything you could to help him out. Unfortunately, he is often away from the office because of his wife's medical treatments, so his performance has not been as good as you would have liked. The third employee is single and the most efficient worker of the three: without his efforts, you're not sure that the branch would be viable at all. What should you do?

(1) Which factor(s) do you weigh most in your decision? (2) Does it matter that one person is your friend and you have made him a promise? (3) Do you also have a duty to your company? (4) How would a feminist ethicist resolve this dilemma? (5) How does this differ from a Kantian or a utilitarian perspective? (6) What might a virtue ethicist advise?

Scenario Two

You are a mother who has just given birth to conjoined twins. You are from an impoverished country where there is minimal prenatal care, so their birth was a surprise to you. Your story made headlines around the world (a *National Geographic* film crew happened to be making a documentary in your area at the time of their birth, and took heart-rending pictures of the girls), and donations flooded in to allow you to take the twins to a highly developed country with an advanced medical system to see whether they can be safely separated, as no such treatments are available at home. After tests are performed, the doctors tell you and your husband that one of the twins is much stronger than the other; the weak one will certainly die if separated from her sister. However, if you do not allow the surgery, the burden on the strong one (whose heart is working for both twins) will be so great that it is likely that both will die in the next year or two. Your husband believes that the operation should not be performed as it would mean choosing to kill the weak one, while letting nature take its course does not involve making the same kind of active choice. You feel the opposite, since it doesn't seem right to let both twins die when one could be saved. What should you do?

(1) Should the twins be left conjoined or should they be separated? Whose decision is this to make? (2) Is there a moral difference between taking an action that will result in the death of one twin and doing nothing that will result in the death of both? (3) What arguments, based on the ethical theories, could you give your husband in support of your position? (4) Do any of the theories support his contention that it is best to do nothing?

Scenario Three

You are an intrepid journalist who has covered stories in many of the world's dangerous hotspots. No one has had as much success as you at befriending tyrannical dictators and vicious warlords in order to tell the *real* story of what is going on in their countries. (They seem oblivious to the fact that your reporting makes them look bad in the eyes of the world, since each believes that the friendship you purport to offer, at least in his particular case, is genuine). You have just managed to make friends with a genocidal warlord, who proudly shows you the 20 women and children he captured in a raid on a small village. He intends to kill them in front of you to demonstrate to you how committed he is to his genocidal campaign. You plead with him to spare his prisoners and tell him that, if he does, you will write a nice story about him in your newspaper. He thinks for a moment, and then says that he will let 19 of the prisoners go if you agree to choose, and then shoot, one; you can then write your story about how merciful he is. If you refuse, he will shoot them all and then shoot you. What should you do?

(1) What would Kant say? What would Mill say? Who provides a better solution? (2) Is there an adequate way to resolve this dilemma? If so, what is it?

Scenario Four

You manage funds for a charity, which works to provide starving children in Africa with food and clean water. You are advised by your friend, a financial advisor, to put the money into an astonishingly productive fund run by a well-respected fund manager. Space for investors is limited and exclusive: not everyone who wants to invest is accepted, but your friend has connections that will get your charity in. Over the past 15 years, returns on this fund have been between 12 and 14 percent, much better than the average. You do some investigating and discover that most people who have invested in the fund are wealthy celebrities; however, since you have a good understanding of how the market works, you suspect that this fund must be a scam: no one else can match these returns. However, you know that, if it is a scam, it is one that can probably continue for several more years and that any money you put into the fund can be retrieved safely. In the meantime, the returns you can generate through the investment could save many lives. Also, the fund manager is so well respected that you think no one would believe you if you were to make your concerns public.

(1) Should you say anything? (2) If you decide not to say anything, should you invest the charity's money in the fund for a limited period of time? (3) What conflict between Kantianism and utilitarianism is illustrated in this case? (4) Can we resolve this conflict, and if so, how? (5) Does the end justify the means in this case?

GLOSSARY

Applied ethics: concerned with the application and evaluation of ethical principles, norms, and values to issues that arise in particular contexts, such as the practice of medicine, business, and the media. The distinction between theoretical and applied ethics, however, should not be seen as absolute: theoretical ethics must be able to address practical questions if it is to be useful, and applied ethics must be shaped and informed by theoretical considerations if it is to justify its conclusions.

Consequentialist ethical theories: theories that assert that it is the consequences of our actions that determine what action we ought to perform, not duties or inclinations. Utilitarianism is an example of a consequentialist ethical theory.

Deontological ethical theories: theories that assert that the proper approach to ethical questions is to determine the duties of moral agents. These duties are understood to take precedence over inclinations, self-interest, and the consequences of actions. Kantianism is an example of a deontological theory.

Ethics: a branch of philosophy that, broadly speaking, examines questions of how human beings ought to treat one another, organize societies, think about moral judgments, and ought to act in particular circumstances. Ethics is often subdivided into two categories: theoretical ethics and applied ethics.

Teleological ethical theories: theories that focus on the aims, purpose, or goal of our actions; the correct action to perform in a given circumstance is the action that will best fulfil that purpose or take us closer to achieving the intended goal. Virtue ethics is an example of a teleological ethical perspective.[77]

Theoretical ethics: considers ethical questions, such as how we ought to treat others and how we ought to organize our societies, on an abstract level, and is concerned with the nature of ethical language, how moral judgments can be justified, and the role of reasoning and argumentation in this process.

FOR FURTHER READING

Blackburn, Simon. *Being Good: A Short Introduction to Ethics*. Oxford: Oxford University Press, 2002.
In this excellent introduction to moral theory, Blackburn connects theoretical ethics to particular elements in our contemporary culture, and challenges the reader to notice the ethical climate that surrounds all of us and to take ethics seriously.

Callahan, Sidney. "The Role of Emotions In Ethical Decisionmaking." *Hastings Center Report*, 18, no. 3 (June-July 1988): 9–14.

Callahan asks what the moral significance is of our emotional responses to moral dilemmas; while there has been a strong tradition in ethical theory of dismissing the importance of the emotions, Callahan proposes "a model for the mutual interaction of thinking and feeling in ethical decisionmaking.... The ideal goal is to come to an ethical decision through a personal equilibrium in which emotion and reason are both activated and in accord" (p. 9). Callahan's position provides an interesting counterpoint to that expressed by Rachels (see below), and encompasses some of the insights of virtue and feminist ethics on the role of the emotions in ethical judgment.

Davis, Dena. "Rich Cases: The Ethics of Thick Description." *Hastings Center Report*, 21, no. 4 (July-August 1991): 12–17.

Davis considers the role that case studies play in the discipline of bioethics. In the course of her discussion, Davis explores the difference between "thin" cases (which are minimalist and factual) and "thick" cases (which provide more details and include elements of character). This paper helpfully demonstrates the importance of case studies in bioethics.

McGinn, Colin. *Moral Literacy, or How to Do the Right Thing*. Indianapolis: Hackett Publishing Company, 1993.

This book is a short, very accessible introduction to moral reasoning. It includes, among others, chapters on abortion, our treatment of animals, and the nature of virtue. McGinn's style is lively and clear, and his discussions are both thoughtful and rooted in "real life" concerns.

Rachels, James. "Can Ethics Provide Answers?" *Hastings Center Report*, 10, no. 3 (June 1980): 32–40.

In this essay, Rachels considers whether ethical arguments can provide answers to hard questions and argues that reason should guide us in determining what to do. In the course of his discussion, Rachels shows some of the problems with relativism and makes some helpful observations about the relationship between ethical behaviour and ethical theory.

RECOMMENDED WEBSITES

The Cryonics Institute

www.cryonic.org

This site provides an interesting glimpse into the concept of cryogenics and the motivations of those who are committed to this approach to life extension.

EthicsWeb.ca

www.ethicsweb.ca

This Canadian site offers links to websites concerned with various branches of applied ethics, including health care ethics.

National Institutes of Health—Bioethics Resources on the Web

www.bioethics.nih.gov/

This website provides links to other sites that cover such topics as case studies, health law, and careers in bioethics as well as those that cover specific issues, such as research on human subjects, genetic testing, and public health issues.

Impact Ethics: Making a Difference in Bioethics

www.impactethics.ca

This Canadian website offers a forum for bioethical commentary and provides a Canadian context for the discussion of current bioethical issues.

NOTES

1. Louis P. Pojman, *Ethics: Discovering Right and Wrong* (Belmont, CA: Wadsworth Publishing, 1995), xv.

2. Quoted in Bernard Williams, *Ethics and the Limits of Philosophy* (Cambridge, MA: Harvard University Press, 1985), 1.

3. A note about terminology: Some philosophers distinguish "ethics" from "morality," and "ethical theory" from "moral philosophy." While the terms "moral" and "ethical" have different origins (the former is from the Latin, the latter from the Greek), and slightly different connotations (with *morality* sometimes used to mean the moral rules of particular societies, while *ethics* is sometimes described as the study of those rules and whether or not they can be justified), we will be using "moral," "ethical," "moral philosophy," and "ethical theory" interchangeably. "The important thing to remember ... is that moral, ethical, immoral, and unethical, essentially mean good, bad, right, and wrong, often depending on whether one is referring to people themselves or to their actions." Jacques Thiroux, *Ethics: Theory and Practice* (Upper Saddle River, NJ: Prentice Hall, 1995), 3.

4. The issue of maternal-fetal conflicts is covered in Chapter 6.

5. Mike W. Martin, *Everyday Morality: An Introduction to Applied Ethics* (Belmont, CA: Wadsworth Publishing, 2001), 21–22.

6. Ruth Benedict, "A Defense of Ethical Relativism," in Christina Sommers and Fred Sommers, *Vice and Virtue in Everyday Life* (Orlando, FL: Harcourt College Publishers, 2001), 212.

7. Benedict, 216.

8. Pojman, 243.

9. Thomas H. Murray, "What Do We Mean By 'Narrative Ethics'?" in Hilde Lindeman Nelson, *Stories and Their Limits: Narrative Approaches to Bioethics* (New York: Routledge, 1997), 9.

10. This characterization of ethical theory adopts and expands on a suggestion made by Nina Rosenstand in *The Moral of the Story* (New York: McGraw-Hill, 2006), 263.

11. James Rachels, *The Elements of Moral Philosophy* (New York: McGraw-Hill, 1993), 92.

12. Michael C. Brannigan and Judith A. Boss, *Healthcare Ethics in a Diverse Society* (Mountain View, CA: Mayfield Publishing Company, 2001), 26.

13. Jeremy Bentham, quoted in Rosenstand, 217.

14. Quoted in *The Encyclopedia of Philosophy*, Vol. 1, ed. Paul Edwards (London: MacMillan, 1967), 183.

15. J.S. Mill, *Utilitarianism, On Liberty, and Considerations on Representative Government*, ed. H.B. Acton (London: Everyman's Library, 1972), 7.

16. Mill, 7.

17. Mill, 7.

18. Mill, 8.

19. Martin, 25.

20. Mill, 10, 11.

21. Rosenstand, 231.

22. Rosenstand, 231.

23. Mill, 17.

24. Martin, 26.

25. Stephen J. Freeman, *Ethics: An Introduction to Philosophy and Practice* (Belmont, CA: Wadsworth Publishing, 2000), 53.

26. Atul Gawande, *Complications* (New York: Metropolitan Books, 2002), 27–28.

27. Immanuel Kant, *Foundations of the Metaphysics of Morals*, trans. Lewis White Beck, with critical essays ed. Robert Paul Wolff (Indianapolis, IN: Bobbs-Merrill Educational Publishing, 1969), 11.

28. Kant, 12.
29. Kant, 12–13.
30. Jacques Thiroux, *Ethics: Theory and Practice* (Englewood Cliffs, NJ: Prentice Hall, 1995), 68.
31. Kant, 20.
32. Kant, 36.
33. Pojman, 139.
34. Kant, 44.
35. Thiroux, 68.
36. Kant, 54.
37. Kant, 64.
38. Tom L. Beauchamp and LeRoy Walters, *Contemporary Issues in Bioethics* (Belmont, CA: Thomson Wadsworth, 2003), 16.
39. Rachels, 126.
40. Kate Atkinson, *Case Histories* (New York: Doubleday, 2004), 25.
41. This sense is hard to articulate in the language of philosophy, but often illuminated by fiction. Martha Nussbaum has argued that the *way* in which we say things is an important part of *what* we say, that form and content work together. And "this suggests … that there may be some views of the world and how one should live in it … that cannot be fully and adequately stated in the language of conventional philosophical prose, a style remarkably flat and lacking in wonder … but only in a form [like a literary text] that itself implies that life contains significant surprises, that our task, as agents, is to live as good characters in a good story do, caring about what happens, resourcefully confronting each new thing." Martha C. Nussbaum, *Love's Knowledge: Essays on Philosophy and Literature* (Oxford: Oxford University Press, 1990), 3–4.
42. K. Cox, "Nova Scotians Asking Why Doctor Charged With Murder," *The Globe and Mail* (March 2, 1998), A10.
43. Cox, A10.
44. Cox, A10.
45. Aristotle, *The Nicomachean Ethics*, trans. David Ross (Oxford: Oxford University Press, 1986), 1.
46. Aristotle, 1.
47. Aristotle, 2.
48. Robert B. Talisse, *On Rawls* (Belmont, CA: Wadsworth Publishing, 2001), 7.
49. Aristotle, 24.
50. Aristotle, 14.
51. Gawande, 19.
52. Gawande, 21.
53. Aristotle, 38.
54. Aristotle, 46.
55. Aristotle, 12.
56. Rachels, 176.
57. Johnna Fisher, *Biomedical Ethics* (Don Mills, ON: Oxford University Press, 2009), 17.
58. Ronald Munson, *Intervention and Reflection: Basic Issues in Medical Ethics*, 7th ed. (Belmont, CA: Thomson Wadsworth, 2000), 789.
59. Virginia Held, *The Ethics of Care* (Oxford: Oxford University Press, 2006), 10.
60. Held, 10.
61. Held, 12.

62. Held, 13.

63. Held, 13.

64. Kathleen Oberle and Shelley Raffin Bonchal, *Ethics in Canadian Nursing Practice* (Toronto: Pearson-Prentice Hall, 2009), 18.

65. Oberle and Bonchal, 18.

66. See, for instance, Walter Glannon, who states that "[f]eminist ethics is considered by some to be an extension of virtue ethics, in the sense that it emphasizes an ethics of care involving human connectedness and the importance of interpersonal relationships." *Biomedical Ethics* (New York: Oxford University Press, 2005), 14–15.

67. Alasdair MacIntyre, *After Virtue* (Notre Dame, IN: University of Notre Dame, 1981), 147.

68. Diana Fritz Cates and Paul Lauritzen, *Medicine and the Ethics of Care* (Washington, DC: Georgetown University Press, 2001), xvi–xvii.

69. Susan Sherwin, *No Longer Patient: Feminist Ethics and Health Care* (Philadelphia: Temple University Press, 1992), 50.

70. Sherwin, 50.

71. Sherwin, 54.

72. Sherwin, 115.

73. Sidney Callahan, "A Case for Pro-Life Feminism," in John D. Arras and Bonnie Steinbock (eds.), *Ethical Issues in Modern Medicine*, 5th ed. (Mountain View, CA: Mayfield Publishing Company, 1999), 366.

74. Sherwin, 57.

75. Tom L. Beauchamp and James F. Childress, *Principles of Biomedical Ethics* (Oxford, UK: Oxford University Press, 1994), 111.

76. These case studies have been designed to encourage readers to think about and apply the ethical theories in situations; consequently they are not necessarily related to biomedical ethics.

77. Utilitarianism is also considered by some commentators to be a teleological theory because it makes the achievement of human happiness the goal of ethics.

Chapter 2

DISTRIBUTIVE JUSTICE

LANDMARK CASE: JACQUES CHAOULLI

George Zeliotis was a patient of Dr. Jacques Chaoulli. Mr. Zeliotis had been in and out of hospital for various health problems over a number of years. He frequently experienced delays in obtaining treatment and eventually joined together with Dr. Chaoulli, who tried and failed to obtain a licence to offer his services in an independent private hospital. The two hoped to challenge the provisions of Quebec's Health Insurance Act and Hospital Insurance Act, which prohibits private insurance for health care services that are available in the public health care system. Zeliotis and Chaoulli held that, in effectively prohibiting private delivery of health care services, the prohibition violates the rights to life, liberty, personal security, and inviolability guaranteed by section 1 of the Quebec Charter of Human Rights and Freedoms (the "Quebec Charter") and sections 7, 12, and 15 of the Canadian Charter of Rights and Freedoms (the "Canadian Charter").

Dr. Chaoulli and Mr. Zeliotis were unsuccessful in their challenge before both the Quebec Superior Court and the Quebec Court of Appeal. Their appeal to the Supreme Court of Canada was heard by a panel of seven judges in 2005, who decided four to three in their favour. In making their decision, the Chief Justice and Justice Major, the authors of the Reasons for Judgment, focused primarily on the section 7 analysis.

Section 7 of the Canadian Charter guarantees all persons the "right to life, liberty and security of the person and the right not to be deprived thereof except in accordance with the principles of fundamental justice."[1] In examining the evidence adduced in the lower courts, the Chief Justice and Justice Major found that many Quebec residents face significant delays in receiving medical treatment in the public health care system, resulting in adverse physical and psychological effects. This amounts to a violation of the right of life, liberty, and security of person guaranteed by section 7 of the Canadian Charter:

> Access to a waiting list is not access to health care.... [T]here is unchallenged evidence that in some serious cases, patients die as a result of waiting lists for public health care. Where lack of timely health care can result in death, section 7 protection of life itself is engaged. The evidence here demonstrates that the prohibition on health insurance results in physical and psychological suffering that meets the threshold requirement of seriousness.

> We conclude, based on the evidence, that prohibiting health insurance
> that would permit ordinary Canadians to access health care, in circum-
> stances where the government is failing to deliver health care in a rea-
> sonable manner, thereby increasing the risk of complications and death,
> interferes with life and security of the person as protected by section 7 of
> the Charter.[2]

Having found that the prohibition on private insurance violates the individual's right to life, liberty, and security of person, the Chief Justice and Justice Major then had to decide whether such a deprivation was in accordance with the principles of fundamental justice. Given, in their view, the arbitrariness of the prohibition, it was found that it is indeed inconsistent with the principles of fundamental justice.

The finding of arbitrariness, and thus the inconsistency with the principles of funda-mental justice, was based primarily on what the Chief Justice and Justice Major considered an absence of clear evidence establishing that a prohibition against private insurance was necessary to properly sustain the public system. They held that the experts testifying in favour of the prohibition in the lower courts based their arguments on "common sense" arguments without any clear evidentiary foundation. In contrast to the sorts of assumptions and arguments made by these experts, the Chief Justice and Justice Major looked to the actual evidence of the types of health systems in place in other Western democracies. In particular, the Court found that Sweden, Germany, and the United Kingdom each provided an example of how a universal public health care system could be combined with private health care insurance in order to strengthen the public system, rather than undermine it, and broaden the services available.

Having concluded that the prohibition violates section 7 of the Canadian Charter, the Chief Justice and Justice Major then went on to consider whether the violation could be permitted under section 1, which permits the government to justify measures that might otherwise violate the Char-ter if it can be shown that the offending provision is a "reasonable limit demonstrably justified in a free and democratic society."[3] The requirements for a measure to be saved under section 1 are as follows: "[T]he government must demonstrate that the objective underlying the measure is pressing and substantial and further that the measure is proportionate in the sense that (i) there is a rational connection between the measure in question and the legislative objective; (ii) the measure impairs the guaranteed right as minimally as possible and (iii) the benefits of the measure outweigh the deleterious effects."[4] Given the absence of evidence that this prohibition protects the public health care system, and the failure of the prohibition to meet the minimum impairment test, the Chief Justice and Justice Major concluded that the offending provisions of the Quebec legislation must be struck down.

In their concluding remarks, it is important to note that the Chief Justice and Justice Major do not consider a ban on private insurance unconstitutional in all circumstances. They ended their Reasons for Judgment with the following statement: "In sum, the prohibition on obtaining private health insurance, while it might be constitutional in circumstances where health care services are reasonable as to both quality and timeliness, is not constitutional where the public system fails to deliver reasonable services. Life, liberty and security of the person must prevail."[5] Thus, it was found that a ban on private insurance is unconstitutional where the public health care system is not meet-ing the needs of the public.[6]

Passengers flee the sinking *Titanic*. Distributive justice is concerned with the question of who gets what, and on what basis. Decisions about who gets a seat in a lifeboat and who is left to go down with the sinking ship dramatically illustrate both the importance of distributive decisions and the difficulty of making them fairly.

INTRODUCTION

In Chapter 1, we began our consideration of the ethical issues that arise in the context of health care with a consideration of a particularly complex case, "The Ultimate Case Study," in which a cryogenics technician in a situation of pandemic disease was forced to choose who should live and who should die. We noted that this case raises a number of significant ethical issues and demonstrates both the complexity of ethical decision making and its necessity: many of our choices have significant ethical dimensions. We also considered the assistance that ethical theories and principles can provide in helping us make sure that our choices are ethically sound, that they are ones that we can defend to others. Our discussion of ethical theory focused on the guidance it can provide to individuals who must make choices in situations of moral complexity. There is, however, another important dimension to ethical theory, a dimension that is especially important within the context of medical decision making: how should scarce goods, including medical goods, be distributed? In other words, bioethical choices have not only personal and medical dimensions, but social and political ones as well. While we benefit from medical goods (whether they consist of a physician's time, a hospital bed, or an organ transplant) as individuals, these goods would be unavailable were it not for the fact that societal resources have been used to create them. The education of physicians is largely funded by taxpayers, hospitals require government funds for construction and maintenance, and most individuals would be unable to pay for all their lifetime health care needs out of their own pockets. Even in countries like the United States, in which individuals, largely through health insurance plans connected to their jobs, are expected to pay for their own health care, health care remains a public good that would be largely unavailable without the contribution of communal resources. Poor countries, which lack the resources to create and maintain the infrastructure required by a well-functioning health care system, have much lower life expectancies and much higher rates of infectious disease than countries that can afford to provide their citizens with medical goods. In short, health care, like roads, clean water, and sewers, while beneficial to us as individuals, is largely only available to us because of political and communal choices and commitments.

This social or public dimension to health care means that we must consider issues related to **distributive justice** when we examine the ethical issues that arise in a medical context. Distributive justice is concerned with the question of how scarce goods can be distributed most fairly within a society, or within particular societal institutions. As members of a society, we have some interests that coincide with the interests of others (for instance, we all have an interest in the provision of clean water, the existence of good roads, an adequate health care system, and the creation and maintenance of universities), and some that conflict (not everyone can go to university, and while an adequate health care system—it might be argued—will cover organ transplants, not everyone who needs one can be provided with one). We can see the way in which interests sometime coincide and sometimes conflict more clearly if we consider, once again, the situation facing the cryogenics technician. Everyone has an interest in having the cryogenics chambers maintained, since they offer the only hope of survival for anyone. However, there are not enough chambers to go around, and one of the two technicians must remain outside the chambers during the freezing process to make sure that it proceeds properly. This means that distributive choices have to be made and that some people will benefit and others will lose out.

Questions of justice arise when we consider how these choices should be made. If we wish to be ethical, as individuals and as societies, we must not be arbitrary or careless in our distributive decisions, our decisions about who gets what and on what basis. Political philosopher Rawls calls the combination of shared interests and potential conflicts the "circumstances of justice,"[7] because questions about the just distribution of resources arise when co-operation is both necessary and possible. Distributive justice would be an unnecessary virtue if there were such an abundance of goods that our interests never came into conflict (no hard decisions would have to be made about the distribution of the cryogenics chambers if there were more than enough to go around). Likewise, this form of justice might be impossible to obtain were it not for the fact that "social cooperation makes possible a better life than any would have if each were to try to live solely by his own efforts."[8] (For all their power, the politicians need the services of the cryogenics technicians as much as anyone else does.)

The situation facing the cryogenics technician reflects, in microcosm, the situation within the Canadian health care system. Costs are rising, goods are scarce, and difficult choices need to be made, both within the system itself (Who gets the hospital bed, and who gets sent home? Who gets the kidney, and who remains on dialysis?), and by social decision-makers, who must balance medical goods with other social goods. In 2006, *The Globe and Mail* reported, "Health care in Ontario … [consumed] 46 cents of every dollar spent on provincial programmes, up from 33 cents a decade ago,"[9] and in 2013, an op-ed by the Fraser Institute published in the *National Post* stated that, in Canada, "some 68% of personal income taxes paid in aggregate are needed to cover the cost of health care."[10] Finally, the Canadian Institute for Health Information reported that, in 2014, "total health care spending … is projected to exceed $214.9 billion … [and] to consume 11% of Canada's gross domestic product.[11] As increasing amounts of social resources are put into health care, they must be taken from other important spheres, such as education and physical infrastructure. And health care costs continue to rise at rates that are unsustainable, because they exceed the revenue growth of most provinces. This means that the challenge for those who must make allocation decisions at all levels of the system must strive to do so in ways that are as fair and justifiable as possible.

Health care systems are commonly divided into three levels: the macro level, the meso level, and the micro level. The macro level is the governmental level of the system, the level at which public health care priorities are identified, policies developed, and budget allocation decisions made. The meso level is the middle level of the system, the level at which local health care initiatives are developed and hospital administrative decisions made. The micro level is the level at which patients encounter health care providers. For many people, this is the most significant level of the system, because what matters most to them is whether or not their treatment is beneficial and whether or not they are treated with dignity and respect.

Allocation decisions must be made at each of these levels, and questions of distributive justice must be considered in each part of the system. Policy-makers must ask whether their policies treat fairly those who will be affected by them and whether budget choices are reasonable. Decision-makers at the meso level must consider similar questions as they distribute organizational and institutional resources. Finally, health care providers must ensure that they treat their patients in ways that respect them as individuals, and that, as much as possible, their health care needs are met.

It should be noted that decisions made for good reasons at different levels of the system can sometimes be in tension with one another. For example, while governments must put resources into health care, they must also meet other obligations, such as providing an effective school system and safe roads for their citizens. Consequently, even governments that are deeply committed to a flourishing health care system must limit the public resources they commit to it. They may decide, for example, that their province can only fund a small number of positron emission tomography (PET) scanners, no matter how useful these scanners may be for the diagnosis and treatment of certain diseases. These macro allocation decisions have an effect on the resources available to people at the meso level, such as hospital administrators, who must decide how to distribute the resources available to them: should they invest in a PET scanner or in more ICU beds? Finally, health care professionals, such as doctors and nurses, have the well-being of their patients as their primary moral obligation. They may sometimes find that what a particular patient needs is unavailable or rationed, and they must decide how to distribute resources, including their own time, to best satisfy their primary goal of enhancing the well-being of their patients. Their challenge becomes one of doing what is best for their patients, despite (for example) the limited availability of hospital beds, or the governmental and administrative policies that restrict the services they can provide.

It is likely that difficult allocation decisions will always have to be made within any health care system, because demand for medical services usually exceeds supply and costs continue to rise. There are a number of reasons for this continual increase in health care costs. The most significant include: technological developments, demographics, new treatments, public attitudes, and the difficulty of defining medical needs. We will examine each in turn.

Technological Developments

The increasing use of technology in medicine has led to improvements in a number of areas, including diagnosis and life extension. At the same time, however, new technology is expensive to develop and purchase, requires that technologists be hired and trained in its use, and may lead to an increased number of tests being performed. New technology is usually more expensive to use than the technology that came before it, technologists must be adequately paid for their specialized services, and technology itself is often more costly than the non-technological treatments it replaced.

Demographics

In Canada, as in many parts of the industrialized world, the percentage of the population that is elderly is increasing and will continue to do so for the foreseeable future. While this demonstrates a welcome improvement in life expectancy, it is also the case that the older we are, the more health care we are likely to require. Moreover, many of the ways in which life can be extended involve the use of the technologies just considered. Garrett, Baillie, and Garrett note that technological means of prolonging life can be tremendously expensive and are not always beneficial to the patient or to society: "[O]ne-quarter of all [health care] ... funds are spent during the last year of a person's life, and most of that is spent during the last month.... Much of this money is spent prolonging dying, and represents scarce resources that could be used to maintain and improve health."[12]

The difficulty, of course, is that it is difficult to determine in advance whether someone is indeed dying, in which case the issue of what treatment is truly beneficial arises (Should it be aggressive and intense, or would palliative treatment be more helpful?), or simply suffering from an illness from which they can recover well enough to live several more satisfactory years. Callahan, for instance, in a discussion of medical treatment decisions and the elderly, asks us to imagine a Mr. Smith, who has a heart attack at 65, colon cancer at 75, another heart attack at 80, a stroke at 82 that leaves him alive but in poor health, and who finally dies at 88. At all these stages, he was treated with the available technology. And, Callahan asks, "When, in that continuum, was he dying? There is no straightforward answer to that question, for he was—but for the technology—dying at many points. Each crisis presented the need to make a choice for or against initiating treatment."[13] When we have a choice to use technology to prolong someone's life, it is very hard to choose not to.

New Treatments

New treatments for diseases and medical conditions are continually being developed. While these new treatments improve health and save lives, they—like new technologies—create choices and generate costs. Consider, for instance, the development of the surgical techniques that allow organ transplantation and the creation of drugs that allow someone to use someone else's organ without his or her body rejecting it. Even though organ transplantation is tremendously costly, once it exists as a treatment, many will desire it. From the perspective of distributive justice, however, what is important to note is that all medical treatments require that trade-offs be made: even if we consider organs to be resources, it is clear that there are not enough available to give them to everyone who might desire one, which means that we have to make choices between individuals (just as the cryogenics technician must choose who will get a chamber). Furthermore, there are larger medical and social implications here as well. Since organ transplantation is so expensive, decision-makers within the health care system must choose to put resources into this form of treatment, rather than, say, into more long-term care beds or into a neonatal ICU, or into preventing health problems in the first place.

Public Attitudes

It is interesting to note, from the perspective of distributive justice as it relates to health care, that there is a reluctance on the part of individuals and of many social commentators to acknowledge that these trade-offs within a health care system are inevitable. The demand for health care resources will always exceed the supply available, and in addition, social commitments to health care must be balanced with other priorities.

In part, this reluctance can be traced to questions about the goals of medicine. Is the purpose of medical treatment to relieve suffering, to allow individuals to achieve their own goals and desires, to prolong life, or something else altogether? Each of these goals suggests different priorities for the medical system and for the individuals who use it; consequently, the way in which the goal is defined has implications for what is understood to be a fair and just distribution of health care resources. If the purpose of health care is to prolong life (as many appear to believe it is), then any technological and treatment advances that achieve this will be employed. As Callahan puts it, "Mr. Smith [his hypothetical patient] lived on because we expect medicine to continue to devise ever-more-ingenious ways to save our lives."[14] If this is the goal we see embodied in the practice of medicine, any limits on the use of available technology or treatments will be difficult to justify. Likewise, if we understand the purpose of medicine to be that of allowing people to maximize their own desires and goals, we will have a difficult time placing any limits on their choices: we will fund procedures that are not clearly medically required, such as sex reassignment surgery and Caesareans planned for convenience rather than safety. If, however, we see the goal of medicine as being primarily to relieve suffering, then natural limits will be placed on what we do; the epistemological difficulty, however, will remain: it will not always be clear when treatments will prolong suffering and when they will heal.

The fact that, for many, the goal of medicine seems most clearly connected to the prolongation of life at all costs is arguably connected to the way in which we view science and our modern understanding of medicine as a straightforward practical application of scientific knowledge. Studies have shown, for instance, that North Americans

> have exaggerated ideas of the power of health care and medical knowledge, because they have a dubious concept of science in general and of medical knowledge in particular. Many people believe that health care is simply a matter of … identifying the cause of a problem and treating it with a scientifically validated drug or procedure. They expect that this cause can be identified by a diagnostic procedure that will give a clear and unambiguous answer. They further expect that the treatment will be equally precise and straightforward. It is as though medicine, in particular, is a kind of magic that offers cures and restoration beyond the frustrations and limits we find in other areas of human life.[15]

This view of medicine and what it can accomplish is, Jecker suggests, connected to the rise of Baconian science, in which the purpose of scientific exploration—and the technologies it generates—is "to exercise dominion and control over nature."[16] This is in marked contrast to the ancient model of Hippocratic medicine in which "medicine conceived its task to be one of working with human nature to assist in restoring disruptions in the natural order."[17] Hippocratic medicine had natural limits built into it: the wise doctor was the one who knew when to intervene and when to let nature take its course; and it recognized that human life itself has natural and appropriate limits. Baconian-influenced medicine, in contrast, sees these natural limits as things that medicine ought to overcome. However, Jecker argues, this approach damages our ability to place ethical limits on medical treatment and is harmful both to our ability to restrain health care costs and to patients themselves: "So long as the myth of a value-free science distorts medical and ethical thinking, no final resolution of ethical problems in medicine can be achieved…. The values of modern Baconian science are more troubling where the battleground for dominating nature is an animate being, and the nature to be conquered is our own."[18] For example, a consequence of this model is that we will continue treatment even in cases in which there is clearly no possibility of cure. Garrett, Baillie, and Garrett echo this sentiment: "The limits of medical diagnosis and of all forms of health care need to be acknowledged if we are to have a realistic view of the extent to which they can satisfy needs and should be supported by society."[19]

Defining Needs

It might be thought that the concept of **need** can fill the gaps between what is desired, what is medically possible, and what society can afford to provide. That is to say, perhaps the best way to deal with issues of distribution might be to identify genuine and serious needs that can be satisfied medically and then ensure that these are the first priority; if resources are left over, less urgent needs could then be met; and, finally, if there are any resources available after these two sets of needs have been met, desires can be satisfied. For example, those seriously injured in car accidents will be treated before those who need a hip replacement but who are currently functioning quite well; and those who need hip replacements will be treated before those who want cosmetic facelifts. The difficulty with this proposal, however, is that needs themselves are difficult to define in clear and non-controversial ways. Needs fall into different categories, including inherent, subjective, and socially induced.[20] **Inherent needs** exist whatever we happen to think about them. Biological needs fall into this category: all humans need food and water to survive and function. These needs are the most basic and the least controversial to define.

Subjective needs, in contrast, arise from the desires of particular individuals: framed in this way, someone who desires to have a planned Caesarean because she wants to know exactly when she will begin her maternity leave is articulating a subjective need. Subjective needs, then, are often difficult to distinguish from desires and, in fact, might indeed be considered a kind of desire: while an individual can feel them very deeply, and believe that he is damaged if these needs are not met, other people might not desire them at all or believe that anyone should want them.

Finally, some needs are **socially induced**. According to Garrett and colleagues, "Socially induced needs are a result of a historical development of material and social conditions coupled with a social consensus that some things are necessary for happiness, social life, or some other goal."[21] In Canadian society, for example, electricity, running water, and a telephone can be described as socially induced needs. Socially induced needs are context-dependent: needs that exist within a particular society, at a particular time in history. Consequently, socially induced needs change over time. For example, 20 years ago, Canadian university students could function in that role perfectly well without a computer; now, however, access to a computer has become a need.

Medical needs can fall into any of these categories of need. Inherent needs, of course, are the most necessary and the easiest to justify meeting: anyone whose appendix bursts needs to have it removed. Subjective needs, in contrast, vary from person to person, and this has implications for the distribution of health care. Given that it is a public and communal good, if at least some subjective needs can be met through medical treatment, should they not be met? Do you, as a taxpayer, have an obligation to fund my deeply desired but medically unnecessary planned Caesarean? If I am morbidly obese, are you required to pay for my stomach stapling, or should I be told, instead, that it's my responsibility to go on a diet? If we consider stomach stapling to be medical treatment, what about liposuction?

In addition, many medical needs are socially induced. Needs that, for instance, can only be met through the use of technology or new medical discoveries are socially induced: they become needs only when the technologies and treatments exist to satisfy them. Once respirators were invented, sick people needed them; once antibiotics were discovered, children with strep throat and ear infections needed them; once protease inhibitors were invented, AIDS sufferers needed them; and once in vitro fertilization was developed, those who are infertile needed it in order to reproduce. It must be noted that to say that these needs are socially induced is *not* to say that they are not genuine or valid. It is merely to say that they only exist within a particular context.

Given our social, political, historical, and economic context, access to health care can be described as a need. Indeed, it can even be described as a right, as something that just societies like our own should provide and which citizens can legitimately expect to have provided for them. Daniels puts the point this way: "[I]n nearly every advanced industrial democracy in the world, there is a right to health care, since institutions exist in them that assure everyone access to needed services regardless of ability to pay."[22] To claim that something is a *right* is simultaneously to claim the existence of particular obligations, those necessary for the achievement of the content of that right. A right to free speech, for instance, imposes obligations on all of us not to interfere with others when they express their views, even when those views are ones we disagree with. Consequently, the claim that a there is a right to health care simultaneously generates obligations on the part of society—on the part of all of us—to ensure that the requirements of this right are met. As Daniels observes,

> [A] right to health care imposes an obligation on others to assist the rights-bearers in obtaining needed and appropriate services. Specifically, claiming a right to health care includes these other claims: society has the duty to its members to allocate an adequate share of its total resources to health-related needs; society has the duty to provide a just allocation of different types of health care services taking into account the competing claims of different types of health care needs; each person is entitled to a fair share of such services....[23]

But to say that, given the context, health care can be considered a right does not tell us very much about the scope of that right, as the different decisions of the lower courts and the Supreme Court in the Chaoulli case, presented at the beginning of this chapter, demonstrates. Is it a right to basic health care, for instance, or does it cover all health care needs? Is it a right to purchase health care? What constitutes a just allocation of health care services? How, and on what basis, are competing claims to be balanced with one another? In short, to assert that a right to health care exists is only to begin the discussion, not to conclude it. From the perspective of distributive justice, it tells us only that health care resources are resources that a society ought to provide, among other communal goods, but not how they should be distributed. We will consider the most influential approaches that have been put forward as distributive principles in the next section.

METHODS FOR THE DISTRIBUTION OF HEALTH CARE RESOURCES

There are a number of approaches to the distribution of health care goods. Broadly speaking, they commonly fall into utilitarian and Kantian approaches, although methods suggested by both feminist ethics and virtue ethics may also be considered. Before exploring these proposals in more detail, however, we need to consider one other possibility.

Distribution According to the Market

If distribution is based on the marketplace, then those who can pay for medical goods and services will receive them, and those who cannot will have to go without. While, as Daniels points out, most industrialized nations view health care as something that societies have an obligation to provide to their citizens, the United States, which expects its citizens to be largely responsible for funding their own health care, is a notable exception. Since, as we have seen, health care can be understood to be a public good because it costs more than most individuals can afford, what this means is that, in the United States, people pay for health insurance that is usually connected to their jobs. Consequently, people can lose coverage if they lose their job, and a number of people are not covered at all. In September 2014, the U.S. Census Bureau reported that 42 million Americans were uninsured in 2013. The same report noted that 53.9 percent of the population had health insurance that was employment-based.[24] As a result, when health outcomes in the United States are compared to those in other industrialized economies, the United States does not fare very well. For instance, according to the World Health Organization's "Healthy Life Expectancy Index," in 2012, citizens of the United States could expect 70 healthy years, while those in Canada could expect 72 years, and those in Japan could expect 75 years.[25] In 2014, the United States ranked 26th in the world in terms of its infant mortality rate, behind Slovakia, Hungary, and Poland.[26] Ironically enough, despite these poor results, more money is spent on health care in the United States, as a percentage of GDP, than many other countries that provide universal coverage to their citizens.[27] Goldhill observes that the federal government in the United States "spends eight times as much on health care as it does on education, 12 times what it spends on food aid to children and families, 30 times what it spends on law enforcement, 78 times what it spends on land management and conservation, 87 times the spending on water supply, and 830 times the spending on energy conservation."[28] The main beneficiaries of all this spending on health care have been for-profit insurance companies: "From 2000 to 2007, the annual profits of America's top 15 health-insurance companies increased from $3.5 billion to $15 billion."[29] In the U.S., a new Health Care Act was passed in 2010, and its provisions continue to come into effect. While it increases the number of citizens covered by Medicaid, it leaves a significant role in the system for insurance companies and still connects many health care benefits to employment. The long-term effects of this bill on American health care remain to be seen.

Some commentators have argued that that the free market is inefficient as a distributor of health care resources because it makes medicine a business that is as driven by the profit motive as any other business. The need to make a profit contributes to the increased use of technology, increased tests, and increased drug prescriptions. While these things all increase the cost of health care, there is little evidence that they lead to better health outcomes for Americans when compared to those for citizens in other industrialized nations.

While some theorists argue that a system that requires people to pay for the health care they can afford is a fair approach that is consistent with the values of a market economy and free enterprise (since it reflects individual contribution and encourages personal responsibility), a strong case can be made that distributing health care benefits on this basis is in tension with the obligations of a just state. It puts the poor at an even greater disadvantage; in the United States, those who are poor are disproportionately members of minority groups, which can make the lack of a universal, publicly funded health care system a form of socially sanctioned racism.[30] Further, since health insurance is connected to the ability to work, "the free-market approach ignores the needs of those who are disadvantaged due to illness. For instance, the disabled are placed at a disadvantage because they are not able to compete on a market basis with those who are healthier. In other words, a free-market approach may be fair only if there is a level playing field, yet this is not possible."[31]

In short, then, distribution of health care goods and services in accordance with the principles of the free market, it can be argued, is an unsatisfactory approach from the perspective of justice, the values internal to the practice of medicine, and efficiency. In the first case, distributive justice attempts to distribute goods fairly; distribution according to the market, however, creates "two kinds of medicine—one for the rich and one for the poor. And it too often happens that the medicine for the poor is none at all."[32] From the perspective of fairness, it is hard to claim that the poor somehow deserve to have a smaller share of the health care goods available than the rich—particularly given the fact, as already noted, that health care is a public good, rather than a private one. In terms of the values central to the practice of medicine, it is an unsatisfactory outcome when those most in need of care, such as the disabled, have difficulty affording it. Finally, it is inefficient, since, as noted above, the United States spends more on health care than most industrialized nations while benefiting a lower percentage of its citizens.

Even if we reject the free market method of distribution, the problem of scarcity—and therefore the need to determine a method of distribution—remains. How should the cryogenics chambers be distributed?

ETHICAL THEORY AND DISTRIBUTIVE JUSTICE

Ethical theories not only provide guidance when we must make difficult personal choices, they also provide assistance for distributive ones as well. Indeed, most of the approaches to questions of distributive justice draw, to a greater or lesser extent, on the ethical theories that were explored in Chapter 1.

Utilitarian Approaches

Utilitarians focus on the promotion of the greatest good for the greatest number. While this can serve as an ethical principle that guides personal choices (each of us ought to act in such a way that we promote the greatest good for the greatest number, not weighing our own interests more heavily in our calculations than the interests of others), utilitarian thinking has an important (and perhaps inescapable) role to play as a guide for the most efficient distribution of social goods, where "efficient" means using them in a way which benefits the greatest number. In practice, what this might mean is that scarce medical goods and services would (a) be used to ensure that everyone has access to some socially determined level of basic health care; and, (b) that distribution above this level, or in emergency situations, would be in accordance with **social worth**. We can explore what this might mean by applying it to the situation facing the cryogenics technician. Recall that the candidates for the cryogenics chamber include: two politicians, a doctor, a novelist, a water-treatment specialist, an environmental scientist, a spiritual leader, two cryogenics technicians, a farmer and his wife, their handicapped daughter, and the daughter of one of the technicians. The threat posed by the gangster, who wants a chamber, must also be considered. (For the purposes of this discussion, we will not consider the dog.) Which of these people has the greatest social worth, and so should receive a chamber?

What we should notice immediately is that social worth is *not* synonymous with wealth or power: what is important from the perspective of social worth is the contributions a person can make to the happiness and well-being of others. From this perspective, an ambitious politician may not be as worthy of a cryogenics chamber as a farmer who has the skills to ensure that people are fed. It is also important to note, however, that social worth is also not synonymous with **moral worth**: even if the doctor is an unrepentant pedophile, it may still be important to give him a chamber because he may be able to save the lives of others as a result of his medical training. On the other hand, the technician's daughter and the handicapped infant have little social worth, however morally blameless they are, because they can contribute little to the well-being of others.

This social worth approach has been criticized on the ground that it violates a fundamental ethical principle, namely, the commitment to the equal worth of all individuals. Instead, so the objection goes, it replaces this commitment with subjective and questionable social judgments that are as likely to reflect prejudices and biases as they are to capture genuine social contributions. In short, critics suggest, this approach is unethical because it perpetuates existing social injustices (those who are rich, for instance, are also likely to be powerful, and will ensure that they receive the best treatment), and because this approach rejects a basic ethical principle that all persons should be treated with equal dignity and respect.

Kantian Approaches

The alternatives suggested by these critics reflect Kantian, rather than utilitarian, intuitions. Kantians emphasize the equality and autonomy of individuals, and place moral weight on intentions and obligations rather than on consequences. In practice, Kantians, like utilitarians, would arguably support a universally available, publicly funded level of basic health care; where they would differ from utilitarians is in how they would distribute scarce goods above this level, or in emergency situations. Kantians commonly advocate two similar methods for distribution at this level or in emergency circumstances: first-come, first-served, or random selection (also known as the lottery method). According to Miller, "Defenders of this view advocate that who receives the scarce medical resource in question should be a matter of luck, not deliberate human choice."[33] (Like random selection, first-come, first-served depends on luck to determine the order in which people receive a scarce resource.) In terms of the decision facing the technician, this approach would suggest that who receives the chambers might be decided by lot:

all persons would have an equal chance of receiving a chamber, and no one would be required to make a judgment about the social worth of someone else's life—or of his or her own.

Advocates of this approach argue that it not only better reflects the ethical commitment to the equality of persons than the utilitarian approach, but will have positive consequences as well. First, people will be much happier if this method of distribution is used, because they won't feel that they have been unfairly discriminated against when these decisions are made. Second, they argue that it will promote a healthy relationship between physician and patient, a relationship that is based on trust: "Trust requires a belief that one will be dealt with fairly; and if in situations of scarcity resources are allocated by a method of random selection, then candidates can be confident that they have been treated impartially."[34] Third, advocates hope that those who do not receive the scarce medical resource will feel better if they know that they lost out as a result of an impartial process: "It is one thing to lose because of bad luck; it is much more devastating to be told that you are unqualified."[35] And, finally, some believe that this approach will lead to a quicker resolution of the shortage of the resource than the social worth approach, because those who have the power to make changes in the way in which societal resources are distributed will want to ensure that their chance of getting the resource, if they should need it, is increased. If politicians, for instance, knew that their access to scarce medical goods was dependent on a lottery, they would work to put policies in place to ensure that supplies of the resource in question were increased. For all these reasons, both ethical and practical, the variations on the random selection approach have much to recommend them.

Despite this, however, questions have been asked about whether this approach can really be kept free of at least some social worth criteria, and whether, indeed, it should be. Consider, again, the situation facing the cryogenics technician. Suppose that a decision is made to remove the five people already occupying the chambers (thus ensuring their certain death), so that 10 chambers are now available. It is then decided to choose who will be placed in the chambers by drawing lots. Both cryogenics technicians get spots, as do the handicapped infant, the young girl, the elderly novelist, the spiritual leader, the farmer's wife, the two politicians, and the doctor. The farmer, the water-treatment specialist, and the environmental scientist are left out. As a consequence, the cryogenics process, which can be started automatically, is not supervised, and unexpected technical difficulties occur. These problems are exacerbated by the attempts of the gangster to destroy the machinery. As a result of the flawed cryogenics process, all of those inside the chambers die, and everyone outside them succumbs to the pandemic. Rather than saving 10 people by making difficult choices based on social worth criteria, the possibly fairer method of drawing lots leads to the deaths of everyone. This suggests that the random selection approach requires at least some exceptions, or scarce resources will end up being used in ways that are detrimental to everyone. And, as McConnell points out, "allowing for one exception may open Pandora's box; once the first is allowed, many others will follow, and the merits of the lottery method will be lost."[36] For instance, once we allow that it makes sense to make sure that one of the technicians is left outside the chambers to ensure that the process goes smoothly, and that it might make more sense from the perspective of survival to save the farmer rather than the novelist, we have to ask whether we are not "wasting" a precious chamber if we use it on the infant, who has only a small chance of surviving because of her handicaps.

The pandemic situation, while contrived, has close parallels in real-world decision making, whether these decisions are made in an emergency room, a long-term care facility, or by policy-makers. The emergence of Ebola as a global concern demonstrates how quickly diseases can appear, that they are unlikely to remain within national borders, and that difficult decisions must be made about how medical resources are distributed. Ebola also highlights the issue of global disparities in health care, and the tendency of individuals and governments in the developed world to pay attention to diseases only when they pose a threat to themselves. In addition, there are concerns that we are long overdue for a worldwide flu pandemic; recent potential candidates have included avian influenza, SARS, and H1N1, the so-called "swine flu." According to an article in the journal *Science*, the costs of an actual flu pandemic would be immense in both human and economic terms: in the U.S., it is estimated that 90 million people would become ill, 1.9 million would die, and 10 million would be hospitalized. Of those hospitalized, 1.5 million are likely to need intensive care beds.[37] Furthermore, there would not be enough vaccine available to vaccinate everyone if a flu pandemic were to occur, and the question, of course, becomes: on what basis should these scarce medical resources be distributed?

In an attempt to avoid making controversial social worth judgments, the U.S. National Vaccine Advisory Committee (NVAC) and the Advisory Committee on Immunization Policy (ACIP) have recommended a save-the-most-lives policy. Using this approach, workers engaged in vaccine production and front-line health care workers would receive top priority, followed by the ill elderly; healthy individuals between the ages of 2 to 64 are at the very bottom of the list, below embalmers. According to advocates of this approach, those at the top of the list "get higher priority not because they are intrinsically more valuable people or of greater 'social worth', but because giving them first priority ensures that maximal life-saving vaccine is produced and so that health care is provided to the sick. Consequently, it values all human life equally, giving each person equal consideration in who gets priority, regardless of age, disability, social class, or employment."[38]

Two questions can be asked about this proposal. First, has it really avoided making social worth judgments? And, second, is it an approach that makes the best use of a scarce medical resource? In terms of the first question, a case can be made that it does not avoid making social worth judgments, but, rather, explicitly embodies them: to give priority to those who produce vaccines, front-line health care workers, and embalmers before other healthy individuals is precisely to make a judgment about what they can contribute to others—in other words, to make a social worth judgment that most utilitarians would have no difficulty accepting! In fact, it is arguably the case that *any* prioritization that goes beyond that of first-come, first-served or random selection involves a social worth judgment of some sort. The confusion here seems to be that judgments of social worth are being correlated with judgments of moral worth; in fact, however, the two are quite distinct.

Once this point is made, we can ask the second question. If this approach cannot be simply defended on the ground that it avoids morally problematic judgments about the social worth of particular individuals, do its recommendations provide for the best use of a scarce resource? Should the elderly and those who are already ill be vaccinated before those who are young and healthy? Emmanuel and Wertheimer suggest that this approach does not make good use of a scarce resource, and we will consider their arguments in the next section. What it is important to note, however, is that some judgments must be made. Pure random selection, or first-come, first-served approaches, seem to generate an inefficient and, therefore, ethically problematic (more harm is done than good) distribution of scarce resources, at least on occasion. Consequently, while it may have a place at some stage in decisions about the use of scarce resources (once we have determined who ought to receive the resources, based on criteria such as who is likely to benefit, we might then choose randomly if the demand for the resource still exceeds the supply), we must find a method of distribution that allows us to make choices that both use scarce resources efficiently and avoid the more ethically problematic aspects of social worth criteria. Such an approach is difficult to find, and will probably remain controversial, because most people would like to believe that these hard choices can be avoided. Despite our inclinations, however, such an approach needs to be found because health care resources are limited, while needs—whether inherent, subjective, or socially constructed—are limitless.

Virtue Ethics–Based Approaches

While not much has been written about health care allocation decisions and virtue ethics, virtue ethics, arguably, offers a potentially fruitful approach to those decisions. First, what such an approach would do is encourage us to ask different questions about medical resource allocation than those asked by Kantians and utilitarians. It would connect medical choices to the concept of a whole human life, and what it is appropriate for the system to provide, and users to expect, given the different stages into which our lives normally fall. Moreover, a virtue ethicist would recognize that part of what gives our lives form and purpose lies in their impermanence: part of what it means to be human is that we are mortal, that our lives will come to an end, and that at least some suffering is part of the human condition. The question for a virtue ethicist, when considering what medical care is appropriate for those who are close to the end of life (whether young or old), would be not so much how to postpone death and eliminate suffering, but, rather, how to help people die well and how to make suffering meaningful.

Second, a virtue ethicist would encourage decision-makers to strive for excellence at all levels of the system. Those who make choices at the macro level would have to ask themselves what being excellent stewards of public resources requires of them; those at the meso level would have to consider the teleological purposes built into the organizations that they are responsible for, and would have to make allocation decisions that best accord with those goals; and, finally, both patients and health care providers would have to strive for excellence in their use of resources. How many resources should an excellent patient expect or demand from the system? How would an excellent doctor or nurse distribute those resources to patients?

Rather than making hard-and-fast rules about what medical services should be provided by a health care system (as both Kantians and utilitarians are likely to do, though on different grounds and for different reasons), a virtue ethicist is likely to argue that what is provided to particular patients (and what particular patients should expect from the system) should be tied to norms built in by nature. Consider a procedure such as in vitro fertilization (IVF), which some jurisdictions provide within their health care systems and others exclude. Rather than simply arguing that such a procedure should be included or excluded, a virtue ethicist would assert that it is inappropriate to provide IVF to a 60-year-old woman (who is clearly beyond the age at which pregnancy could occur naturally), but would claim (perhaps) that it should be provided to women who fall within the age range in which pregnancy should normally occur.

In addition, because virtue ethics places a requirement on all of us to strive for excellence (as individuals, as citizens, as patients, and so forth), a virtue ethicist would expect a 60-year-old woman to recognize that a demand to become a mother, given the risks to her own health and the health of her child, as well as the likelihood that she will not be able to care adequately (as an excellent parent should) for that child until it reaches maturity, is unreasonable. To expect such treatment at her age would not indicate a virtuous character, even though the same request from a 25-year-old woman might.

Feminist Approaches

While utilitarian and Kantian approaches are used most often in allocation decisions, feminist ethics would remind us to think, in particular, about the ways in which distributive choices (whether made on utilitarian or Kantian grounds) affect those who are already oppressed and marginalized. This has profound implications for medicine and for how we might understand the choices made in this context. Medicine is one of the most important and powerful institutions in our society, and feminist bioethicists ask probing questions about the patriarchal assumptions that may be built into its practice and how the larger sexist assumptions prevalent in society might manifest themselves in decisions about the best use of medical resources. This point can be best illustrated through an example. Imagine a 76-year-old woman, suffering from cancer, who is considering whether she should go through another round of treatment. With the encouragement of the doctors treating her, she is moving toward the decision not to accept chemotherapy and to switch to (less expensive) palliative care instead.[39] While Kantians and utilitarians would view this as a case of an autonomous individual making a medical decision with the help of her doctors, feminist ethics would ask us to look more deeply. We might ask, for instance, whether the woman is reluctant to continue treatment because she fears being a burden to her children or a cost to the medical system in a way that a man her age might not, and whether her doctors are treating her differently than they might a man in her situation because they perceive her life to be less valuable than his. Feminists might also ask why, given that women tend to live longer than men, so few resources are committed by society to meeting their particular needs. Suppose, further, that the woman is a member of a minority group that has suffered from overt discrimination in the recent past: might this also have some bearing on how the medical staff are treating her, even if they are not consciously aware that they are biased in any way? Feminist ethicists, in short, try to make visible the power structures that may affect our thinking about resource allocation in ways we are not conscious of.

Diego Rivera, *The History of Medicine in Mexico: The People's Demand for Better Health*, 1953. Medical resources are limited, and the way in which they are distributed within a society through its medical system raises important ethical questions. Medical systems are themselves shaped by social values and political commitments.

GUIDELINES FOR LIMITING HEALTH CARE

Discussions of distributive choices within the context of health care often situate the choice within a narrow framework: Given this particular group of people who need a kidney transplant, who should receive it? Who should receive a cryogenics chamber? This perspective arguably encourages us to think that we are making moral judgments about the human worth of particular individuals when we make distributive decisions, rather than decisions about the policies that should guide our choices. However, since the demand for health care resources will probably always exceed the supply, the challenge is to find some morally defensible—rather than morally non-controversial—basis for our distributive choices. We will consider three proposals in this section, all of which try to situate distributive decisions about health care within a broader context than they are sometimes considered: the context of a whole life lived within a human community. Once these considerations are located within this broad context, we can see more clearly the natural limitations that might guide our choices: limitations imposed by our biology and by the obligations we have to other members of our shared society. We can then begin a discussion about how our recognition of these limits might be incorporated into the practice of medicine.

Callahan's Proposal: Age as a Standard

One of the most influential proposals for limiting treatment has been put forward by Callahan. In an essay entitled "Aging and the Ends of Medicine," Callahan begins by asking whether a 76-year-old should receive a liver transplant. In order to answer this question, he places the choice within the context of the costs of health care, the social dimensions of the choices we make, and the goals of medicine. He believes that, when these considerations are taken into account, not only can we not continue on our present path, but we also *should* not: "Even if we could find a way to radically increase the proportion of our health care dollar going to the elderly, it is not clear that that would be a good social investment."[40]

We need to recognize, Callahan believes, that spending increasing amounts of money on research and treatments that extend the lives of the elderly involves trade-offs: money spent for these purposes is money diverted from other areas—including "decent long-term care"[41] that might better meet their needs. Moreover, not only does it divert resources from areas that might better meet the needs of the elderly themselves, it also means that these funds cannot be used by other groups within society, particularly children: "The federal government ... spends six times as much on health care for those over 65 as for those under 18."[42] While these economic concerns are significant, they should not, Callahan believes, be our sole focus: rather, they should prompt us to ask deeper questions about the goals of medicine, the inevitability of death, and the normal correlation of aging with death. Unlike other cultures, which have accepted the process of aging and accord great respect to those who are old, contemporary Western culture, rather than seeing old age as being, in part, "a time of preparation for death,"[43] tends to deny the reality of death. This means that we are reluctant to ask important questions about the meaning and significance of the process of aging, given the inevitability of death: "Our culture seems increasingly ... to think of aging as hardly more than another disease, to be fought and rejected."[44]

What we need to do, Callahan believes, is first understand that aging, and even dying, can be meaningful and significant, and then understand that medicine should not attempt to avert this natural process at all costs. Callahan notes, however, that acceptance of this view will require a major shift in our cultural thinking, both about medicine and about aging. It will require, first of all, that the elderly themselves recognize that they have obligations to others and that they should not demand that an unfair share of societal resources be devoted to them. This is, of course, contrary to the cultural message that the elderly are currently being sent, in which old age is characterized as a time of liberation and self-fulfilment uncontaminated by obligations and filled with possibilities for cruises, cottages, and golf. When this is the way that old age is portrayed, Callahan believes, the elderly themselves are done a disservice, because "by pretending that old age can be turned into a kind of endless middle age, we rob it of meaning and significance for the elderly themselves. It is a way of saying that old age can be acceptable only to the extent that it can mimic the vitality of the younger years."[45]

What we should focus on, instead, is the concept of a "natural lifespan." Humans are biological organisms, and we are not designed to last forever. We have a difficult time accepting this fact, however, because technology has been very successful in prolonging life. But prolongation of life—perhaps of life that is filled with suffering and decline—is not what we should aim for. A natural lifespan, as Callahan understands it, incorporates both chronological age (he believes that someone has lived out a natural lifespan by their late seventies, or sometime in their eighties), and what he calls a biographical standard, in which aging means that a person has passed through the normal stages and experiences of life and consequently has less of a future than a past. He writes: "We would not make long-term plans with an elderly person, nor would we likely invite him to take charge of strenuous long-term projects, even if he were highly talented. For his part, he would not be likely to undertake a total change of his way of life, such as immigrating to another country, or undertaking extensive training for a new career."[46]

BOX 2.1

DANIEL CALLAHAN, "AGING AND THE ENDS OF MEDICINE"

The future goal of medicine in the care of the aged should be that of improving the quality of life, not in seeking ways to extend that life. In its longstanding ambition to forestall death, medicine has in the care of the aged reached its last frontier. That is hardly because death is absent elsewhere—children and young adults obviously still die of maladies that are open to potential cure—but because the largest number of deaths (some 70%) now occur among those over the age of 65, with the largest proportion in those over 85. If death is ever to be humbled, that is where the essentially endless work remains to be done. But however tempting that challenge, medicine should now restrain its ambition at that frontier. To do otherwise will, I believe, be to court harm to the needs of other age groups and to the old themselves.

Yet to ask medicine to restrain itself in the face of aging and death is to ask more than it, or the public that sustains it, is likely to find agreeable. Only a fresh understanding of the ends and meaning of aging, encompassing two conditions, are likely to make a plausible stance. The first is that we—both young and old—need to understand that it is possible to live out a meaningful old age that is limited in time, one that does not require a compulsive effort to turn to medicine for more life to make it bearable. The second condition is that, as a culture, we need a more supportive context for aging and death, one that cherishes and respects the elderly while at the same time recognizing that their primary orientation should be to the young and the generations to come, not to their own age group. It will be no less necessary to recognize that in the passing of the generations lies the constant reinvigoration of biological life....

Earlier generations accepted the idea that there was a natural life span—the biblical norm of three score years and ten captures that notion (even though, in fact, that was a much longer life span than was then typically the case). It is an idea well worth reconsidering, and would provide us with a meaningful and realizable goal. Modern medicine and biology have done much, however, to wean us away from that kind of thinking. They have insinuated the belief that the average life span is not a natural fact at all, but instead one that is strictly dependent upon the state of medical knowledge and skill....

But that is not what I think we ought to mean by a natural life span. We need a notion of a full life that is based on some deeper understanding of human need and sensible possibility, not the latest state of medical technology or medical possibility. We should instead think of a natural lifespan as the achievement of a life long enough to accomplish for the most part those opportunities that life typically affords people and which we ordinarily take to be the prime benefits of enjoying a life at all—that of loving and living, of raising a family, of finding and carrying out work that is satisfying, of reading and thinking, and of cherishing our friends and families....

A longer life does not guarantee a better life—there is no inherent connection between the two. No matter how long medicine enabled people to live, death at any time—at age 90, or 100, or 110—would frustrate some possibility, some as-yet-unrealized goal. There is sadness in that realization, but not tragedy. An easily preventable death of a young child is an outrage. The death from an incurable disease of someone in the prime of young adulthood is a tragedy. But death at an old age, after a long and full life, is simply sad, a part of life itself.

As it confronts aging, medicine should have as its specific goal that of averting premature death, understood as death prior to a natural life span, and the relief of suffering thereafter. It should pursue those goals in order that the elderly can finish out their years with as little needless pain as possible, and with as much vigor as can be generated in contributing to the welfare of younger age groups and to the community of which they are a part.

Source: Daniel Callahan, "Aging and the Ends of Medicine," *Annals of the New York Academy of Sciences*, 530 (June 15, 1988): 125–132.

The notion of a natural lifespan in connection with this biographical standard has implications for health care, in that, once this point is reached, Callahan believes that medical treatment should not be oriented toward prolonging life at all costs, but, rather, to ensuring that what time remains is as satisfying and free from pain as possible. Moreover, the death of someone after this natural lifespan is achieved is sad, not tragic: "An easily preventable death of a young child is an outrage. The death from an incurable disease of someone in the prime of young adulthood is a tragedy. But death from old age, after a long and full life, is simply sad, a part of life itself."[47]

Callahan's proposals have implications for the development and use of medical technology. As we have seen, one of the reasons health care costs are continually rising is the development and use of new technologies. Callahan observes that, while this technology can often prolong the lives of the elderly, it does so at a very high cost, both economically and personally. He proposes three principles that can serve as guidelines for the limitation of treatment (thus saving scarce health care resources) while simultaneously respecting the dignity of elderly persons. First, he believes, "government has a duty, based in our collective social obligations to each other, to help people live out a natural lifespan, but not actively to help medically extend life beyond that point."[48] Second, government obligations to provide health care extend only to the provision of "life-extending technology necessary for medicine to achieve and serve the end of a natural lifespan."[49] And, third, once someone has achieved a natural lifespan, government is obligated only to provide medical care that relieves suffering. To make—and follow—these recommendations does not, Callahan believes, mean that we are making ethically problematic judgments about the social worth of the elderly. If the reason for limiting the medical care provided was because we judge that the life of the person in question is not worth prolonging, we would be making precisely this sort of judgment. However, Callahan argues, age can serve as a reasonable criterion for decisions about goals and plans of care because, when these decisions are made appropriately, they both respect the dignity of the elderly person and allow for the responsible use of a shared, but limited, social resource. He writes, "For many people, beginning with the aged themselves, old age is a reason in itself to think about medical care in a different way, whether in foregoing its lifesaving powers when death is clearly imminent, or in foregoing its use even when death may be distant but life has become a blight rather than a blessing."[50]

The Life-Cycle Allocation Principle

Emmanuel and Wertheimer suggest a different principle for distribution, a modified "life-cycle allocation principle." This principle, like Callahan's, situates the particular medical decisions we make within the context of a person's whole life. Unlike Callahan's principle, however, it allows for limitations in the use of health care resources at both the lower and upper ends of life. This principle takes, as its starting point, an acceptance of the fact that medical resources are limited: as noted above, Emmanuel and Wertheimer apply it to the question of who should receive scarce flu vaccine in the case of a pandemic.

The life-cycle allocation principle extrapolates societal distribution from a principle most of us would use in our own lives—namely, that, if given the choice, "we would prioritize our resources to ensure that we could live past the illnesses of childhood and into young adulthood and would allocate fewer resources to living even longer once we reached old age."[51] So far, this sounds similar to Callahan's proposal; like his, the life-cycle allocation principle also suggests that a responsible use of resources would involve limiting them in the case of those who have achieved a full lifespan. They continue: "Death seems more tragic when a child or young adult dies than an elderly person—not because the lives of older people are less valuable, but because the younger person has not had the opportunity to live and develop through all stages of life."[52] This distributive principle, they believe, is morally defensible because it is strictly egalitarian and not based on problematic judgments of social worth: every person who does not die prematurely will, over the course of their lives, have an equal opportunity to benefit from the resources available.

There is, however, one significant difference between the proposal put forward by Callahan and the one put forward by Emanuel and Wertheimer: the latter believe that the pure form of the principle, which would give priority to the very youngest, and then to the next youngest, and so on (the baby would receive a chamber first, then the young girl, and so on), should be supplemented by what they call an investment refinement.

This investment refinement considers not only the years a person (probably) has left to live, but, also, the amount already invested in creating a life. When these things—the life-cycle allocation principle and the investment refinement principle—are balanced with one another, further gradations within a lifespan can be made: "Within this framework, 20-year-old adults are valued more than 1-year-old toddlers because the older individuals have more developed interests, hopes, and plans, but have not had the opportunity to realize them."[53]

BOX 2.2

EZEKIEL J. EMMANUEL AND ALAN WERTHEIMER, "WHO SHOULD GET INFLUENZA VACCINE WHEN NOT ALL CAN?"

The potential threat of pandemic influenza is staggering: 1.9 million deaths, 90 million people sick, and nearly 10 million people hospitalized, with almost 1.5 million requiring intensive-care units (ICUs) in the United States. The National Vaccine Advisory Committee ... and the Advisory Committee on Immunization Policy ... have jointly recommended a prioritization scheme that places vaccine workers, health-care providers, and the ill elderly at the top, and healthy people aged 2 to 64 at the very bottom, even under embalmers.... The primary goal informing the recommendation was to "decrease health impacts including severe morbidity and death"; a secondary goal was minimizing societal and economic impacts. As the NVAC and ACIP acknowledge, such important policy decisions require broad national discussion. In this spirit, we believe an alternative ethical framework should be considered....

Many potential ethical principles for rationing health care have been proposed. "Save the most lives" is commonly used in emergencies, such as burning buildings, although "women and children first" played a role on the *Titanic*. "First come, first served" operates in other emergencies and in ICUs when admitted patients retain beds despite the presentation of another patient who is equally or even more sick; "Save the most quality life years" is central to cost-effectiveness rationing. "Save the worst-off" plays a role in allocating organs for transplantation. "Reciprocity"—giving priority to people willing to donate their own organs—has been proposed. "Save those most likely to fully recover" guided priorities for giving penicillin to soldiers with syphilis in World War Ii. Save those "instrumental in making society flourish" through economic productivity or by "contributing to the well-being of others" has been proposed....

The save-the-most-lives principle was invoked by NVAC and ACIP. It justifies giving top priority to workers engaged in vaccine production and distribution and health-care workers. They get higher priority not because they are intrinsically more valuable people or of greater "social worth," but because giving them first priority ensures that maximal life-saving vaccine is produced and so that health care is provided to the sick. Consequently, it values all human life equally, giving every person equal consideration in who gets priority regardless of age, disability, social class, or employment. After these groups, the save-the-most-lives principle justifies priority for those predicted to be at highest risk of hospitalization and dying. We disagree with this prioritization....

The save-the-most-lives principle may be justified in some emergencies when decision urgency makes it infeasible to deliberate about priority rankings and impractical to categorize individuals into priority groups. We believe that a life-cycle allocation principle ... based on the idea that each person should have an opportunity to live through all the stages of life is more appropriate for a pandemic. There is a great value in being able to pass through each life stage—to be a child, a young adult, and to then develop a career and family, and to grow old—and to enjoy a wide range of the opportunities during each stage.

Multiple considerations and intuitions support this ethical principle. Most people endorse this principle for themselves. We would prioritize our own resources to ensure we could live past the illnesses of childhood and young adulthood and would allocate fewer resources to living ever longer once we reached old age. People strongly prefer maximizing the chance of living to a ripe old age, rather than being struck down as a young person.

Death seems more tragic when a child or young adult dies than an elderly person—not because the lives of older people are less valuable, but because the younger person has not had the opportunity to live and develop through all stages of life. Although the life-cycle principle favors some ages, it is also intrinsically egalitarian. Unlike being productive or contributing to others' well-being, every person will live to be older unless their life is cut short....

A pure version of the life-cycle principle would grant priority to 6-month-olds over 1-year-olds who have priority over 2-year-olds, and on. An alternative, the investment refinement, emphasizes gradations within a life span. It gives priority to people between early adolescence and middle age on the basis of the amount the person invested in his or her life balanced by the amount left to live. Within this framework, 20-year-olds are valued more than 1-year-olds because the older individuals have more developed interests, hopes and plans but have not had an opportunity to realize them....

Source: Ezekiel J. Emmanuel and Alan Wertheimer, "Who Should Get Influenza Vaccine When Not All Can?" *Science*, 312, no. 5775 (May 12, 2006):1 854–855.

In addition, Emanuel and Wertheimer think that, in emergency situations (such as a flu pandemic) at least, priority should be given to maintaining public order. This means that those who are necessary to ensure the safety and well-being of others should have medical priority. For example, if a flu pandemic were to occur, this principle would suggest that health care workers and vaccine manufacturers would have priority; however, given the other two principles, vaccinating the sick elderly and infants would be a lesser priority than ensuring that healthy teenagers and adults are vaccinated. Interestingly enough, Emanuel and Wertheimer suggest a consequentialist defence of this approach as well: it may save more lives, in practice, than the save-the-most-lives principle they are critiquing, given that most victims of the 1918 flu pandemic were healthy young adults!

Of course, while they are considering these rationing principles in the context of a flu pandemic situation—an obvious medical emergency—these principles can be applied to health care decision making more generally. While the scenario they are considering (like the situation facing the cryogenics technician) makes it clear that hard choices are unavoidable, this is actually the case within all health care systems. As many observers have pointed out, in the United States, Canada, and elsewhere, health care is approaching a crisis, and this crisis cannot be resolved by simply putting more money into the system at the cost of other obligations and social priorities. Rather, it will require a shift in our attitudes about the uses of medical technology, about aging, and about death, along with some form of rationing. Whether the proposals we have just considered are the appropriate ones to guide this rationing is a matter of debate. (Callahan's proposals, for instance, have been criticized on the ground that they disproportionately disadvantage women, who make up a majority of older citizens; and any attempt to limit the health care given to the very young, outside of the most dire and immediate emergencies, is likely to lead to howls of protest and would probably be politically unacceptable.) However, the fact remains that some transparent guidelines for distributing scarce health care resources will have to be found, and a public debate about this distributive principle is ultimately unavoidable. From this perspective, Callahan's proposal is promising, since it respects the dignity of the elderly, is egalitarian (all of those who achieve a full lifespan can expect similar treatment), and requires what is arguably a necessary rethinking of our almost unquestioned reliance on medical technology and our reluctance to acknowledge the limits of our own biology.

Daniels' Prudential Lifespan Account

Daniels makes a third proposal, one that locates our thinking about appropriate health care within larger questions about the nature of a just society and the obligations of citizenship. He uses Rawls' theory of justice[54] to argue that access to health care is a requirement of justice under the principle of "fair equality of opportunity." Equality of opportunity is the concept that "[i]nequalities of income and prestige etc. are assumed to be justified if and only if there was fair competition in the awarding of the offices and positions that yield those benefits."[55] No one, therefore, should be disadvantaged by his sex, race, or social background. While theoretical disagreement exists about what is needed to ensure fair equality of opportunity, all accounts share the idea that "it is fair for individuals to have unequal shares of social goods if those inequalities are earned and deserved by the individual, that is, if they are the product of the individual's actions and choices. But it is unfair for individuals to be disadvantaged or privileged by arbitrary and undeserved differences in their social circumstances."[56] Daniels connects this concept to health care by arguing that fair equality of opportunity requires us to "include health care institutions among those basic institutions of a society [encompassed by a theory of justice because] … social obligations to provide health care services that protect and restore normal functioning [exist]."[57] By normal functioning, Daniels understands the capacities that are appropriate and expected for individuals in particular age groups. These capacities would be different for a 20-year-old person, a 50-year-old person, and a 90-year-old person.

Daniels argues that Rawls' theory of justice has implications both for access to a health care system and for resource allocation within it. In terms of access, it "implies that there should be no financial, geographical, or discriminatory barriers to a level of care that promotes normal functioning."[58] In terms of allocation, Daniels says, it "implies that resources be allocated in ways that are effective in promoting normal functioning,"[59] which places some limits on which health care needs are met. Given the reality of moderate scarcity of resources, in order to protect equal access to health care that promotes normal functioning, "we must weigh new technologies against alternatives to judge the overall impact of introducing them on fair equality of opportunity."[60]

On this basis, Daniels argues for what he calls "the Prudential Lifespan Account," a concept that asks us to "imagine that each of us has a lifetime allocation of health care services, which we can claim only if the appropriate need arises.... Our task now is to allocate that fair share over the lifespan—and to do so prudently."[61] In order to determine what a prudential use of health care resources might be, Daniels says, we should "pretend that we do not know how old we are. We must allocate these resources imagining that we must live our whole lives with the result of our choices."[62] Daniels also believes that age is relevant to considerations of distributive justice within a health care system, because the fact that we all age is something that we all share; it is not, therefore, a morally arbitrary characteristic of an individual in the way that sex and race are. Consequently, according to Daniels, "[I]f I treat the old one way, and the young another, and I do so over their whole lives, then I treat all persons the same way. No inequality is produced."[63] Therefore, Daniels believes, we should be conscious of what needs people are likely to have at each stage of life and which of these are most important; this will, in turn, help us determine what needs the health care system must meet to ensure normal functioning at each stage of life and which it can treat as less important.

This approach suggests, for instance, that facelifts for 60-year-old women would not need to be covered by a public health care system because they are not required for normal functioning. Likewise, treatments thought appropriate for 30-year-old men, such as open heart surgery, might not be thought necessary for 90-year-old males with the same heart problems. It also suggests that individuals should themselves take some responsibility for the demands they make on the health care system, as they keep the concept of a lifetime prudential account—which can be understood as each person's fair share of communal health care resources—in mind.

DISTRIBUTION AND PROCEDURAL JUSTICE

Whatever the merits of the proposals we have considered, and any others that might be advanced, it is unlikely that any one allocation model will be accepted as just and fair by everyone. Moreover, the application of any particular guideline for resource limitation within a health care system creates winners and losers: those who benefit from the guideline chosen, and those who are disadvantaged by it. This fact, Daniels argues, raises what he calls "the legitimacy problem." It is a fundamental principle of justice, many believe, that those who exercise power must be seen as legitimate authorities in the eyes of those who are affected by their decisions. Daniels asks: "Under what conditions do decision makers have the *moral authority* to set the limits they impose?"[64] It is not enough, Daniels believes, that decision-makers simply come up with defensible guidelines for the limitations they impose; rather, they have an additional moral requirement to ensure that the process by which they determined that guideline meets certain conditions. In the case of health care, what this means is that decision-makers at all levels of the system must engage in processes that can be seen as fair and reasonable even by those who "lose out" in the resulting allocation choices. Daniels calls this process "accountability for reasonableness."

Accountability for reasonableness, as Daniels envisages it, must demonstrate four features. First, it must meet the *Publicity Condition*: this requires that the decisions made about how health care goods and services are allocated must be accessible to the public, not made behind closed doors or by secretive committees. The second condition is the *Relevance Condition*. By this, Daniels means that the "rationales for limit-setting decisions should aim to provide a *reasonable* explanation of how the organization seeks to provide 'value for money' in meeting the varied health needs of a defined population under reasonable resource constraints."[65] By "reasonable," Daniels means that the rationale must be one that calls on evidence in its support, and relies on principles that "fair-minded" individuals—"people who are disposed to finding mutually justifiable terms of cooperation"[66]— would be likely to accept. That is to say, a decision-making process is legitimate as long as people who are co-operative, reasonable, and share a commitment to fairness agree that it is; however, this condition does not require that there be universal agreement on the distributive principles chosen.

Third, Daniels lists the *Revisions and Appeals Condition*. This condition requires that the process contain mechanisms by which challenges to whatever decisions have been made can be lodged, and that procedures for dispute resolution and the revision of policies are available. These policies and decisions should be responsive to rational arguments and new evidence. The final condition is the *Regulative Condition*. It requires that the process be regulated to ensure that the first three conditions are met.

While meeting the requirements of "accountability for reasonableness" will not resolve all disagreements about the appropriate uses of health care resources, it will both impose requirements on those who make decisions about their distribution and allow them to defend those decisions to the people who are affected by them and, in particular, to those who benefit the least from them. This, in turn, may make it easier for those who are most disadvantaged by particular choices to accept that, despite this, the decisions made were fair and accessible, and that the people who made them are accountable to those who are affected by them.

DISTRIBUTIVE JUSTICE AND GLOBAL CONCERNS

Anyone living in one of the world's industrialized societies in the 1970s had reason for great optimism: all the infectious diseases such as polio, tuberculosis, and syphilis that had plagued earlier generations were under control, and cures for the remaining common killers, cancer and heart disease, seemed just around the corner. This optimism had social consequences: because people could assume that any children they had would live to grow up, people began to have smaller families; and because sexually transmitted diseases, such as syphilis, could be cured by antibiotics, they lost much of the stigma that had previously accompanied a diagnosis. This, along with the development of reliable methods of birth control, led to a change in attitudes toward sexual behaviour. Many people felt free to experiment sexually, with a number of different partners.

This optimism was shattered in the early 1980s. In June 1981, the Centers for Disease Control (CDC) in the United States reported the first cases of young men suffering from a mysterious and apparently new disease. Shortly after, more cases were reported in New York City. These patients appeared to have received a devastating attack on their immune systems; as a result, they were suffering from a variety of unusual diseases, including a previously rare form of pneumonia (pneumocystis carinii) and a form of cancer called Kaposi's Sarcoma, which previously was most commonly found in older men from particular ethnic backgrounds.

What these first victims had in common appeared to be what might be called lifestyle factors: they were homosexual, bisexual, or intravenous drug users, and it was speculated that these factors might be responsible for the disease itself. This possibility led to discrimination directed toward people who fell into these categories, because the identification of a new disease with an unknown mode of transmission generated a great deal of fear. In this period, many of the ethical issues generated by the disease centred on the need to prevent discriminatory practices directed at those who were suffering from it.

BOX 2.3

LEIGH TURNER, "BIOETHICS NEEDS TO RETHINK ITS AGENDA"

What issues belong at the top of the agenda in bioethics? What important topics are commonly ignored? Does bioethics matter?... Bioethicists commonly address ethical issues arising in wealthy developed countries. Discussions about priority setting and resource allocation typically occur within the context of a particular developed state. While analyses of globalization and international inequity in access to basic goods such as food, clean water, and shelter are beginning to appear in bioethics scholarship, bioethicists have traditionally tended not to think at the transnational level of analysis or addressed issues relating to the developing world.

Perhaps one reason bioethicists are reluctant to address global ethical issues related to health, illness, and poverty is that bioethics are deeply embedded in a global economic system that depends on the continued existence of impoverished societies.... Many of the goods enjoyed by citizens of wealthy nations are available for consumption because of the continued existence of massive economic disparities between wealthy and poor nations.

Most of us would prefer not to confront the incredible disparity between living as a professor or clinician in a smart apartment in Manhattan and eking out a living in one of China's rapidly industrializing districts or a shantytown in South Africa.... Many bioethicists ... see these questions as macrosocial economic issues falling outside the proper scope of bioethics. And yet questions of health and illness—and ethical issues related to health systems, social institutions, and economic policies—are connected to global markets and financial institutions.

Source: Adapted from Leigh Turner, "Bioethics Needs to Rethink Its Agenda," *British Medical Journal*, 328 (January 17, 2004): 175.

In 1984, the virus now understood to be responsible for the disease was discovered, and given the name "human immunodeficiency virus," or HIV. This virus can be transmitted in three ways: through blood, semen, and breast milk. While there is presently no cure for Acquired Immune Deficiency Syndrome (or AIDS), the disease caused by infection with the virus, relatively effective treatments have been developed. As a result, for a number of those infected, the disease has been converted into a chronic condition rather than a terminal one: "The new drugs may make it possible for someone to be infected with HIV and stay alive without symptoms for decades, living long enough to die of something besides AIDS. Those infected with HIV can now contemplate a future that includes them. Instead of studying about death and dying, they can now think about living."[67]

A caveat, however, needs to be added to this claim: it should read, "Those living in a wealthy, industrialized society can now contemplate a future that includes them." These people form only a small percentage of those infected with HIV in the world, and for most sufferers—who live in Sub-Saharan Africa, and, increasingly, in parts of Asia—such treatments are unavailable. Africa has been the hardest hit: in fact, if current rates of disease spread continue, life expectancy in a number of African countries will be below 50. For example, in Angola, it is predicted to be 43; in Botswana, 51; in Rwanda, 46; in Sierra Leone, 43; in Zambia, 42; and in Zimbabwe, 43.[68] Although Sub-Saharan Africa contains only about 10 percent of the world's population, two-thirds of the people currently living with AIDS are found here, and fewer than one in three are receiving antiretroviral treatment.[69] Moreover, since HIV attacks the immune system, other diseases are spreading as well. The number of deaths from AIDS has already had devastating social and economic impacts: millions of children have been orphaned, food production has plummeted, and educational and health care systems are failing as many of those working in them die. The only hope for these people is international funding. However, such funding has often been inadequate.

CONCLUSION

If you don't know anything about a woman, except where she lives,[70] you can—despite this minimal amount of information—make an educated guess about what her life is likely to be like, how long she is likely to live, and what she is likely to die from. For instance, if she lives in a wealthy industrialized society such as Canada, the United States, or Great Britain, you can, with relative confidence, predict that she will be literate, well-nourished, drive a car, have access to advanced medical treatments, and live into her seventies or even her eighties. She will probably die of a non-infectious disease connected to aging, and, perhaps, lifestyle, such as cancer or heart disease. On the other hand, if she lives in Sub-Saharan Africa, if she has survived the infectious diseases of childhood, she is likely to have had a difficult time getting an education, sufficient food, or access to health care. She has a good chance of dying of AIDS; depending on which country she lives in, she may well die before she is 45.

This observation is deeply troubling from an ethical perspective. One of the central claims of the most important ethical theories is that, from the ethical perspective, each person matters: utilitarianism captures this insight in its assertion that each is to count for one and only one, while Kantianism reflects it in its claims about human dignity. From this perspective, a person living in Sub-Saharan Africa (or any other part of the world) is no less important than a Canadian or an American. Yet, the world functions as though some people's lives are, indeed, worth more than others.

A case can be made that the discipline of bioethics, in its present form, does not take global concerns about distribution adequately into account. Most of the issues considered by bioethicists—from the implications of the genetic revolution, to organ transplantation, to reproductive technologies—only have application within the context of a wealthy society with a well-developed and well-funded health care system. Even the issues around the just distribution of scarce health care goods that we have been considering in this chapter are usually situated within this context, within a world in which we can actually consider whether or not people in their eighties should have access to all available medical technologies, and not a world in which the life expectancy for many people is less than 50 years.

Some bioethicists are beginning to ask whether bioethics should not ask deeper and more global ethical questions: as Turner puts it,

> Some of the favourite topics of bioethicists seem trivial compared with the important health issues facing people in the world's poor countries and in impoverished regions in rich countries. Greater consideration of global ethical issues related to health, illness, and suffering might generate a richer, more meaningful research agenda for bioethics. Otherwise bioethics risks becoming a source of entertainment and spectacle in wealthy societies whose inhabitants overlook the poverty and suffering found throughout most of the world.[71]

Concerns about distributive justice are as important; indeed, questions of just distribution arise in connection with most bioethical issues, whether the question is who receives the organ, the physician's time, the infertility treatment, or the life-prolonging technology. If Turner's concerns are correct, however, the context within which we consider these concerns needs to be global rather than local if bioethics is to serve as something more than a source of "entertainment and spectacle." Those of us who are fortunate enough to live in a wealthy industrialized society with abundant resources and a well-functioning health care system are like a multi-billionaire on the lifeboat of our shared planet: our wealth far exceeds what most humans could ever aspire to. However, the lifeboat does not belong to the multibillionaire alone; if we think or act as though it does, we are committing an injustice toward those who share it with us.

PHILOSOPHICAL REFLECTION ON THOUGHT EXPERIMENTS, JOHN RAWLS, AND DISTRIBUTIVE JUSTICE

Thought experiments are imaginary scenarios designed to test and clarify ideas; they play an important role in both philosophy and science. Baggini notes that the purpose of thought experiments "is to strip away the things that complicate matters in real life in order to focus clearly on the essence of the problem."[72] As a result of this stripping away, thought experiments can allow us to test our assumptions, help confirm or refute theoretical claims, and help make ideas visible to us. Like scientific experiments, "they aim to isolate the key variables, the specific factors under examination, to see what difference they, and they alone, make to our understanding of the world."[73]

Some thought experiments are highly contrived and fanciful, while others attempt to be more realistic. Case studies, which play such an important role in thinking about bioethical issues, can be understood as a kind of thought experiment. Some thought experiments can "require us to imagine what is impractical or even impossible, either for us right now or for all people at all times," in order "to keep our focus on one core concept or problem."[74] As long as they succeed in achieving this goal, their impracticality or impossibility is not a problem.

The most successful thought experiments change how we think and how we understand the world: they show something to us that we did not see before, and after them, there is no way of going back to exactly what we thought before we encountered them. Recent political philosophy has been transformed by a thought experiment, namely, the one that underpins John Rawls' influential book *A Theory of Justice*. As Talisse observes, the political philosophy that is articulated by Rawls, called liberalism,

> sets the vocabulary with which we discuss political issues. We may say then that liberalism provides the "framework" within which our contemporary political discourse is conducted ... today's most contentious social and political issues— abortion, affirmative action, gun control, capital punishment, drug prohibition, for example—are debated in terms of individual rights and competing interests and thus presume the liberal framework.[75]

This fact is largely attributable to the success of Rawls' thought experiment.

Rawls' account of distributive justice centres on the profound moral insight that no one "deserves his greater natural capacity nor merits a more favourable place in society."[76] The notion of "just deserts" is a moral one that is closely connected to what it is in our power to do—you deserve your good mark if you worked hard in a course and did well on the assignments and the exam; he deserves praise for the contributions he makes to charity; she deserves to be punished for running a Ponzi scheme that bankrupted her victims and led to several suicides. None of us, however, deserves to be intelligent or stupid, talented or untalented, good-looking or ugly, born into a wealthy family or a poor one, and so on. These things are beyond our control and therefore morally arbitrary, which means that we can take no credit for positive attributes of this sort and no blame for negative ones.

We currently live in a world, though, that rewards people for precisely those characteristics that are beyond our control. For example, even in Canada, a child born into a poor family will have a very different life than a child born into a rich one; those who are beautiful will be treated very differently than those who are plain (some studies have even correlated physical attractiveness with career success); and those who are intelligent will have opportunities that are unavailable to those who are not. While Rawls confines his claims about justice to social arrangements that hold in particular societies, it is clear that this discrepancy between desert and success is multiplied when we consider matters from a global perspective.

This discrepancy between what individuals can expect from life and what they deserve means, Rawls argues, that the fundamental problem of justice is to regulate those particular inequalities that arise from the fact that the basic structure of society "favours some starting places over others in the division of the benefits of social cooperation."[77] Consequently, principles of justice must be chosen that "attempt to mitigate the arbitrariness of natural contingency and social fortune"[78] if a society is to consider itself just. In short, Rawls believes that society as it is presently structured is unjust (some people disproportionately benefit from their place in the natural lottery), and he sets himself the task of designing a just alternative. He asks us to consider questions such as: What might a just society look like? How can we go about answering this question? What incentive can we give people to work toward its creation, given that those who have the power to make changes in any society are often those who have benefited the most from these unfair social arrangements?

This is where Rawls' thought experiment comes in. He asks us to imagine that all of us come together for a meeting in which we will decide how our shared society will be arranged. He calls this meeting the "Original Position," and believes that it is reasonable to suppose that any principles of justice that are chosen here will not be ones that benefit some people more than others as a result of their particular circumstances. Likewise, he believes that the principles adopted should not reflect the views and aspirations of particular individuals. Morally arbitrary distinctions between individuals must not be allowed to affect the outcome of the deliberations, and all must be equally represented as moral persons. The aim of the Original Position, Rawls states, "is to rule out those principles that it would be rational to propose for acceptance, however little chance of success, only if one knew certain things that are irrelevant from the standpoint of justice."[79] That is to say, Rawls wants to rule out principles of justice that would unfairly benefit some people at the expense of others. For example, it might be rational for someone who knew that he was a powerful orator with a great deal of charisma to try to persuade other people to endorse principles of justice that lead to his gaining power in society, even though this would not be beneficial to anyone except the orator himself.

Rawls ensures that individuals in the Original Position will not propose principles of justice that benefit them because of facts that they know about themselves (many of which are completely arbitrary from the moral perspective) by adding a further element to his thought experiment. We are, he says, to imagine that we are meeting behind a "Veil of Ignorance." What this means is that, when we go to this meeting, we will not know any of the facts about ourselves that are irrelevant from the moral perspective. This means that we will not know things such as our race or ethnicity, gender, sexual orientation, religious beliefs, conceptions of the good, marital status, wealth, intelligence, athletic ability, or appearance.

John Rawls argues that the distributive choices we make will be fairer for everyone when the decision-makers can imagine not knowing personal facts about themselves that might affect their judgments. This image of justice blindfolded captures this idea, which Rawls develops through his concept of the Veil of Ignorance.

If we don't know these things, Rawls believes, we will not choose principles that would lead to a racist or theocratic society, or ones that benefited women more than men (or vice versa), because, when we came out from behind the Veil, we might find ourselves at a severe disadvantage. Instead, we would choose two principles of justice. The first principle holds that "[e]ach person is to have an equal right to the most extensive total system of equal basic liberties compatible with a similar system of liberty for all."[80] The second principle states that "[s]ocial and economic inequalities are to be arranged so that they are both: (a) to the greatest benefit of the least advantaged ... and (b) attached to offices and positions open to all under conditions of fair equality of opportunity."[81]

In short, individuals meeting in the original position behind the Veil of Ignorance will agree to principles of justice that ensure that, if, when they emerge from behind the Veil, they turn out to be the least advantaged person in that society (the person who is at the very bottom of the social scale), they will be better off in this society than they would be in any other. Of course, both the Original Position and the Veil of Ignorance are imaginary. However, this thought experiment is one that we can all engage in, and many political philosophers and ethicists believe that it reveals some important insights into the nature of justice.

While Rawls himself did not say much about the implications of his theory for health care, a number of philosophers have used it as a basis for their deliberations about the fair distribution of goods, including health care, within a society. One of the best known is the account presented by Daniels, discussed above. While some scholars disagree with Daniels' application of Rawls' theory to health care, Daniels' account demonstrates the way in which engaging in Rawls' thought experiment can be a useful exercise. It allows us to not only think about the role that health care might play in a just society (arguably, a case can be made that individuals meeting behind the Veil would design a society that included a health care system that was easily accessible to all, including the worst-off member of society, in case they turned out to be that person), but also provides those of us living in the developed world with a way to think about our privileged position with respect to those who live in other parts of the globe. If we take Rawls' moral insight seriously, and extend his thinking to all human beings rather than confining it to the institutional arrangements of particular societies, global disparities in health and life expectations can be understood as injustices that can legitimately be considered by bioethicists.

CASE STUDIES

Scenario One

The annual budget from the provincial Ministry of Finance is usually delivered in the spring. The budget sums up the government's plans for the coming fiscal year. Imagine that you are the Minister of Finance in your province, faced with drawing up this year's budget. Unfortunately, the economy has not been doing well, and revenues have fallen short of predictions. You are aware of the failing health care system. There are many cases where patients have been turned away or put on a long waiting list due to the shortage of health care resources. You also have to deal with long-term care facilities. This sector is becoming increasingly important as the population of the province ages, and requires more and more money every year.

There are also needs for infrastructure spending on roads and bridges, as well as education. Universities, colleges, and school boards are all asking for increased funding. However, you do not have enough money to meet all these needs. You must choose how to allocate this money.

(1) How much of your budget should go to health care and why? (2) How do you weigh the competing demands of each of these sectors? (3) What might Callahan advise you to think about?

Scenario Two

Andrea Darrow has a six-year-old child who suffers from an orphan disease[82] and who will die if not treated with a very expensive medication ($25,000 a month). Because this disease is so rare, affecting less than 1500 people in all of Canada, it has received little attention from either provincial governments or pharmaceutical companies. One company does manufacture a medication, but this treatment is very expensive and not covered under any public or private health plans. Andrea has petitioned the provincial government to provide the drug and has been very successful in launching a media campaign highlighting her child's plight: all the major media outlets have been covering her daughter's story, and some commentators have called on you to support Andrea's request. The petition has landed on your desk. As Minister of Health, how should you respond?

(1) What do you tell Andrea and her supporters? (2) Do you attempt to get this disease covered under provincial health care? If so, where do you get the money? What other services are you willing to cut? (3) How should you respond to the media campaign if you decide not to fund the drug?

Scenario Three

You are in charge of the six beds in your hospital's ICU. Three are currently occupied (one by a 72-year-old man with a long history of civic involvement, including a stint as mayor; one by a young mother with two children; one by a 12-year-old victim of a car accident). All have a good chance of recovering from their conditions, but only if they remain in the ICU for at least another week. You receive word that a serious car accident has occurred: two vehicles were involved, and five people have been seriously injured. (The roads were treacherous after a recent and unforeseen freezing rain storm.) In one car were a young couple and their six-year old child; in the other, one of your hospital's leading oncologists and her husband. All five need beds in the ICU; what should you do?

(1) How will you allocate the beds? (2) What might a Kantian advise? What might a utilitarian recommend? (3) How would Callahan perceive this situation? What might Emanuel and Wertheimer advise you to do? (3) Could you justify discharging one of the patients currently occupying an ICU bed? (4) Do you feel obliged to accommodate your hospital's leading oncologist over any of the others?

Scenario Four

Rick Morris is 59 years old and in need of a hip replacement. His day job involves fairly heavy manual labour, and he is becoming increasingly crippled by his hip problems. He has come to see you, his family doctor, to discuss his increasing difficulties. He has been on a waiting list for a hip replacement for nearly two years, and he is concerned about his ability to continue working.

"I'm fed up with waiting," says Rick. "I have a family that I need to provide for. My wife works full time in retail already, but we're concerned about saving for retirement, and helping our kids and our grandkids. I'd like to retire comfortably and help my children provide for their children—better education, for instance, so that they have more choice about their careers.

"I've done some research online and I've found a hospital in India that caters to North Americans. They can do the hip replacement for a very reasonable price. I'd like you to send them my medical records." He hands you a sheet with the clinic information on it.

You look at the information Rick has handed to you. You have done some work in developing countries and feel that there is something immoral about hospitals designed to cater to the needs of wealthy foreigners when many citizens lack basic health care. Yet you also recognize that these medical services bring in much-needed revenue and that wait times for hip replacements in your province are longer than they ought to be.

(1) What ethical issues (if any) does Rick's request raise? (2) Should you send the information?

Why or why not? (3) If Rick develops complications as a result of his surgery, should he be responsible for his medical costs, or should they be covered by the Canadian health care system?

Scenario Five

Steven Charron is a recent graduate from Dalhousie University's Faculty of Medicine, specializing in infectious diseases. He has been looking for a job both in Canada and abroad. He has received a few offers near home that look attractive; they pay well and he would be working in his field. He has also learned of an opportunity to go to Africa and work with a charity that provides medical services to very impoverished people; in this case, he would get paid next to nothing. He has no student debt to pay off, as he has received large scholarships for most of his education, supplemented by a Registered Education Savings Plan and a savings account that his parents started for him in his infancy.

(1) Should Steven take the job in Africa or remain in Canada? (2) Does he have an obligation to stay, since he is needed in Canada and his education has been subsidized by the Canadian taxpayer? Or does he have a greater obligation to help those who need help the most (those in developing countries who would not otherwise have access to modern medicine)? (3) Could either Kant or Mill adequately resolve this conflict?

Scenario Six

You are a city official selected to work on a task force that has been created to recruit new medical practitioners to your community. The city is currently suffering from a doctor shortage: there are many people without family doctors, and the hospitals are severely understaffed. Some of your peers have suggested that you restrict your efforts to Canada and other first-world countries, as recruiting doctors from third-world nations could be considered as "poaching" highly trained medical specialists who are much needed in their home countries.

There are a few dissenters, however, who emphasize that recruiting doctors from third-world countries would provide those recruited with a higher standard of living and allow entire families to benefit from the higher salaries that doctors receive in Canada. Moreover, some people emphasize that the decision over where to work is a decision to be made by the doctors themselves, not by those recruiting medical specialists. Further, a few people insist that you have a duty to your own city and your own country, and to the people suffering here and now, rather than to people suffering in Africa. It is not your responsibility to look out for people in third-world nations, but rather to look out for your family, friends, acquaintances, and fellow citizens.

(1) What position should you take? Do you recruit doctors from third-world nations as well as first-world nations, or do you restrict your search to the latter? (2) Do you have responsibilities first and foremost to those closest to you, rather than those halfway around the world who have no relation to you? Do you have an equal responsibility for all people? Or do you have a primary responsibility for those who are the worst off? (3) Are there any ethical problems associated with "poaching" highly trained third-world doctors?

Scenario Seven

You are a doctor working in a local hospital. Last spring, a new strain of the flu emerged in China and affected a number of people worldwide, eventually becoming a pandemic. Although this first wave of the flu was not very virulent, there is a consensus among the medical community that there will likely be a second wave in the fall that will spread much faster and be significantly more virulent. As the fall months approach, a vaccine for the virus is found and pharmaceutical companies begin to manufacture it in large quantities. However, at the time the first cases of the flu begin to emerge, there are not enough vaccines for everyone worldwide; only about one million doses have been manufactured so far. You are asked to sit on a committee to decide what to do with the doses your municipality receives. Among your peers are other health care workers, ethicists, and civil servants.

(1) How do you decide who gets the vaccines? (2) Which of the methods described by Emanuel and Wertheimer would you use? Why? (3) Assume that the hospital is given a certain number of doses, but not enough to cover all the employees, volunteers, and medical practitioners who work within it. How do you determine which health care workers get vaccines? Do you vaccinate the worker and his/her family or just the worker? (4) As a doctor sitting on this committee, do you push for more vaccines for the hospital or do you consider all portions of the population? (5) Do you try to get yourself vaccinated? (6) Should you consider whether or not people want the vaccine? What do you do about those who want it but aren't in one of the selected categories? Should you force people in the selected categories who don't want the vaccine to receive it?

GLOSSARY

Distributive justice: a branch of justice that is concerned with the distribution of goods and services within a society, or within particular institutions. Concerns about what constitutes a just distribution of these resources are particularly acute when they are limited or scarce. This is the kind of justice that is usually at issue in bioethical dilemmas, in which the demand for medical resources exceeds the supply.

Inherent needs: needs that exist as a matter of fact, whatever we happen to think about them. Biological needs, such as a need for food and water, fall into this category.

Moral worth: a concept that suggests that all persons are equally worthy of being treated with respect, simply because they are human beings. A variation on this idea holds that the degree of respect individuals are owed is connected to the moral choices they have made, or failed to make.

Need: a situation or condition in which something is required.

Socially induced needs: needs that are created within particular social contexts.

Social worth: a concept often used by utilitarians that holds that individuals can be evaluated according to the contributions they can make to the happiness and well-being of others.

Subjective needs: needs that arise from the desires of particular individuals. Different people will experience different subjective needs.

FOR FURTHER READING

Annas, George. "The Prostitute, the Playboy, and the Poet: Rationing Schemes for Organ Transplantation." *American Journal of Public Health*, 75, no. 2 (1985): 187–189.

In this well-known paper, Annas considers various approaches that can be taken in order to decide who should receive an organ for transplant when organs are scarce. While he focuses his attention on organs, the distributive approaches he discusses apply to other scarce resources as well.

Callahan, Daniel. "Terminating Treatment: Age As a Standard." *Hastings Center Report*, 17, no. 5 (October-November 1987): 21–25.

In this essay, Callahan makes a case for using age as a criterion for treatment decisions. He argues that the proper goal of medicine for those who have lived a full biographical lifespan should be to relieve suffering rather than to prolong life. He also considers the challenge posed by medical technology: it can both prolong life and increase suffering.

Daniels, Norman. "Four Unsolved Rationing Problems." *Hastings Center Report*, 24, no. 4 (July-August 1994): 27–29.

In this essay, Daniels offers a challenge to bioethicists to solve four rationing problems that have proven to be difficult to resolve. He identifies each, and then sums up the issue it raises in a question. The first is the Fair Chances/Best Outcomes Problem, which is captured in the question

"How much should we favor producing the best outcome with limited resources?" The second is the Priorities Problem, which he sums up in the question "How much priority should we give to treating the sickest or most disabled patients?" The third is the Aggregation Problem, which is reflected in the question "When should we allow an aggregation of modest benefits to larger numbers of people to outweigh more significant benefits to fewer people?" Finally, he identifies the Democracy Problem, articulated in the question "When must we rely on a fair democratic process as the only way to determine what constitutes a fair rationing outcome?"

Dwyer, James. "What's Wrong with the Global Migration of Health Care Professionals? Individual Rights and International Justice." *Hastings Center Report*, 37, no. 3 (September-October 2007): 36–43.

This paper considers an issue that raises questions about international justice, as well as the tension between individual freedoms and social responsibility: this is the movement of skilled and highly trained health care workers from poor countries to rich ones. The author usefully places the concern that rich nations (including Canada) have about a shortage of medical professionals within the larger framework of global social justice.

Gawande, Atul. "Piecework: Medicine's Money Problem." *The New Yorker*, April 4, 2005. (Available at www.newyorker.com/archive/2005/04/04/050404fa_fact.)

In this essay, Gawande, an American surgeon, examines the way in which doctors are paid and the role played by insurance companies in the medical process. This essay provides some interesting insights into the American health care system and the discrepancies in the treatments available to those who are insured and the care given to those who are not.

Jecker, Nancy S. "Knowing When to Stop: The Limits of Medicine." *Hastings Center Report*, 21, no. 3 (May-June 1991): 5–8.

In this interesting account of the origin of values that are embodied in modern medicine, and which are generally accepted uncritically, Jecker argues that some of the ethical problems facing medical practitioners could be alleviated if they took seriously some of the values that were embodied in the older Hippocratic tradition.

Kenny, Nuala P., and Roger Chafe. "Pushing Right Against the Evidence: Turbulent Times for Canadian Health Care." *Hastings Center Report*, 37, no. 5 (September 2007): 24–26.

There are growing concerns with some aspects of Canadian health care, including the length of time required to access medical services and inadequate out-of-hospital drug coverage. This has led some commentators to call for more privatization within the health care system. However, the authors argue, the wisdom of such a shift is not supported by the evidence. This paper also explores the impact of the *Chaoulli* decision on the debate, and compares the Canadian health care system to those in other countries.

RECOMMENDED WEBSITES

Bioethics Web

www.intute.ac.uk/bioethicsweb/

This site provides a "gateway to evaluated, high quality internet resources relating to biomedical ethics," including sites concerned with distributive justice in a medical context.

Family Care Foundation: If the World Were a Village of 100 People

www.familycare.org//news/if_the_world.htm

This site provides a useful place to start thinking about global discrepancies in the distribution of goods and services. It is predicated on the idea that we can imagine reducing the world's population to a village of 100 people while keeping global ratios (age, nationality, religion) accurate. In doing so, we can more clearly see how global resources are distributed.

A Guide to Bioethics Resources on the Web

www.onlyhealthy.com/a-guide-to-bioethics-resources-on-the-web/

This site provides links to bioethics resources on the web, with a particular focus on sites that "are designed to clear up fact from fiction, open a constructive dialogue on bioethics subjects, and spread the word on what is actually happening in the fields of science, technology, and medicine."

Public Health Agency of Canada Pandemic Preparedness

www.phac-aspc.gc/influenza/plans-eng.php

This site provides information on Canada's pandemic influenza plan, as well as the plans of a number of provinces.

World Life Expectancy

www.worldlifeexpectancy.com/

This site provides a map showing the rates of life expectancy around the world. It also shows global causes of death and allows users to calculate their own life expectancies.

NOTES

1. HG.Org Worldwide Legal Directories, found at www.hg.org/articles/article_698.html (September 24, 2009).

2. HG. Org Worldwide Legal Directories, paras. 123, 124.

3. HG. Org Worldwide Legal Directories.

4. HG. Org Worldwide Legal Directories.

5. HG. Org Worldwide Legal Directories.

6. *Chaoulli v. Quebec*, Judgments of the Supreme Court of Canada, found at csc.lexum.umontreal.ca/en/2oo5/2005scc35/2005scc35.html (September 24, 2009).

7. John Rawls, *A Theory of Justice* (Cambridge, MA: Harvard University Press, 1971), 128.

8. Rawls, 126.

9. Karen Howlett, "So Many Patients and Too Few Dollars," *The Globe and Mail* (June 5, 2006), A11.

10. Nadeem Esmail, "Top Dollar for Bargain Health Care in Canada," *National Post*, May 13, 2013, found at fullcomment.nationalpost.com/2013/13/05/fraser-institute-for Monday/ (May 7, 2014).

11. Canadian Institute for Health Information, "National Health Expenditures and MIS Reporting," found at www.cihi.ca/ (November 26, 2014).

12. Thomas M. Garrett, Harold W. Baillie, and Rosellen M. Garrett, *Health Care Ethics: Principles and Problems*, 4th ed. (Upper Saddle River, NJ: Prentice Hall, 1998), 87.

13. Daniel Callahan, "Terminating Treatment: Age as a Standard," in Joseph H. Howell and William Frederick Sale (eds.), *Life Choices: A Hastings Center Introduction to Bioethics* (Washington, DC: Georgetown University Press, 1995), 151.

14. Callahan, "Terminating Treatment," 152.

15. Garrett, Baillie, and Garrett, 89.

16. Nancy S. Jecker, "Knowing When to Stop: The Limits of Medicine," in Howell and Sale, 141.

17. Jecker, 140.

18. Jecker, 144–146.

19. Garrett, Baillie, and Garrett, 90.

20. Garrett, Baillie, and Garrett, 91.

21. Garrett, Baillie, and Garrett, 92.

22. Norman Daniels, "Is There a Right to Health Care and, If So, What Does It Encompass?" in Tom L. Beauchamp and LeRoy Walters (eds.), *Contemporary Issues in Bioethics*, 6th ed. (Belmont, CA: Thomson Wadsworth, 2003), 46.

23. Daniels, 47.

24. Jessica C. Smith and Carla Medelia, "Health Insurance Coverage in the United States: 2013," found at census.gov (November 26, 2014).

25. World Health Organization, "Life Expectancy Data by Country," Global Health Observatory Data Repository, found at apps.who.int (Novmeber 26, 2014).

26. Tara Haelle, "U.S. Infant Mortality Rate Worse than Other Countries," found at www.cbsnews.com/news/u-s-infant-mortality-rate-worse-than-other-countries/ (November 26, 2014).

27. In 2008, Dykman reports, health care spending as a percentage of GDP was 16 percent in the United States, or the equivalent of $7026 per person. *Time*, December 1, 2008, 28–29.

28. David Goldhill, "How American Health Care Killed My Father," *The Atlantic*, September 2009, 41.

29. Goldhill, 45.

30. Michael C. Brannigan and Judith A. Boss, *Healthcare Ethics in a Diverse Society* (Mountain View, CA: Mayfield, 2001), 620.

31. Brannigan and Boss, 620.

32. *Munson*, 809.

33. Terrance McConnell, *Moral Issues in Health Care* (Belmont, CA: Wadsworth Publishing, 1997), 222.

34. McConnell, 224.

35. McConnell, 224.

36. McConnell, 225.

37. Ezekiel J. Emmanuel and Alan Wertheimer, "Who Should Get Influenza Vaccine When Not All Can?" *Science*, May 12, 2006, 854.

38. Emmanuel and Wertheimer, 854.

39. Munson presents a similar example in his discussion of feminist ethics, 791.

40. Daniel Callahan, "Aging and the Ends of Medicine," in Munson, 839.

41. Callahan, "Aging," 839.

42. Callahan, "Aging," 840.

43. Callahan, "Aging," 840.

44. Callahan, "Aging," 841.

45. Callahan, "Aging," 841.

46. Callahan, "Terminating Treatment," 154.

47. Callahan, "Aging," 842.

48. Callahan, "Aging," 842.

49. Callahan, "Aging," 842.

50. Callahan, "Terminating Treatment," 157.

51. Emanuel and Wertheimer, 855.

52. Emanuel and Wertheimer, 855.

53. Emanuel and Wertheimer, 855.

54. For a more extensive discussion of Rawls' theory, see the "Philosophical Reflection" at the end of this chapter.

55. Will Kymlicka, *Contemporary Political Philosophy* (Oxford, UK: Oxford University Press, 1990), 55.

56. Kymlicka, 56.

57. Norman Daniels, "A Lifespan Approach to Health Care," in Walter Glannon, *Contemporary Readings in Biomedical Ethics* (Orlando, FL: Harcourt, 2002), 421.

58. Daniels, "A Lifespan Approach," 421.

59. Daniels, "A Lifespan Approach," 421.

60. Daniels, "A Lifespan Approach," 421.

61. Daniels, "A Lifespan Approach," 422.

62. Daniels, "A Lifespan Approach," 422.

63. Daniels, "A Lifespan Approach," 422.

64. Norman Daniels, *Just Health: Meeting Health Needs Fairly* (Cambridge, UK: Cambridge University Press, 2008), 103.

65. Daniels, *Just Health*, 118.

66. Daniels, *Just Health*, 118.

67. Munson, 332.

68. Found at siteresources.worldbank.org/DATASTATISTICS/Resources/ssa_wdi.pdf (October 1, 2009).

69. Found at www.avert.org/aidsimpact.htm (October 1, 2009).

70. This way of thinking about the issue draws on the approach Daniel Callahan uses in "Terminating Treatment."

71. Leigh Turner, "Bioethics Needs to Rethink Its Agenda," *British Medical Journal*, 328 (January 17, 2004): 175.

72. Julian Baggini, *The Pig That Wants to Be Eaten and Ninety-Nine Other Thought Experiments* (London: Granta Books, 2005), ix.

73. Baggini, ix.

74. Baggini, x.

75. Robert B. Talisse, *On Rawls: A Liberal Theory of Justice and Justification* (Belmont, CA: Thomson Wadsworth, 2001), 15.

76. John Rawls, *A Theory of Justice* (Cambridge, MA: Harvard University Press, 1971), 102.

77. Rawls, 102.

78. Rawls, 96.

79. Rawls, 18.

80. Rawls, 302.

81. Rawls, 302.

82. "An 'orphan disease' is a disease that has not been 'adopted' by the pharmaceutical industry because it provides little financial incentive for the private sector to make and market new medications to treat or prevent it." Found at www.medterms.com/script/main/art.asp?articlekey+11418 (October 1, 2009).

Chapter 3

THE HEALTH CARE PROFESSIONAL–PATIENT RELATIONSHIP

LANDMARK CASE: SCOTT STARSON

In 2005, a detainee at the Brockville Psychiatric Hospital named Scott Starson was injected against his will with an antipsychotic drug designed to treat his schizo-affective disorder.[1] At the time, Scott had been kept in various psychiatric institutions for seven years.

His mother, as substitute decision-maker, gave permission for this treatment. She was concerned, as were the doctors caring for him, about his physical health: as a result of hallucinations and para-noid delusions, Scott believed that the hospital was trying to poison him, and he was refusing to eat and drink. He was dying. As one of his doctors put it, "We thought we were going to lose him."[2] Consequently, his doctors went to Ontario's Consent and Capacity Board and got a ruling that said that Scott was incapable, as a result of his mental illness, of making treatment decisions for himself.

This would have seemed a sad, though not unusual, set of circumstances but for one thing: Starson had, two years previously, won a Supreme Court of Canada case upholding his right to refuse treatment.

Starson was first detained at a forensic psychiatric facility in 1998, after he was found not crimi-nally responsible for uttering death threats because he suffered from a mental disorder. This disorder first revealed itself in the mid-1980s. At the time, Scott Schutzman (as he was then called) was a suc-cessful salesman, a handsome and charming man, with a number of friends. He lived in a penthouse in Toronto, which he shared with his pet bird, Mumbles, who had a room to himself.[3] His friends began to notice that Scott's behaviour was becoming odd. He expected his friends to communicate with Mumbles, and he began to show up for work in a dirty and dishevelled state.

Between 1985 and 1998, Scott was arrested a number of times for trespassing, making harassing phone calls, and uttering death threats; in this period, he was placed in psychiatric institutions at least 15 times, 14 times by court order. He also changed his name to "Starson," because he believed he was the son of the stars.

Despite his illness, Scott displayed a keen interest in physics and demonstrated significant abilities in this area. He co-authored several articles in this field that were published in peer-reviewed academic journals, and his insights were described by some as both important and inspired. It was primarily this interest in physics that led Scott to refuse treatment for his mental illness, because he believed that medication would make his thinking sluggish and disorient him. Even if medication could make him "normal," he stated that "[b]eing 'normal' would be like death for me, because I have always considered normal to be a term so boring it would be like death."[4] He also asserted that he would rather be physically detained indefinitely than accept treatment, even if that treatment might allow him to be released back into the community.

His psychiatrists argued that he was incapable of making treatment decisions, and Scott appealed to the Consent and Capacity Board in Ontario, which upheld the determination of the psychiatrists. This Board ruling was overturned by the Ontario Superior Court in 1999, a ruling that was upheld in 2001. This decision was then appealed to the Supreme Court of Canada. The question that the Court needed to decide was "whether the Ontario Consent and capacity Board had properly deemed Mr. Starson incapable of making a treatment decision."[5] In other words, did Scott understand his condition well enough to make rational decisions about appropriate treatment?

Before the trial, some commentators noted that Scott faced a "classic Catch-22: If he admits to a serious illness, it opens him to the possibility of being treated against his will. But if he denies it, psychiatrists can conclude that he lacks insight and forcibly treat him."[6] And a second Catch-22 can also be identified: with treatment, Scott might be able to recover sufficiently to be released from the psychiatric institutions in which he was being held, but perhaps at the cost of his intelligence and creativity; without treatment, he might retain his intelligence and creativity, but would remain physically incarcerated for an indefinite term.

The Supreme Court of Canada upheld Scott's right to refuse treatment in a 6-3 decision. Justice Major, writing for the majority, made the following points:

> [P]atients with mental disorders are presumptively entitled to make their own treatment decisions. The presumption of capacity can be displaced only by evidence that a patient lacks the requisite elements of capacity provided by the [Health Care Consent] Act. Capacity involves two criteria: first, a person must be able to understand the information that is relevant to making a treatment decision and second, a person must be able to appreciate the reasonably foreseeable consequences of the decision or lack of one.[7]

Further, given that the only question to be decided was whether Scott had the capacity to refuse treatment, the question of whether or not such treatment might be in his best interests was irrelevant. The majority concluded that, while the Consent and Capacity Board had determined that "the respondent was in 'almost total' denial of a mental disorder, and that he failed to appreciate the consequences of his decision,"[8] a review of the evidence did not support either of these claims.

In contrast, Chief Justice McLachlin, writing the dissenting opinion, held that the Board's decision was reasonable:

> The Board's finding that the respondent's denial of his illness was "almost total" is amply supported by the evidence. While the Board never suggested that the respondent denied all his difficulties and symptoms, it did suggest, entirely accurately, that the respondent did not see his symptoms and difficulties as an illness or problem

relevant to the proposals for treatment. The Board was entitled to conclude from the evidence that the respondent was in denial about his mental illness generally, and not just about his specific diagnosis.... There was also ample evidence to support the Board's finding that the respondent was unable to appreciate the foreseeable consequences of treatment and refusing treatment because he lacked the ability to appreciate (1) the possible benefits of the proposed medication; (2) the fact that absent medication it is unlikely he will ever return to his previous level of functioning and his condition may continue to deteriorate; and (3) the relationship between lack of treatment and future dispositions by the Review Board.[9]

A range of opinions was expressed about the case shortly before the Supreme Court decision was announced. Scott's mother stated: "I hope the Supreme Court decides he should be medicated, otherwise he will remain a dribbling idiot.... [H]e has absolutely no insight into his situation. He can rationalize anything. He always insists he isn't crazy, you are."[10] Dr. Bradford, one of the psychiatrists treating Scott, stated: "I hope the Supreme Court in its wisdom will look not only at the issue of the right to refuse treatment, but the right to treatment. There is tremendous suffering. To pretend that a person is a 'happy psychotic' simply doesn't make sense."[11] Finally, Anita Szigeti, a lawyer appointed by the Court to provide additional arguments in the case, said that the "significance of this ruling relates to our right to refuse any kind of treatment.... It involves safe-guarding the rights of capable individuals to refuse all kinds of medical intervention even when they appear to be in our best interest."[12]

The relationship between health care professionals and patients is a particularly intimate one, as this medieval representation of a hospital illustrates. The way in which this relationship is understood will shape how patients are treated and affect their experience of illness.

INTRODUCTION

Humans live in relationships with one another, and our relationships are complex and dynamic. Parents, who once took care of us, can come to need our care; children, who once needed to be fed and changed, grow up and leave home; marriages, embarked on with hope and enthusiasm, can be empowering or disappointing; and friends can both betray and support us. Within the health care system, patients develop relationships with various health care workers, including doctors, nurses, health care aides, technicians, and therapists of various sorts. Of these relationships, the ones between doctor and patient and nurse and patient are particularly important: doctors diagnose illness and determine appropriate treatment, while nurses are responsible for the ongoing care of patients, including the intimate activities of feeding and washing. In this chapter, we will consider the nature of the doctor-patient relationship, the nature of the nurse-patient relationship, and the types of questions that both doctors and nurses must consider as they determine what treatment and care is appropriate for their patients.

The relationship between doctor and patient is particularly complex. Doctors are required, by the nature of their profession, to do what is best for their patients when they are at their most vulnerable, and to respect their dignity. Patients turn to doctors for help and advice when they are sick and frightened. However, it is not always clear what is best, what is most helpful, or what a respect for dignity requires.

McConnell notes that the way in which health care professionals understand their relationships with patients has "significant ethical implications.... How health care workers conceive their roles in relation to patients will affect all the moral decisions they make in that context."[13] How doctors envision their role will be affected both by the way in which they understand the physician-patient relationship and by what they believe the goals of medicine to be. Philosophical questions can be asked about the purposes of medicine, particularly given the ever-increasing use of technology in health care; and while there is currently something of a consensus on the nature of the doctor-patient relationship, there are a number of ethical issues not adequately resolved by this consensus. We will refer to the Starson case as we consider the complex nature of the issues that can arise as doctors and nurses try to do what is best for their patients, and as patients attempt to retain dignity and to make decisions for themselves when they are ill and must turn to doctors and nurses for help.

THE GOALS OF MEDICINE

It might seem odd to ask what the goals of medicine are: aren't these self-evident? The goals of medicine, it might be thought, simply involve making sick people better. However, the picture is more complicated:

> Is the overarching purpose of the health care professions the prevention of death or the alleviation of suffering? If it is the alleviation of suffering, does this embrace not only a cure of the cause of the suffering, but also the comforting of the sufferer who cannot or will not be cured? Another possibility is that health care, in the context of a specific illness, is only the attempt to optimize the patient's chances for a happy and productive life.[14]

Should the purpose of medicine also be to promote health? If so, then the goals of medicine would encompass the prevention of illness as well as its treatment.

Clearly, it makes a difference to our making of practical ethical decisions which model of medicine we endorse. If, for instance, it is the prevention of death that is held to be the primary purpose of medicine, then we will do whatever we can to keep people alive, with the use of any available technologies and treatments, even when there is clearly no hope of recovery. If, on the other hand, we see the purpose of medicine to be to maximize the patient's own goals in the context of illness, then we will be inclined to do whatever patients ask, including facilitating choices that we don't agree with and that may hasten their deaths. We will, for example, support Starson's desire not to be treated for his mental illness, even if this means that he must remain in a psychiatric institution for an indefinite period of time.

It is not entirely clear how the goals of medicine should be characterized, and the issue remains a matter of some debate. Indeed, when the Hastings Institute, a well-known bioethics centre, conducted a project to identify the purposes of medicine, the results were uncertain and indecisive.[15] Any answers given to these questions will be more than simple statements of fact and will themselves involve a considerable degree of ethical judgment. That there is little agreement about what constitutes the goals of medicine is demonstrated in the language used in discussions of these issues. Some commentators refer to "physicians," or "doctors," and "patients"; others to "health care workers" and "clients"; or even to "health care providers" and "consumers." The terminology used reflects different ideas about the goals of medicine and the nature of the relationship between those who seek medical assistance and those who provide it. The terms "doctor" and "patient" suggest a special relationship based on a calling. Doctors, Tauber notes, who reflect this understanding of medicine, are not like members of other professions; they are not, for instance, like plumbers. "A plumber may show up a day late or not at all; the physician was [sic] accountable to another principle, and with good reason. A blocked-up toilet was [sic] a problem; illness or threat of death was [sic] a calamity."[16] At the core of the relationship between physician and patient, he argues, "lies an ethical commitment to make each of us whole when diseased."[17] This commitment is demonstrated through the compassionate care that is given to patients who are sick and vulnerable. Likewise, in their book on nursing ethics, Oberle and Bouchal argue that the term "patient" better captures the ethical nature of the relationship between nurses and those they seek to help than do any of its competitors: "We prefer the term patient to client because it reminds us that there is often a power imbalance: the nurse has services that the patient requires, and hence the patient is in a vulnerable position."[18]

Tauber uses the past tense in the quote above because he believes that these ideals are being lost as a result of economic and political pressures. Politicians want efficient and cost-effective health care systems; at the same time, medicine is a very big business—the largest industry in the U.S., and, in Canada, something that absorbs an ever-increasing proportion of government budgets. According to Health Canada, over 1 million Canadians work in health care and related services, representing 6 percent of the total Canadian workforce.[19] Furthermore, while total Canadian health care costs consumed 7 percent of Gross Domestic Product (GDP) in 1975, by 2010, they had risen to an estimated 11.7 percent of GDP, or $4614 per person.[20] In addition, the pharmaceutical industry makes billions of dollars every year and has a role to play, not only in the treatment of disease, but also in its very construction and identification.[21] The terminology of "health care providers" and "clients" reflects these political and economic dimensions of health care: "clients" go to "health care providers" for specific services, rather than existing in a special ethical relationship with them (banks and hairdressers also have clients). The move to "health care consumer" takes us even further away from Tauber's notion of a special relationship based on compassionate care: consumers buy products, and health care becomes simply one more commodity. This terminology suggests, Tauber argues, that the norms of the marketplace are what should govern the practice of medicine, and leaves little space for the committed and caring relationships that seem integral to sound medical practice; in essence, it moves us from an ethic based on caring within a relationship between two people who know each other to a commercial exchange between strangers. Health care becomes a product that can be sold "just as one might sell a vacation to Bermuda or a sneaker called Air Jordan."[22] Groopman also believes that clinical care is compromised by the marketplace model of medicine: "In healthcare planning, it is natural that each service might be seen as a commodity or product. The calculus involved in determining the cost of providing the service, the factors affecting reimbursement, the required numbers of such services, and other factors all promote the commodity view.... [However], medical care ... is a human interaction between patient and doctor within a context and in a social system. As such it is not a commodity."[23]

We will use the terminology of "nurse," "doctor," or "physician" and "patient" because these terms best reflect the ethical dimensions of these relationships. In addition, the terminology of "providers" and "clients" or "consumers" doesn't readily allow us to notice some of the ethical issues that exist, let alone help to resolve them: consumers and clients buy services, and their choices might reflect nothing more than their unconsidered desires; providers give them what they want without asking them why they want it, and without considering whether what they want is something that should be desired. If this is the nature of the relationship between those who seek medical attention and those who offer it, then many ethical issues will simply be resolved by finding out what people want and giving it to them. But this is arguably unsatisfactory: it ignores the possibility that doctors, nurses, and patients can have shared goals that are bound up in the practice of medicine itself (however difficult these goals might be to articulate); it gives doctors no basis on which to make decisions for those who are unable to make them for themselves; and it assumes that patients always know what they want and have the capacity to judge what is in their own best interests correctly (even as they define them). It does not, that is to say, help us determine what ought to be done in the Starson case.

Arguably, then, the language of clients and consumers cannot adequately account for the complex nature of the issues that can arise in the medical context, nor for the special nature of the relationship that should exist between those who care for the sick and vulnerable and those who need this care. The latter are, as Tauber reminds us, all of us: "Each of us has been and will at some time in the future be ill. At these times we seek and expect compassionate care."[24]

MODELS OF THE DOCTOR-PATIENT RELATIONSHIP

However, even if the terminology of doctors and patients is more helpful for a consideration of the ethical issues that arise in health care than the terminology of clients and consumers, this, in itself, does not tell us what the appropriate model of that relationship should be. Likewise, to say that there may be goals that are shared by doctors and patients, or goals internal to the practice of medicine, does not tell us what those goals are (to promote health? to relieve suffering? to prolong life?). Even to say that doctors (and other health care practitioners) should demonstrate care and compassion toward their patients does not tell us what this should mean in practice: Should they do whatever patients say they want done? Should they influence their health care choices in any way? Should they make decisions for them in what appears to be their best interests? Consider the Starson case: what did care and compassion demand of his medical practitioners? That his wishes not to be treated be respected, even if he refuses to eat and drink, and might die as a result? Or that he be treated against his will, on the basis of what many might consider to be his best interests, even if he, himself, disagrees about what those interests are?

Veatch has distinguished three models of the doctor-patient relationship. Each of these models describes an ideal of the relationship and is designed to help us work through some of these questions in theory and then in practice. The three models Veatch identifies are the Engineering Model, the Paternalistic Model, and the Contractual Model.[25] We will consider each of these models in turn and will conclude with an examination of May's Covenantal Model.

The Engineering Model

According to this model, doctors should think of themselves as applied scientists, who "must deal only with facts and divorce themselves from all questions of value. The role of physicians ... is to present the facts to patients, and then let them make their own decisions. Or, more accurately, physicians must not let their value judgments affect their actions in medical contexts."[26] While this model does a fine job of allowing patients to make decisions about their treatment, it is problematic. This becomes immediately apparent when we consider that it provides little guidance for how Starson should be treated, because deciding either to treat him or not to treat him requires that a moral judgment, not simply a factual judgment, be made. What makes many medical situations difficult is that the physician cannot avoid making a value judgment, and the question then becomes: what judgment and on what basis should it be made? This model provides no answers to these questions.

The Engineering Model fails, arguably, to provide a persuasive articulation of the ideal doctor-patient relationship. First, in any relationship, value judgments must be made, and the domain of medicine is no exception. Second, it is both unfair and undesirable to ask doctors to leave their moral views out of their medical judgments: unfair, because it can't be done, and undesirable, because it suggests that the practice of medicine, rather than being an inherently ethical enterprise, is merely a domain of facts. Doctors should be highly aware, given the vulnerability of their patients, and their own power, of the central role that value judgments must play in their decisions. Finally, it is not at all clear that physicians should always do whatever their patients wish: some of their desires may be harmful, as, for instance, when a patient asks for unnecessary antibiotics.

The Paternalistic Model

The second model Veatch identifies is the paternalistic or priestly model, in which "patients come to health care practitioners for treatment, counsel, and comfort. The ideal portrayed here is that decision-making is placed entirely in the hands of health care professionals, and patients are expected to follow their orders."[27] This model was, until recently, the dominant model of medicine. It suggests that, just as a parent knows what is best for a child, so a doctor knows what is best for a patient. If a doctor, for instance, believed that it was not in a patient's best interest to know her diagnosis and prognosis, then the doctor could lie to her about both. In a defence of this model, Lipkin argues that it is often not in a patient's best interest to be told the truth about her condition, since she may not even fully understand the information presented: "[T]houghtful physicians know that transmittal of accurate information to patients is often impossible. Patients rarely know how the body functions in health and disease, but instead have inaccurate ideas of what is going on; this hampers attempts to 'tell the truth.'"[28] Not only should doctors decide what courses of treatment are best for their patients, Lipkin believes, they can also deceive them—as long as this deception is intended to benefit the patient and not the doctor.

This model would simply allow doctors to make judgments and provide treatments on the basis of their assessments of what the patients need. (It should be noted that, given the difficulty of pinning down universally agreed-upon goals of medicine, different doctors might well make very different judgments about what this is.) This model would not see the Starson case as presenting any ethical challenges: of course psychiatrists are justified in treating patients such as Starson with antipsychotic medications, even if those patients believe that such treatment would diminish their intelligence and hinder their creativity.

The Paternalistic Model has been largely rejected, and for good reason. First, it relies on three problematic assumptions: that the goals of medicine are clear, so that doctors will know what is best for their patients; that giving a diagnosis and prognosis, and determining the correct treatment is an exact science; and, finally, that all physicians are competent and know what is in their patient's best interests. None of these assumptions holds up under examination: the goals of medicine are hard to articulate; doctors are fallible, and each patient is different; and deciding for others what is in their best interests is perhaps impossible. For instance, while most patients might agree that a life-saving blood transfusion is in their best interests, a Jehovah's Witness will feel very differently. As Dworkin observes, it's very hard to find any goods that all rational individuals can agree on, including seemingly obvious candidates such as life and health: if someone's religious views rule out blood transfusions, "it may be more important for him to reject 'impure substances' than to go on living."[29] In addition, as Mill famously puts it, "Each of us is the proper guardian of his own health, whether bodily, or mental and spiritual."[30] Following this line of thinking, then, it is arguably the case that it is precisely because medical decisions are so significant and potentially life-altering that patients should make them for themselves, rather than leaving them in the hands of doctors.

The Paternalistic Model has two other failings: it puts too much power in the hands of physicians, and it demonstrates a lack of respect toward patients. As Cullen and Klein state, "Treating humans with respect means recognizing their autonomy by allowing them the freedom to make choices about their lives. By contrast, to disrespect people means taking away their freedom to live as they choose."[31] Patients care the most about what happens to them and know what is most important to them: competent patients should be permitted to make their own decisions, and doctors should provide them with sufficient and accurate information so that these decisions can be informed ones.

The Contractual Model

The final model Veatch identifies attempts to capture the strengths of each of the previous models while avoiding their weaknesses. In the Contractual Model, the guidance provided by the Paternalistic Model is tempered by respect for the **autonomy** of the patient. This model has the following features. First, it suggests that "the relationship between patients and health care providers is best conceived as a tacit contract between the two. The relationship involves a true sharing, and each party has a role to play in the decision-making process."[32] The model also stipulates that both doctors and patients have obligations to share information; that patients should be given sufficient information to make informed decisions on important matters, and must give their consent before treatment; that doctors can make minor decisions for patients; and that if agreement cannot be reached, either party can opt out of the relationship.

This model can be useful when it comes to decisions made by patients who are informed and competent; it is not so helpful when it comes to making decisions for those who are not so well placed. What should be done in emergency situations, when no agreement has been reached about what should be done? What should be done when decisions have to be made for someone who is incompetent and the caregivers disagree? This model does not tell us whether Starson should be treated or not: does the fact that he is an intelligent man with a deep interest in physics mean that he is capable of entering into this kind of relationship with his doctors, a relationship built on the capacity to give—or to refuse to give—**informed consent** to medical procedures, despite his medical condition? Or does the particular nature of his medical condition make such a relationship impossible? The comments from Scott's mother, his doctor, and the court-appointed lawyer, as well as the different conclusions reached by the judges on the Supreme Court, demonstrate how difficult questions such as these are to answer in particular cases.

While the Contractual Model counterbalances **paternalism** by emphasizing the autonomy of both doctor and patient, it seems to ignore some of the virtues that should characterize the doctor-patient relationship, as well as the vulnerabilities and power differentials that are an integral part of it. It envisages two autonomous people engaged in a mutually beneficial exchange, rather than a relationship based on compassionate care. It is ill-equipped to deal with the limitations that illness and infirmity place on our ability to be autonomous choosers.

The Covenantal Model

A fourth model of the doctor-patient relationship is the Covenantal Model described by May. Like the Contractual Model, the Covenantal Model asks the patient to be an active participant in the medical treatment that he or she receives. Unlike the Contractual Model, however, the Covenantal Model emphasizes the concept of reciprocity in the doctor-patient relationship, and understands the relationship to be ongoing rather than episodic. Unlike other models, which suggest that the doctor gives the patient more than she receives from the patient, the Covenantal Model places the doctor within a societal context that also acknowledges the benefits the doctor receives from the larger community, and from the patient.

May points out that the picture we are usually given of the doctor presents her as an essentially self-sufficient individual who virtuously, even heroically, chooses a life of service to others. As May puts it, "[T]he medical profession imitates God not so much because it exercises power of life and death over others, but because it does not really think itself beholden, even partially, to anyone for those duties to patients which it lays on itself."[33] In fact, however, the physician owes much to the community. First, the physician benefits from the public good of education, which is subsidized by the community. Second, the physician benefits from a number of social privileges that accompany the medical profession, including a relatively high social status and income. Third, the physician benefits from patients who serve as both research subjects and teaching material; as May observes, "Early practice includes, after all, the element of increased risk for patients who lay their bodies on the line as the doctor 'practices' on them. The pun in the word but reflects the inevitable social price of training."[34] Finally, the physician remains indebted to his patients over the course of his career. The relationship between doctor and patient is one of mutual giving and receiving, and this reciprocity needs to be acknowledged. May compares the doctor to the professor:

> In the profession of teaching … the student needs the teacher to assist him in learning, but so also the professor needs his students. They provide him with regular occasion and forum in which to work out what he has to say and to rediscover his subject afresh through the discipline of sharing it with others. Likewise, the doctor needs his patients…. A covenantal ethics helps acknowledge this full context of need and indebtedness in which professional duties are undertaken and discharged.[35]

May asserts that this model has distinct advantages over its rivals. For example, because it emphasizes an ongoing relationship between doctor and patient, it has the capacity to frame health and disease differently. Rather than seeing health and disease as polar opposites, with disease as a discrete and episodic condition that requires the patient to submit to the authority of the medical profession, the Covenantal Model would emphasize disease prevention, as well as, presumably, the role that chronic illness can play in people's lives. In addition, while the Covenantal Model avoids paternalism, it also covers more than either the Engineering Model or the Contractual Model does by adding the virtue of fidelity, which encompasses the requirement that doctors be responsive to the justified expectations that patients have of them because of their professional role. As May notes, "Covenant fidelity includes the code obligation to become technically proficient; it reinforces the legal obligation to meet the minimal terms of contract; but it also requires much more,"[36] namely, an acknowledgment of the reciprocal nature of the doctor-patient relationship.

BOX 3.1 **SHERWIN B. NULAND, *THE UNCERTAIN ART***

It is judgment that lies at the heart of diagnosis, of therapy, and of all that is gathered under the umbrella of what clinicians call case management. Inherent in the nature of clinical decision making is the realization that, perforce, it must always be accomplished in the face of incomplete and largely ambiguous information. The process is one of sifting, weighing, and judging.... Disease never reveals all of itself; the path toward healing may appear visible, but it is always poorly lit and subject to changes in direction. No matter what biomedical advances may realistically be expected in the future, no one who has spent more than a few months at the bedside of the sick could find it conceivable that this imperfect state of affairs will ever change. Uncertainty is more than a constant.... Without uncertainty there would be no need for judgment; without judgment, medicine would be a career for technicians, and, given the intrinsic nature of illness, an impossibility....

For as long as there is individual variability in human biology; in the specific manifestations of any given disease; in the social setting in which the disease occurs; in the psychological response to disease; and, in turn, the feedback effect of that response on the disease and the patient's perception of it—as long as all those differentiating and problematic factors exist, as they will forever, there can be no certainty in medicine, and medicine will remain an art rather than a science.

Source: Adapted from Sherwin B. Nuland, M.D., *The Uncertain Art: Thoughts on a Life in Medicine* (New York: Random House, 2008), xv.

Brannigan and Boss argue that this Covenantal Model is the most satisfying of the models of the doctor-patient relationship that have yet been proposed. They believe that this model captures the fundamental insight of virtue ethics, namely, that actions cannot be separated from character: "[A] genuinely moral relationship between physician and patient is not simply a matter of following rules, acknowledging rights, and performing duties. A covenantal relationship is a mutual expression of the character of both the physician and the patient. It is not a matter of doing the right things; it involves good persons."[37]

As May observes, every model of the doctor-patient relationship describes not only a vision of what a doctor is, but also of what a patient is. Is a patient like a child, dependent on the doctor? Like a contractor, buying goods and services? Or a partner, motivated by the shared goals of preventing, treating, and curing disease? Each of these possibilities establishes not only a conceptual framework within which medical decisions can be made, but articulates a moral vision as well. There is, consequently, no morally neutral, simply descriptive account of the nature of the doctor-patient relationship that can be given. Therefore, when we choose which model to endorse, the choice must be made on the basis of which best captures and describes our moral judgments about the nature of this relationship.

THE NURSE-PATIENT RELATIONSHIP: AN EVOLVING ETHIC

Doctors are not the only professionals whose role in health care is vitally important; nurses too occupy a significant place and often have closer and more prolonged contact with patients than physicians do. Consequently, the ethical dimensions of the nurse-patient relationship must also be examined. While doctors and nurses must consider the same issues with respect to the patient—namely, how to respect the patient's autonomy, how to ascertain **competency**, and how to ensure that the consent a patient gives for medical treatment is fully informed—the ethical issues facing nurses are distinct from those facing doctors because of the different places members of these professions occupy within the health care system.

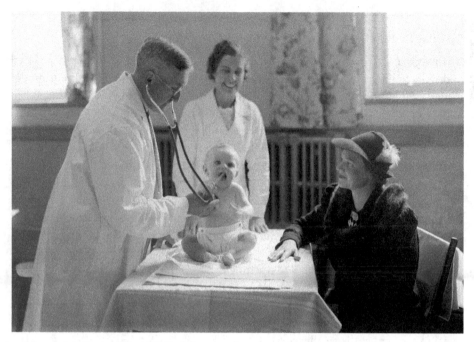

Doctor and nurse doing home visit, c.1940. Both doctors and nurses care for patients. Their roles, however, are distinct, and the ethical challenges they face may be different.

The different role of doctors and nurses is often summed up in the claim that "doctors cure and nurses care." This simple statement suggests that doctors diagnose illness and make medical decisions about how patients should be treated, while the job of nurses is to take care of patients in other ways: by administering the medicine ordered by physicians, by keeping patients clean and comfortable, and by talking to them and reassuring them. These different roles are supported and entrenched by the hierarchical structures that exist within complex organizations such as hospitals, which place doctors above nurses in that hierarchy. The hierarchical structure of health care, in itself, is the source of a number of ethical conflicts. As Chambliss puts it, "[T]he hospital as an organization is not merely the setting for moral crises: the hospital's organizational form actively generates such crises."[38]

Consider the following scenario. Mr. T is admitted to hospital for an operation on his fractured ankle. He complains of acute pain, a "10" on a 1–10 pain scale. Dr. U prescribes Extra Strength Tylenol, and tells Nurse V that he will not prescribe anything stronger because Mr. T is a recovering narcotics addict; his addiction began after he was prescribed narcotic pain medication for severe headaches. Mr. T continues to complain about the pain he is experiencing. After the nurse brings this to the attention of the doctor, the doctor orders a placebo[39] to be given by injection. Mr. T's acute pain remains, and he asks what pain medication he is getting. Mr. V, the nurse, tells him that he is receiving "what the doctor ordered." The nurse believes that his patient is not receiving adequate care and is unsure of what he should do.[40]

The dilemma facing the nurse in the scenario illustrates this point nicely: while the nurse disagrees with the doctor's orders and thinks that they are harmful to the patient, he must nonetheless carry them out, and, further, he must implicitly, though not directly, lie to the patient as he does so. The physician, in contrast, faces no such moral difficulties: he believes that he has made the correct medical decision for the patient and does not have to deal directly with the consequences for the patient of that decision.

This hierarchical relationship between doctors and nurses has several dimensions. Its origins lie both in the histories of their respective professions and in the gender differentials that have, until very recently, been inherent components of each: the nursing profession has been primarily the preserve of women, while the medical profession has until recently been dominated by men.

Nursing, historically, was done by women in the home and included such tasks as bathing, feeding, and some forms of medical treatment. In the 17th, 18th, and even 19th centuries, physicians would only infrequently be called upon. As Jecker and Self observe, "[T]he popular 18th century book, *Domestic Medicine*, assured readers that physicians need be consulted rarely, and that most people underestimate their own abilities and knowledge."[41] The domestic origins of nursing are apparent even today in that the kind of care provided by nurses to patients closely reflects the kind of care a parent might provide to a sick child (keeping them clean, monitoring their temperature, changing bed linens), while the role played by doctors maintains a more "professional" distance, just as it did historically.

In addition, the professional status now occupied by doctors is importantly linked to deliberate attempts made by physicians to distinguish themselves from other health care practitioners. Doctors in the 17th and 18th centuries had to compete with other health care providers, such as midwives and homeopaths; consequently, in an attempt to gain respect and social prestige, the medical profession found ways to set itself apart from its competitors. Duffin points out that the "American Medical Association was founded in 1847 partly as a professional lobby to protect the market share of doctors against homeopathists"[42] and observes that the "history of medical professionalization is the shift from pluralistic health care to a monopoly of a powerful orthodoxy."[43] In other words, doctors gained prestige and power through deliberate efforts to delegitimize other health care workers, and this is still reflected in medical practice.[44] An important part of this process was the development of specialized techniques, theories, and language, which set physicians apart from both laypersons and their health care competitors. The emotional well-being of patients, as well with their mundane bodily needs for food and bathing, became the preserve of nurses. This process of distinguishing doctors from other health care practitioners was further consolidated by the acceptance of a mechanistic view of the body, where illness is understood to be simply something that interferes with the effective working of the body-machine, and the mental and emotional states of the patient are seen to be largely irrelevant to the determination of appropriate treatment.

As many feminist scholars have observed, the hierarchical relationship between doctors and nurses was further entrenched by the fact that, until very recently, most doctors were men and most nurses were women. A number of suggestions have been made as to why this has traditionally been the case, including, of course, the historical reasons just considered. In addition, it has been suggested that, if Kohlberg's and Gilligan's psychological analysis of the different ways in which males and females view ethical dilemmas and the appropriate ways to resolve them is at all correct, this gender divide is not at all surprising.[45] Females, who tend to want to help others in concrete and intimate ways, and to think of themselves primarily in relational terms, will be attracted to nursing because it allows them to exercise their capacity to care for others. Males, in contrast, are likely to be attracted to abstract scientific principles and will see in medicine an opportunity to test them out on the human body. Keller, for example, argues that, culturally speaking, scientific objectivity can be seen as a masculine trait, while the identification felt by nurses with their patients' subjective experiences matches well with societal expectations about how women should behave.[46] Moreover, as Brannigan and Boss point out, "[E]ven though more men are becoming nurses, in the mind of the general public the nursing profession is still 'feminine.'"[47]

This dimension of the doctor-nurse relationship is reflected in the case of the nurse who disagrees with the doctor's orders to prescribe a placebo for pain relief: even though the nurse in the scenario is male, his "caring" activities seem to place him in a subordinate position, not only in the mind of the doctor, but also in the hierarchy of the institution in which he works. In the book in which the full version of this case appears,[48] two nurses and one physician provide commentaries. While the physician argues that the doctor's use of a placebo is itself ethically problematic, the only advice he can offer the nurse is that he ask his superior for assistance, and he states that, in a properly managed hospital, "the nurse raising the concern should … be protected from retribution from the attending physician for raising such complaints as a matter of conscience."[49] Likewise, the two nurses state that the doctor's orders are not ethically acceptable since they violate the patient's medical need for adequate pain relief and involve deception, and they suggest that the nurse make an appeal to a higher authority in an effort to deal with the matter. One nurse, in her analysis, puts it this way: "He [the nurse] needs to start by addressing Dr. U directly with his concerns about the moral conflict inherent in the situation.… [I]f Dr. U continues to insist on placebo use, Mr. V needs to refuse to participate and must take his concerns up the chain of command in his organization"[50] and should try to find other ways to relieve the patient's pain. The second nurse goes even further, and states that the nurse "is responsible and accountable for his nursing practice, and that includes the undertreatment of pain. He may consider consulting his immediate supervisor to see what could be done to alleviate the patient's pain. And, if appeals to the appropriate officials in the hierarchy of authority are unsuccessful, he could, as a final step, present the case to the ethics committee."[51] In short, there is agreement among the three commentators that the doctor's actions are morally questionable and that the nurse has an ethical obligation to take care of his patient, which he is violating if he simply does what the doctor tells him. Yet, it is equally clear that his ability to act as an accountable moral agent is compromised by the hierarchical structures of the institution in which he works, and by the power differential that exists between nurse and doctor.

It has sometimes been suggested (and as this scenario illustrates) that doctors and nurses see ethical dilemmas differently: the doctor in this case (rightly or wrongly) believes that it would be wrong to prescribe any painkilling medication that might re-establish the patient's addictive dependency on narcotics. The nurse, on the other hand, sees the ethical concern as residing in his being asked to deceive the patient and being prevented from treating his acute pain adequately. As Oberle and Bouchal point out, however, the issue here is not simply a matter of differing perceptions that result from different professional roles; rather, and much more fundamentally, because of the power differential that exists between doctors and nurses, nurses seldom experience true ethical dilemmas. According to White and Zimbelman, "*An ethical dilemma* is a situation that requires a choice between two mutually exclusive courses of action. For example, if I decide to stop treatment, I cannot at the same time continue treatment. The reason nurses may not experience true ethical dilemmas as often as doctors is that the kinds of decisions that are required in such situations are not often nursing decisions."[52] Instead, nurses experience different parts of the moral landscape than doctors do and consequently face distinct concerns, including moral distress, moral uncertainty, and difficulties in exercising moral agency.

First, moral distress is felt when a nurse believes that "something should be done but is constrained by institutional pressures from acting on that belief."[53] Nurse V, who cannot treat his patient's pain adequately or even tell the patient that he is receiving a placebo, is experiencing moral distress. Moral uncertainty is slightly different: it occurs when a nurse believes that something is morally wrong, or that something should be done differently, but is not sure what should be done instead. This, too, occurs as a direct result of the hierarchical nature of health care. As Oberle and Bouchal succinctly put it, "Physicians write orders for nurses to carry out; the reverse is not true."[54] Finally, concerns about moral agency arise from the presence of moral distress and moral uncertainty. Nurses often have moral beliefs that they are unable to act on because of the fact that "there is an imbalance of power in the health care system itself."[55]

To these three ethical concerns, a fourth has recently been added, namely, moral residue, which has been defined as "the long standing feelings of guilt, remorse or inadequacy an individual experiences because of unresolved ethical conflicts or morally distressing situations."[56] If Nurse V is unable to get support from his superiors when he expresses his concerns, he is likely to experience moral residue.

For these reasons, while the principles of bioethics became an important part of professional nursing ethics during the 1980s and after, there has recently been a move away from the principle-based bioethical approach and toward the creation of a distinctive nursing ethics. While this distinctive nursing ethics is still developing, and will continue to develop until it reaches a standard form, certain features of what it is likely to look like are already apparent. First, it will begin with the recognition of the importance of relationships for nursing practice (consequently, it has been termed a relational ethics). Second, it will suggest that "principled reasoning is inadequate for the kinds of issues nurses face."[57] Third, following feminist critiques, it will emphasize the roles of hierarchical structures and differential power relationships within medicine; in fact, while nursing ethics is still evolving, it is clear that it will probably be built on a feminist base and will focus on the unique nature of the nurse-patient relationship. Unlike doctors, "nurses do not simply care for patients' physical bodies. Rather, nurses pay attention to the patient's whole experience: mind, spirit, and social connections."[58] In addition, this relational ethics will be a kind of virtue ethics informed by feminist concerns and situated within the context of the health care system, embodied in traditions of professional practice, and guided by codes of ethics: it will be a "virtue-based approach [that] … encourages us to consider the kind of person the nurse ought to be in his or her practice."[59]

While the move to a distinctive nursing ethics is an interesting and potentially fruitful shift, it is not entirely clear that it will resolve all of the ethical issues explored here. First, it is not clear how it will address the differential power relationships that give rise to ethical conflict between doctors and nurses. These structural arrangements seem to require both a shift in the way in which hospitals and health care agencies are organized and a sea-change in the way in which doctors view themselves and the nurses they work with. In *Hospital*, her account of one year in the life of a large American hospital, Salamon reports that, when the institution conducted a survey of employees to determine how respectfully they treated one another, it was discovered that doctors "were the worst offenders in every category. It was believed by only 46 percent of the respondents that doctors treated other doctors with respect; only 39 percent felt that doctors treated nurses and technicians with respect."[60] Even if Nurse V were to employ this relational nursing ethics in his deliberations, it is unclear whether Dr. U would respect his opinion or that any courses of action would be open to him that were not already available, namely, reporting the situation to his superiors.

Second, if the ethical training received by doctors and nurses diverges significantly—if, for instance, the principled approach accepted by most bioethicists and applied in texts like this one is taught to medical students and employed by ethically aware doctors, while nurses increasingly use a relational ethics approach—this in itself might further contribute to ethical conflict and all the negative effects that result from it, as doctors and nurses will view, describe, and attempt to resolve the ethical dilemmas of medicine in very different ways. That is to say, if all health care professionals were to use a common ethical approach (such as that provided by the principled approach to bioethics), they would be likely to use the same principles to describe ethical concerns, and would perhaps be able to communicate better than if their ethical approaches are distinctively different in both focus and emphasis.

These concerns are hypothetical at present, as this distinctive relational ethics is not yet fully formed and its effects within the health care system are not yet completely known. It can be said with some certainty, however, that there is a shared consensus that both doctors and nurses are morally required to pay attention to the needs, desires, and choices of their patients. At the heart of both relational ethics and currently acceptable models of the doctor-patient relationship lies a commitment to autonomy.[61] We will, therefore, turn our attention to the patient, and to the concept of autonomy, along with its related concepts of competency, harm, and informed consent.

BOX 3.2

JOHN STUART MILL, *ON LIBERTY*

The object of this Essay is to assert one very simple principle, as entitled to govern absolutely the dealings of society with the individual in the way of compulsion and control, whether the means used be physical force in the form of legal penalties, or the moral coercion of public opinion. That principle is, that the sole end for which mankind are warranted, individually or collectively, in interfering with the liberty of action of any of their number, is self-protection. That the only purpose for which power can be rightfully exercised over any member of a civilized community, against his will, is to prevent harm to others. His own good, either physical or moral, is not a sufficient warrant. He cannot rightfully be compelled to do or forbear because it will be better for him to do so, because it will make him happier, because, in the opinions of others, to do so would be wise, or even right. These are good reasons for remonstrating with him, but not for compelling him, or visiting him with any evil in case he do otherwise. To justify that, the conduct from which it is desired to deter him must be calculated to produce evil to someone else. The only part of conduct of any one, for which he is amenable to society, is that which concerns others. In the part which merely concerns himself, his independence is, of right, absolute. Over himself, over his own body and mind, the individual is sovereign.

It is, perhaps, hardly necessary to say that this doctrine is meant to apply only to human beings in the maturity of their faculties. We are not speaking of children, or of young persons below the age which the law may fix as that of manhood or womanhood. Those who are still in a state to require being taken care of by others may be protected against their own actions as well as against external injury....

This, then, is the appropriate domain of human liberty. It comprises first, the inward domain of consciousness; demanding liberty of conscience in the most comprehensive sense; liberty of thought and feeling; absolute freedom of opinion and sentiment on all subjects, practical or speculative, scientific, moral, or theological. The liberty of expressing and publishing opinions may seem to fall under a different principle, since it belongs to that part of the conduct of the individual which concerns other people; but, being almost of as much importance as the liberty of thought itself, and resting in great part on the same reasons, is practically inseparable from it. Secondly, the principle requires liberty of tastes and pursuits; of framing the plan of our life to suit our own character; of doing as we like, subject to such consequences as may follow: without impediment from our fellow creatures, so long as what we do does not harm them, even though they should think our conduct foolish, perverse, or wrong. Thirdly, from this liberty of each individual, follows the same liberty, within the same limits, of combination among individuals; freedom to unite, for any purpose not involving harm to others: the persons combining being supposed to be of full age, and not forced or deceived.

No society in which these liberties are not, on the whole, respected, is free, whatever may be its form of government; and none is completely free in which they do not exist absolute and unqualified. The only freedom which deserves the name, is that of pursuing our own good in our own way, so long as we do not attempt to deprive others of theirs, or impede their efforts to obtain it. Each is the proper guardian of his own health, whether bodily, or mental and spiritual. Mankind are the greater gainers by suffering each other to live as seems good to themselves, than by compelling each to live as seems good to the rest.

Source: John Stuart Mill, *Utilitarianism, On Liberty, and Considerations on Representative Government*, ed. H.B. Acton (London: Everyman's Library, 1972), 78–81.

AUTONOMY: THEORETICAL CONSIDERATIONS

While there is no consensus about which model of the doctor-patient relationship is most satisfactory, it is important to note that three of the four models considered above share a commitment to autonomy; the Paternalistic Model has been largely rejected in recent decades. This emphasis on autonomy, however, raises other questions. How do we treat those who cannot make decisions for themselves? What ought caring doctors do if they see patients making choices that clearly seem wrong? How do we treat children and adolescents who have some decision-making capacity, but are not yet autonomous? Who should make decisions for those who cannot make them for themselves, and on what basis should those decisions be made? Can we agree on any objective goals of medicine that all doctors should pursue and all patients acknowledge? And, finally, despite the dominance of autonomy, are we nonetheless morally required, on occasion, to act paternalistically?

In order to make sense of questions such as these, the concept of autonomy needs to be explored more fully. Autonomy acts both as a moral principle that can guide ethical decision making and as an ideal of human flourishing. In bioethical discussions, there is sometimes a tendency to conflate autonomy and competence, and to use these terms interchangeably (for example, "Competent patients should make their own medical decisions," and "Autonomous patients should make their own medical decisions"). Competency and autonomy, however, while related concepts, should be kept distinct: to confuse them obscures our ability to see the ethical issues at stake, let alone resolve them. Moreover, while autonomy is one of the fundamental principles of bioethics, competency is not a principle at all. We will proceed by making some theoretical observations about autonomy, and then explore the implications these observations have for informed consent, for morally justified paternalism, and for **surrogate decision-makers**.

Autonomy and Choice

While a commitment to autonomy has come to dominate both our self-understanding and our relations with others, the concept is theoretically complex. In terms of our self-understanding, it tells us that we should make choices for ourselves, whatever these choices happen to be and whatever anyone else thinks about them. Autonomy suggests that our lives go best when we shape them in accordance with a plan of our own choosing. It follows from this that others should not interfere with our choices as long as they concern only ourselves: if I decide to engage in dangerous extreme sports that may kill me, that is my business. However, there is a theoretical ambiguity in the concept: If it is good to live autonomously, in accordance with individual determinations of what is important, is autonomy itself valuable because it facilitates the making of good choices? Or is autonomy valuable merely because it allows us to choose for ourselves, to actively engage in creating a life as we see fit, whatever particular choices are made? The first possibility suggests that we can identify worthwhile desires and choices, and distinguish them from worthless ones; and it follows from this that some choices, no matter how strongly someone desires them, are simply mistaken. The problem with this approach, however, is that it leads to the difficulty noted above, that rational goals that everyone can agree on are very difficult, if not impossible, to find.

The second possibility suggests that it is the act of choosing that makes a choice valuable. But this does not make sense: it is hard to make a moral case for autonomy on this basis, given that some choices clearly seem to be misguided, wasteful, useless, or harmful, even if general claims about what makes choices fall into these categories are difficult to make. In short, we cannot explain why autonomy is thought valuable (and why we should respect the autonomous choices that others make) unless we can connect the exercise of autonomy to the achievement of valuable goals. However, we simultaneously have a difficult time identifying goals that ought to be considered valuable and articulating what it is that makes them so; thus, it is unlikely that we could come up with a list that almost everyone could agree on.

Autonomy as Capacity and as Achievement

It should also be noted that while many discussions of autonomy focus on actions, this emphasis can be misleading. To identify an action as "autonomous" means more than that it was not subject to interference from others, was not forced or demanded; it means, as well, that the person who performed that action was herself autonomous. In order to get at what "being autonomous" means, it is helpful to think of autonomy as both a capacity and an achievement. To be fully autonomous, one must have sufficient mental abilities to make choices and to understand what the consequences of those choices are likely to be. This capacity is not simply intellectual; it also requires that one not be in the grip of a compulsion, addiction, or mental disorder that would interfere with one's ability to identify what one truly desires. For example, in the Starson case, if it were clearly established that Scott lacked the capacity to understand and appreciate the consequences of his choices, then his desire not to be treated would not be seen as an expression of his autonomy, nor would treating him against his will—however problematic it might be on other grounds—be seen as a violation of his autonomy.

Furthermore, to make an autonomous choice, one must have sufficient information; we cannot judge the likely consequences of our choices, or be expected to take responsibility for them, if we are lacking information relevant to that choice. Finally, the exercise of autonomy requires that the political or social setting be one that permits individuals to choose freely; one can have the mental and psychological capacity to make choices and take responsibility for them, and yet be unable to act autonomously. As Raz observes,

> No one can control all aspects of his life. How much control is needed for life to be autonomous ... is an enormously difficult problem.... [What] has to be accepted is that to be autonomous, a person must not only be given a choice but he must be given an adequate range of choices. A person whose every decision is extracted from him by coercion is not an autonomous person. Nor is a person autonomous if he is paralysed and therefore cannot take advantage of the options which are offered to him.[62]

Our capacity to act autonomously, then, can be interfered with both internally (if we lack the intellectual and psychological capacities to truly choose for ourselves, and to understand the consequences of those choices) and externally (if the circumstances within which we find ourselves do not allow free choice from a range of options, or if we do not have sufficient information to make reasonable judgments about those options). When considering the role that autonomy should play within the doctor-patient relationship, then, we need to consider both the abilities of the patient and the obligations of the doctor to fully inform that patient of her diagnosis or prognosis. Someone suffering from advanced dementia, for instance, cannot make an autonomous choice to accept or refuse treatment, even if her doctors ask her what she wants; nor, however, can a patient who is not fully informed about the risks of a proposed treatment.

Autonomy and the Concept of a Whole Life

The concept of autonomy is also complicated by the fact that we need to think in terms of a whole life (rather than merely in terms of actions, desires, and choices) to understand some of its dimensions. Autonomy, as noted, should be seen as an achievement as well as a capacity: it is something we work toward (small children are not autonomous), gain when we are mature adults, and then perhaps lose again as illness and infirmity take their toll. For example, a person suffering from advanced Alzheimer's, while once autonomous, is autonomous no longer. Further, we should also notice that one may have the capacity (intellectual, psychological, social, and political) to make autonomous choices, be a competent adult, and yet not be in a position to make a choice that is fully autonomous. Illness itself may interfere with our ability to choose autonomously. In a study of seriously ill patients, Schneider found that the ill are often in a poor position to make good choices: "[T]hey were frequently exhausted, irritable, shattered, or despondent. Often, they were just trying to get through their immediate pain, nausea, and fatigue; they could hardly think about major decisions."[63] As Mill puts it,

> It is, perhaps, hardly necessary to say that this doctrine [that we should be free to make our own choices] is meant to apply only to human beings in the maturity of their faculties. We are not speaking of children, or of young persons below the age which the law may fix as that of manhood or womanhood. Those who are still in a state to require being taken care of by others, must be protected against their own actions as well as against external injury.[64]

This adds enormous complexity to the role given to autonomy in medicine and generates questions that are very difficult to answer. When, for instance, does a teenager become autonomous? At what point does someone suffering from dementia cease to be autonomous? In the case of individuals such as Starson, do antipsychotic medications restore autonomy, even when they are imposed on people against their will? On what basis should we make decisions for those who cannot make them for themselves if we cannot identify any goals that are uncontroversial?

THE ETHICAL LIMITS OF AUTONOMY

The four most important bioethical principles are autonomy, justice, beneficence, and non-malfeasance, and these principles need to be balanced with one another. Within the context of the health care professional–patient relationship, the principle of autonomy needs to be balanced with the principle of beneficence—the requirement that we ought to do good—and the principle of non-malfeasance—the requirement that we ought to prevent harm. Finally, autonomy and justice can come into tension with one another when individuals ask for more than their fair share (however this is defined) of the available health care resources. These principles are demonstrated in the following limitations on the exercise of autonomy.

The Harm Principle

First, the exercise of autonomy can legitimately be constrained by the **Harm Principle**, which can be understood, in part, as an elaboration of the principle of non-malfeasance. Mill states the principle in this way: "The only purpose for which power can be rightfully exercised over any member of a civilized community against his will is to prevent harm to others."[65] Consider a doctor who has a husband and wife as patients and knows that the husband is infected with HIV, that his wife is unaware of this, and that they are trying to have a child. If the husband (autonomously) refuses to tell his wife about his HIV status, according to the principle of non-malfeasance, the doctor would be justified in violating confidentiality since the harms that will result from breaking this rule are outweighed by the harms that will result if she (and perhaps her hoped-for child) are infected. In the case of Starson, if he were to be considered an autonomous agent, while both detaining him in a psychiatric institution and giving him medication against his will interfere with his autonomy, the former can be justified on the grounds that, because of the death threats he uttered, he is a danger to others. Following Mill's line of thinking, however, Starson should not be detained or medicated if he is simply a danger to himself. The "if," of course, is crucially important; as noted in the quote above, if it is determined instead that he is in "a state to require being taken care of by others," then he must be protected from himself: the delusions that made him believe that he was being poisoned and his consequent refusal to eat, if taken to indicate a lack of autonomy, would justify treatment even for Mill according to the principles of beneficence and non-malfeasance.

The Common Good

Second, according to the principles of beneficence, non-malfeasance, and justice, autonomy can sometimes be limited for the sake of the common good. On occasion, it is justifiable to limit the exercise of an individual's autonomy, even when that exercise is not clearly or directly harmful to others. Take, for example, the issue of scarce medical resources and how they might be distributed to ensure maximum benefit. A particular person may need and desire a heart-lung transplant, which is very expensive; but a case can be made that the money would be more fairly spent on additional long-term care beds, since more people would benefit. Or imagine a terminally ill person who wants doctor-assisted suicide to be legalized; this request might be turned down on the grounds that such legalization will have long-term undesirable affects on society as a whole: it will make people less caring of those who are sick, more prone to view them as expensive burdens on the health care system, more eager to euthanize those who might not desire it.[66]

Ethically Justifiable Paternalism

Third, while paternalism has been superseded by autonomy, there remain some circumstances in which we think our autonomy can be limited for our own good. Paternalism draws on both the principles of beneficence and non-malfeasance, and suggests that, on some occasions, autonomy can legitimately be interfered with in order to do good or to prevent harm. We accept, for instance, laws that require us to wear seat belts, life jackets, or motorcycle helmets on this basis. While a case can be made that such laws are beneficial to society as well (because they reduce medical costs), their primary purpose is to force us to do something that we know is good for us but that we might otherwise fail to do. Dworkin notes that there are situations in which we can recognize that we ought to do something, desire the good consequences that will result if we do it, and yet still need some coercion if we are to do what we know we should. Dworkin writes: "I ... neglect to fasten my seat-belt and I concede such behaviour is not rational but not because I weigh the inconvenience differently from those who fasten the belts. It is just that having made (roughly) the same calculation as everybody else I ignore it in my actions."[67]

Moreover, it should be noted that paternalistic interference with the choices of those who are incompetent and thus not autonomous is not only morally acceptable but required, because such interference upholds the principles of beneficence and, more importantly perhaps, of non-malfeasance: someone must take care of those with advanced Alzheimer's and those in a persistent vegetative state. Given the theoretical triumph of autonomy, the challenge becomes to distinguish those who can make their own decisions from those who cannot. Can a 16-year-old girl make decisions for herself, even if we think that an 11-year-old girl cannot? Should Starson's desire not to be medicated be respected once he stops eating?

Miniature from Avicenna's *Canon of Medicine*: "The Doctor's Visit." When people are sick, they turn to health care professionals for help. It is now recognized that the ethical practice of medicine requires that competent patients give informed consent to any treatment they receive.

INFORMED CONSENT

The way in which the theoretical triumph of autonomy has been translated into medical practice is through the principle of informed consent. This principle can be defined in this way: "You shall not treat a patient without the informed consent of the patient or his or her lawful surrogate except in narrowly defined emergencies."[68] This principle places requirements on both doctors and patients. On the part of the doctor, it requires, first, that she provide the patient with sufficient information about his diagnosis, prognosis, and treatment options so that an informed decision can be made; second, that she not lie to the patient or withhold information that the patient might find important in making that decision; third, that she make an effort to establish whether or not this information has, in fact, been understood; and, finally, that she not coerce or pressure the patient to accept a particular treatment.

As already pointed out, illness can interfere with a person's capacity to make autonomous decisions. Indeed, a case can be made that someone who is seriously ill, whether that illness is temporary or terminal, is no longer fully autonomous. The illness itself limits the extent to which the ill person can shape his life. Moreover, as Frank observes, serious illness can irrevocably alter how one experiences one's life. Once one has been seriously ill, he argues, one becomes a member of the "remission society," a group of people who have been saved by modern medicine but who are neither sick nor well.

> Members of the remission society include those who have had almost any cancer, those living in cardiac recovery programmes, diabetics, those whose allergies and environmental sensitivities require dietary and other self-monitoring, those with prostheses and mechanical body regulators, the chronically ill, the disabled, those "recovering" from abuses and addictions, and for all these people, the families that share the worries and daily triumph of staying well.[69]

Members of the remission society, then, are forever shaped by the experience of illness and by an awareness of their own fragility; they know that complete autonomy is a myth and that any plans humans make for themselves can be overturned in an instant by forces beyond their control.

Competence

The doctrine of informed consent, while drawing on the concept of autonomy, does not, therefore, require that patients be autonomous; rather, it requires merely that they be competent. Competence can be described as "the ability to perform a certain task. In the context of health care ethics ... [this means] the ability to make choices based on an understanding of the *relevant consequences* of that choice on oneself and others."[70] Competence should be judged by a commonsensical standard, rather than by a professional or technical one:

> According to the common sense standard, the patient must be able to understand such things as the fact that he or she will die or get sicker without treatment or that the treatment will be painful and will result in the patient being out of action for a number of weeks. The competent patient is not to be judged by his or her educational level, nor does the competent patient have to understand everything about the condition or the treatments proposed.... The competent patient must understand the consequences of his or her decision to accept or reject a particular treatment. In particular, the patient should understand that she or he is authorizing or refusing to authorize treatment....[71]

It is important to note that a patient can make decisions that go against what the doctor recommends, or are different from the ones most people would make, without being considered incompetent. For example, consider the case of a Jehovah's Witness who is suffering from leukemia and refuses a blood transfusion. While not everyone shares her religious beliefs, these beliefs are of central importance to her, and she is not rendered incompetent by the fact that most people would choose a blood transfusion rather than death.

Children and the Incompetent

The requirements of informed consent are relatively easy to meet in two situations: when the patient is clearly competent and can understand the information being presented; or when the patient is clearly incompetent so that others must make decisions for her. Meeting the requirements of informed consent becomes more difficult, however, when it is not clear whether or not a patient is competent, and in emergency situations in which decisions must be made quickly and consent is difficult or impossible to obtain. Is an 11-year-old able to understand and appreciate medical information well enough to make his own medical decisions, particularly when a likely consequence of refusing treatment is death? At what point does someone who develops Alzheimer's disease move from competency to incompetency? These questions are not easy to answer, and a consideration of them requires that we revisit the concept of paternalism and the circumstances in which paternalism can be morally justified.

Paternalism is a principle that justifies interference with a person's choices or actions for that person's sake. While the doctrine of informed consent requires that doctors must presume that a patient is competent (even if the patient makes a treatment choice the doctor thinks mistaken), "there are times when our intuition clearly tells us that this person ought not to be making important decisions for himself. The problem is establishing when our intuitions are correct."[72] If they are, then paternalistic interference is justified on the basis of beneficence and non-malfeasance: we have a moral obligation to take care of those who cannot take care of themselves and to prevent harm from coming to them. This can be seen clearly when we consider one class of the unquestionably incompetent, small children. Parents have an obligation to do what is in the best interests of their children and must make decisions for them. Incompetence can be temporary or permanent. Someone who lapses into unconsciousness is, for that period, incompetent. Some philosophers argue that paternalistic actions can be justified if their goal is to restore competence. For those who are permanently incompetent, someone else—called a surrogate or substitute decision-maker—must make decisions for them.

The most difficult challenge, then, is to determine whether or not someone is so incompetent that medical decisions must be made for him or her by others. Competency exists along a spectrum,[73] with those at one end being able to understand and appreciate the information being presented to them, and those at the other end having no understanding or appreciation whatsoever. In the middle lies understanding, but not appreciation. Dworkin describes the difference between understanding and appreciation in his discussion of his own failure to use a seat belt, even though he knows intellectually that this failure is irrational: "A plausible explanation for this deplorable habit is that although I know in some intellectual sense what the probabilities and risks are I do not fully appreciate them in an emotionally genuine manner."[74] For instance, a 13-year-old boy[75] with bone cancer might understand that he needs treatment, but not be able to appreciate the consequences of treating his illness through prayer and alternative medicine rather than with an amputation, especially if his parents encourage him to reject the latter option. An adult in the same position, however, might make the same choice with a clear understanding of the alternatives and a good appreciation of the likely consequences of opting for either approach. The Supreme Court of Canada recently ruled that what it termed mature children under the age of 16 should have their treatment wishes taken seriously. The case concerned a 15-year-old Jehovah's Witness who had been given a blood transfusion against her will in order to save her life. The Court said that what must be considered include the maturity level of the child, the child's best interests, and the seriousness of the procedure being contemplated. The ruling stated: "The more serious the nature of the decision, and the more severe its potential impact on the life or health of the child, the greater the degree of scrutiny that will be required."[76] Unfortunately, this ruling does not really clarify matters practically or theoretically. In practical terms, a judgment still has to be made in any given case about whether that particular child meets the competency requirements to be considered a mature minor. In theoretical terms, particularly when children and adolescents are making medical decisions on the basis of the religious beliefs that their parents have taught them, it is not clear that those beliefs should be considered their own in the way that they might be for adults. In other words, it might be argued that, rather than supporting the autonomy of mature children, what the Court ruling does is simply uphold the autonomy of the parents to follow their own religious practices and to impose those practices on their offspring.

Clearly, while we can identify those who exist at either end of the spectrum, those who fall in between are less easy to place, since degrees of ability (and inability) shade into one another almost imperceptibly. As the Starson case demonstrates, determinations of competency are difficult to make and sometimes controversial; the disagreement between the Supreme Court majority and the dissenters was precisely with respect to whether Starson had the capacity to make treatment decisions and understand their consequences, and each side drew different conclusions from the same factual evidence.

STRONG AND WEAK PATERNALISM

Paternalism holds that we can interfere with a person's choices if, by doing so, we can prevent harm coming to them or can benefit them. Interference, too, exists along a continuum: the mildest form is explanation (a required part of informed consent), and this can shade into argumentation, pressure, and, finally and most seriously, physical coercion. Consider someone who refuses to be placed on a ventilator. His doctor can explain to him the likely consequences of his refusal. He can argue with him about his choice. He can pressure him if he still refuses. Or he could simply place him on the machine against his will. Likewise, detention in a psychiatric facility falls at the serious end of the spectrum of degrees of interference, as does forcibly injecting antipsychotic medication.

The purpose of paternalistic interference is to prevent avoidable harm. Harms, too, can be distinguished from one another on the basis of their degree of seriousness: they can be permanent and serious (for instance, death); permanent, but less serious (losing a finger); serious, but not permanent (treatable pneumonia); and neither permanent nor serious (a bad cold). Paternalists can be divided into strong and weak in terms of how they approach these distinctions.[77] For a **weak paternalist**, as long as a patient understands, or understands and appreciates, the nature of her diagnosis, prognosis, and treatment options (including the likely consequences of non-treatment), then, with respect to even serious harm, the only interferences that are morally justified are explanation and argumentation. For example, in the case of a competent Jehovah's Witness with leukemia who does not want a blood transfusion, doctors might try to talk her out of her refusal to have a blood transfusion, but if they are weak paternalists, this is all that they will do. In cases in which a weak paternalist can be confident that a patient does not have the capacity to understand, she will move more coercively to prevent harm coming to her patient. For example, if a weak paternalist decides that an Alzheimer's patient who needs a heart operation does not understand the information that is being presented to him, she will pressure him to accept the operation. Likewise, if a weak paternalist believes that Starson is incompetent, she would have no difficulty medicating him against his expressed wishes.

A **strong paternalist** agrees with the weak paternalist that the incompetent can be legitimately pressured or coerced but also believes that, sometimes, paternalistic behaviour can be justified in the case of the competent. There are two sorts of justifications the strong paternalist can use. First, the strong paternalist can argue that the patient will be subsequently grateful for the interference. Second, the strong paternalist might appeal to some objective standard of well-being, even if this standard is not accepted by a particular patient: a strong paternalist might, on this basis, give an unwanted blood transfusion to a Jehovah's Witness. Given the dominance of autonomy and its translation in medical practice into the doctrine of informed consent, strong paternalism is difficult to ethically justify.

Surrogate Decision-Makers

Once incompetency is established, it becomes clear that someone else must make decisions for the patient. These surrogate decision-makers can include parents, close relatives, or legally appointed guardians. The challenge they face is how they should make those decisions. There are two possibilities: they can make a substituted judgment or a best interests judgment. A substituted judgment requires them to make a decision on the basis of what they think that particular person would have wanted; if someone who becomes incompetent made her wishes known before this occurred, those wishes should guide treatment decisions. A best interests judgment, in contrast, is based on what most people, in those circumstances, would think desirable. For example, if most patients who develop pneumonia would want to be treated, then treatment would be provided to the incompetent who develop pneumonia. However, since weak paternalism has triumphed in medicine and strong paternalism has been largely banished, if a substituted judgment can be made (if, that is, enough is known about what the patient would probably have wanted), then it takes precedence over a best interests one. Finally, in accordance with the requirements of informed consent, a surrogate decision-maker must be fully informed and must consent to any treatment provided (except, of course, in emergency situations).

ADVANCE DIRECTIVES

Given these complexities, **advance directives** (sometimes known as "living wills") can be very helpful. Advance directives allow people to determine, while competent, the treatments they would and would not like to receive if they became incompetent and unable to make their desires known. While advance directives can be helpful, determining in advance exactly what any of us would or would not want in the way of treatment is very difficult. For example, most people find it difficult to know what treatment they would want if they were to have a car accident and slip into a coma. In addition, as Hebert notes, not only are we faced with the problem that advance instruction directives "cannot cover every possible situation and may draw attention away from setting goals for appropriate treatment,"[78] but (as when a person becomes incompetent as a result of dementia) personhood may change.

Someone who is young and in good health may find it hard to imagine how he or she—as patient or surrogate—would view life and the burdens of care when older and less fit. Indeed, this is a thorny problem with living wills generally: why should they be followed if the patient's personhood has totally changed? Therefore, in difficult cases such as continued treatment of a "hopeless case," living wills may give us the view from the patient's past, but they do not tell us if it is the right thing to do in the present.[79] Consequently, it is important that advance directives be updated as people age, in the light of changing interests and as developments in medicine open up new possibilities for treatment.

FEMINIST CHALLENGES TO THE AUTONOMY-BASED CONCEPT OF THE DOCTOR-PATIENT RELATIONSHIP

While the autonomy-based model of human flourishing is widely accepted, and currently plays a central role in any morally acceptable description of the relationship between health care professional and patient, this model has been challenged on a number of fronts. The most important of these challenges, arguably, is the one presented by feminists, who have asked questions about the understanding of autonomy that is most frequently used in contemporary bioethics. These concerns can be summed up in the question: what conception of autonomy is being employed, and does it match the realities of lived experience, particularly the lived experience of women and members of oppressed groups?

While most feminist bioethicists acknowledge both the importance of autonomy in medicine (it provides a crucial defence against medical paternalism) and its appeal (it is hard to argue convincingly against the claim that competent individuals should be left free to make their own decisions in matters as deeply and crucially important to them as their own health), a number of feminist scholars have expressed concerns about the way in which autonomy and its exercise within the medical context are currently understood. These concerns fall into two broad categories. First, feminist scholars examine the multiple ways in which women and members of marginalized groups are oppressed and ask whether, given this context, the choices that these people make in the medical setting can be considered truly autonomous. Second, feminist critics have argued that the model of autonomy that is most commonly invoked in bioethics (and elsewhere) assumes an unencumbered, individualistic male moral agent, whose characteristics do not fit well with the experiences of most women. Rather than this individualistic model of autonomy, many feminists suggest that autonomy should be understood as a relational concept. (This approach, as we saw above, is now being incorporated into nursing ethics.) Each of these concerns will be considered in turn, and then the implications of a feminist approach to the issues that arise in health care will be considered.

The way in which the ideal of autonomy has been translated into medical practice and patient choice is through the concept of informed consent: competent individuals are assumed to have had their autonomy respected when the appropriate range of medical options and information about their risks and benefits is provided to them, and they are left free to make an uncoerced choice about which treatment they prefer. However, as Dodds notes,

> [I]dentifying respect for autonomy with informed consent presupposes that ethical concern should be directed to the actions *of the physician* in obtaining consent (whether the physician gives full and adequate information, whether the physician has unduly influenced the decision of the patient, whether the physician explains the information clearly, etc.) and not to the decision-making process *of the patient*.[80]

This is significant because it obscures or ignores questions about the extent to which the patient is able to make genuinely autonomous choices, given the social, political, and medical context within which those choices are made.

Sherwin observes that the concept of informed consent suggests that patients make autonomous choices when four conditions are met. First, the patient is deemed to be competent, to have the rational capacity to make the choice. Second, the choice should be a reasonable one, given the options available. Third, the patient has been given sufficient information about the possibilities available and has understood that information. And, finally, the choice of any of these options is free and uncoerced.

However, Sherwin argues, given the larger context within which these choices are made, each of these requirements, even if ostensibly met, is nonetheless problematic. In terms of the competency requirement, it should be noted that competency is usually connected to rationality, "yet the rationality of women and members of other oppressed groups is frequently denied."[81] In terms of the second requirement, it is important to note, Sherwin believes, that "the set of available options is constructed in ways that may already seriously limit the patient's autonomy by prematurely excluding options the patient might have preferred."[82] For example, consider a pregnant woman who is told that, during birth, she can choose whether or not to have an epidural (an anaesthetic administered into the spine to control pain during labour). However, her real preference—to have a home birth—is not one of the options available to her. In terms of the third condition, the requirement that sufficient information be provided to allow an informed choice, a similar concern exists: the only information that will be presented will be "the information that has been deemed worthy of study and that is considered relevant by the health care providers involved."[83] Finally, Sherwin believes that the appearance of choice is actually a deceptive mask for the exercise of medical authority in ways that surpass even that envisaged in the old-fashioned paternalistic model. What patients are provided with is not genuine choice, or self-evident physician paternalism, but, rather, the appearance of choice that actually disguises the fact that powerful medical forces that lie well beyond the patient's control are actually at work. As Sherwin concludes, "Thus, informed consent procedures aimed simply at protecting autonomy in the narrow sense of specific choice among preselected options may ultimately serve to secure the compliance of docile patients who operate under the illusion of being invited to consent to procedures they are socially encouraged to choose."[84]

Models of the Self

In addition to asking questions about the nature of patient choice, feminist bioethicists have also observed that embedded at the heart of the concept of autonomy is a model of the self. In contemporary thought, particularly in North America, the self is assumed to be individualistic, able to make whatever choices it feels like as long as they are not harmful to others; unencumbered by obligations or commitments to others; and rational, with the capacity both to articulate goals and determine the ways in which they might be achieved. This concept of autonomy, Friedman argues, is epitomized in the life of the painter Gauguin, who abandoned his wife and five children in order to "paint pictures in sunny locales."[85] This conception, she believes, is largely irrelevant to women who, even today, define themselves primarily in terms of their relationships: it is a model that, we might say, fits Gauguin but not his wife, who presumably was left to take care of their children regardless of what else she might have wanted to do with her life. Consequently, Friedman observes, "Many feminist philosophers have recently suggested that women find autonomy to be a notion inhospitable to women, one that represents a masculine-style preoccupation with self-sufficiency and self-realization at the expense of human connection."[86]

Both feminist ethics and the ethics of care emphasize that humans exist in relationships with one another. Likewise, as noted above, the distinctive form of health care ethics that is emerging in nursing emphasizes the centrality of concrete relationships in ethical thought and practice. Consequently, rather than emphasizing our individuality and distinctiveness from one another, feminist scholars suggest that we should conceive of autonomy itself relationally; that is to say, however we conceive of the individual and the choices she makes, we should notice that all of us, both male and female, exist in a web of relationships and that these relationships provide the context within which any of our choices are made. Furthermore, on occasion at least, we are morally obliged to consider the consequences for others of the choices we make. However much we may admire Gauguin's paintings, we cannot ignore the fact that he had moral obligations to his wife and children that he ignored. Finally, in addition to having obligations to others because of the relationships we have with them, we also become autonomous agents through our relationships with others. Each of us is dependent on others, which means that we exist in interdependent networks that are essential for autonomous personhood. As Barclay puts it, "The very precondition of our being able to develop and sustain our capacity for autonomy is attributable to our developing and remaining embedded within a network of social relationships. The capacity and aspiration for autonomy is not something we are born with but something we develop only in society. The fact that any of us has the capacity for autonomous agency is a debt we each owe to others."[87]

Feminist ethics emphasizes the significance of power structures and sources of oppression; consequently, ethical considerations are intimately bound up in social and political ones. This means that a feminist approach to the issues that arise in a health care context will be distinctively different from the standard approaches, which tend to construct ethical issues in terms of individuals and the particular choices they make. This point can best be illustrated through the use of examples. First, in the standard bioethical approach, a number of illnesses are attributed to the individual and to the choices he or she has made. Consider a condition such as skin cancer, a disease that is on the increase. Skin cancer can be attributed to an individual's failure to apply sufficient sunscreen, to stay out of the sun at certain times of the day, and to stay in the shade when the UV index is high. A feminist approach, in contrast, might ask why so little attention has been paid by the medical profession to the causes of the thinning of the ozone layer, which is largely responsible for the rise in skin cancer rates.

Second, consider in vitro fertilization, a reproductive technology that has made it possible for individuals who might not otherwise be able to conceive to have children. This technology is often presented as a way in which the autonomy of the involuntarily infertile can be enhanced, because it provides a way in which their goal of parenthood can be achieved. Feminist bioethicists, however, will ask why it is that so few public resources are committed to preventing infertility in the first place and why so many women feel such intense social pressure to become mothers that they are willing to risk their health to undergo such a potentially dangerous medical procedure.[88]

Finally, consider prenatal genetic testing, which offers pregnant women the opportunity to test their fetuses to see whether they carry genetic mutations that may result in handicaps. These tests are often viewed as adding to the information available to pregnant women and thus facilitating autonomous, informed choice about whether or not they should continue with their pregnancies. Feminists, though, would ask why so much money is spent on developing and providing these tests when so few social resources are provided to help families with handicapped children. They would also ask whether, in the absence of this help, the choice that many women make to take these tests, and to abort when an abnormality is discovered, is really freely executed and autonomously chosen.

In conclusion, feminist bioethicists ask questions about the nature of patient choice and about the model of autonomy that is often used in bioethics. They suggest that this model needs to be adjusted so that it acknowledges the web of social relationships within which human beings live and choose, rather than emphasizing our individuality and separateness. Finally, feminists suggest that bioethical issues should be considered broadly so that they encompass not only the dimension of individual choice within health care, but also the larger social, political, and medical context that determines what choices are available in the first place, who they benefit, and who they may leave out. Only when all these dimensions are considered, feminists believe, can we create the conditions necessary for everyone to make genuinely autonomous choices.

AUTONOMY AND THE EXPERIENCE OF ILLNESS

While autonomy has, for good reason, been placed at the heart of the ethical practice of medicine, it is a complex concept that will almost certainly continue to develop. Feminist challenges to the individualistic model of autonomy are already being incorporated into the evolving description of the nurse-patient relationship, and may, in time, be incorporated into the doctor-patient model as well. We noted at the beginning of this chapter that relationships are dynamic, not static. The challenge for bioethicists, now, is not to assume that, since medical paternalism has been replaced by an ethically superior model based on autonomy and structured around the requirements of informed consent, all the work has been completed. One area in which work still remains to be done is suggested by first-person accounts of illness, which indicate that, while autonomy is fundamentally important in the medical context, doctors (and other health care professionals) need to do more than respect patients' autonomy if they are to feel that they have been ethically treated. A second area in which standard assumptions about the place of autonomy in health care are challenged relates to the diverse expectations of patients in multicultural societies. We will conclude with an exploration of these challenges, and suggest that the Covenantal Model of the doctor-patient relationship seems better placed than its rivals to accommodate the concerns expressed by ill people and to provide a context for the multicultural dimensions of health care in pluralistic societies.

In his account of what it is like to be a member of the "remission society," Frank argues that the successes of modern medicine for people like him have come at a high cost. They live longer, but feel that they have been "colonized," that their stories are no longer their own:

> [A] core social expectation of being sick is surrendering oneself to the care of a physician. I understand this obligation of seeking medical care as a *narrative surrender*.... The ill person not only agrees to follow physical regimens that are prescribed; she also agrees, tacitly but with no less implication, to tell her story in medical terms.... The physician becomes the spokesperson for the disease, and the ill person's stories come to depend heavily on repetition of what the physician has said.[89]

What ill patients need, Frank believes, is some way to reclaim their voice, to talk about their experiences in ways that go beyond the things that the medical story can encompass. As Frank states, "The loss of a life's map and destination are not medical symptoms.... The scope of modernist medicine—defined in practices ranging from medical school curricula to billing categories—does not include helping patients learn to think differently about their post-illness worlds and construct new relationships to those worlds."[90] Frank's concern is not that people like him were not given choices or allowed to make their own medical decisions; rather, it is that the context within which those choices were provided did nothing to help him make sense of what he was going through and how this would alter his understanding of himself for the rest of his life, even if he never became seriously ill again.

Likewise, Carel argues that the conceptions of illness and health, as they are used in the medical world, are impoverished and incomplete. Like Frank, she discovered after being diagnosed with a degenerative, untreatable, and potentially fatal condition that her lived experience was at odds with medical descriptions and expectations. Again, the problem was not that her autonomy was not respected; it was, ironically, that many of the health care professionals, including physicians, whom she encountered appeared to be made uncomfortable by sick people, and this translated into the way in which they treated her. She describes, for example, her experiences with doctors and nurses:

> Very few people were explicitly rude to me; no one ignored my questions or requests. But few cared to make the encounter more comfortable and less frightening for me. No one asked me how I feel about my illness. I quickly learned that when doctors ask "How are you?" they mean "How is your body?"; that when an X-ray of my lungs is up on the screen and several doctors stand around it discussing my "case," they will not include me in the discussion. That they will not want to know how my life has changed because of my illness, how they could make it easier for me.[91]

Carel wonders whether doctors (and nurses) need to maintain a sharp dividing line between themselves and their patients in order to preserve their sanity. Even if this is the case, she notes, it makes the experience of patients much more difficult than it needs to be as they navigate through a world of medical tests and procedures while grappling with their own fears of disability and death. Carel asks whether "the encounter must be so impersonal, so guarded. Could some genuine care be introduced into the exchange?" She continues: "I often wondered why it is that not a single medical practitioner ever said they are sorry to hear I am ill. Such a banal social convention: I am sorry to hear about your illness. Why does this convention cease to apply as soon as one enters a hospital ward or a doctor's clinic?"[92] She also asks other questions that point to the importance of developing an ongoing relationship with particular health care practitioners: "I wonder … if a dedicated nurse could do my breathing tests, rather than a new person each time. Wouldn't such a system actually be more efficient, if the nurse knew my name and details, if we had a routine way of doing things? And if I felt comfortable with her, surely that would save rather than waste time?"[93]

MULTICULTURAL CHALLENGES IN PLURALISTIC SOCIETIES

In 2013, the Society of Obstetricians and Gynecologists of Canada (SOGC) released a position statement on how their members should respond to patient requests to be treated by a physician of a particular ethnicity or gender. According to a *National Post* article about the statement, the Society insisted that time-sensitive services, such as attending to a woman who is in labour, "should be provided by the most qualified professional available—with no heed to personal background."[94] Further, "Providing such services should 'not ever' be based on gender, race, sexual orientation, age or religion, and facilities 'should not be expected to provide alternative care providers.'"[95] While some medical practitioners applauded the Society's position, others were not so certain that it was an appropriate response to such requests, which are often made for religious or cultural reasons. The article quoted one doctor who noted that "some studies suggest that newcomers to a country are more likely to obtain potentially life-saving services—from contraception to diabetes prevention—if it is culturally sensitive."[96]

Those who place themselves on this side of the debate believe that the provision of good health care includes a responsiveness to the cultural and religious backgrounds of patients—a responsiveness that need not be limited to preventative and ongoing treatment but should also encompass, whenever possible, the provision of time-sensitive treatment. For example, Leonard argues that ethical nurses practice requires that nurses demonstrate cultural competence in their dealings with patients from diverse backgrounds. Consequently, she argues, patient assessments should include not only information about their health, but also their "birth place, time since immigration if appropriate, ethnic affiliation and its strength, primary and secondary languages, speaking and reading ability, people (family members and friends) who support them, religion and its importance in daily life and current practices, food preferences and prohibitions, health and illness beliefs and practices as well as customs around such transitions as birth, illness, and death,"[97] and nurses should strive to accommodate those beliefs, practices, and customs at all stages of treatment.

The views expressed in the SOGC position statement, and the mixed responses to the reality that patients come from diverse backgrounds, reflect the challenges of medical practice in a multicultural and pluralistic society. Patients who enter into health care settings bring very different social, cultural, and medical expectations with them, and the challenge this can pose for bioethics in both practical and theoretical terms is acute.

As Turner observes, this challenge is perhaps most clearly exemplified in "the dispute surrounding the provision of female genital 'circumcision' in North American hospitals."[98] As he puts it, "What is interpreted as responsible, caring conduct within one community is sometimes regarded as callous and cruel behaviour by individuals encultured into different moral norms and patterns of social life."[99] In the case of female genital circumcision, the divide between these two positions is particularly stark: "What is a morally defensible, culturally significant rite of passage for the defenders ... is regarded by opponents as an act of mutilation, an assault on the bodily integrity of vulnerable female children by adult members of patriarchal societies, and a violation of basic human rights."[100]

Surprisingly, Turner notes, despite the fact that many societies today are both pluralistic and multicultural, the moral theories and approaches used by bioethicists offer little guidance for how such cross-cultural conflicts should be dealt with. "Instead," Turner adds, "the regnant moral theories continue to obscure variations in communal understandings of moral practice, and foster idealistic, 'decontextualized' accounts of moral reasoning that pay little attention to changing patterns of social life and moral experience throughout Canada and the United States."[101]

The reasons for this are arguably historical, and they go to the heart of contemporary bioethics. Many scholars trace the origins of modern bioethics to the revelation of the atrocities committed by physicians in the Nazi regime. Revolted, the early bioethicists sought to create a form of bioethics that allowed for the making of moral judgments uncoloured by particular cultural perspectives and ideologies, those that were cross-culturally and cross-temporally valid. That is, no Nazi doctor should be able to defend his actions on the grounds that they were compatible with the cultural, legal, and ethical standards of his community at the particular period in history in which they were performed. Consequently, the "international bioethics" that emerged in response to the medical practices of the Nazi regime was founded on the idea that fundamental ethical principles—including the informed consent of research subjects and a commitment to the concept of human rights—are shared by all civilized societies.

Baker labels the beliefs on which contemporary bioethics is predicated a form of "moral fundamentalism": "As the label 'fundamentalism' suggests, the central tenet of this position is that certain basic or *fundamental* moral principles are accepted in all eras and cultures and thus are universally applicable to agents and actions in any era or culture."[102] Recently, however, the belief that an international form of bioethics—one that is free of cultural, national, ideological, and religious presuppositions—has been challenged both theoretically and practically.

Theoretically speaking, a number of issues with which bioethicists need to grapple are global in scope. Ryan, for instance, identifies AIDS, drug pricing, and medical research as issues that can only be adequately explored in a global context. Consequently, she asserts, the "moral geography" of bioethics must shift, and bioethicists must begin to listen to the voices of those who live in the "two-thirds world,"[103] the voices of those who live in Africa, Asia, and South America, rather than Europe and North America.

When we start "listening to these voices," a number of scholars have begun to argue, we can no longer be so certain that an international form of bioethics can be found. For example, Alora and Lumitao draw a distinction between the assumptions that are made about the nature of bioethics from a Filipino perspective and from a Western one: "The very character of ethics in the West contrasts with ethics in the Philippines not just in terms of the issues and solutions, as well as the context in which each is embedded, but also in the very language and character of moral concern."[104] In support of this claim, they note that Western bioethics is focused on the individual, while Filipino bioethics is focused on communal concerns. In addition, "Western bioethics often is oriented to principles; Filipino bioethics, on the other hand, is not articulated primarily in principles but in lived moral virtues. Whereas Western bioethics is almost always expressed in discursive terms, Filipino bioethics is part of the phenomenological world of lived experience."[105] In short, they conclude, while Western bioethics "is a framework for thought, a conceptual system," in the Philippines "it is a way of life, an embodied activity of virtue."[106]

Likewise, Ndebele, Mfutso-Bengo, and Masiye argue that the application of Western ideals of medical confidentiality to the Bantu peoples of Southern Africa is not only inappropriate but actually harmful to their health if they have been diagnosed as HIV-positive. In Bantu culture, family is fundamentally important, and communal values take precedence over individual ones. Consequently, "[w]hen a person is sick, the whole extended family has to be informed about the nature of the illness so that they can participate in decisions as well as in the illness.... Together, the family members decide where to go for treatment."[107]

Similarly, studies have shown that the Navajo view the provision of medical information very differently than do most North Americans. In particular, they have beliefs about "the cosmic power of thoughts and words for how it is appropriate to conduct discussions about medical treatment or non-treatment, the risks that they entail, the expected course of a patient's condition, and the prognosis about its outcome"[108] that challenge the standard expectations around informed consent that are now built into bioethics. Since the Navajo believe that negative thoughts about illness and the possibility of death can actually create those outcomes, some bioethicists have concluded that it would be harmful to provide the kind of information about diagnosis and prognosis that patients drawn from other cultural groups would expect.

These cultural differences in the way in which illness, medicine, and bioethics are perceived suggest that ethical medical practice might look very different in different cultural contexts. Given this, bioethicists like Baker are skeptical about the possibility that a universally applicable, cross-cultural, and cross-temporal form of bioethics has been, or could be, developed: "[E]ven if fundamental principles could be found, they necessarily would be read through different conceptual-interpretive-perceptual gazes or narrative frameworks.... Thus, even the long-sought panacea of universally accepted fundamental moral principles does *not* suffice to guarantee universal agreement in moral judgment."[109] In light of these kinds of observations, some bioethicists argue that, rather than seeking to develop an international form of bioethics, theorists should instead work to create national culturally based forms of bioethics that respond better to specific cultural circumstances than the form that currently dominates in the bioethical literature and in "standard" bioethical discourse.

Moreover, some bioethicists go a step further and argue that the "standard" version of bioethics is itself a cultural construct, despite its claims to universality—namely, a Western approach to bioethical questions and concerns. As Ndebele and his colleagues put it, "Bantu cultures do not share many of the assumptions implicit in the Western autonomy-based approach to deliberations,"[110] and they argue that bioethical discussions of concepts such as patient confidentiality need to be broadened "by lessening the emphasis on the individual patient and including the family."[111]

It seems both fair and uncontroversial to acknowledge that cultural differences exist and that the practice of medicine, understood, at least in part, as a set of practices, is culturally and temporally embedded. It follows that culture will influence the expectations that individuals bring to their encounters with the health care system and with the professionals who work within it, and that these differing expectations may pose a challenge for medical practitioners (and bioethicists) working in multicultural societies.

Two challenges are particularly important. The first concerns the central place occupied by autonomy, the individualistic conception of the person that underpins it and the ability of this concept to mediate the encounter between health care professionals and patients. The second challenge follows from the first, in the sense that, if autonomy is not always capable of mediating these encounters satisfactorily, then cultural and religious differences take on a new and altered importance; the question then becomes how the cultural and religious values of patients can—and cannot—be accommodated within health care settings and by the practitioners who work in them.

First, then, let us once again examine the nature of autonomy. This principle has become so powerful in contemporary bioethics, in part, because it is often assumed to allow us to sidestep or even avoid the difficult questions that can arise when patients are drawn from a multiplicity of cultural and religious backgrounds that influence the medical treatments they desire and their interactions with health care professionals. That is to say, autonomy is thought by many bioethicists to be a principle that is capable of transcending cultural and religious differences. In effect, it allows us to have a common bioethical approach in health care *and* to respect and accommodate divergent religious and cultural perspectives.

Consider, for instance, the acknowledged right of patients who are Jehovah's Witnesses to refuse blood transfusions even when such transfusions may save their lives, a right that has been upheld by the courts and is now an accepted part of medical practice. In terms of the theoretical underpinnings of autonomy, explored earlier in this chapter, we can acknowledge that the theory allows for the possibility that an individual can autonomously choose, to a greater or lesser degree, to accept limitations on her exercise of autonomy (as, for instance, when she chooses to have a child, get married, or take a vow of obedience upon entering a religious order). In the case of a Jehovah's Witness, then, we can accept that she has voluntarily chosen to adhere to a particular set of religious beliefs that limit the range of medical options open to her (they no longer include, that is to say, blood transfusions). When the medical system and its practitioners respect this right of refusal, they are, in fact, respecting an autonomously made choice.

Similarly, Macklin argues that, when medical practitioners withhold negative information from their Navajo patients, they are not violating their autonomy (as we would normally think) but respecting it: "Navajos holding traditional beliefs can act autonomously only when they are not thinking in a negative way, so physicians who withhold bad news are not being paternalistic in the usual sense (acting in what *they* believe to be in the patient's best interest). Instead, they are acting in what the Navajo patients believe is in their own best interest, and that shows respect for autonomy."[112]

Understanding the choices of patients who come from cultures termed non-autonomy supporting and non-individualistic in this way is thought by some bioethicists to seriously misconstrue what is at issue. They argue that medical practitioners working in multicultural societies cannot easily navigate cultural and religious differences by appealing to the principle of autonomy in the way suggested by the Jehovah's Witnesses, right to refuse blood transfusions considered above.

Fagan, for example, asserts that autonomy is not a neutral concept that can provide a shared language between patients from all cultures and those who give them medical treatment. First, he states, "[T]he existence of a diverse collection of ethnic, cultural, and religious communities within a single society raises fundamental questions concerning the basis for a common, public moral discourse."[113] Second, he continues, "[T]hese concerns bear directly on norms capable of regulating relationships between clinicians and patients."[114] Fagan's argument is simple, but its implications are profound. There are, he says, some cultures that do not support the development of autonomy, do not assume the individualistic principles that it requires, and do not value the exercise of certain choices. It is not that individuals from such cultures autonomously choose to act in ways that accord with their cultural commitments and the beliefs that are shaped by these; it is, far more fundamentally, that their continued membership in the culture precludes them from thinking of themselves as autonomous persons in the first place. As Fagan puts it, "[O]ne must not assume that personal autonomy is an ideal that is universally recognized and espoused by all of those communities one aims to address and legislate for"[115] and, he goes on to say, "One cannot ... simply assume that respecting patients' beliefs and commitments is necessarily consistent with respecting patients' autonomy."[116] Some religious beliefs and some cultural commitments, in short, impose constraints that cannot be overcome by the exercise of autonomy—at least, not if one wants to remain a member of that community. In some situations, then, Fagan argues,

"Remaining within the fold will ... require of the individual precisely that she should not deliberate upon the fundamental tenets of her community. Her opinion remains valid only as long as it conforms to the expectations of the community. One is therefore 'free' to choose only so long as one chooses to act in the prescribed manner."[117]

If Fagan's position is at all plausible, it is likely that medical professionals working in multicultural societies will sometimes face practical challenges in their interactions with at least some of their patients. The language of autonomy, and the concepts that follow from the central place now given to it within ethical medical practice—such as individualism, informed consent, privacy, and confidentiality—will simply not resonate with patients who come from non-individualistic, family-oriented, and religiously based cultures.

The second challenge follows from the first. If autonomy and its related concepts cannot always be counted upon to provide a common, shared, non-culturally situated context for the encounter between health care providers and patients—if the religious beliefs and cultural commitments of some patients "go all the way down," and cannot be evaluated from some outside standpoint by the patient, and accepted or rejected—this will be reflected in the requests and choices these patients make, some of which may be difficult for health care providers to accommodate or even accept.

Consider, again, the problem that the position statement of the Society of Obstetricians and Gynecologists discussed above is trying to address, that of requests by patients to be treated by physicians of a particular gender, ethnicity, or cultural background. How should such requests be viewed? Do they represent an autonomy-based request that should be accommodated whenever possible because of the commitment to the values of informed consent and patient-centred care? Are they representative of cultural beliefs and religious values that medical professionals should try to respect, given their commitment to patient choice, even if they personally disagree with them and even if the patients who make these requests do not conceive of themselves as autonomous choosers when they make them? Or are they requests that simply do not fit within the ethical framework that is assumed by most health care providers and by many of their patients? Do they, in other words, reflect culturally based assumptions that ought not to be accommodated because they are predicated on sexist, racist, or religiously intolerant beliefs that have no place within the ethical provision of health care?

There are no easy answers to these questions, and bioethicists have not yet reached a consensus on the place of cultural differences in their analysis of the health care professional–patient relationship. It should also be noted that not all members of particular communities believe that such requests ought to be respected. Aruna Papp, a counsellor and educator who describes herself as "a South Asian immigrant to Canada ... [and] who has worked intimately with South Asian victims of abuse for 30 years,"[118] argues that such requests should not be accommodated. In her view, "in health units where the patients and medical personnel are diverse, patients should not have the right of refusal of service based on race, culture, or religion. We would have no sympathy for white people who refused medical care from black people—and according to many physicians, that too is a common phenomenon—even if they insisted their healthcare depended on it."[119] She concludes that "the position taken by the Society of Obstetricians and Gynecologists is both fair and reasonable."[120] And, it might be added, 50 years ago, many Canadian men might not have wanted to be treated by a female physician and many white patients might not have wanted to be treated by non-white medical practitioners. We have rightly decided that such prejudices, however deeply and sincerely felt, should not be respected. There is a very thin line between respecting a patient's cultural and religious beliefs and reinforcing their prejudices, and it does not seem unreasonable to expect newcomers to adapt to the prevailing expectations about who provides medical care in North American medical practice.

BOX 3.3

ANNE FADIMAN, *THE SPIRIT CATCHES YOU AND YOU FALL DOWN*

In a fascinating exploration of the clash between cross-cultural expectations in medicine, Anne Fadiman compares the beliefs of Hmong parents to those of doctors regarding the medical treatment received by their daughter, who suffered from serious epilepsy. Her exploration suggests that health care professionals working in multicultural societies should strive to understand the belief systems held by patients from different cultures.

Almost every discussion of cross-cultural medicine that I had ever read quoted a set of eight questions, designed to illicit a patient's "explanatory model," which were developed by Arthur Kleinman, a psychiatrist and medical anthropologist who chairs the department of social medicine at Harvard Medical School. The first few times I read these questions they seemed so obvious I hardly noticed them; around the fiftieth time, I began to think that, like many obvious things, they might actually be a work of genius. I recently decided to call Kleinman to tell him how I thought the Lees might have answered his questions after Lia's earliest seizures, before any medications had been administered, resisted or blamed, if they had had a good interpreter and felt sufficiently at ease to tell the truth. To wit:

1. *What do you call the problem?*
   Quag dab peg. That means the spirit catches you and you fall down.
2. *What do you think has caused this problem?*
   Soul loss.
3. *Why do you think it started when it did?*
   Lia's sister Yer slammed the door and Lia's soul was frightened out of her body.
4. *What do you think the sickness does? How does it work?*
   It makes Lia shake and fall down. It works because a spirit called a *dab* is catching her.
5. *How severe is the sickness? Will it have a short or a long course?*
   Why are you asking us those questions? If you are a good doctor, you should know the answers yourself.
6. *What kind of treatment do you think the patient should receive? What are the most important results you hope she receives from this treatment?*
   You should give Lia medicine to take for a week but no longer. After she is well, she should stop taking the medicine. You should not treat her by taking her blood or the fluid from her backbone. Lia should also be treated at home with our Hmong medicines and by sacrificing pigs and chickens. We hope Lia will be healthy, but we are not sure we want her to stop shaking forever because it makes her noble in our culture, and when she grows up she might become a shaman.
7. *What are the chief problems the sickness has caused?*
   It has made us sad to see Lia hurt, and it has made us angry at Yer.
8. *What do you fear most about the sickness?*
   That Lia's soul will never return.
   I thought Kleinman would consider these responses so bizarre that he would be at a loss for words. (When I had presented this same material, more or less, to Neil and Peggy [Lia's doctors], they had said, "Mr. and Mrs. Lee thought *what?*") But after each answer, he said, with great enthusiasm, "Right!"...

Then I told him what had happened later—the Lees' noncompliance with Lia's anticonvulsant regimen, the foster home, the neurological catastrophe—and asked him if he had any retroactive suggestions for her pediatricians.

"I have three," he said briskly. "First, get rid of the term 'compliance.' It's a lousy term. It implies moral hegemony. You don't want a command from a general, you want a colloquy. Second, instead of looking at a model of coercion, look at a model of mediation. Go find a member of the Hmong community, or go find a medical anthropologist, who can help you negotiate. Remember that a stance of mediation, like a divorce proceeding, requires compromise on both sides. Decide what's critical, and be willing to compromise on everything else. Third, you need to understand that as powerful an influence as the culture of the Hmong patient and her family is on this case, the culture of biomedicine is equally powerful. If you can't see that your own culture has its own set of interests, emotions, and biases, how can you expect to deal successfully with someone else's culture?"

Source: Anne Fadiman, *The Spirit Catches You and You Fall Down* (New York: Farrar, Straus, and Giroux, 2012), 260–261.

CONCLUSION

What first person accounts of illness indicate is that, while respect for autonomy may be necessary for any ethically satisfactory description of the relationship between health care professional and patient, it is not sufficient to ensure that the practice of medicine will be as beneficial to the patient as it should be. Likewise, the diverse cultural values of patients in pluralistic and multicultural societies raise questions about whether the concept of autonomy can serve as a culturally neutral value in health care. These challenges suggest that respect for autonomy needs to be carefully balanced with other ethical principles. While paternalism directed at the competent is considered by most bioethicists to be morally problematic, the principles of beneficence and non-malfeasance are important counterbalances to autonomy and can be expressed in non-paternalistic ways. Nursing ethics appears to be in the process of incorporating additional features that draw on these principles and may go some distance toward addressing patient needs more holistically. A case can be made, however, that the doctor-patient relationship needs to more easily incorporate ways for patients to not only make their own medical decisions, but also allow them to tell their own stories in their own voices, to be heard and listened to, so that they can come to grips with and make sense of what they are experiencing. It is in this context that the strengths of the Covenantal Model become most evident. Since this model emphasizes a reciprocal and ongoing relationship between physician and patient, if widely adopted, it would encourage physicians to make a genuine effort to know their patients, to listen to their fears and dreams, and to treat them as whole persons rather than as a collection of symptoms embodied in an autonomous decision-maker.

All models of the doctor-patient relationship are idealistic and incorporate ethical judgments: they describe not what actually is the case, but rather reveal a vision of what ought to be the case. While the Covenantal Model seems to capture more of the ethical dimensions of the physician-patient relationship than do its competitors, a gap remains between its theoretical articulation and its practical application in contemporary medical practice. Considering ways in which this gap can be bridged might go some distance toward both accommodating the feminist insight that we should sometimes think of autonomy in relational rather than individualistic terms and overcoming the alienation that patients often feel when they are ill and must place themselves in the care of medical professionals.

PHILOSOPHICAL REFLECTION ON THE CONCEPT OF AUTONOMY AND MODERN PERSPECTIVES ON HUMAN FLOURISHING

Suppose someone were to tell you that you are not living the best life possible because your religious beliefs are mistaken and your choices foolish and misguided: rather than making these decisions for yourself, you should allow her to tell you how to behave and what to believe. You would almost certainly feel that she had no right to say these things, and would probably be offended by the suggestion that your life would be better if someone else decided for you how you should live. Those of us living in this time and part of the world tend to believe that what matters most is how our lives feel to us, not what other people think about our choices and beliefs. As Kymlicka puts it, even if our beliefs about what is valuable are incorrect, no one should tell us what to do because we flourish when we "lead our lives from the inside, in accordance with our beliefs about what gives value to life."[121]

This seems so self-evident that it is hardly worth remarking on. When we are adults, we feel that no one, not even our parents or best friends, should tell us how to live. But the belief that we live best when we determine for ourselves what is most meaningful and valuable, and that each of our determinations may lead us in very different directions (I feel that a life spent in front of the television eating junk food is a life well spent, while you get satisfaction from reading great literature and helping the poor), is actually very modern and the result of a philosophical debate about what is involved in living well.

The idea that we should be free to make choices for ourselves, according to our own beliefs about what is valuable and what is not, can, in large part, be traced to the writings of two very different philosophers, Kant and Mill. In addition to his writings on utilitarianism, Mill is equally well known for his deliberations on the subject of freedom. In *On Liberty*, Mill makes an impassioned case for freedom of speech, thought, and action; he argues that we should be free to think, speak, and do as we want as long as our activities are not harmful to others and that no one, including the government, should interfere with these choices even if they are harmful to ourselves. For Mill (and some other thinkers), autonomy is primarily a political concept, an idea about the way in which the just state should treat its citizens. Kant, as we saw in Chapter 1, believes that humans are, by virtue of our rationality, self-governing creatures. It is only because we are self-governing that we can be held morally accountable for the choices we make.

When we combine these two perspectives, as a number of modern philosophers have done, autonomy becomes not only a political concept but an ethical one as well. This combination provides the theoretical underpinnings of some of our most important contemporary self-understandings: each of us as self-governing creatures should be free to make our own choices, and it is inappropriate for anyone to interfere with these choices as long as they do not cause harm to anyone else.

However, the idea that it should be left up to each of us to determine for ourselves what to believe and how to live has not been common to all philosophers or all societies, and it is not accepted everywhere even today. For instance, as we saw in Chapter 1, Aristotle believed that there *were* human purposes and that our happiness as individuals depends on living in accordance with those purposes. This view is shared with other ancient thinkers, including Socrates. In the *Apology*, Socrates tells the jurors at his trial that "the unexamined life is not worth living for a human being."[122] By this he means not only that he, Socrates, would not want to live a life that did not involve such examination, but that no one should. According to this older perspective there are objectively good ways to live, and we are mistaken if we do not live in accordance with them, even if our choices give us pleasure. That is to say, even if I enjoy my life sitting in front of the television and eating junk food, I am wasting it from a Socratic perspective because I am not engaged in the sort of examination he thinks all humans should engage in. On this view, questions about how we can best flourish as individuals cannot be detached from an objective account of how we flourish as human beings.

The shift from the ancient account to the modern one has profound political, social, and ethical implications. In political terms, the triumph of autonomy—the idea that competent adults should be self-determining—leads to the idea that the state should be neutral between competing conceptions of how we should live: it should allow freedom of religion rather than promote a particular faith; it should allow free speech even when what is said is controversial; and it should ensure that these freedoms are protected by laws and policies. In Canada, we have a Charter of Rights and Freedoms, which serves this protective role. In the name, we see elements of Kant's thought (rights) and Mill's (freedoms).

In social terms, if the state gives us the freedom that makes extensive exploration and experimentation possible, then our societies will permit a multiplicity of beliefs, commitments, and ways of living. Individuals brought up in such societies will be reluctant to interfere with the choices made by others and will resent any interference with their own choices.

Finally, when it comes to making ethical decisions, the most common way to determine what should be done will be to first establish what someone wants and then determine whether providing them with what they desire will be harmful to anyone else. The "right thing to do" will be whatever best accommodates this desire without doing harm to others. This is in marked contrast with the older perspective, in which determining what should be done involves a consideration of the issue in a way that abstracts it from the wants and desires of particular persons and relates it to larger questions about how human beings ought to live. Take, for example, the question of whether physician-assisted suicide should be legalized. In the contemporary form of the debate, the strongest arguments in support of legalization revolve around the fact that there are people who desire it, and the strongest arguments against it are that legalization would be harmful to those who might not want it, such as the elderly, and the incompetent, who might be unable to make their desires known. From the older perspective, however, the focus would be on the appropriateness of this sort of act within the context of the doctor-patient relationship, given the purposes, practices, and values built into it.

Have we taken the concept of autonomy too far? It is worth noting that both Kant and Mill would probably be astounded to see what we have done with their ideas and concerned about the ways in which we have applied them. Consider again the choice to spend a life in front of the television eating junk food: how might Kant and Mill view this? Kant gave a central place to rationality within his account and believed that rationality would show us what we ought to do; Kant would likely argue that the decision to live in this way is irrational, a waste of potential, and a poor use of natural talents. Moreover, Kant emphasized duties as well as rights. In his view, we have duties to ourselves (that are violated when we waste our talents) and duties to others, and it is only when duties (what we owe to others) are acknowledged that rights (what others owe to us) have a place. Contemporary applications of his views, however, often emphasize rights (to free speech, freedom of religion, freedom of thought, and so on) at the expense of the corresponding duties to use these rights responsibly.

Likewise, Mill believed that we should be free to think, speak, and act because these freedoms would allow us to discover valuable things that we would not otherwise notice. With freedom, he believed, we would make better choices, both as individuals and as societies. Neither Kant nor Mill, arguably, would endorse the view that the identification of desires and the freedom to pursue them is sufficient for full human flourishing: each would believe that we should be concerned about the content of our desires as well. And we can see the force of this argument when we consider our own choices. Each of us may want to be free to decide for ourselves how to live, but we also want the choices we make to be genuinely valuable. Flourishing involves both choosing freely and choosing well. The freedom to choose to spend a life in front of the television and the pleasure we might feel as we do so is not sufficient to make that a life well lived.

CASES OF INTEREST

Sarah Bahris

Sarah Bahris was diagnosed with a rare form of bone cancer at age 14. While undergoing chemo-therapy, doctors at the BC Children's Hospital in Vancouver, where she was being treated, pressed her to accept a blood transfusion. Sarah, a Jehovah's Witness, refused the transfusion on religious grounds. At this point, B.C. child welfare authorities stepped in and obtained a court order to ensure Sarah received a blood transfusion if doctors deemed it necessary as part of her treatment. Sarah's family then took her to Ontario, where another court case ensued, ending with Ms. Bahris being ordered to return to B.C. Provincial authorities there, however, negotiated a settlement in which Sarah would be admitted to Schneider Children's Hospital in New York, which offers chemotherapy without transfusions. After treatment at Schneider Children's Hospital, Sarah appeared to be cancer-free. The disease returned, however, and Sarah died, at age 19, in July 2009.

In similar cases, child welfare authorities have repeatedly stepped in and asked the courts to order that the transfusions be allowed. In June 2009, however, after a review of one such case, the Supreme Court of Canada ruled that the wishes of minors who are mature and capable of making their own decisions must be taken into account and in some cases a mature minor must be allowed the right to refuse blood transfusions.[123]

Reibl v. Hughes

In late 1968, John Reibl, a 43-year-old assembly line worker at the Ford Motor Company of Canada plant in Oakville, developed severe headaches that appeared to him to be aggravated by the constant bending down required of him for work. He consulted a physician whose examination revealed that high blood pressure, a medical condition known as hypertension, was likely causing the headaches. When Reibl's condition did not respond to medication, he was admitted to St. Joseph's Hospital in Hamilton in the spring of 1969. Further tests failed to determine the origin of the hypertension, so Reibl was referred to Dr. Hughes, the chief of neurosurgery at the hospital.

Dr. Hughes discovered a buildup of plaque in the left carotid artery of the plaintiff's neck, significantly narrowing the artery. It was determined that the blockage was unrelated to Reibl's hypertension and head-aches and that it was not presently causing any detectable neurological dysfunction or abnormality. Dr. Hughes nonetheless formed the opinion that it should be surgically removed in order to reduce the risk of a stroke over the next several years. On March 18, 1970, Dr. Hughes performed the procedure, which left Reibl paralyzed on the right side of his body, impotent, and unfit for work for the rest of his life.

Although Reibl consented to the surgery, Dr. Hughes did not inform him of the risk of a stroke. At trial, Reibl argued that, had he been made aware of the risk of a stroke, he would have waited a year and a half to earn his pension and extended disability benefits before consenting to the surgery. The trial judge ruled that Dr. Hughes did not properly inform Reibl of the risks involved and awarded him $225,000 in damages. A new trial was then awarded on appeal. The Supreme Court of Canada (SCC), however, restored the trial judgment and held that a physician must inform a patient about all potential risks, especially with respect to death and strokes, irrespective of how small the risks are. The SCC imposed liability on the basis of Dr. Hughes' negligence; he failed to provide sufficient information about the nature of the surgery, and so Reibl was unable to make an informed decision.[124]

A.C. v. Manitoba

A.C., a devout Jehovah's Witness, was two months shy of her 15th birthday when she was admitted to a Winnipeg hospital in 2006 for lower gastrointestinal bleeding as a result of Crohn's disease. Some months before, she completed an advance medical directive with clear instructions that she not receive any blood transfusions, even in the case of an emergency. A psychiatric assessment conducted at the hospital revealed that she did not suffer from a mental illness, and that she understood the reason for the proposed transfusion and the potential result of refusing the transfusion. She was deemed a "mature minor."

As her condition worsened, she persisted in her refusal to receive blood. She was soon apprehended by the Director of Child and Family Services as a child in need of protection under section 25(8) of Manitoba's Child and Family Services Act. This effectively enabled the courts to order any kind of medical treatment deemed to be in her "best interests." Soon after, the application judge granted a treatment order, and A.C. made a successful recovery after having received three units of blood against her wishes.

Despite her full recovery, A.C. appealed the application judge's decision on the grounds that it violated sections 2(1), 7, and 15 of the Charter. In 2009, the Supreme Court majority upheld the lower court's decision, reasoning that there are no legislated restrictions on the court's ability to order medical treatment for children who are under 16 years of age. Despite losing the constitutional challenge, however, A.C. convinced the top court that children under the age of 16 should be given the opportunity to demonstrate sufficient maturity to have their medical decisions respected. Writing for the majority, Justice Abella stated that "if, after a careful and sophisticated analysis of the young person's ability to exercise mature, independent judgment, the court is persuaded that the necessary level of maturity exists, it seems to me necessarily to follow that the adolescent's views ought to be respected."[125]

CASE STUDIES
Scenario One
Jason Simonetti was admitted to the hospital several times over the last few months complaining of severe nausea, dizziness, and headaches. He initially came in to the emergency department complaining of a severe headache, but the emergency physician could find nothing wrong with him. His headaches continued, and he returned again and again to his family doctor's office. His family doctor, Dr. Ross, ordered a number of tests. Eventually, a CT scan revealed a tumour in Jason's brain. The results were sent to Dr. Ross. Jason's doctor knows that he has been married to his wife for 49 years. Their 50th wedding anniversary is coming up, and they have booked a Caribbean cruise. Jason and his wife plan to leave in a week. He has told his doctor all about these plans.

The tumour is malignant and there is nothing that can be done for Jason. His doctor has already prescribed medication to relieve the pain that Jason is experiencing, but Jason's cancer is terminal. He will not recover, no matter what treatment he receives.

Melanie, Dr. Ross' secretary, calls him into the reception area. "Jason Simonetti is on the phone. He wants to know if his test results are in."

Dr. Ross knows that if he tells Jason that he has terminal brain cancer, the news will ruin his anniversary and the trip. If he keeps quiet, Jason can enjoy the trip and come into the office when he returns. He also does not expect Jason to experience any new symptoms within the next couple of weeks. His only symptoms so far have been the headaches, for which Dr. Ross has already prescribed pain medication. If Dr. Ross does not give Jason the news, he should be able to enjoy his vacation in peace.

(1) What should Dr. Ross do? (2) Can he justify lying to his patient in this case? How might Kantians and utilitarians answer this question? (3) Does virtue ethics have anything to add to this analysis? (4) Would your decision change if Jason were not terminally ill?

Scenario Two
Anna Sommer is a 23-year-old woman entering her last year of university, who is soon to be a single mother. When Anna became pregnant, she was in a long-term relationship, but her boyfriend has

since left her for another woman. A routine ultrasound revealed possible fetal abnormalities, which were later confirmed through amniocentesis: the child Anna is carrying has Down's syndrome. She met with her family doctor and discussed the responsibility involved in raising a Down's syndrome child. She has decided that she wants to keep the baby.

Shortly after learning of her baby's impairment, Anna went into premature labour and was rushed to the hospital. She is only 26 weeks pregnant. Dr. Brown, her family doctor, who has extensive hospital duties and is able to participate in her new treatment, gives Anna something to slow down her labour and then discusses her options with her. He recommends that they do not initiate treatment when the baby is born, but instead allow the infant to die. Given the severe prematurity, Anna's child has only a 44 percent chance of surviving and about a 30 percent chance of suffering no additional impairments. Anna, however, insists that the medical team do all they can to save her child. She claims that she can raise this child, regardless of the severity of his handicaps. However, Dr. Brown, who is familiar with Anna's personal circumstances, is concerned that she will not be able to handle this responsibility. If the child does survive long enough to leave the hospital, Anna will have to devote enormous amounts of time and effort to him, possibly putting a halt to her studies. She has no immediate family to help her. Her doctor reminds her that once she postpones her education, she may not be able to go back to finish her degree. Without a degree, her employment options are limited.

Anna clearly understands the risks and the responsibility of raising a severely impaired child. She claims that she will have help from her friends and that she can seek out community resources. Although young, she seems resourceful, intelligent, and capable of making informed decisions. Dr. Brown, however, is not convinced that she fully understands what is involved in caring for a severely handicapped child and is discouraged by the baby's poor prognosis.

(1) Is Dr. Brown being paternalistic? (2) Is Anna being realistic in thinking she can manage to take care of this child as a single mother? Is her autonomy being threatened by Dr. Brown's attitude? (3) How might a feminist view this situation? Would a Kantian or a utilitarian agree?

Scenario Three

Madalyn is a 65-year-old woman who is suffering from rheumatoid arthritis. The pain and deformation of her joints have been getting progressively worse, and she is losing mobility. You, Madalyn's doctor, have been trying different medications, none of which seem to be slowing the disease's progression or relieving her pain. You want to put Madalyn on leflunomide, which has been known, in rare instances (less than 1 percent of all cases), to cause fibrosis of the lungs. If Madalyn does develop this side effect, she will suffer from inflammation and scarring of the alveoli and interstitial tissues of the lungs. The scarring may proceed gradually or run a rapid course. There is a slim possibility that this would prove fatal. You are hesitant to tell Madalyn about this potential side effect, as you know she has a history of overreacting. You have given her information about serious but unlikely risks before, and each time she became convinced that she would experience these side effects. You also believe that this treatment offers the best chance of slowing the disease and relieving its painful symptoms, and you fear that without this medication, Madalyn may become confined to a wheelchair or even become housebound.

(1) Do you have an obligation to tell Madalyn about the slim possibility of fibrosis of the lungs? (2) Would you feel differently if you were in Madalyn's place? Would you want your doctor to reveal or withhold this information? (3) Would your decision be any different if the probably of contracting fibrosis of the lungs were higher? Is there a point beyond which it is unacceptable to withhold information? (4) What would a utilitarian recommend? What would a Kantian say?

Scenario Four

Eliza Abel is a home care worker who makes daily trips to the home of Mark Addison. Mark is an ALS patient, sick enough to require daily care but not sick enough for hospitalization. Mark lives alone and has no one else to care for him. Eliza has been going to Mark's home for the past three weeks, but she is becoming increasingly uncomfortable around him. She has complained to her employer that he is verbally abusive. He also smokes in his home, even though he has repeatedly been asked not to do so while Eliza is there, since this is her work environment and she has a mild allergy. She has also told her employer that he is unpleasant, unnecessarily demanding, and crude. He has made sexual advances toward her on more than one occasion, despite her requests that he stop. He makes sexist remarks and constantly treats her disrespectfully, yelling at her when he thinks she has done something wrong and questioning her competence on the grounds that she is "just a woman." He has threatened to report her to the College of Nurses for not doing her job, although she has done nothing wrong.

Eliza is not the first home care worker to demand reassignment after caring for Mark. Her supervisor is now considering whether to pull home care from Mr. Addison until he complies with their wishes to treat their workers with more respect.

(1) How should the supervisor respond to this situation? (2) Eliza has a duty to provide care to her client, but does Mark Addison also have a duty to treat her with respect? (3) Does Mark Addison have a right to health care? Does he have a right to home care? Does this right come with certain responsibilities?

Scenario Five

Sandra Rimmer is a nurse in a small hospital in northern Manitoba. She has been spending much time with Deborah Prescott, an elderly woman who was brought into the hospital a few days ago suffering from heat stroke. When Deborah first entered the hospital, she was still conscious and able to converse with Sandra and the other nurses. Her body temperature continued to rise, however, for a significant period before the medical staff was able to bring it down, and, as a result, she has suffered permanent damage and is now in a coma. Although Sandra tells the doctor on duty that Deborah expressly stated that she did not want any heroic measures undertaken should her condition worsen, he insists on doing everything possible. At present Deborah is not responding to stimuli, but she is still breathing on her own. The doctor on duty, however, has arranged to have a respirator ready in case her breathing fails. Sandra knows that this is not what Deborah would have wanted. Deborah was brought into the hospital by a neighbour, but has no family or friends who could act as surrogates in this situation.

(1) What should Sandra do if the doctor places Deborah on the respirator? Does she know Deborah well enough to be certain of what she really wants or what is best for her? (2) Would the situation be different if it were not a matter of life and death? (3) Whose views should prevail in this case, Sandra's or the doctor's?

Scenario Six

You are a doctor who has been treating Mateo Ramirez, a young Latin American, for several years. You know that Mateo has been HIV-positive for some time. When he told you last year that he was planning to get married, you asked him whether he had informed his future wife of his status. When he admitted that he had not, you advised him to inform his fiancée and to practise safe sex. He assured you that he would do so, and when the marriage took place, you assumed that the information had been passed on to his wife.

Once Mateo and Sara were married, you agreed to accept her as a new patient. Mateo, his wife, and his mother are now in the office because she is pregnant; blood tests have revealed that she, too, is now HIV-positive, although this was not the case when she had her initial patient checkup that you provide to all new patients. You want to speak with her alone, but she insists that she is happy to have her husband and her mother-in-law come into the examination room with her, because family input to medical decisions is important in Hispanic culture. You agree to her request.

She is flabbergasted when she is told that she is HIV-positive, because, she asserts, she was a virgin when she got married. Her husband accuses her of cheating on him and states that he has never tested positive for HIV, and her mother-in-law reacts angrily and begins shouting insults at her. How should you respond? And should you have insisted that you speak to her alone? You are vaguely familiar with the practice of family-based decision making from your encounters with other patients. You know that there is a practice of placing a strong emphasis on family input in Hispanic culture and of valuing familial needs over those of the individual. In some cases, loyalty to the extended family outranks the needs of the individual.[126]

(1) Does your obligation to uphold confidentiality override your obligation to tell the truth to Sara, who is also your patient? (2) Can you respect her autonomy without providing this information? (3) What should you do?

Scenario Seven

A woman, suffering from advanced dementia, develops pneumonia. Before developing pneumonia, she seemed happy enough while going through her simple, repetitive daily routines. You are the physician on call at the long-term care facility where she lives. You ask her children what should be done to treat her pneumonia, since she did not make an advance directive before she developed dementia. Her son says that the pneumonia should not be treated, because he knows that she would not like to go on living in her present state (she is unable to read or enjoy television programs while, prior to succumbing to her dementia, she was a much-respected professor and public intellectual). He believes that if she were aware of her present state, she would think her worst nightmare had come true. Her daughter disagrees, saying that she made a promise to her mother to take care of her no matter what, and she states that she does not believe that "taking care of her means letting her die." She believes that her mother is happy and that she has no memories of her earlier years and no conception that she was once different.

(1) What should you do? (2) Whose decision is this to make? (3) What decision would you come to if you were a Kantian? A utilitarian? A virtue ethicist? A feminist? Which perspective is the most helpful?

GLOSSARY

Advanced directive: a document in which individuals set out the medical treatments they would and would not like to have performed on them if they reach a stage in their lives in which their capacity to make these decisions for themselves is seriously diminished. It may also include the name of the person who is to make these decisions for them should such incapacity occur.

Autonomy: a term used to describe a modern conception of human flourishing that holds that we live best when we are free to make decisions for ourselves in matters that concern us, and an ethical principle that places a limit on what others may do to us. It is perhaps the most important ethical principle in bioethics, and it requires that health care practitioners respect the decisions patients make about the medical treatments they do and don't want as much as possible.

Harm Principle: a principle, famously articulated by John Stuart Mill in *On Liberty*, that places an ethical limit on the exercise of autonomous choice. This principle holds that, while we should be left free to do as we wish in matters that concern only ourselves, when our actions are harmful to others, we ought not to perform them and can legitimately be constrained if we refuse to take the interests of others into account.

Informed consent: the idea that patients should be given adequate and truthful information about their diagnosis, prognosis, and the risks and benefits of possible treatment and that they must give permission before any treatment is begun or discontinued.

Competency: a patient's capacity to understand the consequences of accepting or rejecting particular medical treatments and that he or she is giving, or refusing to give, consent for treatment. Since illness and infirmity can interfere with autonomy, all that is required for informed consent to be ethically valid is for the patient to be able to understand the relevant consequences of the medical choices she makes and the capacity to weigh potential benefits and risks of treatment in the context of her own values and preferences.

Substitute/surrogate decision-maker: an individual who has been designated to make medical decisions for someone who has been deemed incompetent. Substitute or surrogate decision-makers can make decisions on the basis of a substituted judgment, which tries to duplicate the decision that that particular person would have made if capable; a best interests judgment, in contrast, is a decision made on the basis of what most people, in similar circumstances, would have chosen.

Paternalism: The idea that some people should make choices for others, either because the decision-maker possesses a specialized expertise, or because the person for whom the decision is being made is too young or lacking the intellectual capacity to make the decision for themselves. Historically, medicine was paternalistic and held that the doctor knew what was best for his patients and should, therefore, make medical decisions for them. While paternalism in medicine has been largely rejected, paternalism is included in the list of bioethical principles in recognition of the fact that there are some people who must be taken care of by others in the medical context because they are unable to take care of themselves.

Strong paternalism: a principle that holds that we are morally justified in coercively interfering with the choices of even those who are competent if by doing so we can benefit them or prevent harm coming to them. Forcing a competent adult to undergo a life-saving blood transfusion that he has rejected for religious reasons is an example of strong paternalism.

Weak paternalism: a principle that holds that it would be wrong to coercively interfere with the choices made by those who are competent, even if we believe that those choices are misguided and harmful. Instead, all we are morally permitted to do is give them advice or argue with them. Health warnings on cigarette packages are an example of weak paternalism.

FOR FURTHER READING

Blustein, Jeffrey. "The Family in Medical Decisionmaking." *Hastings Center Report*, 23, no. 4 (May-June 1993): 6–13.

This essay defends the right of individuals to make autonomous decisions and suggests that families can sometimes play an important role in assisting in this process in the context of illness. Blustein's account provides a nuanced and helpful description of the importance of autonomy in medicine.

Brody, Howard. "Transparency: Informed Consent in Primary Care." *Hastings Center Report*, 19, no. 5 (September-October 1989): 5–9.

Informed consent is a crucially important concept in contemporary bioethics, but what informed consent actually requires in practice is not always entirely clear. Brody proposes a transparency standard for informed consent in which sufficient information has been presented to the patient when the patient is able to understand what the doctor is thinking and why.

Capron, Alexander Morgan. "The Burden of Decision." *Hastings Center Report*, 20, no. 3 (May-June 1990): 36–41.

This article usefully considers some aspects of the connection between ethics and the law. While ethical questions and legal ones are separate and distinct from one another, many of the ethical issues that arise in the medical context are referred to the courts for resolution. Capron argues that this tendency undermines the development and practice of sound medical judgment.

Hardwig, John. "What About the Family?" *Hastings Center Report*, 20, no. 2 (March-April 1990): 5–10.

The ideal of autonomy is complex and evolving; this essay adds further considerations to the debate about what it requires in the context of medicine. Hardwig presents a provocative challenge to the standard accounts of autonomy in health care by arguing that the health care system will go bankrupt if we understand autonomy as simply meaning that patients should have any care they want, regardless of the cost.

Macklin, Ruth. "Ethical Relativism in a Multicultural Society." *Kennedy Institute of Ethics Journal*, 8, no. 1 (1998): 1–22.

In this comprehensive essay, Macklin considers the challenge posed to the principles of autonomy and informed consent in the multicultural and pluralistic societies of North America that are committed to respecting cultural differences. Macklin argues that the requirements of informed consent and respect for autonomy can usually be adapted to accommodate cultural differences, except when it comes to children.

Mappes, Thomas A., and Jane S. Zembaty. "Patient Choices, Family Interests, and Physician Obligations." *Kennedy Institute of Ethics Journal*, 4, no. 1 (1994): 27–46.

This article considers the nature of the concept of autonomy both theoretically and as it relates to medical practice and to the obligations physicians have toward their patients. In the course of their discussion, the authors consider the arguments made by Hardwig and Nelson in the essays recommended in this section and critically assess the positions they present.

May, William F. "Code, Covenant, Contract, or Philanthropy?" *Hastings Center Report*, 5, no. 6 (December 1975): 29–38.

In this essay, May considers the nature of the Hippocratic Oath, and argues that it has two parts, a Code and a Covenant. He relates this distinction to models of the physician-patient relationship and argues that it is best understood as being governed not by a code, but by a covenant.

Nelson, James Lindemann. "Taking Families Seriously." *Hastings Center Report*, 22, no. 4 (July-August 1992): 6–12.

Nelson argues that medical decision making is much more complex than the widely accepted individualistic model that dominates contemporary bioethical theory. This model considers, he believes, individual patients in isolation from their social contexts, and a model that takes this social context into account could accommodate a broader range of values.

RECOMMENDED WEBSITES

American Medical Association

www.ama.assn.org/

This website contains resources for physicians and patients. An interesting feature of this website is that it allows users to create their own "iHealth Record," in which their health information can be electronically stored. The site claims that the record will be private and secure, and that users will control access.

British Medical Association

www.bma.org.uk/

The official website of the British Medical Association, this site has information on ethical issues ranging from the plight of asylum seekers to the nature of the doctor-patient relationship, as well as on consent and capacity issues and human rights concerns. It also provides links to other websites concerned with medical ethics and the doctor-patient relationship.

Canadian Medical Association

www.cma.ca

This website contains information on the Code of Ethics of the CMA, as well as information on advanced directives. It provides PDF versions of two related policies on advance directives, the first being the Policy on Advance Directives for Resuscitation and Other Life Saving or Sustaining Measures and, the second, The Joint Statement of Resuscitative Intervention, which was approved by the Canadian Healthcare Association, the CMA, the Canadian Nurse's Association, and the Catholic Health Association of Canada.

Canadian Nurses Association

www.cna-nurses.ca/CAN/default_e.aspx

This website presents information on nursing practice in Canada, including a Code of Ethics, a vision statement setting out the way in which nursing may develop in the future, and information for those interested in pursuing a career in nursing.

The Hastings Center of Bioethics and Public Policy

www.thehastingscenter.org/

The Hastings Center is arguably the best-known bioethics centre in North America and is a place in which most of the issues discussed in this chapter (and, indeed, in this or any other bioethics text) are considered, debated, and even shaped. This site contains information about the centre, its activities, its publications, a bioethics forum, and news about jobs and fellowships.

National Aboriginal Health Organization (NAHO)

www.naho.ca/English/

This is a website dedicated to advancing the health and well-being of First Nations, Inuit, and Metis Canadians. It contains, among other things, guidelines for interviewing elders and links to resources aimed at preserving and promoting traditional healing practices.

NOTES

1. Juliet O'Neill and Doug Fischer, "Fighting for the Right to Refuse Treatment," *The Ottawa Citizen*, June 11, 2005, n.p.
2. O'Neill and Fischer, n.p.
3. O'Neill and Fischer, n.p.
4. Kirk Makin, "Brilliant Man in an Asylum Fights Doctors to Top Court: Physics Expert with Bipolar Disorder Tells Judges He'd Rather Stay Locked Up for Life Than Be Forced to Take Medication," *The Globe and Mail*, May 8, 2003, n.p.
5. O'Neill and Fischer, n.p.
6. Makin, n.p.
7. *Starson v. Swayze* 2003 SCC 32 (2003) 225 D.L.R. (4th) 385.
8. *Starson v. Swayze.*
9. *Starson v. Swayze.*
10. Makin, n.p.

11. O'Neill and Fischer, n.p.

12. Makin, n.p.

13. Terrance McConnell, *Moral Issues in Health Care* (Belmont, CA: Wadsworth Publishing, 1997), 29.

14. Thomas M. Garrett, Harold W. Baillie, and Rosellen M. Garrett, *Health Care Ethics: Principles and Problems*, 4th ed. (Upper Saddle River, NJ: Prentice-Hall, 1998), 15.

15. Sherwin B. Nuland, *The Uncertain Art* (New York: Random House, 2008), xviii.

16. Alfred I. Tauber, *Confessions of a Medicine Man* (Boston: MIT Press, 1999), xii.

17. Tauber, xii.

18. Kathleen Oberle and Shelley Raffin Bouchal, *Ethics in Canadian Nursing Practice* (Toronto: Pearson-Prentice Hall, 2009), 30.

19. Health Canada, "Canada's Health Care System"(2012), found at www.hc-sc.gc.ca/hcs-sss/pubs/system-regime/2011-hcs-sss/index-eng.php (October 4, 2014).

20. Health Canada, n.p.

21. Carl Elliot claims that "[p]harmaceutical companies have a powerful financial interest in expanding categories of mental disease, because it is only when a certain condition is recognized as a disease that it can be treated with the products that the companies produce. The bigger the diagnostic category, the more patients who will fit within its boundaries, and the more psychoactive drugs they will be prescribed." See *Better Than Well: American Medicine Meets the American Dream* (London: W.W. Norton & Company, 2003), 124.

22. Tauber, xii–xiii.

23. Jerome Groopman, *How Doctors Think* (New York: Houghton Mifflin Company, 2007), 99.

24. Tauber, xiv.

25. More recently, Veatch has reached the conclusion that all medical judgments involve non-scientific value judgments. Consequently, the person in the best position to know what a patient needs is the patient himself. Consequently, none of the models discussed here fit with the model that he believes should animate the "new medicine": "Physicians can no longer be expected to be able to do what is in their patients' interests just because they are competent physicians. They cannot be expected to do what best serves patients' interests because they cannot be expected to know what patients' interests are.... [In the new medicine] only in very special and unusual circumstances will it be the doctor who knows best what is in either the patients' or the community's interests." Robert M. Veatch, *Patient, Heal Thyself* (New York: Oxford University Press, 2009), 4–5.

26. McConnell, 30.

27. McConnell, 31.

28. Mark Lipkin, "On Telling Patients the Truth," in Ronald Munson, *Intervention and Reflection: Basic Issues in Medical Ethics*, 7th ed. (Belmont, CA: Thomson Wadsworth, 2000), 155.

29. Gerald Dworkin, "Paternalism," in Munson, 132.

30. J.S. Mill, *Utilitarianism, On Liberty, and Considerations on Representative Government*, ed. H.B. Acton (London: Everyman's Library, 1972), 81.

31. Susan Cullen and Margaret Klein, "Respect for Patients, Physicians and the Truth," in Munson, 157.

32. McConnell, 32.

33. William F. May, "Code, Covenant, Contract, or Philanthropy?" *Hastings Center Report*, 5, no. 6 (December 1975): 32.

34. May, 32.

35. May, 33.

36. May, 38.

37. Michael C. Brannigan and Judith A. Boss, *Healthcare Ethics in a Diverse Society* (Mountain View, CA: Mayfield Publishing Company, 2001), 114.

38. Daniel Chambliss, quoted in Brannigan and Boss, 117.

39. Placebos are inactive substances given to patients who believe that they are receiving medication. Placebos occupy a complex place in contemporary medicine; they are seen to have a legitimate place in medical research, as they help researchers determine the efficacy of new drugs. In addition, the so-called "placebo effect" must be considered: this is the therapeutic benefit that has been observed when patients are given placebos that they believe are appropriate medications for their condition. As Nuland points out, "The frequency of beneficial effects of placebos ranges from approximately one in five to almost three in five, depending on the way the study is carried out and the criteria by which success is measured" (Nuland, 100). Consequently, Nuland believes, many of the successes of medicine historically might be attributable to the placebo effect. As he observes, "In 1937, there was still far too little that the average doctor could scientifically do for the average patient with the average complaint. Until antibiotics became generally available after World War II, the likelihood of an individual's being helped by the pharmacologic effects of a doctor's treatment was less than fifty-fifty. Even so, the vast majority of people seeking medical aid recovered from their illnesses" (Nuland, 101). It is now generally accepted, however, that the use of placebos to treat conditions for which effective medication exists is unethical. Moreover, the deception involved with the use of placebos in this case study makes the physician's behaviour ethically problematic.

40. This is a simplified version of a case entitled "Whose Pain Is It Anyway?", presented in Becky Cox White and Joel A. Zimbelman, *Moral Dilemmas in Community Health Care: Cases and Commentaries* (New York: Pearson Longman, 2005), 29–30.

41. Nancy S. Jecker and Donnie J. Self, "Separating Care and Cure: An Analysis of Historical and Contemporary Images of Nursing and Medicine," in Elisabeth Boetzkes and Wilfrid J. Waluchow (eds.), *Readings in Health Care Ethics* (Peterborough, ON: Broadview Press, 2000), 60.

42. Jacalyn Duffin, *History of Medicine* (Toronto: University of Toronto Press, 1999), 120.

43. Duffin, 120.

44. For a more extensive discussion of this process, see Chapter 9.

45. For more discussion of this issue, see Chapter 1 and the discussion of feminist approaches to ethical theory.

46. Jecker and Self, 58.

47. Brannigan and Boss, 115.

48. White and Zimbelman, 29–30.

49. White and Zimbelman, 36.

50. White and Zimbelman, 39.

51. White and Zimbelman, 42.

52. Oberle and Bouchal, 21.

53. Oberle and Bouchal, 21.

54. Oberle and Bouchal, 21.

55. Oberle and Bouchal, 22.

56. Oberle and Bouchal, 22.

57. Oberle and Bouchal, 40.

58. Oberle and Bouchal, 40.

59. Oberle and Bouchal, 48.

60. Judith Salamon, *Hospital* (New York: The Penguin Press, 2008), 236.

61. "Today, nurses work to ensure that patients have autonomy to make their own decisions, respect-ing their rights to choose and protecting those who are not able to decide for themselves. Nurses strive to avoid paternalism and instead enter into dialogues with patients. Decisions about treat-ment or health promotion activities are made through a process of discussion whenever possible." Oberle and Bouchal, 121.

62. Joseph Raz, *The Morality of Freedom* (Oxford: Oxford University Press, 1986), 373.

63. Atul Gawande, *Complications* (New York: Metropolitan Books, 2002), 222.

64. Mill, 78.

65. Mill, 78

66. See the Sue Rodriguez case in Chapter 8.

67. Dworkin, 132–133.

68. Garrett, Baillie, and Garrett, 30.

69. Arthur W. Frank, *The Wounded Storyteller* (Chicago, IL: The University of Chicago Press, 1995), 8.

70. Garrett, Baillie, and Garrett, 31–32.

71. Garrett, Baillie, and Garrett, 32.

72. Garrett, Baillie, and Garrett, 33.

73. Parts of this discussion draw on Healthcare Ethics Notes drawn up by Alister Browne, Vincent P. Sweeney, and Margaret G. Norman for a program in Ethics Committee Education run by the Division of Health Care Ethics at the University of British Columbia, 1996.

74. Dworkin, 133.

75. See the Tyrell Dueck case in Chapter 9.

76. Janice Tibbetts, "Child's Wishes Count, Court Says," *National Post*, June 27, 2009.

77. Some scholars characterize the difference between weak and strong paternalism as lying in whether the paternalist intends to prevent harm (weak) or do good (strong).

78. Philip C. Hebert, *Doing Right: A Practical Guide for Medical Trainees and Physicians* (Toronto: Oxford University Press, 1996), 32.

79. Hebert, 32.

80. Susan Dodds, "Choice and Control in Feminist Bioethics," in Catriona MacKenzie and Natalie Stoljar, *Relational Autonomy: Feminist Perspectives on Autonomy, Agency, and the Social Self* (New York: Oxford University Press, 2000), 214.

81. Susan Sherwin, "Relational Autonomy," in Boetzkes and Waluchow, 73.

82. Sherwin, 73.

83. Sherwin, 73.

84. Sherwin, 74.

85. Marilyn Friedman, "Autonomy, Social Disruption, and Women," in MacKenzie and Stoljar, 35.

86. Friedman, 35.

87. Linda Barclay, "Autonomy and the Social Self," in MacKenzie and Stoljar, 57.

88. Consider, for example, Peggy Orenstein's account of her struggle with infertility, and her use of Clomid, a drug that appears to increase the risk of developing ovarian cancer: "Swallowing that little white pill was the first time I did something I swore I wouldn't in order to get pregnant: I willingly put my health on the line. It was in that moment that desire and denial merged to become obsession; it was then, right then, that doing anything to become pregnant, regardless of the consequences, became possible." Peggy Orenstein, *Waiting For Daisy* (New York: Bloomsbury, 2007), 60.

89. Frank, 5–6.

90. Frank, 6.

91. Havi Carel, *Illness* (Stocksfield, UK: Acumen, 2008), 39.

92. Carel, 41.

93. Carel, 41.

94. Tom Blackwell, "'It Happens All the Time': Patients Shouldn't Be Allowed to Choose Doctor Based on Race, Medical Group Says," *National Post*, October 21, 2013, A1.

95. Blackwell, A2.

96. Blackwell, A2.

97. Barbara J. Leonard, "Quality Nursing Care Celebrates Diversity," *The Online Journal of Issues in Nursing*, 6, no. 2 (2001).

98. Leigh Turner, "Bioethics in a Multicultural World: Medicine and Morality in Pluralistic Settings," *Health Care Analysis*, 11, no. 2 (2003): 102.

99. Turner, 102.

100. Turner, 102–103.

101. Turner, 103.

102. Robert Baker, "A Theory of International Bioethics: Multiculturalism, Postmodernism, and the Bankruptcy of Fundamentalism," *Kennedy Institute of Ethics Journal*, 8, no. 3 (1998): 203.

103. Maura Ryan, "Beyond a Western Bioethics?" *Theological Studies*, 65 (2004): 159.

104. Ryan, 170.

105. Ryan, 170.

106. Ryan, 170.

107. Paul Ndebele, Joseph Mfutso-Bengo, and Francis Masiye, "HIV/AIDS Reduces the Relevance of the Principle of Individual Medical Confidentiality among the Bantu People of Southern Africa," *Theoretical Medicine and Bioethics*, 29 (2008): 336.

108. Renee C. Fox and Judith P. Swazey, *Observing Bioethics* (Oxford: Oxford University Press, 2008), 165.

109. Baker, 224.

110. Ndebele et al., 333.

111. Ndebele et al., 339.

112. Ruth Macklin, quoted in Fox and Swazey, 165.

113. Andrew Fagan, "Challenging the Bioethical Application of the Autonomy Principle within Multicultural Societies," *Journal of Applied Philosophy*, 21, no. 1 (2004): 16.

114. Fagan, 16.

115. Fagan, 20.

116. Fagan, 20.

117. Fagan, 25.

118. Aruna Papp, "Picking Doctors By Colour," found at fullcomment.nationalpost.com/2013/10/25/aruna-papp-picking-doctors-by-colour/

119. Papp, n.p.

120. Papp, n.p.

121. Will Kymlicka, Liberalism, *Community, and Culture* (Oxford: Oxford University Press, 1989), 9.

122. Plato, *Apology*, in *Four Texts on Socrates*, ed. Thomas G. West and Grace Starry West (Ithaca, NY: Cornell University Press, 1995), 92.

123. Normally the issue of Jehovah's Witnesses refusing blood transfusions is treated in bioethics as a question of autonomy and informed consent: adults have the right to refuse any treatment, and provided they are fully informed, we should not judge their reasons (see Chapter 2). They

do not, however, have the right to refuse treatment for their minor children if doing so puts the health and life of the child at risk. This case puts the matter in a different light. The existence and expanding use of alternative methods of surgery or chemotherapy that do not necessitate blood transfusions means that, in cases like this one, the person is not refusing treatment but rather choosing an alternative treatment, and asking that the alternative treatment be recognized by the medical establishment. See Tom Blackwell, "Teen's Death Fuels Debate on Religion's Blood Ban," *National Post*, July 15, 2009.

124. *Reibl v. Hughes* [1980] 2 S.C.R. 880.

125. *A.C. v. Manitoba (Director of Child and Family Services)* [2009] 2 SCR 181.

126. Alissa Hurwitz Swota, *Culture, Ethics, and Advanced Care Planning* (Lanham, MD: Rowman & Littlefield, 2009), 103.

Chapter 4

MEDICAL RESEARCH

LANDMARK CASE: JESSE GELSINGER

Jesse Gelsinger, born on June 18, 1981, was a fairly normal baby until, at the age of two years and eight months, his behaviour became very erratic. After extensive testing, Jesse was diagnosed with ornithine transcarbamylase deficiency syndrome (OTC), a rare metabolic disorder that affects the body's ability to rid itself of the ammonia that builds up from the body's use of protein. Jesse exhibited a mild form of OTC, meaning that his condition could be controlled through medication and diet. After 11 days in hospital, Jesse was sent home where (except for a relapse at age 10 as the result of too much protein) he progressed fairly normally on a strict diet and medications.

In September 1998, Jesse's specialist told Jesse and his father, Paul, of a clinical trial being conducted at a renowned medical facility in Philadelphia to examine the possibility of gene therapy for OTC. Although Jesse and his father were interested, Jesse was told that he could not participate until he turned 18. In the meantime, Jesse's metabolism was under stress because he was taking his medication (nearly 50 pills a day) erratically. Although he was displaying symptoms of his disorder, he kept them hidden from his parents out of fear of having restrictions placed on him. On December 22, his father found him vomiting uncontrollably. Jesse was subsequently admitted to hospital with ammonia levels six times higher than normal. He was allowed to go home for Christmas but collapsed on Christmas night, was admitted to intensive care, and diagnosed with hypoglycemia. Jesse's specialist was sure that this was a side effect of one of his medications. He consequently discontinued the medication and ordered a newer and more effective one. While awaiting this new medication, Jesse suffered another crisis. His condition deteriorated so much that he stopped breathing and was put on a respirator. At this point, Jesse weighed only 97 pounds. However, once he began the new medication, his ammonia levels began to fall, he regained consciousness, and he was moved out of intensive care. Within a week, he was out of the hospital and back attending school full time.

In early April 1999, about three months after the Christmas crisis, Jesse had another appointment at the metabolic clinic where the topic of the clinical trial in Philadelphia came up again. Jesse and his father were both still interested. Paul had already planned a trip to Philadelphia in late June, by which time Jesse would be 18. On June 22, the Gelsinger family headed to Philadelphia to meet with the research team. At the hospital, a doctor, one of the principal investigators, explained the technique that would be used. Jesse would be sedated and two catheters would be placed into his liver: one in the hepatic artery at the inlet to the liver to inject the viral vector,[1] and another to monitor the blood exiting the liver to ensure that all the vector was being absorbed by the liver. It was explained that there would be no long-term benefit to Jesse. Even if the genes worked, their effect would be transient as the body's immune system would attack and kill the virus within six weeks.

The doctor also explained possible side effects of the technique. Jesse would have to remain immobile for about eight hours after the infusion to minimize the risk of a clot breaking free from the infusion site. Other possible side effects included experiencing flu-like symptoms for a few days afterward and a remote possibility of contracting hepatitis. If hepatitis should develop and progress, Jesse could require a liver transplant, but this possibility was seen by Jesse's father as being so remote that "no more alarms went off in my head."[2] A liver biopsy would be performed one week after the infusion, a procedure that carried a 1 in 10,000 chance of death.

After a 45-minute conversation with the doctor, Jesse agreed to undergo an ammonia study to determine his level of enzyme efficiency. He then returned to Tucson where he was later informed that his enzyme efficiency was only 6 percent of the normal level. At this point, Jesse's father asked him if he still wanted to participate. "He hesitated about a moment and said yes."[3] A week later, Paul spoke with another of the principal investigators, a renowned OTC expert, and was told that the treatment had worked temporarily in mice, even preventing death following a lethal injection of ammonia. Further, one of the participants in the study had shown a 50 percent increase in her ability to excrete ammonia following the gene therapy. Paul Gelsinger was impressed and believed that this treatment really worked. And with Jesse at 6 percent efficiency, the lowest rate of the study participants, the researchers would be able to show exactly how well it worked. The doctor agreed, but reiterated that the targeted beneficiaries of the study would be newborn babies with the worst form of OTC and people with 25 other liver diseases that could perhaps be treated with this therapy.

At this point, although Paul had not discussed the risks of the procedure in detail with the OTC expert, Jesse agreed to participate in the study. His father recalls the day that he left Jesse at the airport for his flight to Philadelphia: "Words cannot express how proud I was of this kid. Just eighteen, he was going off to help the world. As I walked him to his gate I gave him a big hug and, as I looked him in the eye, I told him he was my hero."[4]

The trial was a Phase I toxicity trial, meaning that its goal was to test the highest tolerable dose of a genetically modified adenovirus. There would be six different groups of participants, and the dosage would be increased slightly for each group. Jesse had been scheduled as the last patient in the last group, but he was moved forward because of scheduling problems.

Jesse's trial was scheduled for September 13. The evening before the infusion, he was placed on intravenous medications as his ammonia levels were elevated. The next day, the infusion went as scheduled. On the 15th, Jesse's father received a call from the doctor who said Jesse was jaundiced and a bit disoriented. Later that day, Paul received another call informing him that Jesse's blood ammonia levels were rising and his condition was worsening. At this point, he got on a plane to Philadelphia, but by the time he got to the hospital, Jesse was on a ventilator and in a coma. The doctors explained that he was having a blood-clotting problem and his blood pH level was too high. They wanted to induce a deeper coma and Jesse's father agreed. Later that day his lungs began to fail; after two days of complications, the medical team informed Jesse's parents that he had suffered irreparable brain damage and that his vital organs were shutting down. They wanted to shut off life support. Jesse's parents agreed and held a small service for him before removing life support. Paul Gelsinger demanded a full autopsy to determine why his son had died and insisted that this should never have happened. The official cause of Jesse's death, as listed on the death certificate filed by Dr. Steve Raper, was adult respiratory distress syndrome: Jesse's lungs had shut down.

Jesse's therapy consisted of an infusion of corrective genes encased in a dose of weakened cold virus, adenovirus, which functioned as a vector, getting inside the body's cells and "infecting" them with the corrective genes. The researchers involved in the clinical trial had tested the same dose of vector that Jesse received on mice, monkeys, baboons, and one human patient. The side effects, as expected, were flu-like symptoms and some mild liver inflammation, which went away on its own. When Jesse got the vector, however, he suffered an unexpected chain reaction: jaundice, a blood-clotting disorder, kidney failure, lung failure, and brain death, a multiple organ system failure.

During the investigation into Jesse's death, Paul Gelsinger found that this treatment had never had any efficacy in humans as he had been led to believe. Further, the research team in Philadelphia had violated protocol in multiple ways. They had not adequately reported serious adverse events in other patients prior to Jesse and had withheld vital information from the FDA on adverse side effects in animals. Further-more, "[t]he over-enthusiasm of the clinical investigators painted a picture of safety and efficacy of their work. That enthusiasm led them to blind themselves to the ill effects that they were witnessing.... Some of that blindness appears to have been intentional."[5] Both Dr. James Wilson, who was the lead investiga-tor in the clinical trial, and the University of Pennsylvania's Institute for Human Genome Therapy had equity stakes in Genovo, the biotech company that had invested in the genetically altered virus used in the gene therapy experiment. In addition, "Wilson and one of his colleagues also had patents on certain aspects of the procedure. At the time, Genovo contributed a fifth of the $25 million annual budget of the university's gene therapy institute and in return had exclusive rights over any commercial products."[6]

Jesse's family sued the university for wrongful death and settled out of court for an undisclosed sum.

INTRODUCTION

The topic of research on human subjects is one of the foundational issues of the discipline of bio-medical ethics. It was the abuses during and after the Second World War by the Nazis in particular, but also by other countries, including Canada, that brought to the fore the need to establish ethical standards to prevent people from being harmed by the excessive enthusiasm of medical experiment-ers. More recently, some of the same ethical concerns are being expressed by animal rights activists, as well as by serious philosophers, regarding the use and abuse of animals as research subjects.

With respect to research on humans, this is one issue where there is a clear demarcation along Kantian and utilitarian lines. In effect, the autonomy of and respect due to individuals is set against the needs (or, in the eyes of some, the perceived needs) of society in general and medical science in particular. Much of the progress in medicine over the last century has been accomplished as a result of medical research—and most medical research must take place on human subjects before therapies can be approved. Yet some experimentation is risky and, in some cases, a few may suffer so that many may profit as a result of the knowledge gained in an experiment. This conflict between respect for individual autonomy and the needs of science is very apparent in the case of Jesse Gelsinger, above.

Another clear demarcation that we point to in this chapter is one between what can be considered therapy and what must be considered experiment—also an issue in the Gelsinger case. In particular, many see a conflict between the role of the doctor as therapist (seeking the best for a sick patient) and his or her role as scientist (seeking knowledge for future sick patients). This conflict is particularly acute in **randomized clinical trials** where any participating doctor is wearing two hats.

Another issue that we will examine, also raised by our landmark case, is the increasing and uncom-fortable closeness between researchers and pharmaceutical companies whose products are being tested, a situation that is clearly demonstrated by the case of Dr. Nancy Olivieri of the University of Toronto (see Box 4.3). We will also examine the ethical issues involved in randomized clinical trials and discuss whether or not anyone has a moral obligation to participate in such trials or in research of any kind.

Finally, we discuss philosophical questions relating to the difference between humans and animals, and ask whether the latter can be used solely for the benefit of the former. Is it morally acceptable to impose suffering and death on animals in order that humans can accumulate the knowledge that is considered necessary for medical research? How do we justify using animals as a means to human ends? Must we extend our ethical analysis to include animals? Are they part of our moral community? We may not fully answer these questions, but in this chapter we hope to make you think seriously about them.

Nurse Eunice Rivers is photographed here with some of the 400 Southern crop workers who were subjects of the Tuskegee Syphilis Study. The experiment was designed to study the progression of untreated syphilis, a study that continued even after the invention of penicillin, which could have cured them. Nurse Rivers was convinced she was helping "her people," but the study seriously affected the attitude of black Americans toward the government and the health system.

HISTORICAL ASPECTS: USES AND ABUSES OF MEDICAL RESEARCH

It has been pointed out that the "history of medical experimentation is a history of risk vs. benefit,"[7] and the main issue is who undergoes the risk and who gets the benefit. Historically, many people have been subjected to considerable risk in order that others, or future others, might benefit from their suffering. In this respect, the story of experimentation on human subjects is not the most edifying chapter in the history of Western medicine. It is worth noting that the use of the word "experimentation" has declined in bioethical discourse in favour of the word "research," which carries a more positive connotation, both in the scientific community and with the general public. Research on human subjects in the quest for medical progress is not new. In fact, the idea of human experimentation is a very ancient one, and discussions about it are found in the writings of Greek and Roman physicians. According to Rothman, "The most frequently cited cases involve testing the efficacy of poisons on condemned prisoners, but the extent to which other human research was carried on remains obscure."[8] It was an ethical issue early on as well. The famous 12th-century Jewish physician and philosopher Moses Maimonides, for example, held that physicians must always treat patients as ends in themselves, not as a means to medical and scientific ends. So the idea of not using patients as means to an end (a preoccupation of contemporary bioethics) is not new either.

Interestingly, early modern experimenters in the 18th and 19th centuries tended to rely on fellow physicians, neighbours, friends, or even themselves. The English physician Jenner injected swinepox into his one-year-old son but this did not save him from smallpox (although a later injection in another child did succeed). A German physician named Jorg swallowed doses of 17 different drugs in order to analyze their effect, and in one extreme example of self-experiment, a certain Werner Forssman "passed a catheter, guided by radiography, into the right ventricle of his heart, thereby demonstrating the feasibility and the safety of the procedure."[9]

Not all physicians were so altruistic: an American, William Beaumont, signed a contract with a man whose abdominal wound healed in such a way that it left a hole in his stomach. The contract amounted to servitude—in return for room and board and $150 a year, he agreed "to assist and promote by all means in his power such philosophical or medical experiments as the said William shall direct or cause to be made on or in the stomach of him."[10] Through his observations, Beaumont was able to prove that the stomach juices digest food—but the research subject finally ran away.

Even where efforts were taken to treat human subjects as ends in themselves, exceptions were always allowed, especially when they related to prisoners. Claude Bernard, known as the father of modern biology, sanctioned experiments on the dying and on criminals about to be executed on the grounds that "they involve no suffering of harm to the subject of the experiment,"[11] perhaps believing that those who are about to die do not feel pain.

Early in the 20th century, some experiments did raise public criticism when antivivisectionists began to express concern about the use of animals in experiments. In general, however, the question of experiments on humans was not an issue of great public concern, possibly because the victims of experimentation belonged to the disadvantaged classes. In addition, there was an implicit trust in physicians and a belief that they always acted for the benefit of their patients. To the extent that most of the research at that time was actually meant to benefit sick patients, it can be described as being mainly *therapeutic*.

The real change both in the type of research and, eventually, in the public's reaction to it came with the Second World War and its aftermath. Much medical experimentation during the war was done to benefit soldiers—to prevent or cure diseases to which they were vulnerable (for example, malaria, dysentery). In other words, it was *non-therapeutic* in relation to the subjects: one group of people underwent the risks so that another group could benefit. There was a sense of urgency due to the war that allowed researchers to ignore issues such as consent and/or benefits to the subjects being used. After all, if you could draft young, healthy men into the army without their consent, why worry about consent when dealing with the sick, the old, or the mentally infirm? Rothman states: "One part of the war machine conscripted a soldier, another part conscripted a human subject, and the same principles held for both."[12] In other words, a utilitarian ethic predominated over deontological principles, and this was justified because of the high stakes of war.

The other impact of the Second World War on research ethics came in the form of human experimentation conducted by the Nazis. Terrible experiments were conducted on the mentally handicapped, on Jews, and on all the other groups that the Nazis deemed less than human. According to Pence, "[P]hysicians sympathetic to Nazi ideology participated in programs in which disabled, insane, and comatose patients were involuntarily killed; and even some of the most prestigious German professors of medicine supported extermination of racially 'inferior' people. In addition to 'euthanasia,' there was also a great deal of experimentation on human subjects, much of which was at least irregular and at worst almost unimaginably savage and brutal."[13]

Pence cites a research study on typhus involving 1000 homosexual men, convicted criminals, Russian officers, Polish dissidents, Jews, and Gypsies. In other studies, "hormones were implanted to 'cure' homosexuality, inmates were shot to study gunshot wounds, inmates were starved to study the physiology of nutrition, and women's bones and limbs were surgically removed to study regeneration."[14]

Terrible as these were, the Germans were not alone in their wartime experiments. Japanese physicians carried out deadly experiments on Chinese prisoners of war, killing over 3000 by injecting diseases such as anthrax, syphilis, plague, cholera; in one study of the plague, 700 Chinese died. Americans were not exempt from abuses: American researchers experimented on orphans, on mentally handicapped patients, and even on their own military personnel. One director of a cancer hospital "supervised the long secret and now infamous tests where thousands of American troops were intentionally exposed to mustard and other poisonous gases. Rhoads discovered that the mustard gas killed white blood cells and other cells that divided rapidly. After the war he and others began to experiment with mustard gas as a cancer treatment and also to search for other systemic poisons that kill dividing cells."[15]

More Recent Abuses

Other abuses had nothing to do with the war. The infamous Tuskegee study used poor, uneducated Southern black Americans suffering from syphilis to study the progression of the disease *in nature*; in other words, how the disease would progress without treatment. This was government-sponsored research, which went on for 40 years. In order not to threaten the purity of the scientific information coming out of the study, the men were left untreated even after penicillin became available. When the true nature of the study came to light in 1972, it was described as "the longest running nontherapeutic experiment on human beings in medical history and the most notorious case of prolonged and knowing violation of subjects' rights."[16] The American government ultimately paid out over $10 million in compensation to the remaining Tuskegee victims or to the families of those already dead. In 1997, President Clinton formally apologized to the survivors, stating that, while what was done could not be changed, "we can stop turning our heads away. We can look at you in the eye and finally say on behalf of the American people: 'What the United States did was shameful, and I am sorry.'"[17]

Canada too has a large shameful blot on its medical research reputation. Clandestine experiments were carried out in Montreal at McGill's Allan Memorial Institute on mentally ill patients in the 1950s and 1960s. These experiments were performed under the auspices of the CIA as part of a program code-named MK-ULTRA, and implicated about 30 universities and medical institutions, mostly in the U.S.[18] Dr. Ewen Cameron of McGill University was a highly regarded, world-renowned psychiatrist who conducted brainwashing experiments on patients using powerful drugs (including LSD) and shock therapy. In many cases patients were given massive doses of insulin, which put them into a coma (or "sleep") for long periods of time (in one case for 86 days). While in coma, reprogramming tapes played continuously under their pillow in order to erase their disturbed minds and, in some way, create a blank slate for starting over. In many cases, patients' memories were wiped clean; people who had gone to Dr. Cameron with mild (or in some cases postpartum) depression came out with their lives and their futures shattered. Some were reduced to the state of babbling, incontinent toddlers, unable to remember anything of their past lives (one mother of five children could no longer remember giving birth to them).[19] In the 1980s it was revealed that Dr. Cameron had been working for the CIA, using his patients as guinea pigs to conduct brainwashing experiments. It was also revealed that the Canadian government had sanctioned the experiments and even helped to fund the research. A number of Dr. Cameron's victims sued the CIA and received compensation; others settled out of court. Some sought and received compensation from the Canadian government, but unlike the Tuskegee victims, no formal apology has ever been offered. These experiments represented a violation of the Nuremberg Code of research ethics that had only recently been signed when they began. Ironically, Dr. Cameron had been a member of the Nuremburg medical tribunal doing psychiatric assessments of accused Nazis for their crimes of medical experimentation.

Disturbingly, as one virulent critic of the LSD experiments points out, McGill University "has never publicly criticized the fact that [Dr. Cameron's] actions and 'treatments' had been carried out to advance CIA research into torture in unwitting un-consented individuals.... Even today, the description of Cameron in the archives of McGill fails to mention what is now known about his activities there."[20] The same critic states that "MK-ULTRA set the standard for later industrial-university collaboration,"[21] a subject that will be discussed later in the chapter.

Another blot on Canada's medical research reputation came to light in 2013 when Ian Mosby, a post-doctoral researcher at the University of Guelph, published a paper on the nutrition policies of the Canadian government during the Second World War. Mosby discovered that the government was aware of serious malnutrition on Indian reservations, due in large part to the collapse of Native traditional food practices. Instead of providing emergency food relief, the federal government permitted researchers to conduct experiments to test the effect of vitamin supplements on undernourished people. What followed were "two separate long-term studies that went so far as to include controlled experiments conducted, apparently without the subjects' informed consent or knowledge, on malnourished Aboriginal populations in Northern Manitoba and, later, in six Indian residential schools."[22] The food in residential schools was known to be insufficient in both quality and quantity, leading to both malnutrition and hunger. Many survivors of that system have vivid memories of being constantly hungry.[23] Rather than the residents' situation being improved with the recognition of their plight, six of these schools became, in effect, scientific laboratories. According to Mosby, the early architects of Canada's residential school system saw the schools as "social laboratories in which people's beliefs and ways could be refashioned,"[24] and the nutrition experiments thus served a wider government policy of assimilation. The researchers hoped to show that certain characteristics, such as shiftlessness and inertia, were not hereditary traits but the result of malnutrition, and that better nutrition might have a positive effect on their motivation and their living conditions.[25] Whether or not the intention of the experimenters was ultimately to improve the nutrition of the Aboriginal population, the fact remains that the experiments were only possible "because the researchers had access to a population of chronically malnourished and vulnerable children who, as wards of the state, had little say in whether or not they participated in the study." In addition, "the success of the study depended on so-called 'controls' and experimental subjects alike being fed, for anywhere between two and five years, diets known to be nutritionally inadequate."[26] It is also interesting that, like those of the CIA mentioned above, these experiments were government sanctioned and took place during and after the Nuremberg trials and the development of the Nuremberg Code of research ethics.

The results of these abuses, within the wartime context and outside of it, raise the question of how much of our current medical knowledge was gained at the price of human suffering and degradation. As Jonas writes, "We can never rest comfortably in the belief that the soil from which our satisfactions sprout is not watered with the blood of martyrs."[27] Jonas' comment may strike some as extreme, but it does give us reason to pause and to ask who is hurt by, and who benefits from, medical experimentation and research.

THE GOAL OF MEDICAL RESEARCH: HEALING OR KNOWLEDGE?

At the heart of the debate on the ethics of experimentation on human subjects lies a tension between individual rights and societal needs. The practice of medical research is based on the assumptions that research is essential to medical progress and that medical progress is in the best interests of society. Since experimentation on human subjects is an essential component of medical research (research on animals providing only preliminary information), such experimentation serves the common good. Most people simply accept this argument at face value, but Jonas questions the premise that medical progress is in the best interests of society and rejects the conclusion that experimentation always serves the common good. Jonas draws a distinction between the common good in times of disaster, epidemic, or war and the common good as it pertains to the more general goal of improving society. The former presents us with a situation of *urgency* during which society can call on individuals to perform sacrifices for the common good. The latter is what Jonas calls an *expansive* goal, which lacks the urgency necessary to justify demanding such sacrifices: "The destination of research is essentially melioristic. It does not serve the preservation of the existing good from which I profit myself and to which I am obligated. Unless the present state is intolerable, the melioristic goal is in a sense gratuitous, and not only from the vantage point of the present. Our descendants have a right to be left an unplundered planet; they do not have a right to new miracle cures."[28]

That our descendants do not have a right to new miracle cures might strike some as a radical claim. However, Jonas is not saying that miracle cures are not a good thing; rather, he is saying that they are neither urgent nor essential. They are "**melioristic**" goals in the sense that they target what are presently conceived of as future needs and the improvement of the society of the future, rather than immediate, urgent problems. He is saying that such goals cannot justify asking some people to take part in, and perhaps be harmed by, what might be risky research; the notion that an individual should put himself or herself at risk for the common good does not apply in this kind of case. It is difficult to argue, for example, that young Jesse Gelsinger was putting himself at risk for the common good (the potential beneficiaries were a small number of future newborns, not society in general). Jonas would say that the kind of risk this young man undertook was not something that society should demand of anyone: "No one has the right to choose martyrs for science."[29]

Does this mean that no one should take part in medical research experiments? It does not. However, it does mean that those who do take part must be fully informed and absolutely free in making their decision to do so. Moreover, they should be found among those who are the most educated and the most interested in the results of the experiment. For Jonas, the ideal principle of recruitment would be one of complete identification of the research subject and the research purpose; in other words, members of the scientific community itself. In what Jonas refers to as a "descending order of permissibility," the sick and the vulnerable would be the last to be considered as research subjects: "The poorer in knowledge, motivation, and freedom of decision (and that, alas, means the more readily available in terms of numbers and possible manipulation), the more sparingly and indeed reluctantly should the reservoir be used, and the more compelling must therefore become the countervailing justification."[30]

It goes without saying that Jonas' position is not one that is widely held in medicine today. Much progress has been made in trying to correct the abuses of the past, and medical research is generally conducted on a much more ethical basis than it used to be. But the notion that the goal of research is "melioristic," to use Jonas' word, is not widely shared. It is generally accepted both within the medical community and the public at large that medical research is an essential present good for society, that medical progress cannot take place without it, and that people have an obligation to participate in it when the opportunity arises. Many cancer patients, for example, take part in clinical trials to test a new drug and, even though they know they may be given a **placebo** (and thus receive no benefit), feel obliged to participate.

BOX 4.1

HANS JONAS, "PHILOSOPHICAL REFLECTIONS ON EXPERIMENTING WITH HUMAN SUBJECTS"

Experimentation was originally sanctioned by natural science. There it is performed on inanimate objects, and this raises no moral problems. But as soon as animate, feeling beings become the subjects of experiment, as they do in the life sciences and especially in medical research, this innocence of the search for knowledge is lost and questions of conscience arise.... One difference between human experiments and the physical is this: The physical experiment employs small-scale, artificially devised substitutes for that about which knowledge is to be obtained, and the experimenter extrapolates from these models and simulated conditions to nature at large. Something deputizes for the "real thing"— balls rolling down an inclined plane for sun and planets, electric discharges from a condenser for real lightning, and so on. For the most part, no such substitution is possible in the biological sphere. We must operate on the original itself, the real thing in the fullest sense, and perhaps affect it irreversibly.... Up to a point, animals may fulfill the proxy role of the classical physical experiment. But in the end man himself must furnish knowledge about himself, and the comfortable separation of noncommittal experiment and definitive action vanishes. An experiment in education affects the lives of its subjects, perhaps a whole generation of schoolchildren. Human experimentation for whatever purpose is always *also* a responsible, nonexperimental, definitive dealing with the subject himself. And not even the noblest purpose abrogates the obligations this involves.

Can both that purpose and this obligation be satisfied? If not, what would be a just compromise? Which side should give way to the other? The question is inherently philosophical as it concerns not merely pragmatic difficulties and their arbitration, but a genuine conflict of values involving principles of a high order. On principle, it is felt, human beings *ought not* to be dealt with in that way (the "guinea pig" protest); on the other hand, such dealings are increasingly urged on us by considerations, in turn appealing to principle, that claim to override those objections. Such a claim must be carefully assessed, especially when it is swept along by a mighty tide. Putting the matter thus, we have already made one important assumption rooted in our "Western" culture tradition: The prohibitive rule is, to that way of thinking, the primary and axiomatic one; the permissive counter-rule, as qualifying the first, is secondary and stands in need of justification. We must justify the infringement of a primary inviolability, which needs no justification itself; and the justification of its infringement must be by values and needs of a dignity commensurate with those to be sacrificed....

We may observe that averting a disaster always carries greater weight than promoting a good. Extraordinary danger excuses extraordinary means. This covers human experimentation, which we would like to count, as far as possible, among the extraordinary rather than the ordinary means of serving the common good under public auspices....

Much weaker is the case where it is a matter not of saving but of improving society. Much of medical research falls into this category. A permanent death rate from heart failure or cancer does not threaten society. So long as certain statistical ratios are maintained, the incidence of disease and of disease-induced mortality is not (in the strict sense) a "social" misfortune. I hasten to add that it is not therefore less of a human misfortune.... But it is misleading to equate the fundamentally human response to it with what is owed to society....

Nowhere is the melioristic goal more inherent than in medicine. To the physician, it is not gratuitous. He is committed to curing and thus to improving the power to cure. Gratuitous we called it (outside disaster conditions) as a *social* goal, but noble at the same time. Both the nobility and the gratuitousness must influence the manner in which self-sacrifice for it is elicited and even its free offer accepted. Freedom is certainly the first condition to be observed here. The surrender of one's body to medical experimentation is entirely outside the enforceable "social contract."

Source: Hans Jonas, *Philosophical Essays: From Ancient Creed to Technological Man* (Englewood Cliffs, NJ: Prentice Hall, 1974), 236–246.

Harris argues strongly that we all have a moral obligation to participate in medical research if and when the opportunity arises. He argues that the principle of beneficence dictates that we must help other people in need: "Most, if not all diseases create needs.... Because medical research is a necessary component of relieving that need in many circumstances, furthering medical research becomes a moral obligation."[31] Not only should we participate in research projects, we should support such research financially, both personally and politically. Harris also argues from the principle of fairness.

Because, in his view, we all benefit from medical research ("Many of us would not be here if infant mortality had not been brought under control, or antibiotics had not been invented"[32]), it is unfair for some to be what is often referred to as "free riders," enjoying the benefits of medical progress without participating in the risks. According to Harris, "This entails that there are circumstances where an adult, competent person ought to participate in research, even if participating is not in his or her best interests narrowly defined."[33] For Harris, it is not narrow self-interest that prevails here; it is the public interest. Some go even further, suggesting that participation in research should be made a requirement of treatment, at least in cases where the trial is designed to compare established therapies. Echoing Harris' view that those who share society's benefits should share its burdens, Orentlicher states:

> It should be permissible for a physician to condition a patient's access to treatment on the patient's willingness to enter a clinical trial when the trial compares two or more accepted therapies to find out whether they are equivalent or whether one is better than the others. That is, the physician should be able to offer treatment to the patient only in the setting of the clinical trial. Patients who declined to participate in the study would have to receive care from another physician.[34]

Accepting these arguments would of course necessitate agreement about what *is* in the public interest and what benefits are or are not accruing to society as a whole, and Jonas would argue differently.

THERAPEUTIC MISCONCEPTIONS

Jonas' argument is especially compelling in cases where the research in question is non-therapeutic and promises no benefits to the participants. For example, the purpose of Phase I clinical trials is to test the toxicity of a drug. Thus they are, by definition, not designed to benefit the participants; yet sometimes participants believe (or are led to believe) that they could benefit from them. In non-cancer trials healthy volunteers are used, so the question of therapy should not arise. In cancer trials, the side effects of drugs can be extreme, so healthy volunteers are not used. Jesse Gelsinger's case was somewhat ambiguous: he was healthy at the time of the trial, but he did suffer from the disease being researched, and his father seemed to believe that there might be a benefit for him. In this case, it can be said that Jesse's father was exhibiting what some refer to as "therapeutic misconception," meaning that the research subject (or in Jesse's case, his father) does not seem to fully understand that decisions regarding the methodology of the study he is involved in are not made with his best interests in mind, but solely in the interests of the research project and its scientific results. Paul Gelsinger is not alone in having placed more hope in a research study than he should have. In spite of being told that a project is not therapy, but research, research subjects often tend to assume "that decisions about their care are being made solely with their benefit in mind."[35] The term "therapeutic misconception" was coined by Appelbaum, Roth, and Lidz to describe this phenomenon after their study of the attitudes of participants in several different research trials. They found, for example, that in spite of a consent process that emphasized random assignment to one of three groups to receive either one of two different medications or a placebo, most subjects believed that they would be assigned to one group or the other according to their particular needs. As explained by Appel-baum and colleagues, subjects invented "reasonable means by which that could be done. 'They will look over my chart,' noted one patient, while another claimed that the doctors 'decide by talking to you.' A patient who had initially described the purpose of the study as to 'see which medication helps the problem I'm having,' and who thought that his medication would be 'the one that helps me,' became extremely angry at the end of the study when he discovered that he had received a placebo. He indicated that, if he had known at the beginning of the project what he now knew, he would not have agreed to participate."[36]

While the study by Appelbaum and colleagues dealt with the field of psychiatric research, the phenomenon is more generalized, and it has been recognized for some time that research subjects have difficulty believing that their doctor will not do what is best for them even though he is wearing his research hat. Appelbaum and colleagues concluded that research subjects "may have to be told explicitly that scientific goals will have priority over therapeutic goals, that the investigator—because of his dual role as researcher and physician—will be unable to maintain an unadulterated devotion to their well-being ... and that various aspects of the study may turn out not to be in their best interests at all."[37]

Looking specifically at therapeutic misconception in relation to Phase I cancer trials, Miller notes a "collusion of misunderstanding," whereby patients tend to be overly optimistic about possible therapeutic benefit and investigators tend to understate the real objectives of the research trial. Even though the participants sign consent forms stating that they are participating in a toxicity study without therapeutic intent, "patients enrolled in these trials overwhelmingly cite hope of physical benefit (rarely altruism) as their primary motivation for enrolling."[38] Miller recognized his own collusion in this misunderstanding through his tendency to think he was serving his patients' interests by recruiting them into a study. He saw himself as "reinforcing the fiction that we were about to embark on a therapeutic enterprise. An opportunity to unpack research from therapy was transformed into an occasion that conflated the two."[39] From this point of view, both doctor and patient appear to want to preserve the doctor-patient relationship, something that is not possible in these trials.[40]

The misconception that research is actually therapy is not unusual according to Miller, who states that "patients generally fail to understand the nature of phase I trials" and that the investigators themselves believe that "patients enrol in these trials for physical benefit, not for altruistic reasons."[41] Further, the line between therapy and research is often blurred in the eyes of the researchers who tend to see "patient care and research rather as a seamless continuum than as distinct activities with inherently competing claims on physician loyalty," a tendency that can be exacerbated in the context of teaching hospitals.[42] In any experiment using human subjects, the risks must be weighed against the benefits that can be expected for the participant. If the participant stands to gain by the successful results of a research project, then certain risks can be justified, provided that the participant is fully informed and consents to them. However, if by the very nature of the experiment no benefits can be expected to fall on the participant (as in the Jesse Gelsinger case), the risks should be minimal or they cannot be justified.

The Role of the Physician

The role of the physician is at the centre of the ethical debate about therapy and research. The principle of beneficence dictates that a physician has a duty to do good for his patient and to care about his or her well-being. In relation to the patient, the physician is wearing the hat of a therapist. However, when participating in a research trial, he or she puts on another hat, that of the research scientist, whose principal interest or goal becomes the furtherance of knowledge and medical progress. This raises the issue of the physician's conflicting loyalties referred to earlier. Medical research is not designed to help individual patients—that is not its goal. Wearing the first hat, the physician's responsibilities are centred on his own patient; when he puts on the second hat, he extends his responsibility to other patients, to future sufferers of the disease in question, or to the accretion of knowledge, fame, or even profits for a pharmaceutical company. With respect to the latter, the physician actually puts on a third hat, particularly if he has a financial stake in the company involved in the research (as in the Jesse Gelsinger case). Which hat should the physician wear when he or she is encouraging a patient to participate in a clinical trial?

Leaving aside the third hat, which involves a clear conflict of interest and is not justified under any moral theory, the issue of therapeutic versus non-therapeutic research might be analyzed differently depending on whether one takes a utilitarian or a Kantian point of view.

A utilitarian would be prone to accept the melioristic goal of medical research and hold that the cure of disease for existing as well as future sufferers of disease is something that would ensure the greatest good for the greatest number. This would, however, entail the inclusion of future humans among "the greatest number." Most utilitarians could accept that it was morally justifiable for Jesse's physician to encourage him to participate in the experiment because of the potential good that would result from the experiment if it succeeded. Even if there were risks to Jesse himself, it would be the *overall* good resulting from the experiment that would serve as its justification. Knowing all the facts of the case, the utilitarian might object to the casual way in which the information about risks and benefits was treated and would certainly not approve of the conflict of interest involving the researchers and the drug company. However, he or she would not object in principle to asking Jesse to participate in research that would bring him no therapeutic benefit.

A Kantian would look at the matter differently. Jonas takes a Kantian view when he puts the dignity of the individual above the presumed benefits to society as a whole. He does not accept that the melioristic goal is adequate to override human dignity in cases of non-therapeutic experimental research, and he would most likely disapprove of Jesse being conscripted as a subject in the research. A Kantian would think that Jesse was used solely as a means to an end and would find this morally reprehensible under the second formulation of the Categorical Imperative (respect for persons). It is also unlikely that Jesse's case would pass the test of universalization under the first formulation of the Categorical Imperative, especially in light of the ambiguity surrounding the information that Jesse and his father were given.

INFORMED CONSENT

As a result of the abuses performed by Nazi physicians on prisoners in concentration camps during the Second World War—and of the trials at Nuremberg after the war where 15 of these physicians were tried for war crimes—the Nuremberg Code came into being. This is an international statement of principles meant to govern all medical research using human subjects. Its first principle states, in part: "The voluntary consent of the human subject is absolutely essential. This means that the person involved should have the legal capacity to give consent; should be situated as to be able to exercise free power of choice ... and should have sufficient knowledge and comprehension of the elements of the subject matter involved so as to enable him to make an understanding and enlightened decision."[43]

With its clear statement regarding voluntary and informed consent, the Nuremberg Code came down firmly on the side of the subject of experimentation and emphasized individual rights over social goals. Because it was seen as a rigid code, developed in response to the truly horrible abuses of the Nazis, it did not gain universal acceptance in the research community. As a result, the World Medical Association developed a compromise set of principles incorporated in the Declaration of Helsinki (issued in 1964 and amended in 1989, 2000, and again in 2008). This was more flexible in relation to informed consent, allowing proxy consent and permitting physicians to withhold information under the principle of therapeutic privilege, a principle that assumes that doctors can be trusted not to abuse patients in research experiments. However, as information about abuses un-related to the Nazis became public (for example, the Tuskegee study referred to above), the need for stringent guidelines was recognized, resulting in the promulgation of the four principles that eventually became the foundation of bioethics: autonomy, beneficence, non-malfeasance, and justice. Since that time, the need for informed consent (reflecting the principle of autonomy) has, in principle, been accepted internationally as one of the most important prerequisites for medical research and has been incorporated into codes of ethics of countries and medical associations worldwide.[44] In Canada, the Canadian Institutes for Health Research (CIHR) sets out guidelines that govern all federally funded medical research. These guidelines state clearly that research involving human sub-jects cannot be undertaken unless free and informed consent is obtained from participants and is maintained throughout the research project.

> Free and informed consent lies at the heart of ethical research involving human subjects. It encompasses a process that begins with the initial contact and carries through to the end of the involvement of research subjects in the project. As used in this Policy, the process of free and informed consent refers to the dialogue, in-formation sharing and general process through which prospective subjects choose to participate in research involving themselves.[45]

Free and informed consent of the participating subject provides the moral justification for expos-ing subjects to the risks involved in experimentation. The rule of informed consent is rooted in the principle of autonomy: every competent person has the right to make his or her own decisions about medical treatment. This includes the right to make free and informed decisions regarding participation—or non-participation—in medical research experiments.

The question of informed consent has been discussed in Chapter 2, and we will simply give a brief review here in the context of medical research. For a patient to properly agree to participate in a research study (or to undergo a medical treatment that could be considered experimental), we can ask: What constitutes "informed"? And what constitutes "consent"? With respect to the first question, potential research subjects cannot make a free and voluntary choice unless they have all the necessary information concerning the nature of the experiment, its risks and potential benefits, and, most importantly, whether any of the benefits will accrue to themselves as participants, to future sufferers of the disease in question, or simply to the growth of medical knowledge. Some physicians and researchers are *paternalistic* with respect to informed consent to research: they believe that it is impossible to explain to patients all the complex techni-cal information about an experiment and that it is the physician himself who is best able to decide what is best for the patient. Others fear that giving too much information could deter patients from participating. We have already seen that such paternalistic attitudes are highly questionable when it comes to medical therapy; they are even more so in the context of medical experimentation, especially if there are risks involved. The rule of informed consent requires not only that physicians and researchers provide information to their patients, but also that the information be usable. In other words, patients must be able to understand it and act on it. That this may be difficult in some situations does not relieve physicians and researchers of the obligation to make the necessary information available in a format that a reasonably competent person can understand.

BOX 4.2

HALUSHKA V. UNIVERSITY OF SASKATCHEWAN[1]

In 1965, the Saskatchewan Court of Appeal awarded the claimant, a 20-year-old student known only as Halushka, $22,500 on the grounds of trespass to person and negligence on the part of the defendants, the physicians conducting an experimental procedure in which Halushka took part.

The defendants were conducting an experiment with a new anaesthetic drug, floromar. Although he did not expect to gain any therapeutic benefits from the procedure, Halushka had been offered $50 for his participation and agreed to it after being told that the experiment was safe and that it had been carried out numerous times before. In fact, this was a new anaesthetic agent being tested for the first time. Halushka was also not informed about the risks of using the drug, the risks inherent in the procedure, or even the way the experiment would be carried out (he was told that a catheter would be put in his arm, but not that it would go through his heart). During the procedure, Halushka went into cardiac arrest and was unconscious for four days. He had to remain in hospital for 10 days and, following his recovery, was unable to return to his studies because of concentration problems and fatigue.

At the original trial, the jury found the defendants guilty of trespass and negligence on the basis of lack of consent, and awarded Halushka $22,500. The Saskatchewan Court of Appeal upheld the verdict, concluding that consent had not been freely given and therefore trespass had occurred. Justice Hall held that informed consent requires a physician to give a fair and reasonable explanation of the proposed treatment along with any anticipated side effects or risks, and this was not done. The court acknowledged that there might be some exceptions to the rule of informed consent when it comes to treatment, but there are no exceptions in cases of experimentation. The court saw it as a matter of trust between physician and research subject and that trust had been broken in this case. Subsequent courts have followed this example and have required health professionals to provide patients with enough information for the individual to make an informed decision.

Note
1. *Halushka v. University of Saskatchewan*, [1965] 52 W.W.R. 608 (Sask. C.A.).

In looking at the Gelsinger case, it is not unreasonable to ask whether Jesse and his father had the required information to allow informed deliberation and consent. Did Jesse and his father truly understand that this was a Phase I trial designed only to test toxicity and not in any way to benefit Jesse?[46] Did they know that Jesse could, or would, be in the group receiving the highest—or next to highest—dose of the injected virus? Did they have all the necessary information about the unsuccessful animal experiments? Some might argue that Jesse and his father should have asked more questions. However, given the importance of the principle of autonomy and the rule of informed consent, should the onus be on the patient to ask the right questions or on the physicians and researchers to provide all the relevant information?[47]

With respect to the "consent" part of informed consent, we have already seen how the most important criterion for determining consent is that the person be competent. This means that he or she must be capable of acting rationally on the basis of the information given (and must be capable of understanding the information). If a person is not considered competent, proxy consent is obtained from a third party acting on that person's behalf and in his or her best interests.

But even competent people might not be able to give consent freely. This could be the case if the patient or research subject is unduly influenced by another (a doctor, a family member, and so on) or is in a situation where he or she fears that refusing to participate could entail negative consequences regarding future treatment. The Canadian guidelines underline the importance of consent that is voluntarily given, "without manipulation, undue influence or coercion.... Undue influence may take the form of inducement, deprivation or the exercise of control or authority over the prospective subjects."[48]

The courts in Canada have upheld the importance of informed consent in research trials. In particular, in 1965, the Saskatchewan Court of Appeal awarded a Saskatchewan student $22,500 on the grounds that the physicians conducting the experiment in which he had taken part were guilty of trespass to person and negligence because the subject had not been given all the information necessary to make a truly informed decision; in fact, he had been given misleading information about the safety of the test and also was harmed in the experiment (see Box 4.2). Subsequent court decisions in Canada have followed the *Halushka* decision, requiring researchers and health professionals to take seriously the need for free and informed consent on the part of patients and research subjects.

Consent and Vulnerable Populations

The question of free and voluntary consent is especially problematic with respect to what are often called *vulnerable populations*, which can include people living in places such as nursing homes or prisons (for example, a large percentage of drug trials before the 1970s took place within prison populations). These people may be competent, but, living in what some refer to as *total institutions*, their consent may not be entirely free or voluntary. In such institutions, "all aspects of a person's life are connected with the social structure.... [T]here are social forces at work that both pressure and encourage an inmate to do what is expected of him or her."[49] It is very difficult to know whether the consent of such people is truly free, and some would insist that they should never be used as research subjects. Excluding these people from research trials, however, could seriously affect the possibility of furthering research on their particular illness (for example, research on Alzheimer's if residents of homes for the aged were excluded as subjects). According to Canada's Interagency Advisory Panel on Research Ethics, while concern about injustice and unfair treatment have historically been the focus of debate regarding vulnerable populations, "contemporary concerns with justice in research have broadened: are the overall benefits and burdens of research distributed fairly, and have disadvantaged individuals and groups received a fair share of the benefits of research?"[50] The same questions relate to those who lack the capacity to consent for themselves, and these individuals or groups should not automatically be excluded from research. At the same time, however, extreme care must be used in soliciting consent from vulnerable populations.

Children as Medical Research Subjects

Children must be counted among the most vulnerable potential subjects for medical research. Some ethicists think that children should never be used as research subjects, while others argue that research on children is essential for two reasons: some diseases are more common in children than in adults, and it is unreliable (and even dangerous) to base therapy for children on the results of studies on adults.[51] To exclude children as subjects of medical research could severely limit the advancement of pediatric medicine.

At the same time, however, as recognized by the Panel on Research Ethics, children "may be particularly vulnerable as research participants because of their developmental status. Researchers and REBs [research ethics boards] must consider a child's stage of physical, physiological, psychological and social development to ensure adequate protections for a child's welfare. Physical or psychological harms a child experiences in a research setting may have long-lasting effects."[52] And research should only be done on children if such research could not be carried out without their participation.

One of the main ethical issues regarding the use of children as research subjects concerns consent. Informed consent is closely linked to autonomy, and children are, by definition, not fully autonomous persons. The lack of autonomy of babies and small children is clear, but when it comes to older children and adolescents, the line between autonomous and non-autonomous is much more difficult to draw. Some children are more mature than others and, even in cases of serious or terminal illness, might be quite able to make decisions concerning their own treatment. Others might simply not be capable or might be so much under parental influence as to render any consent questionable. When it is a question of using children as research subjects, great care should be taken in soliciting their participation. Many children are altruistic by nature and might be easily convinced that undergoing risks for the benefit of others would be a good thing.

Jesse's case is instructive in this regard. Although he was legally able to make his own decision about participating in the research at the time he entered the trial, he was barely past his 18th birthday, and the solicitation of his participation began the year before. Further, one suspects that he was quite easily influenced both by his father and by his own desire to help others. He was no longer a child, but he was not a fully autonomous adult either.

Parents have a very serious obligation to consider when acting as a proxy for a child or adolescent. They must act responsibly and they must act *in the best interests of the child*—and they must know that their right to decide is not absolute. If they appear to be making a decision that is not in the best interests of the child, or if they are considered to be acting irresponsibly, the courts can step in with an injunction to stop the parents from consenting (or refusing) on the child's behalf. This has often been the case, for example, in situations involving refusal of blood transfusions for children of Jehovah's Witnesses. The responsibility that parents have when making decisions about treatment is great enough; it is even greater when it comes to making decisions about participation in research. Parents have an obligation to ensure that their children are not harmed as a result of being used as subjects of medical research. Even if they might think they would put themselves at risk in a medical research experiment, they cannot assume that such a risk is a good thing for their child. On the other hand, parents themselves are vulnerable to pressure if their children are sick. They may be willing to accept any degree of risk because they are so desperately hoping for a cure. Just as researchers must be careful not to exploit the fear and the hope of the very sick, they must exercise the same care in relation to the parents of a very sick child.

Parental obligation is particularly serious in cases where the research in question does not offer any therapeutic benefit to the child. A certain amount of risk can be tolerated in research involving children if the possibility of therapeutic benefit for the child can be demonstrated. If there is no therapeutic benefit to the child, then the experiment should involve minimal, or no, risk. Parents must resist the urge to assume a high degree of altruism on the part of their child.

Not everyone would agree with this position, however. The advancement of medicine depends on research, including research on children in relation to children's diseases. According to Freedman, Fuks, and Weijer, "Almost by definition, exciting and important research ventures into the unknown. A prohibition on such research involvement would be to the long-term detriment of children, just as a prohibition on new experiences is harmful to children over the long term."[53] Many argue as well that children are moral beings, and if they are capable of understanding the risks and benefits, they should have a say in any decision regarding research on them or their disease. The Declaration of Helsinki states that if a minor child is capable of consent, that consent must be obtained in addition to that of the parent or guardian. By the same token, if such a child refuses, parental consent should not be used to override the child's wish.

A utilitarian could justify exposing some children to risks in order to benefit many more children in the future. A utilitarian might even say that, in making a decision on behalf of their child, parents should weigh the benefits to future children along with the risks and benefits to their own child. A Kantian would be more inclined to see parental autonomy as encompassing particular duties to one's own child over the existing or future children of others.

RANDOMIZED CLINICAL TRIALS AND THE USE OF PLACEBOS

Much medical research today is carried out in the form of randomized clinical trials (RCTs). Such research is usually designed to test the efficacy of new drugs or procedures, sometimes comparing the new with an existing drug or procedure and sometimes testing it against a placebo. Clinical trials fall into one of four categories or phases. Phase I trials, as we have seen, are designed solely to test the toxicity of a drug. They are usually carried out on healthy subjects (except in the case of cancer drugs, which use only terminally ill cancer patients) and do not entail any therapeutic benefits for the research subject. In these trials, which are limited to a small number of research subjects (for example, 20–80), increasingly strong doses are given to different groups of subjects in order to determine the highest tolerable dose (normally such trials escalate only to the level of reversible side effects, although this is not guaranteed as the Gelsinger case shows). Phase II trials, which are administered to a larger, but still limited, number of patients (for example, 100–300), are designed to test the optimal dose and to lay the ground conditions for Phase III trials. Since researchers are looking for positive results from testing in this phase as well as side effects, these trials may or may not be therapeutic. Phase III trials, on the other hand, are administered to a large number of subjects (for example, 1000–3000), are carried out in multiple sites (and often in multiple countries), and can be therapeutic. They are designed to establish whether or not a new drug works as well as an existing one, and they are performed using a control group. The new treatment is given to one set of subjects, and the existing treatment or placebo is given to another group. If this phase demonstrates good results, the drug is approved and marketed. Phase IV trials, carried out after a drug has been approved and is in use, are designed to continue monitoring the benefits and side effects and also to explore the possibility of wider application of the product.

Most of the ethical issues already discussed in relation to medical research in general are equally applicable to clinical trials, in particular, the issue of therapy versus experimentation. Particular care must be taken in obtaining consent for participation in Phase I (and sometimes Phase II) trials *because they are by their nature non-therapeutic.* Phase III and IV trials, on the other hand, raise particular issues because they are, or are deemed possibly to be, therapeutic. Therefore it makes a difference whether one is assigned to the group receiving the therapy (the new treatment) or to the control group. For these trials, the particular ethical problems that arise concern the process of randomization, the use of placebos, and the interpretation of *equipoise.*[54]

Randomization

Since the 1970s the randomized clinical trial has become the gold standard of medical research for testing the safety and efficacy of drug treatments. Randomly placing subjects into groups (that is, the experimental group and the control group) minimizes the chance that other factors (such as state of health or financial status) might actually be the reason the patient gets better and not the administration of the drug therapy. The procedure is meant to be as objective as possible and to go beyond the interest and enthusiasm of physicians for trying a particular new drug—or, in the words of Passamani, to safeguard "current and future patients from our therapeutic passions."[55]

However, as already pointed out, the physician is wearing two hats when it comes to medical research and patients: that of physician or healer and that of researcher or scientist. The obligation of a physician in conformity with the principles of beneficence and non-malfeasance is to do good for the patient and to avoid doing harm. The physician must apply all the knowledge that he or she has in order to recommend the best treatment for the patient. However, in agreeing to enter a patient in a trial, or even encouraging a patient to participate, the physician is consenting to have that patient blindly assigned to the group receiving the new treatment or to the control group. In order for randomization to work properly, the physician *must wilfully remain ignorant* about the treatment the patient is receiving. In effect, when wearing the hat of the researcher-scientist, the physician must remain in a state of ignorance, whereas with the hat of the healer, he or she must apply all of his or her knowledge for the benefit of the patient. Some ethicists see this as a conflict that cannot be resolved and thus do not think that doctors should participate in randomized clinical trials. As Samuel and Deborah Hellman put it: "Even though the therapeutic value of the new agent is unproved, if physicians think that it has promise, are they acting in the best interests of their patients in allowing them to be randomly assigned to the control group? Is persisting in such an assignment consistent with the specific commitments taken on in the doctor-patient relationship?"[56]

This brings us back to the original question asked earlier in this chapter: who undergoes the risks and who receives the benefits of medical research? Looked at from the point of view of a utilitarian, this question does not pose ethical problems. The objective of medical research in general (including clinical trials) is the discovery of treatments and cures for the good of all existing and future sufferers of the disease in question. Thus the greater good accomplished by a successful clinical study would balance out any harm that came to a few patients as a result of being part of the control group. A utilitarian would be assessing the overall good and not the good obtained by any one patient. It is not how pains and pleasures are distributed but the overall pain or pleasure that matters. However, as Hellman and Hellman point out: "Physicians must care very deeply about the distribution of pain and pleasure, for they have entered into a relationship with one or a number of individual patients. They cannot be indifferent to whether it is these patients or others that suffer for the general benefit of society.... [T]he ethical obligation created by the covenant between doctor and patient requires the doctor to see the interests of the individual patient as primary and compelling."[57]

The Use of Placebos

In randomized clinical trials, those in the control group might be treated with either a known standard treatment or a placebo.[58] From an ethical point of view, testing a new treatment against a standard treatment is the least problematic of the two since those in the control group are actually receiving treatment that has, up to that point, been considered effective. This treatment may turn out to be less effective than the new treatment, but it is still acceptable treatment. But pharmaceutical companies often prefer to test their products against a placebo rather than an existing treatment, claiming that the results are purer. The question of using placebos is even more troubling in what are called confirmatory trials, which are often conducted after a treatment has been shown to be effective but further study is deemed necessary. Hellman and Hellman note, "How can one conduct such trials ethically unless one is convinced that the first trial was in error? The ethical problems we have discussed are only exacerbated when a completed randomized clinical trial indicates that a given treatment is preferable."[59] Veatch goes further in pointing out that, in many cases, even completing a trial raises moral problems since it is often evident long before the end of the trial that one treatment is more effective than another, even though the statistical proof may not yet confirm this. In such cases, Veatch says, "[I]t is immoral to complete the trial. Thus, most clinical trials today become immoral before they are completed."[60] According to the Canadian guidelines, an experimental drug or therapy "should be tested against an established effective therapy."[61] Placebos may be used if they do not compromise the safety of the participants, and participants should be informed that they may not be receiving either the experimental therapy or the established effective therapy but a placebo instead. Depending on the health of the patient, the illness being treated, and the current effectiveness of the standard treatment, it is difficult to see how the use of a placebo would not compromise the safety of the participants. This is something that must be assessed by the physician when placing a patient in a clinical trial—and it takes us back to the conflict referred to above regarding responsibilities to patients and responsibilities to medical research.

Equipoise

The third ethical issue concerning randomized clinical trials (RCTs) revolves around the question of equipoise. If, at the start of a clinical trial, there exists "a state of honest, professional disagreement in the community of expert clinicians as to the preferred treatment,"[62] then it can be said that there is a state of **clinical equipoise**. If a doctor honestly does not know which of two treatments is more effective in treating a patient's disease, then there is no ethical problem involved in entering the patient in a trial. But what happens if, as the trial evolves, the doctor truly begins to believe that the treatment being tested is superior to the existing treatment (or placebo)? Some (including Veatch, cited above) would consider it unethical if a doctor knows that a patient is not receiving the treatment that is proving effective and yet continues to keep the patient in the trial. But not everyone agrees with this point of view. Passamani, for example, argues that every physician is part of a "competent medical community" and that it is the consensus of this community (and not the opinion of any one doctor) that determines what is, or is not, an effective therapy. When a doctor is participating in an RCT, he or she "represents this competent medical community in asserting that the community is unpersuaded by existing data that an innovative treatment is superior to standard therapy."[63] In Passamani's view, as long as the medical community as a whole is undecided, equipoise exists, and no ethical line is being crossed by keeping a particular patient in a clinical trial.

For people like Passamani, "randomized trials are in fact the most scientifically sound and ethically correct means of evaluating new therapies."[64] While there have been abuses in the past, regulations governing medical research are in place and are constantly being improved. Thus, clinical trials can be designed in ways that meet adequate standards of science and of ethics. Others, such as Hellman and Hellman, question the fundamental need for, and efficacy of, clinical trials: "It is fallacious to suggest that only the randomized clinical trial can provide valid information or that all information acquired by this technique is valid.... The scientific method is based on increasing probabilities and increasingly refined approximations of truth. Although the randomized clinical trial contributes to these ends, it is neither unique nor perfect. Other techniques may also be useful."[65]

Passamani and Hellman and Hellman hold radically opposed views concerning the need for randomized clinical trials, and their differences can, in part, be traced to different perceptions of the dual role of the physician-healer and to differing ethical perspectives on the meaning and value of medical research. Passamani's position can be defended by a utilitarian ethic, which looks to the greatest overall good for the greatest number. Hellman and Hellman, on the other hand, take a more Kantian perspective of respect for persons and of never using a sick person as a means to an end, no matter how important the end is perceived to be. Ethical theory cannot tell us who is right; it can, however, force us to examine what we may not have thought of questioning before. And it can help us in adapting our practice of medical research to ethical principles, rather than adapting our ethical principles to the needs of medical research.

CONFLICT OF INTEREST IN RESEARCH

It is a growing reality of contemporary medical research that more and more of it is conducted by, or in collaboration with, pharmaceutical companies. Canada's Research-Based Pharmaceutical Companies (Rx&D) member companies, numbering more than 50, invest more than one billion dollars in pharmaceutical research and development (R&D) in Canada annually, and contribute over three billion dollars to the economy.[66] As a result "most clinical trials undertaken to establish the safety and efficacy of [drugs and medical devices] are funded by industry."[67] The trials themselves are often carried out under the auspices of universities and research hospitals, and often in collaboration with federal funding agencies that provide part of the funding needed for the research. This was the case in the research trial conducted by Dr. Nancy Olivieri of the University of Toronto (see Box 4.3), who received funding from the federal government and from the pharmaceutical company Apotex. This case clearly demonstrates a problem that is more and more common in this kind of research collaboration: the manipulation and even suppression of research results by the pharmaceutical companies. According to Hailey, "Findings that support manufacturers' claims are widely disseminated, while others may be withheld.... [S]ome companies appear to be ready to stifle scientific discussion by turning to the courts, seeking injunctions to prevent the release of reports or threatening researchers with legal action."[68]

UNIVERSITY RESEARCH AND PHARMACEUTICAL COMPANIES: NANCY OLIVIERI AND APOTEX

BOX 4.3

In 1987, Nancy Olivieri, a hematologist and researcher at the University of Toronto, was working at the Hospital for Sick Children where she had begun a study on the experimental chelating drug deferiprone. She wanted to find out if deferiprone might be effective in the control of iron loading in patients with severe thalassemia, a disease that causes anemia and, in its severe form, can require regular blood transfusions. Her objective was to test the efficacy of the new drug against the standard treatment, deferoxamine, an intravenous drug with a number of adverse side effects. Deferiprone, an oral medicine, could prove to be a major breakthrough for patients suffering from this disease.

Dr. Olivieri received funding from the Medical Research Council of Canada and Apotex, a major drug company with strong connections to both the hospital and the university. Apotex (then in discussions with the university concerning a proposed $20 million donation for a new research centre) agreed to sponsor Olivieri's research and acquired commercial rights to sell deferiprone. Dr. Olivieri started two research studies to test the safety and effectiveness of deferiprone with the help of Dr. Gideon Koren, a clinical pharmacologist who had contacts with Apotex and who had helped secure the funding.

The contract that Olivieri signed with Apotex included a confidentiality clause giving Apotex the right to control all communication of the results of the studies for one year after completion. While initial results of the research appeared promising, in early 1996, Olivieri discovered a serious problem when some patients who initially had a good response to deferiprone began to get iron buildup again. Olivieri immediately informed Apotex, and consulted with the research ethics review board at the hospital. She felt obliged to continue to offer the drug to those who were still responding to it but believed that all patients should be informed of the potential risks. Dr. Koren and the other researchers agreed with her, but Apotex did not. When Olivieri told Apotex that the research ethics review board had instructed her to inform the patients of the risk, Apotex abruptly cancelled the contract and shut down the research. Since there was no longer any research going on, the research ethics review board had no jurisdiction; thus there could be no enforced public disclosure of information.

Since deferiprone was being used in other studies around the world, Olivieri believed the risks should be made known. When Apotex refused to release the information, she decided she had no choice but to break the confidentiality agreement and publish her data through professional conferences and journals. Under the advice of legal counsel, she informed Apotex of every step she took, but the company continued to threaten her with legal reprisals while insisting that her data were erroneous. Even though the research had been officially stopped, Olivieri continued to provide deferiprone to those patients who still responded to it while monitoring them for possible organ damage, a process that included liver biopsy. In February 1997, she found that a number of patients were developing fibrosis, a scarring of the liver that could lead to serious liver disease, most likely as a result of the drug. This led to another round of denials and threats from Apotex, who demanded the original biopsy slides from Olivieri. They sent these to their own pathologist who contradicted Olivieri's findings.

In spite of faculty support for Olivieri, the university decided that this was a hospital issue and stayed out of the controversy. The hospital joined with Apotex in accusing Dr. Olivieri of wrong-doing and held two disciplinary inquiries, both of which concluded that she was guilty of wrong-doing. Many scientists, shocked by these events, circulated a petition in support of Olivieri—then found themselves victims of anonymous character assassination and administrative harassment.

In January 1999, the Hospital for Sick Children removed Oliveri from her post and placed a gag order on one of her chief defenders, prohibiting both of them from publicizing the case. At this point, the University of Toronto administration stepped in, and, and, defending academic freedom, reinstated Olivieri as director of her program. Apotex then broke off discussions with the university, and withdrew its donation of $20 million for the Centre for Cellular and Biomedical Research at the University of Toronto.

In 2001, as a result of this case, the University of Toronto reached an agreement with its teaching hospitals to harmonize research policies and enforce stringent ethical guidelines and public accountability in research. It reiterated the importance of peer review as fundamental practice, along with the right of researchers to make their research results known.

In 2004, Dr. Olivieri entered into a settlement agreement that stipulated that Apotex pay her $800,000 and that she not "disparage" the company or the drug deferiprone. Apotex has resisted complying with the agreement, however, claiming that Olivieri has disparaged the company, a claim that, according to the Canadian Association of University Teachers, is unfounded. As of 2009, Apotex was continuing to appeal the court decision.

Research scientists are subject to the peer review process, and their methodology and results must pass the assessment of their peers in order to be published in academic journals. They are, therefore, accountable to their peers in the scientific and research community, and to the university of which they are a part. Their goal is, or should be, academic and research excellence in medical research. Pharmaceutical companies are accountable to their shareholders and, while their stated objective is to save lives through their products, ultimately their primary goal is the business goal of profits. This represents a conflict of values and purpose that is built right into the industry-university partnership. While drugs might save lives, they are also big business. Companies are always trying to produce a better (or more saleable) product than their competitors, especially if their competitor has already brought a successful drug to market. Petryna refers to the "profitable and highly competitive 'me-too'" drugs business, whereby drugs are developed that build on or mimic "blockbuster" drugs that have sales of more than a billion dollars a year (such as Prozac or Viagra).[69] Competition for market share can go so far as enticing respected physicians and academics to sign articles ghostwritten by pharmaceutical companies to promote their products.[70]

The participation of pharmaceutical companies in "educating" doctors about their products and promoting these products through "incentives" such as conference funding for medical associations (in desirable vacation locations) has been a concern for some time. But recent reports of ghostwritten articles and even of fake medical journals are more disturbing. Elliott writes about for-profit medical education and/or communications companies (called MECCs) and their role in disseminating information in medical journals:

> Pharma pays the MECC; the MECC puts together the articles; academic physicians are paid to sign onto the articles, and the MECC places the articles in medical journals. Some academics simply sign ghostwritten articles, while others work from a draft supplied by the company.... Some academics have signed on for as little as $1,000 or $1,500 per article, including the two faculty members at the Medical University of South Carolina who recently "authored" a ghostwritten article on Ritalin for Novartis. Others command much higher fees.[71]

There is no question, from a bioethical point of view, that this sort of activity is unethical, and it is satisfying to see the courts looking into it and the universities trying to regain control over academic freedom and excellence (as the University of Toronto eventually did in the Olivieri case). But these activities point to a very disturbing issue in relation to subjects participating in research. If pharmaceutical companies are more interested in market share than in patient health, how can any research participant ensure that his or her interests are being looked after? More importantly, how can it be said that anyone has an *obligation* to participate in research? As pointed out earlier in this chapter, some philosophers believe that we have a duty to participate in research for the public good. If we do not, we are being "free riders" by benefiting from the research and not risking anything for it. However, it is clear that the public good is not the prime motivation for the manufacturers of the drugs being tested; how can a plea to the public good then be used to persuade patients to participate in clinical trials where these manufacturers have control over the results? Further, as seen in the Jesse Gelsinger case, it is not unusual for the researchers themselves to have a financial interest in the outcome of the study. The argument that it is a moral duty to participate in research would be more persuasive if the public sector were running the research; it can hardly be convincing when medical research is an industry and those pulling the strings are multinational corporations.

BOX 4.4

JOHN HARRIS, "SCIENTIFIC RESEARCH IS A MORAL DUTY"

Let me present the question in its starkest form: is there a moral obligation to undertake, support and even to participate in serious scientific research? If there is, does that obligation require not only that beneficial research be undertaken but also that "we" as individuals and "we" as societies be willing to support and even participate in research where necessary?

Thus far the overwhelming answer given to this question has been "no," and research has almost universally been treated with suspicion and even hostility by the vast majority of all those concerned with the ethics and regulation of research. The so-called "precautionary approach" sums up this attitude, requiring dangers to be considered more likely and more serious than benefits, and assuming that no sane person would or should participate in research unless they had a pressing personal reason for so doing, or unless they were motivated by a totally impersonal altruism. International agreements and protocols—for example the *Declaration of Helsinki* … have been directed principally at protecting individuals from the dangers of participation in research and ensuring that, where they participate, their full informed consent is assured. The overwhelming presumption has been and remains that participation in research is a supererogatory, and probably a reckless, act not an obligation.…

We all benefit from living in a society, and, indeed, in a world in which serious scientific research is carried out and which utilises the benefits of past research. It is both of benefit to patients and research subjects and in their interests to be in a society which pursues and actively accepts the benefits of research and where research and its fruits are given a high priority. We all also benefit from the knowledge that research is ongoing into diseases or conditions from which we do not currently suffer but to which we may succumb. It makes us feel more secure and gives us hope for the future, for ourselves and our descendants, and for others for whom we care. If this is right, then I have a strong general interest that there be research.…

Moreover, almost everyone now living, certainly everyone born in high income industrialised societies, has benefited from the fruits of past research. We all benefit—for example, either from having been vaccinated against diseases such as polio, smallpox, and others or because others have been vaccinated we benefit from the so called "herd" immunity; or we benefit (as in the case of smallpox) from the fact that the disease has actually been eradicated.…

In view of these considerations there is a clear moral obligation to participate in medical research in certain specific circumstances.… This entails that there are circumstances where an adult, competent person ought to participate in research, even if participating is not in his or her best interests narrowly defined.…

It is crucial that the powerful moral reasons for conducting science research are not drowned by the powerful reasons we have for protecting research subjects. There is a balance to be struck here, but it is not a balance that must always and inevitably be loaded in favour of the protection of research subjects. They are entitled to our concern, respect, and protection to be sure, but they are no more entitled to it than are, say, the people whom—for example, HIV/AIDS or other major diseases are threatening and killing on a daily basis.…

An interesting limiting case is that in which the risks to research subjects are significant and the burdens onerous but where the benefits to other people are equally significant and large. In such a case the research is both urgent and moral but conscription would almost certainly not be appropriate.… That is not of course to say that individuals should not be willing to bear such burdens nor is it to say that it is not their moral duty so to do. In fact the history of science research is full of examples of people willing to bear significant risks in such circumstances, very often these have been the researchers themselves.…[1]

Note
1. In Jonas' descending order of permissibility for recruitment of research subjects, it is precisely the researchers themselves who should be recruited first because it is they who have the greatest interest in, and knowledge about, the research project.

Source: John Harris, "Scientific Research Is a Moral Duty," *Journal of Medical Ethics*, 31, no. 4 (2005), 242–246.

Research Goes Global

Not surprisingly, there is considerable distrust in North America about the clinical trials process. This, along with a tightening of the rules for conducting ethical trials, has resulted in pharmaceutical companies moving their research offshore to countries with fewer medical resources, fewer restrictions, and populations more willing to participate in research trials. Clinical trials cannot go forward (and pharmaceutical products cannot make it to market) unless there are willing participants. And according to Petryna, who has investigated the international market in clinical trials, "landscapes of experimentation evolve in a kind of give-and-take where people with unmet medical needs are willing to say yes to the movement of global capital and scientific and medical communities."[72] This raises a number of questions, including: Are these trials exploitative "or are they social goods or some combination of both?... Who is ultimately responsible for the experimental subject's immediate and long-term well-being?"[73]

One can also ask who the ultimate beneficiaries are of these drug trials: patients in less-developed nations where they are carried out, or patients in Europe and North America who are more reluctant to be experimented on, and whose countries have developed higher standards to protect principles of autonomy and informed consent? Petryna quotes a Brazilian doctor and critic of the clinical trials system that is used to introduce new drugs into Brazil's already weakened health care system: "After a trial ends, the industry enlists doctors to prescribe and patients to demand drugs from the state.... [O]ften these new drugs have not even been approved here and their benefits are not yet clearly established."[74] In other situations, poor people in countries in Africa are exploited in clinical trials, and they will never see the benefits if the trial is successful since the drugs will be marketed in the developed world.

Writing about a series of clinical trials for AIDS being carried out in the 1990s that involved more than 17,000 pregnant women primarily in Africa, Annas and Grodin raise questions about the ethics of doing medical research on subjects in countries that do not have adequate health services. Specifically, they conclude that unless the drugs being tested "will actually be made available to the impoverished populations that are being used as research subjects, developed countries are simply exploiting them in order to quickly use the knowledge gained from the clinical trials for the developed countries' own benefit."[75]

People who are sick with AIDS and people who live in countries that do not have adequate health care must be considered to be "vulnerable populations," just like the groups referred to earlier (children, prisoners, and so forth). They are not in a position to give free and informed consent, and they are very vulnerable to believing the falsehood that they are being offered medical care. Annas and Grodin believe that any consent in these situations is suspect unless there is a clear plan to make the medical interventions that result from the trials available to the population. This is, once again, a simple matter of asking who is undergoing the risks and who is getting the benefits.

DOES BAD ETHICS MAKE BAD SCIENCE?

The question was raised earlier in this chapter about how much of our current medical knowledge is the result of unethical experimentation. There has been a tendency in the bioethical literature to play down abuses in the field of medical research and to suggest that some of the more blatant instances took place outside the parameters of normal medical research, or even that they did not yield useful knowledge. However, a number of recent articles have shown that this impression is simply not true. Referring to the Tuskegee study, for example, Caplan writes: "Even a cursory glance through the literature of health care reveals that the Tuskegee study was and remains a key source of information about the diagnosis, signs, symptoms, and course of syphilis. No effort has been made to impugn its findings, and the biomedical community has relied upon them for decades."[76]

In spite of this, "the view that the study was immoral and therefore worthless has flourished."[77] This is, in Caplan's view, a dangerous situation since it allows both the medical and the bioethical communities to continue to believe that abuses do not take place within the context of mainstream science or in experiments conducted by reputable scientists and physicians. But the Tuskegee study was in place both before and after the implementation of the Nuremberg and Helsinki declarations and was supervised by reputable physicians and government agencies.[78]

Similarly, while the Nazi experiments in the camps were reprehensible in the extreme, this has not diminished the fact that knowledge was obtained from them and that this knowledge has been extremely useful to science and medicine. Cruel and inhumane experiments were performed on prisoners, many of whom died in the process, in order to determine the limits of human exposure to cold. The results of the Nazi hypothermia experimentation represent a valuable source of information about physiological responses to extreme cold and are "widely known among experts in the physiology of exposure to cold temperatures in the U.S., Canada, Britain, Japan and the Soviet Union."[79] Hypothermia research may seem far removed from ordinary medicine, but the fact that the German company Bayer, the maker of Aspirin, "was one of the companies that enlisted the cooperation of the notorious Dr. Josef Mengele to test its products on twins at Auschwitz"[80] underlines the stark reality that most of us have benefited in some way from the terrible excesses of medical experimentation.

Some ethicists question whether the knowledge gained by unethical experimentation should even be used. This is a difficult question for utilitarian ethicists, who weigh the consequences of an action and for whom the pain and suffering of a few can be justified if it benefits the many (the results of the Nazi hypothermia experiments have probably saved many lives). For a Kantian, however, nothing could make these experiments right. The more practical question, of course, relates to how knowledge can be erased once it is generally known and accepted in the medical community. Perhaps, at the very least, this information should come with a historical note outlining the source of the knowledge obtained and the fate of those who were abused in its pursuit.

Galen performs a surgical procedure on a live pig during a demonstration. Vivisection, or experimentation on living animals, is not a recent phenomenon—Galen lived in Rome in the 2nd century C.E.

RESEARCH ON ANIMALS

Another area of medical experimentation upon which ethical analysis has begun to shed light and ask embarrassing questions in recent years concerns the treatment of animals used in research. Animals are used (and abused) extensively in medical research based on the assumption that, while it would be immoral to use humans for much experimentation, it is not immoral to use animals—and in fact it is important for the good of humans that we do so. This assumption—which is, in turn, based on the assumption that we do not have moral obligations to animals because they are inferior creatures—is now being challenged, not only by so-called animal rights activists, but by philosophers and ethicists as well.

The question of the ethics of experimentation on animals can be posed in three ways: (1) Is research on animals wrong *in itself*? (2) Is it right or wrong depending on the degree of pain inflicted on the animals? (3) Is it right or wrong depending on the value of the research to humans?

Depending on how you answer the above questions, you might find yourself either on the side of the *abolitionists* or the *reformists* in relation to animal experimentation. Those who give an uncompromising answer to the first question, and hold that it is wrong *in itself* to use animals for research purposes, are referred to as abolitionists: they wish to abolish the practice of animal experimentation regardless of the impact of such a choice on the future of medical research (and thus, by extension, on the future of human health). For them, there is simply no justification possible for using animals solely for human ends, which is precisely what research on animals is all about.

BOX 4.5

RICHARD D. RYDER, "SOME SEVERE EXPERIMENTS ON ANIMALS"

Despite improvements in regulation, many experiments on animals continue to cause significant suffering.

- In Maryland, in 1996, in a study of septic shock, permanently tracheotomized beagle dogs were used. *E-coli*-infected clots were surgically placed in the dogs' peritoneum. Over the course of the next twenty-one days, ten of the sixteen dogs died.
- In Taiwan in 1997 spinal injuries were caused by dropping weights onto the spines of rats. It was found that greater injuries were caused by dropping the weights from greater heights.
- In Minneapolis in 1999 scientists studying bone cancer pain demonstrated a correlation between bone destruction, pain, and neurochemical changes in the spinal cord by injecting tumor cells into the femurs of mice. This replicated the symptoms of patients with bone cancer pain.
- Since the 1990s many animals in America have been used to study the effects of high alcohol consumption and withdrawal. In studies of chimpanzees, monkeys, dogs, cats and rodents, severe effects have been observed. These can include vomiting, tremor, anxiety, and seizures. Convulsions have been induced in alcohol-withdrawal animals by lifting animals by the tail, giving electric shocks, or injecting chemicals directly into the brain.[1]

Note
1. The author's sources are: (1) P.Q. Eichacker et al., "Serial Measures of Total Body Oxygen Consumption in an Awake Canine Model of Septic Shock," *American Journal of Respiratory Critical Care Medicine*, 154, no. 1, 68–78; (2) C.C. Hong et al., "Kinematic Principles of Primate Vestibulo Ocular Reflex," *Journal of Chinese Society of Veterinary Science*, 23, no. 5 (1997), 383–394; (3) Matthew J. Schwei et al., "Neurochemical and Cellular Reorganization of the Spinal Cord in a Murine Model of Bone Cancer Pain," *Journal of Neuroscience*, 19, no. 24 (December 1999), 108886–108897; and (4) Howard C. Becker, "Animal Models of Alcohol Withdrawal," *Alcohol Research & Health*, 24, no. 2 (2000), 105–113.

Source: Richard D. Ryder, "Speciesism in the Laboratory," in Peter Singer (ed.), *In Defense of Animals: The Second Wave* (Malden, MA: Blackwell Publishing, 2006), 91.

Others, taking a less radical stand, examine the issue from the point of view of the second and third questions. Research on animals should be permitted as long as it does not cause too much pain to the animal subjects. (This raises the question of how much pain is too much pain.) Alternatively, research on animals should be permitted when that research is considered vital to human health, but animals should not be used for frivolous or unnecessary research (for example, cosmetics research, or, for some, psychological experiments). These people can be referred to as reformists: they are prepared to condone research on animals if that research is strictly regulated and subject to review by ethics boards, for example. They opt for humane methods in the use of animal subjects, and they wish to minimize research on animals through the development of alternative methods of investigation.

Some thinkers point to a basic flaw in the reasoning about the use of animals in research: either animals are like us or they are not like us. If they are so like us that we are able to make inferences about human health based on animal experiments, then we should not treat them in ways that we would not treat humans. And if they are so unlike us that we can feel free to treat them in ways that we would not treat humans, then the information gleaned from animal experimentation is unlikely to be of use when applied to the human context. As one ethicist explains: "A 'good' animal model must be assumed sufficiently 'close' to the human breed to authorize inferences from animal to man, and sufficiently 'distant' to allow guilt to remain unconscious or discharged. Thus the 'genetic distance' is not measured on the same scale for the purpose of science or ethics."[81]

The fundamental question is this: *is it morally justifiable to use animals solely for human ends?* If you are inclined to answer this question positively, then you must provide a *morally relevant criterion* as to why this is so. What is it that makes animals so different from you and me that we can cause them to suffer and die in our pursuit of medical knowledge?

Religious and Philosophical Roots

That animals can be used solely for the good of humans is an assumption that has a long history and is buttressed by both religious and philosophical beliefs. One need look no further than the Book of Genesis to explain the origins of our Western attitude toward animals (and nature in general):

> And God blessed Noah and his sons, and said unto them, Be fruitful and multiply, and replenish the earth. And the fear of you and the dread of you shall be upon every beast of the earth, and upon every fowl of the air, and upon all that moveth upon the earth, and upon the fishes of the sea; into your hand are they delivered. Every moving thing that liveth shall be for meat for you; even as the green herb have I given you all things.[82]

Thomas Aquinas, who was one of the principal philosophers of the Roman Catholic Church, wrote at length about the place of the human species in the hierarchy of life, based on Christian beliefs. In chapter 78 of *Summa Contra Gentiles*, entitled *That Other Creatures are Ruled by God by Means of Intellectual Creatures*, he states that "as the highest creatures are under God and are governed by Him, so the lower creatures are under the higher creatures and are governed by them.... [O]f all creatures the highest are the intellectual ones.... [T]he rational plan of divine providence demands that the other creatures be ruled by rational creatures."[83]

The situation of animals does not improve greatly with rationalist philosophers such as René Descartes, the founder of modern philosophy—if anything, it becomes more extreme. In Descartes' world, Aquinas' hierarchy is collapsed and the universe divides into humans (with minds) and everything else—nature, animals (without minds). Since animals do not have minds (or souls—since for Descartes mind and soul are equivalent), they cannot think and, therefore, they do not feel pain. As he explains in a letter to his good friend and mentor, Marin Mersenne: "I do not explain the feeling of pain without reference to the soul. For in my view pain exists only in the understanding. What I do explain is all the external movements which accompany this feeling in us; in animals it is these movements alone which occur, and not pain in the strict sense."[84]

Kant also emphasized rationality as the defining feature of humans and held that animals do not exist as ends in themselves but only as means to an end—and that end is man. He did not, however, condone cruelty to animals since such behaviour could result in cruel behaviour toward other humans. In other words, if we are kind to animals, we might be kinder to each other.

The only dissenting voice in a long line of philosophical and religious thought comes from the father of utilitarianism, Jeremy Bentham, who believed that it was the possession of sentience rather than rationality or linguistic ability that entitles a being to moral consideration. For Bentham, it was not rationality but sentience that counted. We should not exclude animals from the moral sphere because they can't reason or speak; we should include them because they, like us, can suffer. So the question for Bentham was not whether animals reason, but whether they suffer. Many modern-day utilitarians follow Bentham's belief that animals are beings that can suffer and, as such, have an interest in not suffering, just as humans do. As Matheny puts it, "[P]leasure and pain *matter* to all of us who feel them. As such, it follows that we are obliged to consider, at a minimum, the interests of those who are capable of feeling pleasure and pain—that is, all those who are *sentient*. We can then say that sentience is a sufficient condition for having interests and having those interests considered equally."[85]

Changing Views of Animals

A number of factors have worked to change our traditional attitude toward animals, including growing evidence of animal intellectual and perceptual abilities that are similar to those of humans, along with an increasing awareness of nature and of our interdependence with the creatures of the natural world. Ryder even suggests that the abortion controversy of the last several decades has "moved the concept of a person to the center of the stage,"[86] something that has caused many people to question how so many people attribute personhood to fetuses and not to animals. We have become, as well, "conscious of living in a post-Darwinian age when the moral implications of Darwinism were overdue for serious consideration.... Some members of the younger generation [have] rejected the double standards of their parents and the conspiracy of silence on a whole range of moral issues, among them our abuse of animals."[87]

Few people today would deny that animals feel pain. So if you accept Bentham's argument that sentience, rather than intelligence, is what entitles a being to moral consideration (at least in the limited sense of admitting that they have an interest in not being unnecessarily hurt), then you must accept that at least some animals must be included in our moral calculations. In other words, "if a nonhuman animal can feel pleasure and pain, then that animal possesses interests. To think otherwise is to pervert the sense in which we understand pleasure and pain, feelings that matter to us and to others who experience them. At a minimum, a sentient animal has an interest in a painless, pleasurable life."[88]

BOX 4.6

PAOLA CAVALIERI, "DO ANIMALS SUFFER?"

The view that René Descartes put forward in the seventeenth century is so contrary both to common sense and to empirical findings that one wonders how it could have been formulated at all. Animals do not suffer. Not possessing language, they do not possess reason. Not possessing reason, they are not feeling beings, but mere automata. In the face of such a counter-intuitive claim, some authors have attempted to amend the perspective claiming that, if not in his main works, at least in some private letters, Descartes granted animals some sensations, thereby showing that he did not himself believe his theory.

This is enlightening, but in a sense opposite to the one suggested. Why, in fact, did Descartes argue for a stance he could not really accept? Why did so many of his contemporaries blindly take it at its face value? At least part of the explanation lies not at the level of philosophical thinking, but rather at the level of felt social needs. Through late antiquity and medieval times, when hierarchy and subjection were the rule even among human beings, the status of animals as mere means had never been challenged. They had been exploited in whatever ways humans saw fit—except for an injunction against cruelty. Though usually justified in terms of an ethics of virtue, or of the possible consequences of cruel habits for human beings, this injunction withstood the centuries. But something was changing in Descartes's era. This era saw the establishment of the experimental method in science and, concomitant with it, the spreading of a new area of inquiry, empirical physiology, which embodied a practice requiring the plain abandonment of any qualms about cruelty. The practice was called "**vivisection**," and consisted in studying physiological processes by literally cutting living animals. Occasionally present in antiquity—instances of it are mentioned in the Hellenistic age and during the Roman Empire—"vivisection" had been abandoned in the periods when the appeal to influential authors of the past, rather than autonomous research, dominated even empirical fields of study. But the methodological revolution of the seventeenth century caused a resumption, and a real outburst, of the practice—so much so that public sessions of vivisection were common among experimentalists and the "educated public."

The notion of cruelty has much to do with the intentions of the perpetrator, and with the "gratuitousness" of the infliction of suffering. However, it is also connected with the level of suffering involved. Vivisection did imply extraordinary levels of suffering, inflicted knowingly and openly by some of the most respected members of society. The problem was so evident that something was needed to counteract the budding criticisms, and to allow the unimpeded continuation of the practice. In this light, to advance, or to adhere to, the view that vivisected animals did not suffer offered a good escape route. True, such a view—the beast-machine theory—entailed the implausible idea of a radical discontinuity between humans and animals. Descartes's endeavor, however, was favored by his ability to draw upon two different theoretical sources—classical metaphysics, with its rational, immortal souls for humans, and the new mechanistic view of nature as mere matter for animals. The resulting doctrine allowed investigators to perform vivisection in an even more ruthless manner.

To accept this reconstruction means to accept the idea that the first significant revival of the debate on animals did not stem from a critical reflection on past biases, but from an intensification of human exploitation. In this light, it is no surprise that the new discussion, far from challenging conventional premises, narrowed the focus. Instead of starting from the question, "How much do animals count?" it started from the question, "How much can animals suffer, if at all?" This led to a dispute about animals' mental capacities, with the main normative problem—"Are we entitled to inflict suffering on animals at all?"—disappearing into the background.

Source: Paola Cavalieri, "The Animal Debate: A Reexamination," in Peter Singer (ed.), In Defense of Animals: The Second Wave (Malden, MA: Blackwell Publishing, 2006), 58–59.

To think that only humans matter and that we matter simply because we are *human* is to fall into the error of what some call **speciesism**,[89] which can be defined as "discrimination against or exploitation of certain animal species by human beings, based on an assumption of mankind's superiority."[90] Overcoming speciesism does not mean treating all animals as equal to all humans; it simply means not using species as the criterion by which we determine the moral difference between humans and animals. If it is wrong to inflict pain on sentient humans, it is equally wrong to inflict pain on sentient animals. The fact that animals are not human does not make it right. Further, if we think it is wrong to conduct painful experiments on infants or on brain-damaged humans, then it cannot be right to perform such experiments on intelligent monkeys, cats, or dogs. In Singer's view, if the experimenters "would not be prepared to use a human infant then their readiness to use nonhuman animals reveals an unjustifiable form of discrimination on the basis of species, since adult apes, monkeys, dogs, cats, rats, and other animals are more aware of what is happening to them, more self-directing, and, so far as we can tell, at least as sensitive to pain as a human infant."[91]

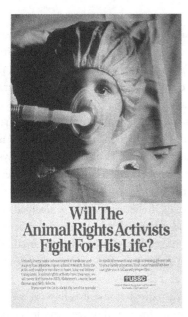

As in all polarized ethical issues, both sides of the "animal rights" debate have strong views that are often put forth publicly in graphic, and often exaggerated, ways. Those in favour of animal experimentation will emphasize its importance to medical progress and saving human lives. Those against will argue that harming and killing animals for better cosmetics is immoral. In such debates it is difficult to find the middle ground. (This PETA ad dates back to 1990. Eye irritancy tests on rabbits are rarely used in cosmetics tests today, thanks to consumer opposition, but are still widely used in chemical tests.)

Are Animals Part of the Moral Community?

Not everyone agrees with the position that sentience is the criterion by which a being becomes part of the human moral calculation. Many who agree that animals have an interest in not suffering do not agree that this necessarily makes them part of the moral community, or that it is immoral to use them for human ends. In their view, to be part of the moral community, it is necessary to be capable of moral judgment. Carl Cohen defends speciesism based on the fact that only humans can be part of the human moral community. Only humans can make and break laws (an animal can never commit a crime, for example). Further, "humans confront choices that are purely moral; humans—but certainly not dogs or mice—lay down moral laws, for others and for themselves. Human beings are self-legislative, morally *autonomous*."[92]

The problem with Cohen's argument is that not all humans are self-legislative, morally autonomous beings. Babies and the mentally impaired, among others, are not capable of making or breaking moral laws, and yet we consider them part of the moral community. We do not eject people with disabilities from the moral community, and we would not dream of substituting an orphan baby for a laboratory rat in a medical experiment. Why is that? Cohen says the issue is one of kind: "Humans are of such a kind that they may be the subject of experiments only with their voluntary consent. The choices they make freely must be respected. Animals are of such a kind that it is impossible for them, in principle, to give or withhold voluntary consent or to make a moral choice."[93] But babies and incompetent adults cannot give or withhold voluntary consent. They cannot make a moral choice. This underlines the difficulty of finding a morally relevant criterion that fits with all humans and no animals. Cohen's opponents would argue that qualities such as rationality, language, or intelligence that are usually used to differentiate humans from animals are qualities that some animals possess and, more importantly, that not all humans possess. For Cohen, however, this argument is not insurmountable: while not *all* humans can in fact make moral choices, humans generally have the capacity to do so while no animal, no matter how intelligent, has this capacity.[94]

Cohen further believes that the use of animals in medical research can be justified on utilitarian grounds since we must include in our calculation "the disadvantageous consequences of not using animals in research, and to all the achievements attained and attainable only through their use."[95] This is a strong argument only if the advantages of this kind of medical research to human life and health are as great as its proponents believe, and this is difficult to prove. However, measuring the utility of every experiment that uses animals could go a long way to eliminating frivolous experiments and causing unnecessary pain and suffering to animals. As Matheny points out, much research may answer interesting questions without necessarily bringing any benefit. "Do we really need to know," he asks, "what happens to kittens after their eyes are removed at birth, or to monkeys when deprived of all maternal contact from infancy? In every case, we should ask if the pain prevented by an experiment is greater than the pain caused by that experiment."[96]

This might sound like a vote in favour of using animals if the experiment is deemed to bring much good to humans, but it is not. Matheny, Singer, and others ask why, if an experiment is that important for human needs, we would not use a brain-damaged baby instead of an animal. That we would not use such a baby (which probably has little or no awareness of what is happening to it) but are willing to use animals that are fully conscious, aware, and capable of great suffering is, for them, simply discrimination based on species. We will not use the baby because it is human; we will use the animal because it is not. This is speciesism, according to Singer and others, and it is a position they vehemently reject.

Many philosophers will say that, while we have some moral responsibility not to cause unnecessary suffering to animals, this does not mean we must consider them part of the human moral community and treat their interests—even if only their interest in not suffering—as equal to ours. This would fit with the reformist position outlined above: reduce the use of animals, reduce the amount of pain inflicted, eliminate frivolous or unnecessary experiments, and so forth. Some reformers refer to the principle of the Three Rs: Replacement, Reduction, and Refinement. This would certainly help solve the practical problem of excessive animal suffering in the name of human need, but it would not solve the philosophical problem of where our moral responsibility to animals comes from. Our responsibilities to other humans are based on the fact that we are all part of the human community. We have a responsibility to help weak or helpless humans (including babies and the mentally incompetent) because we are all humans (or as Cohen would say, we are all part of the moral community). If we extend that moral responsibility to include animals, are we not then making them part of our moral community too? Or do we include them only some of the time, depending on our purposes? Is it a simple question of benevolence, and if so, is this enough?

The philosophical problem raised by the animal rights movement is a very challenging one. Many philosophers in the past 30 years have attempted to counter the position that animals have interests or even rights that humans must take into account in their moral deliberations. But, as Peter Singer points out, "[T]he continuing failure of philosophers to produce a plausible theory of the moral importance of species membership indicates, with increasing probability, that there is no such plausible theory."[97]

ETHICAL THEORY AND MEDICAL RESEARCH

It can be seen from the issues discussed in this chapter that utilitarians and Kantians often have different approaches to determining what is ethical treatment of research subjects, and what is not. This is, in part, because the benefits accruing from medical research very often do not accrue to those who take on the risks of participation. This is not a matter of chance; it is the nature of the practice: the goal of research is the accretion of knowledge in order to prevent disease, or to help present and future sufferers of a disease. It may have a positive effect on those who take part in a research trial, and that is good. But that is not the ultimate goal, nor even a necessary goal. There is, as we have shown, a difference between medical therapy and medical research.

Kantian ethics, with its emphasis on respect for persons, autonomy, and, in the medical context, informed consent, will usually come down on the side of the research subject, insisting on transparency and truth, and rejecting procedures and processes that could result in using research subjects solely as a means to an end. Utilitarians, on the other hand, emphasizing the consequences of an action, will look more to the potential overall good that might come of the research, and would tend to include future sufferers (even those not yet born) in the calculation of benefits. Some utilitarians will go so far as to argue that we all have an *obligation* to participate in research, even if the benefits to ourselves are minimal or non-existent, and that this obligation extends to consideration for those not yet born. That some should be put at risk for the benefit of the many (including some future "many") is not a position a utilitarian would reject—but a Kantian would.

Kantianism cannot be relied upon to argue against using animals as research subjects, since the proscription against using persons as a means to an end applies solely to persons—and animals are not persons in the Kantian world (Kantians would, therefore, have to be numbered among those whom Singer would call "speciesist"). Utilitarians could argue either way on the question of animal research: Singer is a professed utilitarian and he includes animals when he calculates the harms and benefits to "the greatest number." Like Bentham, he believes that animals have an interest in not suffering and that this must be taken into account in calculating harms and benefits. Other utilitarians would argue that animals should not be included in the calculation and that it is the harms and benefits to humans only that must be taken into account.

Jonas has pointed out in another context that traditional ethics dealt only with dealings among human beings—it was not designed to cover our dealings with nature, of which animals are a part: "Ethical significance belonged to the direct dealing of man with man, including the dealing with himself: all traditional ethics is anthropocentric."[98] Thus, what is an accusation on the part of animal activists (our approach to ethics is *anthropocentric*) is true, but it is also a simple fact of philosophical history. It may be that this has to change (and Jonas believed that it must in relation to our dealings with the environment), but until it does, we will have difficulty applying the old theories to the new problems of medical research. The same can be said for the global business of clinical trials: from a utilitarian point of view, whether or not this is ethically justifiable depends on whether the research subjects in developing countries are included in the utilitarian calculus of the "greatest number." It is easier to discount the risks to others if those others are far away and our own needs are great. The stark reality is that, as this practice grows, it could become just another way in which the developed world exploits the rest of the world—for corporate profits and consumer goods.

CONCLUSION

Medical experimentation and the abuse of human subjects was one of the pivotal issues that led to the development of the new discipline of bioethics several decades ago. As can be seen from this chapter, some of the concerns expressed at that time are still a concern both from a medical and from an ethical point of view. It is clear that the drive to know, to experiment, and to progress is strong, and the goal of forever improving humans and society is one that needs to be tempered by serious consideration of the means used to achieve it. This concern has now been broadened to include the abuse of animals and vulnerable populations in the third world. In addition, with the ever-increasing dependence on pharmaceuticals in our search for long and healthy lives, the goal of huge profits for multinational corporations has been added to the mix of ethical conflicts inherent in the practice of research. These conflicts stretch our ethical thinking to its limits and will continue to pose a challenge to the discipline of bioethics as it matures.

PHILOSOPHICAL REFLECTION ON MEDICAL RESEARCH

The practice of medical research is built on the idea of medical progress, and there are debates about just how much medical progress (or at least the increase in the lifespan of us, the inhabitants of the Western world) is due to medical research and how much is due, among other things, to more simple causes such as improved hygiene, better nutrition, decreased poverty, and the decline of infant mortality. Singer cites studies that suggest that as little as "3.5% of the fall in the overall death rate [between 1910 and 1984] can be explained through medical interventions for the major infectious diseases."[99] As for non-infectious diseases such as cancer, for example, we have more medical research than ever before, and yet more cancer than ever before. Granted, we have more and better drugs for combating cancer, but we do not seem to have found ways of preventing cancer in the first place. We have yet to find a cure for the common cold.

So when it comes to medical progress, it can be said that there are believers and there are skeptics, and which group has the greater claim to reason is a question that goes beyond the scope of this book. One thing that is clear from the issues analyzed in this chapter is that there are winners and losers in the ongoing march toward medical progress and in the promise of medical research. As we will see in later chapters, people are living longer, but in the eyes of many, the extension of life often means little more than a prolongation of death as many people spend year after unproductive year in nursing homes waiting to die. Many babies who have been saved by new techniques of treating extreme prematurity end up leading lives of diminished quality, and some will never be autonomous persons. Expensive cancer drugs can extend the lives of some, but often for only a matter of months at an extremely high financial cost (raising ethical controversies in Canada about what drug treatments should be covered at public expense).

If we accept the position of those who believe strongly in medical research, we must still face the reality of the history of abuse that has accompanied our never-ending quest for knowledge. We must also resist believing that this abuse is all in the past. Issues have been raised in this chapter suggesting that the potential for abuse is hovering very close to the surface of the entire enterprise. As medical research is more and more geared toward research for miracle drugs (including those that enhance sexual performance, slow the process of aging, and even, perhaps, conquer death), the discourse of the marketplace takes up more and more room in the conversation. The search for knowledge has become tainted with the search for profits. Some will say that this is simply human nature. Aristotle would likely disagree with this, and it is certainly not an argument in favour of situating medical research among what we like to think of as public goods.

Medical experimentation cannot be accomplished through experiments on things—there is, as Jonas points out, no stand-in for the real thing (as there is, for example, in physics)—it can only be accomplished on people. The challenge is, in the process, to not allow people to be turned into things.

CASES OF INTEREST

Grimes v. Kennedy Krieger Institute

In 1993, researchers at the Kennedy Krieger Institute (KKI), a children's health facility and research institute, initiated a study to determine the effects of different lead abatement methods on urban homes in the Baltimore area. The cost of full lead abatement was too high compared to the worth of the properties in question, so many landlords were abandoning the unprofitable houses. Finding the minimal and affordable level of lead abatement, then, could potentially entice landlords to keep their properties and thus preserve the availability of low-rent housing.

In the study, three groups of houses received less than full lead abatement; the first group received the least, the second had more than the first, and the third more than the second. The two control groups either received full lead abatement or none at all if their homes were constructed without lead paint. The families in the study were paid by KKI to occasionally take dust, soil, water, and blood samples from the children. The effectiveness of the lead abatement procedures was to be assessed based on the extent to which the blood levels of the children in the first three groups were contaminated with lead compared to those in the control groups.

Two of the children who participated in the KKI study, Ericka Grimes and Myron Higgins, later based a negligence claim against KKI on the assertion that the study was carried out in a manner that increased, rather than decreased, the children's exposure to lead, which caused lead-related health injuries. They further held that KKI did not adequately inform the parents of the risks associated with the study. The trial court issued a summary judgment in favour of the defendants on the basis that the researchers owed no legal duty of care to the research subjects, and so the plaintiffs' case could not proceed. The Maryland Court of Appeals overruled the trial court and maintained that a duty of care was owed to the subjects. The case was sent back to the lower court for trial. Most significantly, the appeals court ruled that parents cannot consent to their children's participation in research that does not offer them a prospect of direct therapeutic benefit. [100]

The Nonhuman Rights Project

On December 2, 2013, the Nonhuman Rights Project (NhRP), a group of animal rights lawyers, filed the first of three court cases in Fulton County, New York. They sought to free Tommy, a chimpanzee being held captive in a small cement cage with high temperatures, little room to move, and no social access to other chimpanzees. The current legal status of non-human animals holds them to be pieces of property that can be owned, imprisoned, and used for experiments. The NhRP petitioned the court for a writ of *habeas corpus*, which allows a "person" who has been forcefully detained to challenge their captors and to demand from them a justification for the prisoner's captivity.

Steven Wise, an attorney arguing for NhRP, made it clear that he does not wish to change the legal definition of a human being, but that the legal definition of personhood should be extended to certain non-human animals such that their interests and rights become recognized at law. Chimpanzees, he argued, are fully autonomous beings with complex cognitive capacities who have an awareness of the past and an ability to make choices, and who possess complex emotions such as empathy. Wise cited extensive scientific evidence and affidavits from the world's leading primatologists to make this point. And since chimpanzees should be considered legal persons, Wise argued, Tommy has a right to bodily liberty in the absence of a compelling reason to be detained. As Wise expected, the court denied the petition, but it admitted that Wise's argument was very impressive.

On December 9, 2013, the NhRP completed the first round of court hearings on behalf of the other chimps for which they petitioned the courts for a writ of *habeas corpus*. Kiko lives in a 30 by 30 foot chain link cage, with a tree and steel beam to climb in Niagara Falls, New York. Hercules and Leo are owned by a research centre and are being used in locomotion experiments at Stony Brook University on Long Island. Both petitions were denied. But the appeals are proceeding normally, and the higher courts, Wise maintains, is where new law gets made on contentious issues.[101]

CASE STUDIES

Scenario One

You are a clinician at a major Canadian university, working on research trials at a nearby hospital. The trials are intended to examine the safety and efficacy of a new drug to treat systemic lupus erythematosus (SLE). You are examining two immunosuppressant treatments, hoping to find a more efficacious and less toxic treatment than the current standard treatment, which is serving as the control treatment in your trial. Several weeks into the trial, it appears that the new treatment is both less toxic and more effective than the control. It appears to significantly reduce flare-ups of thrombophlebitis, the inflammation of veins associated with blood clots, which could travel to the lungs and prove fatal. It also seems to reduce the incidence of pleurisy, an inflammation of the pleura surrounding the lungs that makes breathing difficult and painful. Overall, your test group seems to be greatly benefiting from the new treatment, and the control group seems to be experiencing the adverse effects of the standard treatment.

(1) Do you stop the trial at this point and administer the less toxic treatment to the control group, or do you run the trial to its end? Has equipoise been disturbed in this trial? (2) Does the severity of the symptoms affect your decision? If so, how severe must the symptoms be to warrant stopping the trial? (3) Would looking at this from the point of view of the patients in the study change your decision? If so, what might this suggest about the methodology of clinical trials? (4) What would Hellman and Hellman say about your situation?

Scenario Two

You are a doctor working in a local hospital. You have recently received funding for a major research project that you have been pushing for, for nearly a year. You are about to begin clinical trials to examine the safety of a new drug for managing acute attacks of multiple sclerosis (MS). This is a Phase I trial, designed solely to test the toxicity of the drug, and for this you require healthy research subjects.

You have this project in mind when you enter into an examination room to see Mr. Linville, a patient in the early stages of multiple sclerosis, who tells you in the midst of the conversation that he just lost his job; he is in financial difficulty as he waits to find something else. You are planning to pay participants $100 per day for time and travel, and you quickly realize that Mr. Linville could use the money. Although he suffers from a relapsing form of MS, at the moment he is between attacks and has no symptoms. You have some concerns about the toxicity trial, and you know that Mr. Linville can expect no immediate medical benefit from it. However, if this treatment turns out to be effective, you believe that he might benefit in the future as his symptoms get worse. As a researcher, you believe that he is a perfect test subject. Because he is not currently suffering from any complications, you will be able to easily identify the effects of the drug. You are debating whether or not to recruit this patient into your study.

(1) Should you ask Mr. Linville to join your study? How would you reconcile your responsibility as a physician with your responsibility as a researcher in this situation? (2) Would your analysis of the situation be different if the participants were not paid? (3) How would you ensure that you obtained free and informed consent from the patient? (4) Would it make a difference if Mr. Linville were currently experiencing symptoms of his disease? (5) Do you see any similarities between this case and the Jesse Gelsinger case that opens this chapter?

Scenario Three

You are a researcher working on developing a new flu vaccine. At this stage in your research, you are testing the vaccine on beagles. This involves giving the animals the vaccine and then exposing them to the flu virus. You have already tested one round of the vaccine, and it has not proved very effective; since this particular flu virus is very virulent, most of the animals got very sick and a few died. You are currently running a second round of this vaccine, but you suspect it will need to be reformulated to increase its efficacy.

You have been having trouble coping emotionally with this stage of the project, as you have a pet beagle, Bubbles, at home. However, given the potential benefits that may be gained by this research, you have decided to put your personal feelings aside and proceed with the study. You have also been dealing with a local animal rights chapter, which objects to all experimentation on animals. There have been a number of break-ins at your lab, and animals have been let loose. Today, as you enter the lab, you realize that the animal rights group has taken a new tactic: Bubbles is in the cage with the other beagles. Beside the cage is a note: "If you are going to test your vaccine on animals, use *this* animal too!" Your emotional conflict has turned to rage.

(1) How would you explain your willingness to experiment on "stranger" beagles and your anger at the thought of including Bubbles? Is there a moral difference here? If so, why? (2) What message are the animal rights activists trying to get across? What would Singer say? (3) How would you weigh the need for a vaccine for the human population against the pain and suffering animals must endure for us to achieve that end?

Scenario Four

William Acker is a 20-year-old man suffering from phenylketonuria (PKU), an inherited enzyme deficiency that affects approximately 1 in 10,000 people and can result in brain damage if not treated early. The deficiency was detected in William early enough to put him on a low phenylalanine diet shortly after birth, preventing any major developmental damage. However, he still suffers from high levels of phenylalanine and must monitor what he eats. He has been able to keep his condition under control through diet alone.

William has recently learned of a study being done at a nearby hospital, testing a drug that is intended to lower phenylalanine levels in the blood of infants and young children. If he were to participate in this study, he would be exposing himself to the possibility of adverse side effects with no foreseeable benefit to himself. However, by participating he might help develop a treatment for those unable to keep phenylalanine levels under control with diet alone or with current treatments. He feels he has an obligation to participate and to perhaps improve the lives of future sufferers of this malady.

(1) Does William have an obligation to participate in this trial? What would Jonas say? What would Harris say? (2) Does it matter how severe the potential side effects are? (3) Is there a point at which the risks to William could outweigh the potential good he may do? (4) Would it make a difference if someone close to William might benefit from this trial—if, for instance, he had a young niece with the condition?

Scenario Five

You are a prison warden at a minimum-security prison. A medical team at a nearby hospital is conducting research on a new allergy medication, and they are looking for healthy volunteers to participate in a Phase I trial. A representative from the hospital has approached you and asked for your help in recruiting a number of inmates to participate in the study. The risks to the participants in the study are minimal.

You have encountered such requests before and have found that the prisoners are often quite eager to participate for various reasons, ranging from the desire to help others as a way of making up for their previous misdemeanours, to more personal motivations such as participating in research that might benefit a loved one. You know, for example, that one prisoner has a young daughter who has severe allergies, and you believe that he might want to participate in this trial in hopes of some benefit to her.

Typically, prisoners who have participated in clinical trials in the past have been rewarded for good behaviour. You are now debating whether or not to allow these men to be recruited for the study and whether they should be rewarded for doing so.

(1) Should you allow these prisoners to participate in the trial? Are they in a situation that allows them to make a fully autonomous choice about whether to participate not? (2) Would your answer change if this were a maximum-security prison? (3) Should participants be given any kind of reward? Does giving a reward change the ethics of the situation? (4) Are there any other factors that must be considered when looking at informed consent in this population?

Scenario Six

You are a physician working on a neuro-rehabilitation program that you hope will help children with developmental amnesia, a disorder that causes serious problems with remembering everyday events but leaves the ability to learn factual information intact. Developmental amnesia is linked to damage in the hippocampus resulting from loss of oxygen to the brain. This might be caused by extreme prematurity, difficult birth, long epileptic seizures, or temporary arrest of the heartbeat. This disease is progressive and becomes more noticeable as a child ages. You and your colleagues have designed a program that you believe will help these children regain some of their abilities to recall everyday events and may slow the progress of the disease. The risks of participation are minimal. You are now faced with the task of recruiting research subjects.

In your clinical practice, you deal with children on a daily basis. One of your current patients is Tanya, a 10-year-old child with developmental amnesia. She has been in to see you on a number of occasions for other medical concerns. Each time, you notice that she appears absent-minded, gets lost easily, and cannot tell you about her day. At the same time, she has a remarkable ability to retain factual information. During a recent visit, you mentioned to her that you are working on a program that should help children with developmental amnesia reacquire some everyday narrative recall. She spontaneously told you what developmental amnesia is, rattling off the information as in an encyclopaedic definition, and asked to participate in your study.

(1) Should you try to get permission to have Tanya participate in the study? How do you go about getting informed consent from her parents? (2) Should Tanya's enthusiasm and desire to participate influence the way you approach her parents? (3) Is the fact that she cannot remember what she's done on any given day relevant in obtaining consent? If she forgets that she volunteered for this study, is her desire to participate still valid? (4) Is it ethical to use children at all in this situation or are you morally restricted to using adults? Should you have even mentioned your study to the child?

GLOSSARY

Clinical equipoise: a term used in relation to clinical trials, referring to a situation of genuine uncertainty as to the efficacy and/or safety of one therapy (the new one being tested) over another therapy (the existing, or control, therapy). If a bias in favour of one therapy becomes apparent, equipoise is said to be disturbed. Equipoise is usually seen as applying to a community of physicians, rather than to any one individual physician who may actually have a bias in favour of one therapy or another.

Meliorism: a term (from the verb "ameliorate") referring to the belief that the world can be made better through human effort.

Placebo: an inactive substance (e.g., a sugar pill), which is given to the control group in a randomized clinical trial. A placebo might be designed to mimic the effects of the experimental drug or therapy to keep research subjects unaware of which group they are in.

Randomized clinical trial (RCT): the preferred model of experimentation, particularly in relation to drug therapies, whereby participants are randomly assigned to the experimental group (i.e., the group receiving the experimental therapy) or to a control group (i.e., the group receiving either an existing therapy, no therapy, or a placebo). The participant is unaware of which group he or she is in. In a double-blind RCT, neither the participants nor the researchers are aware of which participants are in which group.

Speciesism: a term coined by the Oxford psychologist Richard Ryder in 1970 to indicate the arbitrary discrimination against animals based solely on the fact that they are not human (thus solely on the basis of "species"). It is often used as a parallel to *racism* and *sexism*.

Vivisection: refers to the cutting open of live animals for the purposes of experimentation. It is based on the dubious premise that animals do not feel pain (see Box 4.6).

FOR FURTHER READING

Hellman, Samuel, and Deborah S. Hellman. "Of Mice but Not Men: Problems of the Randomized Clinical Trial." *New England Journal of Medicine*, 324, no. 22 (1991): 1585–1589.

This is a classic article found in many bioethics textbooks that questions the need for, and the ethical justification of, randomized clinical trials.

Lewis, Steven, et al. "Dancing with the Porcupine: Rules for Governing the University-Industry Relationship." In Baylis et al. (eds.), *Health Care Ethics in Canada*, 2nd ed. (pp. 340–343). Toronto: Thomson Nelson, 2004.

This very aptly titled article sets out the difficulties faced by university researchers who must seek funding from the pharmaceutical industry in order to further their research, difficulties that are inherent in the conflicting values of universities and businesses. The article also sets out proposed rules for governing university-industry relationships in Canada.

Passamani, Eugene. "Clinical Trials: Are They Ethical?" *New England Journal of Medicine*, 324, no. 22 (1991): 1589–1591.

Passamani takes an opposing view from the Hellmans, arguing that randomized clinical trials are both necessary and ethical. His article, published at the same time and in the same journal as theirs, is often paired with their article in bioethics texts.

Petryna, Adriana. *When Experiments Travel: Clinical Trials and the Global Search for Human Subjects.* Princeton and Oxford: Princeton University Press, 2009.

A very detailed and disturbing book about the privatization and globalization of clinical trials by the pharmaceutical industry, which shows that the arrangement and carrying out of clinical trials has itself become an industry that has gone offshore. It is based on international field research by the author, an anthropologist, in particular in the U.S., Brazil, and Poland.

Singer, Peter (ed.). *In Defense of Animals: The Second Wave. Malden*, MA: Blackwell Publishing, 2006.

This collection of readings on issues relating to the mistreatment of animals reflects the current state of the animal movement (Singer avoids the use of the term "rights" in relation to animals and thus does not call it the animal rights movement). It balances philosophical and psychological articles with articles by activists in the field, including their strategies.

RECOMMENDED WEBSITES

BBC website: "Animals Ethics"

www.bbc.co.uk/ethics/animals

A very complete website on the issue of the ethical treatment of animals, with pages relating to both sides of the debate and including historical information and religious perspectives. It also includes an audio section with selected discussions.

Canadian Institutes for Health Research

www.cihr.ca

> The CIHR is the Canadian government's funding agency for medical research in Canada, replacing what was formerly the Medical Research Council of Canada. It brings researchers together to work on particular health issues in an integrated fashion through 13 "virtual" institutes. The website outlines the structure, role, and mandate of the CIHR, along with funding criteria and research projects and results.

Panel on Research Ethics

www.pre-ethics.gc.ca

> A creation of Canada's three funding agencies (CIHR, NSERC, and SSHRC[102]), this agency's mandate is to promote ethical conduct in research involving human subjects. The Tri-council policy statement on ethical research involving human subjects (TCPS) can be found on its website.

People for the Ethical Treatment of Animals (PETA)

www.peta.org/

> With three million members worldwide, PETA (based in Norfolk, Virginia) is the largest animal rights organization in the world. Aside from animal experimentation, it focuses on other issues such as factory farming and fur farming, among others. It is an activist organization, claiming to have saved countless animals from their fate of being used and abused by humans, often using unconventional methods including undercover investigations. The website includes videos of animals in cruel experiments.

NOTES

1. Viral vectors are a tool used by molecular biologists to deliver genetic material into cells.
2. Paul Gelsinger, "Jesse's Intent: The Story of Jesse Gelsinger As Written by His Father, Paul," Part 1, found at www.jesse-gelsinger.com/jesses-intent.html (August 25, 2009). This summary of the case relies heavily on Paul Gelsinger's testimony.
3. "Jesse's Intent," Part 1.
4. "Jesse's Intent," Part 1.
5. "Jesse's Intent," Part 2, found at www.jesse-gelsinger.com/jesses-intent2.html (August 25, 2009).
6. Sheldon Krimsky, *Science in the Private Interest* (Lanham, MD: Rowman & Littlefield, 2003), 133.
7. Wanda Teays and Laura Purdy, *Bioethics, Justice & Health Care* (Belmont, CA: Wadsworth Publishing, 2001), 163.
8. David J. Rothman, "Research, Human: Historical Aspects," in Stephen G. Post (ed.), *Encyclopedia of Bioethics*, rev. ed. (New York: MacMillan Reference Books), 2248.
9. Rothman, 2249.
10. Rothman, 2249.
11. Rothman, 2249.
12. Rothman, 2252.
13. Gregory E. Pence, *Classic Cases in Medical Ethics*, 3rd. ed. (Boston and Toronto: McGraw-Hill, 2000), 248.
14. Pence, 248.
15. Pence, 251.
16. Arthur L. Caplan, "When Evil Intrudes," *Hastings Center Report*, 22, no. 6 (November-December 1992): 29.
17. Ronald Munson, *Intervention and Reflection*, 8th ed. (Belmont, CA: Wadsworth Publishing, 2007), 214.

18. MK-ULTRA is a CIA cryptonym, where MK stands for the agency's Technical Services Division and ULTRA was a classification taken from top secret Second World War operations.

19. The stories of nine Canadians who were treated by Dr. Cameron (and who eventually took the CIA to court) can be found in Anne Collins, *In the Sleep Room: The Story of the CIA Brainwashing Experiments in Canada* (Toronto: Lester & Orpen Dennys Limited, 1988).

20. Dr. Aubrey Blumsohn, "LSD and the corruption of medicine (Part III)," Scientific Misconduct Blog (May 2008), found at scientific-misconduct.blogspot.com/ (July 23, 2009).

21. Dr. Aubrey Blumsohn, "LSD and the corruption of medicine (Part I)," Scientific Misconduct Blog (May 2008), found at scientific-misconduct.blogspot.com/ (July 23, 2009).

22. Ian Mosby, "Administering Colonial Science: Nutrition Research and Human Biomedical Experimentation in Aboriginal Communities and Residential Schools, 1942–1952," *Histoire sociale/Social History*, 46, no. 91 (May 2013): 148.

23. Mosby, 149.

24. Mosby, 162.

25. Mosby, 147, 154.

26. Mosby, 165.

27. Hans Jonas, "Philosophical Reflections on Experimenting on Human Subjects," in *Philosophical Essays* (Englewood Cliffs, NJ: Prentice Hall, 1974), 239.

28. Jonas, 246.

29. Jonas, 238.

30. Jonas, 252.

31. John Harris, "Scientific Research Is a Moral Duty," *Journal of Medical Ethics*, 31, no. 4 (2005): 242.

32. Harris, 242.

33. Harris, 243.

34. David Orentlicher, "Making Research a Requirement of Treatment," *Hastings Center Report*, 35, no. 5 (September-October 2005): 21.

35. Paul S. Appelbaum, Loren H. Roth, and Charles Lidz, "The Therapeutic Misconception: Informed Consent in Psychiatric Research," *International Journal of Law and Psychiatry*, 5 (1982): 321.

36. Appelbaum et al., 324.

37. Appelbaum et al., 328.

38. Matthew Miller, "Phase I Cancer Trials: A Collusion of Misunderstanding," *Hastings Center Report*, 30, no. 4 (2000): 34, 36.

39. Miller, 37.

40. The ethical issues surrounding clinical trials are dealt with later in this chapter.

41. Miller, 35.

42. Miller, 37.

43. "The Nuremberg Code," reprinted in Teays and Purdy, 187. The Declaration of Helsinki on research involving human subjects was signed in 1964 and has been revised several times since.

44. The Canadian Medical Association's Code of Ethics states that before proceeding with clinical research, "the physician will obtain the consent of all involved persons or their agents, and proceed only after explaining the purpose of the clinical investigation and any possible health hazard that can be reasonably foreseen." *Canadian Medical Association Journal*, 155, no. 8 (1996): 1176.

45. Canadian Institutes for Health Research, *Tri-Council Policy Statement: Ethical Conduct for Research Involving Humans—TCPS* (Government of Canada, 2003), Article 2.1. This document is available online at Government of Canada, Panel on Research Ethics (July 2009) at www.pre.ethics.gc.ca (August 24, 2009).

46. Commenting on the clinical trial in which Jesse took part, the bioethicist Arthur Caplan is quoted as saying: "Not only is it sad that Jesse Gelsinger died, there was never a chance that anybody would benefit from these experiments. They are safety studies. They are not therapeutic in goal. If I gave it to you, we would try to see if you died, too, or if you did OK." Quoted in "Jesse's Intent," Part 2.

47. It is interesting to note that Paul Gelsinger, who later said he had been naive about the whole experiment, *did* ask Dr. James Wilson (after Jesse's death) about his financial interest in the project and received the answer that he was an "unpaid consultant" to the biotech company sponsoring the research. In fact, he had a 30 percent share in the company. "Jesse's Intent," Part 2.

48. *Tri-Council Policy Statement*, Article 2.2.

49. Munson, 12.

50. *Tri-Council Policy Statement*, Ch. 4: "Inclusion in Research" (modified February 4, 2009), found at www.pre-ethics.gc.ca (September 18, 2009), 1.

51. Munson, 16.

52. *Tri-Council Policy Statement*, Ch. 4, Article 4.4, p. 3.

53. Benjamin Freedman, Abraham Fuks, and Charles Weijer, "*In Loco Parentis*: Minimal Risk as an Ethical Threshold for Research upon Children," *Hastings Center Report*, 23, no. 2 (March-April 1993): 17.

54. *Equipoise* means that there is real uncertainty as to the therapeutic value of the treatments being tested. Once it is known that one treatment is better (or more harmful) than another, equipoise is said to have been disturbed.

55. Eugene Passamani, "Clinical Trials: Are They Ethical?" in Munson, 67.

56. Samuel Hellman and Deborah S. Hellman, "Of Mice but Not Men: Problems of the Randomized Clinical Trial," in Munson, 62.

57. Hellman and Hellman, 63.

58. Munson points out that placebos are not always just "sugar pills": "They often contain active ingredients that produce in patients effects that resemble those caused by the medication being tested—nervousness, vomiting, loss of appetite, and so on" (Munson, 14). So the patients receiving the placebo risk being doubly harmed—first, by not receiving the remedy that might help them, and second, by receiving a remedy that might harm them.

59. Hellman and Hellman, 65.

60. Robert M. Veatch, *Patient, Heal Thyself: How the New Medicine Puts the Patient in Charge* (Oxford and New York: Oxford University Press), 216.

61. *Tri-Council Policy Statement*, Ch. 11, "Clinical Trials," Article 11.10.

62. Charles Weijer, "Placebo Trials and Tribulations" in Eike-Henner W. Kluge (ed.), *Readings in Biomedical Ethics: A Canadian Focus* (Toronto: Pearson Education Canada, 2005), 254.

63. Passamani, 66.

64. Passamani, 67.

65. Hellman and Hellman, 65.

66. Canada's Research-Based Pharmaceutical Companies (Rx&D) Statement, 2013, found at www.canadapharma.org (December 9, 2014).

67. David Hailey, "Scientific Harassment by Pharmaceutical Companies: Time to Stop," *Canadian Medical Association Journal*, 162, no. 2 (January 25, 2000): 212.

68. Hailey, 212.

69. Adriana Petryna, *When Experiments Travel: Clinical Trials and the Global Search for Human Subjects* (Princeton and Oxford: Princeton University Press, 2009), 20.

70. See Leemon McHenry, "On the Origin of Great Ideas: Science in the Age of Big Pharma," *Hastings Center Report*, 35, no. 6 (November-December 2005), for a discussion of the marketing battle carried out by the manufacturer of Paxil (GlaxoSmithKline) and the manufacturer of Prozac (Eli Lilly) using articles in medical journals.

71. Carl Elliott, "Pharma Goes to the Laundry: Public Relations and the Business of Medical Education," *Hastings Center Report*, 34, no. 5 (September-October 2004): 19. (For information on the Ritalin case, see M. Petersen, "Madison Ave. Has Growing Role in the Business of Drug Research," *New York Times*, November 22, 2002.) An article by Stuart Laidlaw in the *Toronto Star*, dated June 22, 2009, reports a civil suit in Australia regarding the creation of fake academic journals, including the *Australasian Journal of Bone and Joint Medicine*, one of nine journals published by Elsevier and paid for by the pharmaceutical company Merck.

72. Petryna, 10.

73. Petryna, 11.

74. Petryna, 11.

75. George J. Annas and Michael A. Grodin, "Human Rights and Maternal-Fetal HIV Transmission Prevention Trials in Africa," in Michael C. Brannigan and Judith A. Boss, *Healthcare Ethics in a Diverse Society* (Mountain View, CA: Mayfield Publishing Company, 2001), 380.

76. Arthur L. Caplan, "When Evil Intrudes," *Hastings Center Report*, 22, no. 6 (November-December 1992): 30.

77. Caplan, 31.

78. The story of the Tuskegee study was made known to the general public through publication of the book by James H. Jones, *Bad Blood: The Tuskegee Syphilis Experiment* (New York: The Free Press, 1981), and by the movie *Miss Evers' Boys*, starring Lawrence Fishburne.

79. Arthur L. Caplan, "How Did Medicine Go So Wrong?" in Brannigan and Boss, 375.

80. Brannigan and Boss, 362.

81. Anne M. Fagot-Largeault, "Epistemological Presuppositions Involved in the Programs of Human Research," in Stuart F. Spicker et al. (eds.), *The Use of Human Beings in Research* (Dordrecht: Kluwer Academic Publishers, c.1988), 173.

82. *The Holy Bible, King James Version* (Toronto: The Canadian Bible Society, 1957), Genesis 9:1–5.

83. St. Thomas Aquinas, *Summa Contre Gentiles, Book Three*, Ch. 78, in Owen Goldin and Patricia Kilroe, *Human Life and the Natural World* (Peterborough, ON: Broadview Press, 1997), 92. It should be noted that not all religions share this view of the animal world (nor do all Christians share the same interpretation of Genesis). Muslims, too, believe that humans are superior to other animals, but they "also believe that other animals possess a psyche and are conscious. All species have moral standing and form one community. Animal experimentation, therefore, is strictly regulated in Islamic countries." See Brannigan and Boss, 357.

84. "Letter to Mersenne, 11 June 1640," in J. Cottingham, R. Stoothoff, D. Murdoch, and A. Kenny (trans. and eds.), *The Philosophical Writings of Descartes, Vol. III* (Cambridge: Cambridge University Press, 1991), 148. Many people deny that Descartes really thought that animals do not feel pain. We do know, however, that Descartes performed vivisection on at least one occasion when he opened a live hare to check the circulation of the heart, so either he truly believed that animals do not feel pain ("in the strict sense") or he was extremely cruel.

85. Gaverick Matheny, "Utilitarianism and Animals," in Peter Singer (ed.), *In Defense of Animals: The Second Wave* (Malden, MA: Blackwell Publishing, 2006), 17.

86. Richard D. Ryder, "Speciesism in the Laboratory," in Singer, 87.

87. Ryder, 88.

88. Matheny, 19. It can be argued, however, that animals used in experiments (or for food, for that matter) only exist because of the use to which they are put. Without medical research, the laboratory rat would have no life at all, raising the question of whether even a painful existence is better than no existence.

89. This term was coined by Ryder in 1970. It is often used as a parallel to *racism* and *sexism*.

90. Peter Singer, *Rethinking Life and Death* (New York: St. Martin's Griffin, 1994), 173.

91. Singer, "Animal Experimentation," in Munson, 85.

92. Carl Cohen, "The Case for the Use of Animals in Biomedical Research" in Munson, 89.

93. Cohen, 90.

94. This could be disputed by apparent moral agency or altruism in apes.

95. Cohen, 91.

96. Matheny, 22.

97. Singer, *In Defense of Animals*, 4.

98. Hans Jonas, "Technology and Responsibility: Reflections on the New Task of Ethics," in *Philosophical Essays*, 6

99. Peter Singer, "Animal Experimentation," in Munson, 85.

100. *Grimes v. Kennedy Krieger Institute, Inc.* [2001] 782A.2d 807.

101. Oral arguments in Kiko's case were made at a hearing on December 2, 2014, and a decision was handed down on January 2, 2015. The Court did not make a determination on the question of legal personhood, but asserted that "*habeas corpus* does not lie where the petitioner seeks only to change the conditions of confinement rather than the confinement itself. We therefore conclude that *habeas corpus* does not lie herein." Nonhuman Rights Project, found at www.nonhumanrightsproject.org/category/courtfilings/ (December 9, 2014).

102. These acronyms stand for: The Canadian Institutes for Health Research; the Natural Sciences and Engineering Research Council of Canada; and the Social Sciences and Humanities Research Council of Canada.

Chapter 5

REPRODUCTIVE TECHNOLOGIES

LANDMARK CASE: JAYCEE BUZZANCA

For a time, Jaycee Buzzanca had no legal parents, despite the fact that eight adults could claim to have had a part in her creation.[1] The embryo that was eventually to become Jaycee was obtained by John and Luanne Buzzanca, a couple who had spent over $200,000 on fertility treatments and surrogacy efforts over the course of six years. They obtained the embryo from the fertility clinic, a leftover from a successful in vitro fertilization (IVF) treatment undertaken by an infertile woman. She and her husband had obtained donor eggs and fertilized them with his sperm. After having twins as a result of the IVF procedure, they gave the fertility clinic permission to donate any remaining embryos to other couples. John and Luanne hired a gestational **surrogate**—a woman who was genetically unrelated to them and to the embryo—to carry the child to term for them.

A month before Jaycee was born, John filed for divorce. He argued that, because he was neither the biological father of Jaycee nor married to her biological or gestational mother, and since Luanne was neither her biological nor her gestational mother, he had no obligation to pay Luanne child support. A lower court agreed with him and, using the same logic, said that Luanne was not Jaycee's mother. Jaycee was rendered parentless, since the surrogate mother, who had signed a contract giving up all maternal rights, was not her mother nor was the surrogate's husband her father. Moreover, at this time, her **genetic parents** were anonymous and had no intention of becoming her social parents when they donated their genes.

Luanne appealed this decision to a higher court, and won; she and John were designated as Jaycee's parents on the basis of the fact that they had signed a legal contract to create her. John pays child support, but insists that Jaycee is not his child.[2]

INTRODUCTION

Historically, individuals have not had much control over whether or not to have children. The absence of effective techniques of birth control other than abstinence meant that most people had children whether or not they wished to, and the absence of medical treatments for infertility meant that little could be done to help those who were involuntarily childless. Moreover, the social context in most societies connected gender roles to reproduction, and the presumption was that marriage and parent-hood went together. Smith observes that a woman was traditionally expected "to get married and to provide reproductive services to her husband. Her pride and destiny consisted in producing and rearing children. That was her purpose in life, and it was a purpose predetermined for all women. It was not a matter of choice. It was not up to individuals."[3] While these social pressures are still present for many individuals in the developing world, for those in developed nations, decisions about whether and when to reproduce have largely moved from the realm of social and physical necessity to the realm of conscious personal choice. This choice is connected to an individual's conception of what is meaningful and valuable in life, rather than to social expectations of how adults should behave. Lauritzen captures this sense that having children (or not) is a matter of conscious choice:

Gustav *Klimt, Hope I*, 1903. For many people, reproduction is important. It is connected both to their self-image and to their life plans.

> Like many in our generation, we had postponed that decision for years as we each produced graduate degrees. But by that summer I had completed my doctoral work, and Lisa had completed her penultimate year of law school. It seemed like a good point to begin a family. If we conceived in July or August, Lisa would be able to complete her final year of law school before the child was born. She might have to delay final examinations and thus graduation, but we had known other women who had done so without difficulty. She would certainly be unable to take the bar examination the following July, but we were willing to make the "sacrifice."[4]

Most people assume that, when they do decide to have a child, they will be able to conceive without difficulty. However, the discovery that this is not always the case can come as a profound shock.

Orenstein describes her feelings after she made a careful, deliberate, and difficult decision to reproduce, and then experienced difficulty getting pregnant: "How could I have been so stupid? Why didn't I realize how much I wanted a baby until that possibility was threatened? Later I would remember that moment as the first time I was ready but my body said no. You can't believe it, not in this age when we control so much of our own destinies."[5] Lauritzen and his wife, who also had difficulty conceiving, look back on their earlier assumptions and now see them very differently: "In retrospect, the combination of naivete and romanticism with which we made our plans is embarrassing"[6] and painful.

When a couple has made the decision to reproduce, the discovery that they may not find this goal easy or even possible to achieve can be very painful. As Murray puts it, for those who want to have children and find it difficult, "*Hunger* is the right word, for it [the desire to have a child] can be felt as a need, a profound longing…. [W]hen we speak of the suffering of people who want to have children but cannot, suffering is neither metaphor nor hyperbole: people who crave children to raise and love but cannot have them suffer because, for many of us, our children are a vital part of our own flourishing."[7] The fact that infertility causes such great suffering provides what Murray calls the "chief moral impetus"[8] behind the development of reproductive technologies: their purpose, at least in part, is to help relieve this profound suffering. Moreover, the reproductive possibilities these technologies open up are often embraced by the infertile, because they appear to restore the very element of personal control over reproduction that was lost along with the diagnosis of infertility.

THE RISE OF REPRODUCTIVE TECHNOLOGIES

Modern reproductive technologies began with the development of in vitro fertilization (IVF), a procedure in which a woman is given a reproductive hormone that causes her ova to ripen. The ova are then extracted and fertilized outside the body. One or more of the resulting embryos are transferred back into the body. Since the birth of Louise Brown (the first so-called "test tube baby") in 1978, more than 3 million babies have been produced by this method or through related procedures. While artificial insemination was performed for a number of years prior to this date, it did not require the highly technological interventions required by IVF and its related technologies, which include: cytoplasmic donation (CD), a procedure that takes cytoplasm from a donor egg and injects it into the egg of an infertile woman to increase the chances of successful implantation and normal embryo development; intra-cytoplasmic sperm injection (ICSI), a technique that injects a single sperm into an egg, and, although it requires a woman to undergo IVF, is primarily a treatment for male infertility; partial zona dissection (PZD), which involves drilling holes in the membrane of an ovum so that sperm can penetrate it more easily; gamete intra-fallopian transfer (GIFT), a procedure that involves inserting ova and sperm into the fallopian tubes so that fertilization takes place inside the body; zygote intrafallopian transfer (ZIFT), a procedure in which zygotes (also sometimes called pre-embryos) are placed into the fallopian tubes; intravaginal culture (IVC), a procedure in which ova "are placed in a tube to which sperm cells are added, and the tube is then inserted into the vagina and kept next to the cervix by a diaphragm…. Two days later, the tube is removed, the contents decanted, and any fertilized ova are transferred into the uterus";[9] uterine lavage embryo retrieval (ULER), a process in which one woman is inseminated with donor sperm, and after about five days, the fertilized egg is washed out and transferred into another woman (the drawback of this particular reproductive technique is that the fertilized egg might implant before it is washed out, in which case the woman must consider an abortion); and DNA transfer, in which the nucleus is taken out of an older woman's egg and replaced with the nucleus taken from the egg of a younger woman.

In addition to the reproductive technologies that are direct offshoots of IVF, there are other methods of assisting reproduction that may or may not draw on these more technological approaches. One of these methods is artificial insemination (termed AID when performed using donor **gametes**, and AIH when the sperm used is from a woman's husband or partner). Another assisted reproductive practice involves surrogacy arrangements in which one woman is contracted to carry a child to term for someone else. The surrogate can be the genetic mother, as well as the gestational mother—the woman who goes through a pregnancy and carries the fetus to term—if the egg used is her own. Or she can be simply the gestational mother, if the egg or embryo used comes from the contracting woman, or from a woman unrelated either to the contracting mother or the surrogate, as in the Buzzanca case. Finally, a woman who can carry a child to term but who has difficulty conceiving might get either an egg or an embryo from a donor and give birth to a child that she intends to raise. In such a case, she would be both the gestational mother and the social mother—the woman who intends to raise the child—but not the genetic mother.

The breaking down of the process of reproduction and childrearing into discrete steps and stages—genetic conception, gestational development, and social rearing—generates most of the ethical concerns that these technologies and practices raise. For the first time in human history, women can give birth to babies who are genetically unrelated to them; as a result of the freezing of sperm and ova, men and women can, with assistance, conceive children after death; and children can have not just one mother, or even two, but three: a genetic mother, a gestational mother, and a social mother. Women can become biological mothers without ever engaging in sexual intercourse, and men can have children with multiple women whom they will never meet. Women and men can sell their reproductive materials in accordance with the demands of the marketplace and be told that they have performed an altruistic act to help an infertile couple. Women in their sixties have given birth with technological help, and multiple births are increasingly common as a result of fertility treatments. It has even been suggested that aborted female fetuses would provide a useful source of eggs; if this were ever to occur, a child could be born whose genetic mother never was. In short, even as these technologies and practices allow infertile people to have children, they sometimes do so in ways that challenge our normal conception of what it means to be a parent and what it means to be someone's child.

It is important to note that these technologies do not exist on a spectrum from least medically intrusive to most medically intrusive; rather, each raises distinct moral issues that are unrelated to their medical complexity. Some, such as IVF between husband and wife, while medically intrusive, generate few ethical questions. Others, particularly those that involve third parties, raise ethical concerns even when they are not—like artificial insemination using donor sperm—medically complicated. The ethical issues raised by at least some of the uses of these technologies are challenging for a number of reasons. First, particular individuals can have different reasons for choosing to have children. Some of these reasons can be ethically justified (such as a couple's desire to have a child together), while others may be morally problematic.

Second, the concept of infertility can be understood in a number of distinct ways. Unlike many other medical conditions, it is not always clear what constitutes a "cure" for the condition: is it to provide people with a child? To fix the physical problem that prevents conception, so that they can then conceive naturally? Or is it to provide a social context within which individuals are left as free as possible to pursue their own reproductive goals, regardless of age, marital status, or sexual orientation?

Finally, while reproductive decisions are decisions made by individuals, they necessarily take place within a social context that provides them with meaning. This means that technologies and practices that may be morally unproblematic in some societies will be considered morally troubling in others. For example, the Canadian Assisted Human Reproduction Act prohibits the purchase of gametes, embryos, and surrogacy services. The United States, though, has developed what Plotz calls a "consumer revolution"[10] in the marketing of gametes: sperm banks and egg donors compete with one another to meet the desires of demanding customers in order to attract the highest prices for their products. Our task will be to disentangle the various threads that constitute the ethical dimensions of assisted reproductive practices.

INFERTILITY AND THE DESIRE TO HAVE CHILDREN

The moral impetus for the development and use of assisted reproductive practices lies in the intention to reduce the genuine suffering experienced by the involuntarily infertile. There is, however, an ambiguity in the desire to have a child; namely, articulating what, precisely, is desired and what would constitute its achievement. Is it a desire to nurture a child? To gestate and give birth to a child? A desire to see one's genes carry on into the future? To have a child with a particular person? While most people will experience a mix of these motivations, it is clearly the case that, while some of the reproductive technologies—such as IVF between a husband and wife, using their own gametes, who intend to raise any resulting child together—can achieve all these goals, others can only meet some of them at the cost of others. Couples who utilize donor sperm or donor eggs to have a child sever the genetic connection between the resulting offspring and one member of the couple. Likewise, surrogacy arrangements, even when an embryo from the contracting couple is used, separate the activities of gestation and birth from the process of raising and nurturing the child. As the Buzzanca case demonstrates, separating the process of reproduction into discrete parts and dividing these parts up among different individuals can create serious difficulties for individuals and raise a number of ethical concerns.

If all the goals embedded in the desire to have children can most easily be met when couples conceive naturally, some commentators have asked why so much money has been spent, research efforts expended, and attention paid to reproductive technologies and so little to preventing infertility in the first place; they argue that we should not simply assume that those who have done the research to create the reproductive technologies are motivated by an altruistic desire to help the suffering infertile have children.

Infertility treatment has become what might be termed an industry. It generates large amounts of money (in the United States, it is estimated that it is worth about $3 billion a year[11]), and functions largely in accordance with the norms of the free market, in which vendors offer products or services to the highest bidder. Human eggs can range in price from $8000 to a reported $65,000, depending on the attributes of the seller.[12] Sperm banks, meanwhile, market sperm with tried-and-true marketing techniques, including glossy catalogues that list the physical attributes, accomplishments, ethnic backgrounds, and interests of their donors, and sometimes include the seller's baby photo.[13] Plotz reports that the average payment for a sperm donor at one sperm bank he investigated is $209 per sale. He observes that, in the United States at least, "sperm banking is a business with 'customers' instead of 'patients' [and] marketing plans instead of doctor's orders."[14]

While the Canadian Assisted Human Reproduction Act, which received Royal Assent in 2006, prohibits the purchase of gametes, embryos, and surrogacy services, most infertility treatments that go beyond testing and surgery are provided by private clinics. Most provinces do not cover the costs of IVF. This means that patients must pay for treatments themselves, including treatments using donor gametes. Although the fees paid are ostensibly for the treatment, not the gametes, it is not always clear how the two can be distinguished. A fertility clinic in Vancouver, for example, currently offers IVF treatment with a donor egg for $5000 a cycle for medication, plus $5800 for each IVF treatment, and donor sperm samples for $250 a shipment.[15] In addition, Canadians can easily access American services. As Haase observes, "[T]he role played by internet communication in the marketing of private [U.S.] fertility clinics and gamete donation banks is … highly relevant for Canadians."[16] She also notes that many Canadian fertility clinics rely on commercial sperm banks in the U.S. for the sperm they provide to their clients.[17] In short, a case can be made that approaches to infertility in Canada, and the responses to this condition, are shaped either directly by the free market in reproductive products and services in the United States (as in the case in which Canadians travel to U.S. clinics) or indirectly (when Canadian clinics use gametes that are imported from the U.S.). Moreover, most fertility clinics in Canada are private, profit-making entities. The fact that the market plays such an important role in infertility treatment means that there is less incentive to prevent infertility than there is to devise methods of profiting from it.

CAUSES AND CONCEPTIONS OF INFERTILITY

The risk factors for infertility are both well known and largely preventable. The Royal Commission on Reproductive Technologies identified the most common risk factors as being smoking, delayed child-bearing, sexually transmitted diseases, alcohol use, eating disorders, toxic agents in the environment and in the workplace, medical interventions, stress, and excessive exercise.[18]

Infertility as a Medical Condition

Infertility can be understood as a medical condition that results from factors such as a low sperm count, blocked fallopian tubes, or a damaged uterus that prevents individuals from conceiving naturally. It follows from this conception of infertility that the solution is to fix the physical problem: raise the sperm count, unblock the fallopian tubes, or repair the uterus. However, an ambiguity immediately reveals itself: is the solution to infertility to resolve the medical problems that make conception and gestation difficult, or is it to ensure that infertile people end up with a child?

One result of this vagueness, as Callahan observes, is that many infertility procedures do not address the medical issues at all: "The concentration of research efforts on spectacular interventive technologies detracts from research on the causes and possible treatments of infertility, an omission which, by implication, leaves the infertile as they were—and directly dependent on the medical community each time a pregnancy is desired."[19] Another is that those undergoing treatment can find it difficult to refuse any of the options that are presented to them, even if they are not entirely comfortable with them. For example, Lauritzen describes his own experience of infertility and his consequent immersion in the world of the infertility industry as an almost inexorable process. He and his wife found themselves pushed to a point at which the only thing that mattered was having a child. He notes: "[O]nce one has become goal oriented in the process of reproduction, choices about interventions tend to get framed exclusively in terms of the likelihood of successfully realizing the goal of producing a healthy child."[20] Consequently, once couples place themselves in the hands of infertility specialists, they may find themselves moved almost imperceptibly toward the belief that the only thing that matters is having a child. They may seriously consider procedures that they would not initially even have contemplated in order to achieve that goal.

The Social Dimension of Infertility

The notion that infertility has been successfully treated once a child has been born suggests that infertility can also be understood as a social condition, one that can sometimes be alleviated through medical interventions and sometimes through social practices. The desire to have children and the means by which that desire can be fulfilled take place within particular contexts that give meaning to the desire itself and legitimize particular ways of fulfilling it. In support of this conception of infertility, we can note that different cultures approach reproduction and assisted reproductive practices very differently. For example, in her examination of third-party assisted reproduction in Israel,

Landau notes that Jewish attitudes toward infertility are shaped by the biblical commandment to "be fruitful and multiply." As a consequence, Israel has the highest per capita rate of IVF clinics of any nation.[21] Jewish citizens of Israel have accepted most assisted reproductive practices, including surrogacy, egg and sperm donation, and even posthumous conception. In contrast, Landau notes, IVF is permissible for Muslims if it involves a husband and wife, but a "third party donor is unacceptable under any circumstances."[22]

Likewise, because Chinese culture emphasizes the importance of blood ties, couples feel that they have an obligation to extend the family tree into the next generation. This obligation can only be met by having children who are their own genetic offspring. Consequently, third-party assisted reproduction, using donor sperm, egg, or embryos, is not widely accepted.[23] We can contrast this perspective with those held by the adults who contributed to the creation of Jaycee Buzzanca. Jaycee could not have come into existence without the technology that allowed for her conception. Equally, she would never have been born if commercial surrogacy arrangements were illegal in the United States; if her genetic parents had felt (as they might have in other social contexts) that genetic ties required them to take responsibility for the care of their biological offspring; and if embryos were not viewed as objects or possessions that could be bought, sold, or given away.

Further evidence that infertility is unavoidably freighted with social meaning is provided by the fact that medically fertile individuals are increasingly accessing reproductive technologies. Their reasons for doing so are connected to larger social issues, such as the fact that many women now feel compelled to postpone child-bearing until they have finished their education and established themselves in a career. This means that, by the time these women are ready to reproduce, they may have passed the age where conception is easy or even possible. Consequently, some women are now freezing their eggs while they are young so that they will be available at some point in the future. As Ms. Hanck, executive director of the Infertility Awareness Association of Canada, puts it, "[W]hat if you couldn't have children? What if you didn't meet Mr. Right and you were 33 years of age? Is there any reason why we shouldn't freeze the eggs?"[24] Hanck argues that there is nothing wrong with such procedures because, while women's fertility peaks in their early twenties, modern societies have made it unrealistic for women to give birth at that age.

Finally, while these procedures and practices are ostensibly designed to allow people to have their own (genetic) offspring, they are often used in ways that separate genetic and social ties. As Mead notes, the discussion surrounding assisted reproductive practices is confused and confusing. In reference to the Buzzanca case, she observes that the reasoning used by the superior court that concluded that John and Luanne were Jaycee's parents because they had intentionally signed a contract to become her parents

> makes for some remarkably slippery values. A woman who bears an egg-donor child is encouraged to believe that carrying the fetus is the crucial component of motherhood. But a woman who hires a surrogate to carry her fertilized egg to term for her is encouraged to think the opposite: that the important thing is the genetic link to the baby, and not the womb out of which the baby came. Biologically, an egg donor's situation is identical to that of a woman who uses a surrogate. But egg donors are encouraged to believe that what makes a woman a mother is the wish to be a mother—to be what is known in the infertility business as the "social parent."[25]

Further, because reproductive choices occur within particular social and political contexts, we must also consider the extent to which reproductive practices should be regulated and what form that regulation should take. Consider, for example, the fact that when third party gametes such as donor sperm are used to produce a child, a question can be asked about who the legal father of the child is; normally, we consider a genetic father to have a moral and even legal responsibility for his offspring. The activity of donor insemination, however, as currently practised in North America, depends on the donor not being held legally or morally responsible for any children conceived with his sperm, even though, genetically speaking, they are as much his children as any children he might have with a wife or partner. Likewise, whether or not a market exists for reproductive materials is something that each society needs to determine.

BOX 5.1 JOHN A. ROBERTSON, "THE PRESUMPTIVE PRIMACY OF PROCREATIVE LIBERTY"

At the most general level, procreative liberty is the freedom either to have children or to avoid having them. Although often expressed or realized in the context of a couple, it is first and foremost an individual interest....

Procreative liberty should enjoy presumptive primacy when conflicts about its exercise arise because control over whether one reproduces or not is central to personal identity, to dignity, and to the meaning of one's life. For example, deprivation of the ability to avoid reproduction determines one's self-definition in the most basic sense. It affects women's bodies in a direct and substantial way. It also centrally affects one's psychological and social identity and one's social and moral responsibilities. The resulting burdens are especially onerous for women, but they affect men as well.

On the other hand, being deprived of the ability to reproduce prevents one from an experience that is central to individual identity and meaning in life. Although the desire to reproduce is in part socially constructed, at the most basic level transmission of one's genes through reproduction is an animal or species urge closely linked to the sex drive. In connecting us with nature and future generations, reproduction gives solace in the face of death. As Shakespeare noted, "nothing 'gainst Time's scythe can make defense / save breed." For many people "breed"—reproduction and the parenting that usually accompanies it—is a central part of their life plan, and the most satisfying and meaningful experience they have. It also has primary importance as an expression of a couple's love or unity. For many persons, reproduction also has religious significance and is experienced as a "gift from God." Its denial—through infertility or governmental restriction—is experienced as a great loss, even if one has already had children or will have little or no rearing role with them.

Decisions to have or to avoid having children are thus personal decisions of great import that determine the shape and meaning of one's life. The person directly involved is best situated to determine whether that meaning should or should not occur. An ethic of personal autonomy as well as an ethics of community or family should then recognize a presumption in favor of most personal reproductive choices. Such a presumption does not mean that reproductive choices are without consequence to others, nor that they should never be limited. Rather, it means that those who would limit procreative choice have the burden of showing that the reproductive actions at issue would create such substantial harm that they could justifiably be limited. Of course, what counts as the "substantial harm" that justifies interference with procreative choices may often be contested....

A closely related reason for protecting reproductive choice is to avoid the highly intrusive measures that governmental control of reproduction usually entails. State interference with reproductive choice may extend beyond exhortation and penalties to gestapo and police state tactics....

If procreative liberty is taken seriously, a strong presumption in favor of using technologies that centrally implicate reproductive interests should be recognized. Although procreative rights are not absolute, those who would limit procreative choice should have the burden of establishing substantial harm.... If an important reproductive interest exists, then use of the technology should be presumptively permitted. Only substantial harm to tangible interests of others should then justify restriction.

In determining whether such harm exists, it will be necessary to distinguish between harms to individuals and harms to personal conceptions of morality, right order, or offense, discounted by their probability of occurrence.... Many objections to reproductive technology rest on differing views of what "proper" or "right" reproduction is aside from tangible effects on others. For example, concerns about the decomposition of parenthood through the use of donors and surrogates, about the temporal alteration of conception, gestation and birth, about the alienation or commercialization of gestational capacity, and about selection and control of offspring characteristics do not directly affect persons so much as they affect notions of right behavior....

To take procreative liberty seriously, then, is to allow it to have presumptive priority in an individual's life. This will give persons directly involved the final say about use of a particular technology, unless tangible harm to the interests of others can be shown.

Source: John A. Robertson, *Children of Choice: Freedom and the New Reproductive Technologies* (Princeton, NJ: Princeton University Press, 1994), 22–42.

THE PROCREATIVE LIBERTY ARGUMENT AND THE HARM PRINCIPLE

A common response to the moral issues presented by assisted reproductive practices is to argue that reproductive decisions are an expression of personal autonomy. Proponents of the **procreative** liberty argument deem it inappropriate for others to make moral judgments about the reproductive choices made by others or for the state to interfere with those choices; they argue that any moral concerns raised must be justified on the basis of the Harm Principle, which holds that we should only interfere with the choices of persons when those choices are clearly harmful to others. If they are harmful only to the individual who freely chooses to engage in them, we have no right to interfere. In addition, any ethical concerns that might be raised about possible harms resulting from assisted reproductive practices pale in comparison to the value we place on autonomy and to the harm we do when we limit the autonomous choices of individuals. Because autonomy is so important, what matters most is that individuals be left free to make their own reproductive decisions on the basis of their understanding of how reproduction fits into the plan of life that they have devised for themselves. As Robertson puts it, what is at issue is **negative liberty**: the right to make choices free from the interference of others in matters that concern only themselves.

> Decisions to have or to avoid having children are ... personal decisions of great import that determine the shape and meaning of one's life. The person directly involved is best situated to determine whether that meaning should or should not occur. An ethic of personal autonomy as well as an ethics of community or family should then recognize a presumption in favor of most personal reproductive choices.... [T]hose who would limit procreative choice have the burden of showing that the reproductive actions at issue would create such substantial harm that they could justifiably be limited.[26]

It is important to note that the procreative liberty argument (sometimes called the reproductive autonomy argument) is drawn from political philosophy. Consequently, it melds moral concerns into a political framework. Most fundamentally, it draws on the concept of negative liberty, which is primarily concerned with the degree to which the institutions of the state can legitimately interfere with the choices made by citizens. As Berlin famously states, "I am normally said to be free to the degree to which no man or body of men interferes with my activity. Political liberty in this sense is simply the area within which a man can act unobstructed by others.... [In order to preserve a sphere for negative liberty] a frontier must be drawn between the area of private life and public authority."[27] Where the line should be drawn between these two spheres remains a contentious issue.

Given that the only legitimate limit on autonomous choice is the Harm Principle, any proponent of this position must determine what role this principle plays in reproductive matters. Robertson asserts that what the Harm Principle requires when it comes to reproductive decisions is "that those who would limit procreative choice have the burden of showing that the reproductive actions at issue would have created such substantial harm that they could conceivably be limited."[28]

Most proponents of the procreative liberty argument believe that such harms cannot be proven, for two reasons. First, any ascriptions of harm rely on what have been termed "perfectionist" accounts of the good—accounts that claim that there is a proper way for people to live, and that any deviations from this way of living are morally problematic—that not everyone can agree on. It follows from this that the state, too, should not interfere with the reproductive choices made by citizens, but should instead leave individuals free to do what they wish. Second, they hold that ascriptions of harm in cases of reproduction rely on a conceptual mistake.

Pence articulates the first position when he states that any attempts to regulate reproductive choice depend on accounts of the good that are contentious and, therefore, involve an unwarranted interference in purely private matters: "I do not tell you how many children to have or whether you should have children at all. Neither does the government. If the ... government attempted to do so—if it attempted to say you should get pregnant, or should have at least five children ... —you would rightly object to this as an offensive, grave violation of your personal liberty."[29] Moreover, most justifications for this sort of interference rely on conceptions of the good that are "essentially religious."[30] Even if they happen to be held by a majority of citizens, they should not be imposed on the minority who disagree with them. Consequently, judgments about reproduction are best left in the hands of individuals.

Just as procreative liberty requires non-interference with reproductive choice, Pence believes, it also requires non-interference with the methods an individual uses to reproduce. If you think that hiring a gestational surrogate to give birth to an embryo that you purchased, as Luanne Buzzanca did, is wrong, then don't follow in her footsteps—but don't think that you have the right to tell her that her choices were wrong or that the state ought to have prevented them.

The second prong in the defence of the procreative liberty argument is the claim that any harms that might be generated by particular reproductive choices, if experienced by the adults involved, are covered by their right to make autonomous decisions in matters that concern only themselves. If, however, the concern is that children produced by the assisted reproductive practices might be harmed by the methods that brought them into existence, the response is that this concern rests on a conceptual mistake. That is to say, if Luanne or John regret the choices they made, that's unfortunate, but that is their responsibility. However, it would be conceptually incoherent to argue that Jaycee was harmed by the manner by which she was created, as, before she existed, there was no one there to be harmed; further, it is always better to exist than not to exist. As Pence puts it, "In a perfectly understandable sense, a person cannot be harmed in being created by IVF because otherwise he would not have existed."[31] Robertson takes the argument a step further by asserting that it is worse not to exist than to exist with defects, even serious ones. He believes that someone can be said to have suffered "substantial harm"—harm serious enough to justify interference with the activities that created her—only when she would be better off not existing. Thus, even if it were the case that children produced with the help of reproductive technologies have a higher incidence of birth defects, this "would not justify banning the technique in order to protect the offspring, because without these techniques these children would not have been born at all. Unless their lives are so full of suffering as to be worse than no life at all, a very unlikely supposition, the defective children … have been born healthy."[32] In other words, to show that a child would be (or had been) substantially harmed by being created through the use of reproductive technology, one would have to show that his existence is worse than non-existence. Robertson continues: "Preventing harm would mean preventing the birth of the child whose interests one is trying to protect. Yet a child's interests are hardly protected by preventing the child's existence. If the child has no way to be born or raised free of harm, a person is not injuring the child by enabling her to be born in the circumstances of concern."[33]

BOX 5.2

THOMAS H. MURRAY, "FAMILIES, THE MARKETPLACE AND VALUES: NEW WAYS OF MAKING BABIES"

There are times when adults hunger for children. *Hunger* is the right word, for it can be felt as a need, a profound longing, not a mere appetite for something pleasant. When we speak of the suffering of people who want to have children but cannot, "suffering" is neither metaphor nor hyperbole: people who crave children to raise and love but cannot have them suffer because, for many of us, our children are a vital part of our own flourishing. The chief moral impetus behind alternative reproductive practices—from medical interventions to surrogacy contracts—is the desire to ease the suffering of infertility.

Despite this worthy purpose, these new arrangements inspire wariness. They are accused of intensifying medical, especially male, control over reproduction; of treating women as nothing more than vehicles for reproduction; of treating children as **commodities** or products; and of threatening the intimacy of natural reproduction. The uneasiness lingers despite responses that can be given to each of the particular complaints.

Rather than rehearsing these arguments, I want to see if it is possible to uncover the root of our discomfort. Could our uneasiness with certain alternative reproductive practices stem from a sense that they threaten to undermine the very values that prompted us to create these alternatives in the first place? In particular, do the values of the marketplace, with their exaltation of individual liberty, control, and choice, endanger what we value in family life?

Suppose the answer to this question is yes. How could such self-defeating practices have emerged? In brief, the story is this: Proponents of alternative reproductive practices defend them as expressions of procreative liberty. This is not surprising. Liberty is a powerful principle with great resonance in our political and moral traditions. We rely heavily on liberty to defend the option *not* to reproduce by using contraception or abortion. If we are free to avoid having children, shouldn't we have equal freedom to pursue parenthood? The fallacy here is a presumption that the choice *to have* a child is morally parallel to the choice *not to have* a child. The former is a choice to initiate a very special relationship; the latter is a choice to decline such a relationship. The values at the core of the parent-child relationship constrain the former in ways they do not affect the latter.

The story also concerns the tapestry in which negative liberty is such a prominent strand. Negative liberty is freedom *from*, the liberty to do as one wishes without the interference of others. Great principles like liberty do not stand in isolation. They draw their strength from a culture's traditions; those same traditions link liberty so closely with other values that they become a kind of web, each strand supporting and supported by the other strands. In the web of values supporting alternative reproductive practices, liberty is interwoven with an emphasis on the individual who bears rights in sometimes isolated splendor. The web also contains strong threads representing the value we place on choice and control. The model of human relationships favored in this web is the contract, the free agreement of independent, autonomous actors. The social institution that best fits with these strands—liberty, individualism, choice, control, contract—is the market. If you frame your response to the needs of the infertile and childless in terms of procreative liberty, you will find yourself in the web that includes these other values. Buying and selling reproductive products and services—sperm, ova, embryos, and gestation—will appear as straightforward expressions of that liberty....

In the realm of commerce, moral relationships are relatively simple. There are owners and property and prospective buyers. The property has no independent moral significance. Its "worth" is measured fully by the price agreed on by buyer and seller.... In the realm of parents and children, of family, the new additions—that is, children—have a more complex moral status than mere property.... And the relationships among the various parties who may be involved in providing babies—suppliers of gametes, gestational services, and those who wish to rear the children—are more complex as well, to say nothing of the relationships between each of those parties and the children they create. Indeed, it could be said that the main point in having a child is to initiate the relationships that will develop between that child, its siblings, and the adults in its life.

Source: Thomas H. Murray, *The Worth of a Child* (Berkeley, CA: University of California Press, 1996), 14–18.

WEAKNESSES OF THE PROCREATIVE LIBERTY ARGUMENT

The procreative liberty argument is very powerful and, initially at least, enormously appealing: it resonates with the values of freedom and choice that underpin democratic societies; it supports modern Western self-understandings and conceptions of human flourishing; and it places responsibility for the choices made in the hands of those who made them—those who are arguably best placed to make informed judgments about them. Despite its appeal, however, some critics argue that it is not entirely convincing.

First, Cohen argues that it utilizes a problematic understanding of harm. The claim that reproductive practices cannot be harmful to children, since no one can be harmed by the way in which he was brought into existence, and that existence, even with defects, is preferable to non-existence, rests on a conceptual mistake. While we might argue that existence is preferable to death for already existing persons, it does not follow that for those not yet conceived existence is preferable to non-existence. Cohen notes that this argument "assumes that children with an interest in existing are waiting in a spectral world of non-existence where their situation is less desirable than it would be if they were released into this world.... Before a person exists, however, he or she does not reside in some other domain. Prior to conception, there is *no one who waits to be brought into this world*."[34] Consequently, Cohen argues, the question of whether assisted reproductive technologies might be harmful to the children that are produced through them is fundamental to any moral evaluation of them.

Second, Murray argues that the procreative liberty argument frames the moral issues around reproductive decisions primarily in terms that fit well with the marketplace but fit badly with the values that, at their best, animate family life. The model of human relationships envisaged in this model "is the contract, the free agreement of independent, autonomous actors…. If you frame your response to the needs of the infertile in terms of procreative liberty…. buying and selling reproductive products and services—sperm, ova, embryos, and gestation—will appear as straightforward expressions of that liberty."[35] However, Murray believes that introducing the values of the market into the sphere of the family will actually undermine the ability of parents to achieve the goals they hoped to achieve by having children in the first place: "the values of the marketplace are ill suited for nurturing the values, institutions, and practices that support the flourishing of children and adults within families."[36]

Third, the procreative liberty argument elevates autonomy to such an extent that it becomes not merely an important moral principle, but essentially the only one; consequently, it can be argued that it does not adequately acknowledge that autonomy needs to be balanced with other principles, such as beneficence and non-malfeasance, the principle that we ought to avoid causing harm. We need, then, to take seriously the possibility that at least some assisted reproductive practices raise moral concerns that cannot be resolved by a simple defence of the right of people to make their own procreative choices. In saying this, however, we need to be clear that the issue is not one of making moral judgments about the motivations of those who use assisted methods of reproduction. As Berg reminds us, infertile individuals are

> held to an idealistic standard which is not required of the fertile. Society questions their reasons for having children, their willingness to pursue reproductive technologies, their reluctance to adopt, and their discomfort with adopting "special needs" children. There is a bias against the infertile that is revealed when we picture ourselves questioning the fertile in the same manner … the fertile are not questioned about why they want to have children, or why they don't adopt a child.[37]

A more productive approach is suggested by Lauritzen, who argues that individuals considering using assisted reproductive practices should consider whether some of the possibilities available to them might be incompatible with what he calls "responsible parenthood"—the ability to properly care for and nurture any resulting child. Just as we might ask all couples who are considering whether to become parents to "consider whether they can properly care for a child at that particular point in time and under some particular set of circumstances, so we should expect a couple considering donor insemination [or any other assisted reproductive practice] to consider whether they can properly care for a child conceived in this way."[38] He suggests that we must take seriously the possibility that at least some of these practices might be a threat to the well-being of future children and thus violations of the principles of beneficence and non-malfeasance. We will next consider some of the moral questions raised by particular reproductive practices.

ETHICAL THEORY AND ASSISTED REPRODUCTION

Assisted reproductive practices raise a number of ethical concerns, including the risk of physical harms, the severing of genetic and social connections, commodification, objectification, secrecy, anonymity, and the potential harms caused by post-menopausal and multiple pregnancies. Some of these concerns fall into what can be termed utilitarian categories; in particular, a utilitarian would ask how particular assisted reproductive practices appear when we apply the principles of beneficence and non-malfeasance to them on either an individual level or a societal level. Some of these practices raise particular concerns for Kantians, as they may appear to involve treating other people as a means rather than as an end in themselves, or may disregard the duties individuals have to themselves. Some of these practices may trouble virtue ethicists, who will consider the place of reproduction within the context of a whole life and the ongoing relationship between a parent and child that begins, not ends, with birth. Moreover, virtue ethicists, with their focus on teleology, will ask what it might mean to separate the genetic, gestational, and social aspects of parenting. They will raise concerns about things such as post-menopausal reproduction and posthumous conception, which abstract assisted human reproduction from anything that would naturally occur. Finally, feminist theorists have asked a number of questions about the implications of assisted reproduction for the women who place their bodies in the hands of the medical profession and for the children who result from these interventions.

Physical Harms

The most straightforward ethical concern raised by reproductive technologies and practices is the possibility that they may be physically harmful to the adults who engage in them and to the children produced by them. Since these technologies disproportionately affect women, the possibility of physical harm is more relevant to women than to men. Women who undergo IVF treatments or serve as egg donors must take drugs that are associated with an increased cancer risk;[39] IVF is physically invasive, and so carries with it all the risks that all such physically invasive treatment does; and some of these procedures are both highly technological and experimental, so we still cannot be certain of all their long-term effects. Gosden, a doctor specializing in the field of reproductive technologies and an unabashed supporter of the reproductive choices these technologies make possible, nonetheless observes that "infertility patients are willing to accept considerable discomfort as they undergo a roller coaster of emotions and medical procedures that would be considered humiliating or even dangerous in other circumstances.... Some patients are all too willing to subject themselves to experimental treatments that stand only a tiny chance of success"[40] and that have known and unknown risks.

It is significant that the question of whether these technologies pose long-term risks to women and children remains difficult to answer with any certainty. Only Australia has kept systematic records at birth on the health of children conceived through IVF and also kept track of their subsequent progress. However, the Australian data do raise some cause for concern: they "indicate that these children are two to three times more likely to suffer such serious defects as spina bifida and transposition of the great vessels (a heart abnormality)."[41] Moreover, the Australian data suggest that the drugs used to stimulate a woman's ovaries as a part of IVF treatment not only carry an increased cancer risk for her, but may also increase the risk of birth defects in children conceived from them.[42] An Australian epidemiologist, Dr. Carol Bower, has analyzed the data and reports that 1 in 10 children produced through IVF had a birth defect, twice the rate of children produced naturally.[43] In addition, many of these defects are serious and include not only heart defects and spina bifida, but also chromosomal abnormalities such as Down's syndrome, gastrointestinal problems, and musculoskeletal defects. Likewise, a shorter-term French study indicated that death rates were higher for infants created through IVF when compared to those conceived naturally.[44] Finally, some studies have shown that children conceived through ICSI may suffer from developmental delays and, if male, might themselves suffer from infertility.

A further source of potential harm arises from IVF and its associated practices, such as egg donation, as these practices have made it possible for post-menopausal women to give birth and have increased the frequency of multiple births. In 2009, two cases that received much attention graphically illustrated these possibilities and their attendant risks. In Canada, a 62-year-old woman, Ranjit Hayer, gave birth to twin boys in Alberta after undergoing IVF treatment using donor eggs in India. She suffered serious health problems during her pregnancy, and her sons spent a number of weeks in the ICU after their birth. In the United States, Nadya Suleman, who was quickly dubbed the Octomom, gave birth to eight infants, all of whom had low birth weights (a condition associated with long-term health problems) and needed treatment in intensive care. As Picard notes, even in Canada, many of the provisions of the Assisted Human Reproduction Act have not been enforced. As a result, he argues, we are seeing the "rapid, uncontrolled proliferation of reproductive technologies.... [T]he lack of monitoring means there is no consistency in the quality of care, and the result is far too many multiple pregnancies and health problems in the children born of those pregnancies."[45]

These facts raise concerns for utilitarians, Kantians, and virtue ethicists, albeit for different reasons. From a utilitarian perspective, these harms violate the principle of non-malfeasance on both an individual and a societal level. If women and children suffer health problems as a result of these technologies, this is clearly harmful to them. And if society then has to cover their health care costs, this means that resources that could be used elsewhere—such as, perhaps, resources dedicated to the prevention of infertility—are unavailable. For Kantians, the fact that few records are being systematically kept about the health of those using these technologies and those conceived through them means that the question of the harms versus the benefits of assisted reproductive practices will remain somewhat speculative at best. This situation impedes the ability of those who might need help in reproducing from making informed and fully autonomous choices about whether or not to employ them. (It should also be noted that this lack of information weakens the procreative liberty argument: one cannot make a fully autonomous choice if one is lacking crucial information relevant to that choice.) Finally, as the examples of Ranjit Hayer and Nadya Suleman demonstrate, these technologies make possible forms of reproduction that are highly unlikely, if not impossible, to occur naturally (in nature, for example, a 62-year-old woman is unlikely to give birth and never to children who are the genetic offspring of another woman). Examples such as these raise questions about teleological norms built in to reproduction.

BOX 5.3 NATURAL LAW THEORY AND ASSISTED REPRODUCTION

The Roman Catholic Church has been one of the fiercest and most public critics of reproductive technologies. The church rejects IVF treatments for married couples and artificial insemination using a husband's sperm, as well as all forms of third-party assisted reproduction. Even though these views are primarily relevant to members of the Roman Catholic Church, they are worth examining because the reasoning used to reach these conclusions draws on a once powerful and widely accepted branch of moral philosophy called natural law theory.

Natural law theory combines aspects of Aristotelianism with Stoic thought, and then gives the result a Christian gloss. The Stoics, who flourished in the 1st century B.C.E., introduced the idea of natural law. They believed that the universe is governed by rational laws, that human beings have the capacity to discover. The closer we come to living in accordance with these laws, as individuals and as creators of human communities, the happier we will be and the more harmonious our societies. The natural law is eternal and unchanging, and its shape can be discerned through the exercise of reason; this eternal law provides a standard against which actual laws can be measured.

St. Thomas Aquinas (1225–1274) combined the natural law account provided by the Stoics with the teleology of Aristotle. Aristotle believed that everything has a function or purpose, and that excellence lies in performing that function well. The purpose of an acorn is to become an oak tree, of a knife is to cut well, of an eye is to see, and of a human is to live in accordance with reason. Aquinas accepts Aristotle's claim that this is the function of human beings, and argues that it is through the exercise of reason that we can discover the natural laws that govern the universe and learn how humans should live. What reason tells us, Aquinas believes, is that humans should seek good and avoid evil: "this is the first precept of law, *that good is to be done or promoted, and evil is to be avoided*."[1] Like Aristotle, Aquinas gives happiness a central place: living in accordance with these laws will make us happy, and "the last end of human life is happiness."[2] For the natural law theorist, the natural world is not composed of a collection of physical objects that have emerged out of random contingencies; rather, it is a rational realm with purposes and values built into its very fabric.

For Aristotle, the purposes built into natural things, whether animate or inanimate, are themselves natural. Likewise, the happiness Aristotle believes will result from humans doing what they are supposed to do is happiness in this world. For Aquinas, in contrast, it is God who builds the purposes into things, and God who sustains the order of the universe: "[I]t is evident ... that the whole community of the universe is governed by divine reason."[3] When we use reason to examine the world around us, the order that we discover is simply the order built into things when God designed and created the universe. Human happiness, as a result of the shift from a natural teleology to a supernatural one, becomes something that cannot be fully achieved in this life. For Aquinas, "the natural purpose of living by reason becomes a supernatural purpose: supreme happiness through communion with God, a happiness imperfectly realizable in this world, and perfected only in life after death."[4] Another consequence of the shift from a natural teleology to a divine one is that we need the assistance of the Church to help us fully understand what God intends for us. Since the rational plan is God's plan, it is not only present in the things we can discover as we explore the world around us, but also something that is revealed in the Scriptures, reflected in Church traditions, and conveyed to us through Church teachings.

Aquinas identified some specific goals that make it easier to determine what is good and what is evil. First, he argues that life must be preserved, and that all creatures desire their own preservation. Second, we must, according to the natural law, act on natural inclinations that we share with other animals, "such as sexual intercourse, the education of offspring, and so forth."[5] This suggests that we should respect the purposes that are built in to such activities. For instance, the purpose of sexual intercourse is reproduction, and even though we can find ways to interfere with this purpose, natural law suggests that we should not do so.

Third, the natural law identifies not only how things are, but also how they ought to be. As humans, we have the capacity to violate the natural law—we can commit suicide, have an abortion, use birth control, choose to remain ignorant—but we ought not to. If we ignore what the natural law requires, we do so out of wilful sinfulness, and demonstrate a failure to do the things that reason tells us we ought to do.

Reproductive technologies are problematic from the perspective of natural law theory, because they allow the process of reproduction to be broken down into discrete parts; have the potential to separate genetic, gestational, and social parenthood; and make possible the participation of third parties in what should properly be the intimate relationship of a married couple. From the perspective of natural law theory, as interpreted by the Catholic Church, teleological purposes are built into sexual intercourse, marriage, and the family, and anything that interferes with these teleological purposes (such as separating sexual intercourse from reproduction) is morally wrong. Moreover, while intercourse, marriage, and the family each have their own telos, their full teleological potential cannot be achieved unless they are manifested together: "the procreation of a new person, whereby the man and woman collaborate with the Power of the Creator, must be the fruit and the sign of the mutual self-giving of the spouses, of their love and their fidelity."[6]

The easiest way to understand the natural law reasoning with respect to reproductive technologies is to see it as essentially the same reasoning that is used by the Church to reject contraception; namely, that the sexual act has two meanings, unitive and procreative, and that the two should not be separated. Consequently, even IVF between husband and wife, or artificial insemination of a woman using her husband's sperm, are seen to separate the intrinsic connection between the unitive (the act of intercourse) and the procreative (the reproductive purpose of intercourse):

> Just as contraception separates what it is never permitted to separate by allowing for union without procreation, so does AIH [or IVF] make possible an impermissible separation by providing for procreation without union. The problem with contraception is that although intercourse and love may be held together, procreation is split away. The problem with artificial insemination with husband's sperm [or IVF] is that although procreation and love may be held together, intercourse is split away.[7]

Moreover, according to this interpretation of the natural law, any intervention by third parties, including infertility specialists, deprives the resulting child of the human dignity that rightfully belongs to it. This intervention both violates the right of the parents "*to become a father and a mother only through each other*"[8] and treats the resulting child as an object: "The one conceived must be the fruit of his parents' love. He cannot be desired or conceived as the production of an intervention of medical or biological techniques; that would be equivalent to reducing him to an object of scientific technology."[9] It follows, of course, that assisted reproduction using donor gametes is also morally unacceptable.

Notes
1. Aquinas, "Concerning the Nature of Law," in Joel Feinberg and Hyman Gross (eds.), *Philosophy of Law* (Belmont, CA: Wadsworth Publishing, 1986), 17.
2. Aquinas, 12.
3. Aquinas, 14.
4. Mike W. Martin, *Everyday Morality: An Introduction to Applied Ethics* (Belmont, CA: Wadsworth Publishing, 2001), 51.
5. Aquinas, 17.
6. Congregation for the Doctrine of the Faith, "Instruction on Respect for Human Life in Its Origin and on the Dignity of Procreation: Replies to Certain Questions of the Day," in Ronald Munson, *Intervention and Reflection: Basic Issues in Medical Ethics, 7th ed.* (Belmont, CA: Thomson Wadsworth, 2004), 398.
7. Paul Lauritzen, *Pursuing Parenthood: Ethical Issues in Assisted Reproduction* (Bloomington: Indiana University Press, 1993), 7.
8. Congregation for the Doctrine of the Faith, 398.
9. Congregation for the Doctrine of the Faith, 398–399.

The Deliberate Severing of Genetic and Social Ties

One of the results of IVF and its related technologies—intentional or not—is the deliberate severing of genetic, gestational, and social ties. In this context, a comparison of the practices allowed by reproductive technologies and adoption can be instructive. While adoption similarly separates genetic and social ties, it does so in different ways than the reproductive technologies allow. In traditional adoption arrangements, children have genetic parents who, for some reason, were unable to raise them; they were not, however, as in the case of surrogacy arrangements, conceived in order to allow someone else to bring them up. In addition, in traditional adoption, neither of the social parents is genetically connected to the child they are raising together; however, with egg and sperm donation, families are created in which one parent is genetically connected to the child while the other parent is not. We now know that the severing of genetic and social ties entailed by adoption, coupled with the secrecy and anonymity that traditionally accompanied it, has been hurtful and damaging to many adopted individuals. Consequently, many jurisdictions have moved away from anonymity and secrecy in adoption toward more open arrangements, including those that allow birth parents and their children to make contact with one another once those children reach adulthood.

Assisted reproductive practices, particularly those involving donor insemination and, to a lesser extent, egg donation, also allow the severing of genetic and social (and even gestational) ties. In many places, these practices have developed in ways that allow donor parents to remain anonymous to their donor offspring. Often, records are not even kept that will allow the children produced through these practices to identify their genetic parent.

The fact that donor gametes often come from anonymous sources generates a contradiction at the heart of these practices: a major moral impetus behind the development and use of techniques of assisted reproduction lies in the assertion that they allow people to have their own children, meaning children who are genetically related to them. While infertile couples in the past might have had no option but childlessness or the adoption of a child who was someone else's genetic offspring, these practices permit the superior option for couples of having children of their own. However, while some forms of assisted reproduction do facilitate this goal (such as IVF used by an infertile couple using their own gametes, or artificial insemination of a woman using her husband's sperm), others sever all genetic, gestational, and social ties, as the Buzzanca case demonstrates. This fact raises a number of significant theoretical and practical moral questions.

First, the arguments used to defend many of these practices are incoherent: they simultaneously assert the importance of genetic connections (a man whose wife is infertile can hire a surrogate to have his child) while denying the importance of such connections (even if the surrogate in question is both the genetic and the gestational mother, the child is not to be considered hers, but, rather, that of the contracting father and his infertile wife). And the list goes on: a single woman can buy sperm from an anonymous donor in order to have her own child, while the donor is told that he has merely provided genetic material and has no moral or legal obligation to the child that might result from its use. This incoherence is illustrated by the Buzzanca case: John Buzzanca is told that he has a moral and legal obligation to pay child support because he signed a contract to hire a surrogate, while Jaycee's biological parents are held to have no responsibilities to ensure her well-being.

What is the meaning and significance of genetic connections? As Alpern notes, the idea of what it means to have "our own" children becomes less clear the more we examine it. He asks: "How do we, how should we, understand the concept of having one's own child, being a real parent, the gene relation, and a child having one's genes? What significance should they have?"[46] Alpern considers the case of a man who received a testicle transplant from his identical twin brother; he and his wife subsequently had three children. Who is the real father of those children? We can ask similar questions about the Buzzanca case: Who is Jaycee's real mother? The egg donor who did not gestate her and, according to reports, has never met her; the surrogate who was not genetically related to her, but without whom she would not have been born; or Luanne, her social mother, who arranged for her birth, loves her, and is raising her? Or should we say, rather, that Jaycee has three mothers?

While these questions are difficult to answer, it is clear that, for many people, genetic connections are very important. In fact, the desire to discover biological connections is so strong that there are sites on the Internet where children created through anonymous sperm donation can register to try to find out information about their genetic origins. For instance, the Donor Sibling Registry site allows individuals to search for their genetic roots using the name of the fertility clinic that supplied the sperm and the donor's number. The site boasts that it has matched several thousand half-siblings. These sites and the stories that can be found on them are testimony to the strong desire that children produced by third parties have to find their biological parent and half-siblings and the importance for many of genetic connections.

Lauritzen argues that the mixed message sent by providers of these technologies—that genetic ties are simultaneously of supreme importance and essentially irrelevant, depending on the reproductive options being presented—generates significant moral concerns. In his own case, he and his wife underwent multiple treatments intended to allow them to have a child together. They were then offered the option of donor insemination as though it were simply another form of treatment for his infertility. As he struggled with the decision, Lauritzen came to believe that the severing of genetic ties entailed by this procedure was morally troubling. He had to take seriously the possibility that producing a child in this way might be incompatible with the requirements of responsible parenting—that is, with the ability of the couple to properly care for and nurture their child.

This introduces another sort of harm, which is relevant to the principle of non-malfeasance: the possibility that children produced through practices that sever the genetic tie to one or both of the social parents might suffer psychological harm as a result, and that, paradoxically, the practice might undermine the stability of the family unit it was used to create.

Kantians might also ask questions about this facet of assisted reproduction, such as whether the children so produced are being treated as ends in themselves or simply as a means to the ends of the adults involved. This is particularly relevant for those who sell their reproductive materials or services. While the purchasers may fully intend to treat any children that result as ends, it is hard to argue that a sperm seller, egg seller, or commercial surrogate are treating those children as ends in themselves.

Finally, virtue ethicists would look at the norms built into the concept of families, with their mix of genetic, legal, and social questions, and ask whether practices that deliberately separate genetic and social connections fit with these norms. They might also ask questions about the virtue of selling or buying reproductive materials and services: are these the sorts of actions that virtuous parents would engage in?

Asymmetry and Secrecy

Asymmetry is a moral concern that arises out of the fact that some assisted reproductive practices—such as genetic surrogacy, egg donation, and donor insemination—create family relationships in which one of the parents is only the social parent while the other parent is both the social and the genetic parent. Moreover, this asymmetrical relationship is often kept secret or is revealed in a moment of anger or during a period of marital breakdown. Both asymmetry and the secrecy that often accompanies it can be damaging to children and to families. In his investigation of sperm banks and the children produced by them, Plotz notes that, in many cases, the marital unit has broken apart and the father is notably absent. He observes that

> [w]hile good studies on [donor insemination] families don't seem to exist ... anecdotes about them suggest that there is frequently a gap between fathers and their putative children.... "Social fathers"—the industry term for the nonbiological dads—have it tough... they are drained by having to pretend that the children are theirs when they aren't; it takes a good actor and an extraordinary man to overlook the fact that his wife has picked another man to father her child.[47]

What is true for men is also likely to be true for women who have used egg donors, whether or not they go through a pregnancy or hire a surrogate.

The secrecy that accompanies third-party assisted conception is often recommended to couples when this reproductive option is presented to them. Lauritzen and his wife were given this advice when they considered donor insemination. The reason for this, Lauritzen suspects, is not primarily to protect the interests of the child, but to protect the ego of the social father: it allows him to appear fertile in the eyes of the world, rather than publicly suffer the embarrassment of infertility.

While utilitarians will ask whether asymmetry and secrecy are harmful, and virtue ethicists will consider whether these factors detract from the telos of the family, the issue of secrecy will be particularly problematic for Kantians because it is the embodiment of a lie, something that is prohibited by the Categorical Imperative. Lauritzen argues that the kind of deception this sort of secrecy requires is particularly corrosive and pernicious because of the family setting in which it takes place. It necessarily involves "not one isolated incident of lying in a close relationship, but a whole relationship built on a lie. Indeed, the notion of 'living a lie' seems particularly apt to capture a father's relation to a donor child from whom he has kept the truth."[48] Consequently, while a Kantian might accept asymmetry between the parents if both freely and autonomously consent to having a child with third-party assistance, she could not accept the secrecy that often accompanies it.

Anonymity

Third-party assisted reproduction is often accompanied by anonymity. Anonymity means that the identity of the donor is not revealed. While certain facts, such as basic medical information, might be provided, the identity of the egg, sperm, or embryo donor, in theory and usually in practice, is both unknown and unknowable. Arguments in support of anonymity assert that this practice is beneficial both for the donors, who want to ensure that they are not forced to take legal or financial responsibility for the resultant children, and for the recipients, who do not want the biological parents to interfere in their lives.

Anonymity too raises ethical questions. First, it seems to violate the principle of non-malfeasance when the matter is considered from the perspective of the child. Brown writes about her experiences as a child produced by an anonymous sperm donation. She states that never being able to identify her genetic father because adequate records were not kept has had a negative impact on her life. She notes: "What is astounding … is that decisions about insemination are made in the interests of the parents' and the physicians' privacy.... That the child deserves the right to know of a biological father is not a consideration."[49] Brown's experiences lead her to suggest that people considering making use of gametes from anonymous sources should think carefully: "It seems no one thought I might want to know of the other half of my genetic makeup.... Future donor-recipient parents must step out of their own shoes and into those of the person they are creating."[50] A similar sentiment is expressed by one of the donor children interviewed by Plotz, who realizes that he will probably never be able to discover who his genetic father is and is deeply troubled by this: "And now I have no father. My father—my mom's husband—isn't my father. My *real* father—the donor—isn't my father because all he did was donate sperm, which is not enough to make him a father. So nobody is my father."[51]

Kantians, too, might raise ethical concerns about anonymity. If we apply the first and the second formulations of the Categorical Imperative, it is not clear that anonymity in assisted reproduction would pass the test. It is unlikely that those who conceive children under this policy (both donors and recipients) would themselves want to have been conceived anonymously, and it is hard to claim that anonymity, given its main purpose of protecting the adults involved, treats children as ends in themselves.

Finally, a virtue ethicist might wonder about whether a practice that is designed to protect donors from taking legal, moral, and financial responsibility for their biological children is a virtuous practice: they are likely to decide that it is not. Given the concerns raised by anonymity, a number of countries, including Great Britain, Australia, Sweden, New Zealand, and the Netherlands, have moved away from anonymity by creating registries for sperm and egg donors. Once children reach the age of 18, they will be able to access information about their biological parent(s). In both Canada and the United States, however, anonymity remains the norm.

Commodification and Objectification

The final two ethical concerns are generated by the intrusion of market values into the sphere of repro-duction, in which the values of the family—loving, nurturing, and acceptance—are ideally supposed to prevail. We saw above that the procreative liberty argument works well with the values of the market. However, critics have noted, to see reproductive materials and services as commodities, as goods that can properly be bought and sold, may undermine the very reasons for which individuals and families reproduce in the first place. As Murray puts it, "Alternative reproductive practices challenge our no-tions of family because they expose what has been at the core of the family—creating and raising children—to values more at home in the marketplace.... In the realm of commerce, moral relation-ships are relatively simple. There are owners and property and prospective buyers. The property has no independent moral significance."[52] Children are not commodities. However, if we view what we might call the raw materials out of which children are made—eggs, sperm, embryos, surrogacy services—as commodities, then we risk seeing the children that are generated from them as commodities as well.

Commodification can lead to objectification; if you buy something, you want to get good value for your money. This is why sperm and egg donors are chosen for their appearance, athletic achieve-ments, and educational accomplishments. This perspective is captured perfectly by an administrator of a donor agency who was interviewed by Mead: "It's like shopping.... If you have the option between a Volkswagen and a Mercedes, you'll select the Mercedes."[53] Objectification raises an im-portant question: what if the child turns out to be a disappointment, a pedestrian Volkswagen rather than an eye-catching Mercedes? Plotz observes that sperm banks use the latest marketing techniques (deluxe catalogues, "top quality" donors, advertising to increase market share), but that there is a fundamental disconnect between what is being sold and what people think they are buying.

> Once you start thinking of sperm as just another product, you start treating it like just another product. As long as customers consider AID [artificial insemination] to be a form of shopping, some of them will inevitably be disappointed.... A customer who is unhappy with a DVD player can replace it. What about a customer who is unhappy with a child?... Women shop carefully for sperm in hopes of certainty with a baby. It does not come with a warranty. In sperm shopping, there is a deposit, but there are no returns, no refunds, no exchanges.[54]

It is also interesting to note that the personal attributes of donors thought desirable are those that are likely to ensure success in a competitive, market-driven setting. Studies have shown, for instance, that people who are physically attractive fare better in the workplace than those who are not. Attri-butes that are arguably equally important and equally dependent on genetics, though, such as admi-rable character traits, are not considered to be valuable in this marketplace. Indeed, some observers have wondered about the characters of those who are willing to sell their gametes in the first place, whatever other attributes they may possess. As Robert Jansen, a fertility doctor interviewed by Mead, puts it, "As the price rises and becomes more and more of a motivating factor, and we also appreciate the genetics of personality and character, you start to ask, 'Do you really want to bring up a little girl whose biological mother was someone who decided to charge ten thousand dollars for eggs?'"[55]

Commodification and objectification are likely to be of particular concern to Kantians, who again

196 Bioethics in Canada

would ask whether the buyers and sellers of reproductive materials are viewing the children that may be conceived as ends in themselves, or merely as means to their own ends. In particular, it is hard from a Kantian perspective to see how the sellers of these materials can possibly be treating potential children as ends in themselves. They receive financial gains from the transaction, and the transaction itself is predicated on the premise that they will not be responsible for the care of any children that might result. When we consider the buyers of reproductive materials from a Kantian perspective, the fact that they make their choice on the basis of particular desirable attributes possessed by the seller, and are willing to pay money in the hope that at least some of those attributes will be embodied in the child they hope to have, seems equally problematic. Again, it does not appear that the child is being primarily treated as an end in itself.

Some have argued, in other contexts, that utilitarians would embrace the market as an efficient way of generating the greatest amount of happiness, since dollars can easily stand in for utiles when individuals decide how much they're willing to spend and on what. A case can be made, though, that utilitarians would have some concerns about commodification and objectification as well. Utilitarians would consider whether these practices are harmful or beneficial for both individuals and for society. And they would be concerned with the fact that so few records are being kept that it is almost impossible to give an accurate answer to this question. This is morally problematic for both individuals and for society. Individuals cannot perform their own utilitarian calculus when trying to decide whether to buy reproductive materials because they cannot know which benefits to measure against which harms. On a societal level, utilitarians would want to know what the likely consequences are for the larger community over the long term before deciding whether or not a sale in reproductive materials should continue. They need at least some facts in order to fairly make this determination.

Finally, virtue ethicists would have little difficulty making the case that the virtues that characterize family life at its best (patience, acceptance, commitment) and the virtues of the market (competition, efficiency) belong to distinct spheres of human activity (just as the virtues required on the battlefield are distinct from the virtues required in a monastery). Consequently, while a virtue ethicist might support genuine (unpaid) donations of reproductive materials and services, she is unlikely to think that their commodification, which introduces the values of the market into family relationships, is a good thing.

FEMINIST CONCERNS ABOUT ASSISTED REPRODUCTIVE PRACTICES

Feminist scholars have been among the most articulate critics of assisted reproductive practices and the medical technologies that many of them require. While their voices are diverse, most feminists begin with a recognition of one inescapable fact: these assisted practices and technologies disproportionately affect women, take place in women's bodies, and are far more risky for women than for men. While sperm donation carries no physical risks (indeed, Plotz notes that one American sperm bank "hands out pens on college campuses that ask, 'Why not get paid for it?'"[56]), egg donation requires much more of women and is physically risky. The women who wish to serve as egg sellers must take potentially carcinogenic drugs to make them ovulate, require invasive surgery to remove the ripened eggs, and may be risking their own future fertility in the process.[57] In vitro fertilization, as well, is a risky procedure for women. As Sherwin notes, IVF technology "requires disruptive and dangerous hormone therapy, intensive monitoring of the woman's blood and urine, surgery, a period of immobility, and a high likelihood of failure."[58] Moreover, treatments for male infertility are more invasive for their female partners than for the men themselves; ICSI, for example, requires that women undergo IVF treatment so that the eggs into which each sperm is injected are available for manipulation.

While feminists agree on these central facts, they do not always agree on how women should respond to them. In order to get an idea of the concerns raised by feminists about assisted reproduction, we will explore three feminist positions that address the issue of surrogacy and the ethical questions this practice raises. Andrews argues that it is perfectly legitimate for women to sell their reproductive services through surrogacy contracts; Anderson asserts that it is the element of commodification in surrogacy arrangements that makes them ethically problematic; and Raymond claims that even altruistic surrogacy raises serious ethical concerns.

Andrews argues that surrogate motherhood (whether genetic and gestational, or simply gestational) poses an enormous problem for feminists. On the one hand, a central tenet of feminist thought is that women have the right to control their own bodies. On the other hand, however, feminists do not want to see women turned into "breeding machines,"[59] even if this is done with their own consent. The first concern suggests that women should be free to act as surrogate mothers if they so choose; the second concern, however, suggests that, if many women choose this option, the results may be harmful for women in general, and so their freedom to enter into surrogacy contracts should be restricted.

Ironically, Andrews believes, the very success of feminism has made many women feel that surrogacy might be a legitimate option for them.

> Feminism taught that not all women relate to all pregnancies in the same way. A woman could choose not to be a rearing mother at all. She could choose to lead a child-free life by not getting pregnant. If she got pregnant, she could choose to abort. Reproduction was a condition of her body over which she, and no one else, should have control. For some women, these developments added up to the freedom to be a surrogate.[60]

Despite this, a number of feminists have argued that commercial surrogacy should be banned. However, according to Andrews, the arguments this group of feminists present in the case of surrogacy are the very same arguments they have criticized in other contexts, such as abortion and contraception. Consequently, she believes there is something self-defeating in using them in the surrogacy case: "The adoption of these rationales could severely undercut the gains previously made in these other areas."[61]

The rationales presented by feminists against surrogacy fall into three main areas: first, the symbolic harm paid surrogacy poses to society; second, the potential risk to women of commercial surrogacy; and, third, the risks to the potential child of allowing this practice.

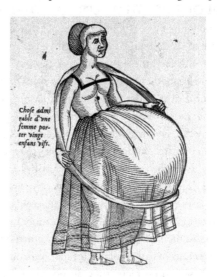

Chose admirable d'vne femme porter vingt enfans vifs.

A 16th-century illustration of a pregnant woman using a hoop to support her burgeoning womb. Feminists argue that paid surrogacy arrangements only affect women's bodies and that pregnancy can be both emotionally and physically stressful.

First, some feminists believe that it is harmful to society to allow women to sell their babies. This argument, Andrews believes, is misguided. For one thing, it is reminiscent of the arguments made against feminists in the abortion context, namely, that it is harmful to society to allow abortions. Moreover, this argument focuses on what Andrews calls "symbolic harms" (predicted harms that tap into visceral fears and deep prejudices), rather than on actual, clearly identified, and established ones. Andrews asserts that one of the "greatest feminist contributions to policy debates on reproduction and the family has been the rejection of arguments relying on tradition and symbolism and an insistence on an understanding of the nature and effects of actual practice in determining how it should be regulated."[62] Many of the arguments presented by feminists against the practice of paid surrogacy—for example, that this practice will reduce women to nothing more than breeding machines and fetal containers whose only value lies in their capacity to reproduce—undermine, in Andrews' opinion, the empirically based arguments that feminists have made against the belief that children must grow up in traditional, two-parent families if they are to flourish.

The second commonly raised argument against paid surrogacy by feminists is the potential physical and psychological harm it poses to women. Andrews believes, however, that the way in which these concerns are often presented is actually demeaning to women: "They focus on protecting women against their own decisions because those decisions might later cause them regret, be unduly influenced by others, or be forced by financial considerations."[63] Andrews points out that this is true of all significant decisions, reproductive or otherwise, whether made by men or women: all important decisions can be regretted, be influenced by others, or be driven by the need to earn money. To suggest that women need to be protected from the decisions that they freely make undermines everything that feminists have fought for. Such a suggestion implies that women are not capable of making their own choices and that, consequently, decisions have to be made for them. Simply because many feminist scholars disapprove of the choice a woman might make to become a surrogate does not mean that she should be prevented from making it, nor does a pro-life person's opposition to abortion legitimate her interference with someone else's decision to have an abortion.

The final claim by feminists that Andrews considers is the possibility that surrogacy arrangements might be harmful to the children produced by them. These arguments suggest, among other things, that surrogacy is equivalent to baby-selling and that parents will expect more of children born through surrogacy because of the money they spent to conceive and gestate them. The first objection, Andrews believes, is mistaken, because laws against child abuse (which prohibit the sale of babies) come into effect at birth, whether a child is conceived naturally or through a surrogacy contract. In terms of the second objection, Andrews points out that the amount paid to a surrogate "is a modest amount compared to what parents will spend on their child over her lifespan."[64]

Andrews concludes that feminists should be very careful about the kinds of arguments they advance against commercial surrogacy; otherwise, they risk "breathing life into arguments [such as the argument that women are not capable of making important decisions for themselves] that feminists have put to rest in other contexts, [or else] the current rationales opposing surrogacy could undermine a larger feminist agenda."[65]

Anderson, in contrast, takes quite a different approach. She argues that commercial surrogacy makes both women's reproductive capacities and the children produced by them into commodities. Moreover, Anderson asserts, neither children nor reproductive capacities are appropriate things to commodify; therefore, it is ethically problematic to apply the norms of the marketplace to them. Anderson's argument against commercial surrogacy is a Kantian one. It is based on the idea that to treat either children or the reproductive capacities of women in accordance with the norms of the market is to fail to value them in the appropriate way, just as slaves are treated inappropriately when they are bought and sold:

> Slaves are treated in accordance with the market norm that owners may use com-
> modities to satisfy their own interests without regard for the interests of the com-
> modities themselves. To treat a person without regard for her interests is to fail to
> respect her.... In Kantian theory, the problem with slavery is that it treats beings
> worthy of *respect* as though they were worthy merely of *use*."[66]

Commodities are appropriately treated in terms of their use value and, consequently, in terms of the norms of the marketplace. Children, and the labour women expend to gestate them, ought to be treated in accordance with the norms of respect, because neither children nor women nor reproductive labour are commodities, but rather things that are beyond price.

Anderson asserts that arguments in support of commercial surrogacy fall into four categories. First, surrogacy is presented as an alternative to adoption. Second, surrogacy arrangements are defended on the grounds that autonomous individuals should be left free to make whatever reproductive arrangements they wish. Third, the "labor of the surrogate mother is said to be a labor of love. Her altruistic acts should be encouraged."[67] Fourth, surrogacy contracts are said to be very similar to activities that are widely accepted, such as donor insemination, adoption, and day care: if we accept these practices, consistency demands that we accept commercial surrogacy arrangements as well.

In opposition to these claims, Anderson argues that paid surrogacy degrades women and children because it substitutes parental love for the norms of the marketplace by treating parental rights, which generate obligations of care and nurturance, as property rights. This is demonstrated, Anderson believes, by the fact that the surrogacy industry treats the characteristics of surrogate mothers who are simultaneously genetic and gestational parents as commodities: those women with higher IQs and more appealing physical attributes command higher prices than women who are less intelligent and attractive.

While this last point is only applicable to genetic surrogates, Anderson argues that commercial surrogacy treats even gestational surrogates—those who are impregnated with an embryo that is not genetically related to them—as objects of use, rather than as persons worthy of respect: "To respect a person is to treat her in accordance with principles she rationally accepts—principles consistent with the protection of her autonomy and her rational interests. To treat a person with consideration is to respond with sensitivity to her and to her emotional relations with others, refraining from manipulating or denigrating these for one's own purposes."[68] Commercial surrogacy does this by requiring a surrogate to refrain from developing feelings of parental love for her offspring, substituting the values of the market for the woman's own perspective on her pregnancy, and leaving the woman open to exploitation. Pregnancy, Anderson observes, involves not only physical labour, but also emotional labour. In non-surrogacy pregnancies, women are encouraged to create a bond with their developing child. In the case of surrogacy, however, the opposite happens: women are actively discouraged from creating these bonds.

Anderson concludes her argument against surrogacy by stating that "[i]f we are to retain the capacity to value children and women in ways consistent with a rich conception of human flourishing, we must resist the encroachment of the market upon the sphere of reproductive labour. Women's labour is *not* a commodity."[69]

In contrast to Andrews, who believes that it is perfectly legitimate for women to sell their reproductive services through surrogacy contracts, and Anderson, who argues that it is the element of commodification in surrogacy arrangements that makes them ethically problematic (suggesting that altruistic surrogacy, in which no money changes hands, might be ethically acceptable), Raymond argues that even altruistic surrogacy raises serious ethical concerns.

Raymond observes that many assisted reproductive practices depend on women. What this means is that those who argue that altruistic surrogacy is morally acceptable in contrast to commercial surrogacy are assuming, without question, that it is perfectly acceptable to ask women to make altruistic sacrifices for others. Women, she argues, are expected to go out of their way to meet the demands and needs of others; men are not. This fact creates a moral double standard that has pernicious effects on the lives of women: "Altruism has been one of the most effective blocks to women's self-awareness and demand for self-determination.... The social relations set up by altruism and the giving of self have been among the most powerful forces that bind women to cultural roles and expectations."[70]

Women can be exploited in reproductive practices, even when no money is involved. In fact, the kind of exploitation and pressure women face to provide a "gift" for a family member, friend, or even a stranger through the use of their reproductive services can be even more insidious than financial inducements. This kind of pressure is difficult for some women to resist both because they have been brought up to believe that they should help others and because altruistic surrogacy "reinforces the perception and use of women as a breeder class and reinforces the gender inequality of women as a group."[71] In short, Raymond believes, altruistic surrogacy reinforces women's inequality just as much as commercial surrogacy does, and in an even more insidious way: "Women are encouraged to offer their bodies in a myriad of ways, so that others may have babies, health, and life. These ... gift-giving arguments reinforce women as self-sacrificing and ontological donors of wombs and what issues from them."[72]

Feminists take a number of distinct positions on assisted reproductive practices, as the arguments considered above demonstrate. While it is not entirely clear which argument is most persuasive—Is it more empowering for women to receive money for reproductive services than to offer them for free, out of the goodness of their hearts?—feminists arguably make a valid observation when they point out that all of the reproductive technologies as well as their associated practices disproportionately affect women's bodies. This is something that many of the arguments made about assisted reproductive practices (whether supportive of them or critical of them) often ignore, or pay insufficient attention to. Any satisfactory ethical perspective on assisted reproduction will, then, at the very least, have to acknowledge the fact that women's experiences with these technologies is very different from men's.

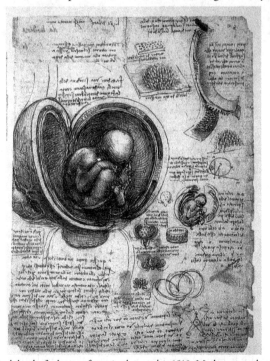

Leonardo da Vinci, *Anatomical sketch of a human foetus in the womb*, c.1510. Modern reproductive technologies have allowed us to control human reproduction in ways that would have been almost unimaginable for most of human history.

CROSS-BORDER REPRODUCTIVE CARE AND THE BABY MANJI CASE

The ethical questions raised by assisted reproductive practices are further complicated by the growth of what is sometimes called "reproductive tourism,"[73] a term that describes the action of purchasing reproductive services (such as IVF treatments, sperm and eggs, and surrogacy contracts) in another country. Usually, the purchasers of these services come from developed countries while the suppliers are from developing ones. In India, for example, the international fertility industry is worth somewhere between $500 million and $2.4 billion,[74] and it is expected to keep growing. The motivation of infertile individuals and couples to seek reproductive care abroad is often financial. Deonandan reports that "India's services can be 10 to 100 times cheaper than in the West."[75] Both the low costs and availability of treatments can be attractive for individuals from countries in which reproductive services are very expensive, or regulated by legislation that prohibits the buying and selling of reproductive materials or outlaws commercial surrogacy.

Cross-border reproductive services present a challenge to our ethical thinking. While they make money for the doctors and clinics that offer them, and provide an affordable means of having a child for those who are unable to have one without assistance, it is not entirely clear whether the women who provide eggs or act as surrogates are empowered by their participation in this industry or are exploited by it. The implications for the children who are produced by it are also unclear.

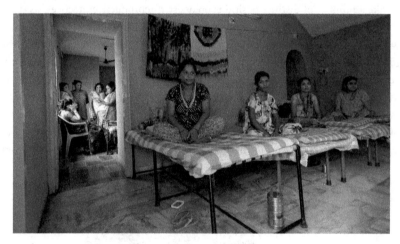

Cross-border reproductive care raises issues of empowerment and exploitation.

These questions gained international attention as a result of what has come to be known as the Baby Manji case. In 2007, Ikufumi and Yuki Yamada, a Japanese couple, travelled to India to arrange a surrogate pregnancy. A married Indian woman with children, Pritiben Mehta, was selected as the surrogate. Under the direction of a fertility specialist, an embryo, which was created from Ikufumi's sperm and an egg harvested from an anonymous Indian donor, was then implanted into Mehta's womb. In June 2008, however, the Yamadas divorced, and when baby Manji was born to the surrogate one month later, Yuki no longer wanted anything to do with the child. As she saw it, she was not related to the child biologically, genetically, or legally.

Baby Manji was left parentless: under the terms of the contract, the egg donor's responsibility ended when the egg was provided, and the surrogate mother's job was completed when she gave birth. And since no Indian law existed at the time to account for children born through surrogacy, Yuki could not be held responsible for the child. While baby Manji could be said to have had three mothers—Yuki (who was the intended mother), the egg donor, and the surrogate mother—she was left without a legal mother. To further complicate matters, Ikufumi wanted to care for the child, but Indian law did not allow single fathers to adopt baby girls. Ikufumi launched a months-long campaign to take baby Manji to Japan. In the meantime, she was cared for by Ikufumi's elderly mother. Ikufumi finally won the legal dispute and now has full custody of baby Manji.[76]

While most children produced through such cross-national arrangements are happily received by those who entered into a contract to create them, the effect of this industry on the women who provide these services remains in question: does it empower or exploit them? Proponents of cross-border reproductive care see it as a win-win situation. For the couples who seek such services, defenders point to "the benefits they enjoy, such as significant cost savings, avoidance of attachment on the part of the surrogate, freedom of choice, and freedom to contract."[77] For the women who act as surrogates, such arrangements benefit them financially. As Parks puts it, "[T]he arguments defending the choices of surrogates emphasize their economic relief (since surrogate mothers in India can earn in nine months what might otherwise take them fifteen years to accumulate), their resultant ability to care for their families, their freedom to use their bodies as they see fit, their freedom of choice and their freedom to contract."[78] In short, defenders argue, infertile couples benefit from the provision of affordable reproductive services, and the women who agree to provide them should be considered autonomous individuals who freely choose to enter into financially beneficial contractual arrangements.

Those who believe that cross-border reproductive arrangements are exploitative, however, are not convinced that the choices made by these women are fully autonomous and freely made, or that the role played by the market that provides the incentive for their participation is beneficial for them. We need, these critics assert, to consider the context within which the women who act as surrogates and egg donors make their choices. As Donchin observes, while it is completely understandable why an impoverished woman might enter in to such a contract, we should not think of this exchange between purchaser and seller as a fair exchange between equals: "Such offers exploit ... [the vulnerabilities] of the seller, extend the reach of market forces, and subvert efforts by the purchasers' home countries to reign in unfair reproductive practices."[79] Moreover, she argues, it is not only the women who provide the services who warrant our attention, but also the infertile women who buy them: "To escape dependence on male wage earners and carve out a career in the workforce, many Western women are postponing reproduction until their careers are well established. But by then their peak childbearing years have passed and conception is more problematic."[80] For critics, then (many of whom analyze the situation from a feminist or care perspective), the global reproductive industry exploits the vulnerabilities of both the women who sell reproductive services and the women who purchase them.

Other critics are concerned about the fact that this industry closely links medicine and commerce, and consequently blurs the line between sound business practices and sound medical ones. Deonandan, for example, points out that "in a business negotiation all parties are required to only consider their own best interests, and whatever they end up agreeing to is by definition ethical—assuming that no one was duplicitous in the negotiation."[81] In medicine, however, the situation is very different. The physician is morally required to do what is in the patient's best interest, and while the infertile woman who buys the reproductive services may view herself as the patient, the real patient is the woman who provides them: "In maternal surrogacy, there's a paying client, a clinician, and a surrogate. It's the latter who's the actual clinical patient, but the business negotiation is between the clinician and the client, with the surrogate essentially acting as an independent contractor."[82]

Deonandan believes that this fact generates a troubling conflict. The medical nature of the services provided by the surrogate means that her health should be of paramount concern to the clinic. However, because the contract is nothing more than a business transaction between the purchaser and the doctor, the health of the surrogate or egg donor is of secondary importance. The more cheaply services can be provided, the better for the purchaser—and one way for the clinic to make more money out of any given contract is to spend as little as possible on the surrogate or egg donor's medical needs. Consequently, critics such as Deonandan believe that to see such arrangements simply as an exchange between freely acting autonomous individuals, without paying attention to the larger social and economic context within which such contracts take place, is to risk ignoring ethical issues that ought to be considered before we can make sound judgments about the benefits and challenges of cross-border reproductive care.

CONCLUSION

Assisted reproductive practices raise ethical questions. While these practices provide additional options for infertile people, they also challenge our understanding of parenthood because they allow the processes of conception, gestation, and nurturing to be separated from one another. Moreover, the ethical issues raised by assisted reproductive practices are both intertwined with one another and deeply embedded in particular social contexts. Consequently, while infertility can be an intensely difficult personal experience for individuals, the social contexts within which individuals make reproductive decisions must be taken into account. The procreative liberty argument, which makes a case for complete freedom of reproductive choice, is as socially embedded as any argument that holds that governments should regulate assisted reproductive technologies and practices. Advocates of this argument assume an individualistic model of autonomy that works well in a free market context, but which seems inadequate from the perspective of reproductive questions that, by their very nature, involve more than one person. Consequently, this perspective is arguably both theoretically unsatisfactory and practically unhelpful for those who must decide how to respond to a diagnosis of infertility.

Theoretically speaking, not only does the procreative liberty argument appear to fit awkwardly with the goals that individuals hope to achieve through reproduction, it also implicitly depends on the societal oversight of individual reproductive choices that it explicitly rejects as morally wrong. Consider, for example, the practice of commercial surrogacy. Advocates of the procreative liberty argument hold that it is wrong for others, or the state, to interfere with the freedom of those who wish to buy and sell this particular reproductive service because they are autonomous individuals who should be left free to make their own reproductive choices. However, if those arrangements go wrong as they sometimes do (for instance, when a surrogate mother decides that she wants to keep the child she has gestated and given birth to), advocates of this approach assert that the state, through the court system, ought to uphold the legitimacy of surrogacy contracts. Robertson, for example, explicitly links procreative liberty to the requirement that contracts be upheld because, "without some contractual assurance, the parties may be unwilling to embark on the complicated enterprise of collaborative reproduction."[83] Before they can make an arrangement with one another, surrogates need to know that they will not get stuck with children they don't want and contracting parents need to know that their parenthood will be legally recognized by the state. The upholding of contracts, then, Robertson believes, is required by a commitment to procreative liberty. But this claim reveals a tension in the argument; more specifically, a tension between the claim that individuals should be left free from government interference to reproduce as they wish, and the claim that governments (through the legal system) are necessary if the arrangements that individuals make with one another are to be respected. In short, those who promote the procreative liberty argument do not really want individuals to be left free from the interference of the state; rather they want them to be left free from certain sorts of interferences while willingly submitting themselves to other sorts.

The Buzzanca case provides an illustration of this point. A law that upholds the legitimacy of paid surrogacy contracts, such as the one John Buzzanca signed, is as much a demonstration of the role of the state in shaping reproductive choice as would be a law (such as exists in Canada and a number of other countries) that makes commercial surrogacy illegal. The appropriate question, then, is not (as the procreative liberty argument holds) whether or not the state is justified in interfering with the reproductive choices made by individuals; it is, rather, what sorts of interferences are justified and on what grounds.

PHILOSOPHICAL REFLECTION ON TECHNOLOGY AND BIOETHICS

When we think of technology, we tend to think of things: inventions such as the computer or the MRI machine. But the word technology covers more than that. Winston speaks of technology as "a systematic and rational way of doing things; it is, in general, *the organization of knowledge, people, and things to accomplish specific practical goals.*"[84] A technological invention, such as the automobile, the computer, or the microscope, is not something that is simply added on to a society; rather, it transforms society. Postman refers to technological change as "ecological" in the sense that one change generates total change: "A new technology does not add or subtract something. It changes everything. In the year 1500, fifty years after the printing press was invented, we did not have old Europe plus the printing press. We had a different Europe."[85] He observes that a similar transformation resulted from the invention of television: "After television, the United States was not America plus television; television gave a new coloration to every political campaign, to every home, to every school, to every church, to every industry."[86]

According to Winston, any technological system is composed of the following six elements:

1. Methods of doing things (know-how);
2. The tools that extend and enhance human capacities;
3. The artifacts (things) that are created which in turn can become tools for creating new things;
4. The use to which the artifacts are put, along with the needs they fill—and the needs that they create;
5. The scientific knowledge that is created and transformed in the process;
6. The social context in which the technology is employed and the new organizational forms that result from it.[87]

These features are apparent in the development and use of reproductive technologies. They have changed what it means to be infertile and what responses are appropriate to this condition. As soon as the technological process of in vitro fertilization was developed, people needed it; and it has allowed us to move away from conceptions of natural reproductive norms, such as the "fact" that humans have two parents and that reproduction cannot take place once women are past menopause, or even dead. Moreover, reproductive technologies pave the way for genetic technologies, perhaps the most powerful technologies ever devised by humans, which may give us the power to shape our descendants.

All of this should convince us that, in spite of what the scientists and inventors might tell us, the development and use of technology is not a neutral enterprise. Of particular importance in the six elements listed above is number four: the uses to which technology is put, the needs (and desires) it serves, as well as the needs (and desires) it creates. Many of the moral debates around medical technology stem from this aspect of the technological system. Questions arise: Should we use this technology? Why do we want to do this? Whose interests will be served? Whose interests will be harmed? How will this technology affect us as individuals, as a society, and even, increasingly, as a species? These are ethical, not scientific, questions, and the way they are answered depends on social goals and values rather than on scientific knowledge and capability.

Unfortunately, scientific knowledge and capability can (and often do) become ends in themselves, rather than means to agreed-upon goals or ends. Thus, the answer to the question "Why should we do this?" is often simply "Because we can." The use and potential impacts of a technology become secondary, and the pursuit of technological capability becomes the only goal. Knowing how becomes more important than knowing why.

This is called the Technological Imperative: using technology just because it exists. When this is seen in the context of the second and third elements listed above, technology becomes something that drives itself: one invention makes possible another, and so on. A strong societal belief in progress helps motivate and justify the process. As we saw with respect to reproductive technologies, this Technological Imperative can place a burden on individuals facing infertility because it generates what Lauritzen terms the coercive choice: once reproductive technologies exist, the expectation is that individuals will use them even if they are uncomfortable with them and even if they do not fully address the needs they are designed to meet.

The Technological Imperative may not be new (some will see it as a manifestation of the innate curiosity of our species), but its impact grows as it drives our ever-increasing power over our environment and, now, over our own biological evolution. This increasing power over Nature, including our own nature, raises questions about our responsibility regarding the use of that power. Until the last century, our impact on the environment was limited (although it was cumulative, and by the time it became evident, much damage had already been done). Now modern technology has the power to destroy the world and us with it. Biological and genetic knowledge is giving us the power to modify the species. As Hans Jonas tells us, "The new order of human action requires a commensurate ethics of foresight and responsibility, which is as new as are the issues with which it has to deal."[88]

One example that Jonas raises is the power over life and death and the quest for immortality. Recent discoveries in cell biology and genetics are driving scientists to look for (and market) the "immortality gene" with a view to prolonging life indefinitely. Jonas writes, "Death no longer appears as a necessity belonging to the nature of life, but as an avoidable, at least in principle tractable and long-delayable organic malfunction."[89] The idea of immortality has long been the stuff of myth and fiction, but if it ever becomes a real possibility, we are faced with questions that have never before arisen: What would this mean for humanity? Is it desirable? Who would benefit from it? Who would be harmed by it? What would be the impact on the young if people could live for 200 years? What would be the impact on the medical system? Does anybody really want to live for 200 years? These are questions that, in Jonas' words, "had never to be asked before in terms of practical choice, and … no principle of former ethics, which took the human constraints for granted, is competent to deal with them."[90]

Many thinkers believe that our ethics have not kept pace with our technological powers and that, while we now know how to do certain things, we don't know why we want to do them.

CASES OF INTEREST

Baby M

A New Jersey Couple, William and Elizabeth Stern, entered into a surrogacy contract with Mary Beth Whitehead. Ms. Whitehead agreed to bear the child of Mr. Stern through artificial insemination, after which she would terminate her rights as a mother and receive $10,000.

Ms. Whitehead gave birth to Baby M on March 27, 1986. Immediately after giving birth, it became apparent that she did not want to part with the child. Ms. Whitehead nonetheless turned Baby M over to the Sterns. However, she appeared at the Stern residence later that evening, claiming to be struck by an unbearable sadness, and convinced them to give her one last week with the child. Fearing that she would otherwise commit suicide, the Sterns handed the child over to Ms. Whitehead. She then fled to Florida with her husband and the baby, where they took evasive measures to avoid detection.

The Sterns filed suit, seeking enforcement of the surrogacy contract and ultimately full custody of Baby M. At trial, the contract was deemed valid, and Baby M was returned to the Sterns. The Supreme Court ruled that the contract was invalid and therefore unenforceable, most importantly because of its baby-selling nature. The Court decreed, however, that it was nonetheless in Baby M's best interests to live under the custody of the Sterns. Ms. Whitehead was granted visitation rights.[91]

Olivia Pratten

Olivia Pratten was conceived in 1982 in British Columbia via anonymous sperm donation. All the records relating to her insemination procedure were destroyed, as is allowed by the College of Physicians and Surgeons. Pratten launched a legal battle in 2008, arguing that certain provisions of British Columbia's Adoption Act were unconstitutional, given that they failed to take into account the rights of people conceived using sperm from an anonymous donor. She claimed that donor off-spring should have the same rights to access information about their biological fathers as do children who are adopted. Namely, they should have the right to know their medical history and to prevent themselves from engaging in a sexual relationship with a half-sibling.

She argued that while the Adoption Act enables adoptees to find their birth parents, it violates the equality rights of section 15 of the Charter because it benefits adoptees only and not donor offspring. Further, she argued that a lack of access to biological information violates a "free-standing" positive right to "know one's past" as is guaranteed by section 7 of the Charter. The British Columbia Supreme Court ruled that the relevant provisions of the Adoption Act violated section 15 of the Charter in that they discriminated against donor offspring on the basis of their "manner of conception." The court also issued a permanent injunction against destroying records with information about the identity of sperm donors. The section 7 claim, however, was dismissed. The British Columbia Attorney General appealed the section 15 decision, while Pratten cross-appealed the section 7 decision. On November 27, 2012, the British Columbia Court of Appeal reversed the lower court's section 15 decision.[92]

The Del Rios Embryos

Mario and Elsa Rios were a wealthy Californian couple and co-owners of a rental property company in Los Angeles. They each had one child from their previous marriages, and they wanted to raise one together. In 1981, they sought help from the Queen Victoria Medical Center fertility clinic in Melbourne, Australia, where Elsa was treated with fertility drugs. Three eggs were subsequently extracted from her ovaries and combined with sperm from an anonymous donor to create three embryos. One embryo was implanted into Elsa's uterus, and the other two underwent cryopreservation. A little over a week later, Elsa spontaneously miscarried. Because of her distress, she decided not to try again for some time.

In 1983, Mario and Elsa were both killed in an airplane accident in South America. They left a multi-million dollar estate with no wills and, of course, no instructions with respect to the use or destruction of the embryos. Elsa's only daughter had died shortly before she underwent IVF, so Michael Rios, Mario's only son, stood in line to inherit his father's estate. The significant question that was raised, however, was whether the preserved embryos had a right to be implanted into a woman's womb and, if so, whether they had a right to the Rios' estate.

Mario's lawyer argued that the embryos are not heirs, while John Noonan, at the time an active member of a California right-to-life organization and law professor, held that they have rights. In Melbourne, a right-to-life organization pressured the government to appoint legal counsel to represent the embryos, and a Roman Catholic theologian argued that a surrogate mother should carry the embryos. A number of women volunteered. In 1984, the Victorian Parliament enacted legislation stipulating that "orphaned" embryos are to be donated to infertile women. The Rios embryos were donated anonymously, and it is unclear what happened to them, although it is unlikely that they survived the thawing.[93]

CASE STUDIES

Scenario One

Olivia Krupin is entering the second year of her Master of Arts degree program at a Canadian university. She has received small scholarships in each year she has been in university, but she is still in debt, owing nearly $40,000 to the provincial and federal governments and another $10,000 to her bank. She is unsure of what she wants to do once she has finished her degree, and she is becoming quite concerned about how she will manage to get out of debt. She recently learned from a friend that, although it is illegal to sell eggs and sperm in Canada, a black market is emerging, and she could potentially earn several thousand dollars by selling her eggs to an infertile couple. Olivia's friend told her that she could post an ad, stating that she is an egg donor seeking to help a couple in need. Olivia begins doing research into the procedure and draws up a potential ad that she could place on the Internet.

(1) Should Olivia go through with her plans to market her eggs? (2) Is donating one's eggs morally acceptable at all? If so, is it morally acceptable to receive money for doing so? Does this amount to putting a price on a child? (3) Is it permissible to be reimbursed only for costs directly related to this process? (4) What advice would a feminist ethicist give to Olivia? What would Robertson say? Would Murray agree?

Scenario Two

Abigail and Daniel Patterson have been trying to have a child for three years without success. Daniel already has one daughter from a previous marriage, and he and Abigail are raising her together. Although Abigail loves and cares for Daniel's daughter, she also wants a child of her own. Because of the difficulty she has had conceiving, she consulted a doctor who told her that she has a problem with her ovaries. She could, however, carry a child to term if she were implanted with an embryo created with a donor egg and her husband's sperm. Abigail likes this option, because, while she will not be providing the genetic material for the child, she will have a biological connection to the child by carrying it to term. She believes that going through a pregnancy will create an emotional bond with the baby growing inside her. Daniel, however, expresses misgivings about the whole thing. He believes that Abigail will feel the same way toward this child that she feels towards her stepdaughter, as both are the genetic offspring of himself and another woman. He doubts that the experience of pregnancy will overcome the lack of genetic connection between mother and child, and that Abigail's desire to have a child of her own will go unfulfilled.

(1) How significant is it that Daniel is uncertain about Abigail's proposal? (2) If Abigail's need to have her own child might not be fulfilled if she uses a donor egg, is this sufficient reason to object to the procedure? (3) Can either Daniel or Abigail make this judgment, given that neither of them can know whether Abigail will be satisfied or not until well after the child is born? (4) Can the procreative liberty argument help Abigail and Daniel make this decision? Why or why not?

Scenario Three

Jennifer Padmore is a 32-year-old single woman. She is a lawyer, working in a successful law office. She currently earns enough money to support herself in a luxurious lifestyle. She has also saved a significant amount of money. Jennifer has come to a point in her life where she wants to have children. She wants a child in order to have a companion, someone she can share her life with, and she does not want to wait until she has a man in her life with whom she can have children. She has already been to a number of fertility clinics and sperm banks, and has found a doctor who will inseminate her. She has told the doctor that she wants to be inseminated with the sperm of an attractive, intelligent man in order to maximize her chances of having an attractive, intelligent child. Since she wants a child for companionship, she believes that only a child who has the capacity to engage with her intellectually will meet her requirements. Further, she is paying good money for the sperm and wants to get value for her purchase. She also wants the child to have a good quality of life, and this is something she believes that she can provide, given her professional accomplishments and her income.

(1) Should Jennifer be allowed to choose sperm based on the qualities of the seller? If so, does it matter what qualities are sought? (2) Does it make a difference to the moral analysis if what Jennifer wanted to avoid was having a child with a serious mental or physical impairment? (3) Is choosing a sperm seller with particular qualities any different from choosing a husband or partner with the qualities one wants to see in one's child? (4) Are there elements of this situation that might be illuminated by a feminist and/or a virtue ethics perspective that might be overlooked by a Kantian or utilitarian one? (5) Would Murray approve of Jennifer's choice?

Scenario Four

Kevin Morgan was conceived through an anonymous sperm donation just over 20 years ago. He recently met a girl, Anna Koziol, whom he has been dating for several months. Kevin and Anna felt an instant bond with one another: they like the same music, have similar political opinions, and even have the same likes and dislikes when it comes to food. He becomes concerned, however, when he learns that she too was conceived by an anonymous sperm donation. The two of them grew up in the same city and are roughly the same age—she is almost a year younger. They were also conceived when it was still legal to pay sperm donors. Kevin has heard a number of stories about half-siblings meeting and becoming romantically involved while unaware of their genetic connection. This is a common concern, as the monetary motivation has often led to a large number of samples being provided by the same man and consequently to a large number of offspring carrying his genetic material.

Kevin contacts his mother and asks for the name of the fertility clinic that she used so he can attempt to track his father; he asks Anna to do the same with the information she gets from her mother. However, Kevin fears that they will have a difficult time finding the information they need since many clinics did not keep adequate records, and some refuse to disclose the information on donors that they do have to protect the donor's anonymity.

(1) Does this scenario reveal problems regarding the practice of anonymous sperm donation? (2) Is there a connection between anonymity and multiple sperm "donation"? Would men make fewer "donations" if they were not paid? (3) Do children conceived through sperm or egg donation have any moral right to know who their genetic parent is?

Scenario Five

Tom Hacker was brought into the hospital with major injuries he sustained after being hit by a speeding driver who lost control of his car. Within hours, Tom slipped into a coma. Due to the seriousness of his injuries, his doctors do not believe that he will come out of the coma; his brain was severely damaged in the accident and it is doubtful that he will ever regain consciousness. Tom's parents, Peter and Jane, have requested that sperm be taken from their son and preserved so that they can find a surrogate to give birth to their grandchild. Tom was their only child, his parents tell the doctors, and if he does not reproduce, then the family line will die with him. Also, he is only 20, and they do not want to let him go. They believe that having a grandchild produced from his sperm would give him the chance to live on through another person. Tom did not give his consent to this procedure before he slipped into the coma, but his parents insist that this is what he would have wanted.

(1) Should the doctors agree to this request? (2) Whose decision is this to make? Do Tom's parents have the right to make this choice? (3) Could Kant, Mill, or Aristotle provide moral guidance to the doctors in this case? What might each say? (4) If we can take reproductive material from a brain-dead person without his or her consent, what might follow from this? (5) Do different ethical concerns arise when we consider this request from the perspective of a child conceived after its parent has died?

Scenario Six
Rosa and Tony Rodriguez had been married for 10 years before they divorced. Only two years into the marriage, Rosa developed thyroid cancer. She and Tony had several embryos frozen before she underwent chemotherapy so that they could still have children if and when she recovered. After she recovered, their relationship began to deteriorate, and they did not implant the embryos. After the divorce, however, Rosa requested the embryos so that she could have a child. As she can no longer conceive, this would be the only way for her to reproduce. Tony, however, wants the embryos destroyed. Although Rosa insists that she will have the embryos implanted only once she is in a relationship with a man willing to raise the child or children, and that she will not ask Tony for child support, Tony insists that he does not want to have a child born of their genetic material.

(1) What should be done with these embryos? Who do they belong to? Would it be permissible to destroy them? (2) Whose decision is this to make? (3) Should moral weight be placed on the fact that this is Rosa's only opportunity to have genetic offspring while Tony can still have genetic children with another partner? (4) Would Robertson be able to provide guidance in this case? Whose side might he take, and why? (5) What might Murray say? (6) What morally significant features of this situation might feminist ethics reveal that otherwise might remain hidden?

Scenario Seven
Baby Kristen was born to Melissa Walker, a gestational and genetic surrogate. Melissa works as a waitress at a café in the small town in which she grew up. She has three children with her husband, a mechanic. Between the two of them, Melissa and her husband can support the family comfortably, and although they would have to tighten their budget, they could afford to raise another child. Melissa was supposed to give up the baby to Sarah and David Allen, the couple who had signed a commercial surrogacy contract with her.

Although Sarah Allen is not infertile, she decided some time ago that, although she wanted to raise a child, she did not want to carry the baby herself. Carrying a child to term would require her to take some time off from her successful career as a corporate lawyer. She also does not want to risk her health by having eggs removed. She was happy to hire a surrogate because this allowed her to have a child without requiring her to go through a pregnancy. Although the child is not genetically related to her, she believes that since it has her husband's genetic material (something which is important to him) and they can provide a good upbringing, they will each have the child they desire. Once the baby moves in with them, Sarah and David plan to hire the best nanny they can find and will spend all their free time with the child. David works for a large commercial airline, and with the money they both earn and the discounts David gets on airfare, they believe that they can provide a good life to the child, one that includes trips to see the world and the best care that money can buy.

Melissa, however, now claims that she has become emotionally attached to the child. She believes the child should stay with her since she is both the genetic and the gestational mother. David and Sarah tell Melissa that she signed a contract and she therefore has no rights to the child. They also tell her that they will hire a lawyer to ensure that she lives up to her contractual obligations.

(1) To whom does this child belong? Does this question in itself raise ethical concerns? (2) What might Andrews say about this situation? How might Anderson respond to it? What problems might Raymond identify? (3) Should a contract like this have been permitted in the first place? Is there anything wrong with enforcing it? (4) Is the educational, social, and financial status of the two couples relevant to the decision about who should get the child? (5) Would it make any difference to an ethical analysis of the situation if Melissa were only the gestational surrogate and had been implanted with an embryo created from Sarah's egg and David's sperm?

Scenario Eight

Bairavi and Tamal Mehta are an Indo-Canadian couple living in Toronto. Bairavi was formerly married in her early twenties to Pranjal, an older man who died of heart failure when Bairavi was 35. Although they tried for many years, Bairavi and Pranjal never had children due to her ovulatory and his fertility problems. Bairavi, who is now 59 years old, has given up on the idea of having a child with her second husband because of her age. Bairavi's sister, Aasha, has recently suggested the possibility of her undergoing IVF treatment. Although clinics in Canada accept referrals of women from 45 to 50 years of age,[94] there is no upper age limit for IVF treatment in India.[95]

There have been numerous cases of women 60 years old and over giving birth as a result of IVF treatment offered in other countries. Upon learning about this possibility, Bairavi regains hope that she may be able to give birth. Although she and Tamal, her current husband, have not been able to conceive, she begins to think that she may be able to give him a child of his own using assisted reproductive technologies and his own sperm. Her physician in Toronto tells her that, if she were to undergo this procedure, she would need an egg donor. However, he informs her that he cannot write a referral for her to a clinic in Canada. She then requests a referral to a clinic in India. "It is my home country," she says. "I still have citizenship in India. And I've always wanted a family of my own, to be able to give children to my husband. I didn't think it was a possibility before." Bairavi further tells the physician that she felt like she was constantly disappointing her husband and their family by not being able to have children of her own. "Being a mother is so important," she tells him. "A woman should be a mother. That's what my parents always told me and my sister. I could finally fulfill my role." Her physician believes that Canada's regulations are medically responsible and has reservations about supporting her request. He is also aware that pregnancy and childbirth for women of advanced age are likely to result in complications for both mother and child that will be costly for the Canadian health care system.

(1) What advice might a utilitarian give the physician? Would a Kantian agree? (2) What features of this situation might a feminist approach focus on? (3) How should the physician respond to Bairavi's request?

GLOSSARY

Commodity: a term used to describe goods and services that can legitimately be bought and sold in the marketplace. Many of the things we value most, such as love and friendship, are not commodities, since they cannot be exchanged for money.

Gamete: a mature reproductive cell that can combine with another reproductive cell to produce an embryo. Gametes from males are called sperm, and gametes from females are called ova, or eggs.

Genetic parent: a person who has generated biological offspring.

Negative liberty: a term describing a concept drawn from political philosophy, which holds that individuals are free to the extent that their actions are not interfered with by other individuals or by the institutions of the state.

Procreative liberty: a term identifying an argument that draws on the concept of negative liberty to assert that individuals should be left free to make whatever reproductive choices seem best to them without the interference of others.

Surrogate mother: a woman who carries to term and gives birth to a child for someone else. Because assisted reproduction allows a woman to give birth to a child who is not genetically related to her, surrogate mothers are termed genetic and gestational mothers when the child is genetically their own, and gestational mothers when the child is the genetic offspring of another woman.

FOR FURTHER READING

Anderson, Elizabeth S. "Is Women's Labour a Commodity?" *Philosophy & Public Affairs*, 19, no. 1 (1990): 71–92.

Anderson addresses the issue of surrogate motherhood in this paper, and makes a Kantian argument against commercial surrogacy. This essay also presents a useful analysis of the concept of a commodity.

Cohen, Cynthia B. "'Give Me Children or I Shall Die!' New Reproductive Technologies and Harm to Children." *Hastings Center Report*, 26, no. 2 (March-April 1996): 19–27.

This essay explores the possibility that IVF might be harmful to children and presents an interesting critique of the procreative liberty argument.

Lauritzen, Paul. "What Price Parenthood?" *Hastings Center Report*, 20, no. 2 (March-April 1990): 38–46.

In this essay, Lauritzen connects his own experiences as a man struggling with infertility to the ethical issues raised by assisted reproduction. The experiences he describes illustrate the ethical dimensions of certain fertility treatments in an accessible and compelling way.

Macklin, Ruth. "Artificial Means of Reproduction and Understanding of the Family." *Hastings Center Report*, 21, no. 1 (January-February 1991): 5–11.

This paper explores some of the implications of assisted reproduction for our understanding of the concept of the family. Macklin argues that the concept of the family can be understood in multiple ways, and, consequently, before we make final judgments about the effect of assisted reproduction on the family, we should explore different possibilities carefully.

Raymond, Janice G. "Reproductive Gifts and Gift Giving: The Altruistic Woman." *Hastings Center Report*, 20, no. 6 (November-December 1990): 1–7.

Most arguments against surrogacy locate the moral concerns in the fact that the surrogate mother is paid for her services. This essay considers surrogate motherhood from a feminist perspective and makes the unusual case that surrogacy arrangements are morally problematic even if no money changes hands.

RECOMMENDED WEBSITES

Donor Sibling Registry
www.donorsiblingregistry.com

This website describes its mandate as consisting of "Educating, connecting, and supporting Donor Families." It was created by a mother and her "donor" son to help other mothers and their donor-conceived children to connect with genetic half-siblings and even genetic fathers. This website provides an interesting window into the world of third-party assisted reproduction.

The Egg Donor Program

www.eggdonation.com/

This American site claims that it is "known for representing the brightest, most beautiful and accomplished donors in the country." It helps connect egg donors with would-be parents, details the physical attributes of the donors, and gives information about the costs of buying donor eggs.

Genesis Fertility Centre

genesis-fertility.com/

This is the website of a Canadian fertility clinic. Genesis claims to be British Columbia's largest IVF centre, and it offers a number of treatment options, including egg and sperm donors and gestational surrogacy services. This site provides an example of the costs of these services in Canada.

The Infertility Network

www.infertilitynetwork.org/home

This website provides information and support for individuals struggling with infertility. It provides access to support groups and information about infertility services, media events, and seminars, as well as serving as a forum for political action and advocacy on infertility issues.

Repromed: The Toronto Institute for Reproductive Medicine

www.repromed.ca/sperm_bank_canada.html

This sperm bank describes itself as a "processor, distributor, importer and exporter of human semen for assisted reproduction," and this website provides an example of what is offered at a Canadian sperm bank. Sperm donors are listed in terms of the following categories: race, paternal and maternal ancestry, hair colour, eye colour, skin tone, height, weight, bone size, education/occupation, and interests.

Surrogate Mother.com

www.surrogatemother.com

This is a social network site for surrogate mothers and intended parents. A number of interesting accounts of the experience of working as a surrogate are accessible through this site.

Women's Bioethics Project

www.womensbioethics.org

The website of the women's Bioethics Project bills itself as "the leading nonprofit, nonpartisan public policy think tank dedicated to ensuring that women's voices, health concerns, and unique life experiences strongly influence ethical issues in health care and biotechnology." Reproductive technologies are of particular interest to participants.

NOTES

1. These adults include: John and Luanne Buzzanca, who hired a surrogate to gestate her; the surrogate and her husband, who agreed to the contract; the egg donor and her husband, who agreed that she should donate; and the sperm donor and his wife, for whom the embryo that became Jaycee was created but was then donated to John and Luanne Buzzanca. Additionally, given the technological expertise that went into her creation, the doctors at the fertility clinic could also be said to have had an important role in bringing her into existence.
2. This account draws on several sources, including a *48 Hours* documentary on the case; Rebecca Mead, "Eggs For Sale," *The New Yorker*, August 9, 1999; and Rick Weiss, "Babies in Limbo: Laws Outpaced by Fertility Advances," *The Washington Post*, February 8, 1998, found at www.washingtonpost.com/wp-srv/national/science/ethical/fertility1.htm (July 23, 2010).

3. Patricia Smith, "The Metamorphosis of Motherhood," in Joan C. Callahan (ed.), *Reproduction, Ethics, and the Law: Feminist Perspectives* (Bloomington: Indiana University Press, 1995), 110.

4. Paul Lauritzen, *Pursuing Parenthood: Ethical Issues in Assisted Reproduction* (Bloomington, IN: Indiana University Press, 1993), ix.

5. Peggy Orenstein, *Waiting for Daisy* (New York: Bloomsbury, 2007), 18.

6. Lauritzen, ix.

7. Thomas H. Murray, *The Worth of a Child* (Berkeley, CA: University of California Press, 1996), 14.

8. Murray, 14.

9. Ronald Munson, *Intervention and Reflection: Basic Issues in Medical Ethics, 7th ed.* (Belmont, CA: Thomson Wadsworth, 2004), 372.

10. David Plotz, *The Genius Factory: The Curious History of the Nobel Sperm Bank* (New York: Random House, 2005), 175.

11. Jim Hopkins, "Egg-donor Business Booms on Campuses," *USA Today*, March 16, 2006, found at www.usatoday.com/money/industries/health/2006-03-15-egg-donors-usat_x.htm (October 6, 2009).

12. Hopkins, n.p.

13. Plotz, 159.

14. Plotz, 159.

15. Genesis Fertility Centre, found at www.genesis-fertility.com/general-information/fees (October 7, 2009).

16. Joan Haase, "Canada: The Long Road to Regulation," in Eric Blyth and Ruth Landau (eds.), *Third Party Assisted Reproduction Across Cultures* (London: Jessica Kingley Publishers, 2004), 56.

17. Haase, 65.

18. "Reproductive Technologies: Royal Commission Final Report," found at dsp-psd.pwgsc.gc.ca/Collection-R/ (July 27, 2009).

19. Callahan, 29.

20. Lauritzen, 19–20.

21. Ruth Landau, "Israel: Every Person Has the Right to Have Children," in Blyth and Landau, 129.

22. Landau, 131.

23. Earnest Ng et al., "Hong Kong: A Social, Legal, and Clinical Overview," in Blythe and Landau, 115.

24. Natalie Alcoba, "Making Baby Wait," *National Post*, July 3, 2009, found at www.nationalpost.com/m/story.html?id=175 7954 (October 6, 2009).

25. Mead, 64.

26. John A. Robertson, *Children of Choice: Freedom and the New Reproductive Technologies* (Princeton, NJ: Princeton University Press, 1994), 24.

27. Isaish Berlin, "Two Concepts of Liberty," in Michael Sandel (ed.), *Liberalism and Its Critics* (New York: New York University Press, 1987), 15–17.

28. Robertson, 24.

29. Gregory E. Pence, *Who's Afraid of Human Cloning?* (Lanham, MD: Rowman & Littlefield Publishers, 1998), 100.

30. Pence, 62.

31. Pence, 28.

32. Robertson, quoted in Cynthia B. Cohen, "'Give Me Children or I Shall Die!' New Reproductive Technologies and Harm to Children," in Munson, 406.

33. Robertson, quoted in Cohen, 407.

34. Cohen, 407.

35. Murray, 15–16.

36. Murray, 33.

37. Barbara J. Berg, "Listening to the Voices of the Infertile," in Callahan, 94–95.

38. Lauritzen, 83.

39. Orenstein, 59–60.

40. Roger Gosden, *Designing Babies: The Brave New World of Reproductive Technology* (London: W.H. Freeman & Company, 2000), 42.

41. Cohen, 405.

42. Cohen, 405.

43. Carol Bower, "IVF Defects," found at www.abc.net.au/catlyst/stories/s904186.htm (October 6, 2009).

44. Cohen, 406.

45. Andre Picard, "Reproduction Watchdog Overdue for Delivery," *The Globe and Mail*, April 20, 2009.

46. Kenneth D. Alpern, "Genetic Puzzles and Stork Stories: On the Meaning and Significance of Having Children," in Kenneth D. Alpern (ed.), *The Ethics of Reproductive Technology* (Oxford: Oxford University Press, 1992), 160.

47. Plotz, 127–128.

48. Lauritzen, 86.

49. Margaret C. Brown, "Whose Eyes Are These, Whose Nose?" *Newsweek*, March 7, 1994, 12.

50. Brown, 12.

51. Plotz, 57.

52. Murray, 17–18.

53. Mead, 62.

54. Plotz, 181.

55. Mead, 63.

56. Plotz, 155.

57. Mead, 60.

58. Susan Sherwin, *No Longer Patient: Feminist Ethics & Health Care* (Philadelphia: Temple University Press, 1992), 129.

59. Lori B. Andrews, "Surrogate Motherhood and the Challenge For Feminists," in Walter Glannon (ed.), *Contemporary Readings in Biomedical Ethics* (Fort Worth, TX: Harcourt College Publishers, 2002), 184.

60. Andrews, 185.

61. Andrews, 186.

62. Andrews, 187.

63. Andrews, 187.

64. Andrews, 191.

65. Andrews, 193.

66. Elizabeth S. Anderson, "Is Women's Labor a Commodity?" in Tom L. Beauchamp and Le Roy Walters (eds.), *Contemporary Issues in Bioethics*, 2nd ed. (Belmont, CA: Wadsworth Publishing, 1999), 656.

67. Anderson, 656–657.

68. Anderson, 659.

69. Anderson, 664.

70. Janice C. Raymond, "Reproductive Gifts and Gift Giving: The Altruistic Women," in Joseph H. Howell and William Frederick Sale (eds.), *Life Choices: A Hastings Center Introduction to Bioethics* (Washington, DC: Georgetown University Press, 1995), 306.

71. Raymond, 311.

72. Raymond, 312.

73. While "reproductive tourism" is a term that is commonly used to describe the purchase of reproductive services in foreign countries, the term itself, Bassan and Michaelsen argue, is ethically loaded and obscures the fact that those who make use of such services view themselves not as "tourists" but rather as "patients." They suggest that a phrase such as "cross-border reproductive care" is simultaneously adequately descriptive and morally neutral. In this section, therefore, we will use this, or similar, terms to avoid the ethical connotations generated by "reproductive tourism." See Sharon Bassan and Merle A. Michaelsen, "Honeymoon, Medical Treatment, or Big Business? An Analysis of the Meaning of the Term 'Reproductive Tourism' in German and Israeli Public Media Discourse," *Philosophy, Ethics, and Humanities in Medicine, 8, no. 9* (2013), found at www.peh-med.com/content/8/1/9 (October 12, 2014).

74. Raywat Deonandan, "Does Reproductive Tourism Treat Women Like Cattle?" *Huffington Post*, October 29, 2012, found at www.huffingtonpost.ca/dr-raywat-deonandan/reproductive-tourism_b_2039343.html (March 17, 2014). See also Raywat Deonandan, Samantha Green, and Amanda van Beinum, "Ethical Conerns for Material Surrogacy and Reproductive Tourism," *Journal of Medical Ethics*, 38 (2012): 742–745.

75. Deonandan, n.p.

76. Information about this case is taken from Kari Points, "Commercial Surrogacy and Fertility Tourism in India: The Case of Baby Manji," Case Studies in Ethics, The Kenan Institute for Ethics and Duke University, found at kenan.ethics.duke.edu/wp-content/uploads/2012/07/Case-Study-Surrogacy.pdf (March 20, 2014); Viveka Roychowdury, "The Curious Case of Baby Manji," *Express Healthcare* [India], December 2011, found at healthcare.financialexpress.com/201112/editorial01.shtml (March 20, 2014); and Jwala D. Thapa, "The 'Babies M': The Relevance of *Baby Manji Yamada v. Union of India (UOI)* and *In the Matter of Baby "M","* *Journal of Indian Law and Society*, 2 (Winter 2011): 83–112, found at jils.ac.in/wp-content/uploads/2011/12/5_Jwala-Thapa_new-style_completed1.pdf.

77. Jennifer A. Parks, "Care Ethics and the Global Practice of Commercial Surrogacy," *Bioethics*, 24, no. 7 (2010): 334.

78. Parks, 334.

79. Anne Donchin, "Reproductive Tourism and the Quest For Global Gender Justice," *Bioethics*, 24, no. 7 (2010): 325.

80. Donchin, 326–327.

81. Deonandan, n.p.

82. Deonandan, n.p.

83. Robertson, 126.

84. Morton Winston, "Children of Invention," in Morton Winston and Ralph Edelbach (eds.), *Society, Ethics, and Technology*, 2nd ed. (Belmont, CA: Thomson Wadsworth, 2003), 1.

85. Neil Postman, *Technopoly: The Surrender of Culture to Technology* (New York: Vintage Books, 1992), 18.

86. Postman, 18.

87. Winston, 2–4.

88. Hans Jonas, "Technology and Responsibility: Reflections on the New Task of Ethics," in *Philosophical Essays: From Ancient Creed to Technological Man* (Englewood Cliffs, NJ: Prentice Hall, 1974), 14.

89. Jonas, 15.

90. Jonas, 16.

91. Clyde Haberman, "Baby M and The Question of Surrogate Motherhood," *The New York Times*, March 23, 2014; "Baby M, in Re," *The Free Dictionary*, found at http://legal-dictionary.thefreedictionary.com/Baby+M,+in+Re (November 26, 2014); and *In the Matter of Baby M*, 109 N.J. 396, 537 A.2d 1227, 1988 N.J.77 A.L.R.4th 1.

92. James Keller, "Olivia Pratten Sperm Donor Case Won't Be Heart by Supreme Court," *Huffpost British Columbia*, July 30, 2013, found at www.huffingtonpost.ca/2013/05/30/olivia-pratten-sperm-case-supreme-court_n_3359567.html (January 16, 2014); *Pratten v. British Columbia* (Attorney General) 2011 BSCS 656; and *Pratten v. British Columbia* (Attorney General) et al. (CA 039124; 2012 BCCA 480).

93. Sandra Blakeslee, "New Issue In Embryo Case Raised Over Use of Donor," *The New York Times*, June 21, 1984; Bernard M. Dicksn and Rebecca J. Cook, "The Legal Status of In Vitro Embryos," *International Journal of Gynecology and Obstetrics*, 111 (2010): 91–94; and Karin Mika and Bonnie Hurst, "One Way to Be Born? Legislative Inaction and the Posthumous Child," *Marquette Law Review*, 79, issue 4 (Summer 1996): 993–1019.

94. For example, Regional Fertility Program, found at www.regionalfertilityprogram.ca/faq-ivf.php (October 12, 2014); and McGill Reproductive Center, found at www.mcgillivf.com/home.html (October 12, 2014).

95. Emily Wax, "In India, Age Often Doesn't Stop Women from Seeking Help to Become pregnant," *The Washington Post*, August 13, 2010, found at www.washingtonpost.com/wp-dyn/content/article/2010/08/12/AR2010081206876.html (October 12, 2014).

Chapter 6

THE GENETIC REVOLUTION

LANDMARK CASE: NANCY WEXLER

One of the most terrible genetic diseases that someone can inherit is Huntington's disease (HD), which causes those afflicted to suffer a torturous and lingering death. Over the course of 15 to 25 years, the afflicted person will gradually decline, first suffering from a deterioration of the intellectual capacities, then jerking of the limbs, followed by depression, hallucinations, delusions, and, finally, a complete inability to function physically and mentally. The HD gene, moreover, is a dominant **gene**, which means that one copy of the defective gene is all that is needed to produce the disease. In addition, if someone has the gene, it is inevitable that he or she will, at some point in life, get the disease. Ridley names this gene "fate": "The cause [of HD] is in the genes and nowhere else. Either you have the Huntington's mutation and will get the disease, or not ... the genes are in charge and ... there is nothing we can do about it. It does not matter if you smoke, or take vitamin pills, if you work out or become a couch potato."[1] There is no treatment or cure for the disease.

Nancy and Alice Wexler watched their mother die of Huntington's disease. Their father, Milton, started the Hereditary Disease Foundation in 1968, and in the same year, Nancy entered a doctoral program in clinical psychology. She made it her life's work to identify the gene for Huntington's. She had several reasons for her pursuit of the gene. First, she believed that if the gene were discovered, people at risk could be tested before the disease began to manifest itself (the range of onset is usually from the mid-twenties to the mid-seventies). This would, she believed, allow them to take charge of their lives, rather than worrying about whether they were afflicted or not. She has said that there's not one day in which she has not thought about HD: "You become aware of all kinds of things you never noticed before—little muscle jerks in bed, or clumsiness. I remember dropping a carton of eggs and thinking 'Oh, no! Is this the beginning?'"[2] Anything, she believed, even knowing that she had the gene, would be better than uncertainty. Second, a test for the gene would be helpful in preventing its transmission to future generations. Since the first signs of the disease don't usually appear until adulthood (and sometimes late in life) most people with the gene reproduced before they knew that they had it. A test would allow them to know their genetic status before they had children.

Given the length of the genome, finding the HD gene was no easy task—akin to identifying 1 word in 60,000 to 80,000. In order to narrow the possibilities, Wexler needed to find a large number of people who were afflicted with the disease, or at risk, so that their genes could be compared with the genes of those who were not affected. She found just such a large group in Venezuela, whose members shared a common ancestor. She and her team created a family tree of almost 10,000 people and began taking blood samples. In 1983, a marker for HD was found, and in 1987, a linkage test was developed. Finally, in 1993, the gene itself was identified, and a test for it is now available.

Interestingly, despite Wexler's certainty that she would take the test once it was developed, as of this writing, she has not—and only a fraction of those who are at risk have done so.[3] It is one thing to know that you *might* get a disease, and another to know, in advance of its onset, that you *will* get it. Wexler now has become an advocate for the choice "not to know now," and is disturbed by the attitude of some physicians and journalists that those who take the test are braver and more worthy than those who don't.[4] Science, she believes, is in the position of Tiresias, the seer of Thebes who was struck blind by the goddess Athena after he saw her bathing. She felt sorry for what she had done, and, since she was unable to give him back his sight, gave him the power to see the future. Ridley writes: "But seeing the future was a terrible fate, since he could see it but not change it. 'It is but sorrow,' said Tiresias to Oedipus, 'to be wise when wisdom profits not.' Or as Wexler puts it, 'Do you want to know when you are going to die, especially if you have no power to change the outcome?'"[5]

INTRODUCTION

The human **genome** is an autobiography of the human species. It contains genes that go back to the very dawn of life on earth, genes that are shared with other living creatures (including ones very different from us, such as seaweed, bacteria, and yeast). It contains the history of human development and a record of patterns of migration. And it provides the recipe for traits that will be passed on to future generations.

Like a book, the genome is composed of chapters, sections, words, and letters. Ridley describes it in this way: "There are twenty-three chapters, called CHROMOSOMES. Each chapter contains several thousand stories, called GENES. Each story is made up of paragraphs, called EXONS, which are interrupted by advertisements called INTRONS. Each paragraph is made up of words, called CODONS. Each word is written in letters, called BASES."[6]

The genome is as long as 800 Bibles. It contains one billion words, but it all fits within the nucleus of a cell. It is a very smart book; it has the ability to photocopy itself (replication) and read itself (translation). However, sometimes in the process of replication, mistakes are made: letters are left out, or wrong ones inserted. These mistakes are known as mutations, and most are harmless. However, a small number cause terrible diseases, which can be passed on to offspring.

While it is likely that we all have mutations in our genetic code, most of us are **heterozygous** for the mutation: because we receive genes from both parents that pair up at conception, these pairs are usually dissimilar. This means that unless the defective gene is **dominant**, it will not be expressed in the form of genetic disease, although that person may be a **carrier** who can pass the gene on to offspring. If two people who are carriers for the same defective gene have a child together, and each passes the defective copy on, the child will be **homozygous** and will have the disease or trait.

The genetic revolution is perhaps the most significant revolution in human history: unlike previous revolutions, which reorganized political structures (as the French, American, and Russian revolutions did), or altered the shape of the material and intellectual world (as the industrial and computer revolutions did), the genetic revolution has the potential to transform humanity. Along with the knowledge of our genes, "we have gained the power to control the destiny of our species."[7] The genetic revolution has this transformative potential because it brings together two different scientific disciplines, reproductive biology (and the reproductive technologies developed in this area) and genetics. Together, these form a new field, **reprogenetics**, which will give us the ability to shape the characteristics of our offspring. Apart from scientific curiosity, the main motivation behind developments in reprogenetics is to reduce human suffering: once we identify the genes that are causal or contributing factors in the development of disease, we may be able to find ways to treat or prevent it.

With knowledge, however, comes choice, and with choice comes moral responsibility. The revolution is so recent (our ability to find the location and function of particular genes has developed only over the last several decades, and there is still much that we do not know) that it is not always clear how we should use our knowledge. Furthermore, the genetic revolution is overshadowed by our eugenic past: by attempts in the 20th century to improve the human race, which led to violations of human rights and culminated in the atrocities committed by the Nazis.[8] This is where the ethical issues lie: increased understanding of how our genes work does not tell us how this knowledge should be used. For example, in the past, when a woman was pregnant, all she could do to try to ensure a healthy baby was hope, pray, cut out alcohol and cigarettes, and eat nutritious food. Now that a fetus can be genetically tested prenatally, however, she has other options and must make some hard decisions. Should she have the fetus tested, and for what conditions? If she decides not to, and her baby is afflicted with a genetic defect, is she responsible in a way that she wouldn't have been before a test was available? If she is tested, and the test reveals a fetal abnormality, she may have only two choices—to give birth to a handicapped child or to have an abortion: which is the morally responsible choice?

In addition, the genetic revolution not only gives us the potential power to eliminate certain diseases, it also raises the possibility that we might be able to enhance the genetic potential of our offspring and descendants. Genes thought to be associated with intelligence, height, sexual orientation, and even mood[9] have been identified. If we can shape our offspring by inserting genes associated with valued traits while deleting those associated with negative ones, should we? Would we be harming those who come after us if we make these changes? Would we be harming them if we refuse to give them valuable traits? If the ethical questions raised by identifying and treating genetic disease are difficult to answer, the issues raised by enhancement are even more challenging. They go beyond the usual parameters of medicine, which encompass the treatment or cure of existing persons, into interventions that "predate the existence of any individual who might be identified as a patient."[10]

It would be useful if we could find some objective, disease-based criterion that would help us make decisions; however, any attempt to find such guidelines quickly reveals itself to be a failure, as subject to moral judgments as the decisions it was meant to help facilitate. Glannon, for instance, suggests four criteria to determine which conditions we should test embryos for so that we can choose which to implant and which to use in research. His criteria include: "(1) [t]he probability of genotype penetrance, or how likely it is that a genetic mutation will cause a disease; (2) [t]he severity of the symptoms of the disease; (3) [t]he time of onset of the symptoms; and (4) [t]he time between onset and death."[11]

However, the mapping of the human genome (completed in 2003) has revealed that things are much more complex than geneticists (and ethicists) had initially hoped: the Huntington's case, in which penetrance is 100 percent (if someone has the gene, he will get the disease), turns out to be the exception, not the rule. Some genetic diseases require the interaction of more than one gene; some genes do not lead to disease in all those who possess them; and some genes may require environmental inputs to do their worst. Moreover, the social context in which genes are expressed can have an effect on how debilitating the resulting conditions are: a gene that causes people to put on weight easily may lead to obesity in a society with material abundance, but be very useful in a society with frequent food shortages. Even Glannon's fourth criterion, upon examination, is less helpful than it first appears. Consider Huntington's again, in which the period between the first symptoms and death may be as long as 25 years. Is this a good thing, because it means that someone with the gene can live many years, or is it one of the worst features of the disease, since this long period simply prolongs their suffering? The central, unavoidable, and recurring questions raised by genetic knowledge are: What should we test or screen for, and on what basis should we make this decision? If we gain enough knowledge to shape our offspring, should we? Who decides whether genetic screening is done? Who decides what is done with the information? And, what is—or should be—the social context within which these decisions are made? Should society regulate the extent to which people can use enhancement technologies, or should these choices be left to individuals?

Since the revolution is so recent, we don't know where it might take us; consequently, many of the ethical concerns are speculative and future-oriented, and concerned with what might happen, what is likely to happen, and what possible futures we want to avoid. We have the power to shape the future, but we need to use this power wisely: the challenge is to determine what "wisely" means when considering possibilities that have not yet occurred, that may never happen, and about which no ethical consensus has yet been reached.

CONFLICTING VISIONS OF THE FUTURE

Speculations about where the genetic revolution might take us conflict with one another. Some (whom we might term optimists) see a future free from genetic disease, in which we have the power to eliminate the conditions that cause profound suffering and can enhance human capabilities. Silver, for instance, imagines a future in which genetic enhancement will allow humans to colonize space.

> In the twenty-first century, overcrowding on earth had reduced the quality of life so much that many ... parents decided to give their children special gifts to help them survive on worlds that were inhospitable to the unenhanced.... [Genetic] engineers had achieved human symbiosis with plants through the successful incorporation of photosynthetic units into embryos. Not only could symbiotic humans receive energy directly from the sun, but they were now able to self-produce some of their own oxygen and water and carbon monoxide, just like plants.[12]

While the future may unfold differently than Silver imagines, Baylis and Robert suggest that the use of genetic enhancement technologies is inevitable; humans are competitive, and we cannot resist shaping the future if we have the power to do so.[13] If they are correct, we cannot simply reject genetic enhancements; rather, we must ask, instead, which enhancements we should seek and which we should refuse.

BOX 6.1

RECREATING EXTINCT SPECIES

One of the most astounding features of the genetic revolution is that it is transforming ideas that were the stuff of science fiction into reality. In *Jurassic Park*, Michael Crichton imagined InGen, a company that cloned dinosaurs:

> What they have done ... is build the biggest tourist attraction in the history of the world. As you know, zoos are extremely popular. Last year more Americans visited zoos than all professional baseball and football games combined ... [a]nd for this zoo, InGen can charge whatever they want. Two thousand dollars a day, ten thousand dollars a day.... And then there is the *merchandising.* The picture books, T-shirts, video games, caps, stuffed toys, comic books and pets.... If InGen can make full-size dinosaurs, they can also make pygmy dinosaurs as household pets. What child wouldn't want a little dinosaur as a pet? A little patented animal for their very own. InGen will sell millions of them. And InGen will engineer them so that these pet dinosaurs can only eat InGen pet food....[1]

This brief excerpt, while entirely fictional, captures both the amazing power of the genetic revolution and the motivations and context that make its use appealing. Moreover, real-world developments indicate the almost unimaginable possibilities unleashed by the genetic revolution. First, on June 16, 1980, "the Supreme Court in the United States ruled that a living microorganism was a patentable matter,"[2] a decision that made possible commercial applications of genetic technology such as the pet dinosaurs envisaged by Crichton. Many of the subsequent developments in genetics have been driven by the profit motive as much as they have by the values of science and medicine.

Second, rapid improvements in DNA sequencing machines have made it possible to decode ancient DNA; *The New York Times* reported in 2008 that "[s]cientists are talking for the first time about the old idea of resurrecting extinct species as if this staple of science fiction is a realistic possibility."[3] The same article states that a woolly mammoth could be recreated for about $10 million. There are also projects underway to recreate more recently extinct animals, including the burcado, and the Tasmanian tiger.[4] Even more significantly, scientists are talking about sequencing the Neanderthal genome, and then reconstructing this extinct human species; one molecular geneticist thinks that the process would not be too difficult. He would "start with the human genome, which is highly similar to that of Neanderthals, and change the few DNA units required to convert it into the Neanderthal version."[5] Using cloning techniques, the Neanderthal genome could then be inserted into a human or chimpanzee egg, and implanted in a human or chimpanzee surrogate mother.

Kaebnick states that he finds "the idea of meeting a live Neanderthal ... fascinating.... Think what we could learn. Could they speak? Could they learn a language?"[6] And using chimpanzees as egg donors and surrogate mothers seems to raise fewer ethical issues than using human ones, since we experiment on chimpanzees all the time. Nonetheless, while he is unable to come up with a decisive argument against recreating a Neanderthal, Kaebnick finds the prospect morally troubling: a Neanderthal would be human, but not a type of human that we are familiar with, which means that none of the ethical principles we currently use to judge our treatment of animals or humans seems to apply. On the one hand, Neanderthals would not be like other animals—"we'd have to care about ... [them], and we couldn't kill them afterwards ... maybe they'd integrate into modern urban life. Or maybe they'd be permanently unhappy, no matter where we put them up."[7] On the other hand, they wouldn't be like designer babies, either; how would a concept such as "the right to an open future" apply to them? "The concept of an open future might be unique to *Homo sapiens sapiens*—it might even be unique to very modern members of our subspecies. And what would we say about the future of a newly created Neanderthal? In some ways, it might seem closed; in some ways it might seem wide open—particularly compared to every other Neanderthal who ever lived."[8] Given that the current principles of bioethics seem unable to help us here, however intriguing the possibility of meeting a Neanderthal might be, Kaebnick thinks it would be unwise to attempt such a resurrection: "[W]e don't know enough to do it right."[9]

Why would we want to do this?

Notes

1. Michael Crichton, *Jurassic Park* (New York: Ballantine Books, 1990), 67.
2. Leon Kass, "Patenting Life," *Commentary*, 72, no. 6 (December 1981): 45.
3. Nicholas Wade, "Regenerating a Mammoth for $10 Million," *The New York Times*, November 19, 2008, found at www.nytimes.com/2008/11/20/science/20mammoth.html (September 17, 2009).
4. Wayne Grady, *Bringing Back the Dodo: Lessons in Natural and Unnatural History* (Toronto: McClelland & Stewart, 2006), 164–165.
5. Gregory E. Kaebnick, "Designing Baby Neanderthals," *Science Progress*, March 10, 2009, found at www.scienceprogress.org/2009/03/designing-baby-neanderthals/ (September 17, 2009), 1.
6. Kaebnick, 1.
7. Kaebnick, 2.
8. Kaebnick, 3.
9. Kaebnick, 3.

A second perspective frames the genetic revolution in terms of more modest, personal goals: knowledge of the human genome will empower individuals in their own lives. This knowledge will provide choice and allow people to have healthy children. Gosden captures this intermediate perspective when he asks, "Why shouldn't all parents be able to count on having a baby who gets off to an excellent start in life, free of inherited disabilities and with full assurance of health and longevity?"[14] Proponents of this position typically focus on possible therapies for genetic diseases and place genetic discoveries within the domain of medicine.

Finally, there are pessimists, who agree with the optimists that the genetic revolution will take us beyond natural limitations, but imagine a very different future. They see a world in which pregnant women feel coerced into taking prenatal tests and into selectively aborting those fetuses that "fail" them;[15] a world in which employers require would-be employees to be genetically screened before they are hired, so that their susceptibilities to environmental conditions within the workplace can be determined; and a world that is profoundly unjust, in which the genetically lucky (who can access therapies and technologies) possess wealth and power while the genetically "unfit" cannot get jobs, life insurance, or marriage partners. For the pessimists, whatever the purported benefits of the genetic revolution, there is something unsettling about the kind of control it offers. Kass, for example, states that "the price to be paid for producing optimum or even genetically sound babies will be the transfer of procreation from the home to the laboratory. Increasing control over the product can only be purchased by the increasing depersonalization of the entire process and its coincident transformation into manufacture. Such an arrangement will be profoundly dehumanizing."[16]

We are, Kitcher suggests, faced with kaleidoscopic images of possible futures:

> We sense that the ... revolution will make large differences—how large, we do not know—in the lives our children will lead, we sense that we have the power now to channel the impact the new biology will have on society, but the kaleidoscope shifts too quickly. We do not know how to stop it, how to bring these images into focus, how to decide which of them represents something for which we should genuinely hope or of which we have reason to be afraid.[17]

We will sort through these images in this chapter as we examine pre-symptomatic testing, selective abortion, pre-implantation testing, cloning, and genetic engineering (therapeutic and enhancement). The challenge facing us, individually and socially, is to maximize the beneficial potential of the revolution while minimizing the potential for abuse. This task is complicated by our inability to find value-neutral criteria on which to base our choices. We cannot find some uncontroversial definition of disease or normal functioning that will tell us which fetuses should be aborted and which shouldn't, or some objective description of the qualities that make a life worth living that will tell us in some decisive way which embryos should be implanted and which used for experiments. We cannot find any objective account of what the fundamental characteristics of a human being are in order to determine which enhancements make better people and which move us into a non-human future.[18] Rather, any judgments will unavoidably be moral judgments, not simply medical or scientific ones, and we need to keep in mind that they may be influenced by ignorance, prejudices, and social and political beliefs and commitments.

BOX 6.2

NICHOLAS AGAR, "TWO KINDS OF EUGENICS"

Human cloning and the genetic engineering of human embryos are technologies of the future. But the idea of human improvement has a past.... Those whose vision of human enhancement emphasizes individual choice tend to avoid the term "eugenics." They want a language that clearly distinguishes them from the Nazis. But this smacks of Orwellian redefinition.... Anyone advocating such a programme must demonstrate an awareness of the errors of the past....

Hitler showed us exactly where eugenics in pursuit of a racial ideal could lead us. However, I ... argue that switching attention from races and classes of humans to individuals provides a version of eugenics worthy of defence. We would be rejecting *authoritarian eugenics*, the idea that the state should have sole responsibility for determining what counts as a good human life, in favour of what I will call *liberal eugenics*. On the liberal approach to human improvement, the state would not presume to make any eugenic choices. Rather it would foster the development of a wide range of technologies of enhancement ensuring that prospective parents were fully informed about what kinds of people these technologies would make. Parents' particular conceptions of the good life would guide them in their selection of enhancements for their children.

The freedoms that define liberal eugenics will be defended in the same fashion as other liberal freedoms. Liberal societies are founded on the insight that there are many different, often incompatible ideas about the good life. Some seek huge wealth, others enlightenment; some devote themselves to their families, others to their careers; some commit to political causes, others to football teams; some worship God(s), others would rather go fishing. And this is only to begin to describe the variation in the kinds of lives that people choose for themselves. Living well in a liberal society involves acknowledging the right of others to make choices that do not appeal to us. John Robertson defends a procreative liberty, which he understands as individuals' freedom to decide whether or not they will become parents and to exercise control over their reproductive capacities. His arguments are motivated by the recognition that one of the most significant choices that people make about their lives concerns whether or not, with whom, when, and how often they reproduce. We have invented a range of technologies to assist us in making these choices. Contraceptive technologies help those who want sex without reproduction. Infertility treatments help those who want reproduction but cannot use sex to achieve it. Genetic technologies currently being developed may give us the power to choose some of the characteristics of our children. Nazi eugenicists would have used these technologies to dramatically curtail reproductive choice. Only a narrow range of human beings would have been deemed worthy of cloning; genetic engineering would have been imposed on couples whose reproductive efforts were deemed incapable of producing children sufficiently close to the Nazi ideal. But liberal eugenicists propose that these same technologies be used to dramatically enlarge reproductive choice. Prospective parents may ask genetic engineers to introduce into their embryos combinations of genes that correspond with their particular conceptions of good life. Yet they will acknowledge the right of their fellow citizens to make completely different eugenic choices. No one will be forced to clone themselves or to genetically engineer their embryos.

Source: Nicholas Agar, *Liberal Eugenics: In Defence of Human Enhancement* (Oxford: Blackwell Publishing, 2004), 3–6.

Eugenics: Past and Future

Given the complexity of the challenge before us, many argue that we must remember the eugenicists of the past and the mirror they hold up to us: we can see that their science was inadequate, their methods inhumane, and their judgments coloured by the assumptions of their time and place. However, we must ask ourselves the extent to which we are better placed to make sound judgments and whether our usage of this new knowledge is also eugenic—and, if so, whether this makes contemporary uses of genetic knowledge morally problematic.[19]

Some commentators try to sidestep this last question. Pence, for instance, believes that "eugenics" is such a loaded term that it has little value when considering the implications of genetic screening tests.[20] However, in recent discussions about enhancements, it is not only those critical of attempts to alter the human genome who use the term "eugenics" but defenders of such manipulation as well.[21] Agar, for example, who endorses enhancement, argues that the past cannot be ignored and that an avoidance of the term "eugenics" when referring to altering the genetic makeup of individuals "smacks of Orwellian redefinition."[22] To acknowledge that "eugenics" is a loaded term, in his view, does not mean that it is an inappropriate term to use.

It is the free choices of many individuals that will almost certainly shape the course of the genetic revolution. Given the role autonomy plays in modern self-understandings and contemporary bioethics, any limitations on the free choices of individuals is difficult to justify—even when those choices will determine the sorts of people who are reproduced. It is the element of free choice that many bioethicists believe distinguishes morally unacceptable eugenics from morally acceptable attempts to shape human beings. Agar asserts that what was wrong with the eugenics of the past was its authoritarian nature: the fact that it was forced on individuals by the state and was intended to produce a particular type of human by weeding out those deemed inferior. He presents arguments in support of what he terms "liberal eugenics," in which the role of the state is to encourage the development of a wide range of genetic possibilities that parents could choose to employ in accordance with their own particular conceptions of the good life.[23] Harris, likewise, argues that democratic societies must allow individuals to make their own choices with respect to genetic technologies.[24] This adds additional complexity to our considerations: can we both respect autonomy and place limits on how genetic knowledge is applied?

Kitcher argues that we cannot escape the spectre of eugenics, however distressing the term, when we consider the freely made choices of individuals, because eugenics is simply the attempt to affect the kind of people who will be born: "[E]ugenics responds to our conviction that it is irresponsible not to do what can be done to prevent deep human suffering, yet it must face the challenge of showing that its claims about the value of lives are not the arrogant judgments of an elite group."[25] The challenge is to ensure that the judgments we make are sound, and that the practices that follow from these judgments are beneficial in intention and morally defensible in application. First and foremost, autonomy requires that individuals not be coerced into using genetic knowledge in particular ways.

Laissez-faire Eugenics

Kitcher distinguishes two varieties of voluntary eugenics. The first form is laissez-faire eugenics, which means letting individuals do as they see fit for whatever reasons they think relevant: deciding what to test for, when, and what follows from the results.[26] Silver points to the power of this form of eugenics when he observes that "in a society which values freedom above all else, it is hard to find any legitimate basis for restricting the use of reprogenetics in any way."[27] He consequently envisages a future in which the free choices of individuals to shape the genetic makeup of their offspring leads to profound changes in the human race. While laissez-faire eugenics initially appears attractive,

Kitcher argues that it loses much of its appeal upon closer examination. It requires no standards besides the most subjective on which these decisions might be based, it ignores the social context within which judgments are made, and it provides no guidelines that would help individuals make choices. If we endorse this kind of eugenics, he believes, it is difficult to raise objections if, for instance, people use prenatal testing and selective abortion for the purposes of sex selection or, in the future, to get rid of fetuses with a genetic propensity for obesity, brown eyes, or mediocre athletic ability. It does not help a woman decide which conditions to screen for prenatally or what to do with the results; and it ignores the need to have a public and informed discussion of the practices society should and should not support. Paradoxically, without such a discussion, the free choices of individuals may generate a situation that is coercive. Imagine, for instance, that many people freely choose to enhance their children's intelligence, and that IQs that now make someone exceptional become average. In such a context, those who might not have freely chosen such an enhancement will feel that they are handicapping their children if they don't do so. As Baylis and Robert put it, "If the context includes the widespread use of a particular enhancement technology, personal freedom may be seriously threatened as people feel obliged to avail themselves of the technology."[28]

Utopian Eugenics

Kitcher suggests, instead, that we should strive for utopian eugenics: freely made reproductive and personal genetic choices informed by an educated analysis of the conditions that should be tested for, why, under what social conditions, and what should be done with the results. Utopian eugenics tries to balance individual freedom, scientific knowledge, and social context; for instance, a society that embraced utopian eugenics would ensure that genetic tests would be available to all who desire them. In addition, while "there would be widespread public discussion of values and of the social consequences of individual decisions, there would be no societally imposed restrictions on reproductive choices—citizens would be educated but not coerced. Finally, there would be universally shared respect for differences coupled with a public commitment to realizing the potential of all those who are born."[29] Anyone who argues both that individual autonomy must be respected and that, nonetheless, some morally legitimate limits may be placed on the uses of reprogenetics can be considered a utopian eugenicist. Consequently, there is no one utopian eugenicist account but, rather, competing conceptions about where lines should be drawn between acceptable and unacceptable uses of genetic technology.

PRE-SYMPTOMATIC TESTING AND THE KNOWLEDGE OF TIRESIAS

Genetic diseases result from the particular combination of genes an individual possesses, and they exist along a spectrum. Some genetic diseases, such as Huntington's, require only one copy of the defective gene from one parent to make the disease inevitable. Other diseases, such as Tay-Sachs (which causes nervous system degeneration and death by the age of four) and sickle-cell anemia (which causes the red blood cells to become sickle-shaped so that they cannot move freely), require a copy of the defective gene from each parent. Finally, still other genetic diseases (such as some forms of lung and breast cancer) appear to require both a particular combination of genes and environmental factors to manifest themselves in individuals.

We can test for an increasing number of defective genes pre-symptomatically, before the disease manifests itself. Pre-symptomatic testing can be done at an embryonic stage (if used in connection with IVF), at a fetal stage, and on existing individuals. The stage of life at which testing is done raises particular issues: which embryos should be implanted? Is selective abortion justified if a fetus tests positive for a certain condition? In this section, we will consider the issues that arise in connection with pre-symptomatically testing living individuals.

The list of medical conditions that can be screened for is growing rapidly; it now includes phenylketonuria (PKU); XYY Syndrome; Tay-Sachs disease; sickle-cell disease; Down's syndrome; Huntington's; BRCA1 and BRCA2 (genes associated with increased breast cancer risk); and cystic fibrosis. This list is not exhaustive, and new genes are identified regularly.

A perfect screening test would be one that identified a gene connected to a disease that could be prevented through treatment, a modified lifestyle, or other preventative measures. The closest we have come to such a test—and, therefore, the example that is usually cited in support of widespread genetic screening—is PKU. Persons with PKU have an excess of phenylalanine, an amino acid. Untreated, it causes mental retardation; however, if those with the condition are identified at birth, they can be put on a special diet that will allow them to develop normally. PKU thus appears to provide a clear-cut case in which genetic screening does exactly what its advocates hope it will do: identify those at risk for a condition that can be treated.

However, genetic testing for most medical conditions is not like this. Usually, all tests can do is reveal conditions that are untreatable; if done at the prenatal stage, selective abortion might be considered; if performed after birth, then little can be done. In a case such as Huntington's, the situation is bleak: people who take the test may discover that they have a disease that is untreatable and unavoidable, even though they presently have no symptoms. This knowledge can blight the healthy period of their lives. Even PKU screening looks less perfect upon closer examination. The special diet that is beneficial to people with PKU is harmful to those without it, and, because of a number of false positive test results (results that falsely indicate that the child suffers from the condition), some children were seriously harmed by being put on the diet unnecessarily. In addition,

> because nobody knew how long children needed to stay on the diet, many of them were returned to normal foods too soon, with serious effects on their development; because girls with the two mutant alleles had only reproduced rarely (if ever), nobody foresaw that pregnant women who had been liberated from the PKU diet would give birth to babies with catastrophic neurological defects.... [As a result, some have asked if], even today, we know just how much good—and how much harm—testing for PKU has done.[30]

To Know or Not to Know

Knowledge of someone's genetic propensities does not tell us what should be done. This means that, sometimes, the knowledge itself can be considered harmful. We will consider this dimension of genetic testing in connection with Huntington's disease and the genes associated with hereditary breast cancer. In the former case, as Ridley states, the gene is "fate": there is nothing that anyone who possesses the gene can do to prevent the disease. In the latter, women at risk can have a "prophylactic mastectomy and oophorectomy (removal of the ovaries)."[31] However, even with this treatment, there is no "guarantee that all risks of breast cancer can be removed: It is almost impossible to guarantee that all breast tissue has been removed, and any tissue left behind retains the possibility ... to cause breast cancer."[32] Indeed, studies suggest that a prophylactic mastectomy is likely to result in only a few extra years of life. For some women, this may be enough to justify the surgery while for others it may not. However, it is difficult to argue that the surgery really constitutes treatment or prevention, as we would normally understand the terms. Gessen was diagnosed with the gene associated with an increased risk of breast and ovarian cancers and was advised to have both a mastectomy and an oophorectomy. She discovered that the latter creates increased risks of osteoporosis, high blood pressure, depression, heart disease, and cognitive problems; moreover, one study that she saw "concluded that a prophylactic oophorectomy would extend the average life expectancy of a mutant like me by between 0.03 and 1.7 years."[33]

For conditions such as hereditary breast cancer and Huntington's, in which the possession of the gene is closely correlated with the appearance of the disease,[34] the ethical issues surrounding pre-symptomatic testing centre around the desirability of knowing versus the desirability of not knowing.

The Case for Not Knowing

After Wexler and her team discovered the gene for HD, she sat down with her father, and they talked about the implications of getting tested:

> And as we started to talk … my father said, "I don't know how I feel about this test. I'm really having a lot of misgivings.… It's up to you; it's your DNA. But for me, it would be tragic if either one or both of you [referring to Nancy and her sister Alice] was diagnosed with Huntington's Disease, and we really need to think very carefully about what we're doing here." His words hit me like a thunderbolt because certainly, my sister and I have thought about Huntington's every day of our life, probably every moment, since 21.… But there is a huge, huge mega-difference between thinking about something and … when you actually put yourself in the position of saying, "I am going to open that Pandora's box and find out if my life is over as I know it, as I want it to be." And I started to think to myself: "How would I go to Venezuela? How would I see all these people? How would I write? How would I be cheerful?"[35]

The case for not knowing has both personal and social dimensions. On a personal level, it is difficult to predict people's reaction to finding out that they have the gene. At the very least, they are likely to feel differently about their lives; at worst, they may contemplate or commit suicide. On one of her visits to Venezuela, Wexler met a woman who wanted to be examined for neurological signs associated with the disease, even though she was currently well. Some signs of the disease were evident to the doctors. The doctors asked:

> What do you think? She thought she was all right. The doctors avoided saying what they thought, mentioning the need to get to know people better before they gave diagnoses. As soon as the woman left the room, her friend came running in, almost hysterical. What did you tell her? The doctors recounted what they had said. "Thank God," replied the friend and explained: the woman had said to the friend that she would ask for the diagnosis, and if it turned out she had the disease, she would immediately go and commit suicide.[36]

On a social level, with a positive test comes the potential for discrimination. There is a possibility that, if such results are not kept confidential, people will lose jobs, life insurance, and other things that they value. In the 1970s, for example, the U.S. Department of Defense had a policy of excluding people who were carriers of the sickle cell gene from the Air Force Academy, effectively restricting their opportunities for advancement;[37] and "an at-risk patient for HD was a candidate for an organ transplant and one physician wanted to do the test so as to not 'waste' an organ on someone testing positive."[38]

The Case for Knowing

The case for knowing, likewise, has personal and social dimensions. Some people just want to know: they feel that nothing, even a positive result, is worse than not knowing. Knowledge, whether good or bad, will allow them to take charge of their lives and to plan for the future. For these people, knowing enhances their autonomy.

The strongest arguments for knowing, however, concern obligations to other people. Consider, for instance, someone who comes from a family with a history of Huntington's, sickle-cell anemia, or breast cancer; they may be thought to have a moral obligation to find out their status before they get married or before they reproduce. Indeed, Purdy suggests that such individuals have an obligation not to reproduce if they have a chance of passing on a disease such as Huntington's: "Wanting to see the genetic line continued is not particularly rational when it brings a sinister legacy of illness and death."[39] According to this line of thinking, choosing to remain ignorant of one's genetic risks is immoral if one wants to be married or have children—and one should refrain from reproducing if one is opposed to abortion. Wexler appears to endorse this view. There is only one thing, she has said, that would make taking the test worthwhile for her: children. According to Wexler, "[M]y sister and I had both decided ... [that] we weren't going to have children unless we could guarantee that they wouldn't get sick."[40]

These considerations relate to the principles of bioethics. Autonomy suggests that the social context within which testing decisions are made is important: testing should be voluntary, since individuals should be able to decide for themselves whether to get tested without coercion or social pressure. Decisions to test (or not) should ideally be accompanied by counselling, so that individuals understand clearly the nature of the choice they are making and its implications. Non-malfeasance requires that society not discriminate against those who test positive for genetic conditions, and justice requires that tests should be available to all who desire them.

GENETIC THERAPY

The main ethical challenge created by genetic testing arises from the fact that there is a gap between what can be diagnosed and what can be prevented, treated, or cured. If treatments were available for the genes that cause disease, the ethical issues surrounding pre-symptomatic diagnosis would substantially diminish. Genetic therapy (somatic or germ-line) has the potential to allow genetic defects to be corrected and their impacts on the individuals who possess them to be minimized. Unfortunately, the present reality of this form of therapy is far removed from the hope that it may offer effective treatments in the future; so far removed, indeed, that many applications of it to those suffering from genetic disorders itself raises ethical questions.

Somatic Cell Gene Therapy

Somatic cell **gene therapy** "involves correcting a mutated copy of a gene or inserting an additional copy of a gene into the cells of a person's body. The aim is to treat genetically caused diseases in existing people."[41] The challenge is to find a way of inserting the therapeutic gene into cells; viral vectors have been tried, with limited success. And, since genetic therapy is in its infancy, research is inherently and unavoidably experimental. Consequently, it carries a risk of harm, and the principle of non-malfeasance suggests that caution is warranted. Individuals who volunteer to be test subjects are taking risks that even the researchers themselves may be unaware of. This means that it is impossible for researchers to provide all the information necessary to allow consent to be informed. Moreover, this type of experimentation has resulted in death;[42] and in January 2003, the American Food and Drug Administration suspended 27 gene therapy trials after two French children who underwent gene therapy developed a leukemia-like condition.[43] More recently, a 36-year-old woman who suffered from rheumatoid arthritis died after receiving an experimental gene therapy treatment. While the cuase of death remains unclear, an investigation concluded that the gene therapy treatment cannot be ruled out as a contributing factor.[44] In short, all the ethical issues that surround human experimentation of any sort are present in any current applications of genetic therapy. However, as with other forms of human experimentation, as long as the ethical requirements are met, if individuals suffering from genetic conditions believe that such experimentation may be helpful to them given their own analysis of the benefits and risks, they may wish to consent to participate in clinical trials. This can be seen as an expression of their autonomy, and their choice may also be supported by the principle of beneficence if they are also motivated by the hope that what is learned from their participation may be helpful to others.

Germ-Line Gene Therapy

A second form of gene therapy is known as germ-line genetic therapy. This form of genetic altera-tion involves "modifying the cells of gametes (sperm and egg). The aim … is to delete or correct mutations that may be passed on to offspring. In this regard, germ-line therapy is a form of disease prevention rather than therapy."[45] With germ-line therapy, the gametes of those at risk for passing on genetic diseases would be modified so that the individuals who might develop from them would be neither affected by the disease, nor carriers of it. Advocates believe germ-line therapy is desirable because "medical intervention need occur only once around the time of conception, and the benefits would be inherited by the child and its descendants."[46]

However, some concerns have been raised. First, germ-line therapy involves conducting experi-ments on human beings. Second, there is an element of unavoidable risk that is beyond the control of even the most conscientious researcher: we do not know everything about how genes interact with one another or the consequences of our interference for future generations (who cannot give their consent to such experimentation). Consequently, while the principle of autonomy may support forms of genetic therapy designed to help currently affected individuals, it arguably does not support germ-line therapy. As Glannon notes, genes "interact in complex ways. Because of this complexity, it would be difficult to weigh the potential health-benefits of germ-line intervention to people in the present against any health burdens of this intervention to people in the future."[47] For instance, by altering one gene we may simultaneously alter others, which may lead to increased cancer rates in the future.

In addition, what counts as a "bad gene" is, to some extent, context-dependent. Consider sickle-cell anemia and Tay-Sachs disease: carriers of these genes may have protection against other diseases—in the case of sickle-cell, against malaria, and in the case of Tay-Sachs, against tuberculosis. As Gosden observes, carriers of the sickle-cell gene "have all the advantages of resistance to malaria without its serious consequences. This enhanced the survival of these people, and therefore of their genes, in the past."[48] If we had the ability to get rid of particular genes with germ-line therapy and chose the sickle-cell gene as a target, we would be assuming both that malaria is no longer a problem and that it will not be a problem in the future. However, millions of people die from malaria every year, and the virus is becoming resistant to common therapies—and, furthermore, the areas in which malaria is a concern are expected to increase if global warming occurs.

In short, we don't know how germ-line interventions might affect the health of future generations or what kind of world they will inherit. These considerations suggest that, at present, germ-line therapy is difficult to ethically justify: we cannot know that we will not do more harm than good, and the principles of non-malfeasance and beneficence suggest that we should wait until we have a clearer understanding of the consequences of interfering in the genome in this way.

BOX 6.3

CAN THE EXPERIENCES OF YOUR ANCESTORS LEAVE THEIR MARK ON YOUR GENES?

Recent discoveries about the role played by **epigenetics** in shaping the psychological and behavioural tendencies of human beings demonstrate that the way in which genes and environment interact is far more complex than was first realized when we began to consider the possibilities offered by the genetic revolution. The study of epigenetics reveals not only that our genes can change in response to environmental factors such as diet and exposure to chemicals, to experiences such as drug abuse and upbringing, and to historical events, such as living in a time of war or famine, but that, in addition, some of these changes can be passed on to our descendants. While discoveries in epigenetics may, in the future, provide new treatments for various conditions—indeed, some of those who are interested in life extension believe that epigenetic discoveries may allow us to slow, or even halt, the aging process[1]—they also reveal that many of the elements that shape us as individuals and as a species are beyond our control, ranging as they do from the ways in which our grandparents were treated by their parents, to global events such as armed conflicts, periods of food scarcity, and large-scale industrial and technological developments. This means that the hope that the genetic revolution would allow us to shape the physical and mental capacities of our children and grandchildren—and, indeed, human evolution itself—were overly optimistic. As Hurley puts it, "Like silt deposited on the cogs of a finely tuned machine after the seawater of a tsunami recedes, our experiences, and those of our forebears, are never gone, even if they have been forgotten. They become a part of us, a molecular residue holding fast to our genetic scaffolding."[2]

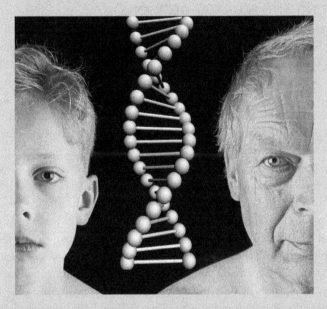

The hope that we might be able to shape the physical and mental characteristics of our descendants through genetic manipulation is challenged by the discovery of epigenetics.

Hurley observes that discoveries in epigenetics reveal that if your grandmother was neglected as a child, you may inherit her tendency toward depression; conversely, if she was raised by loving parents, you may enjoy her resilience and optimism.[3] The fact that epigenetic changes in our genes can affect our children and grandchildren means that, in order to shape the personalities and capabilities of our descendants, we would have to be able to control not only their genetic makeup, but also how we respond to our own children (which is, in turn, influenced by the epigenetic inheritance we receive), as well as their other experiences, from how they are treated in school, to whether they grow up in a period of war and conflict or peace and prosperity. Many of these things, clearly, are beyond anyone's control. Consequently, the discovery that epigenetic changes can be passed on arguably suggests that we should think very carefully before we attempt to deliberately shape the human genome, since any alterations we make may have consequences that are both undesirable and impossible to predict. Ironically, the more we learn about genetics, the less reasonable it seems to try to shape our descendants through advanced technological interventions such as genetic enhancement or genetic therapy, and the more important it becomes to address the social, economic, and political inequalities that shape the possibilities open to individuals and have a profound effect on the way in which they experience their lives.

Notes
1. For more on the technologies that may allow us to extend life, please see Chapter 8, "Death and Dying," in this text, particularly the section "Death as a Medical Failure: Seeking Immortality."
2. Dan Hurley, "Grandma's Experiences Leave a Mark on Your Genes," *Discover Magazine*, May 2013, found at dicovermagazine.com/2013/may/13-grandmas-experiences-leave-epigenetic-mark-on-your-genes#. UyxQm79CYII (March 25, 2014).
3. Hurley, n.p.

PRENATAL TESTING AND PRENATAL DECISIONS

Testing for disorders (genetic or otherwise) can be done prenatally. Tests include ultrasound, which allows the fetus to be examined by high frequency sound waves that produce echoes. These echoes are converted into electrical signals that produce an image of the fetus (ultrasounds have become routine tests for most pregnancies in North America). Another prenatal test is amniocentesis, which requires the extraction of amniotic fluid through a needle inserted through the abdominal wall of the pregnant woman. Amniotic fluid contains fetal cells, which can be examined for chromosomal abnormalities. It is usually performed around the 14th week of pregnancy, and results are not available for two to five weeks after that. This is a weakness of the test, because it means that results are only available when the pregnancy is quite advanced; amniocentesis also carries with it a slight risk of miscarriage. Chorionic Villus Sampling (CVS) requires the extraction of a small amount of placental tissue through the cervix. The cells in the placental tissue are genetically identical to those of the fetus. CVS can be performed earlier in pregnancy than amniocentesis, but may increase the chance of a miscarriage and may produce fetal defects. Maternal serum testing measures levels of hormones in the pregnant woman's blood; these can indicate the possibility of fetal problems, in which case further tests can be performed. Finally, tests are being developed that will allow fetal cells to be distinguished from the mother's blood cells; these cells can be examined for genetic abnormalities. The last two tests have the advantage of being non-invasive and harmless to the fetus.

In prenatal testing, we move from a context in which people make decisions for themselves to one in which they are making decisions about the lives of others. These decisions are complicated by the fact that the choice facing parents may be a choice between two evils—the abortion of a desired child, or the birth of an unhealthy and suffering one. The moral motivation behind prenatal testing is the principle of non-malfeasance, to prevent harm: harm to the fetus, to the parents and family, and perhaps to society. However, this morally sound motive is overshadowed by the spectre of selective abortion. As Shenk observes, there is usually no point in testing unless one would be willing to abort: "[W]hen my wife and I went in for amniocentesis, we did so with the tacit understanding that we would abort our child if we discovered that he or she was carrying the extra **chromosome**.... The fact that we did not abort our child, that she was born healthy, with forty-six chromosomes and four chambers in her heart and two lungs ... is morally beside the point. We had made our if-then choice to terminate."[49]

SELECTIVE ABORTION AND THE SPECTRUM OF CONDITIONS

The conditions that can be tested for prenatally, again, fall along a spectrum. There are conditions at one end that are incompatible with life, or that shorten life so radically or cause so much pain and suffering for those afflicted that a decision to abort, some believe, is morally responsible. Tay-Sachs disease and Lesch-Nyhan syndrome (which causes boys afflicted to suffer intense pain, mental retardation, and an irresistible urge to self-mutilate) fall at this end of the spectrum. For these conditions, some ethicists believe, a case can be made that a person afflicted would be better off not existing. At the other end of the spectrum are conditions that might not be considered serious, such as some forms of polydactylism, which result in extra fingers or toes. Aborting for this condition appears to many to be less morally justifiable. Finally, and most ethically problematic for many ethicists, prenatal testing can also be used to identify the sex of the fetus, which can lead to selective abortion because, while the fetus is healthy, it is not of the desired sex (usually female).

Prenatal Testing and Selective Abortion[50]

Most conditions fall somewhere in between the extremes presented by, at one end, conditions such as Tay-Sachs, and, at the other, a fetus being of an unwanted gender. However, there is no objective account of disease and suffering that we can appeal to as an easy guide for decisions about when selective abortion may be justified or unjustified on the ground of non-malfeasance. Moreover, people disagree even about particular conditions. For example, some people argue that Down's syndrome is a condition that should lead to selective abortion while others believe that it is not incompatible with a worthwhile and happy life;[51] and people who suffer from sickle-cell disease can have very different experiences and life expectancies. We cannot, therefore, avoid making value judgments about the quality of someone else's life—and the challenge becomes (to paraphrase Aristotle) to the make the right judgments, on the right grounds, and for the right reasons. But what these are is difficult to articulate and may require a condition-to-condition analysis, as well as an examination of the social context.

Some advocates of prenatal testing and parental choice in reproductive matters argue that concerns about selective abortion are entirely beside the point: healthy fetuses are aborted all the time, for any reason the pregnant woman deems fit. As long as these decisions are freely made, Gosden argues, concern about selective abortion "pales into insignificance in comparison to the real moral dilemma that abortion poses. In 1995, 1.2 million medical terminations were carried out in America, and probably only 1–2% of the fetuses would have had any abnormality. It would be incongruous to condemn actions based on personal preferences if we accept the destruction of so many normal fetuses."[52] This is arguably a valid point. So the question becomes: does selective abortion raise ethical questions in spite of the fact that we already accept abortion for almost any reason?

Concerns Raised by Selective Abortion

Two main concerns are raised by selective abortion. First, that the decision to selectively abort may be coerced and that women may feel pressured into taking prenatal tests and then terminating fetuses that "fail": in the absence of such coercion, they would choose to have the child the fetus will become. Second, since these decisions are inextricably bound up in judgments about what makes a life worthwhile, selective abortion has implications that extend beyond the particular practice: implications for those who already exist with the conditions we are aborting to prevent and, ultimately, implications for our capacity to be compassionate moral agents.

A Coerced Choice?

First, let us consider the claim that decisions around selective abortion are coerced, not free. Lippman argues that the technologies that allow prenatal diagnosis, and the context within which prenatal tests are offered and performed, are coercive: far from pregnant women autonomously choosing these tests, as advocates claim, they feel compelled to use them. Lippman believes that the very existence of the tests means that women who might want to refuse them find it hard to do so: "This technology perversely creates a burden of not doing enough [to ensure the health of one's child when the technology is not used]."[53] In addition, far from giving women more control over reproduction, these tests actually give them less. Rather than providing information that will allow them to make informed and autonomous decisions, they actually make women vulnerable to social control: "Geneticists and their obstetrician colleagues are deciding which fetuses are healthy, what healthy means, and who should be born, thus gaining power over decisions to continue or terminate pregnancies that pregnant women themselves may not always be permitted to make."[54] Lippman believes these tests are coercive along several dimensions: women who care about the well-being of their future children feel compelled to take them; the conditions which are tested for are chosen for woman by geneticists and obstetricians; and, finally, women whose fetuses test positive for a defect will feel pressure to abort, even if they would rather continue the pregnancy.

Wertz and Fletcher, in contrast, argue that many women welcome these tests, feel reproductively empowered by them, and believe that they contribute to their ability to have healthy children. Many women believe prenatal testing enhances their capacity to act autonomously because it both presents them with information and allows them to make a decision about how to respond to it; for at least some women, while the decision to abort may be difficult and painful, it may nonetheless be morally justifiable. Given the importance placed on autonomy, it is hard to argue that information about the health of their fetus should be kept from women. And given the case that feminists have made that women should be able to decide to have abortions for whatever reason they deem appropriate, it is difficult to argue that they should be prevented from having an abortion when they are told that their fetus has been diagnosed with an abnormal genetic condition—or even because it is of an unwanted gender.

Arguably, then, the claim that these tests are coercive is too strong. However, critics might nonetheless argue that choices around these tests are forced in that the larger social context, within which they are provided and why, makes certain choices more rational than others. Coercion involves a direct interference with autonomy because it means that one is subject to the will and desires of another person. One is forced to make certain choices, however, if the circumstances within which one is choosing are such that only certain choices seem rational or reasonable. If one is a member of a culture that devalues women, pregnant women may feel forced to undergo testing to determine the sex of the child and abort it if it is female.[55] Moreover, in most societies, the birth of an unhealthy child causes great hardship for families because society provides very little support to them: "It is now virtually impossible for parents in many areas to place a newborn or infant in an institution no matter how severe the retardation. In home care, even occasional respite care, is difficult to obtain. Under these conditions, the choice of not having prenatal diagnosis appears to be no choice at all, unless a woman is opposed to abortion under most conditions."[56] Additionally, Sandel claims that prenatal tests increase parental responsibility. He notes that there are reports that some parents of handicapped children feel blamed and judged because having a child with a genetic defect is now seen to be a matter of choice, rather than of chance: "Prospective parents remain free to choose whether to use prenatal testing and whether to act on the results. But they are not free to escape the burden of choice that the new technology creates. Nor can they avoid being implicated in the enlarged frame of moral responsibility that accompanies new habits of control."[57]

Selective Abortion and People with Disabilities

It is this social context that concerns people with disabilities who have argued against the increasing use of prenatal diagnostic tests. If prospective parents are strongly encouraged for the sake of their future child's health to undergo prenatal testing, and if the social circumstances in which tests are offered are such that giving birth to a child with a disability is costly, then what does this say about the value we place on those who already exist with the conditions for which parents are encouraged to abort? For some commentators, this indicates nothing less than that we see their lives as having little or no value—and see them as costly burdens for society.

On this issue, there is a divide between optimists and pessimists. Optimists distinguish the condition from the person and say that the person is valued. In addition, they argue that "if the number of people coming into existence with disabilities were smaller, society would be better able to meet their needs."[58] Optimists can point to the example of thalassemia (an inherited blood disorder) in Cyprus as evidence in support of this position: "As the incidence of thalassemia has diminished, help for the afflicted has increased: because there is now less demand for blood transfusions and other treatments, the lives of thalassemia sufferers are now better than they were."[59]

Pessimists, in contrast, argue that the distinction between the condition and the person is spurious: it makes no sense to say, for example, that one values the person with Down's syndrome but not the syndrome itself, since this is so intricately bound up in who they are, in their abilities, personalities, and physical traits. Likewise, some people with hereditary deafness have argued that this is so much a part of them—and a valuable part—that it has allowed them to create their own unique culture.[60] Such people reject the use of cochlear implants that would allow them to hear better. In one widely reported case, a deaf lesbian couple chose a deaf sperm donor for their child in the hope that the child, too, would be deaf; for them, their disability defines who they are.[61]

In addition, pessimists argue that as medical costs rise and as government budgets get tighter, a refusal of prenatal diagnostic testing or a decision to carry a fetus to term after a positive test will be choices that will be held against the parents. They will have deliberately chosen to have this child, and therefore the responsibility for taking care of it should be theirs alone. Thus, pessimists fear that the result could be a decrease in the resources directed at the disabled as fewer are born.

PRE-IMPLANTATION TESTING AND THE MORAL STATUS OF THE HUMAN EMBRYO

The development of in vitro fertilization (IVF) has given us the ability to manipulate the human embryo. It is possible to remove a cell from an embryo at an early stage in its development and analyze its genes. If done with IVF, only those embryos that are free of genetic defects would be implanted. Such an analysis can be considered a kind of treatment: preventative treatment, not for the embryo itself, but for the person that embryo might become. Consider Purdy's concern about the responsibility that some persons have not to reproduce if they carry genes that would cause serious harm if passed on to offspring: pre-implantation testing, some believe, is a responsible way to respond to this danger—more responsible, indeed, than prenatal testing, since it avoids the need to consider selective abortion.

Our access to embryos opens up a very different possibility as well, not of preventative treatment for the person the embryo might become, but, rather, embryos-as-treatments. Embryos may be a source of therapies for existing persons since early embryonic cells have unusual abilities compared to most cells: they have the capacity to develop into almost any kind of cell. For about four days after fertilization, the cells are totipotent. Their potential is unlimited, and cells separated during this period have the ability to develop into genetically identical but separate individuals. (Identical twins are the result of the separation of two totipotent cells at this stage.)

After about four days following fertilization, the cells start to specialize, and a blastocyst is formed. A blastocyst is composed of an outer layer of cells that will develop into the placenta and related tissues, and an inner cluster of cells that have the capacity to develop into almost all the cells that make up a human body. These inner cells are no longer totipotent, but, rather, have become pluripotent: while they can grow into many types of cells, they do not have the potential to grow into all the kinds of cells necessary to become a fetus. These pluripotent cells are stem cells, and they can produce cells that have a particular function, such as skin cells, hair cells, liver cells, and so on. Multipotent stem cells—stem cells that are more specialized than pluripotent stem cells but less specialized than skin or liver cells—can be found in children and adults. Bone marrow, for instance, contains blood stem cells, and these cells give rise to new blood cells throughout the life of the person.

Embryos—whether created through normal fertilization, or by somatic cell nuclear transfer (SCNT), a process whereby the nucleus is removed from an egg and into which a somatic cell is fused—can be a source of pluripotent stem cells. (SCNT can be said to produce embryos, because what results from the process is a cell that has the potential to develop into an entire individual organism.) This has important medical and scientific implications. Pluripotent stem cells have the ability to aid in research on cancer; help determine why certain birth defects occur; be used for drug testing; and offer a source of cells that might treat diseases and conditions, including Alzheimer's, Parkinson's, stroke, burns, spinal cord injuries, diabetes, heart disease, and arthritis. In addition, SCNT gives rise to the possibility of custom-designed treatments: the pluripotent cells created by this technique would be essentially genetically identical to the cells of the person from whom the somatic cell was taken, which means that there would be little risk of rejection.

The Status of the Embryo

While the identification of stem cells and the discovery of their therapeutic potential are tremendously exciting, questions have been raised about the moral status of the human embryo. What sort of entity is it? On the one hand, an embryo has the potential to become a human being, and all existing human beings were once embryos: does this mean we ought to treat it with the respect due to all human beings? On the other hand, embryos are clearly not yet human beings, and, indeed, most embryos, even those fertilized naturally within a woman's body, never develop into persons. (A large number of embryos are spontaneously aborted, probably because of chromosomal abnormalities. This fact forms the basis for one of the arguments that have been used in support of selective abortion, namely, that defective fetuses have evaded nature's own genetic screening system, and selective abortion merely corrects nature's mistake.)

Opinions on the status of the embryo vary. Some believe that an embryo has the same moral status as an already existing human being. For them, since there is no point at which we can definitively say that a fetus becomes a being worthy of respect, so we cannot find a particular point at which an embryo develops moral worth. The fact that embryos have the potential to become persons, and the fact that we believe that persons deserve respect, means that we must accord embryos—"tiny human beings"[62]—the same respect that we accord existing people. This means, advocates of this position assert, that there are few, if any, morally legitimate uses we can make of embryos.

Others believe that there is nothing in an embryo that carries moral weight. Most embryos, they point out, never become persons. It is as absurd to equate a cluster of cells with an already existing human being as it is to equate an acorn with an oak tree.[63] Moreover, the potential for research on embryos to relieve the suffering of actual human beings should take precedence over concerns about the moral status of particular cells. This position is represented by some members of the President's Council on Bioethics, a committee set up in the United States to consider bioethical issues: "Because we accord no special moral status to the early-stage embryo and believe it should be treated essentially like all other human cells, we believe that the moral issues involved in this research are no different from those that accompany any biomedical research."[64]

A final group fall somewhere in between; they accept the absurdity of equating an embryo with an already existing person, but believe, simultaneously, that there is something of moral significance present in the human embryo. As Glannon puts it, "[E]ven if they lack moral status, embryos seem to have a moral value, a symbolic value for what they represent. This value may prescribe limits on what we are permitted to do with them."[65] It would not be morally permissible, for instance, to eat an embryo or to destroy it wastefully. However, holders of this intermediate position believe that appropriate limits permit research under certain restrictions; for instance, some suggest that research should be limited "to the first fourteen days after development—a point near when the primitive streak is formed, and before organ differentiation occurs."[66]

On balance, the intermediate position appears most easily defensible. While there is clearly a significant moral difference between an embryo and an existing person—and even between an embryo and a six-month-old fetus—an embryo arguably has some moral value, even if this value is only symbolic. The difficulty is to determine what follows from the attribution of even this limited form of moral value: what is permitted, and what is not? For instance, even if we accept the limitation that research should occur only in the first 14 days, are there further limitations that should be placed on the kind of research that should be done? Might it be impermissible to create human and animal chimeras (embryos that contain both human and animal cells)? And what are the implications for couples who undergo IVF treatment and then break up and disagree about what should be done with the embryos? There have been several cases in which women have desired to have their embryos implanted while their ex-partners have refused to give permission. So far, these cases have been decided in favour of the partner who does not want to reproduce. However, arguments can be made in support of the other side as well. And what ought to happen to the embryos about which disagreements of this sort exist?

While these questions remain ethically challenging, it appears increasingly likely that, while research on embryonic stem cells will continue, they will not have the treatment potential they were initially expected to have. There is mounting evidence that the very features that made them look so useful—namely, their ability to become any number of organ or tissues—may also increase the risk of cancer in those who are treated with them.[67] Moreover, researchers are learning how to generate stem cells from adult cells (such as skin cells), thus creating a source of stem cells that does not raise the same ethical questions that using embryonic stem cells generates.

Pre-implantation Testing

IVF has made it possible to genetically screen embryos created for reproductive purposes before implantation. Is there any reason why a woman undergoing IVF should not use such testing to ensure that only the healthiest embryos are implanted? Initially, it appears that the only reasonable answer is no; upon closer examination, however, this question is more complicated. We first need to know what we are testing for and how this information will be used.

Suppose, for the sake of argument, that we avoid the moral issues that surround genetic testing at the fetal and after-birth stages by testing embryos. Let us assume that it would be preferable to avoid both the selective abortion of an unhealthy fetus and the birth of an afflicted child. This is Glannon's position:

> Given that gene therapy and other medical interventions have not been effective in treating most genetic disorders, parents may be morally obligated to select against genetic mutations that cause the most severe of these disorders. This is a means of preventing diseases by preventing the lives of those who would have them. Such a practice can be morally justified on grounds of nonmaleficence and justice. Nonmaleficence requires that we not harm people by causing them to experience significant pain and suffering over the balance of their lives. Justice requires that we not deny people the same opportunities for achievement and well being that are open to others who are healthy or have only moderate diseases. Together, these principles imply that it can be morally wrong to cause a person to exist with a severe disease when it is possible to cause a different person to exist without the disease.[68]

The first step in Glannon's argument, then, is to suggest that a moral obligation exists and that it requires the use of testing.

This argument relies on our ability to find objective criteria of disease and health to tell us which conditions to screen for and which to weed out when we find them. But this is very difficult: there are only a small number of genetic diseases for which the diagnosis and prognosis are clear. Most conditions are far less predictable. As Kitcher points out, two people can both have sickle-cell anemia, and yet the degree of disease, and the extent to which it affects their lives, can be very different: "When the attacks will come and how severe they will be depend on features of the environment that are currently unfathomed."[69] Consequently, again, we must make value judgments rather than scientific or medical ones. In addition, increased genetic knowledge is likely to make decisions harder to make, not easier. Shenk captures the nature of the dilemma well as he imagines his daughter, at some point in the future, planning her first child:

> In keeping with the social mores of the day, she and her partner have fertilized a number of eggs in vitro, intending to implant the one with the best apparent chance for a successful gestation. The doctor calls with the karyotype results. It seems that embryos number 1 and 6 reveal a strong manic-depressive tendency. Will my daughter exclude them from possible implantation? The choice seems obvious, until the doctor tells her that embryos 1 and 6 are also quick-witted, whereas 2 and 3 are likely to be intellectually sluggish. The fourth and fifth embryos, by the way, are marked for ordinary intelligence, early-onset hearing impairment, and a high potential for pancreatic cancer. Which, if any, should be implanted?[70]

In Shenk's and Kitcher's view, then, we cannot look to the genes alone as we try to make responsible judgments about which lives are worth living and which ones are not.[71] The questions we ask and the judgments we make about embryos are the same questions we need to ask about the genetic revolution itself: What are the social consequences of our genetic knowledge? How do the choices we make reflect how we understand ourselves, and how will they affect what we become? What is the context within which information is obtained and applied?

Embryo Cloning

The very early embryo contains totipotent cells: if these cells are split from one another, each has the potential to grow into a genetically identical individual. Embryos can be twinned at this stage, and it is possible to make multiple copies of the same genome. This is a kind of cloning, the deliberate duplication of a particular genome. In addition, the designer therapies envisioned, in which somatic cells are fused into enucleated eggs, can also be described as a kind of cloning, since the genetic makeup of the resulting embryo is nearly identical to that of the somatic cell donor.

Embryos might be twinned or cloned for a number of therapeutic reasons: to increase the number of embryos during IVF treatments; to increase the number of embryos available for research; and to create designer genetic therapies. Once research protocols have been developed, and providing that embryos created by SCNT are not allowed to develop into individuals, the most difficult ethical issues raised by the twinning of embryos arise in connection with IVF. Having multiple identical embryos raises a number of new possibilities: genetically identical people born years apart; genetically identical individuals born from different mothers; an identical embryo being used to replace a dead child; identical embryos being stored to serve as a source of therapies for one that was implanted and carried to term; and so on. The implications of these possibilities are unclear, but they seem morally significant, particularly as they have relevance for current understandings of personal identity. For instance, some have argued that two identical persons born years apart would simply be twins separated in time. But in this case—unlike the normal case—we would already have a good idea of how that particular genome is likely to develop. This might lead the parents to treat the child differently than they otherwise would have, or to have particular expectations that inhibit the child's ability to discover for herself who she is and who she wants to be.

Having a Child for Another Child's Benefit

Six-year-old Molly Nash suffered from Fanconi anemia, a potentially fatal genetic disease that meant that she was unable to produce her own bone marrow. Her parents wanted more children, and they wanted to be sure that the children would be free of the disease; in addition, however, they wanted their next child to be a stem cell donor for their already existing one. The Nashes used in vitro fertilization and genetic testing to guarantee that the embryo used would be free from genetic defects and also a good match for Molly. When their son, Adam, was born, stem cells were taken from his umbilical cord and transfused into Molly. The doctor who performed the transfusion made it clear that the parents' motivations were good. They wanted to have a healthy child and to help their sick one. Furthermore, no genetic engineering was involved; Adam's genome was not changed in any way. Moreover, Adam was not harmed by having the stem cells from his umbilical cord used, and his parents valued him for himself, as well as for what he could do to help Molly.[72]

While all these facts may be true, what some find troubling about this case is not so much its specific details, but its larger implications. First, there is the issue of creating a child to benefit another. Even if we accept that the Nashes' motivations were morally sound, how far should parents go to help their sick children? If it is harmless to use umbilical cord stem cells, more dangerous to use bone marrow, would it be acceptable to take a kidney? A lung? These actions too might be justified on similar grounds. Second, there is the issue of consent. Organ and tissue donors are expected to give consent before their body parts are used. Clearly, however, consent cannot be obtained from babies or from small children. What limits are there on the extent to which parents can make choices for and about their children, particularly when the choice being made is not to benefit that child but a different one? Third, the selection of an embryo, not only to ensure that the resulting child is healthy, but also because it might possess other traits the parents deem desirable (even if those traits were not implanted through genetic manipulation) opens the door to "designer children": to the possibility that reprogenetics might not only allow parents to increase the odds of having healthy children, but children with particular traits chosen by the parent. It is this possibility that has the most potential to unleash the real power of the genetic revolution—and it is this possibility, more than any other, that raises the most extravagant hopes of those who are optimistic about the revolution, and the deepest fears of those who worry about our ability to use our new powers wisely.

UNLEASHING THE POWER OF THE GENETIC REVOLUTION: CHOICE AND CONTROL

The figure that most clearly symbolizes the genetic revolution and demonstrates its power is an unlikely one: Dolly, the cloned sheep. Dolly was introduced to the world as a six-month-old lamb on February 23, 1997. The means by which she had been brought into existence overturned almost unquestioned scientific "truths" and opened the door, for the first time in history, to the possibility of human asexual reproduction. Dolly was created by a process that most scientists believed impossible: she was cloned from an adult cell. (She was named after Dolly Parton, because the cell used came from a mammary gland.) While embryo cells are undifferentiated and have the potential to grow into any of the cells in the body, adult cells have become specialized. Before Dolly was created, it was believed that there was no way to reprogram a differentiated cell so that it became undifferentiated again. As a result, it was thought to be impossible to create a new individual with the same genome as one that had grown beyond the early embryo stage, when splitting can occur.

Dr. Ian Wilmut with Dolly, the cloned sheep, a humble and unlikely symbol of the genetic revolution.

What Dolly's creators, Ian Wilmut and his team, managed to do was remarkable: they managed to get an adult cell to switch off its active genes, thus returning it to its embryological state. Their technique was relatively simple. They took a cell and placed it in a culture with a very low concentration of nutrients. The starved cell stopped dividing and switched off its active genes. At the same time, an unfertilized egg was removed from another sheep, and its nucleus was extracted. The cells were placed together, and several electrical pulses were passed through them. The first fused the two cells together, while the second started the process of cell division. When cell division was advanced enough, the embryo was placed into the uterus of a third sheep, who gave birth to Dolly. Since Dolly's birth, other mammals have been successfully cloned from adult cells, which means that, in principle, there is no reason why a human being could not be similarly cloned. Cloning joins a collection of other technologies that are designed to not merely limit disease and minimize suffering. They are designed to actually control the genetic makeup of our offspring through the techniques of reproductive cloning, or by enhancing their genes.

Arguments for and against Human Reproductive Cloning

While human reproductive cloning has not yet emerged as the serious ethical challenge many predicted, the ethical arguments presented about this possibility demonstrate, in perhaps their clearest form, the positive and negative arguments about the potential of the genetic revolution to transform humanity. They also set the stage for the arguments about human enhancement that will be considered in the next section.

One of the best known arguments against human reproductive cloning is presented by Kass, who asserts that, when we are presented with the possibilities opened up by human reproductive cloning (conceiving children to replace those who have died, mass-production clones, women giving birth to genetic copies of themselves, their husbands, or even their dead parents), most people feel revulsion and repugnance. These feelings, Kass believes, while not in themselves arguments against human cloning, nonetheless should be understood as "the emotional expression of deep wisdom, beyond reason's power fully to articulate it."[73] He compares the feelings generated by the prospect of human cloning to those people feel when confronted with such things as father-daughter incest, cannibalism, or rape-murder, and says that, in such cases, as with cloning, "we intuit and feel, immediately and without argument, the violation of things we rightfully hold dear."[74]

In contrast, advocates of human reproductive cloning (who tend to be supporters of genetic enhancement as well) argue that many of the arguments against cloning rest on misconceptions and, moreover, that the right to reproduce by cloning is protected under the right to procreative liberty. For example, in response to fears such as those articulated by Kass, Pence claims that cloned individuals would not be zombie-like drones, devoid of humanity; rather, "they would just as much be persons as children born from in vitro fertilization. They would be gestated by normal women over nine months. They would be raised by normal parents in normal neighborhoods. The only difference between them and other children is that they would inherit one set of (chosen) genes rather than a randomly mixed set."[75] Moreover, even if we were to reproduce our own genetic makeup, or those of our parents, or of some famous individual, the person who resulted would not be a duplicate of the genome donor: a clone of a 50-year-old man, who is born today, would grow up in a different world, with different parents, different interests, different expectations, and different technologies. As Pence puts it, "[I]f I wanted to clone myself, I would be disappointed."[76]

In addition, Harris claims that the feelings of disgust and revulsion felt by some people at the prospect of human cloning, even if those people are in a majority, are not a sufficient reason to ban the procedure. The freedom to reproduce is "guaranteed by the constitution (written or not) of any democratic society,"[77] and it encompasses the right to choose the means by which we reproduce.

While it is arguably the case that Kass is right to believe that many find the prospect of human cloning to be repugnant, some commentators are suspicious of his appeal to emotion, rather than to argument. Agar, for example, says it "sounds like cheating" because it places the rejection of human cloning "beyond reason's reach [which] goes against the grain for those who are used to rationally justifying their moral conclusions."[78] Agar believes that, while we would be disgusted by the other examples Kass gives (incest, rape-murder) we can provide arguments, if called on to do so, to explain why we feel this way. Agar suggests that Kass conflates disgust with the procedure by which a cloned individual is brought into existence with disgust for that individual. If we could demonstrate that cloning was harmful to the persons it created (for instance, if it shortened their lifespans or produced defects), then we would be able to give a stronger argument against cloning. However, if "we lack a rationally persuasive reason to find their [the clones'] existence wrongful, we should not translate queasiness into moral condemnation."[79]

A more compelling argument against human cloning can perhaps be generated if we consider the perspective of the (potentially) cloned person, and what has been called "**the right to an open future**": the right of a child to have the capacity, when an adult, to choose for himself or herself how to live. This right can be violated when parents exercise too much control over their children, including control over their genome. Davis argues that what is morally troubling about parents' attempts to control the genes of their children is that this can "limit the child's own individual flourishing. The more we are able to control our children's characteristics (and the more time, energy, and money we invest in the outcome), the more invested we will be in our hopes and dreams for them."[80] While Davis does not consider the case of reproductive cloning, her argument appears relevant: the only reason to choose to replicate a particular individual's genes is because you hope (however misguidedly) to produce a particular type of person through this action. Even if this is not directly harmful to the cloned child, it does suggest, if we follow Davis's line of reasoning, an unhealthy degree of parental control over that child.

Enhancement Technologies

Enhancement technologies include "any technology that directly alters the expression of genes that are already present in humans, or that involve the addition of genes that have not previously appeared within the human population (including plant, animal, or custom-designed genes), for the purposes of human physical, intellectual, psychological, or moral improvement."[81] Enhancement technologies, like reproductive cloning, demonstrate the potential of the genetic revolution to alter our understanding of what it means to be human. It may allow us to overcome our genetic limitations, change the way we reproduce and how we view reproduction, and shape humanity into a design of our own choosing. The power that this will give us, many believe, is likely to prove irresistible. Moreover, while these technologies and their applications raise serious ethical questions, they are hard to resist with the normal ethical tools of bioethics (which focus on moral principles such as autonomy, informed consent, and choice). These technologies, some have suggested, go so far beyond the scope of "normal" bioethics that we need to ask questions that are simultaneously deeper and broader than those we might consider in connection with other bioethical topics.[82]

Reproductive Liberty and the Use of Enhancement Technology

The two most commonly cited arguments in support of enhancement technologies are, first, that they are similar to activities we already engage in and do not find particularly morally problematic and, second, that their use is covered by reproductive liberty and the value we place on autonomy.

First, those who support the use of enhancement technologies assert that they fall into an unproblematic continuum. We choose particular procreative partners because we see in them characteristics that we would like our children to have, and parents have always tried to control the way in which their children develop by providing them with everything from piano lessons to religious beliefs. In addition, parents have a responsibility not to pass genetic diseases on to their offspring, and good parents have always tried to give their children advantages: why not ensure that they have good genes as well? We live in a society that "accepts the rights of parents to control every other aspect of their children's lives from the time they are born until they reach adulthood. If one accepts the parental prerogative after birth, it is hard to argue against it before birth."[83] Harris makes the case that, not only should enhancements be permitted, but they can even be a parental responsibility. Imagine that the ozone layer is so depleted that skin cancer becomes a common problem against which green skin offers protection. And suppose, moreover, that genetic enhancements can create green skin of just the right shade. Harris states: "I am sure that I would go green, and if I had to make the intervention in newborns, I would do it for my children. Others might prefer their children normal and cancerous. I would not impose on them, but I hope they would permit me to save … my kids. My kids … would have the last laugh."[84]

Against this claim, it can be argued that there is a difference between providing your child with piano lessons and trying to control his very nature. Far from falling along an unproblematic continuum, some argue that we can draw clear distinctions between legitimate and unjustified uses of our genetic knowledge and, consequently, of acceptable degrees of parental choice in these matters. Glannon, for instance, distinguishes gene therapy (which he believes is morally legitimate) from enhancement (which is morally problematic):

> The first is an intervention aimed at restoring physical and mental functioning at an adequate level. The second is an intervention aimed at improving already adequate functioning. Genetic enhancement augments functions and capacities that otherwise would be considered normal. Insofar as the goals of medicine are to treat and prevent disease and thereby restore and ensure adequate functioning, gene therapy falls within these goals. Genetic enhancement falls outside of them.[85]

BOX 6.4

MICHAEL J. SANDEL, "LIBERAL EUGENICS"

In the age of the genome, the language of eugenics is making a comeback, not only among critics but also among defenders of enhancement. An influential school of Anglo-American political philosophers calls for a new "liberal eugenics," by which they mean non-coercive genetic enhancements that do not restrict the autonomy of the child. "While old-fashioned authoritarian eugenicists sought to produce citizens out of a centrally designed mould," writes Nicholas Agar, "the distinguishing mark of the new liberal eugenics is state neutrality." Governments may not tell parents what sort of children to design, and parents may engineer in their children only those traits that improve their capacities without biasing their choice of life plans.…

While liberal eugenics is a less dangerous doctrine than the old eugenics, it is also less idealistic. For all its folly and darkness, the eugenics movement of the twentieth century was born of the aspiration to improve humankind, or to promote the collective welfare. Liberal eugenics shrinks from collective ambitions. It is not a movement of social reform but rather a way for privileged parents to have the kind of children they want and to arm them for success in a competitive society.

But despite its emphasis on individual choice, liberal eugenics implies more state compulsion than first appears. Defenders of enhancement see no moral difference between improving a child's intellectual capacities through education and doing so through genetic alteration. All that matters, from the liberal-eugenics standpoint, is that neither the education nor the genetic alteration violates the child's autonomy, or "right to an open future." Provided the enhanced capacity is an "all-purpose" means, and so does not point the child toward any particular career or life plan, it is morally permissible.

However, given the duty of parents to promote the well-being of their children (while respecting their right to an open future), such enhancement becomes not only permissible but obligatory. Just as the state can require parents to send their children to school, so it can require parents to use genetic technologies (provided they are safe) to boost their child's I.Q.... Properly understood, the liberal "principle of ethical individualism" not only permits but "commands the struggle" to "make the lives of future generations of human beings longer and more full of talent and hence achievement." So liberal eugenics does not reject state-imposed genetic engineering after all; it simply requires that the engineering respect the autonomy of the child being designed.

Although liberal eugenics finds support among many Anglo-American ... philosophers, Jurgen Habermas, Germany's most prominent political philosopher, opposes it.... His case against liberal eugenics is especially intriguing because he believes it rests solely on liberal premises and need not invoke spiritual or theological notions. His critique of genetic engineering "does not relinquish the premises of post-metaphysical thinking," by which he means it does not depend on any particular conception of the good life. Habermas agrees [with liberals] ... that, since people in modern pluralistic societies disagree about morality and religion, a just society should not take sides in such disputes but should instead accord each person the freedom to choose and pursue his or her own conception of the good life.

Genetic intervention to select or improve children is objectionable, Habermas argues, because it violates the liberal principles of autonomy and equality. It violates autonomy because genetically programmed persons cannot regard themselves as "the sole authors of their own life history." And it undermines equality by destroying "the essentially symmetrical relations between free and equal human beings" across generations. One measure of this asymmetry is that, once parents become the designers of their children, they inevitably incur a responsibility for their children's lives that cannot possibly be reciprocal....

Habermas is on to something important, I think, when he asserts a "connection between the contingency of a life's beginning that is not at our disposal and the freedom to give one's life an ethical shape." For him, this connection matters because it explains why a genetically designed child is beholden and subordinate to another person (the designing parent) in a way that a child born of a contingent ... beginning is not. But the notion that our freedom is bound up with "a beginning we cannot control" also carries a broader significance: Whatever its effect on the autonomy of the child, the drive to banish contingency and to master the mystery of birth diminishes the designing parent and corrupts parenting as a social practice governed by norms of unconditional love.

Source: Michael J. Sandel, *The Case Against Perfection: Ethics in the Age of Genetic Engineering* (Cambridge, MA: Harvard University Press, 2007), 75–83.

Sandel makes a different case against enhancement. He agrees with defenders of enhancement that there is a marked similarity between what some parents already do to shape their children and the control that technology may allow. However, he argues, we should reason in the opposite direction: "[T]his similarity does not give us a reason to embrace the genetic manipulation of children. Instead, it gives us reason to question the low-tech, high-pressure child-rearing practices we commonly accept."[86]

Second, advocates of procreative liberty argue that persons should not only be free to decide whether, how, and with whom to reproduce, but also to choose the characteristics of their offspring. Indeed, choice in these matters is necessary in a free society: "The best way to both avoid totalitarianism and to escape the possibility of racial (or gender) prejudice, either individual or social, dictating what sort of children people have, is to permit free parental choice in these matters. And to do so whether that choice is exercised by choice of procreational partner or by choice of gamete or embryo, or by genetic engineering."[87] Or, as Silver succinctly puts it, "[I]n a society that values freedom above all else, it is hard to find any legitimate basis for restricting the use of reprogenetics [including enhancement technologies]."[88]

In response to the claim that it is hard to find a legitimate basis for restricting the use of these technologies given our commitment to freedom, it can be argued that there are legitimate limitations on the exercise of autonomy: I can't drive my car at any speed I choose, I can't hit you in the face just because I feel like it, and I can't control your choices. When parental autonomy/procreative liberty arguments are made in support of choosing designer offspring, a paradox is generated: the parent's exercise of autonomous choice is used as an argument in support of engaging in practices that may undermine the ability of the resulting child to be an autonomous chooser. Suppose, for instance, that a woman is a basketball fan, and she wants to have a child who is a professional basketball player. If she genetically engineers the child to have the physical characteristics that make it likely that this is what he will become, the child will be deprived of the opportunity (which is central to the concept of autonomy) of discovering for himself what it is that he wants to be.

The exercise of one person's freedom, then, some critics believe, cannot coherently be used as a justification for limiting another person's freedom. As Putnam argues, "The task of good parents is precisely to *prepare children for autonomy*. The good parent ... looks forward to having children who will live independently of the parents, not just in a physical or economic sense, but in the sense of thinking for themselves, even if that means that they will inevitably disagree on some matters, and may disagree on matters that both parent and child regard as important."[89] Habermas likewise believes that there is something paradoxical about using the concept of autonomy to justify the genetic shaping of children because this threatens the future autonomy of those children who will not be able to see themselves "as the sole authors of their own life history."[90]

In his defence of liberal eugenics, Agar is acutely aware of this paradox. Drawing on the concept of a child's right to an open future, he argues that limits can be placed on morally acceptable enhancements at precisely the point at which the exercise of parental autonomy threatens to limit the eventual autonomy of the child. Whatever enhancements the parents choose must be capable not only of allowing the child to live the life his parents want for him, but also of living a very different life. In Agar's words, "It must be possible for a person to completely reject the ideals motivating her enhancement. Furthermore, if she does reject these ideals she must have a reasonable chance of successfully pursuing her chosen plan."[91]

Sandel is not convinced that what makes enhancements ethically troubling is that they may affect the autonomy of the child; non-designed children, like designed ones, have no control over their genetic inheritance. He states: "The alternative to a cloned or genetically enhanced child is not one whose future is unbiased and unbound by particular talents, but a child at the mercy of the genetic lottery."[92] However, he does think that there is something wrong with enhancing children and that what this is cannot be captured with the moral vocabulary we currently use, which consists largely of the "language of autonomy and rights."[93] The genetic revolution, he believes, has "induced a kind of moral vertigo. To grapple with the ethics of enhancement, we need to confront questions largely lost from view in the modern world—questions about the moral status of nature, and about the proper stance of human beings towards the given world."[94]

It is in these terms that Sandel tries to articulate what he believes is ethically problematic about enhancement technologies, namely, that they replace an appreciation of the "gifted character of human powers and achievements"—the belief that not everything we do is, or should be, within our control—with "the drive to mastery."[95] He argues that this drive, demonstrated in the genetic enhancement of children, will have far-reaching implications. It will distort the parent-child relationship; it will make parents even more responsible for their children than they already are; and it will shape how we view the world and its contingencies. In response to defenders of the procreative liberty argument, who see enhancement as part of the exercise of parental freedom, Sandel asserts, "[C]hanging our nature to fit the world, rather than the other way round, is actually the deepest form of disempowerment. It distracts us from reflecting critically on the world, and deadens the impulse to social and political improvement."[96] In response to Harris' claim that he would enhance his own children by giving them green skin if this would protect them from a depleted ozone layer, Sandel would probably say that our energies would be better spent preventing the ozone depletion in the first place: this would benefit everyone, not only those who are able and willing to enhance their children.

A CHIP OF THE OLD BLOCK.
My gracious! here's a likeness,— why its Daddy all over bless its little soul.

While the idea that a "peg-leg" could be inherited is clearly absurd, this image illustrates the challenge of limited genetic knowledge. Even today, there is still much that we do not know about our genes and the effects that our manipulation of them might have on our descendants.

ETHICAL THEORY AND GENETIC TECHNOLOGIES

The genetic revolution may give us the power not only to control our offspring (as we can now do with pre-implantation embryo diagnosis and prenatal testing) but also to shape our descendants and even humanity itself (as germ-line therapy and genetic enhancements are designed to do). This poses ethical challenges that some scholars believe our current ethical theories are unable to resolve.

In a prescient essay, Jonas points out that the purpose of all traditional ethics was to guide action. Moreover, the agent—the one performing the action—and the "other"—the person who was affected by the action—shared a common physical and temporal space. Jonas writes, "It is those alive now and in some commerce with me that have a claim on my conduct as it affects them by deed or omission. The ethical universe is composed of contemporaries, and its horizon is confined to the conceivable span of their lives."[97]

Jonas argues that modern technology is novel in the powers it gives us, and it is this novelty that renders traditional ethics helpless. He identifies four features of older technology that no longer hold: first, with the exception of medicine, all dealings with the non-human world were ethically neutral; second, ethics was concerned with the way in which human beings dealt directly with one another; third, human beings were considered to be "constant in essence"[98] and not subject to technological control; and, fourth, the good and evil results of an action were not matters "for remote planning,"[99] either in time or space.

The challenges to traditional ethics posed by the genetic revolution can be summarized into two main points. First, the ability to shape human beings means that the concept of "natural norms" (such as "human nature," "normal lifespan," "human intelligence," and so on) that provided a context for ethical action no longer apply. Second, the ethical theories are designed to deal with our obligations to already existing people. Determining how they apply to fetuses and embryos is difficult enough, but they seem to lead either to absurdities or to have nothing to say when it comes to future persons.

This can be illustrated when we consider enhancements directed at characteristics such as the intellectual capacities, psychological tendencies, and moral proclivities of future people. Studies on animals reveal what might be possible. Gessen reports on experiments carried out by Russian scientists designed to determine how wolves became dogs, a process that happened far faster than the normal rate of genetic mutations. How does a large wild animal, with a blocky muzzle and a limited range of colours, evolve into breeds as diverse as poodles, golden retrievers, chihuahuas? Even if humans bred dogs to exhibit particular traits, these traits had to begin as spontaneous mutations.

The Russian scientists worked with foxes to answer this question, since they were easy to obtain and closely related to wolves. They divided the foxes into two groups, those that seemed the most friendly and those that seemed the most aggressive. They then bred the friendly ones with friendly ones and the aggressive ones with aggressive ones. Within nine generations, they had a "small population of silver foxes that were unlike any silver fox that had gone before. They loved people. They loved to be given attention by people. They loved to be handled by people. They were, from all appearances, ready to leave their cages and go live with humans in their homes, becoming fully domesticated."[100] Gessen observes that genes correlating with moods and behaviour have been identified in humans, including antisocial and addictive tendencies, risk-taking, depression, and altruism, which suggests that humans too could have particular emotional traits enhanced through genetic selection and manipulation.

How might utilitarians and Kantians respond to these facts? Consider that utilitarians believe that we should strive to increase happiness and decrease unhappiness, and that genes may influence temperament. In some interpretations of utilitarianism, it would not only be morally acceptable, but morally required, for parents to engineer their offspring so that they possessed more of the "happiness genes." On the one hand, the "notion that we must genetically engineer every human being to be as emotionally upbeat as possible is absurd."[101] On the other hand, critics argue, the only way for utilitarians to avoid this kind of conclusion is "by offering no guidance on how we should use enhancement technologies."[102]

Kantians, likewise, seem caught between "absurdity and silence"[103] when it comes to enhancing descendants. For example, how does the Kantian requirement that we ought to treat rational beings as ends in themselves apply here? Would we be violating or respecting this requirement if we took steps to ensure that our descendants were even more rational than we are? Or what if we decided to engineer non-rational human beings who would be capable of doing certain forms of manual labour, and we did this simply by manipulating embryos, so that no already existing rational humans were harmed? Beyond telling us that rational beings need to be treated as ends while non-rational ones can be treated as means, Kantianism seems to have little to tell us about what we should do.[104]

Virtue ethics, moreover, seems equally unhelpful, since it connects action to emotion, and both to character, within the framework of one human life. On the one hand, our understanding of human excellence seems challenged if it can be achieved through genetic manipulation. On the other hand, it is not clear that virtue ethics tells us that it would be wrong to achieve moral excellence through genetic manipulation, either. In fact, it is not clear what a virtue ethicist might say about obligations to future and as yet non-existent persons. Finally, while feminist ethicists would draw our attention to the power structures that shape the way in which genetic technologies are developed and used, it is not clear what more and what else they would say about genetic enhancements whose effects would only be felt in the future, and are presently both unpredictable and unknowable. None of the ethical approaches currently available to us, then, seem fully adequate to address all of the questions raised by the genetic revolution.

With respect to genetic technologies, Jonas asserts that serious questions, such as what right we have to experiment on future human beings, what standards we would use to shape them, and on the basis of what knowledge, "demand an answer before we embark on a journey into the unknown."[105] This assertion seems particularly relevant when it comes to enhancement technologies, which may affect future generations in ways we do not know and so cannot predict. Gessen discovers that breeding foxes for behaviour (not genetically manipulating them through the use of technology) seems to have "thrown the … genome out of whack, causing new mutations to appear faster than normal and activating and deactivating various genes."[106] While the researchers were careful to avoid inbreeding, the physical features of the foxes began to change along with their behaviour, including the shape of their ears and snouts, and their colouring. It is likely that unexpected changes would also occur with human enhancements, which makes any ethical judgments based on traditional ethical theories even more problematic. We cannot determine whether or not we should engage in such enhancements if we do not, and cannot, know what the outcomes of our interference might be or who might be affected by our actions, and this is a problem for both advocates and critics of these technologies.

CONCLUSION

The genetic revolution raises new possibilities for human beings, including the possibility of shaping our descendants and altering humanity. With this power comes enormous responsibility to use it wisely. However, because so many of the potential applications are speculative and future-oriented, it is difficult to determine what a wise use of genetic technology requires of us. Moreover, because our actions today may affect people who are many generations removed from us, both our traditional ethical theories, and the concepts (such as autonomy, utility, and rights) that we have derived from them, may not be fully adequate to guide us. The novel ethical questions raised by the genetic revolution may require a new ethics that is adequate to address them. In the meantime, they suggest that we should exercise caution as we determine how to proceed.

PHILOSOPHICAL REFLECTION ON EUGENICS

Ideas shape our understanding. The most powerful ideas are the ones we don't even notice; they seem not ideas at all, but simple and obvious truths. One of the most powerful of these ideas is the idea of progress, the belief that history demonstrates a continuous and inevitable improvement of the human lot, materially, socially, and politically. Increased scientific knowledge is commonly understood to be an important contributor to progress; science allows us to understand and control the natural world, and provides a basis for the technological tools we employ to improve our lives. No longer are we defenceless in the face of natural phenomena such as disease, famine, and natural disasters. Scientific progress gives us the power to predict, prevent, and ameliorate conditions and situations that our ancestors could do little about. In short, scientific and technological progress allows us to reduce human suffering.[107]

One of the most stunning examples of scientific progress is our new understanding of molecular genetics. We are in the middle of a genetic revolution, "a transformation of our ideas about nature whose only equivalents are the birth of modern science in the seventeenth century and the upheavals in physics of the early twentieth century."[108] Revolutions, however, often have their dark side, and in order to use our new knowledge wisely, we need to pay attention to our (recent) past.

Scientific developments are not always clear-cut, and the application of scientific knowledge is seldom value-neutral. Scientific theories are proposed, tested, and sometimes discredited, and our understanding of nuclear physics led to the development of the atom bomb. What counts as an undisputed scientific truth at one point in time can, in retrospect, reveal itself to be a mistaken interpretation of the evidence. Likewise, the application of scientific developments, while appearing initially to respond to humane purposes, can later reveal themselves to reflect contemporary prejudices. Looking backward, then, can teach us important lessons about our own time, reveal unquestioned assumptions, and allow us to avoid repeating mistakes.

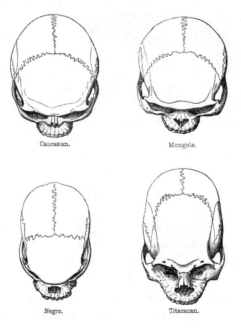

"The vertical configuration of the skull," an engraving from James Cowles Prichard's *Natural History of Man*, 1848. The history of eugenics—a misguided approach to genetics endorsed by many "enlightened" and educated people—reminds us that we should be careful in the way in which we use genetic knowledge. In particular, we need to ensure that we do not simply reinforce existing prejudices concerning which human lives have value and which do not.

One of the most significant of these mistakes was the eugenics movement, which flourished in North and South America, parts of Europe, and Japan from around the 1890s to the 1930s. Eugenicists were inspired by Darwin's evolutionary theory (it was Darwin's cousin, Francis Galton, who coined the term "eugenics," which means "well born") and by the goal of social progress; they believed that they had a moral duty to improve humanity by ensuring that only the most "genetically fit" reproduced. As a result, they believed, they would reduce human suffering, increase the number of intelligent and healthy people, and save scarce societal resources that were being wasted on taking care of the "genetically unfit" who were unable to take care of themselves. In order to achieve these goals, however, it was not enough to encourage the genetically fit to have more children; in addition, the genetically unfit had to be discouraged from breeding—by force, and without their consent if necessary.

Eugenics in this form is now recognized as a pseudo-science (the principles on which it was based were scientifically confused, and eugenicists were unable to clearly distinguish social conditions from genetic ones). However, it is important to note that, at the time, its purposes—to make humanity healthier and happier by weeding out those who suffered from genetic and other defects—were supported by the most enlightened and progressive people, who believed that they were doing what was best for future generations and that their policies were based on "sound" scientific principles. As Gould observes, "[E]ugenics, touted in its day as the latest in scientific modernism, attracted many liberals and numbered among its most vociferous critics groups often labelled as reactionary and unscientific."[109]

The headquarters of the eugenics movement was at Cold Springs Harbor, New York, home of the Eugenics Record Office. The Centre's director was Charles Davenport. Some of his ideas about heredity were so absurd that they seem laughable today. For instance, he was convinced "that the large number of naval officers in some families pointed to a hereditary yen for the sea.... [He] earnestly sought the allele for what he called 'thalassophilia' (literally, 'love of the sea'), which he took to be a sex-linked **recessive** expressed only in males."[110] However, his activities were not laughable at all; he campaigned tirelessly to have legislation put in place to ensure that the genetically unfit were not permitted to immigrate to the U.S., and that those in this category already in the country be prevented from reproducing through compulsory sterilization. His colleague, Harry Laughlin, included in his category of the "most worthless" the "blind, including those with seriously impaired vision; the deaf, including those with seriously impaired hearing; and the dependent, including orphans, ne'er-do-wells, the homeless, tramps, and paupers."[111] As a result of the campaign led by the Eugenics Record Office, the U.S. government restricted immigration from "undesirable" parts of the world such as Southern and Eastern Europe (would-be immigrants were given IQ tests at Ellis Island, and those who performed poorly—often because they did not understand English or knew nothing about the recent "history of baseball"[112]—were sent back from whence they came). And by the 1930s, 30 states had passed eugenic legislation, allowing for compulsory sterilization of those judged defective and feeble-minded.

The eugenics movement also had an influence in Canada. Ironically, proponents of eugenic legislation were among the most enlightened and progressive of social reformers. These included leaders of the suffrage movement, such as Canada's first female magistrate, Emily Murphy (who said, "Insane people ... are not entitled to progeny"[113]), and Nellie McClung (famous for getting women recognized as "persons" under the law), who promoted the sterilization of "young simple-minded girls."[114] As a result of their efforts, the Alberta Sexual Sterilization Act was passed on March 7, 1928. The Eugenics Board created by the act had the power to authorize compulsory sterilization of those brought before it. Among those considered unfit to bear children were Native people, immigrants, epileptics, alcoholics, the poor, and unwed mothers. Consequently, 2822 people were eventually sterilized. (British Columbia also passed a similar act, but did not implement its provisions as rigorously.) The Alberta Sexual Sterilization Act was not repealed until 1972. The eugenics movement was finally discredited by the application of eugenic ideas in Nazi Germany, which began by sterilizing 375,000 people in the 1930s and culminated in the murder of millions deemed "inferior" in the gas chambers.

We can learn a number of lessons from this sobering history. First, even when our goals are laudable—who can argue against reducing human suffering?—the methods we use to achieve them must be subject to ethical scrutiny. Second, we need to be conscious of human fallibility and of our tendency to make judgments about the worth of other people's lives. While we might laugh at some of the beliefs of the eugenicists (though not at their application of those beliefs), our increased knowledge of genetics does not free us from the necessity of making value judgments about how this knowledge is used. Science will not tell us what genes we should test for, or what we should do with the results. Finally, since the history of eugenics demonstrates both coercion and discrimination, the social context within which genetic knowledge is gained and applied is also important.

CASES OF INTEREST

Jones v. Rostvig

Liam Jones was born April 11, 1997, in Chilliwack, B.C., and diagnosed with Down's syndrome a few days later. He has a life expectancy of about 57 years. His parents, Kelly Short and Leonard Jones, were surprised by the diagnosis. Soon after, they advanced claims of negligence against Dr. Rostvig, Ms. Short's family physician. They sought non-pecuniary damages for the cost of Liam's care from birth to the end of his life, based on the assertion that Dr. Rostvig failed to caution them of the potential risk of Down's syndrome and the advisability of Kelly undergoing an amniocentesis. Ms. Short also advanced a claim for past and future wage losses.

Dr. Rostvig admitted liability and conceded that, had he met the appropriate standard of care and provided proper advice to Liam's parents, the pregnancy would have been terminated. The task of the court, then, was to assess and allocate the appropriate damages. Liam is not safety-conscious and cannot be left alone. Unless he is watching a favourite TV program, Liam has an attention span of from 2 to 4 minutes. Dr. Joschko, the psychologist called by the defendant, classified Liam as having a moderate intellectual disability, with an IQ of about 50. He is expected to reach the cognitive capacity of a six- to eight-year-old. In 1999, Mr. Jones fell off a ladder at work and suffered brain damage as a result. Although he loves Liam dearly, he maintains that his level of tolerance and patience is significantly lower than what it was prior to the accident, so he cannot be left to supervise Liam for more than three hours at a time.

The most significant damages were allocated as follows: Ms. Short received $75,000 in non-pecuniary damages, while Mr. Jones received $45,000; Ms. Short received $46,000 for past wage losses; together they received $33,000 for respite care workers; and Liam's daily care is paid for until the age of 25.[115]

Moore v. Regents of the University of California

John Moore, who was suffering from hairy cell leukemia, visited the UCLA Medical Center on October 5, 1976, and was treated by Dr. Golde. Tests administered by Dr. Golde revealed that Moore's cells would be useful for genetic research. On October 8, 1976, Dr. Golde recommended that Moore's spleen be removed. After the surgery, Golde falsely informed Moore that further tests and treatment were required, which must be conducted at the UCLA Medical Center. Over a seven-year period,

Moore travelled from his home in Seattle to the Medical Center where Dr. Golde took blood and tissue samples from him. Dr. Golde also retained his spleen for research without Moore's knowledge.

In August 1979, Dr. Golde established a cell line from the tissue taken from Moore's body. On March 20, 1984, Dr. Golde and his researcher, Shirley Quan, received a patent for the "Mo cell-line," which was developed solely from Moore's tissue. The patent was assigned to the University of California, who then entered into an agreement with Genetics Institute and Sandez Pharmaceutical to develop commercial products from the Mo cell-line. The defendants received significant royalties from licensing the technology, which included cash and stock options.

Moore learned of these activities and sued on 13 counts, the most significant being a claim for conversion, arguing that his blood and tissues and the cell line[116] developed from them were his tangible personal property, and a claim that Dr. Golde had a duty to disclose his intent to use Moore's tissue for economic gain. The Supreme Court of California ruled that Moore had no reason to expect to retain possession of his cells. Since he retained no ownership interest, a conversion claim could not be sustained. They ruled, however, that Dr. Golde breached his fiduciary duty to disclose material facts. A reasonable patient would expect to be made aware that his physician's judgment may be impaired by economic interests.[117]

Zhang v. Kan

Ms. Zhang, a resident of Hong Kong, was 37 when she became pregnant in 1996. She was aware of the increased risks of giving birth to a Down's syndrome child, given her age. Ms. Zhang and her partner, Mr. Fung, planned to give birth to their child in Canada because of what they considered to be its superior health care system. They flew to Vancouver in November 1996, where they stayed with one of Mr. Fung's employees, Ms. Chai. She recommended that the couple consult Dr. Kan. On November 26, 1996, Dr. Kan informed Ms. Zhang that it was too late to perform an amniocentesis. Given her prior research on the subject and her consultations with her physician in Hong Kong, Ms. Zhang doubted this, but reluctantly accepted her partner's suggestion to trust Dr. Kan's professional judgment. Sherry Fung was born in the spring of 1997, and diagnosed with Down's syndrome shortly thereafter. Ms. Zhang and Mr. Fung separated soon after the diagnosis. Sherry now lives with her father.

The co-plaintiffs advanced a claim of medical negligence, arguing that Dr. Kan negligently advised the couple that amniocentesis was no longer an option at the then-current stage of pregnancy. Both plaintiffs claimed that, had they been made aware of the fetus's condition, they would have terminated the pregnancy. The Supreme Court of British Columbia found that Ms. Zhang was a sophisticated and successful businesswoman who had conducted thorough research on the subject and knew that Dr. Kan gave poor advice and that he could have arranged for an amniocentesis on an expedited basis. The couple could have returned to Hong Kong for the test or consulted another physician. Given that Dr. Kan's advice fell below the accepted standard of care expected of a physician, however, the judge found the co-plaintiffs' and defendant's contributory negligence to be 50 percent. Ms. Zhang was awarded $10,000 in non-pecuniary damages. Mr. Fung was awarded $5,000 in non-pecuniary damages, $5,000 for past compensation, $171,926 for future care costs, and $21,845 for the possibility that certain state benefits and services will not be available for Sherry.[118]

CASE STUDIES

Scenario One

Alice Lange is four months' pregnant. During a routine visit to the doctor's office, she learns that her fetus has 22q11.2 deletion syndrome. The symptoms of this syndrome range in severity from mild to very serious and may include heart defects, thymus gland abnormality, increased susceptibility to infections, cleft palate, delayed acquisition of speech, difficulty in feeding and swallowing, renal abnormalities, hearing loss, autoimmune disorders, seizures, learning disabilities, behavioural problems, and hyperactivity. There is no cure, but there are treatments available to manage the symptoms. Given that the child may develop serious mental and physical impairments, Alice wants to abort the fetus. She believes it would be better not to have a child who would face a lifetime of medical problems. However, her husband, Jesse, believes that the possibility of this child leading a relatively normal life with only mild symptoms requires them to carry the child to term. If the child is severely impaired, he believes they could care for it. If the child has only mild impairments, then it could live a relatively normal life, and they should give it this chance.

(1) Should Alice carry the child to term? (2) Is this Alice's decision to make? Or does Jesse have a say? (3) Should she be thinking of aborting this fetus at all? (4) Does the potential child have any interests? Does its future quality of life count in the equation? (5) How might Kantians and utilitarians answer this question? (6) Could a feminist ethicist resolve this dilemma, and if so, how?

Scenario Two

You are an editor at a major newspaper. This morning, some employees in your advertising department brought to your attention an advertisement that caused them concern. The advertisement was from a private clinic in Vancouver, offering sex determination tests. You have heard rumours that this clinic caters to a community in which male children are more highly valued than female children, and while the advertisement says nothing about sex-selective abortion, you are concerned that this is what these tests will lead to.

(1) Should you run the advertisement? (2) Can you make a case for not running it? (3) Ought we to limit public communication that promotes a particular discriminatory practice, even if indirectly? (4) Is it permissible to limit access to abortion services in order to combat systemic gender discrimination? (5) What recommendation might a feminist ethicist make in this case? (6) Would Agar support printing this advertisement? What would Sandel say?

Scenario Three

Nicole Abbey was 37 when she developed symptoms of Huntington's disease. Her mother died of Huntington's, and her daughter, Michelle, is at risk of having the disease. Michelle is now 23 years old. She is asymptomatic and has never been tested. She now wants children of her own. She has been debating whether she is morally obligated to have pre-symptomatic testing before she tries to conceive. She does not want to know if she is a carrier, as she fears that with a positive test result her life will be blighted much earlier than it would be if she does not get tested but later develops the disease. However, she knows that there is a 50 percent chance that she is a carrier, and if she has the gene, then there is a 50 percent chance that her offspring will inherit it.

Michelle discusses her dilemma with a genetic counsellor, who tells her that she could get pregnant and then have the fetus tested for the disease. If it tests negative, then she can continue with the pregnancy without finding out about her own status. If it tests positive, however, then Michelle will learn indirectly that she will develop the disease, and she will also have to decide whether to have a selective abortion. Given that both of these events are likely to be very traumatic, he recommends that she think carefully about what she wants to do.

(1) What should Michelle do? (2) Is Michelle morally obligated to get tested for Huntington's before trying to get pregnant? (3) Should she get pregnant and then have the fetus tested? (4) If she follows this plan, should she abort the fetus if it tests positive?

Scenario Four

You are the Director of a Reprogenetics Institute, which offers clients the opportunity to use cloning technology to produce offspring. So far, the couples that have pursued this reproductive option are parents who have lost children as a result of accidents and want to replace them. You feel that you perform a valuable service to grieving people when you honour these requests. Today, however, the couple you are meeting with present you with an unforeseen dilemma. Jacob Nicholson is 37 years old and married to Lauren, 33. When Jacob was 10, his parents died in a car accident. He was raised by his grandfather. While Jacob was in university, his grandfather died. Jacob was devastated and asked that doctors preserve samples of his grandfather's genetic material. Now that Jacob is married and financially secure, he wants you to implant a clone of his grandfather in his wife. Lauren is reluctant to go through with this plan. She tells you that she is concerned that Jacob will be disappointed as this new person will not be his grandfather. It will merely be a genetic copy, which, she knows, is like having a twin; the clone is an entirely different person with a different personality and interests. Moreover, she is squeamish about giving birth to a clone of her husband's grandfather and fears that she will not be comfortable with the resulting child. She is willing, however, to go through with the pregnancy since it is so important to Jacob. Jacob states that he believes that she will bond with the fetus during pregnancy, and that this procedure will make their marriage stronger; he would also be happy to have normally conceived children with her after this clone of his grandfather is born.

(1) Should you agree to Jacob's request? (2) What are the ethical difficulties created by this situation? (3) If Lauren were enthusiastic about the procedure, would there be any ethical difficulties? (4) Would the situation be different if the person to be cloned were still alive? (5) Do we need a person's consent in order to clone him or her, whether dead or alive?

Scenario Five

Sarah and Peter live in a small northern community. Because Sarah was in her late thirties when she became pregnant, she decided to undergo prenatal testing. When they return to the doctor's office to hear the test results, they learn that their fetus has Down's syndrome. The doctor explains their options. If they have the child, they will face medical costs that are not entirely covered by Medicare and must pay for the special schooling their child may require. As a result of government cutbacks, money that used to go to community programs for mentally and physically disabled children is no longer available. If they decide not to have the child, the doctor can schedule Sarah for an abortion. Sarah and Peter object to abortion on religious grounds. They are, however, concerned about how they will raise the child.

(1) If society allows physically and mentally impaired children to be born when their birth can be prevented, must it also provide funding for their care afterward? (2) Can the parents of an impaired infant make a fully autonomous choice about continuing a pregnancy when they know that they will have to bear financial responsibility for all the child's special needs? (3) Given that Sarah and her husband are opposed to abortion, should she have had prenatal testing in the first place? (4) Does the availability of prenatal testing entail that parents are responsible for the handicaps of their children in a way that they weren't before such testing was developed?

Scenario Six

You are a scientist working in a genetics lab that is considering cloning a Neanderthal using DNA retrieved from a frozen specimen. The idea has long been on the table, and the technology has recently developed sufficiently to make this feasible. The technology requires you to inject Neanderthal DNA into an egg taken from a close species relative (human or chimpanzee) and then place it in a surrogate mother, also either human or chimpanzee. You are to evaluate the ethical issues this possibility generates and make a recommendation about whether the experiment should proceed.

(1) Which do you choose as the egg donor: the chimpanzee or the human? Which do you choose as the surrogate mother? (2) Since Neanderthals were a human species, would they have an interest in which egg and which surrogate you use? (3) Should extinct species be resurrected? (4) Do you agree with Kaebnick, who believes that we should not recreate Neanderthals, even if we could, because we do not know enough about them? (5) If we were to successfully clone a Neanderthal, would it be part of the moral community? (6) What features of this situation would a feminist approach illuminate that might otherwise be missed? (7) Would you recommend that the experiment proceed?

Scenario Seven

"Honey," Jaden Smith called, as she perused a genetic databank online. "I was thinking we should have a little girl with blond hair." Jaden and her husband had an appointment the following week at the reprogenetics clinic, which would enable them to pick certain traits, have their eggs and sperm screened for the appropriate genes, have any necessary genetic alterations made, and implant the perfect embryo.

Her husband passed in and out of the room, obviously doing two things at once and preoccupied with his other task. "Sure," he responded.

"She should be smart, but not too smart. Smart enough to get a business degree, and earn a lot of money. But we don't want her to be so abnormally intelligent that she gets teased and taunted by her classmates until she graduates high school." Jaden flipped to the section on inherited illnesses and the genetic causes. "We should make sure that she doesn't inherit any illnesses from us, either. We don't want her getting diabetes, or having to deal with some sort of physical or mental disability. I want her to be totally healthy, slightly athletic, smart, good with numbers. She should have outstanding social skills. She'll need those if she's going to succeed in the world of business. And she should be clever and cunning. We also don't want her being too moral. You need to exploit people in order to succeed in this world. With blond hair and green eyes. She'll be perfect."

(1) Is anything wrong with this picture? Does such a scenario necessarily follow from genetic and prenatal screening? (2) Do Jaden's planned alterations meet the test of ensuring that the enhanced child has an open future? (3) What might Harris say about these plans? Would Sandel agree? (4) Could Kantians, utilitarians, and virtue ethicists make a recommendation for or against the preselection of desired traits in a child?

GLOSSARY

Carrier: someone who has one copy of a gene for a recessive trait. Carriers can pass the gene on to their offspring but do not express it themselves.

Chromosome: a building block of the genome; chromosomes include DNA, nucleotide sequences, and genes.

Dominant trait: a trait that will appear, or be expressed, in an individual if he or she receives a single copy of a gene (from one parent) for this trait.

Epigenetics: the study of changes in gene expression in response to external factors, such as diet and exposure to chemicals, and the ways in which these changes are passed on to descendants.

Gene: the basic unit of heredity in a living organism.

Gene therapy: experimental therapy involving the insertion of genes into individuals to replace defective ones in order to treat or cure genetic diseases.

Genome: all the hereditary information encoded in the DNA of an organism.

Heterozygous: a term used to describe an organism that inherited dissimilar copies of a gene responsible for a particular trait. If one of the genes is defective, a heterozygote may be a carrier for a genetic disease but will not usually suffer from that disease.

Homozygous: a term used to describe an organism that inherited two similar copies (one from each parent) of a gene responsible for a particular trait. If both copies are defective, that organism may suffer from a genetic disease.

Recessive trait: a trait that requires a copy of a gene from both parents to be expressed in the offspring.

Reprogenetics: a term coined to describe the merging of genetic technologies with reproductive ones. Many of the outcomes expected to result from reprogenetics have not yet been realized.

Right to an open future: an argument that is often used to place a limit on the exercise of parental autonomy when it comes to shaping their children. According to this argument, parents cannot shape their children in ways that will prevent them from choosing for themselves, when they grow up, how they want to live.

FOR FURTHER READING

Bonnicksen, Andrea. "Genetic Diagnosis of Human Embryos." *Hastings Center Report*, 22, no. 4 (1992): S5–S11.

The combination of IVF and increased genetic knowledge has made it possible to identify the genetic traits of embryos before they are implanted. While, for many, pre-implantation diagnosis seems ethically preferable to selective abortion as a means of reducing genetic disease, it raises a number of ethical questions, some of which Bonnicksen explores in this essay.

Davis, Dena S. "Genetic Dilemmas and the Child's Right to an Open Future." *Hastings Center Report*, 27, no. 2 (1997): 7–15.

The moral expectations of contemporary genetic counselling require counsellors to be non-directive (not to tell their clients what to do) and to respect their clients' autonomy. Davis notes that these expectations are challenged when prospective parents ask to have a child with traits normally considered to be disabilities, such as deafness and dwarfism, and argues that counsellors should refuse such requests because they will limit the future child's autonomy.

Gessen, Masha. *Blood Matters*. Orlando, FL: Harcourt Inc., 2008.

In this very accessible book, Gessen explores recent discoveries and developments in genetics. She intersperses her discussion of them with a personal account of her own struggle to decide how to respond after undergoing pre-symptomatic genetic testing and finding out that she possessed the BRCA1 gene mutation associated with an increased risk of breast and ovarian cancer.

Harris, John. "'Goodbye, Dolly?' The Ethics of Human Cloning." *Journal of Medical Ethics*, 23, no. 6 (December 1997): 353–360.

In this defence of human reproductive cloning, Harris examines a number of arguments commonly presented against this form of cloning and finds them unpersuasive. He then argues that procreative autonomy protects not only the right to reproduce without interference, but also the right to choose the means by which reproduction is accomplished.

Ishiguro, Kazuo. *Never Let Me Go*. Toronto: Knopf, 2005.

In this chilling and thoughtful novel, Ishiguro imagines a world in which cloned humans have been created to serve as organ donors for non-cloned ones. The story is told from the perspective of one of the "carers" and reveals, in degrees, both how completely human the clones are and how ethically problematic their treatment is.

Kass, Leon. "The Wisdom of Repugnance." *The New Republic*, 216, no. 22 (June 2, 1997). (Available at www.catholiceducation.org/articles/medical_ethics/me0006.html.)

In this well-known essay, Kass makes a case against human reproductive cloning on the grounds that it elicits feelings of repugnance and revulsion in most people who consider it. In the course of his discussion, Kass makes some interesting claims about the state of contemporary bioethics.

Picoult, Jodi. *My Sister's Keeper*. New York: Washington Square Press, 2004.

This novel tells the story of a young girl who was conceived through pre-implantation genetic diagnosis to be a form of medical treatment for her older sister who is suffering from leukemia. The narrative is told from multiple perspectives, and reveals the way in which parents with the best of intentions can find themselves caught up in unintended ethical dilemmas as a result of their choice to make use of one of the possibilities opened up by the genetic revolution. This book illustrates, in a dramatic way, some of the ethical issues considered by Bonnicksen and Rothman.

Rothman, Barbara Katz. "Not All That Glitters Is Gold." *Hastings Center Report*, 22, no. 4 (1992): S11–S15.

Rothman also considers the ethical issues raised by pre-implantation diagnosis. She argues that women are disproportionately affected by the technologies that allow this form of genetic testing and by the consequences of having a handicapped child. Far from offering women more choice, Rothman suggests that pre-implantation diagnosis may compel them to undergo unwanted IVF and embryo diagnosis.

RECOMMENDED WEBSITES

Genethics.ca

genethics.ca

This site serves as "a clearing house for information on the social, ethical and policy issues associated with genetic and genomic knowledge and technology." It provides links to stories about issues raised by genetic technology, and covers topics ranging from biobanks and cloning to genetic testing and the Human Genome Project.

Genetic Genealogy

www.dnaancestryproject.com

Genes can provide some evidence of the origins of our ancestors. This website claims to help users discover their "deep ancestral roots using genetic genealogy. Find out where your ancestors came from, discover their ethnic background, and trace the roots of your surname." Users can order a DNA kit (for a cost), and send it back after obtaining a genetic sample. Results are analyzed and can then be accessed online.

Humanity+

humanityplus.org/

This site provides an interesting introduction to the transhumanist movement, which is dedicated to improving human beings through the use of technologies, including genetic technologies. Transhumanists represented here hope that these technologies will increase the human lifespan, erase limits on intelligence, and even free humans from our "confinement to the planet earth."

National Institutes of Health

www.nih.gov/

This website provides information on current American guidelines for medical research, including research using embryonic stem cells. The site also includes a section on the ethical issues raised by such research, as well as links to related sites.

NOTES

1. Matt Ridley, *Genome: The Autobiography of a Species in 23 Chapters* (New York: Harper-Collins, 1999), 56.
2. Gregory E. Pence, *Classic Cases in Medical Ethics*, 3rd ed. (New York: McGraw-Hill, 2000), 399.
3. Gessen reports that in "Western countries where predictive testing for Huntington's is available, roughly one in five at-risk people choose to find out if they carry the mutant gene." Masha Gessen, *Blood Matters* (Orlando, FL: Harcourt, 2008), 162.
4. Pence, *Classic Cases*, 403.

5. Ridley, 63.

6. Ridley, 6.

7. Lee M. Silver, *Remaking Eden: Cloning and Beyond in a Brave New World* (New York: Avon Books, 1997), 15.

8. For example, Nicholas Agar states that "evil" was done in the name of eugenics, and it "took its most concentrated form in the racist doctrine of human perfection promoted by the Nazis." Nicholas Agar, *Liberal Eugenics: In Defense of Human Enhancement* (Oxford: Blackwell Publishing, 2004), 3.

9. Agar, 40.

10. Agar, 68.

11. Walter Glannon, *Biomedical Ethics* (Oxford: Oxford University Press, 2005), 103–104.

12. Silver, 246. Lest this sound too much like pure, unadulterated science fiction, Silver observes that people have always said that many of the things we are currently doing were impossible: "'Understanding the true nature of the gene is beyond the capabilities of mortal man,' they said in 1935; it is *impossible* to determine the sequence of the complete human genome they said in 1984 ... it is *impossible* to read the information present in single embryonic cells, they said in 1985; it is *impossible* to clone ... from adult cells, they said in 1986. And all of these impossibilities not only became possible but were accomplished while the early naysayers were still alive." Silver, 245.

13. Francoise Baylis and Jason Scott Robert, "The Inevitability of Genetic Enhancement Technologies," in Francoise Baylis et al. (eds.), *Health Care Ethics in Canada* (Toronto: Thomson Wadsworth, 2004), 448–460.

14. Roger Gosden, *Designing Babies: The Brave New World of Reproductive Technology* (London: W.H. Freeman & Company, 2000), 67.

15. See, for instance, Abby Lippman, "Prenatal Genetic Testing and Screening: Constructing Needs and Reinforcing Inequities," in Baylis et al., 401–411.

16. Leon Kass, quoted in Agar, 115.

17. Philip Kitcher, *The Lives to Come: The Genetic Revolution and Human Possibilities* (New York: Simon and Schuster, 1996), 18.

18. Silver imagines that the reprogenetic revolution may eventually produce beings who can "trace their ancestry back directly to *homo sapiens*, [but are] ... as different from humans as humans are from the primitive worms with tiny brains that first crawled along the earth's surface." Silver, 249.

19. Gessen observes that many contemporary applications of genetic knowledge share a number of features with the eugenics of the past, including: similar area of study; public health measures; economic arguments given in support of genetic testing; and "wrongful birth" lawsuits, which are predicated on the idea that some lives are not worth living. Gessen, 65–68.

20. Pence, *Classic Cases*, 395.

21. Michael J. Sandel, *The Case Against Perfection* (Cambridge, MA: Harvard University Press, 2007), 75.

22. Agar, 5.

23. Agar, 5.

24. "The presumption is that citizens should be free to make their own choices in the light of their own values...." John Harris, *Enhancing Evolution: The Ethical Case for Making Better People* (Princeton, NJ: Princeton University Press, 2003), 72.

25. Kitcher, 192.

26. This position can also be termed "eugenic consumerism": allowing "individuals to pick and choose from what is on offer in the reproductive marketplace, according to personal tastes and circumstances." Gosden, 5.

27. Silver, 9.
28. Baylis and Robert, 453.
29. Kitcher, 202.
30. Kitcher, 66–67.
31. Pence, *Classic Cases*, 404.
32. Pence, *Classic Cases*, 404.
33. Gessen, 82.
34. The correlation is much tighter with Huntington's than with the BRCA genes: in the former case, possession of the gene means the disease is inevitable, while in the latter, possession of the gene makes the disease highly probable.
35. Nancy Wexler, interviewed in the *Australian Huntington's Disease Association Newsletter*, December 2004, found at www.qahda.com/Dec 2004.html (September 3, 2009).
36. Ridley, 62.
37. Kitcher, 130.
38. Pence, *Classic Cases*, 407.
39. Laura M. Purdy, "Genetics and Reproductive Risk: Can Having Children Be Immoral?" in Wanda Teays and Laura M. Purdy (eds.), *Bioethics, Justice, and Health Care* (Belmont, CA: Thomson Wadsworth, 2001), 632.
40. Wexler, n.p.
41. Glannon, 106.
42. See the case of Jesse Gelsinger, which opens Chapter 3.
43. Glannon, 108.
44. Christopher H. Evans, Steven C. Ghivizzani, and Paul D. Robbins, "Arthritis Gene Therapy's First Death," *Arthritis Research & Therapy*, 10 (2008): 110.
45. Glannon, 106.
46. Gosden, 116.
47. Glannon, 109.
48. Gosden, 76.
49. David Shenk, "Biocapitalism: What Price the Genetic Revolution?" in Lawrence M. Hinman, *Contemporary Moral Issues: Diversity and Consensus* (Upper Saddle River, NJ: Prentice Hall, 2000), 85.
50. This chapter deals only with selective abortion. The general issue of abortion is treated in Chapter 7.
51. See, for example, the website of the National Down Syndrome Society, which presents a very positive picture of the possibilities open to individuals with this condition.
52. Gosden, 232.
53. Abby Lippman, "Prenatal Genetic Testing and Screening: Constructing Needs and Reinforcing Inequities," in Baylis et al., 403.
54. Lippman, 402.
55. Kitcher observes that this may be the situation for some women: "Northern Indian uses of prenatal technology to reduce the number of daughters are morally repellent if they are inspired by parental contempt for women. But it is not necessary to conjure up moral monsters in the Punjab. Many of those who go to the new medical centres may do so reluctantly, bowing to the combined pressures of the caste system and their economic situation, or, perhaps, recognizing that the lot of women in their local society is so hard that it would be better not to give birth to girls doomed to be brutalized. Victims of a tradition whose effects they are powerless to undo, they must choose between evils." Kitchner, 216–217.
56. Dorothy C. Wertz and John C. Fletcher, "A Critique of Some Challenges to Prenatal Diagnosis," in Baylis et al., 414.

57. Sandel, 89.

58. Glannon, 116.

59. Kitcher, 85.

60. For more on this point, refer to Chapter 9.

61. The issue of Deaf Culture is discussed at length in Chapter 9.

62. Gregory Pence, *Who's Afraid of Human Cloning?* (Lanham, MD: Rowman & Littlefield, 1998), 89. It should be noted that much of the debate around stem-cell research is set within the context of the debate on abortion.

63. Pence, *Cloning*, 88.

64. President's Council on Bioethics, "Cloning and Stem Cells," in Ronald Munson, *Intervention and Reflection: Basic Issues in Medical Ethics*, 7th ed. (Belmont, CA: Thomson Wadsworth, 2004), 315.

65. Glannon, 82.

66. President's Council on Bioethics, 315.

67. Healy claims that "embryonic stem cells, once thought to hold the cure for Alzheimer's, Parkinson's, and diabetes, are obsolete" because of increasing evidence that embryonic stem cells can cause tumors. A recent medical report, for example, "describes young boy with a fatal neuromuscular disease ... who was treated with embryonic stem cells. Within four years, he developed headaches and was found to have multiple tumors in his brain and spinal cord that genetically matched the female embryos used in his therapy." Bernadine Healy, "Why Embryonic Stem Cells Are Obsolete," *U.S. News and World Report*, March 4, 2009, found at www.usnews.com (September 3, 2009).

68. Glannon, 101.

69. Kitcher, 242.

70. Shenk, 86.

71. Kitcher, 290.

72. For more on this case, go to "Stem Cell Siblings" at www.sciencecentral.com/articles/view (September 3, 2009).

73. Leon Kass, "The Wisdom of Repugnance," in Michael C. Brannigan and Judith A. Boss, *Healthcare Ethics in a Diverse Society* (Mountain View, CA: Mayfield Publishing Company, 2001), 306.

74. Kass, 306.

75. Pence, *Cloning*, 47.

76. Pence, *Cloning*, 50.

77. John Harris, "'Goodbye, Dolly?' The Ethics of Human Cloning," in Brannigan and Boss, 303.

78. Agar, 56.

79. Agar, 58.

80. Dena S. Davis, "Genetic Dilemmas and the Child's Right to an Open Future," in Munson, 337.

81. Baylis and Robert, 449. Methods of enhancement might include: somatic and germ-line therapy; gene transfer; cosmetic gene insertion; somatic cell nuclear transfer; cosmetic stem cell transfer; and the creation of chimeras and hybrids.

82. As Lauritzen puts it, "These matters are not easily considered from within the typical framework of bioethics ... the conceptual tools available in bioethics are not well suited to the task." Paul Lauritzen, "Stem Cells, Biotechnology, and Human Rights: Implications for a Posthuman Future," *Hastings Center Report*, 35, no. 2 (March-April 2005): 30.

83. Silver, 9.

84. John Harris, *Enhancing Evolution: The Ethical Case for Making Better People* (Princeton, NJ: Princeton University Press, 2007), 38.

85. Glannon, 110.

86. Sandel, 61-62.

87. John Harris, "The Case for Cloning," in James P. Sterba (ed.), *Morality in Practice* (Belmont, CA: Thomson Wadsworth, 2004), 202.

88. Silver, 9.

89. Hilary Putnam, "The Case Against Cloning," in Sterba, 196.

90. Jurgen Habermas, quoted in Sandel, 78.

91. Agar, 106.

92. Sandel, 7.

93. Sandel, 9.

94. Sandel, 9.

95. Sandel, 27.

96. Sandel, 97.

97. Hans Jonas, "Technology and Responsibility: Reflections on the New Tasks of Ethics," in *Philosophical Essays: From Ancient Creed to Technological Man* (Englewood Cliffs, NJ: Prentice Hall, 1974), 7.

98. Jonas, 7.

99. Jonas, 7.

100. Gessen, 241.

101. Agar, 41.

102. Agar, 42.

103. Agar, 42.

104. Agar, 43.

105. Jonas, 18.

106. Gessen, 260.

107. For a more sustained discussion of the idea of progress and its implications see Ronald Wright, *A Short History of Progress* (Toronto: Anansi, 2004).

108. Kitcher, 15.

109. Stephen J. Gould, "Carrie Buck's Daughter," in *The Flamingo's Smile* (New York: W.W Norton & Company, 1985), 310–311.

110. Kitcher, 188.

111. Gould, 309.

112. Kitcher, 194.

113. "Eugenics: Keeping Canada Sane," *The Canadian Encyclopedia*, found at www.thecanadianencyclopedia.com/index.cfm?PgNm=ArchievedFeatures (September 22, 2009).

114. "Eugenics: Keeping Canada Sane."

115. *Jones (Guardian of) v. Rostvig*, 1999, 6400 (BC SC).

116. See also the Henrietta Lacks case. A nice discussion can be found in Tom McCarthy, "Henrietta Lacks formally recognized as source of HeLa Research Cells," *The Guardian*, August 7, 2013.

117. "Moore v. Regents of the University of California – Case Brief Summary" found at www.lawnix.com/cases/moore-regents-california.html (November 20, 2014) and "Moore v. Regents of the University of California," *Case Briefs*, found at www.casebriefs.com/blog/law/torts/torts-keyed-to-epstein/traditional-strict-liability/moore-v-regents-of-the-university-of-california/ (November 30, 2014).

118. *Zhang v. Kan*, 2003 BCSC 5.

Chapter 7

ABORTION AND MATERNAL-FETAL CONFLICTS

LANDMARK CASE: DR. HENRY MORGENTALER

On October 19, 1967, Dr. Henry Morgentaler appeared before the House of Commons' Standing Committee on Health and Welfare and argued strongly for the legalization of **abortion** in Canada. At the time, women were harming themselves and even dying as a result of illegal and self-induced abortions. The only other choice for a woman with an unwanted pregnancy was to carry the **fetus** to term and give the baby up for adoption (keeping the child was not an option for a young, unmarried woman, for both economic and social reasons). The Criminal Code was amended as a result of these 1967 hearings in order to decriminalize contraception and certain abortions, but this did not solve the problem of access to abortion for most women. The new law only allowed abortions performed in an approved hospital with the consent of a hospital-based therapeutic abortion committee.

In June 1968, Dr. Morgentaler performed his first illegal abortion, and in 1969 he opened a private abortion clinic in Montreal, openly defying the law. He was charged with the crime of committing abortions, went to trial, and was acquitted. In 1973 he was tried again, admitting at the trial that he had performed over 5000 abortions. He was acquitted by a jury of 10 men and 1 woman. The acquittal was later overturned by the Quebec Court of Appeal and Dr. Morgentaler was sentenced to 18 months in prison. While in jail, he appealed the Appeal Court Decision. He was tried again, this time pleading "necessity" as the reason for performing abortions and was once again acquitted. This acquittal was upheld by the Quebec Court of Appeal; the Minister of Justice ordered a new trial, Dr. Morgentaler was released on bail, and, once again (by this time it was September 1976), he was acquitted. In December 1976, the Quebec government ordered a halt to prosecutions against Dr. Morgentaler and recommended that the federal government amend the law on abortion. All outstanding charges against him were dropped.

In May 1983, Dr. Morgentaler opened an abortion clinic in Winnipeg, which was raided and shut down by the police. He then opened a clinic in Toronto and was once again arrested and once again acquitted, this time by an Ontario Supreme Court jury. During this trial the defence lawyer told the jury to ignore the law. As a result, the Ontario Court of Appeal ordered a new trial, and Dr. Morgentaler appealed to the Supreme Court of Canada. Finally, in January 1988, almost 20 years after Dr. Morgentaler performed his first illegal abortion, the Supreme Court struck down Canada's abortion law, ruling that it violated the Charter of Rights and Freedoms by denying women timely and equal access to abortion across the country. The Supreme Court asked Parliament to create a new law on abortion that would meet the standards of the Charter, but due to political pressures on both sides of the question, Parliament has not succeeded in doing so. Since January 1988, there has been no law on abortion in Canada.

INTRODUCTION

Twenty years of legal battles in the Morgentaler case, including the refusal of several juries in two different provinces to convict Dr. Morgentaler of breaking the law and repeated efforts of the courts to uphold the law, are symptomatic of the complexity of the abortion question. They also clearly demonstrate the fact that the legal and moral dimensions of this issue do not coincide. Abortion is a difficult moral question, and the law is perhaps too blunt an instrument for the resolution of such complex conflicts of values. In this chapter we will analyze the arguments on both sides of this question primarily from a moral point of view. While recognizing that the legal question, if not resolved, is not currently an issue in Canada, we will emphasize that the moral question is in need of elaboration and clarification. The legal void leaves the question of abortion in the realm of personal morality. This, in itself, is a matter of debate for many people. At the very least, there is a need for reflection on the values and principles underlying the moral arguments as a guide to making considered moral decisions, however personal. This is what this chapter attempts to do.

Nurse outside a Marie Stopes mobile birth control clinic, London, 1928. In the 1920s birth control came to be seen as a health issue, concerned with both relieving women of the burden of so many children and ensuring that every child was a wanted child who would be adequately cared for. Like later advocates for abortion rights, birth control advocates had to fight both the law and conservative public opinion.

RELIGIOUS AND HISTORICAL PERSPECTIVES

Given the religious dimension of the current abortion debate, especially in the U.S., many people believe that the proscription of the practice has strong religious and/or biblical roots, but this is not actually the case. There is no notion of fetal rights in the Bible and "life, in biblical terms, commences only when the breath enters the nostrils."[1] Nor is it discussed in the Gospels. One biblical scholar notes that the Bible is silent on the question of abortion and suggests that, "whatever views one may hold about abortion, no straightforward appeal can be made to the teaching of the Bible, for the Bible simply does not discuss it."[2]

While there may not be any direct reference to abortion in the Bible, there is an indirect reference often appealed to by pro-life advocates. A passage of Exodus (21:22–23) deems what punishment should befall a man who, as a result of fighting with another man, harms a pregnant woman and thus causes a miscarriage. If her child "comes out *while not fully formed*, he will be forced to pay a fine…. But *if it is fully formed*, he will give life *[psyche]* for life, eye for eye."[3] This brought into usage the distinction between a formed and unformed fetus (meaning an ensouled fetus or one without a soul) that was often appealed to in later teachings on abortion. According to this teaching, often attributed to Aristotle but more likely a common one in the ancient world, ensoulment was believed to come at 40 days for a male fetus and 90 days for a female fetus.[4]

Even Augustine (for whom celibacy was the highest calling and sexual intercourse was allowed only within marriage with the intention of having children) accepted this teaching and this interpretation of the Exodus text: "If what is brought forth is unformed *(informe)*, but at this stage some sort of living, shapeless thing *(informiter)*, then the law of homicide would not apply, for it could not be said that there was a living soul in that body, for it lacks all sense, if it be such as is not yet formed *(nondum formata)* and therefore not yet endowed with its senses."[5]

In the 13th century, Thomas Aquinas reinforced the church's stance on restricting sexual relations to married couples expressly for the procreation of children. Although he believed that abortion was wrong because it violated natural law principles about propagation of the species and was thus contrary to reason, he did not change the accepted definition of abortion. Rather, "he held to the convention of the age and those before it: abortion was the termination of pregnancy after the fetus was formed. So had said Augustine."[6] According to Riddle, the period prior to formation of the fetus was not perceived as a pregnancy. During this period, women often took drugs to abort or, more precisely, to bring on delayed menstruation. Riddle states: "Thus, there was an indefinite but fairly certain time, a window of opportunity as it were, during which a woman could end what we call a pregnancy, and neither she nor her contemporaries regarded the act as an abortion. Taking a drug for delayed menstruation was just that and nothing more."[7]

The distinction between a formed and unformed fetus became the basis of church law and remained so until the 19th century when biological knowledge overturned the embryology of Aristotle and Aquinas. As a result, Pope Pius IX did away with the notion of ensoulment and extended the prohibition to abortion at any time during a pregnancy from the moment of conception. This is the position of the Catholic Church today.

The only exception to this proscription is the need to save the life of the mother, and only if the action conforms to the *doctrine of double effect*. This allows *indirect* abortion, whereby an operation to save the life of the mother results indirectly in the death of the fetus. In other words, the death of the fetus is not the primary intent, but a secondary effect, of the necessary operation. Thus the removal of a cancerous uterus that results also in the death of the fetus would be permitted. However, aborting the fetus because the pregnant woman's health (or even life) is threatened by the pregnancy would not be allowed. In the first case, it is the removal of the cancer that is the primary intention; in the second case, it is the removal of the fetus. Even if both the fetus and the pregnant woman will die unless the fetus is aborted, it is still unacceptable to abort the fetus, according to Catholic Church doctrine.

While it is difficult (and inadvisable) to lump all Protestant denominations together, historically, the position of the various Protestant churches has been less official and less extreme than that of the Catholic Church. Abortion was not an issue at the time of the Reformation, in part because of the early Reformers' emphasis on scripture for resolving theological and moral disputes. As has already been pointed out, scripture is largely silent on the issue. In addition, morality was considered more a matter of rational discernment than of revealed truth. This does not suggest that abortion meets with approval in Protestant churches, which have tended to see pregnancy as a sign of God's blessing and its deliberate denial as at least impious. Harrison writes: "The most typical contemporary Protestant attitude toward abortion remains a traditionalist, pronatalist negativity toward the practice, with a reluctant recognition that abortions do occur frequently, even within the Protestant communities of faith."[8]

That being said, there is a growing fundamentalist Christian movement in both the U.S. and Canada that takes strong positions on questions of sexuality and reproduction and emphasizes the importance of the family, of sexual relations only within marriage, and of traditional gender roles. The primary goal of this movement seems to be a return to a pre-modern interpretation of sex and gender roles, rooted in divine decree and a literal interpretation of the Bible (although as the discussion above demonstrates, what this actually means is open to interpretation). This movement is strongly anti-abortion and "aims to make even the discussion of abortion taboo in Protestant theological and moral discourses, to make it literally unthinkable."[9]

Although the Jewish faith is generally pro-natalist and is not in favour of casual abortion, it is tolerant of the practice where it is considered necessary. Only the right to life of existing persons is absolute while the right to be born is relative, depending on the mother. According to Feldman, "Rabbinic law has determined that human life begins with birth."[10] It should be noted, however, that in the state of Israel, abortion is legal in certain circumstances (young age or single status of the mother, rape or incest, danger to health, fetal deformity) but is not allowed for economic reasons (that is, financial hardship).

Like Christianity, Islamic teaching holds that life is sacred because it comes from God. Like the Christians up to pre-modern times, it proposes a moment of ensoulment when God breathes a soul into the fetus and the fetus becomes a human being. This is taken to happen around the fourth month of pregnancy, after which abortion is prohibited. However, there are differing interpretations about the permissibility of abortion in the pre-ensoulment period, and some schools of Islam prohibit it completely. In others, abortion is permitted if the pregnancy poses a threat to the health of mother and, in particular, if she is nursing another infant who might be harmed by the pregnancy. Bakar points out that Islam has yet to develop a "well-defined response" to the contemporary reality of increasing numbers of abortions as well as "the challenge to traditional Islamic doctrines on abortion and contraception arising from advances in genetics and biomedical technology."[11]

LEGAL PERSPECTIVES

In spite of the religious strictures noted above, the law was more lenient than the churches, and few countries had laws prohibiting abortion until the late 19th century—and after that time, most did. For centuries, the cultural practice of midwifery kept the issue out of mainstream medical—and legal—practice. This changed considerably with the medicalization of pregnancy and reproduction in the 19th century. Whereas in the 17th century, even aborting a quickened fetus was not an offence, in 1803, in England, it became a capital crime to abort a quickened fetus (although abortion before quickening was considered a lesser offence). Even so, at the time of *Roe v. Wade* in the U.S. (discussed below), the Court pointed out that, from the time of the American Constitution through most of the 19th century, a woman enjoyed a substantially broader right to terminate a pregnancy than she did in 1973 at the time of the decision. The legal proscription of abortion is often seen as a reaction to early feminist movements and their promotion of women's rights in the 19th century. As Pence states, "The prevailing public prudery and anti-sexual moralism condemned feminism and considered sex for pleasure evil, with pregnancy as punishment."[12] But the proscription of abortion was also the result of the medicalization of pregnancy and the development of methods for determining, through a medical examination, whether or not a woman was pregnant. Thus, it was no longer the woman, but the doctor, who determined when a pregnancy had begun. Physicians began to reject the old concept of quickening and to see themselves as responsible for protecting the fetus from the moment of conception. Riddle quotes a New York physician summing up the new view of the fetus when he stated that the idea of quickening "is absurd and false; that there is no time from the moment of conception to the moment of birth when the fetus is not a human being; and that its life is as sacred at one period as at another."[13] Gradually this position became codified in the laws of various countries so that, by the beginning of the 20th century, abortion was universally outlawed in the Western world except where the life of the mother was threatened.

It is important to note that during the century of restrictive abortion laws, the practice did not cease; it just went underground. Hundreds of thousands of illegal abortions were performed in the U.S. during the 1950s and 1960s, and many women died (more than 1000 during the 1960s alone).[14] In Canada it is estimated that the rate of abortions prior to 1969, when abortion was legalized, was about the same as after, and that many women died as a result of botched illegal abortions.[15] Apart from the risk of death, the experience was costly and humiliating to the woman and dangerous for the doctor, who was liable to imprisonment for life (the pregnant woman herself being liable to seven years' imprisonment for procuring an abortion).

The movement against restrictive abortion laws that began in the 1960s can be attributed to a number of factors, including the rising feminist movement and the sexual revolution. At the centre of the sexual revolution was the notion that women enjoyed sexual relations as much as men did, and the arrival of the contraceptive pill allowed this idea of sexual freedom to become a reality. Free love, including that of homosexual men and lesbians, became the watchword of the decade (make love, not war, sang the anti-war protestors), and a growing resistance to authority created an awareness of the oppression and paternalism of many existing laws. The famous statement by Canada's then Justice Minister (and future Prime Minister) Pierre Elliott Trudeau that the state has no business in the bedrooms of the nation encapsulated the feeling of the times as he brought in legislation decriminalizing homosexuality, contraception, and, to a limited extent, abortion.

During the same period an outbreak of deformities in babies of mothers who had taken the drug thalidomide (a drug widely prescribed to pregnant women to combat morning sickness) raised the profile of laws that prevented women who had taken the drug from having abortions.[16] A well-publicized case in the U.S. involving Sherri Finkbane, who was refused an abortion after taking thalidomide, created public sympathy for changing restrictive laws on abortion (Finkbane went to Sweden to obtain an abortion). The case of thalidomide brought to the fore the issue of quality of life versus the sanctity of life, allowing space for the former at the expense of the latter. At the same time, recognizing that women could achieve equality with men only by controlling their fertility, the feminist movement put a high priority on the legalization of abortion, and the pro-choice movement began. Since that time, the laws of most Western nations have been modified to allow safe and legal abortions with varying restrictions, depending on the country.

Two Countries, Two Laws

The current legal situation in both Canada and the U.S. is the result of a decision of each country's Supreme Court. In the U.S., the definitive decision was *Roe v. Wade* in 1973; in Canada, it was the *R. v. Morgentaler* decision of 1988, referred to above. While these decisions made access to abortion easier in each country, the actual decisions and the reasoning behind them are quite different.

Roe v. Wade

In *Roe v. Wade*, the U.S. Supreme Court ruled that no state could restrict abortion during the first 12 weeks (first trimester) of a pregnancy. During the second trimester, it ruled, states could restrict abortion, but only to protect the health of the woman (for example, by regulating abortion procedures or licensing practitioners). Finally, it ruled that in the third trimester, after the fetus is considered viable, states could restrict abortions to those considered necessary to the life or health of the woman. The part of the decision dealing with the first trimester was based on the right to privacy—the Court recognized a guarantee of certain areas of privacy under the Constitution, and this included a woman's right to decide whether or not to terminate a pregnancy, at least in the early stages. At the other end of the scale, however, the Court recognized that individual states have an interest in potential life at the point of **viability**, because the fetus at that point has the capacity to survive outside the womb. Thus the Court ruled that state regulation to protect fetal life at that point was justified. As for the middle trimester, the Court recognized that abortion is more dangerous as the pregnancy progresses and that states may intervene only to protect maternal health.

The Supreme Court decision did not end the abortion debate in the U.S. In fact, in the years since *Roe v. Wade*, there have been numerous cases before the Supreme Court attempting to restrict access to abortion. These include attempts to limit abortions to those performed in hospitals; to require a husband's consent for a married woman's abortion; and to require that a woman receive counselling before an abortion. The Supreme Court rejected all of these cases. On the other hand, the Court did recognize that states do not have an obligation to pay for abortions for the poor and supported a federal law banning the use of Medicaid funds to pay for abortions. Further, in recent years, a debate has raged in the U.S. about late-term abortions as abortion opponents have attempted to have them outlawed completely. More than 40 years after *Roe v. Wade*, the issue is not settled. Daniel Callahan has observed that *Roe v. Wade* "served primarily to galvanize and generate a more organized opposition to abortion; and it led those favorable to the option of abortion to dig in their heels, to defend the notion of free choice all the more tenaciously."[17]

Further, the U.S. Supreme Court decision has been criticized from both sides of the abortion debate. From a pro-life point of view, the exception regarding proscription of abortion in the third trimester (preservation of the life or health of the mother) is open to such a wide interpretation as to be meaningless. From a pro-choice point of view, the reliance on viability as the point of allowing legislation against abortion is problematic, since, as a result of neonatal technology, the line of viability is shifting constantly downward. At the time of *Roe*, viability was about 28 weeks; currently it is between 22 and 24 weeks, depending on the technology available. Justice Sandra Day O'Connor recognized this problem when she remarked a decade after *Roe v. Wade* that the decision "was on a collision course with itself"[18] as the point of viability moves further and further back toward conception. While it is legal to abort at 24 weeks' gestation, such a fetus is now viable and, depending on the hospital and the technology involved, one could have a neonatal team in a hospital struggling to save a premature infant while an obstetrical team in another part of the hospital is aborting a fetus of the same gestational age. Thus technology is blurring both the legal and the moral distinctions that served as a guide for *Roe v. Wade*.

Morgentaler

The landmark case in Canada was the *R. v. Morgentaler* decision of 1988, as outlined at the beginning of this chapter. The reasoning behind the Canadian case was different from the reasoning behind the American case. Here the Court decided that the existing law, requiring approval by a hospital committee, went against the Charter of Rights because it did not allow equal access to abortion for all women in the country. The Court ruled that the restriction of abortion to certain hospitals and to abortions approved by a therapeutic abortion committee interfered with a woman's physical and bodily integrity. As articulated by the Chief Justice in the majority opinion of the Court, "Forcing a woman, by threat of criminal sanction, to carry a fetus to term unless she meets certain criteria unrelated to her own priorities and aspirations, is a profound interference with a woman's body and thus a violation of security of the person."[19] This might be justified, the Court reasoned, if it were in accordance with the principles of fundamental justice. However, the Court went on to point out that the practical application of the therapeutic abortion committee requirements "meant in practice that abortions would be absolutely unavailable in almost one quarter of all hospitals in Canada."[20] The lack of a definition about what was meant by health of the pregnant woman led to widely differing interpretations regarding psychological, as opposed to physical, harm; and the system for obtaining a therapeutic abortion certificate often resulted in serious delays, ultimately affecting the availability of abortion for many women. As a result of these and other problems relating to the application of the existing law, the Court ruled that the law did, in fact, violate the principles of fundamental justice and thus should be struck down. The Court instructed Parliament to develop a law that respected the equality rights of the Charter. A bill was passed by the House of Commons in 1990 requiring that a doctor determine that continuing a pregnancy threatened a woman's physical, mental, or psychological health, but it was defeated by the Senate in 1991, and there has been no further attempt to reinsert abortion into the Criminal Code. Thus, as pointed out earlier, there is no federal law on abortion in Canada at the present time, a situation that makes Canada unique in the world. This does not mean, however, that there is universal access to abortion in Canada, since each province has different regulations about where abortions can be performed and whether or not the service is covered by the provincial health plan. Access to abortion varies from province to province and is often not available at all outside of major centres.

SOCIAL AND POLITICAL PERSPECTIVES

Abortion is an issue that raises heated debate on both pro-life and pro-choice sides of the question. It is also a debate that has become more polarized in the last 20 years in spite of, or perhaps because of, the different legal decisions that attempted to settle the matter. One of the reasons for the polarization is the fact that abortion is not *one* issue: it is imbued with social, political, and even economic factors. In other words, when one is discussing abortion, one is often discussing much more than abortion itself. As sociologist Kristin Luker pointed out in her comprehensive study of abortion activists, pro-life and pro-choice people come from very different parts of the social world, with diametrically opposed views on the status of women, sex, marriage, and morality.[21] As summed up by Daniel and Sidney Callahan, Luker's study showed that there is "a prolife movement dedicated to the preservation of the nuclear family, the centrality of childbearing in the life of women, and a religious rather than a secular view of life," and a "pro-choice ideology dedicated to female emancipation from the body and a repressive nuclear family, a subordination of child-bearing to other personal goals, a celebration of rational control of self in place of the acceptance of fate, and a secular rather than a religious view of life."[22] Given that for these people the question of abortion is rooted in such fundamental world views, it is no wonder that finding common ground is so difficult.

Not everybody holds one or the other of these extreme views; however, the extremists set the tone and help polarize the debate. People who hold a more moderate view of abortion are often uncomfortable if they feel pressured into supporting one side or the other—and are even more uncomfortable with the rhetoric that surrounds the two positions, including the labels themselves. The label *pro-life* suggests that only those who are absolutely against abortion are concerned about life. It also assumes what it has not proved—that fetal life is an absolute value that trumps the life, health, or situation of the pregnant woman. The label *pro-choice* suggests that those who are against abortion do not care about choice (or freedom). It also assumes what it has not proved—that free choice is an absolute value in all circumstances. To assume what you should be proving in an argument is called *begging the question* and this is what these labels do.

In assessing the arguments on both sides of this issue, it is important to pay close attention to the language that is being used. For example, pro-life proponents will often refer to their opponents as pro-abortion. This is very misleading. One might be personally against abortion but think that a woman has a right to make her own choice if she finds herself pregnant in a difficult situation. Similarly, one can be against abortion and, at the same time, be against making it illegal. For example, a January 2000 Gallup poll in the U.S. showed that 44 percent of people considered themselves pro-life (up from 33 percent in 1995), but only 19 percent wanted to see abortion outlawed, seemingly indicating that not everyone who is against abortion is in favour of its criminalization. Caroline Whitbeck sheds light on this rhetorical issue by referring to what she calls the "grim option," an option that one chooses, not because one wants it, but because the alternative is worse: "The distinction between what one wants and what one *wants to be available* is crucial for understanding the resort to a grim option."[23] People who are pro-choice are not necessarily pro-abortion; they simply want those who need it to be able to choose the grim option. However, in the battle of labels, those who hold a pro-choice position are labelled pro-abortion (and, to balance out the equation, those on the pro-choice side often refer to their opponents as anti-choice).

Aside from the false dichotomy of the pro-life and pro-choice labels, there are other language traps on both sides of the debate. In pro-life rhetoric, the contents of the uterus—whether zygote, embryo, or fetus—are referred to as a baby (or even a *child*); abortion is *murder* and the pregnant woman is always a *mother*. In pro-choice rhetoric, the fetus may be referred to as an **embryo** (no matter what the stage); the pregnant woman may be just a *woman*; and abortion is a *procedure*, often likened to an appendectomy or the removal of a tumour. Like the labels "pro-choice" and "pro-life" themselves, this language is often question-begging: to call abortion murder is to presuppose—and not prove—that the fetus is a person with the same moral status as a living person. To liken abortion to the removal of a tumour is to presuppose the opposite: that the fetus is just tissue with no moral status at all. But the status of the fetus is largely what the whole debate is about! One cannot simply push the debate aside by assuming a position about the status of the fetus as a starting point and then declaring that the other side is simply wrong (or immoral).

Another aspect of the debate where rhetoric plays a major role is in the presentation (or rather the misrepresentation) of the facts. Pro-life advocates, especially in recent years, place the emphasis on the gruesome procedure involved in late-term abortions (which they call, for rhetorical purposes, partial-birth abortions). While they are right in pointing out that late-term abortions are gruesome (even most pro-choice advocates would agree), the fact is that only about 2.2 percent of abortions take place after 20 weeks (and many of these late abortions are performed because of a serious threat to the life of the pregnant woman or because of severe fetal defects such as anencephaly). Moreover, almost 30 percent of abortions take place in the first 8 weeks and another 44 percent before the end of the 12th week.[24] It may be a legitimate position to hold that late-term abortions should be banned, but it is not legitimate to apply the rhetorical discourse of late-term abortion to all abortions.

Further, pro-life advocates often frame their discourse in terms of young women taking responsibility for their actions, suggesting that if they find themselves pregnant, they deserve to be forced to have the child. There is little room in their analysis for the admission that sometimes women find themselves pregnant against their will, through rape or incest, or through failed contraception, and that forced pregnancy in these situations is cruel and unusual punishment. An analysis of the pro-choice position, however, could lead one to believe that no woman ever had sexual relations of her own free will—and that women are never irresponsible in matters of sex and contraception. Further, by insisting that the fetus is simply tumour-like tissue, pro-choice advocates suggest that all abortions take place in the early weeks and downplay the facts relating to later abortions.

A further rhetorical device of the pro-life advocates is the proliferation of images of fetuses as free-floating beings (in Monica Casper's words, "resembling out-of-control balloons at a Macy's parade"), as if they had a life of their own, unattached to a pregnant woman. Casper refers to this as one of many contemporary ways of *culturing the fetus*: "Where fetuses were once confined to anonymity and invisibility inside pregnant women's bodies, the fetus has now gone solo." This has the result of erasing the woman from the picture, oversimplifying the debate about the moral status of the fetus and promoting the notion of the fetus as a person or patient separate from its mother. Casper continues: "In the new cultural discourse, fetuses are increasingly represented as free agents with their own needs and interests, and even their own doctors and lawyers."[25] This helps to set up a situation of conflict between the pregnant woman and the developing fetus that will be discussed later in this chapter.

MORAL QUESTIONS AND ARGUMENTS

It can be seen from the above that the debate on abortion is in need of more thoughtful analysis than the political arena (in both Canada and the U.S.) has allowed thus far. We need to step back from the extreme positions and from the emotions that colour them, take a look at what both sides are saying, and examine what values both sides hold in common. It is important to remember that where there is an ethical dilemma, there is a conflict of values and principles, and it is this conflict that must be brought out into the open.

Further, much of the debate about abortion is centred on the question of whether or not abortion should be regulated by law—and if so, to what extent the state should intervene. In other words, the debate focuses on political and legal issues. Our purpose here is to put the emphasis on the moral issues. Therefore, it will be important for the reader to try to analyze these issues without feeling that he or she must take a position on matters of public policy or legislation. Taking a stand immediately on the legal issue (for example, for or against criminalization of abortion) can prejudice the *moral* analysis, which is something we want to avoid. The main moral questions concern the moral status of the fetus (Does the fetus have rights? Is the fetus a person?) and the rights of the pregnant woman (Should a woman be forced to carry an unwanted fetus to term? Does a woman lose her autonomy because she is pregnant?). Other issues relate to the rights and obligations of the father, as well as to the question of maternal-fetal conflicts (relating to potentially harmful behaviour of pregnant women and to the emerging field of fetal surgery).

The discovery of an unwanted pregnancy is a traumatic moment, weighted with personal, social, and moral choices.

The Moral Status of the Fetus

The extreme positions that have been discussed above as pro-life and pro-choice can be more accurately labelled *conservative* or *abolitionist* on the one hand and *liberal* or *libertarian* on the other. For the abolitionists, abortion is never morally acceptable except (for some) to save the life of the pregnant woman. For the libertarians, abortion is morally acceptable at any time during the pregnancy and for any reason, and the decision to abort belongs ultimately to the woman (and her doctor). This is often referred to as abortion on demand.

BOX 7.1

DAVID BOONIN, "THE SLIPPERY SLOPE ARGUMENT"

The difference between a developing fetus at one moment and the fetus a moment later is always very small, but if you add enough such moments, you eventually get an individual just like you and me. I will refer to this as the relation of continuity.…

So why should the fact of continuity between the zygote and us be taken as support for the conclusion that if we have a right to life, then so does the zygote? The most familiar way of putting the answer to this question takes the form of a slippery slope argument.… Suppose that you deny that the conceptus immediately following conception has a right to life. Then since there is no significant difference between the conceptus at this moment and at the very next moment, you must conclude that the conceptus at the very next moment also lacks a right to life. But since you will continue to find no significant difference between the conceptus at each moment and the next, and since you will eventually reach an adult just like you and me, you will then have to conclude that the adult just like you and me lacks a right to life … we must surely concede that this conclusion in unacceptable. Since the conclusion that you and I lack a right to life must therefore be rejected, and since the slippery slope argument seems to show that the claim that a zygote lacks a right to life entails this conclusion, the slippery slope argument seems to show that the claim that a zygote lacks a right to life must also be rejected.... This slippery slope argument appeals to many people. Indeed it is perhaps the single most common argument against abortion.... [T]he slippery slope argument is subject to a commonly noted but not commonly appreciated rebuttal by *reductio ad absurdum*. As one writer has put it, the development from acorn to oak tree is equally continuous, but "it does not follow that acorns are oak trees, or that we had better say they are."[1] Now defenders of the slippery slope argument often claim to have an answer to this objection: The two cases are disanalogous, they insist, because people are important in a way that oak trees are not. If we cared about oak trees as much as we care about people, they say, then the facts about oak development really would force us to conclude that acorns have the same sort of value as oaks. "If oaks had a serious right to life in their own right, so would oak saplings and germinating acorns."[2] And the point is often cast in terms of the tree-loving Druid: "For the Druid, the life-force which exists in the oak tree and which makes it divine, also exists in the acorn."[3] But critics of the acorn objection ... are mistaken in claiming that once the analogy is suitably mended the slippery slope argument is rescued from the objection. For let us suppose that we do value oak trees morally in just the way that we value people morally: We think that they have just the same right to life that you and I have. What will follow from this about the moral status of acorns?

The answer depends entirely on what it is about oak trees that we think confers upon them this right in the first place. If we value oak trees ... because of their "life-force," then since this is a property they share with acorns it will follow that acorns have the same right to life as mature oak trees. And if we confer a right to life on oak trees because they are members of an "appropriate species" ... then we will grant that right to acorns since they are members of the oak species as well. But notice that in either case our attributing a right to life to the acorn will do absolutely nothing to vindicate the slippery slope argument: We will be led to attribute a right to life to the acorn ... because we agree that acorns themselves already possess a property (a certain kind of life force, membership in an appropriate species) that is itself sufficient to warrant such an attribution.

And in the case of fetal development, of course, this will simply beg the question. The slippery slope argument was supposed to show that the claim that the fetus has a right to life from its conception follows from the conjunction of the fact that there is a relation of continuity between it and the adult it gradually develops into and the claim that the adult itself has a right to life. But the right to life of the acorn does not follow from the fact that there is a relation of continuity between it and the oak tree it gradually develops into even if we assume that oak trees have such a right. The acorn objection to the slippery slope argument therefore survives the objections that have been aimed at it.

Notes
1. Judith Jarvis Thomson, "A Defense of Abortion," *Philosophy and Public Affairs*, 1, no. 1 (Fall 1971): 131.
2. Philip E. Devine, *Ethics of Homicide* (Notre Dame: University of Notre Dame Press, 1990), 52.
3. William Cooney, "The Fallacy of All Person-Denying Arguments for Abortion," *Journal of Applied Philosophy*, 8, no. 2 (1991): 162.
Source: David Boonin, *A Defense of Abortion* (Cambridge, UK: Cambridge University Press, 2003), 33–41.

The abolitionist argument is based on the premise that the fetus is a person from the moment of conception and, as such, has the same right to life as any living person. Thus killing of a fetus through abortion is morally equivalent to killing any living human being and is considered murder.

For people holding this view, the right to life of the fetus trumps any rights the pregnant woman might have (or thinks she has) relating to her body, her health, or her economic or social situation. The only exception would be her right to life when it is directly threatened by the pregnancy (and, for some, only following the doctrine of double effect referred to earlier).

The libertarian argument is based on the premise that the fetus is not a person until it is born and thus does not have the same right to life as living persons. In this view a woman's autonomy (which includes her right to control her body) trumps any concern about fetal right to life. The fetus is not a person in its own right; rather, it is a part of the woman's body until birth. Further, refusing abortion to a pregnant woman amounts to forced pregnancy and childbirth, a serious affront to her autonomy.

What Is a Person?

Proponents of both sides of the question are operating on the assumption that they know what a *person* is. However, this is a complex philosophical question that needs to be analyzed, and clear reasons must be given for any conclusion that the fetus is, or is not, a person. The notion of "person-hood" is often used as a way of defining the moral community and thus what is and what is not considered to be a full human being with moral status. If it can be shown that the fetus is a person, the case can be made that it has the same rights as any living person; if the opposite is shown, then the notion of a fetus having rights is negated. Not surprisingly, there are disagreements about what criteria should be used, and depending on the criteria established, some animals could count as persons and some humans would not. Warren takes the position that only persons can be a part of the moral community and suggests a number of characteristics that human beings must have in order to be considered persons: consciousness and the capacity to feel pain; reasoning (the capacity to solve relatively complex problems); self-motivated (as opposed to reflexive) activity; the capacity to communicate; and the presence of self-awareness.[26]

One could argue about the items on this list and insist on subtracting some or adding others, but it is a reasonable list for the purposes of our discussion in this chapter. Warren does not suggest that to be considered a person a being must have *all* of these characteristics, but she does insist that any being that satisfies none of them cannot be considered a person. Many would argue that the first criterion, consciousness and the capacity to feel pain, should force us to include the later fetus in the class of persons. However, Warren does not agree. For her, a fetus of seven or eight months can be seen as somewhat more person-like than an early fetus, having what she refers to as "a rudimentary form of consciousness." Nevertheless, she maintains, "in the *relevant* respects, a fetus, even a fully developed one, is considerably less personlike than is the average mature mammal, indeed the average fish."[27]

Warren's argument might leave the reader feeling uneasy and with good reason. The term "con-sciousness" is a very slippery one, and Warren is not on strong ground when she states, without definition or argument, that a seven- or eight-month-old fetus has a rudimentary form of conscious-ness. What does she mean? Further, she does not show how a human being with the capacity to feel pain can be excluded from the moral community; this is particularly important since the capacity to feel pain is one of her own criteria. Finally, her criteria do not clearly allow a distinction between a very late fetus and a newborn baby, which would appear to make infanticide morally permissible for her. If the difference is simply that the former has not been born and the latter has, then it would be simpler to argue that the moment of birth is the moment at which a human being enters the moral community (which is, in fact, the Jewish stance on abortion as we saw earlier), and leave the question of personhood out of the equation.[28]

BOX 7.2

DON MARQUIS, "WHY ABORTION IS IMMORAL"

A necessary condition of resolving the abortion controversy is a more theoretical account of the wrongness of killing. After all, if we merely believe, but do not understand, why killing adult human beings such as ourselves is wrong, how could we conceivably show that abortion is either immoral or permissible?... The loss of one's life is one of the greatest losses one can suffer. The loss of one's life deprives one of all the experiences, activities, projects, and enjoyments that would otherwise have constituted one's future.... When I am killed, I am deprived both of what I now value which would have been part of my future personal life, but also what I would come to value. Therefore, when I die, I am deprived of all the value of my future. Inflicting this loss on me is ultimately what makes killing me wrong. This being the case, it would seem that what makes killing *any* adult human being prima facie seriously wrong is the loss of his or her future....

The view that what makes killing wrong is the loss to the victim of the value of the victim's future gains some additional support when some of its implications are examined. In the first place, it is incompatible with the view that it is wrong to kill only beings who are biologically human. It is possible that there exists a different species from another planet whose members have a future like ours.... In the second place, the claim ... entails the possibility that the futures of some actual nonhuman mammals on our own planet are sufficiently like ours that it is seriously wrong to kill them also....

In the third place, the claim that the loss of one's future is the wrong-making feature of one's being killed does not entail, as sanctity of human life theories do, that active euthanasia is wrong.... It is, strictly speaking, the value of a human's future which makes killing wrong in this theory. This being so, killing does not necessarily wrong some persons who are sick or dying.... In the fourth place, the account of the wrongness of killing defended in this essay does straightforwardly entail that it is prima facie seriously wrong to kill children and infants, for we do presume that they have futures of value. Since we do believe that it is wrong to kill defenseless little babies, it is important that the theory of the wrongness of killing easily account for this. Personhood theories of the wrongness of killing, on the other hand, cannot straightforwardly account for the wrongness of killing infants and young children.... Accordingly, it seems that this value of a future-like-ours theory of the wrongness of killing shares the strengths of both sanctity-of-life and personhood accounts while avoiding weaknesses of both.... [It] has obvious consequences for the ethics of abortion. The future of a standard fetus includes a set of experiences, projects, activities, and such which are identical with the futures of adult human beings and are identical with the future of young children....

This argument does not rely on the invalid inference that, since it is wrong to kill persons, it is wrong to kill potential persons also. The category that is morally central to this analysis is the category of having a valuable future like ours; it is not the category of personhood. The argument ... proceeded independently of the notion of person or potential person or any equivalent....

[This argument], if sound, shows only that abortion is prima facie wrong, not that it is wrong in any and all circumstances. Since the loss of the future to a standard fetus, if killed is, however, at least as great a loss as the loss of the future to a standard adult human being who is killed, abortion, like ordinary killing, could be justified only by the most compelling reasons.... Accordingly, morally permissible abortions will be rare indeed unless, perhaps, they occur so early in pregnancy that a fetus is not yet definitely an individual....

Source: Don Marquis, "Why Abortion Is Immoral," *The Journal of Philosophy*, 86, no. 4 (April 1989): 189–194.

Gestation as a Developmental *Process*

In assuming that the fetus is, or is not, a person from conception to birth, proponents of both sides of the debate ignore one indisputable fact: the growth of the fetus (from zygote to baby) is a developmental process. In fact, it is not a fetus, but first a **blastocyst** and then an embryo, until eight weeks' gestation. Up to two weeks after conception, in the pre-embryonic stage, the blastocyst could actually split and become two embryos, not just one. The early embryo is about the size of the head of a pin (surely this is not a child) while a fetus after 22–24 weeks is capable of survival outside of the womb (surely this is not just tissue). Most people who hold a moderate view of abortion recognize that the developmental stage of the fetus is an important factor in determining whether or not it has the moral status of a person and whether or not an abortion is morally justified. This can be seen as *drawing a line* before which abortion would be considered morally justified and after which it would not, except in very serious situations (for example, threat to the life of the mother or serious deformity of the fetus). A conservative might want to draw the line at implantation (about 2 weeks) while a liberal might draw the line at viability (currently about 23–24 weeks).

The problem with attempts to draw a line is that, from an ethical perspective, one should be able to argue that the place where the line is drawn is not arbitrary. This is difficult in a process as continuous as fetal development, but it is not impossible. For example, a line could be drawn at the points mentioned above (implantation or viability), at the point of sentience (where the fetus is able to feel pain—believed to be at 13 weeks[29]), or even at the point of consciousness (where brain waves are detected, which could be as early as 6 weeks). The moral line, however, could find itself shifting as scientific knowledge shifts (as the line of fetal viability has shifted in the last few decades). Further, if the line can be drawn according to any of the above standards (in effect, 2 weeks, 6 weeks, 13 weeks, 21–24 weeks), how is moral consensus to be achieved? Can it simply be considered a matter of personal opinion? If we are looking for a moral ground for establishing a line, personal opinion does not suffice.

The difficulty of drawing a line in the development of the fetus raises a version of the slippery slope argument, which Boonin refers to as "the single most common argument against abortion." According to this argument, the development from conception to birth to adult is continuous; thus the zygote has the same right to life as any adult human being. There is simply no point in the process at which it can be said that there is a significant difference in the growing fetus—or even in the growing child—between any moment and the moment before. Thus, the argument concludes, "in virtue of the continuity relation, we must attribute a right to life to the zygote in order to avoid starting down a path that leads inexorably to the denial of our own right to life."[30] The absurdity of this argument is shown by the rebuttal that the same continuity exists between an acorn and an oak tree, but we do not call acorns oak trees.[31] Continuity itself does not prove that zygotes have the same rights as adult human beings. The problem relates to giving good reasons as to why one can draw a line between one point in the process and another. That such a line should not be arbitrary does not entail that there can be no line.

Accepting gestation as a developmental process allows us to see the moral status of the fetus as developmental, but it also suggests that the moral rights of the pregnant woman should also be weighed in light of that development. This seems to be consistent with much public opinion that tends to see late abortions as much more problematic than early ones. From this point of view the rights of the woman would decrease as the rights of the fetus increase, and abortions during the third trimester could be severely restricted. This is already the legal situation in many countries and is the de facto practice in Canada where it is extremely difficult to get an abortion after 22 weeks' gestation.

Another way of moderating the extreme views regarding the moral status of the fetus is to assign some kind of *partial moral status* to the fetus. Such a position, while circumventing the issue of personhood, raises other questions because of the vagueness of what is meant by partial. However, this is the position taken by the ethicist Daniel Callahan, who does not grant the fetus the moral status of a person, but still believes that it is a valuable form of life that should not be destroyed lightly. Abortion is the destruction of a potential human life and this fact should be admitted: "It is not the destruction of a human person … but it is the destruction of an important and valuable form of human life."[32]

At the same time, Callahan believes that a decision in favour of abortion "can be a responsible moral decision, worthy neither of the condemnation of others nor of self-condemnation."[33] This position is echoed by Naomi Wolf, a feminist writer, who had an abortion when she was a young single mother with a two-year-old daughter. She defends the feminist pro-choice position but believes that pretending that abortion is justifiable because a fetus has no moral status is a form of dehumanization. Further, she states, "[W]hen we defend abortion rights by emptying the act of moral gravity, we find ourselves cultivating a hardness of heart."[34] While a woman should be free to choose—and to choose in favour of her own interests when she considers it necessary, she should realize that the death of the fetus is a real death, even if it does not equal the death of what we recognize as a person: "There is no easy way to deny the powerful argument that a woman's equality in society must give her some irreducible rights unique to her biology, including the right to take the life within her life. But we don't have to lie to ourselves about what we are doing at such a moment."[35]

In Wolf's view, the effort of the pro-choice lobby to refuse any moral status to the developing fetus forces a false choice on those who may morally disapprove of abortion but still want it to be legal. These people reflect Boonin's separation of the question of whether or not abortion is morally *impermissible* from the question of whether or not it is morally *criticizable*.[36] Many people may want to talk about values and morals in relation to abortion, but this is seen as putting them in the pro-life camp. This is the only side willing to speak about good and evil, but its position is simply too black and white for them. Wolf's position (as well as Callahan's) suggests that it is possible to see abortion as undesirable, and criticizable, without seeing it as murder. It can be seen as a necessary evil, or the lesser of two evils, the "grim option" of Whitbeck referred to above.

Writing about the biological development of the fetus, Grobstein suggests the possibility of subcategories such as "nonpersons, prepersons, protopersons, quasi persons and neopersons," which would recognize the different stages of prenatal human development. This development, in his view, should be seen as a gradual process with "special emphasis on the maturation of the brain.… [T]he definitive realization of the moral status of a person would seem to await appropriate maturation of the brain, which is achieved only marginally even in the newborn."[37] The notion of partial moral status fits nicely with the notion of subcategories of personhood and allows room to move away from the extreme positions of either complete moral status from conception or no moral status until birth. It also gives more concrete expression to Callahan's notion of partial moral status, mentioned earlier.

BOX 7.3   L.W. SUMNER, "A THIRD WAY"

An adequate view of the fetus promises a morally significant division between early abortions (before the threshold stage) and late abortions (after the threshold stage). It also promises borderline cases (during the threshold stage). Wherever that stage is located, abortions that precede it will be private matters, since the fetus will at that stage lack moral standing. Thus the provisions of the liberal view will apply to early abortions: they will be morally innocent … and ought to be legally unregulated.… Early abortion will have the same moral status as contraception.

Abortions that follow the threshold stage will be interpersonal matters, since the fetus will at that stage possess moral standing.... [T]hey must be assessed on a case-by-case basis and they ought to be legally permitted only on appropriate grounds. Late abortions will have the same moral status as infanticide, except for the difference made by the physical connection between fetus and mother.... A third way with abortion is thus a moderate and differential view, combining elements of the liberal view for early abortions with elements of (a weakened version of) the conservative view for late abortions....

We have thus far assumed that for a creature to have moral standing is for it to have a right to life.... To have full moral standing is to have the strongest right to life possessed by anyone, the right to life of the paradigm person.... The paradigm bearer of moral standing is an adult human being with normal capacities of intellect, emotion, perception, sensation, decision, action, and the like. If we think of such a person as a complex bundle of natural properties, then in principle we could employ as a criterion any of the properties common to all normal and mature members of our species....

That rationality is sufficient for moral standing is not controversial.... As a necessary condition, however, rationality will exclude a good many sentient beings.... A criterion of sentience can ... allow for the gradual emergence of moral standing in the order of nature. It can explain why no moral issues arise (directly) in our dealings with inanimate objects, plants, and the simpler forms of animal life. It ... also requires gentle usage of the severely abnormal. Cognitive disabilities and disorders may impair a person's range of sensibility, but they do not generally reduce that person to the level of a nonsentient being.... Since sentience admits of degrees, we can in principle construct a continuum ranging from fully sentient creatures at one extreme to completely nonsentient creatures at the other.... Human ontogenesis ... presents us with a continuum from adult to zygote. The threshold area will be the stage at which sentience first emerges, but where is that to be located?

There is no doubt that a newborn infant is sentient—that it feels hunger, thirst, physical pain, the pleasure of sucking, and other agreeable and disagreeable sensations. There is also no doubt that a zygote, and also an embryo, are presentient. It is difficult to locate with accuracy the stage during which feeling first emerges in fetal development.... Because there is no quantum leap into consciousness during fetal development, there is no clean and sharp boundary between sentient and nonsentient fetuses.... A fetus is ... probably sentient by the conventional stage of viability (around the end of the second trimester). Viability can therefore serve as a (rough) indicator of moral standing.[1]

We may define an early abortion as one performed sometime during the first trimester or early in the second, and a late abortion as one performed sometime late in the second trimester or during the third.... The threshold of sentience thus extends the morality of contraception forward to cover early abortion and extends the morality of infanticide backward to cover late abortion.... For most people, qualms about abortion are qualms about late abortion. It is a virtue of the sentience criterion that it explains and supports this differential approach.

Note

1. Although this book was written in 1981, the comments on the threshold of sentience are not out of date; there is still no agreement on the point at which a fetus becomes sentient. There is some medical consensus that the fetus definitely feels pain between 24 and 26 weeks, a threshold not far off from Sumner's analysis, although viability is a shifting point that has moved below 24 weeks.

Source: L.W. Sumner, *Abortion and Moral Theory* (Princeton, NJ: Princeton University Press, 1981), 126–151.

Autonomy and the Rights of Women

To treat the fetus as a person with full moral status, equivalent to that of the pregnant woman, is, in the eyes of many, to treat the pregnant woman as less than an autonomous person. Rights for the fetus are purchased at the expense of the rights of women. Autonomy is an important principle in our society. It is also the dominant principle in bioethics. Is a woman to be denied her autonomy because she is pregnant? Many would hold that this is paternalism in the highest degree and that it treats the woman as a means and not an end.

The principle of autonomy in bioethics holds that people have the right to make their own decisions about treatment. It is based on the premise that each person has, or should have, control over his or her own body. If this principle is accepted, how can it be denied in the case of a pregnant woman? Opponents such as Sidney Callahan, a pro-life feminist, will argue that our right to control our bodies does not extend to controlling the bodies of others and thus the pregnant woman does not have the right to control the body within her: "The same legal tradition which in our society guarantees the right to control one's own body firmly recognizes the wrongfulness of harming other bodies, however immature, dependent, different looking, or powerless. The handicapped, the retarded, and newborns are legally protected from deliberate harm. Pro-life feminists reject the supposition that would except the unborn from this protection."[38]

A pro-choice feminist would, however, insist on the exception on the grounds that a fetus is not in the same moral class as the handicapped, the retarded, and newborns—all of whom are living persons (at the very least considered part of the moral community). Sidney Callahan's position begs the question: to say that the fetus is another body, in the sense of the examples of other bodies that she gives, is to presuppose that the fetus is a person. This, as we have seen, is the major issue under debate. Admittedly, the pro-choice feminist is doing the same thing by presupposing that the fetus is not another body within the normal meaning of that term. But it would certainly seem that she is on stronger ground than Sidney Callahan, at least for a very early embryo or fetus. As long as the fetus cannot live outside the woman's body, it is difficult to insist that it is the body of another. When it comes to a late-term fetus, however, to insist that there is only the woman's own body involved is perhaps stretching the point. This brings us back to the question of *drawing the line* and the problems already outlined.

Women's autonomy is used to defend abortion from another perspective, that of equality in society. It is argued, with strong justification, that women cannot achieve economic and social equality if they do not have control over their fertility. Contraception cannot be relied on alone since it does not always work. And women are often coerced into sexual relations that they do not consent to, resulting in pregnancies that they do not want. From this point of view, enforced pregnancy is the ultimate denial of women's autonomy. Sidney Callahan, however, does not believe that women can achieve equality and freedom through permissive abortion laws. In her view, both society in general and men in particular need to support women in bearing and raising children. Her argument here is not without merit: "[I]f a woman claims the right to decide by herself whether the fetus becomes a child or not, what does this do to paternal and communal responsibility? Why should men share responsibility for child support or childrearing if they cannot share in what is asserted to be the woman's sole decision?"[39] This reflects a fear of many in the pro-life movement: relieving men of responsibility for the babies they create.

The Role of the Father

Sidney Callahan's argument raises another important issue in relation to abortion: If one grants that an abortion is morally permissible, who should be involved in the decision to abort? What if a wife wants an abortion and her husband wants the baby? What if the couple is not married and the boyfriend wants the baby but the woman wants to abort? This was the situation in a well-known

Quebec case that ended up in the Supreme Court of Canada in 1989 (the case of Chantal Daigle and Jean-Guy Tremblay). Daigle was pregnant and Tremblay, her former boyfriend, asked for and obtained an injunction to prevent her from having an abortion. The Quebec Court of Appeal declared that the fetus had constitutional rights apart from its mother (it did not declare it a person, however) and upheld the decision of the lower court. Daigle appealed to the Supreme Court of Canada, which lifted the injunction (by which time she had already ended the pregnancy), stating that "no court in Quebec or elsewhere has ever accepted the argument that a father's interest in a fetus he helped create could support a right to veto a woman's decision in respect of the fetus she is carrying."[40]

Only the pro-choice side needs to be considered on this question, since the pro-life side would be against Daigle's abortion as a matter of principle. Given that arguments in favour of choice rely heavily on considerations of a woman's autonomy and equality within society, it follows that her decision to abort (or not abort) a fetus should not be subject to a veto by the man who is the presumed father of the future child. The primacy of choice would automatically mean the choice of the pregnant woman. This does not seem fair to the man who has no say in the abortion decision, but who can be held financially responsible for the child in case the woman decides to go through with the pregnancy. From this point of view, Sidney Callahan's argument is a legitimate one. However, it would seem a greater injustice for a man to be able to force a woman to have a child, especially if he is no longer in a relationship with the woman (as in the Tremblay case) or if the pregnancy was the result of unwanted sexual relations. And it would be unacceptable (both morally and legally) for a man to be able to force a woman to have an abortion in a situation where she wanted to continue a pregnancy. However, one can argue that the current situation amounts to forced paternity, and that the question of a man's responsibility for a child that a woman insists on having against his will is perhaps in need of re-examination.

In the case of a married couple, the situation is more complex. If a married couple cannot agree on whether or not to continue an unplanned pregnancy, especially if one person is morally opposed to abortion, the conflict of values goes right to the heart of the marriage—and a decision either way could threaten the relationship. However, objectively speaking, from a pro-choice point of view the decision ultimately rests with the woman alone. This was recognized as a legal right by the U.S. Supreme Court in 1976 when it struck down a Missouri law requiring a husband's consent for an abortion. In a Canadian situation, the *Tremblay v. Daigle* decision would apply and the pregnant woman would be the sole decision-maker with respect to an abortion.[41]

Abortion is a polarized social and political issue that raises emotions on both sides of the debate. Violence has often been part of the scene when the two sides confront each other, often in front of abortion clinics.

Finding Common Ground

Anthony Weston believes that, with respect to any polarized ethical debate, there is room for common ground, and he tries to find that common ground in the abortion debate.[42] For example, with respect to the importance of *life*, we can all agree that life has value and is precious. So in that sense, he points out, we are all pro-life. When a woman has a miscarriage, it is usually perceived (by her, her spouse, family, and friends) as a loss. Is an abortion, too, not a loss? Further, Weston points out that pro-choice people are almost as uneasy as pro-life people about repeat abortions—and with women who rely on abortion as a form of birth control. While the first abortion can be blamed on lack of information, the second, third, or fourth cannot. Women who take repeated recourse in abortion (in Canada, in 2012, about 40 percent of the women were aborting for the second, third, or even fourth time[43]) are seen as being irresponsible. Margaret Somerville would agree. In her view, people may be free to indulge in casual sex (and even here they might want to think more carefully about what they are doing), but if they "knowingly and deliberately take the risk of conceiving a child they would abort if pregnancy resulted [they] are not, in my view, acting ethically with respect to the transmission of life."[44]

With respect to the question of choice, Weston points out that generally we all value choice and, outside of the abortion debate, "choice is almost axiomatic."[45] Further, even most pro-lifers would allow abortion in cases of rape (as well as in cases where a woman's life is in danger), which means that even people on the pro-life side can accept that sometimes something matters more than fetal right to life. Weston also points out that there are many areas where free-choice advocates on abortion do not condone free choice (for example, gun ownership, speed limits, food safety, to mention only a few). So pro-choice people have to admit that there are situations where freedom of choice is not the ultimate value. He concludes that, "despite painful and persistent debate between two single-minded sides, most people recognize that abortion choices pit two genuine values against each other in a case where *both of them count*."[46]

Many people who supported abortion 40 years ago, when some women were dying from botched illegal abortions and others were suffering through enforced pregnancy and giving their babies up for adoption, are shocked today at the casualness that surrounds abortion for a lot of people. So there is some common ground to be found on the issue of acting responsibly in sexual relations and in taking steps to prevent unwanted pregnancies in the first place. This is the responsibility of all sexually active women and men whether they find themselves on the pro-life or the pro-choice side of the abortion question. It is encouraging to note that the number of abortions in Canada has been declining slowly but steadily: over 98,000 abortions were performed in 2007 with a steady decline to just under 84,000 in 2012.[47]

BOX 7.4

JUNE O'CONNOR, "THE WATER CHILDREN OF JAPAN"

In Japan, a fetus is considered part of the family and its life, however short, becomes part of the family's lineage. If the fetus is aborted, either by miscarriage or induced abortion, it is considered necessary and important to recognize this death through ceremonies and rituals. The fetus is called *mizugo*, which means "water child," and a ceremony in its honour is known as *mizuko kuyo* (meaning "paying respect to the water child"). Memorial gardens with statues resembling tiny gravestones commemorate the water children, and families bring offerings to Jizo, the patron saint of the water children. June O'Connor explains the purpose of these rituals:

Mizuko kuyo enables the woman who has lost or terminated her offspring to process her total experience of a past abortion ritually, in a home or temple religious ceremony, at the same time as it provides the larger community—husband, children and siblings, extended family and others—an opportunity to mourn the loss of the fetus and to reflect on the ways they suffer or benefit from this loss. The family participation in the ritual provides communal recognition of the social and bodily kinship relation to the fetus who is regarded as a member of the family who will not be forgotten. Remembrance is regularly expressed by giving the water-child a posthumously-awarded name and by symbolizing the water-child with a Jizo statue on a temple hillside....

Although the *mizuko kuyo* rites are themselves peculiar to Japanese culture and religion in both form and meaning, these rites disclose meanings germane to abortion that do have cross-cultural import. One is that, while abortion is, indeed, a matter of "choice" that is widely protected by the American legal system, induced abortions are invasive bodily interventions that effect the cessation of bodily life, facts that often have powerful, enduring and sometimes surprising impact even on those who choose abortion. Myriad, conflicting and enduring feelings attend and follow the physical experience of abortion. For some, these feelings beg sustained attention and formal, at times even ritual, recognition.

Source: June O'Connor, "Ritual Recognition of Abortion: Japanese Buddhist Practices and U.S. Jewish and Christian Proposals," in Lisa Sowle Cahill and Margaret A. Fawley (eds.), Embodiment, *Morality and Medicine* (Dordrecht, The Netherlands: Kluwer Academic Publishers, 1995), 94.

In Japan, the fetus is called *mizugo* (water child), and if it dies through abortion, miscarriage, or stillbirth, it is still considered part of the family lineage. Memorial gardens such as the one shown here commemorate the water children, and families come to pay tribute, just as we pay tribute to our buried relatives in cemeteries.

ETHICAL THEORY AND ABORTION

As the above discussion demonstrates, abortion is a complex moral issue that does not admit of easy solutions. It is difficult to look to ethical theory for an answer for one very good reason: ethical theories deal largely with the way people treat each other in society; in other words, they presume a moral community. But the whole issue around abortion is whether or not a fetus is part of the moral community, which is why the question of whether or not the fetus is a person is seen as so central.

The question of personhood with respect to the fetus is relevant to a Kantian analysis of abortion. The second formulation of the Categorical Imperative dealing with respect for persons is based on the premise that individuals are rational, self-legislating agents, something that cannot be said of a fetus (but then it cannot be said of an infant or a child either). For this reason it is difficult to defend a view of fetal rights based on Kantian ethics. Kant's notion of autonomy is applicable, however, to the pregnant woman, who, as a rational and self-legislating agent, has the right to determine for herself if she wants to continue an unwanted pregnancy. Forcing her to have a baby against her will would be an infringement of her autonomy. On the other hand, Kant's notion of duties to self would raise moral questions for the woman who, while not harming a person in Kant's view, would be intentionally harming her body, which could be seen as morally wrong.

Utilitarianism can be applied to the question of abortion, and the issue of personhood is not necessarily relevant here. Using the hedonistic calculus, if a woman determines that a forced pregnancy would bring more unhappiness than happiness for all concerned, an abortion could be justified under this theory. This would necessitate, however, that the interests of the father or husband as well as other children and even the community[48] be taken into consideration, and not just the interests of the pregnant woman herself. So a woman's autonomy could be infringed upon for the greater good. Further, using rule utilitarianism one could argue that a permissive abortion policy might have more negative than positive consequences for society and thus justify restriction on abortion by legislation. So while utilitarianism could be used to justify abortion, it could also be used to justify its restriction.

It is rare to find an analysis of virtue ethics in the abortion literature or in the bioethical literature in general, but Rosalind Hursthouse makes an interesting case for using this ethical theory. In her view, this theory allows us to think beyond the usual issues of the moral status of the fetus and the rights of the pregnant woman.[49] As we have seen, virtue ethics puts the emphasis on the agent rather than the action, and considers an action to be morally right if it is what a virtuous agent (one who has or exercises certain virtues) would do in the circumstances. A virtue, according to Hursthouse, can be seen as "a character trait a human being needs to flourish or live well."[50] The exercise of rights is not the best way of ensuring a flourishing life, since "[l]ove and friendship do not survive their parties' constantly insisting on their rights, nor do people live well when they think that getting what they have a right to is of pre-eminent importance; they harm others, and they harm themselves."[51]

While Hursthouse admits that abortion cuts off a new life and is not something that should be done lightly, the moral status of the fetus is not the main question for moral analysis; the real question concerns whether or not the woman is acting virtuously. And this question must be answered in the context of the woman's own particular life as a whole. A virtuous woman would be one who has "such character traits as strength, independence, resoluteness, decisiveness, self-confidence, responsibility, serious-mindedness, and self-determination"[52] and, exercising these virtues, may know in her own wisdom that having a baby at this time, in these circumstances—or, in some cases, having a baby at all—is simply not something she can do. This could be a very responsible and moral decision. Another woman's decision to abort might be morally justifiable precisely because she is lacking in many of those virtues so that, in Hursthouse's view, "even in the cases where the decision to have an abortion is the right one, it can still be the reflection of a moral failing."[53] And even when the decision to abort may be the right one from the point of view of virtue ethics, this does not mean that no harm has been done or that guilt about it is inappropriate. This somewhat reflects the conclusions of Daniel Callahan and Naomi Wolf cited above that abortion might be a responsible moral decision but that one should not forget the harm involved in the destruction of a life.

Hursthouse has, of course, chosen her virtues carefully when she describes the virtuous woman. In other societies, and at other times in our own, these were not considered ideal virtues for a woman who was expected to be, among other things, humble, submissive, and accepting of life's misfortunes. Many pro-life advocates, too, might have trouble with Hursthouse's list. As discussed earlier in this chapter, the abortion issue is intensely coloured by social values, especially regarding the role of women in society and in the family, and those values will colour one's belief about what constitutes a virtuous woman as well as one's answer to the question of what a virtuous agent would do in this situation.

While virtue ethics might not be helpful in the context of public policy, its emphasis on situating actions within a whole life, and its insistence on framing moral decisions around the question of what kind of person one wants to be, can be useful for any woman trying to make a difficult moral choice regarding abortion.

From the perspective of bioethicists working from within a feminist framework, however, much of what is said about abortion by proponents of these standard ethical approaches is entirely beside the point. As Lindemann puts it, "If you were a Martian unfamiliar with human life forms and you happened to be reading a typical non-feminist bioethicist's argument regarding abortion, you would have no idea that fetuses grow inside women's bodies."[54] Consequently, feminist bioethicists see their role as reuniting "what non-feminists have put asunder"[55] by insisting that any examination of abortion must begin and end with the recognition that fetuses do not exist without women and that this fact is not morally irrelevant but morally primary.

As a result, feminist bioethicists do two things when considering the issues raised by abortion. First, they take pregnant women's experiences seriously, treating them not simply as perspectives that must be balanced with other perspectives and that can perhaps be outweighed by them, but as central to any adequate ethical analysis. This means, as Sherwin observes, that feminists do not believe that abstract moral rules are helpful for determining when an abortion can be morally justified. Rather, according to Sherwin, while feminist bioethicists believe "that it is possible for a woman to make a mistake in her judgment on this matter (i.e., it is possible that a woman may come to believe that she was wrong about her decision to continue or terminate a pregnancy), the intimate nature of this sort of decision makes it unlikely that anyone else is in a position to arrive at a more reliable conclusion."[56]

Second, feminists believe that any examination of abortion must take the connection between gender and power very seriously. The burdens of child-bearing and child-rearing fall disproportionately on women; indeed, we live in societies in which "a grossly disproportionate amount of the exhausting, demanding, self-sacrificing, and socially unrecognized work of reproducing and caring for children [is assigned] to women."[57] These two points, feminists believe, mean that not only is it inappropriate for others to tell a pregnant woman what choice she should make in a matter so intimately connected with her body and so crucially important for her life, but that abortion services should be legal, safe, and easily accessible.

MATERNAL-FETAL CONFLICTS OR THE FETUS AS PATIENT

In some ways, abortion is the original case of maternal-fetal conflict, as it sets the needs of the pregnant woman against the needs of the developing fetus. However, what is meant by this term is different from—although an extension of—the abortion debate: it refers instead to issues about the relationship between the pregnant woman and her fetus *once she has decided to bring the pregnancy to term*.

For those on the pro-life side, pregnant women have the same moral obligations to their fetuses as they do to their born children and, as we have seen, for them abortion is as wrong as killing a child. They also agree that it is wrong to engage in behaviours that could result in harm to the fetus (which is always, for them, an unborn child). From their point of view the issue is quite straightforward: pregnant women have responsibilities toward the fetus as such that override their own personal or professional interests.

The issue is a little more complicated for those who hold a pro-choice position. For them, a pregnant woman does not have moral obligations to the fetus as such, since the fetus has no moral status. However, *having decided to carry a pregnancy to term*, she has obligations to not harm the *future child*. This argument draws the moral line regarding obligations to the fetus not at the stage of development (as in the abortion debate), but at the point of decision to have the child. At this point, the interests of the fetus, *as a future child*, come into play.

BOX 7.5

BONNIE STEINBOCK, "COMPULSORY MEDICAL TREATMENT OF PREGNANT WOMEN"

The principle that pregnant women should not be compelled to undergo any additional risks for the sake of the unborn, even after viability, can be given an equal protection basis. Outside pregnancy, there are virtually no circumstances in which the body of one person could be required to save the life of another. One famous [American] case is *McFall v. Shimp*, in which Robert McFall, who was dying of aplastic anemia, asked the court to order his cousin, David Shimp, the only family member with potentially compatible bone marrow, to donate bone marrow to him. Bone marrow extraction is not an especially risky procedure—far less risky than major surgery—but it is painful and invasive. Shimp apparently believed that the medical risk to him was greater than his cousin's doctors assessed it. On a balancing-interests approach, McFall's interest in survival might well outweigh Shimp's interests in avoiding pain and minimal risk. The court rejected this approach. Although the court found Shimp's behavior to be morally reprehensible, it refused to order him to donate. The court emphasized that there was no legal duty to rescue others, and stated that to require this would change every concept and principle upon which our society is founded....

McFall and Shimp were only cousins, but there is no doubt that the outcome would have been the same even had they been father and child. Angela Holder states, "In no case is an adult ever ordered to surrender a kidney, bone marrow, or any other part of his body for donation to his child, to another relative, or to anyone else."[1] In fact, it is doubtful that a parent could be legally compelled to donate a pint of blood necessary to save his or her child's life.... This principle of our legal system must be remembered in assessing compulsory cesareans. To force women to undergo major surgery, even relatively safe major surgery, is to impose an unequal and unjustified burden on pregnant women. Even if we accept—as I do—the premise that women have moral obligations to the children they plan to bear, and even if these moral obligations include undergoing risks and making sacrifices to secure the health and wellbeing of the children they have decided to bear, it is quite another matter to think that these moral obligations should be legally coerced. I think we can agree that it would be appallingly selfish for a woman to expose her nearly born baby to the risk of an irreversible handicap simply to avoid an abdominal scar. But even in such a case, the woman should not be legally compelled to undergo surgery.

The above argument is based on the injustice of imposing burdens on pregnant women that are not imposed on other people. But what if the burdens were not unequally imposed? Would the state be justified in legally compelling all citizens, men and women, to undergo bodily risk and invasion where necessary to save a life? The answer to this question depends on one's general political outlook. Those who lean toward a more libertarian perspective will be opposed to "Good Samaritan" laws in general, and find the idea of compulsory donation of bodily parts especially repellent. Those who take a more communitarian approach may argue that all members of a community have a duty to make sacrifices for the good of the whole. For example, requiring healthy adults to make occasional blood donations might be considered justifiable. Communitarians might also argue that women should be legally compelled to undergo cesarean sections, where this is necessary to spare the child lifelong disability or death, given the relatively small objective risk to the woman and the enormous benefit to the child....

an improvement over earlier attitudes toward pregnancy that often restricted a woman's behaviour), most pregnant women (and even pre-pregnant women) now refuse all potentially harmful substances, from coffee and alcohol to aspirin and antibiotics.[58]

However, some women do not (or cannot) stop drinking, smoking, or taking drugs, and the question is raised as to whether or not they should be *coerced* into doing so and their behaviour controlled or punished. Like the abortion issue, this one has two extremes. In the U.S., some states have "fetal rights" legislation that deems any behaviour during pregnancy that puts the fetus at risk of damage or death a form of child abuse. At the other extreme, some feminists and libertarians believe that privacy and autonomy concerns dictate that whatever a woman does during pregnancy is her business. Bearing in mind that most women do act responsibly when they are pregnant, the question still remains: is it right to enforce this responsibility through legislation and, ultimately, arrest and punishment?

A Canadian case involving a glue-sniffing pregnant woman in Winnipeg went to the Supreme Court in 1997. The woman, known as Ms. G., was five months' pregnant and addicted to glue sniffing, and refused to go to a treatment centre. Winnipeg Child and Family Services obtained a court order to keep Ms. G in detention until the birth of the baby. The case ended up in the Supreme Court. In its decision, the Court held that the state does not have the authority to order a woman into custody for the purpose of rectifying her conduct. The Court gave three reasons in support of its decision: the "live birth rule," which holds that the law recognizes only the rights of the born person; the fact that the life of the fetus and that of the pregnant woman are intimately connected and must be treated as one; and the fact that setting up an antagonistic dichotomy between mother and fetus would deprive mothers of control of their bodies and their autonomy. With respect to the issue of the lifestyle risks of pregnant women, the Supreme Court held that there is no clear line between offensive and allowable behaviour; that certain risks are not choices (for example, drug abuse or poor nutrition may be products of circumstances and illness); and that imposing a duty of care concerning lifestyle choices would increase the level of outside scrutiny on pregnant women.

While that was the decision of the majority of judges, there was a dissenting opinion, which pointed out that it is inconsistent that a person can sue later in life for damages for injuries suffered in utero when the court cannot prevent the damage in the first place. The dissenting judges also said that a woman has the choice of aborting a pregnancy and, by choosing to become a mother, she forfeits her liberty rights to the state's interest in protecting her fetus. They also concluded that, since medical technology can show that a fetus is alive and can be harmed by the mother's conduct, the "born alive rule" is a legal anachronism and should be ignored.

The zeal with which some American states have been prosecuting pregnant women for the crime of "fetal harm" can perhaps be seen as giving credence to the Supreme Court's ruling in the case of Ms. G. In the U.S., pregnant women (especially young African-American women) have been detained, arrested, and sometimes convicted for behaviour (mostly drug-related) that is perceived by authorities to harm the fetus. According to Martin, "An Indiana woman who attempted suicide while pregnant spent a year in jail before murder charges were dropped last year; an Iowa woman was arrested and jailed after falling down the stairs and suffering a miscarriage."[59] In a case that has attracted much attention, 16-year-old Rennie Gibbs, whose baby was stillborn (with its umbilical cord wrapped around its neck), was charged with depraved heart murder. Under Mississippi law, this is defined as an action that is eminently dangerous to others and carries a maximum sentence of life in prison. Gibbs has been in legal limbo since 2007 while the courts decide whether or not the case should go forward. The reason for the charge: an autopsy revealed traces of a cocaine by-product in the baby's blood. Whether or not the young woman is eventually convicted, this case and others like it are seen by many, Martin states, as part of "the backlash to Roe v. Wade and the conservative push to establish 'personhood' for fetuses as part of a broad-based approach to weaken abortion laws."[60]

In an earlier case in South Carolina, a woman named Cornelia Whitner was accused of causing her baby to be born with cocaine metabolites in its system (because she had injected crack cocaine into her own). She was sentenced to eight years in prison. She later petitioned the court on the basis that the article under which she was charged covered children but not fetuses. The court held that the word "child" in South Carolina's Children's Code includes viable fetuses, stating that there was no rational basis for finding that a viable fetus is not a person in this context. The court also argued that parents of born children could be prosecuted for actions that endanger a child (even if the action is legal—for example, drinking), and thus it is not absurd to extend this protection to viable fetuses, a decision that some fear could be extended back to non-viable fetuses.

While most people agree that pregnant women have a responsibility to not harm the fetus, many are disturbed by the suggestion that a woman could lose her right to liberty when she is pregnant. While the cases mentioned above concern drug addiction with the possibility of serious harm to the child, there is concern that the notion of maternal responsibility can be carried too far and that policing the behaviour of pregnant women could become the norm. If we accept that a child has a right to be born unharmed, do we also accept that a child has a right to optimal health? The report of the Royal Commission on Reproductive Technology reads: "At the core of the impulse toward judicial intervention in pregnancy and birth is the view that pregnant women are the means to an end—the birth of healthy children. To the extent that judicial intervention reinforces the notion that a pregnant woman's role is only to carry and deliver a healthy child, it denies her existence as an autonomous individual with legal and constitutional rights and is dangerous to the rights and autonomy of all women."[61]

Fetal Therapies

Similar questions can be raised in relation to the second form of maternal-fetal conflict. There are a number of therapies that may be considered essential for the health or even survival of the fetus, but that may be invasive and even risky for the pregnant woman. At the most benign level, there are medications that help the fetus and do not hurt the mother; these are minimally invasive. Further up the scale we find fetal blood transfusions, which are more invasive and may require birth by Caesarean section. These are also problematic for a woman who does not believe in blood transfusions: she can refuse a blood transfusion herself, but can she refuse one for the fetus? The third type of intervention, and the one that is the most invasive, is in utero fetal surgery. This necessitates abdominal surgery with associated risks, as well as a Caesarean section for the birth of the child and for all future births. Further, many of these procedures are experimental, raising issues related to medical research versus therapy.[62]

These situations raise many of the same questions discussed above relative to a pregnant woman's behaviour. While most women will want to do everything possible to protect the health of their developing baby, others might be inclined to let nature take its course and try again. For example, in the past a woman who went into early labour would likely lose the baby. Now she is faced with the decision of a risky Caesarean section with a 30–50 percent chance of survival for the baby (along with possible neurological and physical damage). The question is, how much risk should a pregnant woman have to take in order to save the life or the health of her fetus? And whose decision should it be? Does she lose her right to informed consent because she is pregnant? As Nancy Milliken puts it, "[I]f obstetricians are given the authority to force pregnant women to follow their recommendations, this force may be used in a very arbitrary way…. The new therapeutic options with their maternal risks have created difficult ethical decisions for the pregnant woman and her obstetrician. A discussion regarding the legitimate use of force against pregnant women for fetal benefit has begun."[63]

The real issue for Casper concerns the creation of a new category of person resulting from the recent tendency to define the fetus as a patient in its own right, and the creation of the new medical specialty of fetal surgery, which "participates in the erasure of pregnant women" as it "fuels rather than resolves ongoing social confusion about where women end and fetuses begin."[64] Since there is no way of gaining access to the fetus except through the body of a pregnant woman, the very existence of this new specialty causes concern for the principle of autonomy (and of informed consent) in relation to pregnant women.

At least at first glance, a Kantian would opt in favour of the pregnant woman in these debates, holding that she is an autonomous person with the right to make her own decisions. But a Kantian would also emphasize that freedom entails responsibility and that an autonomous person's right to make her own decisions is accompanied by a responsibility to act morally and from duty. In addition, Kant's notion of perfect duties to the self would preclude the kind of behaviour that was destructive both to the woman and to the fetus (for example, the glue-sniffing case above). At the same time, it is unlikely that a Kantian would approve of seeing a pregnant woman punished for behaviour that a non-pregnant woman could do with impunity. Further, it is unlikely that a Kantian would want to see a woman coerced into invasive surgery to protect the fetus. This would be an affront to her autonomy.

A utilitarian might see the matter differently. If maternal behaviour during pregnancy threatens to harm the future child, and if society is eventually going to pay the medical, educational, and social costs of that harm, then constraining a pregnant woman's behaviour could easily be seen as justifiable in order to ensure the greater good. The harm to the individual mother would be less than the harm to her child and to society. At the same time, a rule utilitarian might look at the greater harm caused to society if women began to fear losing their autonomy when pregnant, or if society relied on punitive measures to control maternal behaviour. From this point of view, the harm caused to some children (of drug-addicted mothers, for example) might be seen as less important than the harm caused to society by restricting the freedom of its female population.

Similarly, with respect to fetal therapies, a utilitarian would weigh the benefits to the future child against the harms to the pregnant woman and would likely justify coerced medical treatment if it were not too invasive, onerous, or risky for the woman. At the limit, a utilitarian could even justify risky experimental surgery if the potential benefits were great (taking into consideration the benefits to future children of perfecting a new medical or surgical technique). A rule utilitarian, however, would likely look at the larger picture of the harm to medical practice and the public good if women could be coerced into medical and surgical procedures that they did not want in order to ensure the health of their babies, especially if these procedures were experimental. As with maternal behaviour above, the harm caused to society by restricting the freedom of pregnant women might be considered greater than the harm to particular children who may suffer or die as a result of not receiving available medical treatment in utero due to lack of maternal consent.

Many feminists are wary of the tendency toward punishing pregnant women who "misbehave" or of forcing them to undergo medical treatment that they do not want. These tendencies are seen as a return to the past when women's role was perceived as not much more than producing babies. Casper reports one fetal surgeon referring to a pregnant woman as "the best heart-lung machine available for maintaining the unborn patient," a statement that harkens dangerously back to a time when a woman was not much more than a fetal container.[65] Further, the justification for controlling a pregnant woman's behaviour and restricting her freedom is based on perceiving the fetus as a separate person and a separate patient in whom the medical profession and society have an interest. This is a moral leap that most feminists are unwilling to take. While it would be ideal if all pregnant women were, at all times, completely responsible in their behaviour and their decisions (as it would be if all adults were the same way!), we cannot force people to behave in an exemplary manner. It would be nice if everybody always did the right thing. But, in our society, we are all free to make mistakes. Should a pregnant woman be treated any differently?

CONCLUSION

Abortion is somewhat unique among the issues of biomedical ethics being dealt with in this text, since it has not come about as a result of modern medical technology. As we have seen, abortion has been around for about as long as women have been having babies, and while the ways and means of aborting a pregnancy have changed, the fact of abortion has not. Its practice evolved from a long period of benign tolerance (due in part to lack of scientific means of establishing the fact of pregnancy), through a period of strict criminalization (where it did not cease, but went underground), to its current state, which melds varying degrees of legalization and tolerance with varying degrees of controversy and condemnation. The moral issues, as we have seen, are complex and revolve mainly around the difficulty of establishing with any degree of scientific or moral certainty a point at which the fetus can be legitimately seen as a member of the human community with a right to life. This is the issue around which the polarized debates revolve, and it is exacerbated by the development of technologies that allow the fetus to be perceived, at least medically, as a patient if not a person in its own right. Autonomy and beneficence, sanctity of life and quality of life, principles that reflect important values in our society find themselves in conflict as a woman is confronted with the emerging life within her own life. The issues are complex and a great deal of intellectual patience and detachment is required to work through their many threads. There will probably never be a perfect solution but with effort we can, perhaps, arrive at the "least worst option" on a case-by-case basis. The boxed excerpts in this chapter (along with the suggested readings) may help to deepen the reader's understanding of this complex moral issue.

PHILOSOPHICAL REFLECTION ON LIFE, SOUL, AND BODY

It is somewhat ironic that what led the Catholic Church to change its position on abortion, abandoning the distinction between an unformed and a formed (ensouled) fetus, was a new scientific position that, in effect, abandoned the soul. The new science of embryology could find no stage at which one could say that the soul entered the body. As a result, it declared that the fetus was a human being from the moment of conception, and ensoulment (and the soul) disappeared from scientific discourse. The Church took a long time to follow the scientists and did so by simply declaring that the soul was present from the moment of conception. But whereas the scientific and religious authorities were somewhat on the same wavelength with the notion of ensoulment (however inadequate we might perceive the science to be), the new scientific position offered no support for the religious one, and henceforth the two would be on separate explanatory paths. The idea that the soul is present at conception became an article of faith, not science.

For centuries before this, the soul was considered the principle of life. This ancient notion was developed by Aristotle in the 4th century B.C.E. to explain living beings at all levels. In his view, all living things had a soul, but not the same kind of soul. There was a hierarchy of souls or faculties that explained the differences between plants and animals, and animals and humans. The most basic aspect of soul (the vegetative soul) represents the nutritive faculty, a power shared by plants, animals, and humans. This allows for taking in nourishment and for reproduction. At a higher level is the faculty of sense perception and movement, represented by the animal (or sensitive) soul, which is present in both animals and humans, but not plants. At the top of the hierarchy Aristotle posited the rational soul, or faculty of thought, possessed only by humans. Thus all living things were imbued with soul, representing varying degrees of power and awareness. With such a model of soul, it is possible to see the human being moving through the three levels as it gestates in the womb, with the first months of gestation involving only the vegetative or nutritive soul.

Aristotle's notion of the soul was accepted by both Augustine and Aquinas and was part of the official teaching of the Catholic Church for centuries. Arab philosophers accepted and even developed Aristotle's account of the soul, thus influencing the position of Islamic scholars on abortion. A major change came with the philosophy of René Descartes who, influenced by the scientific revolution of the 17th century, developed a mechanistic physiology designed to explain all aspects of animal and human bodies without recourse to any notion of soul. In his universe there were only two substances: matter and mind. What Aristotle meant by vegetative and animal soul, Descartes described in purely material terms. What Aristotle meant by rational soul, Descartes described as immaterial mind, possessed by humans but not by animals. In his treatise on the body he referred to *machines without souls* (animals) and *machines with souls* (humans). Bodies, both human and animal, were purely material, explicable according to the laws of physics. Minds were immaterial, distinct from bodies, immortal, and not subject to the laws of physics. Descartes never managed to explain how mind and body interact, and one of his legacies to the modern philosophical world is known as the mind-body problem, a problem that still awaits a satisfactory solution.

In our day, biologists explain life without any recourse to notions of mind or soul, and psychologists explain mind (or consciousness) often by explaining it away. Outside of religion, there is little or no serious discussion of soul. At the same time, psychologists are unable to agree on just what mind is, and biologists are unable to agree on the origins of life. We know more and more about complex living organisms, including human beings, but in the words of Carl Sagan, "There is no generally accepted definition of life."[66] Centuries after we abandoned Aristotle's hierarchy of souls, we have yet to find anything to match its explanatory power, in particular, in fetal development.

CASES OF INTEREST

Dobson v. Dobson

In 1993, Cynthia Dobson was driving toward Moncton, New Brunswick, in bad weather. She was involved in an automobile collision, resulting in prenatal injuries to her fetus. The child was delivered later that day by Caesarean section, but had sustained serious injuries causing permanent mental and physical impairment, including cerebral palsy. The child's grandfather later brought an action for damages on behalf of the child against Cynthia, claiming that her negligent driving was the cause of the crash and the injuries that the child sustained. This case made it all the way to the Supreme Court of Canada, where the charge of negligence was ultimately rejected. The Court held that an action could not be brought against a mother by a child for damages sustained to the fetus as this would constitute "a severe intrusion into the lives of pregnant women" and would impose additional and unacceptable burdens on pregnant women, interfering in their bodily integrity, right to privacy, and ability to make autonomous decisions. (This was a landmark case since it was the first time the Supreme Court considered the issue of a child suing his mother for negligence during pregnancy.)[67]

R. v. Prince

On January 1, 1981, in Winnipeg, Manitoba, Bernice Daniels, who was six months' pregnant, was stabbed in the abdomen by Sandra Prince. The following day, Prince was charged with the attempted murder of Daniels. On January 6, 1981, Daniels gave birth to a severely premature child who lived for only 19 minutes. The autopsy report later showed that the knife wound inflicted by Prince penetrated the amniotic sac, causing contamination of the amniotic fluid and the subsequent premature birth and death of the child. Prince was tried and acquitted of attempted murder, but found guilty of causing bodily harm to Daniels.

Prior to the trial, however, and following an inquest into the death of the child, Prince was charged with manslaughter with respect to the deceased child. Invoking the Kienapple principle, which holds that an accused cannot be convicted of two charges arising out of the same act, Prince argued that she could not be convicted of both charges. This argument rested on the premise that there was only one victim, and as such, only one person harmed by the stabbing.

In 1986, the Supreme Court of Canada handed down its decision, stating that "[s]ociety, through criminal law, requires Prince to answer for both the injury to Bernice Daniels and the death of the child, just as it would require a person who threw a bomb into a crowded space to answer for the multiple injuries and deaths that might result." Because the child survived outside its mother's womb before dying, it attained the status of personhood and thus the capacity to be victimized. Prince was found guilty of manslaughter.[68]

Keeler v. Keeler

A California couple, Robert and Teresa Keeler, had been married for 16 years before divorcing in September 1968. Unknown to Robert, Teresa was pregnant at the time of the divorce by a man she had met earlier that summer and with whom she was then living. On February 23, 1969, Teresa was driving on a narrow mountain road in Amador County and met Robert, who was driving in the opposite direction. Robert blocked the road with his car, forcing Teresa to pull over, after which he started walking toward her. He appeared calm, so she rolled down the window to talk to him. He mentioned how he had heard that she was pregnant and became very upset upon seeing her belly. He then pulled her out of the car, pinned her against it, and shoved his knee into her abdomen while saying "I'm going to stomp it out of you." He then struck her in the face several times, causing her to lose consciousness. When she woke up, Robert was gone, and she drove home.

She was taken to the hospital where the fetus was examined in utero, found to have a fractured head, and was delivered stillborn by Caesarean section. The pathologist opined that the cause of death was a skull fracture with consequent cerebral haemorrhaging. It was later determined by expert testimony that the fetus had developed to the stage of viability and that, in the event of a premature birth on the date of the attack, it would have had a 75–96 percent chance of survival.

Robert was charged for murder under section 187 of California's Penal Code, which holds murder to be "the unlawful killing of a human being, with malice aforethought." The issue brought before the California Superior Court was whether the fetus was a "human being" protected by the statute. The court concluded that, when formulating this definition of murder, the Legislature had in mind "a person who had been born alive." No case law or statutory amendments had changed this meaning. In June 1970, then, it was held that Robert could not be found guilty for the murder of Teresa's fetus.[69]

CASE STUDIES

Scenario One

Adriana, a 12-year-old girl, lives with her mother, Joanne, and her stepfather, Carl, in a small town in Quebec. Adriana's mother and father (who got married when Joanne was already pregnant with Adriana) divorced 10 years ago when Adriana was only 2 years old, and her mother, an artist, married Carl about 6 years later. While Joanne has exhibited her portraits and sculptures in various galleries in the region, her art is not, at the moment, a reliable source of income, and she and Adriana are financially dependent on Carl.

Adriana began complaining of abdominal pains nearly five months ago. She saw several doctors who gave her different diagnoses, none of which seemed to help. A few weeks ago, the reason for her abdominal pains became clear: she was pregnant. When she received this news, she confided in her mother that she had been raped by her stepfather almost five months earlier. She had been afraid to say anything out of fear that her mother would not believe her and her stepfather would get angry.

When Carl found out that Adriana was pregnant, he was outraged. He denied having raped the girl and accused her of sleeping with one of the boys from school. He threatened to leave if she kept the baby, removing any financial support that Adriana and her mother currently have. He called Adriana a disgrace and said that no stepdaughter of his would have a child out of wedlock. Joanne believed Adriana's story, and has filed for divorce.

Joanne can return to her old job in a local coffee shop and perhaps sell a few paintings, allowing her and Adriana to live modestly, but she cannot afford to support another child. Under the circumstances, she does not want to raise Carl's child, which, given Adriana's age, she will likely have to do if Adriana does not have an abortion or give the baby up for adoption.

Adriana is already 21 weeks pregnant. There are several clinics in Quebec that will perform abortions up to 22 weeks into the pregnancy; after that point she would have to go to the U.S. where abortions are legally permitted up to 24 weeks. This could be arranged through a clinic in Montreal. Adriana is afraid to have an abortion and also afraid to have a baby. Her mother is trying to decide what should be done in the short time frame available to her.

(1) Should Joanne arrange for Adriana to get an abortion whether Adriana agrees or not? Should she encourage her to have the baby and give it up for adoption? (2) How do Joanne's financial circumstances influence the decision? Would it be different if she could easily support the child? If

Adriana had been raped by someone else? If she had not been raped? (3) What is the threshold beyond which it would be morally unacceptable for Adriana to have an abortion? Would it be morally acceptable at 21 weeks but not 22 weeks? (4) What would Sumner say? What would Marquis say? (5) Taking into consideration Hursthouse's virtue ethics point of view, what would you say to Joanne?

Scenario Two

Maria and Jonathan have been married for seven years and often discuss having children. In fact, they have been weighing the pros and cons of having a child for months. While they both know that they want children, they have had difficulty deciding about the right time to take the big step. One day, shortly after their most recent discussion, Maria finds out that she is pregnant. She has been on the pill for years, but tends to be careless about taking it and often forgets.

Both Maria and Jonathan are entrepreneurs. They own and operate a small but quite successful chain of restaurants in town and in surrounding communities, and the business takes up a lot of their time. Outside of work, they have numerous expensive hobbies. They have memberships in the tennis club and the local gym; Maria takes painting and photography classes; Jonathan restores old cars. They regularly go out to the theatre and to dinner. They recently renovated their home and plan on purchasing an elaborate entertainment system, and are even considering installing a home gym. If they decide to have the child, they will have to scale back both their recreation activities and their home renovation plans.

Maria is now nearly four months' pregnant. She and Jonathan have been leaning toward making the necessary sacrifices and having the child, but an opportunity comes up for a Caribbean cruise, which is being offered at a discount. The cruise starts two months from now, when they have both booked time off for a vacation. Maria, however, does not want to go on a Caribbean cruise when she is six months' pregnant. A number of their friends have already jumped at the cruise opportunity and are encouraging the two of them to come along. Maria decides that this factor tips the scales and now wants an abortion.

(1) Should Maria get the abortion? (2) If you hold a pro-choice point of view, do her motives matter to you? Would it be different if she had a more serious reason for wanting an abortion (marriage difficulty, illness, and so forth)? (3) If you hold a pro-life view, do you see the cases of Adriana and Maria in the same light? (4) Would a feminist analyze this case differently from the case of Adriana? What would Sidney Callahan say? What would Hursthouse say?

Scenario Three

About five months ago, Julie, a 25-year-old graduate student in philosophy, attended a party and got very drunk. She does not remember the whole night, but believes that she may have slept with one or more men with whom she had been flirting early in the evening. She spent the night at the home of the host, but woke up alone. Noticing when she got up that the condoms she always carries in her purse were missing, she presumed she must have made use of them. She did not think to take any precautions after the evening, such as going to a clinic to ask for the "morning after" pill.

Julie is a long-distance runner. There have been occasions in the past where she missed her period for months at a time. She had consulted her doctor and was told that this was normal for some athletes. Consequently, when she missed her period for several months after the party, she took no notice. Now, however, she finds herself pregnant and is trying to decide whether to keep the baby or have an abortion. She is not in a serious relationship and is estranged from her parents, making the option of keeping the baby a difficult one to consider seriously. Since she herself has experienced feelings of abandonment in her own life because of her own adoption, she is unwilling to consider having a baby and giving it up for adoption. She is confused and, given how far advanced she is in the pregnancy, sees her situation as somewhat desperate.

(1) Should Julie get the abortion? What would a Kantian say about Julie's exercise of autonomy both at the party and in the months following? (2) Would a pro-life advocate be likely to think that Julie's predicament is her own fault? Would that justify refusing her an abortion and forcing her to carry the fetus to term? (3) What could each ethical theory contribute to an analysis of Julie's situation? (4) Would you be inclined to assess this case in terms of Whitbeck's notion of the "grim option?"

Scenario Four

Chloe Davis is a 35-year-old married woman. She and her husband have been trying to conceive for three years. Three months ago, Chloe finally did become pregnant, and she and her husband were both thrilled at the news. During a routine trip to the doctor's office, however, she learned that she has uterine cancer. Because they have caught it relatively early, the cancer is operable and surgery would save her life, but it would mean losing the fetus. Her doctor tells her that waiting until after she delivers the child would greatly increase her chances of dying of this disease. If they operate now, they can save her, but the longer she waits, the greater the chances are of the cancer spreading. Chloe does not believe in abortion for religious reasons and wants to go ahead and have the baby. Her husband has also been against abortion for religious reasons, but now, fearing for her life, is pushing her to have an abortion. The doctors appear to agree with her husband.

(1) Should Chloe carry the baby to term or should she follow the advice of her husband and the doctors? (2) Can she get around her religious constraints with the help of the principle of double effect? (3) As this would be a fairly early abortion, can Chloe and her husband find ethical support in Sumner's "third way?" (4) How does Chloe's situation differ from the above cases? (5) What would Marquis say if Chloe ends up sacrificing her own future for her baby's?

Scenario Five

Kimberley Wood is seven months' pregnant. As a teenager, Kimberley had unprotected sex with a number of different partners and ended up contracting genital herpes. She has been managing the infection for the past five years, but is currently suffering from an outbreak. Kimberley has been meeting with her family doctor and other medical specialists monthly. Her doctor insists on her having a Caesarean section, as delivering the baby vaginally could pass on the infection to the child. Kimberley, however, is determined to deliver the baby naturally, as she does not want an abdominal scar. The stretch marks, she claims, will be bad enough to deal with; she does not want a scar on top of that. She is willing to take the risk of passing on herpes to her baby. The infection is not that bad, she asserts, and the baby probably won't catch it. Her doctor has told her he is consulting the hospital ethics committee with a view to obtaining a court order for a compulsory Caesarean birth.

(1) Is the risk to the baby great enough to warrant a compulsory Caesarean section? What would Steinbock say? (2) If the doctor obtains a court order and Kimberley still refuses, should she be physically constrained? (3) How are autonomy and beneficence in conflict in this case? (4) How would a Kantian look at this situation? Would a utilitarian be able to justify a forced Caesarean for Kimberley?

Scenario Six

You are a female lawyer who has made her reputation as a defender of the rights of women. You are consulted by a rich young professional basketball player, who wants you to take a woman with whom he had a one-night stand to court to avoid paying child support. "You've taken dead-beat dads to court and won big," he says. "You've defended the right of women to go topless in public since men have this right, and you've negotiated large divorce settlements for your female clients. You have a history of taking on controversial cases, taking the side of the underdog. I need you to take on my case now."

The young man explains that this woman went out of her way to meet him after his multi-million dollar contract was signed and publicized. They spent the night together and she is now in the early stages of pregnancy. "We've discussed it, and she refuses to have an abortion," he says. You're initially shocked at the thought that he would pressure her into such a thing. "She is now insisting that I pay child support commensurate with my salary," he continues. "She says that I don't need to have anything else to do with the child." The real issue now becomes clear. Your potential client explains that he believes that this woman got pregnant deliberately and that she sees this pregnancy as a meal ticket for life. "Why should it be only the woman who decides whether or not to continue with an unexpected or unwanted pregnancy?" he asks. "Yes, it's her body, but the man is expected to pay child support if the woman decides to go through the pregnancy even against his wishes. Is this not a double standard? If she won't have an abortion, could you defend me in my refusal to pay child support?"

You tell the young man that you will have to consider this case before accepting or refusing, at which point he makes one last request of you. If this petition is turned down, he wants to hire you to sue for sole custody of the child. "This woman is a partier and an athlete groupie," he says. "She has not been able to hold down a regular job or maintain a long-term romantic relationship. She is in no condition to be a good parent to this child."

Your feminist commitments encourage you to refuse his request, but the information he has given you about the woman makes you inclined to believe that she did, indeed, get pregnant deliberately and did so because she knew how wealthy he was.

(1) What issues are raised by this situation? (2) Are the young basketball player's arguments about fathers' right convincing? (3) Does he have a right to sole custody of the child? (4) Should you take the case?

GLOSSARY

Abortion: the intentional expulsion of the contents of the uterus by medical, pharmaceutical, or surgical methods, in order to terminate a pregnancy at any stage. A *spontaneous* abortion, also known as a *miscarriage*, is the natural spontaneous end to a pregnancy before viability of the fetus (after which time it is usually referred to as a *preterm delivery* or a *stillbirth*). When an abortion is required to save the life of the pregnant woman, it is often referred to as *therapeutic* abortion.

Blastocyst/zygote: a fusion cell produced by the union between an egg and sperm (or gametes) is known as a *zygote*. The zygote contains the genetic material from both parents. This cell divides and after five days it is known as a *blastocyst*, the inner cell mass of which forms the embryo, while the outer cell mass becomes part of the placenta. This pre-embryonic period is a biologically unstable stage where individuation has not yet taken place (for example, identical twins can spontaneously form during this phase). The blastocyst begins to attach itself to the uterine wall.

Embryo: the point where the conceptus becomes a single multi-cellular individual in the period between two and eight weeks' gestation. Cells begin dividing into specialized cells (for example, eyes and hair begin to form) and brain waves can be detected between six and eight weeks. The heart begins to beat and blood begins to flow.

Fetus: the conceptus at eight weeks of development. This term is used up to the moment of birth of the baby, when the infant is referred to as a *neonate*. The transition between embryo and fetus is marked by the beginnings of bodily movement that can be observed by ultrasound during the sixth and seventh weeks of pregnancy.

Viability: stage at which the fetus can survive outside the womb of the pregnant woman in an extra-uterine environment. The threshold of viability is usually determined by weight, and it is rare for any fetus of less than 500 grams to survive. Due to neonatal technologies the viability threshold has moved downward in recent years, but has rarely gone below 22 weeks' gestation. Many babies under 26 weeks do not survive and many others survive with serious and lifelong handicaps.

FOR FURTHER READING

Callahan, Sidney. "A Case for Pro-Life Feminism." *Commonweal*, 25 (April 1986): 232–238.

In response to pro-choice advocates such as Sherwin, Callahan offers a pro-life feminist analysis of the abortion question, providing substantive arguments against a number of claims of the pro-choice feminists. It is her conviction that women will never achieve equality in society through permissive abortion policies, which, in her view, are inconsistent with feminist demands for justice.

Hursthouse, Rosalind. "Virtue Theory and Abortion." *Philosophy and Public Affairs*, 20, no. 3 (1991): 223–246.

Hursthouse takes a unique approach to the abortion question. She avoids arguments about both the status of the fetus and women's rights, focusing instead on virtue ethics and on what a virtuous woman would do when faced with a decision regarding abortion. Some abortions may be frivolous or foolish while others may represent the right choice in the circumstances and within the context of a woman's whole life, but every discussion will contain "claims about what is worthwhile, serious and important, good and evil, in our lives" (245).

Sherwin, Susan. "Abortion through a Feminist Lens." *Dialogue*, 30, no. 3 (1991): 327–342.

Sherwin provides a pro-choice feminist analysis of the abortion question by situating it within the context of women's lives. A fetus is not an isolated being; it develops as a result of a specific pregnancy in the body and life of a specific woman and thus its moral status is not absolute. It is relational and dependent on the woman's right to choose whether or not she wants to remain pregnant.

Thomson, Judith Jarvis. "A Defense of Abortion." *Philosophy and Public Affairs*, 1, no. 1 (Autumn 1971): 47–66.

This is a very popular article in the philosophical literature on abortion, one that does not rely on arguments about whether or not the fetus is a person. The author uses interesting, if sometimes surprising, analogies in order to show that a right to life does not entail a right to be given the use of another person's body—even if one needs it for life itself.

Tisdale, Sallie. "We Do Abortions Here." *Harper's Magazine*, October 1987.

This is a very personal and gripping account by an abortion clinic worker who describes the day-to-day reality of doing abortions and the circumstances, emotions, pain, and conflict that surround both the women who seek abortions and the people who do them. In spite of what she sees and feels, Tisdale is pro-choice; while wishing that abortions were not necessary, she recognizes that, in our flawed world, they are.

RECOMMENDED WEBSITES

Abortion Rights Coalition of Canada (ARCC)

www.arcc-cdac.ca/home.html

ARCC is a nationwide pro-choice political action group promoting reproductive rights for women in Canada. This website offers links to other pro-choice organizations and provides information on abortion access across the country.

Campaign Life Coalition

www.campaignlifecoalition.com/

This national pro-life political action group promotes sanctity of life from conception to death. The group lobbies against abortion, but also against euthanasia, assisted suicide, eugenics and reproductive technologies, and other "threats to the family." The site explores these issues and encourages visitors to personal activism.

Canadian Institute for Health Information, Therapeutic Abortions Data

www.cihi.ca/

The website of the Canadian Institute for Health Information (CIHI) offers timely and comprehensive therapeutic abortion data and has done so since 1995. There is some debate about the accuracy of its data due to a lack of uniformity on how abortion statistics are gathered and reported by different provinces.

NOTES

1. Gregory Pence, *Classic Cases in Medical Ethics*, 3rd ed. (Boston and Toronto: McGraw-Hill, 2000), 169.
2. Paul Badham, "Christian Belief and the Ethics of In Vitro Fertilization," quoted in Pence, 170.
3. Quoted in John M. Riddle, *Eve's Herbs: A History of Contraception and Abortion in the West* (Cambridge, MA: Harvard University Press, 1997), 80. Riddle points out that there are nuances of interpretation between the Hebrew and Greek texts of the passage but states that the "implication to those who read the passage in Greek was that the formed fetus had a soul, and anyone causing the death of a fully formed fetus was guilty of killing something with a soul; therefore, the deed was a homicide."
4. According to Aristotle's theory of the soul, all living things have a vegetative soul, all animals a sensitive or animal soul, and only humans a rational soul. While the vegetative soul would be present from conception, the moment of movement or "quickening" was seen to be the moment where the rational soul emerged and the fetus was considered a human being (for reasons that are not explained, this "delayed animation," as it is referred to, was more delayed in female than in male fetuses). The 40 and 90 days used for establishing the point of quickening do not fit with our calendar of pregnancy where quickening takes place around the beginning of the fourth month. But we must remember that in his time there was no way of accurately determining the start of a pregnancy and, as Riddle points out, the first two months were not what we would call a pregnancy.
5. Quoted in Riddle, 84, citing Augustine's *Questiones Exodi*, 80, 1439–1445.
6. Riddle, 92.
7. Riddle, 28. Riddle's book examines in detail the many different herbs that were used as abortifacients, knowledge of which was part of what were known as "women's secrets" passed on through generations of midwives and other wise women. According to the author, "people in the Middle Ages knew a lot about birth control. In some ways, they knew more than we do today about natural products as antifertility drugs." Riddle, 34.
8. Beverly Wildung Harrison, "Abortion: Protestant Perspectives," in Stephen G. Post (ed.), *Encyclopedia of Bioethics*, rev. ed. (New York: MacMillan Reference Books), 36.
9. Harrison, 36.
10. David M. Feldman, "Abortion: Jewish Perspectives," in Post, 29.
11. Osman Bakar, "Abortion: Islamic Perspectives," in Post, 39.
12. Pence, 172.

13. Riddle, 224.

14. Pence, 172.

15. Canadian statistics are hard to come by since death by illegal abortion was under-reported. It has been estimated, however, by historians Angus McLaren and Arlene Tigar McLaren, that 4000–6000 Canadian women died from illegal abortions between 1926 and 1947. See *No Choice: Canadian Women Tell Their Stories of Illegal Abortion* (Toronto: Childbirth by Choice Trust, 1998).

16. According to the Thalidomide Victims Association of Canada, there were between 10,000 and 20,000 disabled babies born as a result of thalidomide during the short time it was on the market. There are about 5000 survivors around the world today. The drug, especially if taken during the first trimester, affected whatever part of the fetus was developing at the time of ingestion. Thalidomide Victims Association of Canada (2007), found at www.thalidomide.ca/en/information/whatisthalidomide.html (April 4, 2009).

17. Daniel C. Callahan, "The Abortion Debate: Is Progress Possible?" in Daniel Callahan and Sidney Callahan, *Abortion: Understanding Differences* (New York: Plenum, 1984), 311.

18. Quoted in Leslie Cannold, *The Abortion Myth* (Hanover, NH: University Press of New England, 2000), 49.

19. *R. v. Morgentaler*, [1988] 1 S.C.R., 59.

20. *R. v. Morgentaler*, 66.

21. Kristen Luker, "Abortion and the Meaning of Life," in Callahan and Callahan, 26.

22. Daniel Callahan and Sidney Callahan, "Breaking Through the Stereotypes," in Louis P. Pojman and Francis J. Beckwith, *The Abortion Controversy: 25 Years After* Roe v. Wade (Belmont, CA: Wadsworth Publishing, 1998), 9.

23. Caroline Whitbeck, "Taking Women Seriously as People: The Moral Implications for Abortion," in Pojman and Beckwith, 435.

24. Canadian Institute for Health Information, "Number of Induced Abortions Reported in Canada in 2012," found at www.cihi.ca/CIHI-ext-portal/pdf/internet/TA_11_ALLDATATABLES20140221_en (December 10, 2014).

25. Monica J. Casper, *The Making of the Unborn Patient: A Social Anatomy of Fetal Surgery* (New Brunswick, NJ, and London: Rutgers University Press, 1998), 16, 21.

26. Mary Anne Warren, "On the Moral and Legal Status of Abortion," in Ronald Munson, *Intervention and Reflection: Basic Issues in Medical Ethics*, 8th ed. (Belmont, CA: Thomson Wadsworth, 2007), 590.

27. Warren, 592.

28. Boonin points out that "the claim that the fetus is a person simply *means* that the fetus has a right to life" and thus basing the right to life on arguments about personhood is superfluous. However, much of the literature on abortion is framed in terms of the personhood question and we consider this aspect of the question relevant. See David Boonin, *A Defense of Abortion* (Cambridge: Cambridge University Press, 2003), 14ff.

29. The question of fetal pain has become a focal point in the abortion debate. In 2005, a study done at the University of California—San Francisco concluded that for the fetus "functional pain perception … does not exist before 29 or 30 weeks." Critics maintained the researchers were politically motivated. "Fetus' Early Ability to Feel Pain Disputed," *The Globe and Mail*, August 26, 2005. In April of 2010, the State of Nebraska passed legislation to restrict abortions after 20 weeks based on assumptions about fetal pain at that stage. Since that time a number of states have followed Nebraska on this issue. See John A. Robertson, "Fetal Pain Laws: Scientific and

Constitutional Controversy," found at blogs.law.harvard.edu/billofhealth/2013/06/26/fetal-pain-laws-scientific-and-constitutional-controversy/ (December 10, 2014).

30. Boonin, 34. This argument also explains why many pro-life activists find themselves promoting the pro-life view at the other end of life, in cases relating to euthanasia and assisted suicide (for example, in the case of the Supreme Court decision on Sue Rodriguez described in Chapter 8).

31. The acorn argument was made by Judith Jarvis Thomson in 1971, and although there have been arguments against it, Boonin shows that the acorn argument survives the objections. Boonin, 40–41.

32. Daniel Callahan, "Abortion Decisions: Personal Morality," in Thomas A. Mappes and David Degrazia (eds.), *Biomedical Ethics*, 5th ed. (Boston and Toronto: McGraw-Hill, 2000), 477.

33. Daniel Callahan, "Abortion Decisions," 477.

34. Naomi Wolf, "A Call for Truth," in Lawrence M. Hinman, *Contemporary Moral Issues* (Upper Saddle River, NJ: Prentice Hall, 2000), 32.

35. Wolf, 34.

36. Boonin, 4.

37. Clifford Brobstein, "Human Development from Fertilization to Birth," in Post, 851.

38. Sidney Callahan, "A Case for Pro-life Feminism," in Munson, 607.

39. Sidney Callahan, 609.

40. *Tremblay v. Daigle*, [1989] 2, S.C.R., 530, III (3).

41. A recent American case shows how complicated a situation can become when fathers begin to declare their rights—even before the birth of a baby. A California woman (Sara McKenna) moved to New York to go to college after her brief relationship with a well-known skier (Bode Miller) broke up. She was seven months' pregnant and Miller accused her (and a New York court agreed with him) of absconding with the fetus. This allowed a California court to grant custody to Mr. Miller, who had in the meantime married someone else. The New York decision was overturned by a higher court, which recognized the infringement of the lower court's decision on the autonomy of a pregnant woman, but the custody battle over the child continued long after his birth. See Nathanial Vinton, "Bode Miller's Custody Battle with Sara McKenna over Baby Son Still on as Former Couple Can't Reach Agreement," *NY Daily News*, March 31, 2014, found at www.nydailynews.com/sports/i-team/bode-battle-custody-son-continues-article-1.1741071 (December 11, 2014).

42. Anthony Weston, *An Ethical Toolbox* (New York: Oxford University Press, 2001), 282–286.

43. Canadian Institute for Health Information, "Number and Percentage Distribution of Induced Abortions Reported by Canadian Hospitals (Excluding Quebec) in 2012, by Number of Previous Induced Abortions," Table 6, found at www.cihi.ca/cihi-ext-portal/pdf/internet/ta_11_alldatatables20140221_en (March 29, 2014).

44. Margaret Somerville, *The Ethical Canary* (Toronto: Penguin Books, 2000), 33.

45. Weston, 283.

46. Weston, 286.

47. Canadian Institute for Health Information, "Number of Induced Abortions Reported in Canada in 2012, by Province/Territory of Hospital or Clinic," Table 1, found at www.cihi.ca/cihi-ext-portal/pdf/internet/ta_11_alldatatables20140221_en (March 29, 2014). Some read this decline as evidence of decreasing access to abortion. Others believe CIHI's statistics are incomplete and underestimate the actual situation. Once again the political situation colours the debate.

48. The interest of the community would not be considered relevant by many; however, it could be considered very relevant in cases of selective abortion, in particular, sex selection. The systematic

abortion of female fetuses has caused serious demographic imbalances in some countries and is also of concern in Canada in relation to certain cultural communities that favour male children over female. Selective abortion is discussed in Chapter 6.

49. Rosalind Hursthouse, "Virtue Theory and Abortion," in Howard J. Curzer (ed.), *Ethical Theory and Moral Problems* (Belmont, CA: Wadsworth Publishing, 1999), 473–481.

50. Hursthouse, 474.

51. Hursthouse, 474.

52. Hursthouse, 479.

53. Hursthouse, 479.

54. Hilde Lindemann, *An Invitation to Feminist Ethics* (New York: McGraw-Hill, 2006), 121.

55. Lindemann, 121.

56. Susan Sherwin, "Abortion Through a Feminist Lens," in Ronald Munson, *Intervention and Reflection: Basis Issues in Medical Ethics*, 7th ed. (Belmont, CA: Wadsworth-Thomson Learning, 2004), 613.

57. Lindemann, 23.

58. Technologies such as ultrasound play a role in this situation, since prospective parents are able to *see* their *baby* at a very early gestational age, making them very aware of the growing life within and of their responsibility to give it care and affection.

59. Nina Martin, "A Terrifying Precedent: Woman to Be Tried for Murder for Giving Birth to Stillborn," *Salon*, March 22, 2014, found at www.salon.com/2014/03/22/a_terrifying_precedent_woman_to_be_tried_for_murder_for_giving_birth_to_stillborn/ (March 31, 2014).

60. Martin, n.p.

61. Government of Canada, *Proceed With Care: Final Report of the Royal Commission on New Reproductive Technologies*, Vol. 2 (1993), 959.

62. See Bonnie Steinbock, *Life Before Birth: The Moral and Legal Status of Embryos and Fetuses* (New York: Oxford University Press, 1992), Ch. 4. Steinbock discusses a case of fetal surgery where before performing this successful operation, the doctor had had six failures! At the time of writing her 1998 book, Casper stated that the technology saves very few fetuses and that "fetal mortality rates are as high as 80 percent for certain operations." Casper, 6.

63. Nancy Milliken, "Maternal-Fetal Relationship: Medical Aspects," in Post, 1407.

64. Casper, 5.

65. Casper, 12.

66. Quoted in Sarah Franklin, "Life," in Post, 1348.

67. *Dobson (Litigation Guardian of) v. Dobson*, [1999] 2SCR 753, CanLII 698 (SCC).

68. *R. v. Prince*, [1986] 2 S.C.R. 480, 1986 CanLII 40 (SCC).

69. *Keeler v. Superior Court*, 2 Cal. 3d 619.

Chapter 8

Death and Dying

LANDMARK CASE: HASSAN RASOULI

In October 2012, Hassan Rasouli underwent minor surgery at the Sunnybrook Health Sciences Centre in Toronto for the removal of a benign tumour. Several days after the operation he developed bacterial meningitis, an infection that led to severe and diffuse brain damage. From that time on, Rasouli was kept alive by mechanical ventilation, connected to a tube surgically inserted into his trachea, and by artificial nutrition and hydration delivered through a tube inserted into his stomach. The physicians responsible for Rasouli's care were of the opinion that he was in a persistent vegetative state, that all appropriate treatment had been exhausted, and that there was no reasonable or realistic hope of recovery. They argued that any further treatment was both futile and harmful to the patient. Thus, they wished to remove him from life support and to provide palliative care until his time of death.

Rasouli's wife, Parichehr Salasel, a physician herself, refused to accept the prognosis that her husband's condition was permanent and irreversible. This disagreement led the hospital to arrange for another opinion from a neurologist, one who had not been involved in Mr. Rasouli's care. The neurologist agreed with the original diagnosis. However, after Mr. Rasouli apparently made a "thumbs up" gesture with his hands in response to questions translated into Farsi, his diagnosis was changed from persistent vegetative state to "minimally conscious state." This new diagnosis revived the family's hopes, but did not change the doctors' opinion that the patient's condition was permanent and irreversible and that life support should be withdrawn. Salasel applied to the Ontario Supreme Court to prevent the withdrawal of life support from her husband. The Court supported her position, and the doctors subsequently appealed to the Ontario Court of Appeal, which upheld the lower court decision. The doctors then appealed to the Supreme Court of Canada.

In October 2013, the Supreme Court heard the case of *Cuthbertson v. Rasouli*. Much of the debate focused on Ontario's Health Care Consent Act (HCCA), which, since 1996, provides a legal framework governing the consent to treatment of both competent and incompetent patients. It is carefully premised on the broad public policy rule that patient autonomy should be safeguarded as much as possible. This means that medical treatment should not be administered without consent. If a patient cannot consent, the HHCA transfers this right to a substitute decision-maker who must act according to the patient's previously declared wishes. Where such wishes have not been articulated, the substitute decision-maker must act in the patient's best interests.

When parties disagree about what constitutes a patient's best interests and thus on the appropri-

301

ate treatment to be administered, the HCCA mandates that the dispute be heard before the Consent and Capacity Board, a quasi-judicial body with specialized jurisdiction over such matters. It consists of three people—one doctor, one lawyer, and one layperson—who hear arguments from both sides and try to establish the patient's best interests. Particular attention is paid to religious beliefs where they are relevant. In this case, convinced that continuing life support was not in the patient's best interests, the doctors could have presented their case to the Consent and Capacity Board. However, they chose not to do this because they believed that the withdrawal of treatment is not itself a treatment, the mandate of the Consent and Capacity Board did not apply, and the decision to withdraw life support should be in their hands. In other words, they did not believe that Salasel's consent was required.

The primary issue at stake was the interpretation of the terms "treatment" and "health-related" purpose under the HCCA. Ultimately, if the withdrawal of life support failed to meet the requirements of a "treatment," then Salasel's consent would be irrelevant, and the doctors would have been granted unilateral discretion in deciding whether to remove Rasouli from ventilator support or not.

The Supreme Court majority ruled that the withdrawal of life support aims to prevent suffering and indignity at the end of life and that this is a "health-related" purpose. Further, it often consists of physical interference with the patient's body. The Court therefore concluded that by "removing medical services that are keeping a patient alive, withdrawal of life support impacts patient autonomy in the most fundamental way."[1] Since the withdrawal of life support is included under the definition of "treatment," the Court concluded that the mandate of the Consent and Capacity Board does apply in this case. The doctors must either respect the wishes of Mr. Rasouli's wife, or challenge her position before the Board. If the Board agrees with the doctors, then life support can be withdrawn even if the substitute decision-maker wishes otherwise. Until such a decision is made, doctors must continue life support for their patient.

Two judges dissented from the majority ruling, holding that "[t]he definition of 'treatment' does not include the withdrawal or the withholding of treatment" and that "the court, and not the Board, is the appropriate forum for resolving any disputes between the doctors and the incapable patient's substitute decision-maker."[2]

While this case originated in Ontario, the Supreme Court decision, by giving power of end-of-life decision making to a quasi-judicial body whose members lack adequate experience in medicine, could affect medical decisions beyond that province. Writing in the *Canadian Medical Association Journal*, Sibbald, Chidwick, and Hawryluck note that "[a]n interesting potential outcome is that if the Consent and Capacity Board determines that ongoing ventilation is in the best interests of the patient, then the Board will essentially have the power to mould a medical standard of care contrary to the professional opinion regarding benefit."[3]

Further, the decision avoids what some refer to as the elephant in the room—the conflict between individual autonomy and the just distribution of resources. According to Deans and Flood, "[L]urking in the background and assiduously avoided by all is the elephant of resource allocation. Hard math is not required to realize sustaining Mr. Rasouli's life is an expensive endeavour and resources assigned to his care could be diverted for useful purposes elsewhere."[4]

INTRODUCTION

Euthanasia and suicide have been around for a long time, with varying degrees of acceptance or condemnation, depending on philosophical, religious, and social norms. Although euthanasia was not uncommon in ancient Greece, Plato, who believed in the immortality of the soul, did not condone suicide, believing that a person's life belonged to the gods. The Stoics, however, who did not believe in life after death, accepted that taking one's own life when illness or disease made it unbearable could be a rational act. Christians have always condemned the taking of one's own life, as well as the taking of another's life, even as an act of mercy. In Asian religions, though, suicide is one of three forms of self-willed death, the other two being heroic and religious. The latter category includes "cases of terminal illness or debilitating old age" and is sanctioned by religion and considered to be a rational and public act.[5] Thus one can say that the moral question of voluntary death in the face of old age or disease is not a new one. It has been asked for centuries, and the answers to it are many and varied.

On the other hand, many of the ethical problems relating to death and dying are new. They are the result of new medical technologies, which, along with increased control over life and death, have brought new and more complex dimensions to old questions about euthanasia and suicide. We are now able to save lives in acute situations, extend lives in chronic situations, and even keep partially formed babies alive at only 23–24 weeks' gestation. And, as demonstrated in the Rasouli case outlined above, we are now able to keep comatose patients "alive" with ventilator support and artificial nutrition for years, if not decades. In other words, many people—at the beginning and at the end of life—who would have died a natural death in the past as a result of accident, disease, or premature birth, can now be saved or at the very least have their lives extended. The question becomes: should they all be saved? Or even, should they all be forced to live?

Technology is not an unmixed blessing. It provides us with control over situations that have not traditionally been under our control, and demands choices from us that were never asked, until now, of anyone. It asks us to decide who will live and who will die. It makes us question whether what is possible is always desirable. It raises fears among older people—and people with chronic but fatal illnesses such as ALS—that they will be kept alive against their will. Modern medicine has brought into the realm of human decision making what in former times remained solely in the realm of nature, of God, or of fate.

HISTORICAL AND PHILOSOPHICAL PERSPECTIVES

One of the universal and unavoidable facts about life is that it *ends*. Life comes to an end at some point for each and every one of us. In spite of this fact (or perhaps because of it), philosophers over the centuries have asked questions about the meaning of death: Why does death happen? Is death really final? Is death the worst thing? What meaning does the fact of death give, ultimately, to the fact of living? What is life for, if its only end is death?

In Plato's dialogue *Apology*, Socrates, who has been condemned to die, speaks about death in an ambivalent fashion. He explains that death is either like a night of dreamless sleep or it is a "journey to another place" (where he will meet gods and heroes), a happier place, whose occupants would not put someone to death for speaking up and questioning ideas and values. As he says at the end of the dialogue: "Now the hour to part has come. I go to die; you go to live. Which of us goes to the better lot is known to no one, except the god."[6] For Socrates, death is not the worst thing; certain conditions of living can be worse than dying. In his case, renouncing his beliefs and his right to speak them would be worse than the death to which he was condemned.

In another dialogue, *Phaedo*, Plato discusses the immortality of the soul, which, in his view, pre-exists the body and will survive the death of the body. In Plato's philosophy, this immortality is not a personal immortality as in the Christian sense; rather, the soul will be reincarnated in another body—even an animal body (depending on the life he has led, a man might return as a woman, or even as a donkey). Life, according to this scenario, is a transient place, a period between one death and another. For Plato, the ultimate purpose of wisdom is to prepare for death: the true philosopher does not fear—and even seeks—death.

For over two millennia after Plato, Western philosophers (influenced and dominated by Christian theology) followed the Platonic belief in immortality but not his belief in reincarnation. This view of death did not change much until the modern period, the beginnings of which were co-extensive with the scientific revolution, when at least some philosophers began to question the notion of life after death and to regard life in this world as more important than life in the next. The 18th-century philosopher David Hume was the one who most clearly attacked the notion of an immortal soul (since neither the soul as such, nor its immortality, can be known by experience). He was not an atheist but a skeptic on all matters connected with religion. His skepticism extended to questions of death, the answers to which, in his opinion, could not be known by our finite minds. However, Immanuel Kant (whose ethical theory we discussed in Chapter 1) believed very strongly in immortality. Kant believed that the whole purpose of the moral law is the attainment of perfection. However, it is impossible to attain perfection in this life, and thus it makes sense to believe that human beings will have the opportunity to continue perfecting themselves in an afterlife. While Kant's philosophy has exerted a strong influence on philosophers up to the present day, his idea of immortality has not. Contemporary philosophers have been more influenced by the work of Charles Darwin and the attendant realization that human life, as one form of life among others, cannot rationally claim uniqueness in this life nor immortality in an afterlife.

If philosophers have asked questions about death and its meaning, it has often been religion that has supplied answers (and, in the process, influenced the philosophers). In the West, the dominant view of death that influenced philosophy until the 20th century—and continues either consciously or unconsciously in the Western psyche—has been the Christian one, including a belief in an individual and immortal soul that will be rewarded or punished in an afterlife in heaven or hell and be reunited with its body at the end of time at the resurrection.[7]

Thus, in the Christian view, death is not the end, but a transformation: life is changed but not taken away. This transformation is personal and not (as in some Eastern traditions) the blending into a universal soul or consciousness. Nor is it a temporary state before another incarnation. The meaning of life (and thus of death) is not to be found in this world but in the next. Linked to the idea of salvation is the notion that suffering is not a bad thing—and it may even be a good thing if it leads to purification of the soul before, rather than after, death. Another important element in the Christian belief about death is its *anthropocentrism*: it is a human-centred view of life and death. The immortality of the soul applies only to humans, not to animals, since only humans have a soul. Further, it should be noted that the Christian emphasis on reward or punishment at the end of life fosters a fear of death in the believer. So while death is a personal transformation, it also holds its dangers. The fate of one's soul is determined at the moment of one's death, and that moment, in the life of a Christian, takes on enormous importance.

This traditional Christian view of death has undergone a radical transformation in our society over the last century for a number of reasons, including the diminishing influence of Christianity in the Western world, increasing secularization and pluralism, and increasing faith in science and technology. Advances in medical science have distanced us from the event of death, making it a rare occurrence in the life of most people. Aside from accidental death, most people die in old age, often in hospitals or institutions for the elderly, and are laid out, if at all, in a funeral home rather than in the family salon. For most people, "death used to be a common life event, and death rates among larger families until around the second half of the twentieth century meant bereavement was experienced much more frequently in Canada than it is today."[8] In the latter half of the 20th century, death became an increasingly rare event in the lives of individuals while becoming more and more hidden from public consciousness.

In addition, with its focus on technology, our medical system fosters a goal of conquering illness and, if not conquering, at least staving off death for as long as possible. Death is seen less as an inevitable fact of life and more as a failure of medical technology. The result of this is a society that, individually and collectively, is at war with death. Interestingly, while many people have lost the notion of spiritual immortality that gave meaning to human death and differentiated it from animal death, they have not replaced it with an acceptance of mortality. We have lost the supernatural dimension of death while refusing to fully embrace its natural dimension. Rather than see death as a normal biological condition, we have come to see death as "a correctable biological deficiency" with medicine confusing "its power to alter, control, or eliminate disease with its power to banish mortality."[9]

We have, as many thinkers have pointed out, lost the *moment of death*. As a result of medical technology, the stages of death have been prolonged, and this prolongation has become an end in itself. While we like to think that we have extended our lives, in reality we have often simply lengthened the process of death. What might have happened naturally is now postponed by technologies that keep the body functioning even when there is little or no hope of any reasonable recovery. The moment of death has been wrenched from nature and given to the medical team. Choices must be made about whether to let a patient continue to live or allow him to die; thus, the moment of death itself has become a moral issue. Should the ventilator be turned off? Is it obligatory to keep an unconscious person alive through artificial feeding? Must treatment be continued when it is not having any effect? When can a treatment be called *futile?* What does futile mean? Who decides? Do we kill a patient when we withdraw life-sustaining treatment? When is a person dead? Can a person take charge of the moment of his or her own death? Does a person have a right to die with dignity? And, if so, what does that mean? These are some of the questions raised by technology and its ever-increasing role in our arsenal against death.

TECHNOLOGY AND THE MEANING OF DEATH

A major factor in the moral equation of death and dying concerns our increasing inability to determine when death has actually occurred. We have lost the moment of death because "death (or dying) in our high-tech medical environment is less an event than a process that defies demarcation by a single point."[10] Rather than a single event, death has become a series of small events, each one amenable to further treatment and not one, in itself, being seen as the moment where treatment should be halted.

Until the last century disease was generally acute, not chronic. People who became ill with influenza, pneumonia, or typhoid fever, for example, either recovered fully or died relatively quickly. A heart attack or stroke was likely fatal. According to Callahan, "In the absence of effective medical treatment, it was left to the body to do its own unaided recovery. If it could do so, it did so rapidly. If it could not, death would come quickly."[11] The development of effective drugs, therapies, and technologies to cure or control many formerly fatal diseases and conditions means that increasingly fewer people die when they become seriously ill. But often they do not fully recover, either. The result is that, while death comes much later in life, it comes often after long periods of chronic illness and degenerative disease. We may be living longer, but we are not necessarily living healthier lives. In some cases, the suffering at the end of life is caused by the technologies themselves. Some refer to these technological interventions as "half-way technologies." They both work and do not work at the same time, creating "a sort of medical purgatory of patients confined to wards that [seem] to be a form of long-term storage," leaving patients "alive but not really living."[12]

Generally, chronic diseases evolve slowly and treatment along the way is incremental. It keeps the patient going without improving his or her health. At what point can the doctor say that the patient is dying? At what point is the cessation of treatment both a practical and a morally correct option? An 80-year-old woman on dialysis is never going to be healthy again. Without dialysis she will die quickly. But, given the life-preserving technology, can we say she is dying? At what point should the dialysis be stopped? The same questions can be asked in relation to patients (conscious or not) on ventilators, Alzheimer's patients who contract pneumonia, elderly patients who need an organ transplant. At what point should treatment be refused or withdrawn?

Thus is the line between life and death vanishing, and the prolongation of life slipping into the prolongation of death. As a result, death can no longer be seen as something that *happens* to one, but is seen now as something that is *allowed to happen*—or not. The doctor, not nature, is in charge. It is no longer a matter of destiny but of decision. Because of sophisticated medical technologies, people dying in hospitals can be kept alive indefinitely. According to Warnock and Macdonald, "For such people, death is not a matter of 'nature taking its course,' but a matter of deliberate decision, not their own."[13] The moral question then becomes: whose decision? This is the question driving much of the debate around issues such as euthanasia and assisted suicide. People have always feared death; now they fear being kept alive against their will. When death was in the hands of destiny, people had no choice. But now that death is more often than not a question of human decision, there is a choice. And, when it comes to their own death, more and more people want to make that choice themselves. If there is a human will controlling the technology, why should it not be the will of the dying person?

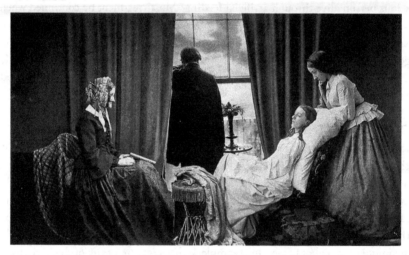

This 19th-century photograph shows a young girl at home on her deathbed surrounded by her family, a rare occurrence today.

When Is a Person Dead? Definitions of Death

Nothing is more indicative of the impact of technology on the blurring line between life and death than the shifting definition of death. Traditionally death was determined by the heart and lung function, that is to say, a person was dead when he stopped breathing and his heart stopped beating. This is generally now referred to as the **cardiopulmonary definition of death**. This method of determining death served us well enough until the late 1960s when two developments rendered it problematic: the invention of the mechanical respirator and the developing practice of organ transplantation.

The availability of the respirator or ventilator[14] made it possible to keep people alive indefinitely through artificially supporting heart and lung function. It was thus considered necessary to determine when it was morally and legally justified to discontinue life support. Because of the growing need for organs for transplant, something that necessitated both dead bodies and live organs, it became important to determine when it was legally acceptable for doctors to remove organs from dying patients without the risk of being accused of murder. These two factors are not unlinked: solving the first problem was perceived as facilitating a solution to the second. If transplant surgery were to progress, then a regular supply of organs would be necessary. But waiting until after cardiopulmonary death to harvest organs results in their deterioration. As Lock notes, "Almost overnight, the organs of the irreversibly comatose had become targets for procurement."[15]

As a result of this situation, the Ad Hoc Committee of the Harvard Medical School was created in 1968 to examine the existing definition of death.[16] The Committee gave two reasons for the need for the revised definition: first, the burden on hospitals (and on patients and their families) created by keeping comatose patients indefinitely on ventilators, and second, the fact that "obsolete criteria for the definition of death can lead to controversy in obtaining organs for transplantation."[17]

The result of the Harvard Committee's work was the establishment of what is called the "whole brain" formulation to determine when death has occurred. This formulation means that a person can be declared dead when the functions of the entire brain have ceased: "An individual who has sustained either (1) irreversible cessation of circulatory and respiratory functions, or (2) irreversible cessation of all functions of the entire brain, including the brain stem, is dead."[18] As a result, the traditional heart and lung determination of death came to be seen as secondary "because the irreversible cessation of [heart and lung] functions shows that the brain has ceased functioning. Other signs customarily employed by physicians in diagnosing death, such as unresponsiveness and absence of papillary light response, are also indicative of loss of the functions of the whole brain."[19] What began as an alternative definition of death has, over the years, become the definition of death. The **whole-brain definition of death** was adopted by the World Medical Association in August of 1968 and by the Canadian Medical Association in November of the same year. The guidelines have been amended over the years,[20] but the basic definition entailing the irreversible cessation of all functions of the entire brain has remained stable among Western countries.[21]

Some ethicists, however, questioned the whole-brain-death definition because they considered it unnecessary for the entire brain to be dead in order to consider the patient dead. According to Veatch, for example, "[O]ne is dead when there is irreversible loss of all 'higher' brain functions."[22] For such thinkers, it would have been better to define death as the irreversible loss of all cognitive brain function, rather than as the irreversible loss of all brain function. In the case of the whole-brain formulation, the brain stem has ceased functioning and heart and lung functions are sustained by a ventilator; in the case of the higher-brain formulation, the brain stem is still functioning, and breathing and heartbeat may continue without technological support. The higher-brain criterion assumes that consciousness is the most relevant factor in determining whether or not a person is alive.[23] Thus, if death had been defined using the higher-brain criterion, those who have permanently lost consciousness but are still breathing on their own would be deemed dead—and their organs would be available for transplantation.[24]

The Status of Brain-Dead Patients

The problematic link between the definition of death and the availability of organs for transplant will be dealt with further in Chapter 9. Here we are more interested in what the new definition of death means for the process of dying and the loss of the moment of death referred to earlier. What is the status of a brain-dead person? Is he or she alive or dead? The fact that the heart is still beating and the patient is still warm and breathing causes many to question whether or not the brain-dead person is really dead.

The following excerpt from a newspaper story underlines the ambiguity surrounding the state of brain-dead people who are considered legally dead: "A brain-dead woman who was kept alive for three months so she could deliver the child she was carrying was removed from life support yesterday and died, a day after giving birth."[25] On the one hand, if this woman's body was capable of nurturing a fetus for three months, can we say that she was "dead"? If she was already dead, how can it be said that she died the day after giving birth? What sense can we attribute to the verb "deliver" in this case? On the other hand, if her body had been needed not to nurture the fetus but to provide organs for others, could this have been done if she was considered to be alive? This is not a question of semantics: that the same body could be considered alive enough to continue a pregnancy and dead enough for its organs to be harvested forces us to face the ambiguity inherent in the revised definition of death.

Hans Jonas had concerns about this ambiguity when he pointed out, very soon after the Harvard Committee had done its work, that "the question is not: has the patient died? But: how should he—still a patient—be dealt with? Now *this* question must be settled, surely not by a definition of death, but by a definition of man and of what life is human. That is to say, the question cannot be answered by decreeing that death has already occurred and the body is therefore in the domain of things."[26]

BOX 8.1

MARTIN S. PERNICK, "EARLY UNCERTAINTIES OVER DEATH AND ORGAN PRESERVATION"

The definition and redefinition of death has been a concern for bioethics for several decades, but as the following excerpt demonstrates, this concern is not entirely new:

> That the pieces of vivisected organisms could be kept alive separately had been demonstrated repeatedly since William Harvey in 1627 maintained the body of a decapitated rooster by inflating the lungs with a bellows. In the 1910s ... perfusion techniques ... enabled Alexis Carrel to maintain isolated cultures of cells, tissues, organs (including the heart), and even preparations of entire organ systems. In the 1930s, Soviet and American scientists used these methods to preserve separate life in the heads and the bodies of decapitated dogs and apes, and in 1963 [two Cleveland researchers] successfully maintained the isolated brains of rhesus monkeys. These experiments also proved crucial to the development of organ transplantation....
>
> Similarly, research on resuscitation, which began with the development of artificial respiration in the mid-1700s, also produced major advances in the first half of [the 20th] century. Three generations of Russian and Soviet scientists from ... 1910 to the 1950s discovered that animals and people with no heart, lung, or brain activity could be revived after prolonged hypothermia, exsanguinations, drug overdose, or other cause of suspended animation....
>
> The mass media avidly reported most of these developments, and, like the scientists, they speculated on the conceptual as well as the diagnostic implications.... Media accounts often adopted the materialist equation of cardiac resuscitation with resurrection.... [M]agazine articles with headlines like "What is Death" reported that science had raised questions about the meaning of death and that physicians lacked both the diagnostic and the conceptual tools to answer them.

Source: Martin S. Pernick, "Brain Death in a Cultural Context," in Stuart J. Youngner, Robert M. Arnold, and Renie Schapiro (eds.), *The Definition of Death: Contemporary Controversies* (Baltimore, MD: The Johns Hopkins University Press, 1999), 5–7.

Once the body is determined to be in the domain of things, there is really no end to the possibility of its use as a means to the ends of others, whether that is for organs (as it has been for the past 40 years) or for experimentation (something that has been slower to develop but is on the horizon).[27] Jonas asks:

> Why turn the respirator off? Once we are assured that we are dealing with a cadaver, there are no logical reasons against (and strong pragmatic reasons for) going

on with the artificial "animation" and keeping the "deceased's" body on call, as a bank for life-fresh organs, possibly also as a plant for manufacturing hormones or other biochemical compounds in demand…. Tempting also is the idea of a self-replenishing blood bank. And that is not all. Let us not forget research. Why shouldn't the most wonderful surgical and grafting experiments be conducted on the complaisant subject-nonsubject, with no limits set to daring?[28]

Jonas wrote this in 1970, but his projections were prescient. In 2004 a number of bioethicists argued that we can, and should, conduct xenotransplantation trials (the transfer of living cells, tissues, and/or organs from non-human animal species into humans) on human subjects in a permanent vegetative state, stating that "[a]s the autonomic and vegetative functions of PVS [persistent-vegetative-state] bodies can often be maintained for years, their use would allow the opportunity to fully test the long term consequences of a solid organ xenotransplantation."[29] In the view of such researchers, it is not the *use* of the brain-dead bodies that raises the ethical questions; rather the *non-use* of this valuable resource would be seen "as the unwarranted loss of an opportunity to achieve good" since "it is illogical to regard or treat a brain-dead individual any differently from a 'conventional' cadaver, i.e. 'brain dead' equals 'dead.'"[30] It has even been suggested that brain-dead women could be used to gestate IVF-produced fetuses.[31] McCulloch puts the issue succinctly when he states that it is a question of "deciding when an individual need no longer be regarded as a live human being but can be considered as a resource that is available for the use of others." He refers to this point as the "reification" of the person and believes that "it is essential that the issue of reification of the individual, the grounds for undertaking it, and the subsequent uses to which the human object may be put require the fullest community consideration attainable."[32] Up to the present time, there has been little public discussion of either brain death or the uses to which brain-dead bodies are put (including procedures for organ transplantation).

Ironically, the goal of solving the problem of patients being kept alive indefinitely on ventilators has not really been solved, and the redefinition of death may have actually exacerbated the problem of withdrawing such treatment from the dying. Fost believes that "[o]vertreatment—the continuation of life-sustaining treatment of patients who have no reasonable prospects for meaningful survival and often no clear interest in or desire for such treatment—is far more widespread today than in 1968, when the redefinition was proposed as a solution to that problem."[33] While the bodies of these half-dead, half-alive people are routinely used as a source of organs and perceived, at least by some researchers, as potential research subjects that should not be allowed to go to waste, they are, at the same time, seen by others as alive, even if unconscious, and disconnecting them from a ventilator or feeding tube is more often than not perceived as killing them. Thus it can be said that there are two sides to the brain-death coin: an almost irreverent use of the not-quite-dead on the one hand, and an almost irrational respect for life, however vegetative it may be, on the other.

Letting Go: Landmark Cases

Two of the most famous cases regarding the ethics of dying, which occurred in the United States but have had implications beyond, are those of Karen Ann Quinlan and Nancy Cruzan. Karen Ann Quinlan went into a coma in April of 1975 at the age of 21. She never regained consciousness but was kept alive (first by a ventilator and, after that was finally unplugged, by a feeding tube) for over 11 years. After a bout with pneumonia and the refusal of antibiotic treatment by her parents, she was finally declared dead in June of 1986. For years she remained in a persistent vegetative state (PVS)—that is, her brain stem was still functioning, allowing respiration and heartbeat to continue. Initially, in order to have her detached from the respirator, her parents went as far as the Supreme Court of New Jersey, which decided on the basis of the right to privacy that the family could decide to let the patient die by disconnecting life support. The doctors, who had fought the parents every step of the way, waited over four months to disconnect—and then they weaned her off the apparatus over many weeks. As a result, she did not die but continued to breathe on her own. A feeding tube kept her alive for another 10 years. While her parents fought to disconnect the ventilator, they would not fight to disconnect the feeding tube, believing that artificial hydration and nutrition was a form of basic care, not a medical treatment. They did, however, refuse to consent to antibiotics to cure pneumonia and their daughter finally died. Or, more precisely, in the words of Pence, "Karen Quinlan's body was declared dead."[34]

Nancy Cruzan's case was slightly different, but no less precedent-setting. Cruzan went into a coma in January of 1983 after an automobile accident. She was revived at the scene but, because of brain damage, was in a persistent vegetative state. Unlike Quinlan, at the time of the court case, she was not on a ventilator but was being kept alive with a feeding tube. According to American law at the time, in order to withdraw the feeding tube, there had to be *clear and convincing evidence* of the patient's wishes to have it withdrawn. No such evidence was available. This case went to the U.S. Supreme Court, which decided that withdrawing a feeding tube was *not* different from withdrawing any other life-sustaining support. On the one hand, therefore, you could not have a law that allowed withdrawal of the ventilator but not a feeding tube. On the other hand, the court upheld the evidence requirement: since clear evidence of Nancy Cruzan's wishes was lacking, the judges ruled that the feeding tube could not be disconnected. Later, however, evidence did come forward through some friends that Cruzan had, in fact, stated while alive that she would never want to be kept alive by a feeding tube, and the feeding tube was finally (and legally) withdrawn. The Cruzan case, according to Pence, "was the first decision by the United States Supreme Court to explicitly recognize the rights of dying patients."[35] However, its decision did not apply to incompetent patients whose wishes were not known (and only applied to Cruzan once her earlier wishes became known).

In a Canadian case in 1992, the Quebec Superior Court ruled that the right to consent to treatment included the right *not* to consent as well as the right "to refuse treatment or to stop treatment when it has begun."[36] A patient, Nancy B., was suffering from Guillain-Barré syndrome, a neurological disease that had caused degeneration to the point where the only life left to her was life on a ventilator. The patient's mental faculties were intact, and in full recognition of the consequences, she requested that she be detached from the respirator so that the progression of her fatal disease could take its course. She went to court requesting an injunction requiring the hospital to remove life support since she was physically incapable of doing it herself. According to Baylis and colleagues, "The judge determined that Nancy B. was competent to make autonomous choices about treatment. She had withdrawn her consent to the use of the respirator and requested that it be removed and her decision was freely given and informed. Therefore Nancy B. was entitled to have her personal autonomy and her right to self-determination respected and the respirator removed as she requested."[37] The judge also ruled that whoever removed life support would not be sanctioned, since this was not a case of killing the patient but of letting nature take its course.

At the time of the Quinlan case, the position of the American Medical Association was that, while it was permissible to *not* connect a patient to a ventilator, it was not permissible to *disconnect* it once the patient was on it. This was changed in 1986 and now, in the U.S., "it is ethically possible for a physician, after consulting with the family, to withdraw a ventilator and feeding tubes from an irreversibly comatose patient."[38] This reflects the Cruzan decision that there is no difference between a ventilator and a feeding tube in the sense that both are seen as medical treatment. While this may be the legal interpretation, it is not always accepted as morally justifiable as was demonstrated in the public outcry over the case of Terry Schiavo in the U.S. in 2005.[39] This public refusal to recognize the futility of continuing to maintain a patient in a persistent vegetative state raises disturbing questions about the limits of technology. When one considers that the thousands of PVS patients in Canada will never regain consciousness and that they require 24-hour-a-day nursing care, it is not unreasonable to ask questions about the moral status of such "persons" and the point of keeping them alive through technology.

KILLING AND LETTING DIE

Callahan points out that "in the former world of nature, some acts and events were our responsibility, others not, and mostly not. In the new world of vanished nature, they are *all* our responsibility."[40] This is the result of the transformation of destiny into decision: in the new world of technology, it is humans who decide when death should take place. This human power is then interpreted as a human responsibility, such that we now see ourselves as morally responsible for the life or death of a person on life support. Thus, in the eyes of many (and in spite of legal decisions to the contrary), withdrawing life support is seen as killing the patient. If the natural progression toward death from disease has been stopped by technology, someone has to make the decision about when to stop the technology. It is this decision, and not the disease itself, that is now seen as the cause of death. And the medical practitioner, whose entire training is geared to the preservation of life, hesitates before the determining power of this life-and-death decision.

This dilemma is at the root of debates about the distinction between *killing* and *letting die*. This distinction has been useful in biomedical ethics because it forms the basis of the distinction between what is often called **passive euthanasia** (letting die) and **active euthanasia** (killing). Passive euthanasia is seen as a way of letting nature take its course through refusal or withdrawal of treatment. This has generally been accepted, both legally and morally, over the years, especially since the landmark cases mentioned above. Active euthanasia entails a direct action to kill the patient, for example, by lethal injection. This is not accepted legally in most jurisdictions and it is considered immoral by many, especially in religious communities. In the bioethical community, some ethicists think that the moral distinction between killing and letting die is artificial and should be done away with; others think it is fundamental and should be maintained.

James Rachels is one philosopher who challenges the distinction. From his point of view, the justification for both active and passive euthanasia is to end a patient's suffering by hastening death. Unfortunately, as he points out, withdrawing treatment and letting the disease take its course can result in prolonged suffering for a patient who is going to die anyway:

> If one simply withholds treatment, it may take the patient longer to die, and so he may suffer more than he would if more direct action were taken and a lethal injection given.... [O]nce the initial decision not to prolong his agony has been made, active euthanasia is actually preferable to passive euthanasia.... [T]he process of being "allowed to die" can be relatively slow and painful, whereas being given a lethal injection is relatively quick and painless.[41]

For Rachels, the intention is the same in both cases: to end the suffering of a person who is dying. While there is a difference in means, this is not where the moral issue lies; the moral issue lies in the intention: "If a doctor lets a patient die, for humane reasons, he is in the same moral position as if he had given the patient a lethal injection for humane reasons."[42]

BOX 8.2

JAMES RACHELS, "ACTIVE AND PASSIVE EUTHANASIA"

One reason why so many people think that there is an important moral difference between active and passive euthanasia is that they think killing someone is morally worse than letting someone die. But is it? Is killing, in itself, worse than letting die? To investigate this issue, two cases may be considered that are exactly alike except that one involves killing whereas the other involves letting someone die. Then, it can be asked whether this difference makes any difference to the moral assessments....

In the first [case], Smith stands to gain a large inheritance if anything should happen to his six-year-old cousin. One evening while the child is taking his bath, Smith sneaks into the bathroom and drowns the child, and then arranges things so that it will look like an accident.

In the second, Jones also stands to gain if anything should happen to his six-year-old cousin. Like Smith, Jones sneaks in planning to drown the child in his bath. However, just as he enters the bathroom Jones sees the child slip and hit his head, and fall face down in the water. Jones is delighted; he stands by, ready to push the child's head back under if it is necessary, but it is not necessary. With only a little thrashing about, the child drowns all by himself, "accidentally," as Jones watches and does nothing.

Now, Smith killed the child, whereas Jones "merely" let the child die. That is the only difference between them. Did either man behave better, from a moral point of view? If the difference between killing and letting die were in itself a morally important matter, one should say that Jones's behavior was less reprehensible than Smith's. But does one really want to say that?...

Now, it may be pointed out, quite properly, that the cases of euthanasia with which doctors are concerned are not like this at all. They do not involve personal gain or the destruction of normal, healthy children. Doctors are concerned only with cases in which the patient's life has become or will soon become a terrible burden. However, the point is the same in these cases: the bare difference between killing and letting die does not, in itself, make a moral difference. If a doctor lets a patient die, for humane reasons, he is in the same moral position as if he had given the patient a lethal injection for humane reasons. If his decision was wrong—if, for example, the patient's illness was in fact curable—the decision would be equally regrettable no matter which method was used to carry it out. And if the doctor's decision was the right one, the method used is not important.

Source: James Rachels, "Active and Passive Euthanasia," *New England Journal of Medicine*, 292, no. 2 (1975), 78–80.

Rachels also rejects the argument that the cessation or withholding of treatment is not an action whereas a lethal injection is. In other words, he does not consider withdrawal or withholding of treatment to be passive, and this, for him, is another reason for dispensing with the moral distinction between passive and active euthanasia. He points out that "one may let a patient die by way of not giving medication, just as one may insult someone by way of not shaking his hand. But for any purpose of moral assessment, it is a type of action nonetheless."[43] He also suggests that a doctor who deliberately withheld treatment from a patient with a treatable illness would be guilty of killing and could not justify it by claiming that he was only letting him die. In such a case, the so-called non-action would be just as serious as any action of killing and just as subject to charges of murder.

This last argument is interesting, but it ignores the fact that in most cases of terminal illness the treatment in question is futile and the patient is not going to get better no matter what treatment is given. So the comparison with a treatable illness is not relevant here. Further, Rachels does not appear to recognize that his argument for blurring the distinction between active and passive euthanasia can work both ways. While he uses it to justify active euthanasia on the basis that, in many circumstances, killing is no worse than letting die, opponents of any form of euthanasia can use this argument to reject even passive euthanasia on the basis that letting die is no better than killing.

Against Rachels, Daniel Callahan argues that the moral distinction between killing and letting die is fundamental and must be preserved, in spite of arguments that withdrawal of treatment may cause a more prolonged and painful death. Callahan believes that the arguments presented by ethicists such as Rachels are based on mistaken assumptions, which result when destiny gives way to decision and the power of technology is interpreted as a responsibility for life and death. Cessation of treatment is then seen as causing the death when, in fact, death is caused by the underlying disease. Callahan emphasizes that "the physician's omission can only bring about death on the condition that the patient's disease will kill him in the absence of treatment.... A lethal injection will kill both a healthy person and a sick person. A physician's omitted treatment will have no effect on a healthy person." With cessation of treatment at the end of life, the natural cause of death is the physical disease. But this has been overlaid, in Callahan's view, with medical ethics and concerns about culpability: "To confuse the judgments of this ethics with the physical causes of death ... is to confuse nature and human action."[44]

Everyone must die at some point and usually of one disease or another. It is not correct to say that a doctor kills a patient by allowing this to happen. These are cases where further treatment will bring no improvement and death will occur whatever the doctor does. In such situations, if a lethal injection is given, death comes about as a result of a human action that does involve issues of morality and culpability. If treatment is simply withdrawn, on the other hand, death comes about as a result of a natural physical reaction to disease, which is not in the realm of morality or culpability. It may very well be, as Rachels suggests, that many cases of letting die cause more suffering than actively bringing on the death, and one may want to argue that both should be permitted. But that does not mean that there is no difference between allowing nature to take its course and actually killing the patient.

Because this distinction is forgotten, physicians have a tendency to believe that they are morally and physically responsible for a patient's death, even if further treatment is futile. Thinking that he is responsible for the death anyway, it is easy to see how the physician can then believe that a quicker death would be a better death, both morally and physically. This is the moral leap that Rachels is ready to take and which Callahan refuses to take. Rachels believes that the mistake made by people like Callahan is in *denying* that the cessation of treatment is really the intentional termination of a life. Callahan would say that the mistake made by people like Rachels is in *accepting* that the cessation of treatment is the intentional termination of a life. For Callahan, the intention is to stop treating—in effect, to stop fighting death. The result is the termination of a life at the hand of disease. For him it is a matter of letting go and letting nature take its course. Some may find this to be no more than an argument about words, but both Callahan and Rachels would disagree. For Callahan, the semantic distinction is essential in order to clarify what is within our power and what is not, and to put an end to the idea that we can control death. For Rachels, the semantic distinction tries to hide the reality that with modern technology we do control at least the timing of death; thus the distinction is artificial and must be done away with in order to put an end to unnecessary suffering at the end of life.

The debate between Rachels and Callahan forces us to ask a few important questions: Once we have the technological means to stave off death, how do we decide when to stop using them (and who decides)? Is the decision to stop using them a *moral* decision, or is it not? If it is a moral decision, where does the dying, suffering patient fit in the moral equation? Is it immoral to want to end that suffering? When we use the power of technology to extend life beyond its so-called natural limits, can we then throw the responsibility for death back onto nature when we pull the plug? In other words, once we have the power of *decision* can we hand it back to *destiny*?

The Grim Reaper has always been seen as the personification of death and a symbol of its inevitability. The new immortalists would put an end to his hold on our collective imagination.

Futile Treatment

The discussion of killing and letting die, particularly those aspects that deal with withholding or cessation of treatment, presumes that there is some consensus on what treatments or interventions can be considered futile. If we are going to accept letting a person die by withdrawing or withholding treatment, we must have a justification, and the usual justification is that further intervention will do no good. This seems simple enough, but it is not. For some, any intervention that keeps the body—or even just an organ—functioning is useful treatment. Those with an extreme view of this position will hold that even continuing to treat PVS patients is not futile. All life is sacred to them, and as long as there is life, there is hope—and if not, there is value in the simple fact of life. Others think that what is futile or not can only be determined by the patient, according to his or her desires and goals. For these people it is a question of individual autonomy: people should not be forced to accept treatment that they do not believe is useful for them, but they should also be able to demand treatment that their physician might consider useless.

It is difficult to talk about medical futility without talking about the ends or goals of medicine.[45] We cannot know if a plan of care is futile unless we know what the medical care is *for*; just treating for the sake of treating is not a good enough reason. According to Saint-Arnaud, we need to spend more time thinking about the *why*, and not just the *how*, of treatment. We need to consider the global benefits to the patient and not just the local or particular benefit of, for example, keeping the heart beating.[46] A ventilator will keep the heart beating, but why do we want to keep the heart beating? Is there a good reason that will be of overall benefit to the patient? Is the prolonging of a strictly biological life a true medical objective?

When Saint-Arnaud talks about the global effects of an intervention she is referring to the effect on the patient as a person and not as a collection of organs. Will the treatment improve the health of the patient? Resuscitation can be a very effective temporary measure to keep someone alive and ultimately restore him or her to health. But if the person can never leave the intensive care unit and will never return to good health (or relatively good health), what is the point? People who argue from this point of view believe that the quality of a life is important in determining the value of treatment and that maintaining a strictly biological existence is not the goal of medicine. For other people, maintaining the biological life of a person is, in itself, an acceptable medical goal. They hold this because they believe that all life, even unconscious or unaware life, is sacred and must be preserved. They are reluctant to define any intervention as futile, believing that the notion of futility is vague and ambiguous and that one should always err on the side of life.

There are two different (and actually opposing) issues relating to medical futility. The first concerns the patient's right to refuse treatment or to insist on the cessation of treatment after it has begun. From this perspective, if a patient believes that treatment is futile, he or she can request that it be withdrawn and the doctor must comply. This is seen as an autonomy issue (under the principle of informed consent, any patient has a right to refuse treatment), and it is often driven by a fear of, or resistance to, the tendency to over-treat patients. Many people are afraid that their doctors will try to keep them alive long past the point where medical treatment is doing them any good. They want to be allowed to die in peace with as much dignity as possible. From this point of view, "the whole notion of futile medical treatment has become an unexpected part of the 'right to die' debate."[47]

The second issue relating to futility concerns the doctor's right to limit treatment that he or she considers unnecessary or useless. This issue results from patient and/or family pressures for treatment (to do absolutely everything possible for their loved one). Some people, often for religious reasons, will not agree to the cessation of any treatment, even if the doctors consider it futile. While this can be seen as an issue of patient autonomy, it is also a question of professional autonomy for the physician. Is a physician obliged to treat a patient even when he or she knows that this treatment is futile? It is also a question of the allocation of scarce resources and whether or not families can demand these resources beyond the point where they are doing any good. Some, invoking the principle of beneficence, argue that one should always err on the side of treating a patient, even if it means over-treatment. Others, invoking the principle of non-malfeasance, argue that interventions that do nothing but prolong death, often in painful or uncomfortable ways, are wrong and, not infrequently, cause harm—either to the dying individual or to others who need what might be the last bed in the ICU.

While the ground-breaking cases of Quinlan, Cruzan, and Nancy B. discussed above paved the way for withdrawal or refusal of life support in the face of resistance by medical doctors, the Rasouli case that opens this chapter outlines the opposite problem: the insistence on continuing life support when the medical doctors consider the patient's situation hopeless and any further treatment futile. At the time of the Supreme Court hearing in 2013, Rasouli had been in a persistent vegetative state for three years. From the point of view of the doctors, the situation was and remains hopeless. But the family does not share this view. For them, Rasouli is still conscious, even if his body cannot respond and he cannot breathe without a ventilator. Their point of view was reinforced when Rasouli was able to give a "thumbs up" in response to questions posed to him in Farsi by his wife. "He is still there," his daughter said. "He can feel us and we can feel him."[48] His diagnosis was upgraded to "minimally conscious," which indicates some level of response to stimuli and is a step above PVS (and one that has only recently been shown to exist).[49]

Dr. Adrian Owen of the University of Western Ontario has been working for a number of years on discovering a method of determining if patients diagnosed as PVS do, in fact, have some level of awareness. He has developed an MRI test that, when applied to certain patients, confirms that some people in this state are in fact able to respond. His test allows a patient to "think" a simple yes or no answer to questions posed by imagining either playing tennis (indicating a yes) or walking through his or her home (indicating a no). A different part of the brain lights up in an MRI scan depending on which scenario is imagined by the patient. Dr. Owen performed his tests on Rasouli in 2012 and reported that his brain responded to some tests and not to others. His report concluded that "the examinations are far from conclusive, but indicate limited brain activity, not a fully functioning mind locked in a frozen body."[50] Dr. Owen's work (and his opinion that up to 20 percent of so-called "vegetative" patients have some cognitive function) has potential ramifications for the question of consent. In one case he was able to get an answer from a minimally conscious patient (using his yes or no test) as to whether or not she was in pain (she was not).[51]

It is not inconceivable that his test could be used to ask the patient whether or not he or she wishes to continue on life support. His work also forces us to question the designation of PVS, especially as it relates to the definition of brain death (and the desire of some to adopt the higher-brain death definition). There is obviously a class of PVS patients who are minimally conscious, and thus assuming they are dead would really be in error. However, none of this resolves the question of futile treatment—the Rasouli case went ahead to the Supreme Court in spite of the change in the patient's diagnosis—nor does it resolve the question of who should decide whether or not to continue what doctors consider futile treatment, a question that the Supreme Court, in referring the issue back to the Consent and Capacity Board, did not accomplish.

One well-known American case deals with the question of who should decide. An 86-year-old woman named Helga Wanglie had been in a persistent vegetative state for over a year and was on a ventilator. Hospital staff wanted to withdraw life support because they believed this was inappropriate treatment for her. Her husband and children disagreed, believing "that life should be maintained as long as possible, no matter what the circumstances" and asserting that Mrs. Wanglie, although unable to speak for herself, shared their belief.[52] The court decided in favour of Mr. Wanglie, and Helga Wanglie was allowed to go on living on life support (although she died several days after the decision). What was important about this case, and disturbing to many, was that in awarding guardianship to Mr. Wanglie, the court "was also giving priority to a patient's right to decide over a physician's professional judgment about the treatment's futility."[53]

While many ethicists dispute the right of a patient (or surrogate) to insist on the continuation of life-sustaining treatment that is considered futile, others believe that this right must be respected if we want to preserve the principle of autonomy and informed consent, and the right to refuse treatment. According to Angell,

> Since the Quinlan case it has gradually been accepted that the particular decision is less important than a clear understanding of who should make it and the Wanglie case underscores this approach. When self-determination is impossible or an unambiguous proxy decision is unavailable, the consensus is that the family should make the decision. To be meaningful, this approach requires that we be willing to accept decisions with which we disagree.[54]

In speaking of medical futility, the language itself is problematic as some ethicists point out: to refer to a treatment as *futile* is meaningless since "one must always ask, 'Futile in relation to what?'" Further, it can be argued that "the decision that certain goals are not worth pursuing is best seen as involving a conflict of values rather than a question of futility."[55] At the same time, some do try to set some objective, quantitative, physiological criteria for futility. For example, one can argue that cardiopulmonary resuscitation is futile if it fails to restore cardiac function. In other words, if the treatment keeps the heart pumping, it is not futile. But that is precisely the type of criterion that Saint-Arnaud would argue against: it is not making the patient better; it is only keeping an organ functioning. It is local, not global, in its effect. It can be argued that any objective, physiological criterion is likely to be local since, by its very nature, the global effect of a treatment (regarding the person, not the organ) is going to be qualitative, not quantitative.

Much of the literature looks at the conflict of values between individual autonomy and the professional autonomy of the physician. But there is a looming conflict between individual autonomy and distributive justice in the face of scarcity of medical resources. Barry points out that Helga Wanglie left behind medical costs of US$75,000. Some defenders of Helga Wanglie's right to be maintained on life support argued that since her insurance was covering the cost, the issue of what resources she was using (or using up) was irrelevant. This is a dubious argument even in the U.S. where, although the costs may be covered by insurance companies, medical resources are not unlimited. But it is definitely not an irrelevant issue in Canada where medical resources are covered by public (taxpayer) funds and where the just distribution of scarce resources is a serious concern. It is less clear in Canada that we must be willing to accept decisions such as the Wanglies' (or the Rasoulis') with which we disagree.[56] Further, moral questions about what constitutes a life or a person are central to this debate. Is the preservation of mere biological life a morally justifiable goal in the face of scarce medical resources? Jecker reminds us that in the time of Hippocrates, doctors were warned "to refuse to treat those who are overmastered by their diseases, realizing that in such cases medicine is powerless," and she points out that in this tradition, "knowing the limits of medicine is related to the physician's appreciation of the art of medicine and the power of nature."[57]

The Feeding Tube

In the Cruzan case discussed above, the U.S. Supreme Court ruled that there was no difference between withdrawing life support in the form of a ventilator and withdrawing life support in the form of a feeding tube. Artificial hydration and nutrition via a feeding tube was considered to be a medical treatment that could be refused or withdrawn under the same conditions as any other life-sustaining treatment. When a person is dying, high-technology treatments such as ventilators are generally considered as extraordinary treatment and thus not obligatory. But many people do not regard feeding tubes as high-tech or extraordinary treatment. Feeding carries an emotional connotation, and even when it is carried out artificially by means of a surgically implanted tube, deprivation of hydration and nutrition is often perceived not as letting a person die, but as killing by starvation. Many people see the provision of food and water as basic patient care and will not allow, or approve of, its cessation, even in the case of comatose patients.

Following the analysis of Callahan above, withdrawal of life support in the form of a ventilator, for example, means that the patient will die of his illness. As Callahan very clearly points out, it is not the doctor, but the disease, that kills the patient. It is more difficult to hold to this point of view in the case of withdrawal of a feeding tube since, in many cases, it is the cessation of feeding that will cause the death of the patient and not the disease, at least not directly. One can argue that it is because of the disease that the patient is unable to eat or drink, and thus the disease is indirectly the cause of death, but many people are horrified by the thought of their loved one dying of starvation. This creates an ethical dilemma, especially in the case of PVS patients (such as Karen Quinlan, described above).

The greatest ethical dilemma surrounding the use or non-use of nutritional support for persons in a PVS arises from the fact that they are not clearly dying. With good nursing care and nutrition, individuals in this condition have survived for up to 35 years. Those who advocate continued nutritional support argue thus: this person is alive and not actively or imminently dying; it is possible to keep him or her alive with minimal effort; this human life is sacred; therefore we are obligated to continue to give artificially administered fluids and nutrition.[58] (It should be kept in mind here that, in relation to PVS patients, at least for those who are not in a "minimally conscious" state, we are referring to the same kind of patients that others—including doctors and researchers—consider already dead according to the **higher-brain-death** criterion, and a valuable resource for medical research and the extraction of organs.)

Callahan points out that the inability to take food and water by mouth is simply part of terminal illness, and it "should be understood as a symptom … one way the dying body shuts down its key systems."[59] Before the advent of the feeding tube, "the inability to take food and water itself helped to induce the final, usually gentle, coma. It led to a peaceful, not a violent death."[60] This natural process of the body shutting down has been circumvented by the invention of the techniques of artificial hydration and nutrition, and in a period of less than 20 years, "a whole new category of morally required treatment was created" and a "whole new moral rule" introduced.[61] This new moral rule is now accompanied by a moral judgment that refusal or withdrawal of artificial feeding is an act of starvation. Those who see withdrawal of artificial feeding as a form of starving a person to death may simply be unable to acknowledge that death is inevitable and that keeping someone alive artificially has its limits.

To a large degree, the debate over feeding tubes encapsulates the problem of technology and the meaning of death discussed above. Technology allows us to keep someone in PVS alive for 35 years, but why do we want to do this? Why did Karen Quinlan's parents insist on keeping her alive by artificial feeding for 10 years? Cases like this elucidate the problem of the vanishing line between life and death, and underline the need to examine our use of medical technologies not just from the point of view of means but, more importantly, from the point of view of ends. That we have a technology—even one as simple as a feeding tube—is not, in itself, a justification for always using it. That something is possible does not mean that it is necessary. When we ask why we are using a technology, the answer must be more than because we can.

Death as a Medical Failure: Seeking Immortality

Much of the discussion so far has dealt with extraordinary efforts to stave off death, to keep people alive as long as possible, even if the result is only to prolong the process of dying. When death does occur, it is often seen as a failure of medicine—as if the role of medicine were not to heal and make well, but to overcome death. Overcoming death is, in fact, the goal of a number of serious researchers working in several different fields. For example, the field of cryopreservation or cryonics represents modern-day hopes of resurrection through freezing the body in a bath of liquid at $-196°C$. The "Ultimate Case Study" that opened this book is fictional, but it is not totally science fiction. More than a hundred people so far have been "cryopreserved." They are legally dead (preservation has to take place *after* cardiac death but *before* brain death[62] so that some cellular brain function remains), but their "life" is being preserved "with the intent of restoring good health when technology becomes available to do so."[63] One should think of them more like frozen embryos than as dead persons; their bodies are suspended in liquid and can be thought of as being suspended in time. However, while frozen embryos can be unfrozen and are used in reproductive technologies today, the technology does not yet exist to unfreeze and reanimate a cryogenically preserved body. The hope of those who have been, or have signed up to be, cryogenically preserved is that future advances in medicine will allow them to be brought back to life and cured of whatever disease has caused their "death."

Others are working to extend life and promote immortality through diet, herbal and vitamin supplements, or by stopping the aging process through genetic research (for example, finding the gene that causes aging and "turning it off")—in short, stopping or turning back the biological clock to prevent both aging and death. Also of note are those working for immortality by disposing of the biological body altogether. Ray Kurzweil, one of the best known of this group, hopes to preserve our personhood in another, more efficient (and deathless) body. He believes that nanotechnology will allow us to overcome the limitations of the biological body. "Ultimately," Kurzweil states, "we will need to port our mental processes to a more suitable computational substrate. Then our minds won't have to be so small, being constrained as they are today to a mere hundred trillion neural connections each operating at a ponderous 200 digitally controlled analog calculations per second."[64] For Kurzweil and others, overcoming death means overcoming not just aging and illness, but the body itself.[65] These thinkers are rightly referred to as *post-humanists*.

A detailed discussion of these efforts to achieve immortality is beyond the scope of this book. They may seem to be more science fiction than science, but even if these visions are based on serious science (as their proponents believe), the questions they raise are more metaphysical than ethical.[66] However, as our discussion at the beginning of this chapter shows, the meaning of death *is* a metaphysical question, one that philosophers and theologians have tried to answer for centuries. For the immortalists, though, there is no meaning in death—only life has meaning, and death must be overcome. And the question arises: will this eventually become the goal of medicine?

EUTHANASIA AND ASSISTED SUICIDE

BOX 8.3

SUE RODRIGUEZ AND GLORIA TAYLOR

In 1991, Sue Rodriguez, a B.C. woman in her early forties, was diagnosed with amyotrophic lateral sclerosis (ALS, also known as Lou Gehrig's disease). This is a degenerative condition that Rodriguez knew would eventually leave her unable to walk, speak, feed herself, or even swallow. She knew she was going to die, possibly through suffocation, and she wanted to end her life at the moment of her choosing. Knowing that euthanasia and assisted suicide were illegal in Canada, she decided to challenge the Criminal Code provisions (section 241b) in the courts, hoping that with a favourable decision she would be allowed to carry out her intention legally. Her case went all the way to the Supreme Court of Canada where she argued that the right to life (section 7 of the Canadian Charter of Rights) includes the right to a dignified death; that it was cruel and unusual punishment for her to be unable to have someone assist her; and that this violated section 15 of the Charter because it discriminated against her based on her disability.

The Court ruled against her, stating that "[i]n order to effectively protect life and those who are vulnerable in society, a prohibition without exception on the giving of assistance to commit suicide is the best approach. Attempts to fine-tune this approach by creating exceptions have been unsatisfactory and have tended to support the theory of the 'slippery slope.' The formulation of safeguards to prevent excesses has been unsatisfactory and has failed to allay fears that a relaxation of the clear standard set by the law will undermine the protection of life and will lead to abuses of the exception."[1]

Nearly 20 years after *Rodriguez*, a similar case was brought to a British Columbia trial court, which again challenged the Criminal Code provisions against assisted suicide and euthanasia. Like Rodriguez, Gloria Taylor was suffering from ALS, and her case made arguments similar to Rodriguez, in particular that the provisions disproportionately affected physically disabled persons who have no means to end their lives without the assistance of others and thus perpetuate a disadvantage. This disadvantage, she held, violates section 15 of the Charter.

Trial Court Justice Lynn Smith found that a number of factors distinguished the case at hand from that of *Rodriguez*. Recent shifts in the Supreme Court's interpretation of the relevant sections of the Charter allowed more credibility to the plaintiff's arguments, and she was thus not bound by the previously affirmed constitutionality of the provisions. Further, the earlier decision did not address whether the provisions against assisted suicide violated the equality rights of physically disabled people. Relieved from being bound by *Rodriguez*, Justice Smith found the Criminal Code provision to be in violation of sections 7 and 15 of the Charter. She declared it invalid and suspended it for one year to give Parliament time to amend the legislation and render it consistent with the Charter. In the meantime, Taylor was granted a constitutional exemption to seek **physician-assisted suicide**.

The federal government appealed, and the B.C. Court of Appeal overturned the decision but not the exemption. However, Taylor did not need to exercise her right to an exemption; she died a quick death due to a severe infection resulting from a perforated colon.

The federal government, holding that *Rodriguez* remains the decisive judgment on the issue, appealed to the Supreme Court of Canada. In January 2014, the Supreme Court agreed to hear the appeal. Although Ms. Taylor was no longer living, the B.C. Civil Liberties Association vowed to continue the fight in the courts. In February 2015, the Supreme Court ruled that the laws prohibiting physician-assisted suicide were unconstitutional, and gave Parliament one year to ammend the law.

Note
1. *Rodriguez v. British Columbia* (Attorney General), [1993] 3 S.C.R. 519. See also *Carter v. Canada (Attorney General)*, 2012 BCSC 886 2015SCCS.

While there are individuals and families such as the Rasoulis and the Wanglies who have difficulty accepting that the end has come, or who wish, perhaps for religious reasons, to continue treatment even when it is considered futile, there are many others who fear over-treatment and, in particular, the possibility of a protracted and painful death. Many believe that when life has become a burden, when cure is hopeless and prolonged suffering the only option, they should be able to end their lives at the moment of their choosing through euthanasia or assisted suicide.

The word "euthanasia" comes from the Greek, meaning "a good death." Like Sue Rodriguez (see Box 8.3), more and more people believe that they have a right to a good death or, as it is more commonly referred to, death with dignity. Rodriguez knew that she was going to die and that death, when it came, would likely be a horrible one brought on by suffocation or choking. She wanted to control the moment of her death, remaining alive so long as she could tolerate the discomfort and the pain associated with her disease while avoiding the devastating end that the natural progression of her disease had in store for her.

Traditionally euthanasia has been referred to in two ways: active euthanasia, or mercy killing, involving the active killing of the sick person usually by lethal injection, and passive euthanasia, brought about by the cessation of life-sustaining treatment. These terms represent the difference between "killing" and "letting die" discussed above. Generally, passive euthanasia is no longer considered euthanasia, since precedent-setting cases such as Quinlan, Cruzan, Nancy B., and others have established a legal right to withhold or withdraw treatment.[67] The traditional distinction is not accepted by everyone as morally relevant (as we have seen in the debate between Rachels and Callahan above). However, for the purposes of this chapter, when we refer to euthanasia, we are referring to active euthanasia.

Euthanasia is also referred to as being voluntary, non-voluntary, and involuntary. "Voluntary" usually means at the request of the dying patient; "non-voluntary" means at the request of a surrogate (usually a family member and usually based on the known wishes of the dying patient). However, sometimes "voluntary" is taken to include a request by a surrogate if there are clear advance directives. This can be problematic, however, if the request for euthanasia is required to be clear and persistent (as it is in jurisdictions that permit it under limited circumstances). It is unclear how a prior request by an incompetent or unconscious patient can be persistent. So there is a certain ambiguity in the use of these terms. "Involuntary" generally means without the consent, or even against the wishes, of the dying patient. It can also include proxy consent, especially if the proxy or surrogate is not aware of the patient's prior wishes. In the case of a clearly competent person, involuntary euthanasia would generally be considered murder. No one who is in favour of euthanasia is recommending involuntary euthanasia; however, those who are against euthanasia in principle see involuntary euthanasia as the inevitable result of any move to legitimate voluntary and non-voluntary euthanasia. For the purposes of this chapter, when referring to arguments for and against euthanasia and assisted suicide, we are generally referring to competent patients who are clearly requesting it.

The difference between euthanasia and assisted suicide is not always acknowledged but it is important. In the case of euthanasia, death is brought about by another person, usually a doctor. With assisted suicide, another person, who may or may not be a doctor, helps the patient set up the conditions for suicide, but the patient brings about the actual death by his or her own action. Sue Rodriguez was asking for help in committing suicide; she was not asking for euthanasia, as it is generally understood.[68] Assisted suicide may come about through a doctor prescribing a lethal dose of barbiturates to a patient, or by a doctor or another party setting up the means by which the person can commit suicide.[69] Since it is the patient himself or herself who performs the death action, assisted suicide is, by definition, voluntary. Suicide was illegal in Canada until 1972 when it was decriminalized. However, assisting in a suicide is still illegal and anyone who helps a dying person bring his or her life to a speedier end is liable to 14 years in prison.

The most common argument in favour of euthanasia and assisted suicide is based on autonomy or self-determination. As we have seen, autonomy is highly valued in our society and in the realm of bioethics:

> Self-determination is valuable because it permits people to form and live in accordance with their own conception of a good life, at least within the bounds of justice and consistent with others doing so as well. In exercising self-determination people take responsibility for their lives and for the kinds of persons they become. A central aspect of human dignity lies in people's capacity to direct their lives in this way.[70]

For proponents of euthanasia, the value of self-determination—and its connection with human dignity—extends to the manner of dying. As Sue Rodriguez and Gloria Taylor tried to convince the Supreme Court of Canada, the right to life includes the right to a dignified death. The principle of autonomy upholds the right of individuals to refuse treatment even if that refusal results in their death. Thus, it is accepted that when patients believe that further treatment will not improve their health and will even destroy their quality of life, they may refuse consent for the treatment. For proponents of euthanasia and assisted suicide, the same principle of autonomy can be extended to justify a request for death when life has become a burden and cure is impossible.

Callahan rejects this argument on the basis that self-determination in such cases involves another person: "Euthanasia is not a private matter of self-determination. It is an act that requires two people to make it possible, and a complicit society to make it acceptable." Further, he asks, "[H]ow are we to make the moral move from my right of self-determination to some doctor's right to kill me—from *my* right to *his* right?"[71] For Callahan, and for others, we cannot give away our right to life to another. We cannot consent to be killed by another any more than we can consent to sell ourselves into slavery. Further, Callahan believes that acceptance of euthanasia in law or morality would introduce a new kind of killing, which he calls "consenting adult killing," something that in his view would represent a turning point in Western thought and practice.

Another argument against euthanasia given by Callahan and others is that the intentional killing of a sick and/or dying person is incompatible with the goals of medicine, which are always directed to the preservation of life. If a doctor consents to a person's wish to die, he or she is accepting that the life of the patient is no longer worth living, a judgment that, in Callahan's view, no doctor has the right to make. Needless to say, proponents of euthanasia disagree with Callahan on this point, holding not only that euthanasia is consistent with the doctor's role as healer, caregiver, and preserver of life, but that only physicians should perform euthanasia and assisted suicide in order to provide social approval of the process.

BOX 8.4

MARY WARNOCK AND ELISABETH MACDONALD, "THE SLIPPERY SLOPE"

The sanctity of life argument purports to be absolute, depending for its force not on any consideration of consequences, but on the intrinsic wrongness of deliberately depriving someone of life. We [have] argued that most people who claim to base their opposition on this argument, though they genuinely believe that human life is of the utmost value, nevertheless go on to reinforce it by pointing to the evil consequences to society that would follow from allowing any weakening of the taboo that forbids the deliberate taking of life. They move from the a priori to the empirical, almost without noticing that they are doing so....

This is the very heart of the slippery slope argument. If you once allow one exception to the law that forbids the deliberate ending of a human life, then inevitably further exceptions will be made, and the supreme value that we accord to human life, whether expressed in terms of its "sanctity" or otherwise, will, as a matter of fact, be eroded. Once that process has begun, there will be no stopping it: it will lead us into nameless horrors.

There is no doubt that this form of argument has an immense appeal to the imagination, and is deployed in many different contexts, wherever a change in a law is proposed, or an exception to a rule contemplated. The argument can be set out formally as follows: it may seem at first sight all right to do x (whatever x may be); but x will inevitably lead to y and y in turn to z; everyone agrees that z is intolerable, therefore, one must not do x. X, which at first appeared relatively harmless, even desirable, has now become wrong on account of the "inevitable" consequences that will flow from it.

The inevitability of the descent down the slope is not a matter of logical necessity. It is not that accepting euthanasia for competent patients who request it actually entails the acceptance of euthanasia for other patients.... To hold that a change in the law would "inevitably" lead to dire consequences ... is to make a prediction about the world of experience. It is based on our knowledge of human nature; on the way things tend to go....

It is sometimes argued that if a law contains terms that are impossible to define precisely, then inevitably that law will become more permissive than was at first proposed.... There is no discernible difference between someone who is likely to die in four weeks time and someone who will die in five. Nor is there a discernible difference between suffering that is very bad and suffering that is intolerable. So the permission for assistance cannot be properly restricted....

In some cases, it is possible to overcome this kind of uncertainty in a law by fixing an arbitrary but precisely calculable limit. A speed limit is of this kind. And ... in the British Human Fertilization and Embryology Act of 1990, a limit was set on the time an embryo might be kept alive in the laboratory.... The limit of fourteen days was in fact not completely arbitrary, in that it corresponded more or less with an important stage in the maturing of an embryo, just as a thirty mile speed limit is not completely arbitrary; it is calculated according to the safe stopping time of motor vehicles....

In those parts of the world where assisted dying has been made lawful, the first condition has been that a patient should formally ask for euthanasia or assisted suicide. However, the most powerfully emotive versions of the slippery slope argument have been those that foresee this condition somehow withering away with the passage of time, so that it will come about that the lives of those who have not asked to die will be deliberately ended. The deliberate ending of life would no longer be taboo, so anyone might be at risk....

Recent evidence has shown that in both Oregon and the Netherlands rates of assisted dying show no evidence of heightened risk for several vulnerable groups, notably the disabled, the elderly, and those with psychiatric illness. Thus, where assisted dying is already legal there is no current evidence for the claim that legalized physician-assisted dying or euthanasia will have a disproportionate impact on patients in vulnerable groups or put these groups at risk of undue pressure to agree to end their lives.

Source: Mary Warnock and Elisabeth Macdonald, "Slippery Slope," Ch. 7 in *Easeful Death: Is There a Case for Assisted Dying?* (Oxford, UK: Oxford University Press, 2008), 75–89.

The Slippery Slope Argument

Many thinkers who may be inclined to accept the morality of euthanasia or assisted suicide in the case of terminally ill patients in great pain are reluctant to approve legalization of the practice in principle because they fear the social consequences. These thinkers rely on what is called a "slippery slope argument" to justify their rejection of euthanasia as accepted social practice. A slippery slope argument generally asserts that even though a preliminary step may be a morally neutral or even good step, if it is accepted, a series of other steps will inevitably be taken and these will lead eventually to a final, morally repugnant result. Often such arguments are made without providing justification for how one step will inevitably lead to another.[72] In the case of euthanasia, for example, people often argue that accepting euthanasia for terminally ill patients in terrible pain who request it will require it to be extended to terminally ill patients who request it but who are not in terrible pain. This in turn will lead to extending it to patients who simply request it, even if their death is not imminent, and so on down the slippery slope until we arrive at a point of euthanizing those who do not request it.

Philosophers are wary of slippery slope arguments (usually classed among the logical fallacies) since those who use them leap from the first—usually acceptable—stage to the final and inevitable last—and very unacceptable—stage without giving clear and sound arguments about how one step would follow from another. Callahan, however, gives a compelling argument showing how, in his view, "the moral logic of the motives for euthanasia contain within them the ingredients of abuse."[73] He points out that, while the two motives for euthanasia—self-determination (autonomy) and easing suffering—are always coupled in the arguments (that is to say, the person must be competent *and* must be in extreme pain), there is no logical reason why these two cannot be uncoupled. For example, he asks why the person must be suffering. To insist on that is to already interfere with the person's autonomy. On the other hand, we can ask why the person must be competent if he or she is really suffering. Is it not unfair to make a dying person suffer simply because they cannot demonstrate that they are willing? In Callahan's words, "If we really believe in self-determination, then any competent person should have a right to be killed by a doctor for any reason that suits him. If we believe in the relief of suffering, then it seems cruel and capricious to deny it to the incompetent. There is, in short, no reasonable or logical stopping point once the turn has been made down the road to euthanasia, which could soon turn into a convenient and commodious expressway."[74]

Many who use the slippery slope argument go so far as to suggest that taking the first step will lead inevitably to forced, involuntary euthanasia. This seems extreme, and those who hold this view do not take the time to consider how safeguards could be put in place that would prevent the slide down the slope. What they see as inevitable, others would insist is easily preventable by clear and strict criteria. However, Callahan's words are worth considering in light of recent Belgian legislation, which will allow euthanasia for dying children who are in great pain if there is parental consent. This is the first time such a law has been passed anywhere in the world (in the Netherlands, for example, a child must be over the age of 12 and request euthanasia), and it does represent a de-linking of the criteria of competence and suffering that Callahan refers to (since children are, by definition, incompetent in relation to medical decisions). However, following the logical argument that Callahan foresees, it would seem quite unfair to allow euthanasia for a suffering adult and not for a suffering child. Thus the first step down the slope (or the expressway) is taken.

Even if adequate safeguards can be put in place to ensure that any request for euthanasia or assisted suicide comes voluntarily from a competent person, it is worth acknowledging the possibility of coercion that could be felt by the elderly and infirm if euthanasia were to become an acceptable practice. Choosing to end one's life could be perceived (by the patient, by the family, by society) not only as a possible option, but even as a preferable option. In such a world, people might feel pressure to justify their continued existence (and their continued suffering) to family and friends who may be thinking (or even asking), "Why are you still here?"

Thus many who use the slippery slope argument fear that the final result will be less a question of forced euthanasia than a matter of the old and dying feeling pressured into asking for euthanasia or assisted suicide in order not to be a burden to their family, friends, and the medical system. In other words, they fear that those who ask for an end to their lives might not be making a truly autonomous decision. Warnock believes that "it is insulting to those who ask to be allowed to die to assume that they are incapable of making a genuinely independent choice, free from influence."[75] She also asks why one should be shocked at what can be perceived as an altruistic act: "Part of what makes a patient's suffering intolerable may be the sense that he is ruining other people's lives" and asking for death for the sake of others can be looked at as worthy of praise.[76]

Women and Euthanasia

Warnock may be ignoring one aspect of the euthanasia debate that is not often addressed, that is, the apparently disproportionate number of women who are ready to take the altruistic route of asking for death at least partly in order to reduce the burden on their families. Keenan points out that those who defend euthanasia usually argue from the case of an old man whose terrible pain cannot be controlled, and who is asking for mercy from a doctor with whom he has a longstanding relationship. In reality, according to Keenan's analysis, the typical case would be an elderly woman facing a chronic illness who fears being dependent on, and a burden to, others; who is depressed; and who is not receiving proper medical attention, including pain management. He points out that the first eight persons that Dr. Kevorkian helped to die were women and that most of the women he aided had not been diagnosed as terminal.[77] Keenan sees this as a gender issue and believes "we are dealing here not with autonomy or rights but with a social failure. Social failure is evident when a woman, who has cared for her husband through his decline and death, elects [physician-assisted suicide] so as not to be a burden to her children and society."[78] Keenan's argument is supported by the fact that women generally live longer than men and that approximately 75 percent of people over 80 are women, many of whom are alone and poor. Keenan's analysis provides a very different perspective to the generally accepted defence of euthanasia based on autonomy and self-determination.

BOX 8.5

SUSAN M. WOLF, "A FEMINIST CRITIQUE OF PHYSICIAN-ASSISTED SUICIDE"

Advocacy of physician-assisted suicide and euthanasia has hinged to a great extent on rights claims.... The strategy is to extend the argument that self-determination entitles the patient to refuse unwanted life-sustaining treatment by maintaining that the same rationale supports patient entitlement to more active physician assistance in death....

Feminist critiques suggest three different sorts of problems with the rights equation offered to justify physician-assisted suicide and euthanasia. First, it ignores context, both the patient's present context and her history. The prior and surrounding failures in her intimate relationships, in her resources to cope with illness and pain, and even in the adequacy of care being offered by the very same physician fade into invisibility next to the bright light of a rights bearer and her demand. In fact, her choices may be severely constrained.

Second, in ignoring context and relationship, the rights equation extols the vision of a rights bearer as an isolated monad and denigrates actual dependencies. Thus it may be seen as improper to ask what family, social, economic, and medical supports she is or is not getting; this insults her individual self-governance. Nor may it be seen as proper to investigate alternatives to acceding to her request for death; this too dilutes self-rule. Yet feminists have reminded us of the actual embeddedness of persons and the descriptive falseness of a vision of each as an isolated individual.... We thereby avoid real scrutiny of the social arrangements, governmental failures, and health coverage exclusions that may underlie these requests. We also ignore the fact that these patients may be seeking improved circumstances more than death. We elect a myopia that makes the patient's request and death seem proper. We construct a story that clothes the patient's terrible despair in the glorious mantle of "rights."...

Finally, the rights argument in favor of physician-assisted suicide and euthanasia confuses two separate questions: what the patient may do, and what the physician may do. After all, the real question in these debates is not what patients may request or even do. It is not at all infrequent for patients to talk about suicide and request assurance that the physician will help or actively bring on death when the patient wants; that is an expected part of reaction to serious disease and discomfort. The real question is what the doctor may do in response to this predictable occurrence. That question is not answered by talk of what patients may ask; patients may and should be encouraged to reveal everything on their minds. Nor is it answered by the fact that decriminalization of suicide permits the patient to take her own life. The physician and the patient are separate moral agents....

Some will find it puzzling that elsewhere we seek to have women's voices heard and moral agency respected, yet here I am urging that physicians not accede to the request for assisted suicide and euthanasia.... I have elsewhere maintained that physicians must honor patients' requests to be free of unwanted life-sustaining treatment. In fact, attention to gender and feminist argument would urge some caution in both realms.... [A]nalysis ... suggests that gender bias may be operating in the realm of the termination of life-sustaining treatment too. Yet finally there is a difference between the two domains ... [and] there is a strong right to be free of unwanted bodily invasion. Indeed, for women, a long history of being harmed specially through unwanted bodily invasion such as rape presents particularly compelling reasons for honoring a woman's refusal of invasion and effort to maintain bodily intactness. When it comes to the question of whether women's suicides should be aided, however, or whether women should be actively killed, there is no right to command physician assistance, the dangers of permitting assistance are immense, and the history of women's subordination cuts the other way. Women have historically been seen as fit objects for bodily invasions, self-sacrifice, and death at the hands of others. The task before us is to challenge all three.

Source: Susan M. Wolf, "A Feminist Critique of Physician-assisted Suicide," in Susan Wolf (ed.), *Feminism and Bioethics* (Oxford, UK: Oxford University Press, 1996), 298–308.

Patient Refusal of Hydration and Nutrition

One option for dying patients who do not want to continue treatment and wish to end their lives sooner is to simply refuse all hydration and nutrition, whether in the form of food and water or in the form of a feeding tube. This is referred to as death by voluntary refusal of food and fluids (VRFF), or patient refusal of hydration and nutrition (PRHN), and it "represents a subject in palliative care that is remarkably understudied."[79] There is a tendency to think that dying from lack of food and water (in other words, from "starvation") is a very difficult and even cruel way to end one's life. However, as pointed out earlier in relation to the feeding tube, it is quite natural for a dying person to not want to eat or drink as the body systems are shutting down, and nurses who have been surveyed on their experience of patients refusing all nutrition and hydration have reported that "most deaths from VRFF were peaceful and involved little suffering."[80]

Some ethicists see this as an alternative to voluntary active euthanasia and physician-assisted suicide, and believe that patients should be told about this possibility and know that they can do it with medical help to ease any discomfort (what is referred to as "mouth care," for example, relieves feelings of hunger and thirst with only the smallest intake of food or fluid, or even ice chips). Thus, "chronically or terminally ill patients who wish to gain more control over their deaths can then refuse to eat and drink and refuse ... feedings or hydration. The failure of the present debate to include this alternative may be the result of confusion [over the distinction between killing and letting die], an erroneous assumption that thirst and hunger remain strong drives in terminal illness, and a misconception that failure to satisfy these drives causes intractable suffering."[81]

Any patient has the right to refuse any treatment as well as the right to refuse artificial feeding and even ordinary food and drink. Thus there is no ethical or legal problem regarding a person's voluntary refusal of food and fluids. It does not compromise the ethics of the physician, the health care worker, or family members, and it does not require a law permitting doctors to hasten the death of their patients through euthanasia and regulating how this would be done. It is both morally and legally permissible. It demands only that families or health care personnel aid in easing the discomfort and any suffering that the patient may undergo, something that is in line with their professional responsibilities. That this is a preferable course to euthanasia or assisted suicide is shown by the fact that one of the American studies on VRFF, which was conducted in the state of Oregon where physician-assisted suicide is legal, showed that "twice as many patients were reported to have chosen VRFF as those who pursued [physician-assisted suicide]."[82]

Advance Directives

It can be seen that the ethical issues around death and dying are complex and that there are many possibilities for conflict between dying patients and their families on the one hand, and the doctors, nurses, and others in the medical profession who are responsible for their care on the other. These situations are difficult enough when the dying patient is conscious and competent and knows what he or she wants, or does not want, in the form of treatment. They are made considerably worse when the patient is either not conscious or is not competent to make a decision regarding his or her care. In these cases, the responsibility for decision rests with a family member or friend who has been designated as a proxy or substitute decision-maker. Anyone acting in this capacity has a responsibility to act in a way that he or she believes the patient would want and to make the decision that most aptly fits with the patient's known wishes and values. Thus it becomes very important for everyone to think ahead and to make their wishes known to their family and close friends long before anyone is hit with the reality of having to make decisions on their behalf, whether in a moment of urgency caused by acute illness, or over a long period of chronic or terminal illness. This is not only a concern for people in the later stages of life, but rather for people of all ages: many of the classic cases (for example, Karen Ann Quinlan or Terri Schiavo) involved young people who were rendered comatose unexpectedly due to accident or other unforeseen incident, and who ended up being kept on life support for years because of uncertainty over what they would have wanted.

Whether it is a good thing or a bad thing (and there are ethicists on both sides of the debate) our medical system has evolved (with the help of the courts and, in Canada, the Charter of Rights) to a place where individual autonomy reigns supreme and where doctors and hospitals can be forced to give treatment they might not think is necessary, or sued if they make the wrong decision. If treatment decisions are left to families of an incompetent patient, conflicts can arise between family members who want absolutely everything done in the way of treatment for their loved one and those who want to let the patient die a peaceful and dignified death. If no one has been designated to speak for the patient, and no one is certain of his or her wishes, the only alternative may be to bring the case to the courts, a situation that is not ideal in what for the family may be a time of private agonizing and grief.

These situations can be avoided to a large extent through advance directives, in the form of a living will or a power of attorney for health care. In the former case, a person sets out specific instructions that he or she wishes to be followed in the case of treatment decisions; in the latter a person designates a substitute decision-maker to make treatment decisions based on his or her wishes (which should be conveyed to the substitute decision-maker ahead of time). While doctors are obliged to honour patients' advance directives when these are known, this is not always possible since the directives may be too narrow or too broad and vague to provide guidance in particular unforeseen circumstances.[83]

MEDICAL FUTILITY AND IMPAIRED NEWBORNS

The discussion of futile treatment above concerned medical futility at the end of life, but the question also pertains to certain cases at the beginning of life. Many babies come into the world with very severe handicaps or deformities such as Down's syndrome, spina bifida, hydrocephaly, anencephaly. Others, born so prematurely that even 20 years ago they would not have survived, are kept alive with aggressive technologies, and only some of them will survive (of those who do survive, many will suffer lifelong impairment). Serious moral questions are raised by such births: Should these babies be treated aggressively with all available technology so that as many as possible survive? If their chance of survival is not high, should they be allowed to die, or even be killed in a merciful manner? How does one know which babies might survive and which ones might not? Who should be making decisions about treatment: parents or doctors? Can attempting to save some of them actually end up harming them?

The moral problem is especially acute in cases where an impaired infant is in need of a normally simple operation in order to survive. A not uncommon example is a Down's syndrome baby who has an intestinal blockage that can be corrected by routine surgery. Without the surgery the baby will die; with the surgery the baby will live, but it will still be a baby with Down's syndrome. In some cases, parents will not consent to the surgery and the baby is allowed to die. Death in such cases is a lingering process with much suffering to the infant. Can one say that treating such an infant is futile? An otherwise healthy infant with an intestinal blockage would be restored to normal health with such an operation; the Down's syndrome baby will be restored to the normal health of a Down's syndrome baby. This is a case of using the distinction between killing and letting die in order to let nature make the decision that neither doctors nor parents could make at the moment of birth but one that, as Rachels points out, causes more, not less, suffering to the baby.

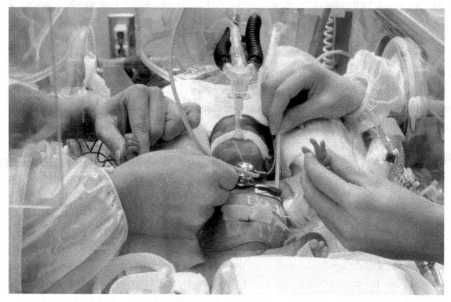

The treatment of very premature babies presents a moral dilemma. Should all be treated when only some will survive to live healthy lives? Should none be treated when some can be saved? Deciding which ones to treat and which ones to let die demands scientific knowledge, moral wisdom, and, ultimately, powers of prediction that go beyond human understanding. It also forces us to ask: who decides?

BOX 8.6

HOW THE NICU CAME TO BE

John D. Lantos reports that the incubator was invented in the 1880s in France, and was designed to keep premature babies warm in the same way that chicken eggs were kept warm before hatching: keeping preemies warm improved their survival rates. One philanthropic physician established Baby Infant Charities in Paris and other cities where visitors could come and pay to watch the preemies being cared for.

In 1896, premature babies in incubators were displayed at the Berlin World's Fair. "Many visitors to the fair were fascinated by the exhibit. While the preemie exhibit was popular, nobody knew quite what to make of it. It was seen more as a curiosity than as a medical breakthrough. For the next few decades nobody seemed to know how to incorporate the curious innovation into everyday life. No interpretive cultural framework helped make sense of the project of keeping premature babies alive. Caring for preemies didn't really seem like medical care.... Incubators for premature babies were thus a technical and scientific curiosity looking for a market. They did not create the sense of personal or societal moral obligation to care for each and every premature baby that would come later.... [N]obody seemed particularly concerned with the moral rights of babies, the moral obligations of their parents or society, or the moral complicity of the viewers in what now appears blatantly outrageous and offensive."

Gradually the new invention began to be used in hospitals, and in 1914 successful units for caring for premature babies were established in the region around Chicago, as techniques developed for feeding the babies, providing them with oxygen, and keeping them warm. This led to the concentration and specialization of perinatal centres serving a larger region. "The creation of a special unit led to the creation of specialized staff with a specialized ethos and mission. The gothic fairy tale of preemies as carnival exhibits became the parable of medical progress that NICUs represent."

Source: Adapted from John D. Lantos, M.D., *The Lazarus Case: Life-and-Death Issues in Neonatal Intensive Care* (Baltimore, MD: The Johns Hopkins University Press, 2001), 12–14.

A case of a different sort is that of Baby Messenger, born prematurely at 25 weeks with only a 25–50 percent chance of survival, and if he survived, a 20–40 percent chance of severe cerebral hemorrhage and neurological damage. His parents asked that no extraordinary measures be taken to keep him alive, but their instructions were ignored and the baby was resuscitated, intubated, and incubated. The baby's father removed the baby from all life support and held him in his arms until he died. He was then charged with manslaughter, but was acquitted.

The statistical nature of the prognosis for infants such as Baby Messenger is particularly problematic from a moral point of view. It means that Baby Messenger might have survived and lived a normal life, or he might have died, or he might have survived and led a life of very low quality due to cerebral and neurological damage. According to Lantos, "Most preemies live and do well. Some die. Worst of all, some end up somewhere in between."[84] Parents and physicians must make decisions about treatment in the face of such grave uncertainty. What are they to do? And how should they decide? Gross points out that a 35 percent risk of severe impairment (in the range of the statistics for Baby Messenger) "is simply one that no parent, physician or policy-maker is prepared to inflict on a newborn.... [However] while this seems a reasonable decision for parents to make, it also means, by extension, that large numbers of healthy infants are sacrificed to avoid fewer numbers of handicapped infants."[85] If all parents made the decision the Messengers made, 65 out of 100 healthy babies would die who could have been saved. At the same time, 35 families would be spared the pain and suffering associated with raising a severely impaired child. A utilitarian could accept this moral equation on the basis that the cost both to parents and to society of saving 35 children (as well as the emotional cost to the families and, likely, to the children themselves) outweighs the benefits of saving the other 65. But this is a quality of life calculation that a defender of the sanctity of life principle could not accept. From that point of view, it is imperative to attempt to save all 100 infants, no matter what the outcome. However, while many people object to considering monetary factors in these cases, Munson points out that the most premature infants may run up bills of more than US$500,000 and that "these infants are also the ones least likely to benefit from the care they are given."[86] Many babies die, and others live with terrible handicaps in spite of, or even because of, the treatment they are given.

Is it a moral imperative to save every infant, no matter how premature, no matter what the odds of healthy survival? Some neonatologists would say yes, insisting that every infant who shows the slightest signs of life must be resuscitated. Others think that the terrible results in some cases and prolonged deaths in others are not worth the price. One doctor, who worked for a time in a neonatal intensive care unit, refers to "the uncertain future faced by premature babies who are resuscitated and treated as part of what we call in medicine the 'learning curve,' babies on whose bodies medicine learns many of its hardest lessons." Another states: "I have been told how some families feel about their fate to provide lifelong care for a blind, deformed, or brain-damaged child kept alive by heroic medical interventions. Some families are ennobled, but too many are boiling with anger."[87]

The references to the "learning curve" and to "babies on whose bodies medicine learns many of its hardest lessons" bring out a seldom-discussed aspect of neonatal technologies: the experimental nature of these interventions. When efforts of heroic proportions are made to keep ever tinier and less developed babies alive (and to extend the threshold of viability ever downward), should we call this therapy or research? Are these struggling little creatures tiny patients or the littlest research subjects? Whose interests are being served along the medical learning curve: those of the babies, of their families, of future babies, of science? Of the doctor who manages to push the threshold of viability down one more notch? The conflict of interest that is present in much clinical research is very apparent here, and Munson points it out quite clearly:

> Does a Neonatal Intensive Care Unit (NICU) physician have an incentive, other than the best interest of a patient, to initiate or continue treatment of a low-birth-weight infant? One rarely mentioned reason for aggressive treatment is that neonatologists want to explore the limits of the modes of treatment and the technology currently used. By understanding the limits, it may be possible to take steps to extend them so that smaller and smaller premature infants can be kept alive. Hence, some neonatologists, motivated by an interest in research, may not give parents an adequate opportunity to take part in treatment decisions.[88]

The hard lessons learned, however, are not restricted to medicine or to the researchers. While the parents of successful cases may be thankful for the risks taken on behalf of their babies in the name of progress, those whose babies are permanently damaged as a result of the efforts to keep them alive bear an enormous burden. Their children have been sacrificed to benefit future children—but they are paying the price. This hard lesson is moral as well as medical and is one that needs to be examined carefully. Does the sanctity of life principle justify such suffering? Is there not a point at which sanctity of life must bow to quality of life and should not parents, who must live with the consequences, have the right to determine how much treatment their baby should have?[89]

Many would answer this last question in the affirmative. However, this does not end the debate, since it returns us to the dilemma of how to determine quality of life! If this question is difficult to address at the end of life, it is doubly difficult to determine at the beginning of life. We referred earlier to consideration of the global effects of treatment as benefiting a patient as a person and not as simply biological life. But what kind of person is a severely premature, severely impaired infant? How can we determine if that baby's life will be worth the effort of trying to save it? Does the neonate have interests? Do family quality of life considerations count? How can we determine with certainty the quality of a future life? And how can we judge its "value"?

Englehardt introduces the notion of the "injury of continued existence," a concept that raises the possibility "that giving life is not always necessarily a good and justifiable action ... one may have a duty *not* to give existence to another person."[90] While a proponent of the sanctity of life view will hold that life itself is a gift and giving it can never be wrong, a proponent of the quality of life view might argue that "certain qualities of life have a negative value, making life an injury, not a gift."[91] In fact, there have been lawsuits in the U.S. based on the notion of "wrongful life" where the plaintiffs have argued that they should never have been born and have held someone (a parent, an institution) responsible for the fact that they are alive. Such cases pose a serious challenge to the notion that any life is better than no life.

The question of whether or not to provide aggressive treatment for severely impaired infants takes us back to our earlier analysis regarding destiny and decision. In the past, these infants would not have survived. In cases of extreme prematurity, the hand of destiny (God or nature) would have decreed, through miscarriage or stillbirth, that the baby would not live. Now the hand of technology offers a choice and necessitates a decision. In the case of dying adults, whatever decision is made, the patient will eventually die of the disease that is killing him. The moral question involves a decision about whether to let nature take its course or to help nature along in the process of dying. With impaired and extremely premature infants, the issue is slightly different: some of these babies might survive and lead fairly normal lives, and some of them might survive and lead terrible lives. So the moral question involves a decision about which ones to treat and which ones to let die. Englehardt states: "The quandaries are in a sense an embarrassment of riches; now that one *can* treat such defective children, *must* one treat them? And, if one need not treat such defective children, may one expedite their death?"[92] Should non-voluntary active euthanasia be an option in some cases? Trying to answer that question brings us back to Rachels and Callahan, to the debate between killing and letting die, and to the dilemmas that confront us as a result of medical technology and the choices it imposes. Reflecting on his own experience in an NICU, Lantos states: "I truly did not know, and neither did [the parents], whether I was a savior or a torturer of babies, whether I offered hope or hubris, whether it was good to use my technology and skills or better to acquiesce gracefully."[93] For those who hold the life and death of these tiny babies in their hands, choice is a mixed blessing.

Egyptian 18th Dynasty mural depicting funeral ceremony, c.1390–1336 B.C.E. Every society has a ceremony to mark the death of one of its members. Rituals and ceremonies differ according to religious practices and beliefs about life after death. But whether death is celebrated or mourned, ritual is part of the process of dying, both for the dead and for the survivors.

ETHICAL THEORY AND DEATH AND DYING

It has already been pointed out in this chapter that the rapidity of technological change has outpaced our ability to think through its ramifications in ethical terms. The ethical theories that we examine in bioethics were developed over centuries and are based on ideas about how human beings living in society should treat each other. When Kant developed his principle of respect for persons, he did not have to think about the status of PVS or brain-dead "persons." And when Mill thought about the harm principle in relation to a person's right to make decisions about his or her own body, he did not have in mind the ethics of using a brain-dead body as a research subject. Even such apparently morally straight-forward duties as looking after one's elderly parents take on a new and perplexing perspective when the prolongation of the dying of the parents can have potentially ruinous effects on the lives of the children and grandchildren. Our ethical theories need to be stretched beyond their conceptual limits in dealing with some of the questions addressed in this chapter. But even if no one theory can give us an answer, each will give us some insight into sorting out our end-of-life dilemmas.

Kantian Ethics

Kantian ethics is, as we have seen, one of the sources of our modern principle of autonomy, so important to bioethics. It can be invoked, for example, in support of a person's right to make his or her own decisions about treatment, including end-of-life treatment. It would seem to support refusal of treatment even if that treatment is necessary to sustain life. Thus one can fairly safely assume that invoking the principle of autonomy to refuse treatment would find moral approval in Kant. However, this would not extend to euthanasia or assisted suicide, as Kantian ethics clearly opposes both killing and suicide. Kant was very clear about suicide, it being, in his view, a contradiction to use one's freedom to snuff out one's life (and freedom).

If one looks at the question of demanding end-of-life treatment that is considered futile, it is unlikely that we can look to Kant's concept of autonomy for support. We do, according to Kant, have duties to ourselves, which would include seeking medical treatment when necessary. But, for Kant, autonomy entails responsibility: we have a duty to do the right thing, and as discussed in Chapter 1, we know what is the right thing to do by applying the Categorical Imperative. Using up scarce medical resources in treatment that is considered futile cannot be universalized under the Categorical Imperative. We cannot treat ourselves as exceptions, and we must treat others as we ourselves would want to be treated. If, in order to slow down our dying, we are using resources that are needed for a person who could actually get well, we (or our surrogates) must be ready to put ourselves in the position of the other and consider if we would want to be treated that way, which is unlikely. Kant's idea of autonomy would, however, support the professional autonomy of a doctor who refuses to treat a patient whom he responsibly believes to be beyond hope. In such a case, giving in to the pressure of a patient or surrogate would diminish the doctor's autonomy.

It is difficult to call on Kant for an ethical answer to the problem of treatment of severely impaired newborns. Newborns, like fetuses, are not persons, and many of the severely impaired newborns will never be what we normally call persons. So it is unlikely that we would have to keep them alive based on Kant's principle of respect for persons. Further, as adults may justify refusal of treatment that is futile or burdensome, then, putting ourselves in place of an infant in this situation might justify withdrawal of treatment (although not direct killing). It would seem as well that parental rights and responsibilities would be supported by the principle of autonomy, and that a Kantian position would support parents as the ultimate decision-makers regarding the treatment of their infant.

Utilitarian Ethics

Utilitarian ethics, with its emphasis on consequences and overall good, can be invoked to restrain the overemphasis on autonomy in bioethical questions about death and dying. In assessing the ethics of a particular situation, the good and bad consequences on all concerned must be weighed. This would mean taking into consideration, along with the needs and wishes of the dying person, the needs of family members, professional health workers and health institutions, and society as a whole. In a country such as Canada with a public health system, the impacts on public medical resources must be taken into consideration. Rule utilitarianism comes into play here in the manner in which jurisdictions (federal, provincial, hospital) allocate resources and in the claim that citizens have upon those resources. Resources must be allocated in a way that maximizes the good and minimizes harm for the greatest number. From this point of view, over-treatment, as well as excessive demands on the system by, or on behalf of, a terminally ill person, could be problematic for a utilitarian.

One of the problems with utilitarianism comes to the fore here, however. In the hedonistic calculus, every person's pains and pleasures are weighed equally. This is a serious drawback, which ignores the responsibilities that families have to family members and that doctors have to their particular patients. Every doctor is going to fight for the ICU bed or the operating room slot in order to serve his or her patients, and we would all have less trust in our doctors if we did not believe they would do this for us. However, a utilitarian analysis can serve as a corrective to the extreme individualism that is more and more apparent in end-of-life treatment.

With respect to euthanasia and assisted suicide, a utilitarian would be more ready than a Kantian to accept both, depending on the consequences. However, although our emphasis on autonomy favours individual decision making and sees suicide, for example, as a self-regarding act, a utilitarian would look at the impacts of euthanasia and assisted suicide on others, including family members and society as a whole. If it could be shown that either or both would have serious long-term negative impacts on society (which is what some people do argue), one could use utilitarian arguments to discourage acceptance of these practices. On the other hand, especially in cases of extreme suffering of a dying patient and his family outweighing any benefits to society, a utilitarian would be inclined to accept voluntary euthanasia or assisted suicide as morally justifiable.

With respect to severely impaired newborns, a utilitarian would be more inclined to look at quality of life arguments rather than sanctity of life arguments in making treatment decisions and would not balk at including the costs and burdens of care of a severely handicapped child on both parents and society in the calculus of pains and pleasures. This could mean supporting a parental decision not to treat if the burden on the family is considered too great; it could also mean overriding parental autonomy and supporting a physician's recommendation to cease treatment if the consequences of continued treatment are considered dire.

Virtue Ethics

Several key and interconnected notions of virtue ethics are relevant to the ethics of end-of-life treatment: its emphasis on situating ethical decision making within a person's whole life; its focus on character; and its goal of leading a flourishing and happy life. From a virtue ethics point of view, death is part of life, and thus a good death should be an integral part of a good life. This, we have seen, was part of argument of both Rodriguez and Taylor regarding the legalization of physician-assisted suicide. Aristotle would likely have more sympathy with the Rodriguez and Taylor argument than the Supreme Court did, and certainly the Stoics would have permitted euthanasia for a dying person whose life has become a source of misery and pain.

From a virtue ethics point of view, our society's war with death would be considered wrong-headed: death is part of life and must be faced, showing the virtues of courage and moderation that are both essential to the good life. Moderation would also dictate against over-treatment, both from the point of view of a patient demanding it and from the point of view of a medical system imposing it, especially when futile treatment can be a source of harm to others through the overuse of scarce medical resources.

By its very nature, virtue ethics is a matter of individual character, not something that can be imposed by legislation or by an ethics committee. The virtuous patient would, however, be inclined to seek what is good for her within the context of her entire life and would rely less on her rights than on what is right for her own flourishing, even if that means dying sooner rather than later. Virtue ethics would be more comfortable in the hospice than the ICU once a patient has reached the point of diminishing medical returns.

CONCLUSION

With the issues raised in this chapter on death and dying, one can see that technological progress is a two-edged sword. It brings with it new possibilities of control over life and death, but also new ethical dilemmas that must be solved. These dilemmas force us to ask questions about the meaning of life, death, and humanity, and to ask whether what is possible is always desirable. They also force us to question an attitude that is prevalent in our society, that is, our refusal to face the reality of death. As a society we are at war with death, and while we must realize that we cannot overcome it, we want to stave it off as long as possible, even if that means prolonging the suffering of our loved ones. Medicine is there to help us get well; when it cannot do this, we must let go. This is not a failure of medicine but a reality of life.

The ethical theories bequeathed to us by the philosophers of the past are not always adequate in addressing the dilemmas of the present—dilemmas that those philosophers could never have imagined. At the same time, the wisdom of Socrates who recognized that death is not the worst thing can still serve us today as we are forced to confront the limits of human knowledge and action. Part of every good life is a good death. The role of medicine should be to aid the endeavour for a good death, not impede it.

PHILOSOPHICAL REFLECTION ON DEATH AND DYING

Any philosophical reflection on death, by its very nature, must be metaphysical. Metaphysics is that branch of philosophy that deals with questions that go beyond the physical world of experience. Since we do not have direct experience through our senses of such things as the soul, life after death, heaven, or hell, any philosophical discussion of such concepts or notions will have to rely on pure thought or religious belief. Philosophers say that such ideas are a priori, that is, not known by experience.

Most Western philosophical views about life after death, since the earliest available writings, have been of this sort. Plato's belief in reincarnation, for example, presupposes an otherworldly place (which he refers to as the world of Forms), a place where the soul can attain pure knowledge of Reality (the earthly realm giving us only appearances—which, for Plato, were not real). It also presupposes an immaterial soul that can be separated from its body and which resides in the other world between its lives (in different mortal bodies) in this one. In other words, our soul exists both before birth and after death. Embodiment, for Plato, is an imperfect state, constraining the soul from attaining true knowledge of the Forms. In some of his writings, he refers to the body as the prison of the soul. Death, then, is a release from this prison and as such is something to be welcomed. Life, in this view, is a preparation for death.

There is a tension in the Western philosophical tradition from its beginnings between seeing death as a continuation of life in some other form, and seeing death as the end of life. In the former, death is a transformation; in the latter, death is final. This tension reflects another tension in philosophy, equally old, between *a priori* reasoning, such as Plato's, and empirical reasoning, based on experience. Since no one has died and come back (in any objective or verifiable manner) to tell us about the other side of death, it is impossible to have an account of death and immortality based on human experience. Empiricists reject accounts such as Plato's out of hand; to them these scenarios represent myth or fiction, not knowledge.

To believe that the soul outlives (and/or pre-exists) the body requires an assumption that the mind and body are essentially different and separable. This was, in fact, what Plato thought; but his pupil, Aristotle, thought differently. For Aristotle, the soul is the form of the body; in the same way that there is no statue without form, there is no living body without soul. And as one cannot separate the form from the statue, one cannot separate the soul from the body, even at death. Thus, for Aristotle, human death was like the death of any other living thing, with body and soul perishing together.[94]

This dichotomy of views regarding body and soul, life and death, persists throughout the history of philosophy with the Platonic view reflected (with modifications) in the work of such later philosophers as Augustine, Descartes, and Kant, and the Aristotelian view of death reflected in the Stoics, Epicureans, Hobbes, Spinoza, and Hume, among others. Interestingly, the philosophical differences about death and immortality did not translate into differences about how to live a good life. In other words, from a philosophical point of view, virtue and happiness in life are not determined by our anticipation of happiness, or our fear of punishment, in an afterlife.

Philosophers whose view of death includes life after death in some other realm and in some other form are relying on *supernatural* explanations (which may or may not be religious in nature) of both life and death. Those who see death as final, on the other hand, are relying on *natural* explanations, and are often called *naturalists*. For them, living a good and virtuous life means living in accordance with nature. Nature, or the cosmos, is orderly and functions according to natural laws; humans must also conform to natural laws—if they are to be happy they must live in harmony with nature. For at least some of these thinkers, the cosmos is both good and ordered and thus there is no difference between the ethical world and the natural world. One must live a good life in order to be happy *in this world*.

Thus whether thinking of death as a transformation or as an end, most philosophers see it as a part of life, and whether or not we anticipate continued life beyond death, part of living a good life is preparing for a good death. This is most obvious in Aristotle's ethics (which we now label virtue ethics and which is covered in Chapter 1). Life is a progression toward completion, that is, becoming what we are meant to be. The good life, the happy life, the successful life (which for Aristotle are one and the same) comes about by practising the virtues. Life has its own end, even if that end is only death: to live is to live well *and* to die well. Thus, from both the supernatural and the naturalist point of view, a good life is a preparation for death, whether as completion or continuation.

CASES OF INTEREST

Munoz v. John Peter Smith Hospital

On November 26, 2013, Erick Munoz walked into his home in Texas to find his wife, Marlise Munoz, who was 14 weeks' pregnant, unconscious on their kitchen floor. Doctors at the John Peter Smith (JPS) Hospital soon determined that she was brain dead and thus both medically and legally dead under Texas law. As paramedics, both Erick and Marlise were familiar with end-of-life issues, and Marlise had repeatedly told her husband that she would never want to be kept alive by life support. Erick and Marlise's family sought to respect her wishes and to withdraw her support, but they were soon prevented by the JPS Hospital, who cited a provision from the Texas Advance Directives Act (1999) that held that a person may not withdraw or withhold life-sustaining treatment from a pregnant woman. Erick quickly launched a legal battle, arguing that the hospital was misreading the legislation. Justice Wallace sided with Erick, reasoning that Marlise was neither terminally nor irreversibly ill, but legally dead. She was removed from life support, thereby terminating the life of the fetus.[95]

This contrasts with a parallel Canadian case in which a 32-year-old B.C. woman, Robyn Benson, gave birth to a baby more than six weeks after she suffered a massive and inexplicable brain hemorrhage when she was 22 weeks' pregnant. On the morning of the hemorrhage, she woke with a fierce headache and asked her husband, Dylan Benson, to go out and buy painkillers. When he returned home, he found his wife unconscious in their bathroom. She was rushed to the hospital and declared brain dead the following day. Mr. Benson asked that her body be kept alive until the fetus was viable. In February 2014, at 28 weeks' gestation, a healthy baby, named Iver, was delivered by Caesarean section. Robyn was disconnected from life support the following day.[96]

Robert Latimer

On November 4, 1993, 40-year-old Saskatchewan farmer Robert Latimer was arrested for the first-degree murder of his 12-year-old daughter, Tracy. She was quadriplegic, weighed only 40 pounds, and functioned at the level of a 3-month-old. She was unable to walk, talk, or feed herself. She was also in a state of constant, agonizing pain. Prior to the events leading to Latimer's arrest, he was informed that Tracy would require further operations to correct a hip dislocation resulting from her advanced state of sclerosis, putting her in even more pain. Moreover, Tracy was administered nothing stronger than regular Tylenol due to the risk of a coma from the anti-convulsive medications she was taking to prevent her epileptic seizures.

Latimer decided to place his daughter in the cab of his Chevy pickup, run a hose from the exhaust to the cab, then climb into the box of his truck and watch his daughter die. A year after his arrest, he was convicted of second-degree murder, which bore a mandatory minimum sentence of life imprisonment with no eligibility for parole for 10–25 years under section 745 of the Criminal

Code. With the consultation of the jury, Justice Ted Noble granted Latimer a constitutional exemption from section 745 and sentenced him to one year in prison followed by one year of probation. He reasoned that Latimer committed a "rare act of homicide" for "caring and altruistic reasons."[97] Moreover, his relationship with his daughter was that of a loving and protective parent, and as such, the mandatory minimum sentence would constitute cruel and unusual punishment under section 12 of the Charter.

Justice Noble's decision was appealed and set aside nearly one year later. The Saskatchewan Court of Appeal handed Latimer a sentence of life imprisonment without the possibility of parole for 10 years. The court ruled that it was up to Parliament to decide whether mercy killing should bear special sentencing. The Supreme Court of Canada later upheld this decision in 2001.

Katie Lynn Baker

Katie Lynn Baker suffered from Rett syndrome, a rare neurological disorder that caused her to develop a severe eating disorder. She was 10 years old, weighed only 22 pounds, was severely disabled, and could not speak. She was virtually non-communicative to all except her closest caregivers. Katie Lynn had already received painful surgeries to help her condition and there was no doubt that there were more to come. Rather than allowing this to happen, Katie Lynn's mother, Cheryl, took her to a favourite spot, a peaceful home of family friends in Slocan Valley, British Columbia, where she died four days later.

An inquest was held in which the coroner summoned a jury to help determine the cause of Katie Lynn's death. The jury found that Katie Lynn had died due to severe malnutrition as a result of inadequate nutritional intake over a period of time, caused directly or indirectly by the actions of other persons. The death was classified as a homicide, but the presiding coroner made it clear that the jury's ruling precluded any assumption of guilt or culpability on anyone's behalf; that is, "homicide" was used as a neutral term. The jury reached this conclusion in spite of the evidence in the Coroner's Report that Cheryl had sought the child's best interests when she brought Katie Lynn to the home of family friends to prevent her from undergoing what she considered to be non-consensual treatment. She later reported to the media that her daughter had been through enough and that she had done what Katie Lynn wanted. On December 2, 1999, it was announced that charges would not be laid as the Crown concluded that there was no likelihood of conviction based on the current evidence.[98]

Maurice Genereux

Dr. Maurice Genereux dedicated much of his medical career to treating the gay and lesbian community in Toronto, particularly those suffering from HIV and AIDS. He was very familiar with their experience, suffering, and sometimes death. In June 1996, he was arrested for assisting in the suicide of two of his patients, Aaron McGinn and Mark Jewitt.

In 1988 Jewitt tested positive for HIV and was living with his partner, who was also one of Dr. Genereux's patients. In 1993 Jewitt found his partner's bottle of Seconal (a barbiturate), prescribed by Dr. Genereux, and was informed that it was a potential method for committing suicide. Shortly thereafter, his partner died of AIDS, and Jewitt was determined to commit suicide before he met the same fate. His condition started to deteriorate, and he mistakenly thought that the AIDS virus had started taking its course. He was also very depressed and struggling financially. In 1995 Jewitt asked Dr. Genereux for Seconal in order to help him sleep. Genereux, knowing that he was suicidal, prescribed Jewitt a lethal dose. Jewitt was found later that day unconscious, next to an empty bottle of Seconal. The friend who found him called 911, and Jewitt managed to survive.

Aaron McGinn tested positive for HIV in 1989. During a meeting in 1995 between McGinn, his best friend, and Dr. Genereux, McGinn asked for Secanol so that he could commit suicide and warned his friend not to interfere. McGinn was given the prescription, and nine months later he ingested the whole bottle, once again warning his friend not to interfere. When McGinn fell unconscious, his friend called Dr. Genereux and asked whether he should call 911. Dr. Genereux responded by saying that death is what McGinn wanted and that he should be left alone. Dr. Genereux later completed the death certificate showing the cause of death to be "AIDS pneumonia."

During his trial, Dr. Genereux pled guilty to two counts of aiding and abetting a patient to commit suicide, making him the first doctor to be convicted of assisted suicide in Canada. He was sentenced to two years' imprisonment less one day followed by three years' probation, and lost his licence to practise.[99]

CASE STUDIES

Scenario One

After a much-publicized case in which a woman asked for the legal right to doctor-assisted suicide, a ruling that went all the way to the Supreme Court, the government is considering legislation that would legalize certain forms of euthanasia in Canada. You have been asked to chair an advisory committee that is to consider the issue and make the proposal more concrete. The committee will be composed of both those who support legalizing certain forms of euthanasia and those who are against all forms of voluntary death. Positions range from maintaining the current criminalization of physician-assisted suicide and euthanasia, to the legalization of physician-assisted suicide only, to the legalization of active euthanasia. The dissenters fear that legalizing any form of euthanasia may open the door to permitting forced active euthanasia for some groups. Even if this is not openly acknowledged, they claim, permitting active euthanasia may put pressure on the seriously ill to request euthanasia to relieve the burden on their family and on society. Supporters of legalization, however, claim that these fears are unfounded and that we need to legalize some form of physician-assisted suicide or euthanasia to prevent the suffering of many terminally ill patients who will otherwise die a slow and painful death. You are expected to come to some sort of conclusion and draft a concrete proposal that takes the concerns of both sides into consideration.

(1) How would you set out, for the benefit of policy-makers, some of the practical concerns that result from consideration of the two sides on the question of legalizing euthanasia? (2) Under what conditions, if any, should physician-assisted suicide or euthanasia be morally permissible? (3) Who should decide and how? (4) What would Warnock say about the slippery slope argument of the dissenters? What would Wolf say? (5) Can both individual autonomy and the public good be accommodated in a legislated policy on euthanasia?

Scenario Two

John Roland sat in a quiet examination room, staring at his doctor's feet. "So I've only got six months to live."

"I'm afraid so." Dr. Cruzo handed John a bottle of pills. "These should help with the pain. You can take up to eight of these in a day. Two pills every four hours."

John took the bottle from Dr. Cruzo. "Can I have something stronger? Something that will kill me? If it comes to that."

Dr. Cruzo shook his head. "I'm afraid I can't do that, John."

"I'm not asking you to help me kill myself. I'm just asking you to prescribe something stronger; something that will help with the pain. I don't even know if I will want to kill myself, before Mother Nature does it for me, that is. I'd just like to keep the door open."

(1) Should Dr. Cruzo accede to John's request and prescribe something stronger? Would you answer differently if the patient's name were Joan rather than John? (2) How would this situation look from a virtue ethics standpoint? From a feminist ethics standpoint? (3) Would Dr. Cruzo be breaking the law if he were to prescribe "something stronger" to John?

Scenario Three

You are a doctor working in the emergency room, and you are currently treating a 23-year-old woman who was severely injured in a car crash and is five months' pregnant. A medical team has been working with her for the past few hours, but it has now declared her brain dead and beyond hope of recovery. You have already spoken with both the young woman's parents and her boyfriend. Her parents have requested that she be kept on life support until the baby can be delivered safely. Her boyfriend objects to this. He is concerned about the welfare of the child, as the fetus would have to be delivered prematurely, and there is no guarantee that the process of life support itself will not be harmful to the developing baby. He is afraid that he will not be able to raise a disabled child if the baby were born with severe impairments.

The young woman's parents, however, insist that they will raise the child if need be. They seem to believe that this young man was never really committed to their daughter and her baby, and that he had no intention of marrying her. However, since their daughter moved out of the house after graduating from high school nearly five years ago, she has been in contact with them erratically; they have not spoken to her in quite some time. Her boyfriend, having spent much more time with her in the past several years, thinks he knows what she would have wanted. The parents insist on going against his wishes, though, claiming that his lack of commitment and fear over the possibility of raising a disabled child are affecting his judgment.

(1) Should you keep this young woman on life support and attempt to deliver the baby, or discontinue life support and let her die, along with the fetus? (2) How would a virtue ethicist analyze this situation? What would a Kantian say? (3) What conflict is revealed when this case is viewed through a feminist lens? (4) Given that there is no designated surrogate decision-maker, whose opinion should you listen to?

Scenario Four

John Gress is an 85-year-old man. He is rushed to the emergency room after suffering a stroke. He is quickly moved to the intensive care unit, where he is placed on a mechanical ventilator. John's doctor has spoken with the family and has told them that John has little or no chance of recovery. Even if he does recover, it is likely that his health will continue to deteriorate and he will find himself back in the hospital, possibly within days. As it stands now, his prognosis is poor. Moreover, there are a number of other patients in need of a bed in the ICU. Many of these patients have much better chances of recovery than John.

The physicians and nurses all believe that John should be taken off the ventilator and allowed to die. John's family, however, disagrees with this decision. They demand that everything possible be done for him. They believe that by removing him from the ventilator, they would be killing him. This amounts to murder, they claim, the deliberate taking of an innocent human life, something that they are deeply opposed to for religious reasons.

(1) What should John's doctor do in this situation? Must he comply with the family's wishes or is it permissible to go against them and remove the ventilator? (2) How would Callahan and Rachels see this situation? Is the family correct to assume that withdrawing life support is murder? (3) How do we weigh the desires of an individual family against the needs of other patients in the hospital?

(4) Who should decide on the use of resources between specific patients? Who should be part of the discussion?

Scenario Five

Sandra Milton and Michael Chang are the parents of a newborn child. Their daughter, Megan, was born very prematurely. The medical team involved in Megan's case recommended that she be treated intensively. They assured her parents that they have had great success in similar cases. Some of the children they treated went home with only mild impairments and are now able to function almost independently, with only minimal support. Megan's parents initially consented to treatment hoping that their child could live a relatively normal life, and their decision was strongly influenced by the recommendations of the medical team.

Several months have passed and it is now clear that Megan suffers from severe handicaps. She is deaf and blind and almost certainly cognitively impaired as well. However, she is no longer in danger of dying. The hospital tells her parents that it is time to take their daughter home; the medical team can do nothing more for her. Megan's parents refuse, claiming that their daughter is still the hospital's responsibility. They state that they would never have agreed to the aggressive treatment of their daughter had they known of the risks of such severe impairment.

Both Sandra and Michael work at minimum-wage jobs. They can barely afford to support themselves, let alone care for a severely impaired child. Further, there is little support available in their community for children with these kinds of handicaps, and neither Sandra's nor Michael's parents are ready to take any responsibility for the child. Michael states that it is unfair that society funds such intensive medical treatment and then offers almost no support for the parents of the severely impaired children it has saved.

(1) Is this child the responsibility of the hospital or the parents? Are the parents obligated to take the child home? (2) Do you accept Michael's argument that a system that keeps severely impaired newborns alive should help provide for them? (3) How would a utilitarian regard this case? Should quality of life arguments be used to justify non-treatment of babies like Megan?

GLOSSARY

Active euthanasia: bringing about the death of a patient directly (for example, through the administration of a lethal dose of a drug that will cause death).

Cardiopulmonary death: traditional definition of death by which a person is considered dead once his or her heart has stopped functioning and he or she is no longer breathing. It is also referred to as the heart-lung criterion for death, as opposed to the whole-brain-death criterion or the higher-brain-death criterion.

Euthanasia: word coming from the Greek *euthanatos* meaning "a good death" and referring to hastening the death of a dying person in order to bring an end to the person's suffering.

Higher-brain death: a definition of death entailing the irreversible loss of function of the upper brain, or cerebral cortex. A person in this state is in an irreversible coma, often referred to as being in a persistent vegetative state (PVS). The brain stem continues to function and heartbeat and breathing continue without the aid of a ventilator. This is not the legal definition of death in most jurisdictions.

Passive euthanasia: allowing death to happen through withholding or withdrawing treatment that is considered futile or even harmful (for example, by not performing cardiopulmonary resuscitation or by disconnecting a ventilator).

Physician-assisted suicide: the death of a person by suicide with the help of a physician. If the help does not come from a physician, then it is simply referred to as "assisted suicide."

Whole-brain death: a definition of death entailing the irreversible cessation of all functions of the entire brain. In other words, no electrical activity can be recorded in the brain with the use of electroencephalographic or imaging machines. The heart and lungs of a person in this state continue to function only with the aid of a ventilator and other forms of life support. A person in this state is considered legally dead in most jurisdictions.

FOR FURTHER READING

Barry, Vincent. *Philosophical Thinking about Death and Dying. Belmont*, CA: Thomson Wadsworth, 2007.

This book raises philosophical questions about death, dying, and the meaning of death. It includes, among others, chapters on the history of death in the West and the possibility of survival of death, as well as a chapter on voluntary death and futile treatment. This is an excellent resource for deeper philosophical analysis of the standard bioethical questions.

Callahan, Daniel. "When Self-Determination Runs Amok." *Hastings Center Report*, 22, no. 2 (March-April 1992): 52–55.

Callahan presents several strong arguments against euthanasia and defends a slippery slope argument, demonstrating how taking the first apparently desirable step would lead to less desirable steps and to adverse social consequences. He also argues in favour of maintaining the distinction between killing and letting die, in opposition to James Rachels and others who would do away with the distinction. (This special issue of the *Hastings Center Report*, entitled "Dying Well: A Colloquy on Euthanasia and Assisted Suicide," contains a number of articles on both sides of the question of euthanasia and assisted suicide.)

Jonas, Hans. "Against the Stream: Comments on the Definition and Redefinition of Death," in *Philosophical Essays: From Ancient Creed to Technological Man*. Englewood Cliffs, NJ: Prentice Hall, Inc., 1974.

An early critic of the redefinition of death, Jonas argues that the brain-death criterion may serve to determine when to stop treating a patient, but not to stipulate that the patient is dead. He warns against the abuses that could result from treating a body that is still warm and breathing as a corpse and is disturbed by using a definition of death as a means of facilitating the retrieval of organs for transplant.

Lantos, John D. *The Lazarus Case: Life-and-Death Issues in Neonatal Intensive Care*. Baltimore and London: The Johns Hopkins University Press, 2001.

Lantos is a physician, an ethicist, and a professor of pediatrics who writes with great sympathy and sensitivity of the gruelling and difficult decisions health workers and families must face in the treatment of severely premature infants. Drawing on his experience as a medical witness in court cases dealing with the negative outcomes of treatment decisions, his book is historical, philosophical, and profoundly disturbing as it explores the minefield of neonatal care where doctors are too often damned if they do and damned if they don't.

Lee, Daniel E. "Physician-Assisted Suicide: A Conservative Critique of Intervention." *Hastings Center Report*, 33, no. 1 (January-February 2003): 17–19.

Lee is personally opposed to physician-assisted suicide for religious reasons, but he does not believe that people who share his religious beliefs have a right to use the power of the law to prevent others from ending their own lives. He also holds that legalizing and strictly regulating the practice is one way of avoiding the slide down the slippery slope to the adverse social consequences that others such as Callahan foresee.

Pojman, Louis P. *Life and Death*, 2nd ed. Belmont, CA: Thomson Wadsworth, 2000.

 Besides several introductory chapters on ethical theory, this book explores sanctity of life versus quality of life, death and dying, euthanasia, criteria of death, and slippery slope arguments.

Warnock, Mary, and Elisabeth Macdonald. *Easeful Death: Is There a Case for Assisted Dying?* Oxford: Oxford University Press, 2008.

 Macdonald is a cancer specialist and expert on medical law, and Warnock is a moral philosopher. Together these two British authors work to clarify and objectively weigh the arguments for and against the legalization of voluntary euthanasia and assisted suicide. Their discussion is equally valid for the Canadian situation.

RECOMMENDED WEBSITES

Alcor Life Extension Foundation: Cryonics
www.alcor.org

 This website provides information about the philosophy and process of cryonics (cryopreservation), including a photo gallery of the procedure used at the Scottsdale, Arizona, facility.

End of Life Law and Policy in Canada, Health Law Institute, Dalhousie University
eol.law.dal.ca/

 This website serves as an information resource on end-of-life treatment policy and practice in Canada and around the world. It also has information regarding advance directives in all the Canadian provinces, as well as summaries of legal judgments on end-of-life court cases.

Library of Parliament, Parliamentary Research and Information Service. Martha Butler et al., Euthanasia and Assisted Suicide in Canada. Publication no. 2010-68-E (revised February 15, 2013)
www.parl.gc.ca/Content/LOP/ResearchPublications/2010-68-e.pdf

 This report provides an historical and legal summary of the issue in Canada, along with a chronology of events (including Parliamentary bills and court decisions).

Ontario Consultants on Religious Tolerance: Euthanasia & Physician Assisted Suicide
www.religioustolerance.org/euthanas.htm

 This group is a non-denominational organization started by several lay people promoting religious tolerance and understanding. Its website on euthanasia and assisted suicide contains detailed information on the legal, religious, and ethical issues involved in this question as well as the legal status of assisted dying in a number of countries. Overall, the site takes a stance in favour of euthanasia and assisted suicide.

NOTES

1. Supreme Court of Canada, *Cuthbertson v. Rasouli*, 2013 SCC 53, found at scc-csc.lexum.com/scc-csc/scc-csc/en/item/13290/index.do (March 19, 2014).
2. *Cuthbertson v. Rasouli.*
3. Robert Sibbald, Paula Chidwick, and Laura Hawryluck, "Standard of Care and Resource Implications of the Cuthbertson v. Rasouli Ruling," *Canadian Medical Association Journal*, 186, no. 5 (March 2014), cited in *ScienceDaily*, February 10, 2014, found at www.sciencedaily.com/releases/2014/02/140210140023.htm (March 19, 2014).
4. Catherine Deans and Colleen M. Flood, "Rasouli and the Elephant in the Room" in *Impact Ethics: Making a Difference in Bioethics*, October 24, 2013, found at www.impactethics.ca/2013/10/24/rasouli-and-the-elephant-in-the-room/ (March 19, 2014).
5. Katherine K. Young, "Death: Eastern Thought," in Stephen G. Post (ed.), *Encyclopedia of Bioethics*, rev. ed. (New York: MacMillan Reference Books), 487.

6. Plato, *Five Dialogues*, trans. G.M.A. Grube, 2nd ed. (Indianapolis, IN: Hackett Publishing Company, 2000), 44.

7. It should be pointed out that not all Christians interpret the notion of the resurrection of the body in the same way, nor do they agree on just what form a resurrected body would take.

8. Herbert C. Northcott and Donna M. Wilson, *Dying and Death in Canada* (Peterborough, ON: Broadview Press, 2008), 20.

9. Daniel Callahan, *The Troubled Dream of Life: In Search of a Peaceful Death* (New York: Touchstone Books, 1993), 58, 59.

10. Vincent Barry, *Philosophical Thinking About Death and Dying* (Belmont, CA: Thomson Wadsworth, 2007), 28.

11. Callahan, *The Troubled Dream*, 43. Callahan is not suggesting such deaths were easy or peaceful; death under such circumstances could be agonizing. But it was rarely prolonged; it was a matter of weeks, not years.

12. John D. Lantos, *The Lazarus Case: Life-and-Death Issues in Neonatal Intensive Care* (Baltimore, MD: The Johns Hopkins University Press, 2001), 70.

13. Mary Warnock and Elisabeth Macdonald, *Easeful Death: Is There a Case for Assisted Dying?* (Oxford: Oxford University Press, 2008), ix.

14. Technically there is a difference between a respirator (which functions to filter or to exchange gases, e.g., oxygen and carbon dioxide) and a ventilator (which moves air in and out), although the two terms are now used interchangeably. We are generally using the term "ventilator" to refer to the life-sustaining mechanism used to aid or restore breathing, although both terms are found in the literature.

15. Margaret Lock, *Twice Dead: Organ Transplants and the Reinvention of Death* (Berkeley, CA: University of California Press, 2002), 65.

16. In fact, a number of other committees and commissions around the world took up the same question. The Harvard Committee was the "most specific and best-publicized of these institutional efforts." Martin S. Pernick, "Brain Death in a Cultural Context," in Stuart J. Youngner, Robert M. Arnold, and Renie Schapiro (eds.), *The Definition of Death: Contemporary Controversies* (Baltimore, MD: The Johns Hopkins University Press, 1999), 8.

17. Lock, 89.

18. President's Commission for the Study of Ethical Problems in Medicine and Biomedical and Behavioral Research, "Defining Death: Medical, Legal, and Ethical Issues in the Definition of Death," in Tom L. Beauchamp and Robert M. Veatch, *Ethical Issues in Death and Dying*, 2nd ed. (Upper Saddle River, NJ: Prentice Hall, 1996), 7.

19. President's Commission, 12.

20. Canadian Congress Committee on Brain Death, "Death and Brain Death: A new Formulation for Canadian Medicine," *Canadian Medical Association Journal*, 138, no. 5, (March 1988), 405–406.

21. Japan and Israel are exceptional in that resistance to the concept of brain death has been strong in both countries. In Japan, brain death does not constitute the legal definition of death; however, since 1997, it has been permissible to declare a brain-dead person dead in order to extract organs if the person has consented in advance. In the Jewish religion, death arrives only with the cessation of heart function. However, in 2008, the Israeli government passed a law that regulates organ donation in accordance with Jewish religious law, under the supervision of religious authorities.

22. R.M. Veatch, "The Impending Collapse of the Whole-Brain Definition of Death," *Hastings Center Report*, 23, no. 4 (July-August 1993): 18–24.

23. Robert D. Truog, "Is It Time to Abandon Brain Death?" in Arthur L. Caplan and Daniel H. Coelho (eds.), *The Ethics of Organ Transplants* (Amherst, NY: Prometheus Books, 1998), 30.

24. Patients in this state are often referred to as being in a persistent vegetative state (PVS), and while they are not always hooked up to a respirator, they are usually hooked up to a feeding tube for what is referred to as artificial nutrition and hydration, without which they could not continue to live.

25. Matthew Barakat, "Brain-Dead Woman Dies after Baby Born," *Toronto Star*, August 4, 2005, A10.

26. Hans Jonas, "Against the Stream: Comments on the Definition and Redefinition of Death," in *Philosophical Essays: From Ancient Creed to Technological Man* (Englewood Cliffs, NJ: Prentice Hall, 1974), 136.

27. Although serious ethical discussions about the perceived need to undertake experimentation on brain-dead (as well as PVS) patients are fairly recent, Pernick reports that this was one of the practical problems (along with organ retrieval and withdrawal of treatment) that concerned the chairman of the Harvard Committee, Dr. Henry K. Beecher: "A third practical problem that played a little-noticed role in shaping Beecher's approach to death was human experimentation.... [He] noted that permanently comatose bodies and their organs might be useful in many other kinds of experiments, such as testing new drugs. Beecher apparently hoped that experimenting on brain-dead bodies could reduce the need for live human guinea pigs and thereby avoid the ethical complications caused by using live human subjects." Beecher's attitude was probably less shocking then than it is now since organ transplantation itself was, at that time, very experimental, "so regulating organ procurement was one part of regulating human experimentation." Pernick, 10.

28. Jonas, 137.

29. A. Ravelingien et al., "Proceeding with Clinical Trials of Animal to Human Organ Transplantation: A Way Out of the Dilemma," *Journal of Medical Ethics*, 30, no. 1 (2004): 92–98. It should be underlined that using PVS patients would require another redefinition of death to encompass cortical death (or "upper-brain death").

30. Peter McCulloch, *Brain Dead, Brain Absent, Brain Donors: Human Subjects or Human Objects* (Rexdale, ON: John Wiley & Sons (Canada) Ltd., 1993), 75.

31. McCulloch, 77. McCulloch quotes Australian bioethicist Dr. Paul Gerber as saying that this was a "wonderful solution for the problem posed by surrogacy, and a magnificent use of a corpse."

32. McCulloch, 2, 3.

33. Norman Fost, "The Unimportance of Death," in Youngner et al., 175.

34. Gregory E. Pence, *Classic Cases in Medical Ethics*, 3rd ed. (Boston: McGraw-Hill, 2000).

35. Pence, 38.

36. Francoise Baylis et al. (eds.), *Health Care Ethics in Canada* (Toronto: Thomson Wadsworth, 2004), 504. The case referred to is: *B. (N.) v. Hotel-Dieu de Québec* (1992), 86 D.L.R. (4th) 385 (C.S.).

37. Baylis et al., 504.

38. Pence, 53.

39. Terri Schiavo had been in a persistent vegetative state for over 10 years when the court battle between her husband, who wanted her feeding tube removed, and her family, who did not, became a sensational public issue in 2005. "By March 2005, the legal history around the Schiavo case included fourteen appeals and numerous motions, petitions, and hearings in the Florida courts; five suits in Federal District Court; Florida legislation struck down by the Supreme Court of Florida; a subpoena by a congressional committee in an attempt to qualify Schiavo for witness

protection; federal legislation (Palm Sunday Compromise); and four denials of certiorari from the Supreme Court of the United States." Wikipedia, "Terri Schiavo case" (February 23, 2009), found at www.en.wikipedia.org/wiki/Terri_Schiavo (February 27, 2009).

40. Callahan, *The Troubled Dream*, 69.

41. James Rachels, "Active and Passive Euthanasia," *New England Journal of Medicine*, 292, no. 2 (1975): 78–80. Reprinted in Michael C. Brannigan and Judith A. Boss, *Healthcare Ethics in a Diverse Society* (Mountain View, CA: Mayfield Publishing Company, 2001), 508.

42. Rachels, 510.

43. Rachels, 511.

44. Daniel Callahan, "When Self-Determination Runs Amok," *Hastings Center Report*, 22, no. 2 (March-April 1992): 53.

45. The goals of medicine are also discussed in Chapter 2.

46. Jocelyne Saint-Arnaud, *Enjeux éthiques et technologies biomédicales* [The Ethical Stakes of Biomedical Technology]. Montreal: Les presses de l'université de Montréal, 1999), Ch. 3.

47. Barry, 215.

48. Quoted in Lisa Priest, "Vegetative Patient Now Able to Give 'Thumbs Up,' Fuelling Debate," *The Globe and Mail*, April 24, 2012.

49. In a permanent vegetative state (PVS) a person can be awake (i.e., have periods of sleep and wakefulness) but is not aware; in a minimally conscious state, a person is aware to different degrees and able to respond to some stimuli. Both of these states differ from that of a coma, where the patient is unconscious, appears to be asleep, and is never awake.

50. Quoted in Tom Blackwell, "Toronto Man at the Heart of a Landmark Life Support Case Has a 'Very Low Level' of Consciousness, Tests Show," *National Post*, December 2, 2012. There is a state, referred to as "locked-in syndrome," where a person is fully conscious but unable to move or speak. The case of Jean-Dominique Bauby, editor-in-chief of the magazine *Elle*, was in such a state after a massive stroke in 1995. He was capable of blinking one eye and was able to dictate his story, which became a book and eventually a movie with the same name. See Jean-Dominique Bauby, *The Diving-Bell and the Butterfly* (London and New York: Harper Perrenial, 2008).

51. This patient eventually recovered (something that is very unusual) and, although she is severely handicapped, is able to communicate—and write emails to Dr. Owen—using a letterboard and a computer. See Pop!Tech, "Adrian Owen: Search for Consciousness," found at www.youtube.com/watch?v=Hz133pdwbOA (March 21, 2014).

52. Marcia Angell, "The Case of Helga Wanglie: A New Kind of 'Right to Die' Case," in Patricia Illingworth and Wendy E. Parmet, *Ethical Health Care* (Upper Saddle River, NJ: Pearson Education, 2006), 210.

53. Barry, 215.

54. Illingworth and Parmet, 212.

55. Robert D. Truog, Allan S. Brett, and Joel Frader, "The Problem with Futility," in Baylis et al., 461.

56. It is estimated that Rasouli's stay at Sunnybrook Hospital has cost $3.5 million. As of early 2014, he was on a waiting list to be moved to another health care facility where the family will have to cover part of that cost of care. See Theresa Boyle, "Hassan Rasouli to Move Out of Sunnybrook after Long End-of-life Court Battle," *Toronto Star*, December 31, 2013.

57. Nancy S. Jecker, "Knowing When to Stop: The Limits of Medicine," *Hastings Center Report*, 21, no. 3 (May-June 1991): 5.

58. Dr. Robert D. Orr and Gilbert Meilaender, "Ethics and Life's Ending: An Exchange," *First Things: A Monthly Journal of Religion and Public Life*, 145 (August-September 2004): 31–35.

59. Callahan, *The Troubled Dream*, 81.

60. Callahan, *The Troubled Dream*, 81.

61. Callahan, *The Troubled Dream*, 81.

62. Cryonics should begin 2–15 minutes after cardiac death; the shorter the delay, the better.

63. Alcor Life Extension Foundation, found at www.alcor.org/ (March 21, 2014).

64. Ray Kurzweil, "The Evolution of Mind in the Twenty-First Century," in Jay W. Richards (ed.), *Are We Spiritual Machines: Ray Kurzweil vs. the Critics of Strong A.I.* (Seattle: Discovery Institute, 2002), 29.

65. For a discussion of some of the philosophical pre-suppositions of Kurzweil's vision, see Carol Collier, *Recovering the Body: A Philosophical Story* (University of Ottawa Press, 2013), 210-214.

66. That being said, if any of these visions actually came to pass, many ethical questions could be raised about access to the technologies involved. In this regard, see the discussion of the genetic revolution in Chapter 6.

67. While laws and court decisions apply only in the country where the case is heard, similar cases relating to refusal and withdrawal of treatment have had similar outcomes in the U.S., in Canada, and in Great Britain. Because the discipline began in the U.S. and much of the literature emanates from there, cases such as Quinlan and Cruzan tend to dominate the discussion of death and dying in biomedical ethics. It is, however, useful to repeat that while legal decisions are often based on moral considerations, the moral issue cannot be reduced to the legal issues.

68. This point has been contested. Since the actual circumstances of Rodriguez' death were never divulged, there is some ambiguity surrounding the question of whether the final act was suicide or euthanasia. She may have been too weak at the end to commit suicide even with assistance, and it may actually have been a case of euthanasia. At any rate, her court applications were based on the former and not the latter.

69. The following describes the 1993 suicide of Thomas W. Hyde Jr., a 31-year-old Michigan construction worker suffering from ALS, enabled by Dr. Jack Kevorkian, an American physician and activist for physician-assisted suicide: "Dr. Kevorkian fitted a respiratory mask over Hyde's face and connected the plastic tubing leading from the mask to a short cylinder of carbon monoxide gas. Dr. Kevorkian placed a string in Hyde's hand. At the opposite end of the string was a paper clip crimping the plastic tubing and shutting off the flow of gas. Hyde jerked on the string, pulled loose the paper clip, then breathed in the carbon monoxide flowing into the mask. Twenty minutes later, he was dead." Ronald Munson, *Intervention and Reflection: Basic Issues in Medical Ethics* (Belmont, CA: Thomson Wadsworth, 2008), 703.

70. Dan W. Brock, *Life and Death: Philosophical Essays in Biomedical Ethics* (Cambridge and New York: Cambridge University Press, 1994), 205.

71. Callahan, "Self-Determination," 53, 52.

72. In logic, slippery slope arguments are considered fallacious unless one can fill in a valid argument to justify each conclusion along the slope. Not all objections to the slippery slope argument are logical ones, however; some people argue that the slide down the slope arises because of purely practical experiences, where exceptions lead to further exceptions, and up to a slide down the slope to more permissive laws or regulations. See the excerpt from Warnock and Macdonald for an argument against this.

73. Callahan, "Self-Determination," 54.

74. Callahan, "Self-Determination," 54.

75. Warnock and Macdonald, 83.

76. Warnock and Macdonald, 83.

77. James F. Keenan, "The Case for Physician-Assisted Suicide?" in Patricia Beattie Jung and Shannon Jung, *Moral Issues and Christian Responses*, 7th ed. (Belmont, CA: Wadsworth Publishing, 2003), 189.

78. Keenan, 189.

79. Stacy Lundin Yale, "Dying Patients Who Refuse Nutrition and Hydration," *Alternative & Complementary Therapies*, 11, no. 2 (April 1, 2005): 100.

80. Yale, 101.

81. James L. Bernat, Bernard Gert, and R. Peter Mogielnicki, "Patient Refusal of Hydration and Nutrition: An Alternative to Physician-Assisted Suicide or Voluntary Active Euthanasia," in Thomas A. Mappes and David DeGrazia (eds.), *Biomedical Ethics*, 6th ed. (New York: McGraw-Hill Higher Education, 2001), 439.

82. Yale, 101.

83. See the website of the Dalhousie Health Law Project listed at the end of the chapter under Recommended Websites for information regarding advance directives and living wills in the different provinces of Canada. Two Ontario court decisions that have upheld the legitimacy of advance directives are *Malette v. Shulman* (1987) and *Flemming v. Reid* (1991). For a summary of these cases see Baylis et al., 501, 502. See also Chapter 2 for a discussion of advance directives in relation to proxy consent.

84. Lantos, 40.

85. Michael L. Gross, "Avoiding Anomalous Newborns," in Munson, 666.

86. Munson, 634. Lantos estimates that the costs of neonatal intensive care in the U.S. are at least $15 billion per year and refers to the "nagging concern" that in many cases "this was not only money down the drain but money that could be spent much better elsewhere for children who would truly benefit from it." But he also points out that the "NICU has become the economic engine that keeps children's hospitals running" and that this drives the commitment to both the technologies and the medical personnel to push for trying to save premature babies. Lantos, 47, 113, 115.

87. Perri Klass, "The Best Intentions," in Marjorie Garber, Beatrice Hanssen, Rebecca L. Walkowitz (eds.), *The Turn to Ethics* (New York and London: Routledge, 2000), 80.

88. Munson, 635. At the same time Lantos reports that while only 20 percent of babies weighing 500–800 grams survived in 1980, in 1995 the number had increased to nearly 60 percent, indicating that many lessons have, in fact, been learned. One can ask where we would be if we had given up on 500-gram babies 20 years ago. Lantos, 76.

89. According to Lantos, parents more often than not are the ones who want to continue treatment of premature babies: "[D]octors need to convince parents that further treatment is futile, while parents persist in believing in a miracle." Lantos, 160.

90. H. Tristram Engelhardt Jr., "Ethical Issues in Aiding the Death of Young Children," in Munson, 649.

91. Engelhardt, 649.

92. Engelhardt, 646.

93. Lantos, 164.

94. It should be noted that, according to some interpreters of Aristotle, he did believe that the rational soul (but not the vegetative or sensitive soul) might live on after death, but he was not specific on this point.

95. Associated Press, "Brain-dead Marlise Munoz Taken Off Life Support in Texas Hospital," January 26, 2014, found at www.cbc.ca/news/world/brain-dead-marlise-munoz-taken-off-life-support-in-texas-hospital-1.2511890 (December 11, 2014).

96. Michael Cook, "Brain-dead Canadian Woman Gives Birth," *BioEdge*, February 16, 2014, found at www.bioedge.org/index.php/bioethics/bioethics_article/10850 (December 11, 2014).

97. *R. v. Latimer*, [2001] 1 S.C.R. 3, 2001 SCC 1, found at scc-csc.lexum.com/scc-csc/scc-csc/en/item/1836/index.do (March 31, 2014).

98. Martha Butler, Marlisa Tiedemann, Julia Nicol, and Dominique Valiquet, "Euthanasia and Assisted Suicide in Canada," Library of Parliament (2013), found at www.parl.gc.ca/Content/LOP/ResearchPublications/2010-68-e.htm (December 11, 2014).

99. Compassionate Healthcare Network, "An Interview with Hugh Scher: Dr. Maurice Genereux: The Darth Vader of Doctors," found at www.chninternational.com/generux_dr._canadian.htm (December 11, 2014). See also Butler et al., 2013.

Chapter 9

Organs and Tissues: Procurement and Transplantation

CASE STUDY: TRANSPLANT TOURISM

Dr. Janice Miller is part of the transplant team at a large metropolitan hospital in British Columbia. Doctors at this hospital have been performing an increasing number of organ transplants and have seen a growing number of patients in need of organs for transplant for whom no suitable donor is available. This situation has caused some patients, desperate for a life-saving operation, to explore other options, including travelling to other countries to buy an organ, sometimes legally in the host country and sometimes illegally in a growing black market in organs. What is commonly known as "transplant tourism" has become a growth industry.

Dr. Miller has observed that some of these patients are open about their plans and ask their physician to provide preoperative treatment. Others simply make arrangements in secret and arrive back in need of emergency care due to botched surgeries, lack of proper post-operative treatment, or serious infection. Both the preoperative and post-operative situations are troubling for Dr. Miller and some of her colleagues. In 2010, the Canadian Society of Transplantation and the Canadian Society of Nephrology published a policy document with a view to establishing a consistent approach to transplant tourism among Canadian health care practitioners (see the discussion under "Transplant Tourism" later in this chapter). Since then, the hospital at which Dr. Miller works has had to navigate increasingly complex issues surrounding the treatment of individuals who go to other countries in search of a life-saving organ.

Today, Dr. Miller brings to the table a case involving post-transplant care for Glen Reed, a 53-year-old civil engineer suffering from end-stage renal disease. He had been on dialysis and was on the waiting list for a new kidney. He knew that the waiting list was long (the median wait time in British Columbia for a kidney transplant is more than five years) and that there was a real likelihood that he would die while waiting for a new kidney. He began to raise the possibility of transplant tourism. In accordance with the document drawn up by the Canadian Society of Transplantation and the Canadian Society of Nephrology, Dr. Miller informed Mr. Reed about the dangers and ethical issues surrounding transplant tourism. She strongly advised against obtaining a kidney for transplant abroad, as it would put him (and perhaps the donor as well) at significant risk. Ignoring her advice, Reed travelled to China and went ahead with the transplant. Upon returning to Canada, he was removed from the transplant list. Since then, however, he has been diagnosed with a severe sepsis syndrome and acute kidney injury, and is in the intensive care unit. His situation is likely related to an injury received during the transplant surgery. Dr. Miller is faced with the question of whether to put Mr. Reed back on the transplant list and what priority to give his case, given the shortage of organs.

"According to the Hippocratic tradition," says Maxime Martin, the hospital administrator, "we are committed to non-judgmental regard. This means that we must remain non-judgmental in caring for our patients and work only for the patient's good. It is not up to us to judge who is worthy of treatment and who is not, nor to make a judgment about how they came to be in the situation they are now in."

"But in placing this patient back on the transplant list, we are implicitly supporting a practice that violates basic human rights," says Jane Anderson, the social worker on the hospital's ethics committee, who always tries to act as the voice of the vulnerable members of society. "The Canadian Medical Association Code of Ethics states that physicians have a fundamental responsibility to refuse to participate or support such practices. In China, there is little regulation or oversight of organ transplantation, and many organs come from executed prisoners, some of whom might have been wrongly imprisoned and may not have given consent. In many countries, individuals are coerced or forced into 'donating' a kidney and often are left worse off than they were before financially and physically. Not only that, the surgical conditions involving such organ transplants are usually suboptimal and carry risks of serious complications for the organ recipient, which appears to be what has happened in this situation. Should we not simply condemn transplant tourism outright?"

"Consent is a non-issue in the case of China," Maxime Martin replies. "Prisoners are denied many rights, including when and how they die. Why should this particular decision about the use of organs after death be an exception to state authority? Our concern here is our patient, not the political system in China. We are bound by professional duty to place our patients' welfare before our own political or moral concerns. We cannot interfere with the autonomy of this patient by denying him care based on our disapproval of his moral choice. I'd go so far as to say that if we are truly concerned about the well-being of our patients (and their 'donors'), we should consider providing training in transplant medicine and surgery to visiting physicians from countries like China who will be performing transplants."

Once the debate dies down, Dr. Miller raises another issue that has been nagging at her. "I know we are bound by professional responsibility to continue to provide care for a patient until it is no longer required or wanted, but I have two other patients who are in at least as dire a situation as Mr. Reed. I cannot agree to give him priority over them, given that he went against my advice and got himself into this situation. We can put him at the bottom of the list and he can go back on dialysis in the meantime."

Maxime looked at her sternly. "We can assess all three of these patients according to our normal medical criteria of urgency, need, and availability. But we cannot rank Mr. Reed lower in priority simply because he was a 'transplant tourist.' That is irrelevant to our decision."

INTRODUCTION

We have chosen to begin this chapter with a fictional case. It is, however, based on several real cases, although none has ended up in the courts. The case illustrates the complexities of the practice of organ transplantation, driven as it is by technological advances that allow for more transplants of more organs along with longer survival rates, with no matching increase in the availability of organs for transplant. In other words, the demand for organs outpaces the supply. Much of this chapter deals with different efforts to bolster the supply side of this equation that raise difficult ethical questions. Our hypothetical case presents one set of dilemmas; there are many more.

Organ transplantation represents the far edge of high-tech medicine, the ultimate in medical progress, and in the eyes of most people, it is an unmitigated good. The many ethical questions raised by organ transplantation in this chapter, however, should cause us to reconsider some of these assumptions. The most obvious, but not generally acknowledged, fact is that for one person to be saved by an organ transplant, another person must die. This is an uncomfortable truth that brings with it the disturbing connection between organ transplants and brain death. The question of brain death was discussed in Chapter 8; here we underline the ethical issues that are raised as the perceived need to increase the supply of available organs for transplant drives efforts to manipulate the definition of death to encompass a wider range of potential donors.

One of the most important philosophical issues raised in this chapter pertains to the commodification and commercialization of the body and its parts. Should human organs and tissues be considered *things* that are valued according to market forces of supply and demand? Who owns my genes or the genetic information gleaned from samples of my blood or tissues collected in the normal course of medical care and treatment? Can they be patented? In the case of living organ transplants (for example, kidneys), is it right for people in rich countries to be able to buy organs from people in poor countries? Is this fair exchange or is it exploitation? Should organs be bought and sold at all? Does the need for an organ on the part of one person create an obligation to donate on the part of another? Further, given that there are not enough organs to go around, what is the best way to determine who gets what in the scramble for available organs?

The issues around organ transplantation go beyond ethical questions regarding consent and the question of fair distribution of the supply of organs available to the many people who need them. Questions can be asked about the high cost of these procedures and whether or not there are more effective ways of dealing with the terminal illnesses that make transplant organs so much in demand.[1] How much is the technological imperative at work in the field? Who profits from the very existence of this practice that demands so many specialized medical resources? We address many of these ethical issues directly or indirectly in this chapter. However, one of our goals is also to help uncover some of the metaphysical assumptions about human bodies that underlie the practice, as well as assumptions about how far our duties to others go when it comes to our bodies. Much current ethical analysis of this issue ignores some of these more fundamental questions, which we raise without, however, having any clear answers.

Andreas Vesalius in the 16th century legitimized the practice of dissection by transforming it into the science of anatomy. Public dissections were very popular events in his time.

HISTORICAL AND PHILOSOPHICAL PERSPECTIVES

Organ transplantation is a surgical procedure by which organs or tissues (for example, kidney, heart, cornea, lung, bones, bone marrow) are removed from one person and transplanted into the body of another (or others). The donor is usually a dead (most often brain-dead) person, although some organs and tissues come from living donors (for example, kidney, partial lung or liver, bone marrow). The recipient of the organ is usually suffering from an incurable or terminal illness, and different types of transplant, with varying success rates, can allow the extension of life for varying periods. The donor is, for the most part, a person who is brain dead as a result of a traumatic event affecting the central nervous system.[2] Organ transplantation has been described as "high-technology medicine in one of its extreme forms," and while it is perceived as a cure, this is only partially true. Depending on the organ in question, many patients "require constant, ongoing treatment with highly sophisticated and often quite dangerous medications."[3]

Organ transplants were on the horizon and thought about long before the technological leap in the area over the last 50 years. There were attempts to transplant kidneys before the 1950s, but none were successful due to the recipient body's rejection of the transplanted organ. The first successful kidney transplant occurred in Boston in 1954 where the donor and recipient of the kidney were identical twins. Because immunosuppressive drugs had not yet been developed, successful transplants were limited for a number of years to kidney transplants between identical twins. The first heart transplant was performed by Dr. Christiaan Barnard, a South African surgeon, in 1967. He transplanted the heart of a 25-year-old woman into the body of a 55-year-old man who lived for 18 days after the operation. The next year, he performed a second heart transplant (using the heart of a 25-year-old man) on a 58-year-old man who lived for 20 months. These early attempts at transplantation have to be seen as experimental, rather than therapeutic. For example, according to Pence, "[O]f 55 liver transplants in 1968 and early 1969 (the 15 months after Barnard's landmark operation), 50 patients failed to live as long as 6 months. Clearly, most of these early transplants were failures."[4] This high failure rate caused many to see these early efforts as experiments, and the debate about their therapeutic value continued until the late 1970s.

Since that time, organ transplantation has expanded to encompass more and more possibilities, success rates have improved, and some types of transplant have become almost routine medical practice. About 15,000 kidney transplants were performed in the U.S. alone in 2003. The five-year survival rate from living donors is almost 90 percent, while heart and liver transplants have a fove-year survival rate of 70–75 percent. However, organ transplantation remains a costly and highly technical procedure, using up what many believe is a disproportionate share of medical resources compared with its overall success. Further, as the practice extends to cover more and more body parts (for example, the first face transplant in France carried out in 2005 and recent attempts at womb transplants), there are continuing concerns about its experimental nature.

BOX 9.1

RENÉE C. FOX, "THE SUBLIMITY AND TYRANNY OF THE GIFT"

The deepest significance of organ transplantation lies in its gift-exchange dimensions— in the nature and magnitude of what is given, taken, and received. The living parts of persons, offered in life or death to known or unknown others, are implanted in the bodies of individuals who have reached the end stages of grave illnesses. This corporeal act of giving, and the surgical process of amputation and transferral through which it is effected, is carried out for the life-sustaining benefit of others. It is what philosopher Hans Jonas has termed a "supererogatory" gift, "beyond duty and claim ... reckoning and rule."[1] Although such a gift of self epitomizes one of my highest values, organ transplantation has always confronted me with the question of how willing and able I would be to give to strangers as well as intimates in this flesh-of-my-flesh way....

Some of the phenomena associated with who offers and who is permitted to be a live donor have continually preoccupied me.... I have given much thought to the biologically deterministic and circumscribed conception of the family that underlies transplanters' refusal until recently to consider as live donors anyone other than parents, children, or siblings of prospective recipients. Is this the most basic and fullest definition of family?... The transplanters' outlook has emanated chiefly from the matching of tissue and blood-type, which they consider integral to managing the rejection reaction triggered by the body's "recognition" of "foreign" tissue, and also by their wariness, on other than biological grounds, about what might motivate persons who are not members of a prospective recipient's nuclear family of origin to make such a sacrificial gift. Irrespective of its sources, this is a very narrow notion of kinship and family, one that I find too psychologically and morally restrictive. The more recent willingness of the transplant community to expand the notion of familial relatedness by considering not only spouses and second-degree relatives but also certain kinlike friends as possible donors is more in keeping with my own philosophical conceptions of a less biologically defined and exclusive view of human relationships and connectedness.

I have given much thought, as well, to the fact that cadaveric organ donations go to, and become part of, individuals whom we do not know—strangers, and perhaps even persons who might have been our enemies. This is a supreme expression of the universalistic values and convictions by which I try to lead my life. It is the antithesis of the particularism that I continually try to surmount. The universalism on which it is premised, however, is somewhat qualified by the strong interest that most recipients of cadaver organs and their kin express in knowing what kind of person the donor was and what type of life he or she lived. The needs of recipients and their families to associate such a lifesaving gift with a human image and to express gratitude to a never-encountered other are involved here. But the desire to learn specific details about the donor also derives from recipients' anxiety about the individual and social attributes that may have been transposed into their bodies along with the transplanted organ....

One of the most chastening insights that years of contemplating the gift dimensions of organ transplantation have afforded me derives from what Judith Swazey and I have called "the tyranny of the gift." The gift that the recipient receives from the organ donor is so extraordinary that it is intrinsically unreciprocal. It has no physical or symbolic equivalent. As a consequence, the giver, the receiver, and their families may find themselves locked in a creditor-debtor vise that binds them painfully to one another. I was raised by my family to be generous to others, particularly to help those in need, in a Jewish subculture in which giving gifts of money and time, concern and care, was regarded as both a moral obligation and a spiritual blessing. Witnessing firsthand the heavy burden and new forms of suffering that being the recipient of an inherently unrepayable gift of an organ can cause has been a soberly edifying experience for me. It has enabled me to qualify and desentimentalize the goodness of the gift without depreciating or belittling it.

Note

1. Hans Jonas, "Philosophical Reflections on Experimenting with Human Subjects," in Paul A. Freund (ed.), *Experimentation with Human Subjects* (New York: George Braziller, 1970), 16.

Source: Renée C. Fox, "Afterthoughts: Continuing Reflections on Organ Transplantation," in Stuart J. Youngner, Renée C. Fox, and Laurence J. O'Connell, *Organ Transplantation: Meanings and Realities* (Madison, WI: University of Wisconsin Press, 1996), 253–254.

That organ transplantation is more successful than it was 40 years ago is, in large part, the result of the development of immunosuppressive drugs that have helped to control (but not eliminate) the rejection phenomenon, a powerful physiological reaction whereby the body of the organ recipient attacks the donor organ. Renée Fox describes the rejection reaction as "a strong biological expression of our individual uniqueness and separateness," which demonstrates "the capacity of the body to distinguish between 'self' and 'not-self'" and results in "aggressive, even violent actions by the body to rid itself of the 'foreign' tissue implanted into it from an alien, threatening not-self."[5] By suppressing the immune response that leads to rejection, these powerful drugs allow organ recipients to live longer; however, they have equally powerful side effects that can have a dramatic effect on the patient's quality of life. For example, the most effective anti-rejection drug to date, cyclosporine, can have a damaging effect on the kidneys, thus causing concern over its long-term use.[6]

The growth in possibilities for new types of transplants, including improved survival rates, has not been matched by an increase in the availability of donor organs; therefore, in the language of the marketplace, the demand considerably outpaces the supply. This has resulted in increased efforts to enlarge what is usually referred to as the pool of donor organs, including the redefinition of death to allow retrieval of organs using the higher-brain criterion and experimenting with different methods of obtaining consent from potential donors and their families. Many of these proposals or practices raise ethical questions that will be discussed later in this chapter. The gap between demand and supply has also resulted in research efforts to find alternative sources of organs (for example, artificial organs, animal organs—from pigs or primates—cloning animals for organs, or even cloning organs). While organ transplantation has been going on for almost 50 years, the many ethical dilemmas posed by the practice (in particular, issues around procurement of transplantable organs) have not disappeared and, in fact, are more complex and difficult than they were at the beginning.

DEATH, BRAIN DEATH, AND ORGAN TRANSPLANTATION

In the previous chapter we discussed the definition of death and the institution of the notion of brain death as a result of the work of the Ad Hoc Committee of the Harvard Medical School in 1968 and of various commissions worldwide that accepted the whole-brain criterion for the determination of death. We also raised the connection between the redefinition of death and the developing practice of organ transplantation, a connection that was not coincidental and is not without its critics.

Peter Singer, for one, refers to the revised definition of death as a convenient fiction: "[I]t makes it possible for us to salvage organs that would otherwise be wasted, and to withdraw medical treatment when it is doing no good."[7] Surprisingly, however, the new definition has been adopted around the world with little resistance from religious, philosophical, or ethical leaders, even though it raises a number of ethical questions. It is surprising that these ethical questions are often avoided in the bioethical literature in which the major ethical problem relating to organ transplants is not the meaning of death, but the procurement and distribution of scarce resources.[8]

Interestingly, while the redefinition of death almost 40 years ago took place in North America and in Europe with little or no public comment, it was quite otherwise in Japan, where mind-body dualism is not part of the metaphysical framework. According to Lock, the whole question of brain death and organ transplantation has caused a great deal of social controversy there, in large part because the Japanese understand death as a process and as an event involving more than the physical body. Lock adds, "What is more, *the cognitive status of the patient is of secondary importance for most people*."[9] Japan resisted legal adoption of the brain-death criterion until 1997. It is still not accepted by the general population, which can accept **living organ donations**, but has difficulty accepting the retrieval of organs from brain-dead patients on ventilators.

Increasing the Supply: Moving to the Higher-Brain Criterion of Death

As pointed out in the last chapter, many thinkers have, from the beginning, preferred the higher-brain definition of death. To a large extent, it is the continuing shortage of organs for transplantation and the accompanying desire to increase the donor pool that motivates the drive to move to the alternative definition. Such a change would allow the retrieval of organs from two classes of patients: those in a persistent vegetative state (PVS) and infants born with anencephaly.[10] PVS patients will never regain consciousness and anencephalic infants will never attain consciousness. However, because in both cases their basic heart and lung functions are intact, they cannot be considered dead under the whole-brain definition. While almost everyone agrees that such patients should not be aggressively treated and should be allowed to die, for some this means that organs are going to waste. If these patients were declared dead, their organs could be retrieved, and lives could be saved.

Thus, the debate about moving to the higher-brain definition of death brings to the fore the connection (not always admitted in brain-death discussions), not between *death* and organ transplantation, but between the *definition* of death and organ transplantation. The basic problem is simple: successful organ transplants require still-living organs from already-dead bodies. The whole-brain criterion of death has facilitated organ transplantation for several decades. But more and more organs are needed, and the supply cannot keep up with the demand. Some wish to solve this problem by moving to the higher-brain criterion; others think this is simply going too far. As Peter Singer comments: "The notion of whole-brain death, I felt, was already something of a deception, an ethical choice masquerading as a medical fact. To move to a higher brain definition of death would stretch an already dubious deception too far."[11] For Singer, it is time to clear up the deception and start asking the right questions.

Instead of asking when a patient is dead, we should be addressing the question: *when is it permissible to retrieve organs from a dying patient?* According to Singer, the Danish Council of Ethics tried to address this question when Denmark was debating the brain death issue. Instead of calling the cessation of all brain functions "brain death," it recommended acceptance of a special stage called "the irreversible process of dying." During this stage it would be permissible to retrieve organs for transplant for up to 48 hours if the dying person had previously consented. The Danish proposal thus attempted to separate the moment of actual death from the moment at which it would be considered acceptable to retrieve organs. However, "the idea that we should be able to take the heart out of a human being who has not been declared dead was too radical for the Danish government. In 1990 it passed a law bringing Denmark into line with other European countries by making brain death a criterion of death."[12] Interestingly, both the Danish proposal of an irreversible process of dying and the current brain-death criterion by which a patient is declared dead are referring *to the same stage between life and death* and to the same action of retrieving organs. The Danish Council of Ethics attempted to bring clarity to a practice that has been going on for years. But their government, and the rest of the Western world, including most ethicists, chose to live with Singer's "dubious deception."[13]

Writing about anencephalic infants as a potential source of pediatric organs, David Lamb states: "Clearly these infants have no hope of benefit, but lacking the prospect of benefit is not a sufficient reason for using them as a form of benefit for others."[14] Lamb makes the point that anencephalic infants cannot be *donors* of organs since they are not in condition to donate anything; they should be referred to as *sources* of organs. Some prefer to use the word "donor" because they are uncomfortable using terms such as "sources" in relation to obtaining needed organs for transplant. However, as Lamb points out, "[Q]uotation marks do not change reality; anencephalic infants are regarded as sources and this is precisely why the issue is ethically controversial."[15] Like Singer, Lamb believes that blending criteria for death with criteria for organ donation runs counter to the theoretical requirement for an objective definition of death based solely on the condition of the dead or dying individual. At the same time, defenders of the use of anencephalic infants for donor organs point to the need for pediatric organs and the lack of supply of small organs. Further, many of the defenders are parents of anencephalic infants themselves, who seek solace in the idea that their dying baby's organs can help save the lives of other babies.

While some wish to solve the problem of anencephalic donors by revising the definition of death, others recommend simply creating an exception to the dead donor rule, making this class of infants a special case. For example, the American Medical Association recommended in 1994 that the use of the anencephalic neonate as a live donor be a "limited exception to the general standard" of brain death.[16] This may not increase the supply as much as some might hope, however. Lamb points out that over 90 percent of cases of anencephaly can now be detected during the second trimester of pregnancy; thus prenatal testing and abortion could result in a drop from 3000 anencephalic births a year to 15. This could eliminate the issue around treatment of anencephalic infants, but it would not solve the problem of the shortage of infant organs.

Increasing the Supply: Cadaver Donations

Most organs for transplantation come from dead or brain-dead bodies and are referred to as **"cadaveric" organ donations**.[17] However, not everyone is willing to donate their organs after death and, at the moment of death, many families refuse consent. Efforts to increase donations have not been overly successful, and some commentators even point out that safety legislation in the past 20 or 30 years has worked against the supply of cadaveric organs: "[L]owering highway speed limits, raising the legal drinking age, enforcing strict drunk-driving laws, and requiring the use of seat belts and child-restraint devices have reduced the number of fatal motor-vehicle accidents and may reduce the potential supply of cadaveric donor organs."[18]

Informed Consent

The retrieval of organs from dead or brain-dead bodies raises ethical issues regarding informed consent, either that of individuals themselves or of their families or proxies. In Canada and the U.S., the principle of individual autonomy and informed consent extends to the dying or dead individual, and organs are not retrieved from bodies without the express prior consent of the patient or the family. The patient may have given consent long before death by signing a donor card or his or her driver's licence or health card, depending on the jurisdiction. Even if a patient has signed a donor card, however, the family is usually consulted at the time of death, and sometimes families do not honour the wishes of their loved one to donate. Many in the transplant community, including ethicists, object to allowing families to override a person's wish to donate organs. They believe that respect for autonomy demands that these wishes be carried out, in the same way that advance directives regarding end-of-life treatment should be respected. However, advance directives are "most persuasive when decisions are being made about life-saving interventions. It is not uniformly accepted by caregivers that the patient's choice should predominate over the family's wishes once the patient has died."[19] Traditionally, the next of kin are responsible for the disposition of a loved one's body; overriding this tradition is not necessarily easy and could also entail legal problems that most hospitals would want to avoid.

Thus the family will be asked about their wishes with respect to the deceased's organs regardless of the existence of a donor card. Further, as a result of "required request" laws in both Canada and the U.S., hospital personnel are required to ask families about the possibility of organ donation, and many hospitals have designated staff that perform this delicate task. According to Caplan, this process "ensures that the burden of decisions concerning donation is equitably allocated among all families whose relatives might serve as organ donors.... Moreover, it removes the option not to inquire, which is often chosen ... because of fears concerning legal and financial consequences."[20] It also separates the attending physician from the process, removing any possibility of conflict of interest and protecting the trust relationship with the family. In spite of required request laws, however, "fully half of potential donations are refused by next of kin when requested in hospital settings."[21]

Mandated Choice and Presumed Consent

Thus there is an apparent resistance to signing donor cards on the part of the general public, and in spite of efforts at public education, the rate of donation has remained remarkably stable over the years. While a majority of people believe in the benefits of organ transplantation, this does not automatically translate into a willingness to agree to donation of their own or their family members' organs, in part because of a "wide range of cultural and religious beliefs about brain death, whole-body burial, and end-of-life decision making," on the one hand, and the emotional effects of the process of harvesting organs from brain-dead patients on ventilators, on the other.[22] This situation has provided the impetus to call for a revision of the rules around informed consent and to move to one of two possible procedures: **mandated choice** or **presumed consent**. In the first case, every citizen would be required to make a choice regarding organ donation using some form of universal registration, depending on the jurisdiction. In other words, "all competent adults would be required to decide and record whether or not they wish to become organ donors upon their deaths."[23] This would have the effect of removing the families from the decision-making process at the time of death. In the second case, rather than relying on express consent either through the prior consent of the patient and/or his family, it would be ethically and legally acceptable to retrieve organs unless there has been an explicit indication or refusal to donate. In other words, unless an individual indicates that he or she does *not* consent to donate organs, consent would be presumed, and organs could be automatically retrieved at death. This has been tried in several European countries, but there is no consensus as to whether or not it actually increases the supply of available organs.[24] The importance of individual autonomy in North America works against any move to presumed consent on this side of the Atlantic, at least at the present time.

A variation on presumed consent that is controversial, but has been tried, might be called "anticipated consent." This entails preparing organs for transplant through the injection of organ-preserving drugs into a dying patient while awaiting permission from the family. This would usually occur in emergency room situations where the patient's wishes are not known, and it represents a kind of presumed consent awaiting confirmation. Such a practice runs the risk of harming a patient who is still living. It also "borders on desecration and denies dignity to individuals whose dead bodies are subjected to an invasive procedure without their prior consent."[25] As with many ethical issues relating to organ transplantation, a utilitarian could respond that this is a small price to pay for the benefits that would accrue to many other sick people who need that dying patient's organs. If the family does not agree to organ retrieval, nothing has been lost; if the family does agree, much has been gained.

The discussion in the bioethical literature concerning opting in (prior consent) and opting out (prior refusal of consent) raises a very fundamental question about the relationship of the individual to the state, as well as to the difference between giving (as in prior consent) and taking (as in presumed consent). There is a difference between giving, or allowing something, for the common good, and society taking, or doing what it deems best, for the common good without the consent of the individual whose body or property is in question. In addition, one can seriously question the notion of "the common good" in the context of organ donation. Whatever the number of organs harvested from any one cadaveric donor, there will be relatively few beneficiaries. This is not the meaning of the common good that might typically be appealed to in order to justify the limitations on the freedom and choices of individuals.

It has further been argued that presumed consent is a misnomer, since lack of a signed donor card does not mean that the person in question consented to anything. Veatch and Pitt take a strong position in this regard: "It is our hypothesis that those who support a societal right to procure organs without consent find it embarrassing to speak bluntly about taking organs without consent, hence they adopt the *language* of presuming consent even when there is no *basis* for such a presumption. In doing so they preserve the appearance of the preferred gift-mode and the guise of respect for individual choice."[26] In their view, presumed consent laws are really routine salvaging laws, and they point out that in most countries that have such laws, the words "presumed consent" are not used. These laws tend to state that unless a refusal has been made known, organs may be removed upon death. This seems to lend credence to Veatch and Pitt's point about routine salvaging, although they do admit that "it is more comforting to use the language of gift-giving and consent" than the language of taking and salvaging, and that the "language of consent … may be necessary to win approval of policies that de facto authorize procurement without donation."[27]

Conscription of Organs

There are many who believe that it is necessary to go even further in the quest to obtain enough organs to meet the demand and who recommend adopting a policy of conscription of organs: "Under conscription, all usable organs would be removed from recently deceased people and made available for transplantation; consent would be neither required nor requested and, with the possible exception of people with religious objections, opting-out would not be possible."[28] Those who recommend this approach believe that the need to save lives through organ transplantation overrides respect for individual autonomy, particularly since, in their view, "it makes little sense to speak of autonomy of a dead person."[29] This last statement is not exactly true since there is a long legal (and moral) tradition built around the last will and testament of a dead person, which indicates acceptance of a principle that a person can have posthumous interests and suffer posthumous harms. Glannon argues that since "the body is so closely associated with who we are, we can have an interest in what is done to it even after we cease to exist" and that respect for individual autonomy means that we cannot "assume that something as closely associated with the essence of the individual as his or her body can be appropriated by the state without permission."[30]

Given the already mentioned difficulty of moving to a policy of presumed consent or mandated choice in North America, it is unlikely that a policy of conscription of organs would be publicly acceptable any time soon (although it is argued that any public outrage would be short-lived and people would get used to the idea). Like presumed consent, such a policy would require a major shift in thinking about the relation of the individual and the state. But it would also require a shift in current thinking about the relationship between donors and recipients of organs, since the very nature of a donation is that it is voluntary. As soon as one speaks of a sick person's *right* to an organ, as some do, then one is implying an obligation on the part of every person to allow the taking of his or her organs upon death. This is, in fact, the view of some writers on the subject: giving one's organs is not an act of charity, or a gift; it is, rather, "a moral duty of substantial stringency."[31]

Glannon rejects the notion of conscription of organs but accepts the idea that people have an obligation to donate their organs, based on a principle of giving back as opposed to simply giving.

He sees the obligation as based, not on the rights of others to obtain organs, but on a concept of mutual benefit, "the idea that one shares common interests, needs, and values with other individuals in a community."[32] Success of this strategy would, however, depend on everyone feeling such a sense of obligation, which, given the resistance to signing donor cards in spite of public education efforts, does not seem to be the case. The French anthropologist David LeBreton writes that one can be informed about and still against giving organs. Attitudes toward organ donation (one's own or those of one's family) are rooted in individual morality and values and thus not totally subject to reason and argument.[33]

One fact that is seldom mentioned in the bioethical discussion about increasing the number of cadaver organs is that not everyone who is dying or dead is a candidate for organ retrieval. Not everyone dies in a hospital, not all hospitals are equipped to retrieve organs from dead bodies, and the majority of patients dying of cancer or other terminal illnesses, or simply of old age, do not have healthy organs that can be used for transplant. As pointed out earlier, the ideal—if unfortunate—situation is an otherwise healthy, preferably young, body that is brain dead and on a ventilator. This is a small fraction of actual deaths.

Financial Incentives

As has already been pointed out, one of the more interesting aspects of the question of organ transplantation, is the fact that, while the public seems to accept and approve of organ transplants, most people are reluctant to donate their organs (or a family member's organs) even after death. As a result of this situation, the transplant community is "awash in a sea of proposals calling for the creation of financial incentives"[34] to encourage individuals to agree to donate after death and to encourage families to agree to the donation of the organs of loved ones who are dying. These range from contracts for selling organs at death, to cash rebates, estate tax discounts, or paying for funeral expenses. The rationale for financial incentives is quite simple. As Murray puts it, "If we were to have a widget shortage, economists would tell us how it could be resolved. What gets people to produce more widgets is an increase in the price of widgets. The ordinary workings of supply and demand in a market would increase the price and, hence, the supply."[35] Murray is actually making the point that organs are not widgets and the public seems to recognize this fact. He points out that if the price of widgets were zero, there would be no supply of widgets. However, thousands of organs are supplied each year, indicating that many people are willing to donate organs without any compensation and thus showing that organs are not like widgets. Further, legislatures, professional organizations, and courts have consistently rejected compensation schemes for cadaver organs, while many religious groups view organ transplantation as being moral only to the extent that it respects the dying and the dead, and does not treat the body as a commodity. Paying for organs is seen as reducing the gift of life to a contractual obligation and transforming donors into mere sources. For most commentators, the rules of the marketplace are not appropriate in the world of organ transplantation. But as Murray points out, the "intuitive appeal of a market solution is strong. Markets celebrate individual preference and choice. In ideal markets, people make their own decisions and live with the consequences of those decisions."[36] This is justification enough for those who value individual autonomy and do not see the body as having any intrinsic value beyond what its "owner" chooses to give it. However, some would be quick to point out that, as with living organ sales, those making "their own decisions" to sell their (or their family member's) organs would be the poor, not the rich. And many worry that moving away from voluntary, altruistic donation to commercial sale would actually decrease the supply of organs: those who might otherwise donate might be reluctant to participate in a system based on commercial transactions.

Saints Cosmas and Damian miraculously transplant the (black) leg of a Moor onto the (white) body of Justinian, c.1600s, artist unknown. The idea of replacing body parts has a long history.

BOX 9.2

RUTH RICHARDSON, "CORPSES FOR ANATOMY; ORGANS FOR TRANSPLANTATION"

The activities involved in the dissection of the dead for anatomical study and for transplantation bear close affinities. Both depend upon an accessible supply of dead bodies. Each damages the dead body for the sake of what is generally seen as a greater good....

The great majority of bodies used for dissection, and most organs used for transplantation ... are gifts. This is, however, a comparatively recent phenomenon. Teaching and research in human anatomy were historically rendered difficult and sometimes impossible by a scarcity of corpses upon which to work. Because mutilation of the dead breaks deep-seated taboos in Western culture, historically anatomists met with noncooperation and sometimes outright hostility from the public in obtaining the basic material for their work....

From the inception of surgery in the early Renaissance, those who sought dead human material for dissection have suffered shortage. Put simply, a perception of shortage is not a new problem. Public hostility to the dissection of the dead ensured that demand for corpses always outstripped the legal supply.... The great anatomist William Harvey, who published his work demonstrating the circulation of the blood in 1628 ... dissected the corpses of both his father and his sister. His case, though probably atypical, offers a lucid illustration of one of my key themes: *once the need for human dissection material was recognized, a supply was obtained; and once the supply was obtained, it was found to fall short of demand.* Shortage both intensified demand and prompted illicit supply....

It was probably in the period 1675–1725 that the human corpse began to be bought and sold like any other commodity. Corpses, skeletons, and preserved body parts were sold behind closed doors. The inadequacy of the legal supply led students and professional surgeons to seek elsewhere, and grave-robbing probably served well in a quiet way for a considerable period of time. Opposition made the work hazardous, however, and a class of entrepreneurs—bodysnatchers, or "resurrectionists"—soon arose to procure merchandise for a lucrative black market. Anatomy schools, being established in this period, sold the dismembered parts to students at a profit....

In the early nineteenth century, a significant number of doctors appear to have been comparatively satisfied with the existing system of "authorized stealth"; after all, financial incentives to bodysnatchers had served to produce an adequate supply of corpses for over a century. Corpse deals with bodysnatchers worked, cemented by a bond of mutual secrecy and interdependence—a sort of honor among thieves. Some doctors, however, found shortage intolerable and supported ideas for alternative sources by which the law could accommodate increasing demand. Such ideas focused mainly upon offering incentives to donate, such as sale during life, the offer of money to the relatives of the dead, or the abrogation of death taxes on the estates of those bequeathing their own corpses for dissection....

Nowadays, cloaked in new titles such as *rewarded gifting* and *futures markets*, the very same mechanisms are being mooted as means to promote organ donation. Those raising such ideas seem to be unaware that their arguments are neither new nor original. They should know that these ideas were disposed of as practical alternatives by doctors and lawmakers 150 years ago....

It is a truism of market economics that goods much sought after, but in short supply, fetch high prices. The scientific and therapeutic importance of the human corpse in the past was reflected in its commercial valuation. The attachment of money value to the human body provided the incentive to crime. High prices, severe shortages, and fierce competition between "consumers" all served to weight events in that direction....

Perhaps one of the most remarkable and chilling of the many affinities between the two eras under consideration is that *all* these factors are to some extent active today in the new field of transplantation. The benefits accruing from the quarrying of a single human body are comparatively as great, or indeed greater, today than they were at the time of the Burke and Hare murders.[1] The theft, or surreptitious removal, of body parts is already known to have occurred. The incentive to procure premature death in order to procure human organs already exists.

Note
1. Burke and Hare were two famous bodysnatchers who procured fresh corpses through murder. Murder for anatomy came to be known as "burking," named after Burke himself.

Source: Ruth Richardson, "Fearful Symmetry: Corpses for Anatomy, Organs for Transplantation?" in Stuart J. Youngner, Renée C. Fox, and Laurence J. O'Connell (eds.), *Organ Transplantation: Meanings and Realities* (Madison, WI: University of Wisconsin Press, 1996), 66–83.

Donation after Cardiac Death

Most of the cadaveric organs available for transplant come from brain-dead patients (this is now referred to as donation after brain death, or DBD). However, there are many people who are dying but not brain dead. They may be on a ventilator but still conscious, or if they are not conscious, their brain may still be functioning—and they may have indicated their desire to donate their organs. In these cases, the patient (or family) can request that life support be removed and, when the patient dies shortly thereafter, the organs be donated for transplant. This is referred to as donation after cardiac death (or DCD).

Until recently such donors were referred to as "non-heart-beating donors," an awkward phraseology that differentiates these donors from brain-dead donors whose hearts are actually still beating due to ventilator support. The former are not yet dead; the latter have been declared dead according to the brain-death criterion. As Youngner explains, "After an elaborate informed-consent process, the patient is taken to the operating room ... prepped for surgery, and the ventilator turned off. Two minutes after the heart stops beating, the surgeons come in and remove the organs as quickly as possible to reduce warm ischemia time."[37]

This procedure (known as the Pittsburgh protocol, since it was first implemented at the University of Pittsburgh Medical Centre) is controversial for several reasons. Many critics do not believe that the time period after removal of life support is long enough to ensure that the patient is really dead (by the heart-lung criterion). But, as Youngner points out, it is controversial for another very important reason: "By controlling the time and place of death, the Pittsburgh protocol takes a critical symbolic step: It links the planned death of one human being to the procurement of organs for another."

While this procedure was initially considered quite controversial, in part because preparation for the harvesting of organs takes place before life support is withdrawn, it is now considered an acceptable practice and a way of increasing the supply of organs. Some believe that use of DCD has the potential to increase the supply of available organs by 10–30 percent. While academics still debate the ethics of the procedure, it is actively promoted on organ donation websites. Ontario's Trillium Gift of Life Network informs us that [i]n Ontario, organ and tissue donation after cardiac death (DCD) is now a possibility for patients who do not meet the strict criteria for neurological or brain death. Patients who meet the criteria for DCD are critically ill and dependent on mechanical ventilation. DCD is a possibility for families who have decided to withdraw life sustaining therapy after a physician has determined that there is no long-term prognosis for recovery."[38]

Competent patients can ask that life support be withdrawn when they know their situation is hopeless, and families of incompetent patients can make the same request. Once life support is withdrawn, the patient dies. None of this is controversial or ethically problematic. And if organs can be retrieved from a brain-dead patient with prior consent, why can a dying (but not brain-dead) patient not agree to donate his or her organs as soon as the life support is withdrawn? Youngner is correct in pointing out the critical symbolic step that is being taken in linking the planned death of one patient with the saving from death of another. He is not against the practice and sees the next logical step as extending it to cover voluntary euthanasia and assisted suicide (if, or in his view, when, such practices are permitted): "If we ask patients, as the Pittsburgh protocol does, to become donors when they ask that their ventilators be turned off, why would we not allow them the same prerogative when we help them to commit suicide or put them to death at their own request?"[39]

While Youngner emphasizes the importance of voluntary and informed consent in these situations, many critics see a potential slippery slope to coerced euthanasia and organ donation. At the very least, this practice (and its potential future application) should cause ethicists to take a serious look at the constant and one-sided obsession with supply that is driving the organ transplantation community. This is what sociologist Renée Fox did when she decided to leave the field after 30 years of research on organ transplantation, stating that the "combined impact of the expansion of transplantation, the ardour that has fostered this expansion, the shortage of donated organs that is felt to exist, and the sense of urgency about alleviating the shortage seem to me to be leading to the profanation of the meaning of giving, taking, and receiving human organs, and of the reverent respect for the dignity of human life and death that ought to undergird these acts."[40]

Increasing the Supply: Living Organ Donations

It can be seen from the above analysis that there is a shortage of cadaveric organs that is not easily remedied in spite of decades of effort to find ways around it worldwide. However, living donors can be used for kidney transplants, for bone-marrow transplantation, and sometimes for liver, lung, pancreas, and bowel transplants, where only a segment of the organ is removed from the donor. In some countries, given religious or social resistance to brain death, most or even all transplants use organs from living donors.[41] Removing organs or parts of organs from healthy living donors is ethically problematic from the point of view of the principle of non-malfeasance: a healthy person is being harmed for the benefit of a sick or dying person. So the practice raises several questions, including how much risk is too much for a healthy donor to undergo? This question is particularly important with respect to living donors who are not related to the beneficiary. One can understand why a family member might want to take the risks involved in donating an organ; a parent might experience enormous emotional satisfaction from donating an organ to his or her own child, for example. But why would a complete stranger undertake the risks involved in donating an organ to another person?

In general, the risks fall on the side of the donor and the benefits on the side of the recipient of the organ in question. Removal of a kidney, a liver lobe, or a section of the pancreas requires major surgery. The donor's liver will regenerate over time, and normal functioning can return. However, with kidney donation or donation of part of pancreas or lung, normal functioning does not return. Thus, there is a long-term physical cost to the donor, and donor deaths, while rare, do occur. Kidney transplants from living, related donors have a very high success rate; as a result, the risks to the donor are often ignored or underplayed.[42] At the same time, while a successful liver transplant is life-saving, a kidney transplant is not: dialysis is an option, albeit an inconvenient one. Thus some ethicists question whether kidney transplants from living donors should be encouraged, and some doctors refuse to perform these operations, especially using unrelated donors. The benefits of pancreas transplantation (for diabetics) are uncertain, and some consider live donations unjustifiable. As with the definition of death, the preoccupation here is supply: how to increase the pool of available organs for transplant. Some physicians and surgeons have questioned the justification for living donation that could potentially harm the donor. Yet, living donations are an important avenue to reduce the organ shortage. Without living donors, many patients would be denied transplantation. Consequently, some transplant programs accept living, unrelated kidney donors who are fully informed of the potential risks, benefits, and alternatives.

This practice clearly relies on a utilitarian argument: the ethical justification of the practice is based solely on the consequences. It is similar to the ethical dilemma involved in medical research, and the question is the same: who undergoes the risks and who gets the benefits? However, with respect to medical research, a utilitarian can address the question by weighing the risks to the research subject against the benefits to society as a whole (medical progress, benefits to future sufferers of a disease). Sometimes the research subject undergoing the risk is very sick and feels he has little to lose. However, in the case of organ transplantation, the utilitarian must weigh the risks being undergone by one perfectly healthy individual for the benefit of another single individual. In this case, any risks to the recipient can be justified because he is very sick and possibly dying, so the recipient has little to lose. In addition, the person who needs the organ may be in that situation because of past lifestyle choices, further complicating the ethical dilemma involved in harming a healthy person to save a sick one.[43]

A Kantian would look not at the consequences but at the act in itself: harming one person in order to save another. On the surface at least, this would seem to violate the principle of respect for persons (the second formulation of the Categorical Imperative). As with using people as research subjects, this can be seen as using a person solely as a means to an end. The only way this can be made morally justifiable is through the absolutely free and informed consent of the person undergoing the risk. But can a person agree to undergo any risk, no matter how severe? Is there a limit to the risks a person can take to save another? Does one have an obligation to undertake the risks? No one would fault someone for jumping in the lake to save a drowning person even if it resulted in the loss of the rescuer's life. And one might even blame a potential rescuer for not jumping in the lake if the risk was small (for example, the water was not very deep and the drowning person was a child). But the analogy does not work very well for organ transplantation because, while the rescuer directly aids the drowning victim, the donor of an organ does not directly give it to the recipient: there is a third party (in the form of the doctor or the medical team) who must do the harm. To put this in the context of the drowning analogy, it would be as if a third person pushed the rescuer into the water to save the victim. The principle of non-malfeasance must be taken into consideration in assessing the ethics of using living donors.

At the same time, some commentators point to the fact that there can be considerable benefits to live donors. According to Levey, Hou, and Bush, "Studies of kidney donors who are related to the recipient have revealed that they experience long-lasting positive feelings about their decision to donate, regardless of the success of the transplantation. Many donors report an increased self-esteem and sense of worth. In addition, some report an indirect benefit from the improved health of the recipient."[44] For this reason, many are encouraging an expansion of living donation to include unrelated donors. In most cases such donors would be spouses or friends, but many believe that the possibility should also be open to anyone who might want to donate to an unknown person who needs a transplant. However, vigilance is needed in accepting organs from unrelated donors, who should be assessed as to their understanding of the risks and the voluntary nature of their consent.

In 2002, a 57-year-old journalist died in New York City after an operation to remove part of his liver for transplant. The recipient, his brother, survived and was reported to be doing well. The case raised questions about violation of the principle of non-malfeasance and about the principle of informed consent. Many people believe that free and voluntary consent is not possible in a family situation where one family member will die unless he or she receives an organ from a sibling or a parent, since the donor may feel coerced. As Munson states, "[P]otential donors must be protected from the overt and subtle pressures of friends and relatives. They must be free to say no as well as yes."[45] This is the only way the potential donor's autonomy can be respected. On the other hand, Elliott points out that "it's an odd notion of autonomy which would count emotional ties and moral commitments as constraints on autonomy."[46] Both Munson and Elliott may be right. In some stable, well-functioning families, the emotional ties and moral commitments may be strong and healthy; in dysfunctional families, however, there could be family members who are used or abused in ways that could make the voluntary nature of the choice to donate an organ problematic. Whatever the individual situation, the fact remains that in the New York case mentioned above, the previously healthy donor is dead and the previously dying recipient is alive and well. Munson refers to the dead brother as a "moral hero," pointing out that until we find other sources of organs, we must rely on the courage of people like him.[47] This focus on the demand side of the equation seems to assume that every person in need of an organ should be able to obtain one. This raises the ethical question, though, of whether one person's need (for an organ) creates another person's obligation (to donate), a question that few ethicists would be willing to answer in the affirmative, at least for living donors.[48] Further, given the enormous gap between supply and demand, the question has a very concrete and practical dimension as well.

A Market in Organs?

The desire to increase the supply of, and meet the demand for, organs for transplant has stimulated a lively ethical debate about the desirability of (and ethical justification for) financial compensation for living organ donations; in other words, allowing a legal market in organs (for the most part this would refer, at least for the time being, to sales of kidneys). We live in a capitalist society where commercial transactions are a way of life and "medical advances are making it possible to buy things that were previously unobtainable at any price."[49] Writing about a Turk who sold a kidney for $4400 because he needed the money for an operation for his daughter, Kinsley states: "Capitalism in action: one person had $4,400 and wanted a kidney, another person had a spare kidney and wanted $4,400; so they did a deal.... The buyer avoided a lifetime of dialysis. The seller provided crucial help to his child, at minimum risk to himself."[50]

People are naturally horrified at the idea of the poor selling their kidneys to the rich, but while agreeing that this can be seen as exploitation, some argue that it is just one form of exploitation among others. Further, Kinsley points out that people put their health at risk in more dangerous ways (for example, working in coal mines) to support their families. So, in effect, the horror that we feel at the injustice of a poor Turk selling a kidney to save his daughter is "a sentimental reaction to the injustice of life."[51]

If donating a kidney is a good thing—an act of altruism and generosity that we even admire—what is wrong with selling a kidney? It is no more dangerous for the donor to donate a kidney than to sell one, so protection of the donor (or seller) cannot be the explanation. Further, many people point out that everybody benefits from an organ transplant (recipient, doctors, hospitals, brokers, pharmaceutical companies) except the donor of the organ who, while gaining nothing, undergoes all the risks. What is it about the exchange of money that changes an altruistic action into a reprehensible one?

The most common answer to this question is that the buying and selling of organs transforms the body and its parts into commodities: "The concept that human organs are spare parts that can be bought and sold can adversely influence respect for the human body and human dignity. It puts organ sale in the same category of such paid human body transactions as prostitution and slavery."[52]

In Kantian terms, it is the difference between a thing having *intrinsic* value, meaning that it has value for what it is in itself, and having *instrumental* or use value, meaning that it is valued solely as a means to some other end. From a Kantian perspective, the human body is something that has intrinsic value and is not something from which pieces can be detached and sold. It is not a commodity. Thinking of bodily organs as objects that can be bought and sold is to treat them solely as means. It is to detach them from any notion of the person. As Leon Kass so vividly puts it, "Selling our bodies, we come perilously close to selling out our souls. There is even a danger in contemplating such a prospect; for if we come to think about ourselves as pork bellies, pork bellies we will become."[53]

The tendency in modern Western thought to see the person as something different from the body entails the tendency to think of one's body as something separate from one's self. It is to see it as something one owns: it's *my* body and I can do what I want with it! Thus many people already see their body and its parts as objects, and as we have seen with reproductive technologies, the idea of buying or selling parts of the body is not necessarily shocking to everyone. We are not all Kantians!

Some philosophers who argue in favour of the commercialization of organs do so based on a difference between objectification of the person and objectification of the body. Wilkinson, for example, says, "[I]t's fairly easy to show why the objectification of persons might be thought to be wrong. Things are not so straightforward, however, when it comes to bodies.... Bodies and body parts are physical objects. Hence, any ethical concerns that we have about the objectification of bodies can't be about whether bodies are treated as objects—since they are objects."[54] The issue is whether or not we treat the body as a *mere* object. Wilkinson argues that what really bothers those who are against a market in organs is the connection between bodies and persons. When we treat a body as a mere object, we act as if it were not the body of a person: "For example, if I act on another person's body without requiring and obtaining her consent, this may amount, in a sense, to treating her body as if it's not 'hers' (as if it's a mere body)."[55] Consent of the person is what acts as a brake on treating someone's body as a *mere* body. From this point of view then, if a person gives valid consent, buying her kidney is not treating either her (the person) or her body as a mere object. Whether this argument would pass muster with Kant is unclear: Kant's discussion of duties to self suggests that consenting to turn oneself into an object for the use of others is wrong—and doing it for money is even more so.[56]

BOX 9.3

J. RADCLIFFE-RICHARDS ET AL., "THE CASE FOR ALLOWING KIDNEY SALES"

Most people will recognize in themselves the feelings of outrage and disgust that led to an outright ban on kidney sales, and such feelings typically have a force that seems to their possessors to need no further justification. Nevertheless, if we are to deny treatment to the suffering and dying we need better reasons than our own feelings of disgust....

The commonest objection to kidney selling is expressed on behalf of the vendors: the exploited poor, who need to be protected against the greedy rich. However, the vendors are themselves anxious to sell, and see this practice as the best option open to them. The worse we think the selling of a kidney, therefore the worse should seem the position of the vendors when that option is removed. Unless this appearance is illusory, the prohibition of sales does even more harm than first seemed, in harming vendors as well as recipients. To this argument it is replied that the vendors' apparent choice is not genuine. It is said that they are likely to be too uneducated to understand the risks, and that this precludes informed consent. It is also claimed that, since they are coerced by their economic circumstances, their consent cannot count as genuine.

Although both these arguments appeal to the importance of autonomous choice, they are quite different. The first claim is that the vendors are not competent to make a genuine choice within a given range of options. The second, by contrast, is that poverty has so restricted the range of options that organ selling has become the best, and therefore, in effect, that the range is too small. Once this distinction is drawn, it can be seen that neither argument works as a justification of prohibition.

If our ground for concern is that the range of choices is too small, we cannot improve matters by removing the best option that poverty has left, and making the range smaller still.... The other line of argument may seem more promising, since ignorance does preclude informed consent. However, the likely ignorance of the subjects is not a reason for banning altogether a procedure for which consent is required. In other contexts, the value we place on autonomy leads us to insist on information and counselling, and that is what it should suggest in the case of organ selling as well....

The risk involved in nephrectomy is not in itself high, and most people regard it as acceptable for living related donors. Since the procedure is, in principle, the same for vendors as for unpaid donors, any systematic difference between the worthwhileness of the risk for vendors and donors presumably lies on the other side of the calculation, in the expected benefit. Nevertheless, the exchange of money cannot in itself turn an acceptable risk into an unacceptable one from the vendor's point of view. It depends entirely on what the money is wanted for.

In general, furthermore, the poorer a potential vendor, the more likely it is that the sale of a kidney will be worth whatever risk there is. If the rich are free to engage in dangerous sports for pleasure, or dangerous jobs for high pay, it is difficult to see why the poor who take the lesser risk of kidney selling for greater rewards—perhaps saving relatives' lives, or extricating themselves from poverty and debt—should be thought so misguided as to need saving from themselves....

Another familiar objection is that it is unfair for the rich to have privileges not available to the poor. This argument, however, is irrelevant to the issue of organ selling as such. If organ selling is wrong for this reason, so are all benefits available to the rich, including all private medicine, and, for that matter, all public provision of medicine in rich countries (including transplantation of donated organs) that is unavailable in poor ones....

It must be stressed that we are not arguing for the positive conclusion that organ sales must always be acceptable, let alone that there should be an unfettered market.... Nevertheless, we claim that the burden of proof remains against the defenders of prohibition, and that until good arguments appear, the presumption must be that the trade should be regulated rather than banned altogether.

Source: J. Radcliffe-Richards et al., "The Case for Allowing Kidney Sales," *The Lancet*, 351 (June 27, 1998): 1950–1952.

Canada has always had an altruistic blood donation system, and it works well. Canada has also, since 2003, made it illegal to buy and sell gametes (sperm and ova) for reproductive purposes and to pay for the services of a surrogate. These policies are based on principles relating to the dignity of the human body: that it is not, or should not be, an object of commerce. The fact that Canada's blood collection is based on altruism is used by many as an example of the positive effects of altruism, and as a reason why we should not allow the principles of the market to infringe on the current altruistic system of organ donation. In the U.S., where the blood collection system is commercialized, there are relatively few voluntary donations of blood. Many fear that altruistic donation of organs would diminish if the collection of organs were commercialized.

Those in favour of a market in organs point to the great need of organs, as evidenced by long waiting lists, and to the fact that an outright ban on organ sales causes harm—both to those who need an organ and are willing to pay for it, and to those who need money and are willing to sell an organ to obtain it. Because of the harm being caused, in their view, the onus is on those who are against organ sales to make the moral case, not on those who are in favour. They also point out that the ban is not working since there is an illegal market in organs operating worldwide: "In spite of being almost universally criminalized and condemned, a 'black market' in organs persists, particularly in 'developing' countries like India. That this is so should hardly be surprising given the desperation which exists on both sides of the transaction: the desperation of Americans and Europeans who urgently need (and can afford to pay for) kidneys and that of the organ vendors who need the money."[57]

The existence of a black market in organs was not openly admitted to for several decades (falling, according to bioethical writers, into the realm of urban myths), but in the last several years it has become too widespread to ignore and discussions are now appearing in the mainstream bioethical literature. Nancy Scheper-Hughes, an American anthropologist who has followed and documented the organ trade (both legal and illegal) for more than a decade, writes that the global demand for organs has brought "strange markets and occult economies" in its wake:

> The ideal conditions of economic globalization have put into circulation mortally sick bodies travelling in one direction and healthy organs (encased in their human packages) in another, creating a bizarre kula ring of international trade in bodies. The emergence of the organs markets, excess capital, renegade surgeons, and local kidney hunters with links to organized crime, have stimulated the growth of a spectacularly lucrative international transplant tourism, much of it illegal and clandestine. In all, these new transplant transactions are a blend of altruism and commerce; of consent and coercion; of gifts and theft; of care and invisible sacrifice.[58]

Transplant Tourism

A serious discussion of the issue of the black market in organs now exists in the bioethical literature under the heading of "transplant tourism." Buying an organ is illegal in Canada, as it is in most countries (except Iran). However, "many destination countries have thriving black markets, either due to their willful failure to police the practice or more good faith lack of resources to detect it."[59] More and more North Americans, desperate for a life-saving organ, are taking advantage of this situation if they can afford the price (which can run as high as $150,000 or more). While by definition it is difficult to measure a black market, the illegal trade in organs is estimated to generate from $600 million to $1.2 billion USD a year in profits.[60]

In Scheper-Hughes' opinion, bioethical arguments in favour of buying and selling organs arise out of European and North American values of autonomy and individual choice, and "create the semblance of ethical choice in an intrinsically unethical context. The choice to sell a kidney in an urban slum of Calcutta or in a Brazilian favela or a Philippine shantytown is often anything but a free and autonomous one."[61] Selling a kidney, for example, is often an act of desperation for the poor of third-world countries, and as badly off as they must be to do this, they can end up even worse off as they find themselves after the surgery shunned by their families, unable to work in jobs that demand heavy labour, and in poor health with no medical care. Such transactions represent exploitation at its worst rather than simple contracts between buyers and sellers providing utility on both sides, as the proponents of an organs market would have us believe. In the words of Scheper-Hughes, "[T]he traffic in kidneys reduces the human content of all the lives it touches."[62]

Others would disagree. De Castro points out that not all exchanges of services that involve money necessarily involve commodification, for example, in cases of reward for exemplary service or for a very important donation.

> We give monetary rewards to citizens for noteworthy accomplishments ... [and] to outstanding and dedicated teachers. We also give special monetary benefits to family members left behind by soldiers killed in battle. It does not usually cross our minds that the giving or acceptance of the reward may commodify the recipient or diminish the value of his or her contribution to society.[63]

De Castro also uses examples such as birthday, condolence, and baptismal gifts that can be in the form of money without anyone thinking that money changing hands makes these activities suspicious: "[o]n the contrary, money has important symbolisms for various practices and traditions."[64] No one would argue against this kind of reward or recognition for special service or for special occasions. Similarly, it would be difficult to argue that recognition, for example, for exemplary service to the community in the form of regular blood donations would amount to the commodification of blood. But this is quite different from financial payment for a kidney arranged in advance through a contract or written agreement. The seller does not provide his kidney and then unexpectedly find himself rewarded for his altruistic act. In the case of transplant tourism, a clear agreement on the financial transaction is made before the sale. On the other hand, de Castro is correct in pointing out that commodification of organs "is not something that is still waiting to happen."[65] It is a fact that an exploitative legal trade and a even more exploitative illegal trade in organs is occurring internationally and that stopping it will likely be impossible.

Given that stopping the illegal trade in organs is likely impossible, we are faced with the very practical issue outlined in our opening case study presentation. People are going abroad for organs; the situation for preoperative as well as post-operative care in the host countries is, as stated in our hypothetical case, "suboptimal"; and people are returning to Canada in dire need of medical care and, in some cases, another organ transplant. How can doctors and hospitals respond to this need without becoming complicit in the illegal trade and the exploitation of which Scheper-Hughes writes? But how can they not respond to this need without violating the principle of beneficence and their duty to treat?

Following the Istanbul Declaration of 2008, a non-binding international agreement to ban organ trafficking, the Canadian Society of Transplantation and the Canadian Society of Nephrology issued a policy statement on organ trafficking and transplant tourism to "provide healthcare professionals with a framework to approach the subject of transplant tourism and organ trafficking with patients."[66]

The policy statement deals with both pre-transplantation and post-transplantation issues relating to patients who decide to go abroad for an organ transplant. It recommends that all patients who are candidates for transplantation be given information about the illegal trade in organs. Anyone considering such a move should be told how those who sell their organs might be harmed through the forceful harvesting of organs (sometimes obtained by killing the "donor"). The statement warns that "[t]he entire transplant tourism industry relies on secrecy, making it impossible to determine whether donor information provided by organ brokers, who are motivated by financial gain, is accurate."[67] Further, doctors are counselled not to "prescribe medications or otherwise facilitate obtainment of medications that will be used during the transplantation of a purchased organ."[68] In addition, they may choose not to provide medical records to patients if they believe the patients are travelling for an illegal transplant. With respect to post-transplant obligations, physicians are reminded of their responsibility to treat in cases of emergency. In relation to ongoing care, physicians who object to being implicated in an illegal transplant situation are required to find a replacement physician for the post-transplant care of the patient, and they should inform the patient ahead of time as to their personal position on the issue.[69]

The policy document attempts to walk a fine line between physicians' complicity in an illegal (and often deadly) practice and their responsibility to treat a patient in need. It is a moral line and one that Canadian law has not attempted to deal with, at least in relation to the illegal trade abroad (organ sales are illegal *in* Canada). However, one MP tried to address the issue through a private member's bill (Bill C-381, sponsored by Liberal MP Borys Wrzesnewskyj, and introduced in the House of Commons in 2009 and again in 2011) that recommended penal sanctions for anyone involved in the illegal obtention of human organs, either inside Canada or abroad. The bill—as with most private member's bills—did not pass.

However, the Instanbul Declaration appears to have had some effect. Several countries (including China) have since instituted legislation against the illegal traffic in organs. Further, in 2013, five people, including two doctors, were put on trial in Kosovo after being charged with organ trafficking, their network having "lured poor people to the country to sell their kidneys and other organs to wealthy transplant recipients from Israel, the United States, Canada and Germany. Organs sold for as much as $130,000 each."[70] Three of the five received sentences of three to eight years' imprisonment. Some commentators argue that a very stringently regulated legal trade in organs might reduce the worst of the current illegal exploitation. For many, however, this is a political or legal solution, not a philosophical or ethical one.

Increasing the Supply: Xenotransplantation

The transplantation of an organ from an animal to a human is called a **xenotransplant** or **xenograft**. One of the first xenotransplants was done in California in 1984 on a human infant known in the bioethical literature as Baby Fae.[71] Several unsuccessful attempts had been made on adults before this one, with recipients living from a few hours to several days.

Born three weeks early and weighing just five pounds, Baby Fae was suffering from hypoplastic left heart syndrome, a fatal condition that affects 1 in 10,000 newborns. Baby Fae underwent a heart transplant, receiving the heart of a young baboon (named Goobers) from a colony kept to supply medical centres with primates. The operation appeared to be successful. Dr. Leonard Bailey, who performed the transplant operation, stated that Goobers' heart would grow along with Baby Fae and that she might live to celebrate her 20th birthday. But just five days later, Baby Fae's body began to reject the organ. She died on November 15, having lived for 21 days with the heart of Goobers. In another milestone case of xenotransplantation in 1992, a 32-year-old man who was HIV positive and suffering from hepatitis B became the first recipient of a baboon liver. He lived for 70 days.[72]

Aside from the experimental nature of these operations, which raises serious ethical questions on its own, xenotransplantation raises other issues, "challenging divisions between individual and public health, human and animal identity and welfare, and scientific progress and public concern about risk."[73] Ethical concerns about xenotransplantation fall into three categories: the impact on our understanding of being human; the question of risk in relation to the experimental nature of the procedure, as well as the problem of the possible transfer of animal disease to humans, called **zoonosis** (or **xenosis**); and the ethics of using animals as a source of spare parts for humans.

Crossing the Species Barrier

The practice of xenotransplantation crosses the species divide between animals and humans in two ways: first, by the implantation of animal organs in human bodies; and second, by the genetic manipulation of animals (the insertion of human genes into pigs, for example) to reduce the rejection phenomenon that is much stronger in animal-to-human transplants than in human-to-human transplants. Hanson states: "The creation of transgenic animals and the placement of their organs and tissues within human beings transgresses boundaries long established and maintained by evolution.… Placing human genes in pigs and pig organs in human beings may not only be scientifically risky, it promotes subtle but not insignificant changes in world view and self-understanding."[74]

Xenotransplantation confronts us with the question of what it means to be human and whether or not it is intrinsically wrong to treat the human body this way. Margaret Somerville sees it as a question of our sense of *identity* as human beings: "Does xenotransplantation take us yet one more step away from an integrated theory of personal identity and towards a modular theory of human identity … towards seeing ourselves simply as a series of interchangeable parts?"[75]

This is a good question but one that has been answered by our general acceptance of human-to-human organ transplantation: we already have a modular theory of human identity and do not see any moral problem in putting the organs of one human being into another. Thus, one must ask whether or not the transplantation of a pig liver is *intrinsically* different from the transplantation of a human liver.[76] Given the philosophical difficulties in determining precisely what makes us human, this question does not receive a great deal of attention in the bioethical literature. Those who think there is something intrinsically wrong in crossing the species divide have difficulty presenting arguments as to why this is so. To say that the human is unique, or sacred, or superior to the animal body is, for some, just another indication of "speciesism" (the discrimination against animals that was raised in Chapter 3) and is not something that is scientifically defensible. To hold to this on purely religious grounds is not acceptable for those who do not share the religious sentiment. To say that crossing the species divide is unnatural is also not seen as a strong argument. Caplan points out that "naturalness is very much a function of familiarity.… [F]acing death, most will probably accept a transplant and decide to deal with the naturalness issue later."[77] Any argument about the sanctity of the human body or the unnaturalness of crossing the species divide must compete with utilitarian arguments about the importance of saving lives and with the recognition, once again, of the dramatic shortage of organs needed to obtain that medical objective.

The Question of Risk

Those who seriously question the ethics of xenotransplantation do so based largely on the possibility of unforeseen negative consequences to the recipients of these organs and to the public in general. There are considerable risks in crossing the human-animal divide that are not philosophical but practical: there are a number of known, as well as the possibility of unknown, dangers that must be overcome before xenotransplantation can be considered ethically justifiable. Further, it is difficult to overcome these dangers without experimenting, and such experimentation is ethically problematic, as already seen in the case of Baby Fae.

The greatest danger is the risk of zoonosis (or xenosis), the transfer of animal disease to humans. Hanson points out that scientists can only screen for known diseases whereas some disease they know nothing about could be transferred. This means that "the consequences of infection by retroviruses from the source animals require rigorous study.... [T]he risk may be extremely small, but the consequences of spawning a new pandemic are catastrophic."[78]

Thus the benefits foreseen by xenotransplantation must be weighed against the risks to public health (not just the health of recipients of the organs, but the health of their families and the public in general). Further, the consequences of inserting human genes into pigs are also unknown. What would happen if the meat from genetically modified pigs entered the human food chain? Given the public's propensity to panic in the face of threats such as vCJD (mad cow disease), bird flu, and, more recently, swine flu, it is remarkable that there is so little public discussion of the potential consequences of xenotransplantation, especially using animals containing human genes.

Given these risks, is it ethical to be experimenting on patients who need a transplant? At the moment, xenotransplantation cannot be considered therapy; it is experimentation. The questions raised earlier in relation to research versus therapy apply here. Is it possible for a dying person to give truly informed consent? And should people who are dying be considered appropriate research subjects? The authors of a recent article on research ethics (referred to in our discussion of brain death in Chapter 8) point out that "there have as yet not been any experiments of solid organ xenotransplantation conducted on humans which can be called successful.... [I]mmunological adverse reactions of xenograft organs have limited the best survival rates of recipients to a few months."[79] The authors recognize that "xenotransplantation trials on living human subjects would intrude upon generally accepted ethical codes and rights regarding experimentation on humans."[80] However, the solution they propose is equally fraught with ethical problems. They suggest using patients in a persistent vegetative state (PVS) as research subjects. As support for their argument, they cite the American Medical Association's Council on Ethical and Judicial Affairs, which recommended the retrieval of organs from anencephalic infants, and the arguments of others who argue in favour of using PVS patients as a source of donor organs. The next logical step, they maintain, is that "not only the donation of organs but of the entire body for scientific research should be permissible for PVS bodies on the condition that former consent has been obtained."[81] Scientific research for them includes xenotransplantation trials. Since people in a persistent vegetative state can be kept alive indefinitely, long-term research on xenotransplantation can be undertaken under conditions that would not threaten family members or the general population. This would allow researchers to fully test the safety issues before undertaking clinical application on a large scale.

It is with this recent recommendation that the connection between brain death and organ transplantation comes full circle: the use of the higher-brain-death criterion to permit the use of "bodies" that would serve either as donors (for human-to-human transplantation) or as research objects (for animal-to-human transplantation), with both practices receiving their ethical justification solely from the inexhaustible need for replacement organs.

What about the Animals?

For many, the most important ethical question that must be faced in relation to xenotransplantation is whether or not it is morally justifiable to use animals in this way, as a means to human ends. Writing about the Baby Fae case, philosopher and animal rights activist Tom Regan argues that Goobers (the baboon) should not have been seen as existing solely as a resource for Baby Fae and that the animal's right to be treated with respect was violated. According to Regan, "That she could do nothing to protest, and that many of us failed to recognize the transplant for the injustice that it was, does not diminish the wrong, a wrong settled before Baby Fae's sad death."[82]

The issues here echo the concerns already raised in our discussion of the use of animals in medical research (see Chapter 4), and as we saw, not everyone would agree with Regan's claim that Goobers had a right to be treated with respect. But the issue of xenotransplantation differs from normal medical research in that it is complicated by the genetic engineering of transplant animals and the need to keep these animals completely free of disease. This requires that they live in unnatural, sterile, and isolated environments, potentially in large-scale breeding colonies. Hundreds of animals are being sacrificed in the research involved in developing the appropriate genetic modifications. Further, research piglets are born by Caesarean section, "the sow is not recovered from the procedure, and the piglets are hand-raised under sterile conditions, with little or no contact with humans and none with other pigs."[83]

Thus the ethical issues go beyond the simple killing of the animal for its organs to encompass the whole life of the animal, as well as the routine destruction of many animals in the research effort needed to perfect the procedures around xenotransplantation. How much animal suffering can be tolerated in our quest to increase the supply of donor organs for transplant, especially when the consequences of transplanting animal organs in human bodies are unknown? This is a case where we must seriously ask whether the risks are worth the benefits.

The Gift of Life. The discourse of organ transplantation veils the reality that organs come from real human bodies and that in order for one person to live, another has to die.

CONTROLLING THE DEMAND: ALLOCATION ISSUES

For many ethicists, the most important ethical question regarding the practice of organ transplants is not related to its questionable connection with brain death, or to the means of increasing the supply, but to the distribution of what is often referred to simply as a scarce resource. Many bioethics textbooks, for example, place the whole issue of organ transplantation within a chapter dealing with the distribution of scarce medical resources and centre their discussion on issues relating to distributive justice. As we have seen, organs for transplant are in short supply, and the demand for them is great. Thus decisions must be made about who gets what organ and when; and since many people die while still on the waiting list, these are life and death decisions. As Caplan and Coelho put it, "[T]he resolution of the terrifying dilemma of who lives and who dies when shortage is a reality is an omnipresent ethical challenge in transplantation."[84]

Does a person's so-called social worth matter in deciding which of two patients should receive the one available organ? Should it go to a man with three children to support rather than an unmarried drifter? Does a woman who has worked for her community all her life deserve an organ more than a young man who has just moved to town and has a criminal record? Does someone in Ontario in desperate need have a right to an organ retrieved in B.C., or should it be reserved for someone on the waiting list in B.C. even though the Ontario person's need is greater? Does an alcoholic have a right to a liver transplant? Should he or she be on the waiting list at all?

Caplan and Coelho point out that one can look at allocation from two different points of view: maximizing the chance of success of a transplant or responding to the most urgent need for a transplant. The first position would favour relatively younger, healthier, and more robust patients who would live longer. The second would favour those who are closer to death and who might be older and sicker, and thus not live as long. For example, someone who has already had a transplant that is now being rejected would be chosen over the younger patient with overall better health if medical necessity were the main criterion. Another medical criterion linked to the chance-of-success point of view is the availability of a supportive family environment to ensure successful aftercare, a serious medical consideration in any organ transplant. However, Annas points out that this supposedly medical criterion actually hides a social worth criterion: it "discriminates against individuals without families and those who have become alienated from their families. The criterion may be relevant, but it is hardly medical."[85] Even criteria relating to compatibility of blood and tissue type are considered by some to be discriminatory. If most of the available organs are from Caucasians, fewer blacks or Asians will be considered compatible recipients due to increased chance of rejection (and thus diminished chance of success).

Thus, it is "not always obvious what is fair when allocating scarce medical resources. Our desire to rescue the sick conflicts with our desire to do the greatest good for the greatest number."[86] However, there is a larger allocation problem that is less often discussed. If we want to do the greatest good for the greatest number, should organ transplantation even be among the services that a public health plan provides? It is hugely expensive and absorbs a disproportionately large portion of hospital resources, often for questionable benefits. Is an extra few years of life for one person a justifiable benefit when the cost is so high and it takes money and other resources away from other health needs? This question was tackled by the State of Oregon in 1987 when it discontinued Medicaid funding for organ transplants in order to expand coverage of basic medical services for low-income women and children. The move was very controversial but was seen by the governor of the time as being necessary: "We all hate it, but we can't walk away from this issue any more. It goes way beyond transplants. How can we spend every nickel in support of a few people when thousands never see a doctor or eat a decent meal?"[87] The demand for organs is not going to diminish with an aging population. The fastest growing group on the waiting lists consists of people over 70, many of them with other health problems, raising the question of how many resources (human and financial) can be allocated to this very costly branch of medicine in a public health system. Should we not be allocating more resources to preventing the very conditions that cause so many people to be on the waiting lists in the first place? Should we not be asking why there are so many people with diabetes and kidney disease? How many of those who need kidneys or livers are in need because of lifestyles that rendered them ill? Should our efforts to educate potential donors not be accompanied by efforts to educate potential recipients long before they become sick? As Mary Midgley points out with her usual candour, "[M]uch of the demand for liver transplants is due to alcohol. But it is a lot harder to think what to do about alcohol than it is to call for research on transplants."[88] Perhaps the single focus on increasing the supply should be shifted to reducing the demand through educating the public to care for its individual and collective health.

TISSUES AND GENES AS PROPERTY

This chapter has been devoted so far to the ethical issues surrounding the procurement and distribution of solid bodily organs. Our chapter on reproductive technologies dealt with the donation and buying and selling of eggs, sperm, and embryos. The development of biotechnology has expanded the scope of body parts and tissues that have become desirable products for commercialization, expanding some of the ethical issues already discussed and, at the same time, raising new ones. Blood has been collected for decades for transfusion and the saving of lives, but now it is collected for developing cell lines for research and for developing pharmaceuticals. Tissue that used to be considered waste (for example, from biopsies or from surgery) can be transformed into genetic material for therapeutic use. According to Nelkin and Andrews, the development of markets in these tissues has "increased the value of human tissue, and institutions with ready access to tissue find they possess a capital resource."[89] Thus hospitals enter into agreements with biotechnology firms to provide them with tissues, for example, from cancer biopsies, and doctors will even sell patient blood samples. Nelkin and Andrews remark, "Human tissue has become so valuable that it is sometimes a target for corporate espionage and theft."[90] People with rare diseases are finding themselves in a position of having samples of their blood, sperm, or other tissues collected, not for their own treatment, but for research purposes (and, ultimately, financial gain for the researchers). The case of John Moore and his spleen cells discussed in Chapter 6 (see "Cases of Interest") is an example of this practice. When Moore discovered that he had become a patent number he stated: "My doctors are claiming that my humanity, my genetic essence, is their invention and their property. They view me as a mine from which to extract biological material. I was harvested."[91]

The problem with what some refer to as biopiracy can only grow as biotechnology firms develop ever more uses for the tissues, cells, and genes of individual human bodies. Questions about autonomy are relevant here, as they are in relation to organ retrieval, but here the issues are more complex. Much of the tissue being used is made available following normal testing and treatment of patients (post-operative waste, blood samples, aborted fetuses, placentas). In the past, it would have been discarded; now it is extremely valuable for research and for the development of pharmaceutical products (and even cosmetic products) that can make some people very rich. So do the ethical problems revolve around using the material itself—material that formerly would have been thrown away? Or do they revolve around questions about who is making how much money from whose body parts? Further, it is fair to ask whether or not a surgically removed tumour or spleen can even be considered a body part in the normal sense of the term. People do not usually reclaim their cysts, tumours, or surgically removed bits of body, and these may have been used in the past for research or educational purposes with nobody objecting. It is difficult to claim ownership in bodily waste. If researchers and pharmaceutical companies were not getting rich (for example, if all the research were done by governments and the resulting products owned by the public), would there be an ethical problem?

In some ways this is nothing more than an extension of medicine as an industry, one that operates more and more in collaboration with the pharmaceutical industry, something that society seems already to accept. Drug companies make profits on the immunosuppressive drugs related to organ transplantation, or the chemotherapy and post-operative drugs of breast cancer survivors. Hospitals (and their doctors) make a lot of money from organ transplantation (and, as seen in Chapter 8, from neonatal intensive care units). People who need an organ are not restrained by arguments of justice from exploiting the poor in third-world countries to get a kidney, so why should we be shocked that researchers should exploit patients by recuperating their tissues and cells when the exploitation does not involve harming the patient? Where should we look for our ethical guidance in the high-technology world of divisible bodies? Scheper-Hughes' comments regarding organ markets are applicable here as well: "[N]either Aristotle nor Aquinas is with us. Instead, we are asked to take counsel from the new discipline of bioethics that has been finely calibrated to meet the needs of advanced biomedical technologies and the desires of postmodern medical consumers."[92] These are strong words that challenge the field of biomedical ethics to stop and take a look at what the body has become in the world of medicine. Perhaps we can begin to balance utilitarian concerns about ends with Kantian concerns about the means used to achieve them, and take more seriously the notion that the human body has intrinsic, as opposed to instrumental, value. But as we have seen in this chapter and in the last, this is very difficult to do. The instrumental value of the body is so apparent and its life-saving benefits so obvious that arguments against such use fall on deaf ears. As Willard Gaylin put it over 40 years ago, "Cost-benefit analysis is always least satisfactory when the costs must be measured in one realm and the benefits in another. The analysis is particularly skewed when the benefits are specific, material, apparent, and immediate, and the price to be paid is general, spiritual, abstract, and of the future."[93] The ethical conflict comes down to the saving of lives on the one hand and a metaphysical discussion of the value of the human body on the other. In the context of society's priority for extending life at any cost, it is not surprising that the arguments in favour of life continue to hold greater weight. Very few of us today agree with Socrates' statement that death is not the worst thing.

BOX 9.4 REBECCA SKLOOT, "HENRIETTA LACKS"

There's a photo on my wall of a woman I've never met, its left corner torn and patched together with tape. She looks straight into the camera and smiles, hands on hips, dress suit neatly pressed, lips painted deep red. It's the late 1940s and she hasn't yet reached the age of thirty....

No one knows who took that picture, but it's appeared hundreds of times in magazines and science textbooks, on blogs and laboratory walls. She's usually identified as Helen Lane, but often she has no name at all. She's simply called HeLa, the code name given to the world's first immortal human cells—*her* cells, cut from her cervix just months before she died. Her real name is Henrietta Lacks.

I've spent years staring at that photo, wondering what kind of life she led, what happened to her children, and what she'd think about cells from her cervix living on forever— bought, sold, packaged, and shipped by the trillions to laboratories around the world. I've tried to imagine how she'd feel knowing that her cells went up in the first space missions to see what would happen to human cells in zero gravity, or that they helped with some of the most important advances in medicine: the polio vaccine, chemotherapy, cloning, gene mapping, in vitro fertilization. I'm pretty sure that she—like most of us—would be shocked to hear that there are trillions more of her cells growing in laboratories now than there ever were in her body....

Henrietta died in 1951 from a vicious case of cervical cancer.... But before she died, a surgeon took samples of her tumor and put them in a petri dish. Scientists had been trying to keep human cells alive in culture for decades, but they all eventually died. Henrietta's were different: they reproduced an entire generation every twenty-four hours, and they never stopped. They became the first immortal human cells ever grown in a laboratory....

Her cells were part of research into the genes that cause cancer and those that suppress it; they helped develop drugs for treating herpes, leukemia, influenza, hemophilia, and Parkinson's disease; and they've been used to study lactose digestion, sexually transmitted diseases, appendicitis, human longevity, mosquito mating, and the negative cellular effects of working in sewers. Their chromosomes and proteins have been studied with such detail and precision that scientists know their every quirk. Like guinea pigs and mice, Henrietta's cells have become the standard laboratory workhorse....

When I tell people the story of Henrietta Lacks and her cells, their first question is usually *Wasn't it illegal for doctors to take Henrietta's cells without her knowledge? Don't doctors have to tell you when they use your cells in research?* The answer is no—not in 1951, and not in 2009, when this book went to press.

Today most Americans [and Canadians] have their tissue on file somewhere. When you go to the doctor for a routine blood test or to have a mole removed, when you have an appendectomy, tonsillectomy, or any other kind of *ectomy*, the stuff you leave behind doesn't always get thrown out. Doctors, hospitals, and laboratories keep it. Often indefinitely....

Scientists use these samples to develop everything from flu vaccines to penis-enlargement products. They put cells in culture dishes and expose them to radiation, drugs, cosmetics, viruses, household chemicals, and biological weapons, and then study their responses. Without these tissues, we would have no tests for diseases like hepatitis and HIV; no vaccines for rabies, smallpox, measles; none of the promising new drugs for leukemia, breast cancer, colon cancer. And developers of the products that rely on human biological materials would be out billions of dollars.

How you should feel about all this isn't obvious. It's not as if scientists are stealing your arm or some vital organ. They're using tissue scraps you parted with voluntarily. Still, that often involves someone taking part of you. And people often have a strong sense of ownership when it comes to their bodies. Even tiny scraps of them. Especially when they hear that someone else might be making money off those scraps, or using them to uncover potentially damaging information about their genes and medical histories. But a *feeling* of ownership doesn't hold up in court. And at this point no case law has fully clarified whether you own or have the right to control your tissues. When they're part of your body, they're clearly yours. Once they're excised, your rights get murky.

Source: Rebecca Skloot, *The Immortal Life of Henrietta Lacks* (New York: Random House, 2010), 1–4, 315–317.

ETHICAL THEORY AND ORGAN TRANSPLANTATION

Once again the ethical theories that have served Western society in the past do not seem adequate to address many of the questions of bioethics, and the complex and ever-changing web of issues relating to organ procurement and transplantation stretches their analytic capacity to the limit. Many approaches to the ethical issues raised have already been discussed within the chapter and we will simply provide a summary here.

Kantianism can address some of the issues relating to autonomy, at least in relation to the procurement of organs. A Kantian would tend to take a hard line in defending autonomy and informed consent in all procurement procedures and policies, and would be unlikely to condone the exploitation of poverty-stricken Asians by rich North Americans in search of a kidney or the use of Chinese prisoners as so-called donors, again for rich North Americans. One might appeal to the Kantian principle of respect for persons in some procurement practices, but this principle is not very helpful in the grey area of brain death and brain-dead bodies—which, because the patients involved have been declared dead, and are thus not "persons," no one is obligated to respect. Further, as we have seen, some thinkers maintain that it is possible to respect a person while making good use of one of his or her body parts—as long as the person consents. This underlines the philosophical reality that many of the issues in this chapter boil down to metaphysical questions that do not have easy—or generally accepted—answers.

One might be inclined to look to utilitarianism for guidance on some of these questions, but this theory also comes up short much of the time. To rely on the principle of the greatest good for the greatest number is not necessarily a secure philosophical position on which to base justification of many of the practices discussed in this chapter. It necessitates acceptance of the premise that saving lives is always the greatest good (something that in a time of aging populations and diminishing health resources cannot be accepted without argument). It also necessitates accepting the premise that organ transplantation serves the greatest number in society, something that is open to question. In reality the practice absorbs extensive medical resources to extend the lives of relatively few people—and not always for a long time or with a good quality of life. Thus, some of the communitarian arguments raised in this chapter (regarding donation of organs—either at death or while still living—as an individual's moral responsibility to society) might not pass the test of the hedonistic calculus. The utilitarian arguments made to support buying and selling organs through a simple and reductionist cost-benefit analysis are also questionable when looked at from the point of view of Bentham's calculus (how do we include in our calculation of benefits and harms, for example, the harm to a small Pakistani village where the majority of healthy young men are in ill health and can no longer do heavy labour because they sold a kidney to get out of debt—and are most likely in debt again?). Further, many utilitarians would have serious problems with xenotransplantation, because of its use (and abuse) of animals and the harm that could result to society in general due to the risk of zoonosis. In such cases, the risks apply to the many and the potential benefits to the few, something that is contrary to the fundamental principle of utilitarianism. Some utilitarians would object to the use of animals for this purpose because they consider them part of the moral community that must be included in the utilitarian calculus; others utilitarians would not have this objection.

As with some of the issues relating to death and dying discussed in Chapter 8, virtue ethics can give some guidance—not necessarily to public policy-makers, but to individuals, especially those in need of an organ. There may be times when extending the life of a very sick person (especially if the sick person is old and has lived a very full life) is not necessarily the best thing—either for that person, his or her family, or society. Recalling Aristotle's dictum that death is not the worst thing, there are times when the demands made on the medical system and its miracle technologies might be best left unmet, and the best person to restrain the use of such technology is the sick person himself or herself. Certainly virtue ethics could serve as a useful ethical guide to any person thinking about travelling to China or India to buy a kidney, since it would pose questions about the meaning, value, and flourishing of the lives of both the buyer and the seller of the organ in question.

CONCLUSION

It can be seen that the issue of organ transplantation has ethical as well as metaphysical dimensions that are often overlooked by the medical community, the general public, and, increasingly, by the bioethical community, or at least by those who see only progress and benefit in this dimension of medicine. Most people tend to be impressed with the possibilities of high-tech medicine and, in particular, with the wonders of organ transplants, as community and government agencies promote both cadaveric donations and, increasingly, living donations. This is also reflected in the media's enthusiastic support, for example, of altruistic donations by living donors.[94] The dark side of the practice is seldom discussed and generally goes unrecognized. But it is useful to keep in mind that, in most cases, in order for one person to survive through organ transplantation, it is necessary that another person dies or is harmed in some way. This, in itself, raises ethical questions that must be examined. How we respond to these questions is an important social indicator of the value we invest in the human body and the human person.

PHILOSOPHICAL REFLECTION ON THE BODY-MACHINE

The question *What is the human body?* might strike you as superfluous, even ridiculous. We are intimately acquainted with our own bodies from our own experience and with the idea of human bodies in general from pictures in books, on television, and in movies. Our minds might be a mystery to us, but our bodies are not. However, if the question is posed in another way it invites further reflection: *Am* I my body? Or, do I *have* a body? Is the "I" with which I am, in spite of its often mysterious nature, intimately acquainted, housed in my body? Is it housed in my brain? Is it identical with my brain? Or is it, perhaps, identical with my body? These are questions that philosophers have asked for hundreds, if not thousands, of years and to which they still do not have answers.

Further, it may come as a surprise to learn that the way in which we perceive, talk about, and act upon the human body in Western society is quite different from the way the body is perceived, talked about, or acted upon in other societies, and even at other times than our own. For example, the body in the East is conceived of quite differently from the body in the West. Eastern medicine understands the body "as an open system connected to the external world … [with] an exchange of life-energy of some sort between the body and the external world, that is, there is an absorption and release of *ki* between them." In contrast, modern Western medicine "first separated the body from the external world, taking it as a closed, self-contained system, and then by dissecting its structure into various organs has attempted to understand their respective functions."[95]

In fact, the notion of a "life-energy of some sort" was part of the Western conception of the body until after the Renaissance. The idea of the body as an "enclosed, self-contained system" came about at the time of the scientific revolution, in particular with the philosophy and science of René Descartes (a large part of whose life work was devoted to applying the methods of science to all fields of study, including medicine). Descartes worked hard to describe the body in mechanistic terms (he actually referred to the human body as a machine), and his conception of the body has endured for 400 years.

The influence of Descartes and his body-machine can be seen by looking at how medical students learn about the human body.[96] For example, in biology, the body is a multitude of cells, ruled by chemical and biophysical laws; in anatomy, the dominant image is of a body made of detachable parts: bones, muscles, joints, tubes, systems (digestive, cardiovascular, pulmonary, and so forth); in physiology, the body appears as a well-oiled tool, with pumps, filtration system, ventilation system, and so on; with the use of cadavers or, more recently, of plastic models of the body, the body is not an individual, but a type.

This teaching reinforces the notion of the body-machine: the heart pumps; the kidneys filter; the lungs ventilate; the digestive tube feeds, cleans, and eliminates; the brain (the highest function, physically and morally) manages and controls. The student learns that the pieces of the machine can break, deteriorate, or wear out and that they can be repaired and, if necessary, replaced. The doctor thus learns to see himself as a mechanic, the fixer of broken parts, the one who must do everything in his power to keep the machine in good working order and to stave off death.

This mechanistic conception of the body reflects another assumption that is also the legacy of Descartes: the mind is not part of the mechanism. For Descartes, the mind and body were two separate and distinct substances. Debates about how this can be so, and, if it is so, how the mind can act upon the body, have raged for years in philosophy and continue today in the field of cognitive science. While Descartes' dualism is roundly rejected today by most philosophers, no philosopher has yet given an adequate answer to the question of what the mind is nor to the question of how it relates to the body. Many just assume that the mind is really the brain and go on from there. Others disagree, but are unable to tell us exactly what the mind is. So, what philosophers call the mind-body problem is still without a solution. Since what we call the "self" is intimately connected to (if not identical with) the mind, it can be said that philosophers also cannot tell us what the self is. Nor can psychologists.

One thing is certain, however: whatever the mind, or self, is, it is generally assumed that it has no place in biological (and thus medical) explanations (it is reserved for psychological explanations only) and that there is no mind or self in any bodily organ. This is a presupposition of the practice of organ transplantation: a kidney is a kidney is a kidney. My kidney, your kidney, your sister's kidney—they are all just kidneys; they are not me, not you, not your sister. From this perspective, in answer to the earlier question, we *are not* our bodies or our organs; we *have* bodies and organs. Whatever we, as selves, are, it is something different from our kidneys and our livers. If everyone did not, at some fundamental level, accept this, the practice of organ transplantation would be more ethically problematic than it is.[97]

The mechanistic conception of the body, and the metaphysical dualism that supported it, allowed the human body to be perceived as an object, originally and ideally an object of science but, increasingly in the biotechnological age, also as an object of commerce. This objectification and commodification of the body has gradually evolved over 400 years, but has, in our day, become part of the presuppositions of biomedical science. Whatever sacredness had been attached to the human body over the course of Western history and culture has now been superseded by technological developments and the needs of medical science. There are ethical debates about buying and selling organs for transplant, for example, but those who argue for keeping the body out of the sphere of commerce are fighting a losing battle: "Body parts are bought and sold for medical research, diagnostics, and therapies ... pieces of people are increasingly being used as raw materials for products—from placenta-enriched shampoos to experimental DNA-run computers."[98] Genes are being patented, often without the knowledge or consent of those from whom the genetic material has been taken. The poor of the third world sell their kidneys to the rich of the first world, giving a whole new meaning to the term exploitation, and as we have seen, many bioethicists defend this practice as morally acceptable. Our bodies, our organs, our tissues, our genes are now "resources" subject to market forces. And pieces of people have become more valuable than people. The question *What is the human body?* is, in our time, neither superfluous nor ridiculous.

CASES OF INTEREST

Medicus Clinic, Kosovo

In November 2008, a young, shaking Turkish man was found at the Pristina airport in Kosovo with a large surgical scar on his abdomen. He told the police that his kidney had been stolen at a medical clinic. When the police raided the clinic, they found a frail, elderly Israeli man who had paid $90,000 for the kidney. Victims started coming forward and evidence gradually emerged that dozens of impoverished people from several countries, including Turkey, Russia, Maldova, and Ukraine, had been lured to Kosovo by the promise of lucrative payments for their organs. Many were promised $15,000, while others were offered payments of up to $26,000. Upon arrival, they were asked to sign fake documents indicating that they were donating organs to relatives for humanitarian purposes. The victims were released with inadequate medical care, many were given substantially less money than they were promised, and some were not compensated at all. The organs were sold to recipients, mostly from Israel, for anywhere between $70,000 and $130,000 USD.

The Medicus clinic was founded by a well-meaning European philanthropist who sought to help local doctors during the Kosovo war. It was later transformed into an illegal organ transplant clinic by Dr. Dervishi, a professor and surgeon at the Pristina University Hospital. Dr. Dervishi, along with numerous other defendants, was tried before a panel of two European judges and one Kosovar judge. In April 2013, Dr. Dervishi was found guilty of organized crime and people-trafficking. He was sentenced to eight years in prison with a fine of €10,000. His son, Arban Dervishi, was found guilty of the same crimes and sentenced to seven years and three months in prison, with a fine of €2,500. The clinic's head anaesthetist, Sokol Hajdini, was sentenced to three years in prison after being found guilty of causing grievous bodily harm. The assistant anaesthetics, Islam Bytyqi and Sylejman Dula, were found guilty of the same crime and were both sentenced to a year's imprisonment, suspended for two years.[99]

Strunk v. Strunk

In 1969, Tommy Strunk, a 28-year-old married man, was suffering from chronic glomerulus nephitis, a fatal kidney disease. He was being kept alive by frequent treatment on an artificial kidney, but the doctors determined that the procedure could not be continued for much longer. They then considered using a kidney from a corpse or a live donor if one could be made available. His mother, father, and a number of collateral relatives were tested, but all were found to be unsuitable donors due to the incompatibility of either blood type or tissue.

As a last resort, they tested Tommy, Jerry's 27-year-old incompetent brother, who had been committed to the Frankfort State Hospital and School, an institution for the feeble-minded. He had an I.Q. of approximately 35, which gave him a mental age similar to that of a 6-year-old. He also had a speech defect, which made it difficult for him to communicate with people who were not well acquainted with him. He was found to be a highly suitable donor for Tommy.

This immediately raised the question of what legal action, if any, could be taken to procure a transplant from Jerry to Tommy. Jerry's mother petitioned the county court within the state of Kentucky for the authority to allow a kidney transplant from her incompetent son. The court ruled that the operation was, in fact, necessary to Jerry's well-being. Given Jerry's strong psychological and emotional dependence on his older brother, it was held that his well-being would be more severely jeopardized by Tommy's death than by the removal of his kidney. The decision was appealed twice, but upheld by both higher courts.[100]

Greenberg v. Miami

Canavan disease is a rare genetic disorder, most common in Ashkenazi Jewish families, that causes progressive damage to nerve cells in the brain. After losing two children to the disease, Daniel and Debbie Greenberg founded the Chicago chapter of the National Tay-Sachs and Allied Diseases Association. They convinced Dr. Matalo, who was then a researcher at the University of Illinois in Chicago, to focus his work on Canavan disease. They hoped that he would be able to isolate the gene responsible for the disease and to later provide accessible and affordable prenatal testing for the public.

The Greenbergs, along with 160 other families, donated tissue (such as urine and autopsy samples) and financial support to Dr. Matalo, and non-profit organizations helped find other families afflicted with the disease internationally. They succeeded in creating the Canavan Registry, a database with epidemiological, medical, and other information about the families. A major breakthrough came in 1993, after Dr. Matalo made use of the tissue samples, financial support, and so on, to successfully isolate the gene responsible for the disease. In 1996 the Canavan Foundation began offering free testing. Unbeknownst to the families who contributed to the research, however, Dr. Matalo submitted an application to patent the gene in 1994. It was granted in October 1997 and gave him the ability to restrict any activity related to the Canavan disease gene, such as carrier and prenatal testing, and gene therapy.

Not only did Dr. Matalo collect royalties, but he also restricted the number of labs that could offer test-

382 Bioethics in Canada

ing and charged a fee beyond the cost of the test. Due to the restrictive licensing, a number of labs stopped offering the test. The families claimed to have been unaware of Dr. Matalo's intention to commercialize their donations. They filed a lawsuit in 2000, alleging a lack of informed consent, breach of fiduciary duty, unjust enrichment, fraudulent concealment, conversion, and misappropriation of trade secrets. All claims were dismissed with the exception of unjust enrichment. The parties settled out of court.[101]

CASE STUDIES

Scenario One

Walter Smith, a 71-year-old man in need of a heart transplant, sat in his kitchen eating breakfast alone. He picked up the phone when it rang.

"I just found the most fantastic information on the Internet!" said his 25-year-old grandson, Jeremy, who had learned about his grandfather's situation a few days ago. Because of his age and other medical conditions, Walter was very low on the transplant list. Jeremy had been visibly upset when he heard the news and has been trying to help his grandfather find a solution. "You can go to China and buy a heart. I looked it up, and for about $200,000 you can travel to China and have the transplant surgery. They take organs from executed prisoners. The transplants are arranged before the execution to ensure donor-recipient compatibility and donor consent. The price includes all related medical expenses." Jeremy was obviously excited about the news.

Walter was sombre. "I know, Jeremy. Your uncle told me about this a few days ago. Did you know that many of the prisoners in China are political prisoners?"

"No. I didn't."

"They're imprisoned because of their political views, not because they committed some heinous crime." In 1964, Walter had taken part in the student demonstrations against the Vietnam War.

"Oh." Jeremy sounded disheartened. "But this is your life on the line. You have the money. Maybe just consider it." Jeremy was right. Walter had invested his money wisely in his youth and now had a small fortune in the bank, most of which would go to his children and grandchildren after his death.

Walter sighed. "I will."

(1) How would a Kantian look at Walter's dilemma? Would a utilitarian react differently? (2) Would it make a moral difference if the organ came from a "common criminal" rather than a political prisoner? (3) What would Radcliffe-Richards et al. say about this situation? (4) How would you assess consent of the donor in such cases? (5) Think about this case in light of the excerpt from Ruth Richardson's article on procuring corpses for anatomy several centuries ago.

Scenario Two

Karen and her husband, Sam, are taking a vacation in India. At the age of 37, Karen is in need of a kidney transplant. She heard from a friend that there are hospitals in India that will perform the surgery, and she found a hospital where she could get it done for $7,000. Only blocks away from the hospital lies one of the poorer parts of India, the Ernavoor slum, which is now a refugee hutment. She knows that the people selling kidneys are desperate and are pushed to extremes due to poverty, but she also knows that by buying a kidney here, a portion of the cost goes to the seller who can support his family for several years on the sum. She needs a kidney if she is going to live past 40, and the seller of the kidney needs the money to support himself and his family. She feels it's a win-win situation. Right now, Karen and Sam are taking a week off work to explore the country and check out the hospital. Karen wants to get a better feel for the situation before she goes through with the transaction.

(1) Should Karen buy the kidney and have the operation? (2) Would a utilitarian agree with her interpretation of this as a "win-win situation?" What would a Kantian say? (3) Is Karen's age a relevant factor in the decision? (4) Does this case point to broader ethical issues regarding poverty and exploitation? What would Radcliffe-Richards et al. say?

Scenario Three

"I've called you all here to discuss the organ transplantation controversy that has come up," began Suzanne Walsh. As head of the organ transplant rehabilitation program, Suzanne was addressing fellow physicians, hospital administration staff, and members of the hospital ethics committee who were meeting in a small conference room.

"As I'm sure you've all heard by now, a famous and wealthy film star has offered to fund a new section of the hospital if he receives a liver transplant here. This man is a long-time abuser of alcohol and drugs. He is a poor candidate for liver transplantation and would otherwise be very low on the transplant list."

One of the physicians spoke up at this point. "Demand for organ transplantation has been steadily increasing across Canada." He held out a small stack of papers. "According to the Trillium Gift of Life Network, in 2007 more than 1700 Ontario patients were waiting for a new organ. In 2005, 283 people died while waiting for a transplant. If we perform this liver transplant, we could use the money to expand the organ transplant rehabilitation program. We could use some of the money to increase awareness of the need for organ donors. We could hire more transplant and rehabilitation specialists."

"But," interjected a member of the ethics committee, "this man doesn't meet the admission criteria. He is not medically stable, and it is unlikely that he will be motivated to participate in rehabilitation. He is addicted to drugs and alcohol and has not taken any steps to remedy this. As far as we know, he has never set foot in a rehabilitation centre."

"It would be unethical to move this man to the top of the transplant list simply because he can donate money to the hospital," another physician agreed. "There are a number of patients on the waiting list who are much better candidates for surgery. They have been waiting for a liver transplant, all the while complying with the admission criteria. It would be unthinkable to move this man ahead of them."

"But if we give this man the transplant," another physician protested, "we will have the funds to increase the number of beds we have available, as well as the number of staff. We could expand our program so that fewer people die every year. Is that not worth sacrificing the one individual who misses out this time?"

(1) As a physician, would you support moving this man to the top of the transplant list? Would your answer be different if you occupied a different role? (2) Is giving a large donation to a hospital in return for a liver transplant any different than paying for a liver transplant operation in China or India? If you agree that Karen should buy a kidney in India (Scenario Two), should you also agree that the film star should get the transplant? (3) Could you make a utilitarian argument to justify moving the film star to the top of the transplant list? What would a Kantian say? (4) How would you explain this to the patient who is next on the waiting list and is desperately waiting for an available organ?

Scenario Four

Marian Winchester brings her husband to the hospital every week for dialysis. Alistair Winchester, a 70-year-old man, suffers from diabetes. He suffered a mild brain injury some years ago and occasionally becomes confused. He can still conduct his life in a fairly normal manner, though he usually needs help remembering where he is and what he should be doing. Marian has taken over responsibility for her husband's care and acts as a de facto surrogate. Alistair jokes and smiles, and seems happy with his life, interacting with friends and family regularly. He has been going to the hospital for renal dialysis for the past six months, but the disease is progressing. Recently, the doctors had to operate to remove one of Alistair's toes. They informed Marian that without a transplant Alistair might need further amputations. Marian is exhausted from the weekly trips to and from the hospital.

Although there are no human organs currently available, there is another option. Geneticists have been able to modify pigs with human genetic material so that they can serve as organ donors for people with reduced risk of rejection by the recipient. Marian's husband is an excellent candidate for such surgery. Such transplants, however, have not yet been performed. This would be an experimental surgery, and Alistair would have to be kept in isolation and closely monitored for several years after the transplant.

The doctors have been encouraging Marian to enrol Alistair in the study. Because he would be kept in isolation at the hospital, the constant trips to and from the hospital would cease. As it stands now, every trip to the hospital is like the first time for Alistair; he is confused and frightened.

The doctors also tell Marian that Alistair would be doing something good for future patients if she agrees to the experimental transplant. It may benefit Alistair himself, and it would certainly benefit future patients. One of Alistair's doctors has assured Marian that he will personally see to it that Alistair is comfortable during his stay at the hospital, as he is one of the key researchers conducting this study.

(1) Should Marian opt for the transplant for her husband? How significant is the fact that Alistair himself is not completely competent to consent? Given her responsibility for her husband's care, might her decision be biased? (2) How are we to weigh the potential good of xenotransplantation against the risk of introducing new diseases into the human population? (3) Must we consider the interests of the pigs if we make a utilitarian analysis? (4) How should we view the fact that one of Alistair's doctors is also a key researcher?

Scenario Five

Melanie and Luke Jolan are parents of a seriously impaired newborn infant, Tracy, who was born prematurely at 25 weeks. She suffers from a number of complications due to extreme prematurity, and she has suffered brain damage due to the loss of oxygen during labour. She is now hooked up to a ventilator, which is keeping her alive.

Tracy's physician, Dr. Crawford, has told Melanie and Luke that the outlook is grim. Tracy is not expected to live more than a few weeks, at most, and she is not expected to ever be able to breathe on her own. Tracy's condition is deteriorating by the day. Dr. Crawford tells Melanie and Luke that they could donate her organs to save another baby. Dr. Crawford assures Melanie and Luke that Tracy's death would be swift if life support is removed, whereas her death will be drawn out and she will continue to suffer if they keep her on the ventilator and under intensive care. If Tracy becomes an organ donor, the medical team must retrieve the organs within 90 seconds after her heart stops in order to prevent deterioration, which would render them useless for transplant.

In the meantime, Melanie and Luke meet another couple at the hospital whose baby will die if she does not receive an infant heart very soon. Melanie urges the doctor to remove life support and donate Tracy's organs; she wants some good to come of her death. She specifically wants Tracy's heart to go to the other couple's baby. Luke, however, objects. Tracy is not property, he claims, and they cannot make decisions over what to do with her body while she is still alive. He agrees with Melanie that life support may be removed once Tracy's suffering becomes too great, but he wants her to die peacefully in her parents arms, and not be opened up for organ removal only seconds after her heart stops beating. Their disagreement about what to do is causing both Melanie and Luke considerable stress.

(1) Should life support be removed? (2) If so, should Tracy's organs be retrieved in order to save another baby's life? Which ethical theory can be called upon to support each parent's position? (3) Is Dr. Crawford in a conflict-of-interest situation? (4) If Luke's wish were followed, would you see Tracy's organs as "going to waste"?

Scenario Six

Dr. Benson sits quietly in the courtroom as his lawyer begins his appeal of the conviction of assault and manslaughter brought against him. Dr. Benson was found guilty of removing life support from PVS patients and using their organs for transplant without the consent of their families; he has been sentenced to 10 years in prison. The judge is listening intently as the lawyer presents his arguments.

Like Henry Morgentaler before him, Dr. Benson hopes to overturn the law in Canada, making it legal to use all PVS patients as organ donors. His argument is that higher-brain death is as good as whole-brain death for determining when a patient has died; thus he did not, in reality, kill his patients: they were already dead. There was never any intent to kill his patients, all of whom had signed organ donor cards before becoming comatose. In his view, and in the view of many in the medical establishment who support him, a PVS patient cannot be said to be a person with interests to protect. These people will never regain consciousness; they are dead, and it is morally justifiable to use them as sources of organs for transplant as long as they have previously consented to donate. Such use of PVS patients, Benson holds, does no harm to the patients themselves and benefits society in general by increasing the pool of organs available for transplant. The patients are no longer a drain on the health care system but instead can contribute to the health and well-being of other patients, giving them a second chance at life. Dr. Benson believes that he caused no harm and that his actions have done a lot of good. He is not guilty of manslaughter since the patients were already dead by the higher-brain-death criterion.

You are the lawyer representing the Crown on this case; you must argue that the initial charge of assault and manslaughter, and the prison sentence, are justified.

(1) Should PVS patients be used as sources of organs for transplant? (2) What argument could you give against Dr. Benson's claim that PVS patients are dead? (3) Can it be said that a PVS patient is still a person with interests to protect? (4) What would Singer say about the link between the definition of death and the harvesting of organs? Would he agree with Dr. Benson? (5) Would the ethical analysis of the situation change if the families had given consent?

GLOSSARY

Cadaveric organ donation: donation of organs after death. This can be done in advance by an individual signing a donor card, or at the time of death through the consent of a family member. The deceased is usually, although not always, brain dead and is thus ventilator-dependent up to the time of the actual retrieval of organs.

Living organ donation: donation of an organ by a living person. In certain cases the donor donates a whole organ (for example, a kidney); in others, part of an organ (for example, a liver lobe). Donations are usually from people related to the transplant recipient (for example, a sibling), although more and more anonymous donors are being encouraged and, in some cases, actively solicited, for example, through the Internet.

Mandated choice: a system whereby every citizen is required to make a decision in advance as to his or her willingness to donate organs at death. Such a system would ensure that the consent (or lack of consent) of every person is recorded in a central registry and relieve both hospitals and families of the burden of decision when a loved one is dying or dead.

Presumed consent: a system whereby consent to donate organs is assumed unless there exist clear indications to the contrary. In such a system the onus is on each individual to refuse to consent to organ retrieval; if there is no refusal, consent is presumed. This system exists in some countries, but not in North America.

Xenotransplant or xenograft: the transplant of an animal organ into a human being.

Zoonosis or xenosis: the transfer of infectious disease from animals to humans and from humans to animals.

FOR FURTHER READING

Caplan, Arthur L., and Daniel H. Coelho. *The Ethics of Organ Transplants: The Current Debate.* Amherst, New York: Prometheus Books, 1998.

This book covers all aspects of the ethics of organ transplantation from different points of view. It covers issues relating to the sources of organs; policies governing procurement, such as informed consent and presumed consent; ethical issues about commodification of the body; and issues of allocation and rationing.

Cohen, I. Glenn. "Transplant Tourism: The Ethics and Regulation of International Markets for Organs." *Global Health and the Law* (Spring 2013): 269–285.

This article provides a comprehensive overview of the transplant tourism issue, including an analysis of the bioethical questions it raises and suggestions for deterring the practice. The article is particularly relevant as it provides data on sellers, recipients, and brokers in the organ trade.

Lauritzen, Paul, et al. "The Gift of Life and the Common Good." *Hastings Center Report*, 31, no. 1 (January-February 2001): 29–35.

As the title states, the authors wish to promote a communal approach to organ donation, putting less emphasis on individual autonomy and more on a communal appeal for beneficent action. They believe that a public that truly understands how donating organs contributes to the common good will be more willing to commit to donating organs upon death.

Midgley, Mary. "Biotechnology and Monstrosity: Why We Should Pay Attention to the 'Yuk Factor.'" *Hastings Center Report*, 30, no. 5 (September-October 2000): 7–15.

In this article, Midgley treats seriously the strong emotional response that people have when they hear about certain issues of biotechnology such as xenotransplantation. The "yuk factor," as this is often called, is dismissed by philosophers as simple unthinking prejudice, but Midgley believes that it can hide legitimate concerns that need to be addressed. When dealing with such technologies that totally reconfigure our world view, we must decipher the message that our emotions are trying to tell us.

Scheper-Hughes, Nancy. "Keeping an Eye on the Global Traffic in Human Organs." *The Lancet*, 361 (May 10, 2003): 1645–1648.

Scheper-Hughes has been keeping track of the international traffic in organs for over a decade and has written an article for the medical world about some of her findings. This article emphasizes the tragic side of a market in body parts, legal or illegal.

Youngner, Stuart J., Renée C. Fox, and Laurence J. O'Connell. *Organ Transplantation: Meaning and Realities.* Madison, WI: University of Wisconsin Press, 1996.

This book is a compendium of essays by people who have been involved in the transplant community from different disciplines (sociology, history, psychiatry) and whose writings bring out the deeper dimensions of the practice of organ transplantation—both negative and positive.

Wilkinson, Stephen. *Bodies for Sale.* New York: Routledge, 2003.

Wilkinson analyzes a number of important concepts in the organ transplantation debate, concepts that tend to be ambiguous and slippery in the literature, including exploitation, harm, objectification, and so forth. He also discusses the ethics of kidney sales and DNA patenting.

RECOMMENDED WEBSITES
Havoscope: Global Black Market Information

www.havocscope.com/

Havocscope (which calls itself "a sort of Consumer Report for the Underworld") is a site designed to provide "accurate and unbiased data" about global black markets, including the black market in organs.

The Organ Donation and Transplant Association of Canada

organdonations.ca

This is an organization devoted to educating the public about organ transplant issues and encouraging Canadians to become organ donors. It provides information on how to become a donor in different Canadian provinces along with downloadable forms.

Trillium Gift of Life Network

www.giftoflife.on.ca

Created in 2000 by the Ontario Government, the Trillium Gift of Life Network is Ontario's central organ and tissue donation agency. A large part of its mandate is to increase the rate of both cadaveric and living organ donation across Ontario.

NOTES
1. That being said, it is generally agreed that with respect to kidney transplants, a transplant is less costly in the long run than dialysis.
2. Many donors are young people dying as a result of auto accidents or head trauma; others, the result of stroke. Age is a factor, with a preference for younger donors, although older donors are now acceptable for certain organs.
3. Jeffrey Pattos, "Organ and Tissue Procurement: Medical and Organization Aspects," in Stephen G. Post (ed.), *Encyclopedia of Bioethics*, rev. ed. (New York: MacMillan Reference Books), 1852.
4. Gregrory E. Pence, *Classic Cases in Medical Ethics*, 3rd ed. (Boston: McGraw-Hill, 2000), 286.
5. Renée C. Fox, "Afterthoughts: Continuing Reflections on Organ Transplantation," in Stuart J. Youngner, Renée C. Fox, and Laurence J. O'Connell (eds.), *Organ Transplantation: Meaning and Realities* (Madison, WI: University of Wisconsin Press, 1996), 255.
6. Some of the known side effects of immunosuppressive drugs (which must be taken for the rest of the organ recipient's life) are: vulnerability to infections; progressive damage to the kidneys; elevated blood cholesterol; increased hairiness; increased risk of cancer in children; osteoporosis; impotence; and facial acne. See Lesley A. Sharp, "Organ Transplantation as a Transformative Experience," *Medical Anthropology Quarterly*, 9 no. 3 (1995): 373. Also Margaret Lock, *Twice Dead: Organ Transplants and the Reinvention of Death* (Berkeley, CA: University of California Press, 2002), 312.
7. Peter Singer, *Rethinking Life and Death* (New York: St. Martin's Griffin, 1994), 35.
8. This, in itself, begs the question of the status of a brain-dead person and his or her organs. If the organs are mere "resources," the question has already been decided.
9. Lock, 4, 8 (emphasis added).
10. Anencephaly is a developmental abnormality of the central nervous system resulting in the absence of a major portion of the brain, skull, and scalp. The brain stem is functioning so that unconscious activity is present (breathing, heart beat, digestion, and so forth), but there is no consciousness and the babies usually die within a few hours or days. See the Council on Ethi-

cal and Judicial Affairs, American Medical Association, "The Use of Anencephalic Neonates as Organ Donors," *Journal of the American Medical Association*, 273, no. 20 (1995), found at jama. jamanetwork.com/article.aspx?articleid=388595 (November 2, 2014); and R. Hoffenberg et al., "Should Organs from Patients in Permanent Vegetative State Be Used for Transplantation?" in Arthur L. Caplan and Daniel H. Coelho, *The Ethics of Organ Transplantation* (Amherst, NY: Prometheus Books, 1998), 80, 116.

11. Singer, 50.

12. Singer, 55.

13. Truog recommends abandoning the notion of brain death altogether and resolving the issue of treatment withdrawal and organ retrieval by debating four questions: When is it permissible to withdraw life support from patients with irreversible neurological damage for the benefit of the patient? When is it permissible to withdraw life support from patients with irreversible neurological damage for the benefit of society, where the benefit is either in the form of economic savings or to make an ICU bed available for someone with a better prognosis? When is it permissible to remove organs from a patient for transplantation? When is a patient ready to be cremated or buried? Caplan and Coelho, 32.

14. David Lamb, *Organ Transplantation and Ethics* (London: Routledge, 1990), 85.

15. Lamb, 85. Some articles refer to "parental donors" since it is the parents' decision to donate the organs.

16. Caplan and Coelho, 90.

17. This is not true in all countries. In Japan, for example (due to issues relating to death and brain death already referred to), 70 percent of kidneys come from living donors who are related to the recipient. In Canada, by contrast, only 15 percent of organs come from living donors.

18. Andrew S. Levey et al., "Kidney Transplantation from Unrelated Living Donors: Time to Reclaim a Discarded Opportunity," in Caplan and Coelho, 49. That this statement is made without any hint of irony or sarcasm is an indication of the truth of another statement by Stuart J. Youngner: "In order for some to live and benefit from transplantation, others: must die." Youngner, "Some Must Die," in Youngner et al., 35. Youngner makes reference to something called "rainy day syndrome" whereby patients awaiting organs for transplant find themselves hoping for bad weather because of the increased chance of fatal accidents (a situation that causes them "significant feelings of guilt"). Youngner, 39.

19. Ann C. Klassen and David K. Klassen, "Who Are the Donors in Organ Donation? The Family's Perspective in Mandated Choice," in Caplan and Coelho, 157.

20. Arthur L. Caplan, "Ethical and Policy Issues in the Procurement of Cadaver Organs for Transplantation," in Caplan and Coelho, 145.

21. Klassen and Klassen, 155.

22. Klassen and Klassen, 155.

23. Aaron Spital, "Mandated Choice for Organ Donation: Time to Give It a Try," in Caplan and Coelho, 147.

24. Ronald Munson, *Intervention and Reflection*, 7th ed. (Belmont, CA: Thomson Wadsworth, 2003), 467.

25. Munson, 7th ed., 465.

26. R.M. Veatch and J.B. Pitt, "The Myth of Presumed Consent: Ethical Problems in New Organ Procurement Strategies," in Caplan and Coelho, 173.

27. Veatch and Pitt, 178. The question of deceptive language was raised earlier in the chapter in relation to anencephalic infants as *donors* as opposed to *sources* of organs, the latter term being

considered unacceptably blunt. In fact, the word "donor" is even used when an organ is actually sold, as when a person goes to Pakistan or elsewhere to buy a kidney from an individual living person. The choice of language is not accidental; using more explicit (and accurate) language could easily have the effect of making people reconsider their view about organ transplantation and feed the general ambivalence that is apparent in the public's attitudes to donation.

28. Aaron Spital and Charles A. Erin, "Conscription of Cadaveric Organs for Transplantation: Let's at Least Talk About It," in Ronald Munson, *Intervention and Reflection*, 8th ed. (Belmont, CA: Thomson Wadsworth, 2008), 490.

29. Spital and Erin, 490.

30. W. Glannon, "Do the Sick Have a Right to Cadaveric Organs?" *Journal of Medical Ethics*, 29 (2003): 153.

31. Spital and Erin, 491.

32. Glannon, 155.

33. David LeBreton, *La Chair à vif: usages médicaux et mondains du corps humain* [Exposed Flesh: the medical and social uses of the human body] (Paris: Éditions Métailié, 1993), 270.

34. A.L. Caplan, C.T. Van Buren, and N.L. Tilney, "Financial Compensation for Cadaver Organ Donation: Good Idea or Anathema?" in Caplan and Coelho, 219.

35. Thomas A. Murray, "Organ Vendors, Families and the Gift of Life," in Youngner et al., 102.

36. Murray, 105.

37. Youngner, 42. "Warm ischemia time" is the time during which the organs begin to deteriorate.

38. Trillium Gift of Life Network, "Determination of Death," found at www.giftoflife.on.ca/en/professionals.htm (April 4, 2014).

39. Youngner, 43.

40. Fox, 262.

41. For example, between 1993 and 1996, there were no brain-dead donors in India, Indonesia, Pakistan, Japan, or China, although in all but China there were transplants from living donors, both related and unrelated to the recipient. See H. Takagi, "Organ Transplantations in Japan and Asian Countries," *Transplantation Proceedings*, 29 (1997): 3199–3202.

42. One can live with only one kidney so this risk is rarely discussed. However, a person with only one kidney is more vulnerable (e.g., in case of accident) than one with two kidneys. Further, any surgery carries risks, which are normally weighed in relation to the benefits to the person being operated on.

43. This is of particular concern in relation to patients with alcohol-related end stage liver disease. This brings up ethical issues regarding the just distribution of resources as well as issues about patient responsibility and illness (e.g., smoking).

44. Andrew S. Levey, Susan Hou, and Harry L. Bush, Jr., "Kidney Transplantation from Unrelated Living Donors: Time to Reclaim a Discarded Opportunity," in Caplan and Coelho, 51.

45. Munson, "The Donor's Right to Take a Risk," in Munson, 7th ed., 484.

46. Carl Elliott, *A Philosophical Disease: Bioethics Culture and Identity* (New York and London: Routledge, 1999), 106.

47. Munson, 7th ed., 484. The New Yorker was not the first hero of this type. In 1912, in Gary, Indiana, a man named Willie Rugh offered to have his leg amputated so the skin could be used for a graft for a young woman named Ethel Smith, who had been seriously burned and would die without a major skin graft: "Donor and recipient met on adjoining tables in the operating room before undergoing chloroform anesthesia. After 150 square inches of skin were removed from the man's leg and grafted onto the girl's body, Rugh received an additional dose of chloroform

before his leg was amputated at the hip. Although Smith was discharged from the hospital after several days, Rugh developed pneumonia … and he died." See Susan E. Lederer, *Flesh and Blood: Organ Transplantation and Blood Transfusion in Twentieth-Century America* (New York: Oxford University Press, 2008), 18.

48. As pointed out above, this shift in thinking is starting to take place in relation to cadaveric organs.

49. Michael Kinsley, "Take My Kidney, Please," in Munson, 7th ed., 489.

50. Kinsley, 489. It is interesting to contemplate the notion of a "spare kidney." Do we refer to anyone as having a "spare eye," a "spare ovary," or a "spare lung" simply because they have two of each?

51. Kinsley, 489. Kinsley believes, however, that this sentiment is one that ought to be encouraged. Others would not agree.

52. Kishore D. Phadke and Umila Anandh, "Ethics of Paid Organ Donation," in Munson, 7th ed., 490.

53. Leon Kass, "Organs for Sale? Propriety, Property and the Price of Progress," *in Life, Liberty and the Defense of Dignity* (San Francisco: Encounter Books, 2002), 195.

54. Stephen Wilkinson, *Bodies for Sale: Ethics and Exploitation in the Human Body Trade* (New York: Routledge, 2003), 53. It can be argued that Wilkinson's premise that bodies and body parts are physical objects is a supposition of Western mechanistic physiology, one that would not be shared by someone in the Eastern tradition (and some pre-Cartesian philosophers of the Western tradition).

55. Wilkinson, 54.

56. "Moreover, if a man offer his body for profit for the sport of others—If, for instance, he agrees in return for a few pints of beer to be knocked about—he throws himself away, and the perpetrators who pay him for it are acting as vilely as he. Neither can we without destroying our person abandon ourselves to others in order to satisfy their desires, even though it be done to save parents and friends from death; still less can this be done for money. If done in order to satisfy one's own desires, it is very immodest and immoral, but yet not so unnatural; but if it be done for money, or for some other reason, a person allows himself to be treated as a thing, and so throws away the worth of his manhood." Immanuel Kant, *Lectures on Ethics*, trans. Louis Infield (Indianapolis, IN: Hackett Publishing Co., 1963), 119.

57. Wilkinson, 107.

58. Nancy Scheper-Hughes, "Keeping an Eye on the Global Traffic in Human Organs," *The Lancet*, 361 (May 10, 2003): 1645. A Kula ring is a ceremonial exchange system from Papua New Guinea.

59. I. Glenn Cohen, "Transplant Tourism: The Ethics and Regulation of International Markets for Organs," *Global Health and the Law* (Spring 2013): 269, found at www.ncbi.nlm.nih.gov/pubmed/23581670 (March 13, 2014).

60. Jeremy Haken, "Transnational Crime in the Developing World," Global Financial Integrity Report (2011): 22, found at www.gfintegrity.org/report/briefing-paper-transnational-crime/ (January 19, 2014).

61. Scheper-Hughes, 1647.

62. Scheper-Hughes, 1648.

63. L.D. de Castro, "Commodification and Exploitation: Arguments in Favour of Compensated Organ Donation," *Journal of Medical Ethics*, 29, no. 3 (2003): 143.

64. De Castro, 143.

65. De Castro, 145.

66. John S. Gill et al., "Policy Statement of Canadian Society of Transplantation and Canadian Society of Nephrology on Organ Trafficking and Transplant Tourism," *Transplantation*, 90, no. 8 (October 27, 2010): 817–820.

67. Gill et al., 818.

68. Gill et al., 819.

69. One possible deterrent could be the refusal of governments to cover the cost of immunosuppressive drugs to returning patients who have participated in transplant tourism. See Cohen, 281.

70. Dan Bilefsky, "5 Are Convicted in Kosovo Organ Trafficking," *The New York Times*, April 29, 2013.

71. Her real name was Stephanie Fae Beauclair, and her story is told in an award-winning documentary entitled *Stephanie's Heart: The Story of Baby Fae*, found at www.youtube.com/watch?v=_wAJ6-fSD-Y (March 14, 2014).

72. He died of an infection apparently due to heavy immunosuppression, but it was later discovered that archived blood and tissue samples of the patient contained baboon cytomegalovirus, raising the spectre of cross-species contamination, to be discussed further on in this section.

73. Mark J. Hanson, "A Xenotransplantation Protocol," *Hastings Center Report*, 29, no. 6 (November-December 1999): 22.

74. Hanson, 23.

75. Margaret Somerville, *The Ethical Canary* (Toronto and London: Penguin Books, 2000), 103.

76. Although baboons have been used in xenotransplantation, pigs are considered the transplant animal of choice. Baboons are genetically closer to humans but this in itself is ethically problematic (and chimpanzees, even closer genetic relatives, are considered out of the question). Pigs are close enough genetically but far enough ethically to be acceptable. (This is similar to the problem raised in the discussion of animal research regarding the question of genetic distance in science and ethics.)

77. Arthur L. Caplan, "Is Xenografting Morally Wrong?" in Caplan and Coelho, 131.

78. Hanson, 22.

79. A. Ravelingien et al., "Proceeding with Clinical Trials of Animal to Human Organ Transplantation: A Way Out of the Dilemma," *Journal of Medical Ethics*, 30, no. 1 (2004): 92.

80. Ravelingien et al., 94.

81. Ravelingien et al., 95. Note the use of the term "PVS bodies" as opposed to "PVS patients," which represents a metaphysical and not just a logical step. (See Chapter 8 regarding the use of brain-dead patients for research.)

82. Quoted in Pence, 343. Regan is only partly correct here: Goobers was part of a colony of baboons raised for use in medical research, and thus existed solely as a resource to be used for human ends. In other words, if it weren't for the research, Goobers would not exist.

83. Hanson, 24.

84. Caplan and Coelho, 247.

85. George J. Annas, "The Prostitute, the Playboy, and the Poet: Rationing Schemes for Organ Transplantation," in Munson, 7th ed., 495. The question of justice and the distribution of scarce medical resources in general is dealt with in more detail in Chapter 10.

86. Caplan and Coelho, 249.

87. H. Gilbert Welch and Eric B. Larson, "Dealing with Limited Resources: The Oregon Decision to Curtail Funding for Organ Transplantation," Caplan and Coelho, 322. The U.S. has a private-public medicare system where medical and hospital expenses are paid by insurance for those that have it, and Medicaid funds medical services for those that do not. Thus the Oregon

decision only affected those citizens who did not have insurance. But the question of distribution of scarce resources is a serious concern for Canada's public health system as well, as medical care expenses absorb almost 50 percent of some provincial budgets. An aging population combined with technological advances ensures that this number will go up, not down.

88. Mary Midgley, "Biotechnology and Monstrosity," *Hastings Center Report*, 30, no. 5 (September-October 2000): 15.

89. Dorothy Nelkin and Lori Andrews, "Homo Economicus: Commercialization of Body Tissue in the Age of Biotechnology," *Hastings Center Report*, 28, no. 5 (September-October 1998): 31.

90. Nelkin and Andrews, 31.

91. Quoted in Nelkin and Andrews, 32. The pharmaceutical company is said to have paid $15 million for the right to develop the Mo cell line.

92. Scheper-Hughes, 1648.

93. Willard Gaylin, "Harvesting the Dead," *Harper's*, 249, no. 1492 (September 1974), 30.

94. See, for example, Marina Jiménez, "Would You Donate Your Kidney to a Stranger," *The Globe and Mail*, September 23, 2009.

95. Yuasa Yasuo, *The Body, Self-Cultivation and Ki-energy* (Albany, NY: State University of New York Press, 1993), 103.

96. Didier Moriau, "Le corps médicalisé," in Michel Beaulieu (ed.), *Quel Corps?* [What Body?] (Paris: Éditions de la Passion, 1986), 128ff. Moriau's article provides an in-depth analysis of the medical school curriculum in France. The following description is a summary of part of his article.

97. That organ transplantation is *physiologically* problematic can be seen from the existence of the rejection phenomenon. It is also *ethically* problematic in some cultures that do not accept the traditional Western notion of mind-body dualism.

98. Lori Andrews and Dorothy Nelkin, *Body Bazaar: The Market for Human Tissue in the Biotechnology Age* (New York: Random House, 2001), 25.

99. Dan Bilefsky, "5 Are Convicted in Kosovos Organ Trafficking," *New York Times*, April 29, 2013.

100. *Strunk v. Strunk* 445 S.W.2d 145 (1969).

101. *Greenberg v. Miami Children's Hospital Research Institute*, Inc. 264 F. Supp. 2d 1064 (S.D. Fla. 2003).

Chapter 10

Medical Paradigms and Non-Standard Treatment

LANDMARK CASE: TYRELL DUECK

In 1999, a young boy from Saskatchewan, Tyrell Dueck, died of cancer after a lengthy battle between his parents and the courts. The only treatment for his osteogenic sarcoma was chemotherapy, along with amputation of his leg. Without this treatment, he would die; with it, the doctors hoped he might live and, in spite of the amputation, lead a normal life. However, the chances of success for the treatment were estimated at only 65 percent. His parents refused to allow the amputation, believing that his condition could be cured with alternative, non-invasive therapies and prayer. Tyrell said that he understood his situation and agreed with his parents about how his condition should be treated.

Public opinion seemed to support the parents' right to decide for their child but Children's Aid officials did not. They sought a court order to ensure that Tyrell would get the treatment his doctors believed he needed. The presiding judge, Madam Justice Rothery, agreed. In her ruling, she stated that Tyrell was not competent to make his own medical decisions and that he needed protection:

> On the evidence I have no hesitation in concluding that Tyrell is not a mature minor. He is far from it. He is a boy deeply under the influence of his father. The information that his father gives him is wrong and could place the child in medical peril. Tyrell does not appreciate or understand the medical treatment he requires. Tyrell does not appreciate or understand that if he discontinues his chemotherapy and refuses surgery he will die within a year from the spreading cancer. Thus, for the purposes of the next seven months, Tyrell's physicians are not required to obtain Tyrell's own consent or to accept any refusal he may give.[1]

Later, when his doctors examined him, however, they discovered that the cancer had already spread and that treatment now would be unlikely to save his life. His parents took him to Mexico for alternative treatments that included laetrile, the extract of apricot pits that is rejected as a cancer treatment by conventional medicine. He subsequently died. His case incited much public controversy with supporters of alternative therapies lauding Tyrell as a hero, and the medical establishment lamenting his death and proclaiming him a victim of medical quackery.[2]

INTRODUCTION

The discipline of biomedical ethics has grown up around, and been shaped by, modern scientific medicine. Modern scientific medicine is itself rooted in scientific, biological, and medical concepts developed over the centuries in Western civilization. Modern ethics is rooted in philosophical and political concepts that are also unique to the history of Western civilization. As we saw in the section on organ transplantation, for example, both the concept of brain death and the practice of organ donation have not found easy acceptance in Japan where our presuppositions about mind, body, and death are not shared. Similarly, the practices of **traditional Chinese medicine** or TCM (with the possible exception of acupuncture, the efficacy of which some doctors are willing to recognize) do not find easy acceptance in the West. Nor are other so-called alternative therapies, such as **Ayurvedic medicine** or **homeopathy** accepted by mainstream medicine, even though millions of people in North America and Europe rely on them to prevent or cure illness. Even something as benign as **naturopathy**, which emphasizes diet, lifestyle, and herbal remedies to maintain health and prevent disease, is looked upon with suspicion by mainstream medicine. Modern biomedicine has its accepted ideas about health and illness, prevention and cure, and these determine how the profession of medicine is structured. This, ultimately, influences how biomedical ethics structures its approach to the profession that it studies.

However, just as there is an historical dimension to science, so there is also an historical dimension to medicine. Further, much as we like to believe in the objectivity and neutrality of science, there are social and political dimensions to medical science that are not often discussed or even admitted. There are also psychological and environmental dimensions to illness that scientific medicine has difficulty accommodating in its diagnoses and treatments. You will see in this chapter that disease is as much about *concepts* as it is about germs and that not every society approaches health and illness (or its treatment) in the same manner. Our current concepts of health and disease have a history, and its concepts and practices have changed over time and will likely continue to do so.

BOX 10.1

MICHAEL H. COHEN, "THE WHEEL OF TIME"

At the First International Congress on Tibetan Medicine in Washington, D.C., the Dalai Lama reminded the audience that the *first, international* congress on Tibetan medicine was actually held in the seventh or eighth century, not the twentieth. Furthermore, the congress was held in Tibet, not in the American capital, and finally the historical conclave focused on the shared medical traditions of India, Nepal, China, Persia, and Tibet, traditions that already reflected an ethic of medical pluralism. The Dalai Lama went on to point out that even at that meeting—long before the notion of "complementary therapies" had become popular in the United States—Tibetan medical culture already represented an amalgamation of influences from other traditions, and it already manifested deep respect for international collaboration and shared research efforts.

With gentle humor, in his keynote address the Dalai Lama reflected on the hubris and ethnocentrism often described as embedded in modern scientific efforts within the Western Hemisphere to understand indigenous and other medical traditions. The medical stance implicitly critiqued by the Dalai Lama has been described by some critics as one of "co-optation" and assimilation, rather than true collaboration between camps. In other words, even when open to exploring other medical systems, clinicians and research scientists adhering too rigidly to the Western, scientific model—that is, without fully appreciating the asserted role of consciousness in mediating healing therapies—tend to imagine that the medical system adopted relatively recently in human history, in part of the globe, authoritatively can filter, understand, and synthesize other medical traditions.

The Dalai Lama's assertion that this approach may suffer from hubris does not deny the power and elegance of the scientific method to probe questions of safety, efficacy, and mechanism. No doubt scientific inquiry represents a powerful method for discerning truth in discovery.... But science is not the whole of authority, and the Dalai Lama was not criticizing the power of medicine and science but, rather, the exclusive claim these disciplines hold on our epistemological framework—on what we hold to be true, real, and valid. Balanced against scientific method are other modes of inquiry, from other disciplines in the humanities and from within human experience.

The lineage within which the Dalai Lama sits represents one of the great contributions to human understanding of the realms of mind and spirit—a technology of consciousness, if you will. His implicit critique of biomedical ethnocentrism suggests a need to balance current scientific inquiry, on one hand, and tolerance and respect for foreign theories and systems of health care, on the other. His challenge is in essence about embracing pluralism: momentarily suspending categorical disbelief, and being willing to try to understand some of the methods in these nonbiomedical healing systems (such as the mysterious "pulse diagnosis" in Tibetan medicine) on their own terms. Those terms of reference may include framing healing as a transfer of consciousness, healing intention, or therapeutic information through the medium of "spiritual energy" ... that is, through as yet unknown mechanisms. Contrary to reductionistic attempts to boil all inner awakening down to biochemical processes ... an opening to pluralism refuses to dismiss phenomena that may not yet be validated under generally accepted frameworks in one cultural frame of reference, as "implausible" and therefore invalid....

Scientific inquiry has a shadow aspect that manifests as dominance, exploitation, subjugation, and arrogant imposition of authority. The opposite involves a posture of humility and surrender in the face of what is unknown and what is given in stewardship. In his keynote the Dalai Lama did not suggest either abdicating science for religion, on one hand, or abdicating religion for science, on the other; rather, he expressed his respect for science alongside religion, and he offered his hope that our age would find a union between scientific and religious perspectives in the search for knowledge of the healing traditions.

Source: Michael H. Cohen, *Healing at the Borderland of Medicine and Religion* (Chapel Hill, NC: University of North Carolina Press, 2006), 1–7.

Many of our Western philosophical and ethical concepts have no resonance in other cultures. For example, many immigrants to our country who may have strong beliefs about an individual's responsibility to family and community do not easily understand or accept the importance we place on individual autonomy in our approach to medical decisions. The notion of paternalism, which has a negative connotation in our modern society, still has a place in many cultures (as it had a place in our own until fairly recently). The question of justice in relation to health and medical care is resolved differently in different cultures. Even within Western culture there is no consensus on this important principle, as debates over private medicine in the U.S. and public medicine in Canada demonstrate. The principles of biomedical ethics are not universal. Nor are the principles and practices of modern medicine.

In this chapter we will briefly examine methods of treatment that diverge from the norms of medicine, raising the issue of complementary and alternative medicine (CAM). The ethical problems relating to treatment that goes outside of the accepted medical norms are clearly demonstrated by the Dueck case described above. If our concepts of health and disease and our ways of treating them are historical and subject to change, is it justifiable to treat any therapy that falls outside mainstream medicine as misguided and wrong? This is an issue of epistemology: how do we know what we know, and how do we know it is right? Were Tyrell and his parents wrong? Or were they just following a different healing path?

We also raise questions about what we call normal versus what we call pathological. The very notion of illness necessitates an idea of a norm or a standard of health from which the diseased body represents a departure. But just what does normal mean in relation to the human body, the human mind, human health? Who decides what is normal? Two issues are discussed in order to illustrate current debates about what is pathological as opposed to being simply a variation of particular human traits: the intersexed and Deaf Culture. In both cases that which is usually referred to as pathological is seen by many (usually those who suffer from their divergence from the norm) as a normal human variation. The arguments made here force us to question our standards or norms of health as well as the way we treat people who don't meet them. At the same time, questions are raised about going too far in the other direction, for example, by allowing deaf people to create deaf children in furtherance of their ideal of Deaf Culture.

CONCEPTS OF HEALTH AND ILLNESS
Consider the following:

> Health and disease are among the fundamental experiences of human life. The concepts that people in various cultures have used in an attempt to understand and respond to those experiences have to do with the way humans relate to nature and culture. The concepts of health and disease have far-reaching consequences for diagnosis and therapy, the attitude and behavior of physicians, how patients deal with disease, social attitudes and structures, the shape of moral choices, and the cultural significance of sickness and wellness behaviors.[3]

As the above quotation illustrates, health and illness do not exist in a vacuum. What it means to be sick, how one is cured, who does the curing and how, all are concepts that are determined by the way humans relate to nature and culture. They also help to define what it means to be human and what it means to be a person. As we have seen in relation to many issues explored in this book, our approach to medicine carries many assumptions about the person and what we call the self. Further, while medical theories change over time, the changes do not necessarily represent an orderly evolution, but should be seen as "discontinuous steps, the direction of which was determined by the prevailing view of man's nature and of his relation to the cosmos."[4] Since the 17th century, science has framed our relationship to nature, which it portrays as an objective reality separate from the human mind and its purposes, and medicine has followed this paradigm. Our mechanistic view of nature and the human body has given us a mechanistic and technology-driven medicine that "fixes" disease in much the same way that one fixes a broken machine. At the same time, our political structures both reflect and shape our relationship to culture, and through them we have developed an approach to health care governed by public policy, public and private institutions, regulatory frameworks, and legal judgments that determine not only how one is treated when one is sick, but even whether or not one is sick. Thus, how we define health and disease will determine health care policy in general, as well as how we treat individuals—or even if we treat them (for example, if homosexuality or menopause are considered diseases, then resources will be devoted to them and treatments sought to cure them).[5] Whether you are sick or not is more than a question of how you feel!

Some Disease Concepts

It is useful to note that generally the word "illness" refers to the subjective aspect of disease while "disease" itself usually refers to the objective aspect as seen through the lens of medicine and medical doctors. Engelhardt writes: "It is possible for a person to feel ill without having a disease, and, conversely, to have a disease without feeling ill."[6] The importance of this distinction will become evident as we analyze issues relating to alternative medicine.

With respect to disease, one can ask where it comes from or what its cause is. In general, there are two ways of answering this question: disease comes from outside the patient, or it comes from inside the patient. The first perspective, called the *ontological* theory, "holds that the causes come from outside the patient, that diseases vary one from another, and that they exist separate from the patient."[7] The second perspective, called the *physiological* theory, "holds that causes emerge from inside the patient, that patients vary, and that diseases do not exist separate from patients."[8] If disease is seen from the ontological perspective, two different people who have the same symptoms will be treated in the same way. What is being treated is the disease, not the person. If, on the other hand, disease is seen from the physiological perspective, two different patients with the same symptoms may receive two different treatments. What is being treated is the patient, not the disease. As Duffin puts it, in the first case the doctor is concerned with what the patient *has*; in the second case, with who or what the patient *is*.[9] Under these two broad causal theories a number of specific views of illness can be subsumed, some of which clearly reflect one theory or the other and some of which reflect a mix of the two theories.

In the West at the time of Hippocrates, for example, health was seen as living in harmony with nature, and disease was considered to be a state of disharmony. Both the body and nature were seen as being composed of certain energies, forces, and humours that could become unbalanced either within the person or in the person's relation with the exterior world (for example, environmental influences). Concepts of balance and imbalance are fundamental to medical systems of other civilizations such as the Chinese and the Indian (and these systems are still practised today). They are also present in what is often called alternative medicine, much of which relies on ancient concepts of health from both the Eastern and the Western traditions. The goal of medicine in this case is to restore harmony, something that is accomplished by treating the whole person rather than a specific organ or symptom. These accounts of disease are physiological as opposed to ontological.

The influence of the Greek Hippocrates, and his Roman successor Galen, lasted for centuries but gradually diminished with the rise of the science of nosology, which, according to Duffin, "was self-consciously based on the careful observation of symptoms."[10] Diseases began to be classified and catalogued according to symptoms, and nosologists classified them "into conceptual trees with branches for classes, orders, genera, and species. Symptoms and their sequence categorized diseases as if they were entities, or 'beings.'"[11] This stage represented a clear shift to an ontological theory of the cause of disease, and with this development, medical students worked more from books than from the bedside.

A further shift took place with the development of the science of anatomy, followed by the discovery of abnormalities that showed up as a result of dissection and its refinement through the use of the microscope. Descriptions of disease were made in terms of altered anatomy: microscopic and submicroscopic changes in structure were linked to diseases, a form of analysis that is still part of medical practice today: "To determine what disease a patient has, doctors seek lesions, be they anatomical, chemical (such as high blood sugar), or physical (such as elevated blood pressure). The clue to diagnosis is not so much how the patient feels but *what the doctor finds*. A person no longer needs to feel sick to have a disease."[12] The search for lesions appears to favour the ontological theory of causes, but the fact that lesions seem to emerge from within the patient tends to favour the physiological theory of causes. So this theory of disease can be seen as encompassing both ontological and physiological explanations.

However, following the discoveries of Louis Pasteur linking bacteria and disease, the emphasis shifted to a more clearly ontological perspective with the development of a germ theory of disease. Diseases were seen as invading organisms, and vaccines were developed to kill them, shifting the emphasis away from internal causes and focusing on the foreign invaders. At the same time, this clear ontological view has been tempered in recent years by the shift to genetic explanations, which tend to put the emphasis back on physiological views of disease origins; thus both disease concepts can be found in current approaches to medicine.

Unfortunately, the science of genetics has turned out to be much more complicated than was originally thought. In spite of this fact, "biological science typically strives to identify all of the characteristics of an organism with its genetic code, and all deviations from 'normal' structure and function come to be regarded as errors of arrangement of these coded molecular chains which make up the chromosomes."[13] This overreliance on genetic explanation leaves many questions unanswered. It also tends to relieve us of our responsibility for our own health while intensifying the already common attitude of reliance on experts to tell us what is wrong with us. A genetic explanation carries a connotation of destiny with it and seems to suggest that there is nothing we can do to change our fundamental genetic flaws.[14] This is somewhat different from earlier physiological explanations of disease that looked for ways of reinstating balance or harmony within the organism and/or with its environment.

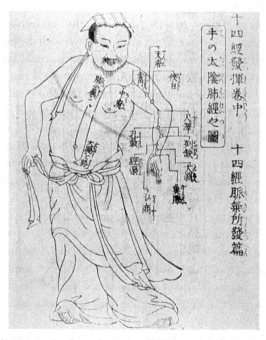

Although acupuncture meridians cannot be observed with the naked eye, they are believed to be channels of energy that flow through the body. The insertion of needles at particular points is believed to help rebalance a person's energy and return them to a state of health and harmony. This illustration shows the lung meridian.

Alternative Approaches

Given that so many different concepts of disease have woven their way through the history of Western medicine alone, how can anyone say that any particular disease concept is the right one? From our modern Western point of view, it is tempting to see the shifts in thinking of disease concepts as a progression—to see our medical system as advanced and those of a few centuries ago as primitive (and, in some respects, this is justifiable). But some thinkers warn us against interpreting the history of medicine in a linear fashion: "The ancient and traditional systems of medicine are not embryonic forms of Western medicine. Instead, they have followed their own evolution along separate lines."[15] Earlier medicine was not so much primitive as different, and the history of medicine has different branches and different political and cultural influences. Further, while the history of medicine can be seen as a story of development and progress, it is also a story of the loss of ideas and practices that had meaning and value, and there is much that we can learn (and, in fact, have learned) from earlier medical practice. For example, the notion of "like cures like" (one of the fundamental principles of homeopathy) comes from the Greeks, and Hahnneman, the father of homeopathy, developed his principles of homeopathic remedies as a result of translating Hippocrates. Principal among the ideas that have been lost to modern medicine is that of health as a harmonious relation between the human organism and its environment. This pre-modern view may seem unscientific to us, but Dubos believes, in fact, that "the scientific medicine of our time is not scientific enough because it neglects, and at times completely ignores, the multifarious environmental and emotional factors that affect the human organism in health and in disease, and to which the organism can consciously respond in an adaptive, creative way."[16]

Dubos' point is echoed by Foss who argues that, if medicine is truly scientific, it should be able to account for the full range of findings in the experimental literature, and its basic premises should "accord with what more basic sciences (on which an applied science like medicine depends for its validity) tell us about both the behavior of matter, notably complex systems (like patients), and the nature of scientific explanation."[17] In his view, the current medical model fails on both counts: too many findings cannot be explained, and the premises upon which medicine is based (mechanism, objectivism) have been overturned in the very sciences from which it takes its basic principles (for example, physics, evolutionary biology).

The viewpoints of Dubos and Foss (among others) echo the following account of the levels of healing in Native American medicine:

> In the Native American traditions, the notion of healing takes on broader dimensions. Healing occurs on various levels that interact with one another: bodily, emotional, social, and spiritual. The last two levels are especially important. Illness is brought on not only by physical ailments, but also by the quality of one's interrelationships with family, friends, coworkers, and so on. Furthermore, illness is produced by an individual's state of spirituality, not in a church-going sense but in terms of one's relationship with one's own self, or spirit. An imbalance among these various levels acts as a catalyst for the development of symptoms of illness.[18]

Our high-technology medicine, in contrast, has become very dependent on measuring pathologies. As Duffin says, "[M]icroscopic anatomy, bacteriology, immunology, and genetics, carried pathology into the laboratory, where it remains."[19] From the perspective of your doctor, if there is no pathology, there is no disease. In fact, our only true measure of health is the absence of disease. This is a far cry from the Native American conception of disease referred to above, where good health means more than the proper functioning of the body as measured by innumerable laboratory tests. The ideal of our scientific medicine, following the ideal of the scientific method itself, is "to subdivide every anatomic structure, physiological function, and biochemical process into smaller and smaller subunits so that each can be studied in greater and greater detail. The most sophisticated and successful application of this analytical approach is the reduction of medical problems to phenomena of molecular biology."[20]

BOX 10.2

BONNIE B. O'CONNOR, "TRADITIONAL CHINESE MEDICINE"

Traditional Chinese medicine (TCM), with a pedigree of several thousand years, conceptualizes every aspect of the body and its functions radically differently from anything found in Western biomedicine. Reflecting the philosophical orientation of its cultural milieu—as all healing systems, including biomedicine, do—TCM focuses its diagnostic and therapeutic attention on pattern and process rather than linear causality. The human body is conceptualized as a microcosm, linked with, reflecting, and manifesting the same processes as those acting in the physical and social environment and in the cosmos. The cosmos is understood as "an integral whole, a web of interrelated things and events. Within this web of relationships and change, any entity can be defined only by its function, and has significance only as part of the whole pattern.…"[1]

The essential cosmological qualities of *yin* and *yang* characterize all aspects of the body and its subsystems and functions, as they characterize everything in the cosmos. *Yin* and *yang* correspond, respectively, with "cold, rest, responsiveness, passivity, darkness, downwardness, inwardness, and decrease;" and with "heat, stimulation, movement, activity, excitement, vigour, light, upwardness, outwardness, and increase," among other properties."[2] *Yin* and *yang* are complementary, rather than oppositional … and are mutually generative, each giving rise to the other … and each can transform into the other, as the shady side of a hill in the morning hours becomes the sunny side in late day.… Having no separable or discrete existence of identities, *yin* and *yang* qualities can only be defined or identified in relation to, or by comparison with, each other.

The human body in TCM is animated, nourished, sustained, and cleansed by five fundamental substances: *qi*, blood, *jing*, *shen*, and fluids. Only one of these, *blood*, has a correlate in the biomedical model; however, its composition, properties, behaviour, and functions are far from identical with those assigned to blood in biomedicine. The primary animating substance is *qi*, which is an elemental force of the universe. Being both substantive and ethereal, *qi* can be conceptualized (in rough translation to terms intelligible to Western thought) as "matter on the verge of becoming energy, or energy at the point of materializing."…[3]

Of these fundamental elements, the one which receives the most attention in Anglo-European cultures is *qi*, reconceptualized in these cultures' terms as a variant form of vital energy. *Qi* circulates through the body through a series of channels called (in English) meridians. These are understood to be actual physical channels of conductivity. The fact that they have no corresponding anatomical structures and could not be located on dissection is a non-issue in the Chinese framework, focused as it is on function and relationality, rather than structure, as the crucial aspects of anatomy and physiology. The system of meridians interconnects and unifies all parts of the body, providing the pathways through which the harmonious balance of health is maintained or regained.

Organs are defined and intelligible in terms of their functions and their relationships with each other, with the meridian system, and with the fundamental substances. They are classified as *yin* or *yang* according to their functions....

The human body is conceptualized as a dynamic and self-regulating complex system whose characteristics are like those of a landscape, an ecology, or a garden.... In this system health is defined in terms of harmony and balance among the various aspects and elements of the body (including mental, emotional, and spiritual aspects, among others), seen within its environmental and cosmological contexts. Disease is not an entity, but a pattern of disharmony that eventuates from a confluence of contributing conditions. The therapeutic goal is therefore not eradication of disease *per se*, but modification of perturbing underlying conditions and influences so as to remove imbalance, resulting in a return to the harmonious state which is health.....

The models of bodily compositions, organization, and function of TCM and Western biomedicine cannot be mapped onto each other in any set of direct correspondences.... Any conceptual model, by determining the identification and classification of problems, strongly shapes the kinds of solutions that suggest themselves. Many contemporary Americans whose symptoms are classified as unrelated or "non-specific" under the biomedical model, find that TCM recognizes their illness experience as a clear diagnostic category with specific corollary treatment options.

Notes
1. T. Kaptchuk, *The Web That Has No Weaver: Understanding Chinese Medicine* (New York: Congdon and Weed, 1983), 15.
2. Kaptchuk, 8.
3. Kaptchuk, 35.

Source: Bonnie B. O'Connor, "Conceptions of the Body in Complementary and Alternative Medicine," in Merrijoy Kelner and Beverly Wellman (eds.), *Complementary and Alternative Medicine* (Amsterdam: Harwood Academic Publishers, 2000), 43–48.

Western scientific medicine is "largely concerned with objective, nonpersonal, physico-chemical explanations of *disease* as well as its technical control. In contrast, many traditional systems of healing are centered on the phenomenon of *illness*, namely, the personal and social experience of disease."[21] Traditional Chinese medicine, for example, is not focused (as is Western scientific medicine) on the body and its components, but on *processes* of vital dynamics, "upon the biological, psychic, social, and cosmic functions."[22] The science of anatomy, so important in the development of Western medicine, has no counterpart in Chinese medicine. Likewise, the science of phase energetics, which reflects the connection between macrocosm and microcosm so important to Chinese medicine, has no counterpart in modern Western medicine. What is important to realize, however, is that each system is backed up by a different view of science, supported by a different mode of cognition; further, "we should always keep in mind that Western science is not more rational than Chinese science, merely more analytical."[23]

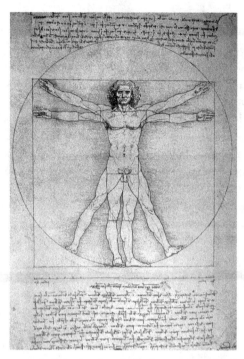

Leonardo's *Vitruvian Man*, drawn around 1487, is based on the ideal proportions of the human body, which he saw as determining the proportions of Classical architecture (he named his drawing after the Roman architect Vitruvius). It also symbolizes the idea of macrocosm-microcosm, with the human body being an analogy for the universe as a whole. Many alternative therapies today are returning to the notion of macrocosm-microcosm in their description of the relation between body, soul, and cosmos.

Homeopathy

Like Traditional Chinese medicine, homeopathic medicine describes health and illness in vitalistic terms, having as its basic assumption the notion of a vital or natural force of the body that reacts to the environment. The form that this reactive force takes constitutes the symptom or symptoms of disease. In other words, what we normally consider an illness or a disease is, in the eyes of homeopathy, a symptom of an imbalance in the organism's vital force. Symptoms are signs of the body's effort to cure itself, and the role of the homeopath is to encourage that effort, not suppress it.

> Regardless of how disagreeable or even painful it may be, the symptom is still the visible manifestation of the organism's reactive power. And since this reactive power always strives for cure, for harmony in the functioning of the organism, and always strives to adjust the balance between the body and its environment, *the symptoms are not the signs of a morbific, but of a curative, process....* The curative medicine is the one which supports and stimulates the organism's incipient and inchoate healing effort.[24]

In stimulating the body's healing effort, homeopathy often uses extremely diluted forms of substances whose effects on a healthy person mimic the sick person's symptoms (the principle of like cures like). These dilutions often contain nothing more than the energy of the substance in question; this is sufficient, according to homeopathic explanation, to work on the vital force that is trying to rebalance itself. However, since our scientific medicine concentrates on disease entities and cannot accommodate explanations relating to anything like a vital force, it is unable to accept the homeopathic explanation; it rejects not only its remedies, but also its fundamental principles. And since the homeopath sees the disease (whatever it is) as a *symptom* of a deeper problem, he cannot accept the explanation of our scientific medicine. Homeopathic medicine and **allopathic medicine**[25] explain disease through different cognitive and explanatory systems. For example,

> the homeopath disapproves of the use of bactericidal medicines, feeling that killing the assumed bacterial or viral disease "cause" within the body does not lead to a true or permanent cure, since it in no way strengthens the organism. In fact, this type of medication may well weaken the organism and affect adversely its inherent recuperative powers.... Killing the germ inside the body does not eliminate the disease cause. The "cause" is not the germ but the preexisting state of the organism which permits the germ to exist and multiply there. Enhancing or blocking some physiological function does not remove the disease cause but only diverts the vital force into different channels. The "cause" ... is non-material and cannot be cognized directly. Knowledge of it is obtained only through the minute homeopathic analysis of the patient's symptoms. This cause can be removed only through administration of the similar remedy.[26]

Thus it can be seen that not only the homeopathic treatment, but also the *rationale* underlying the treatment, is different from that of conventional medicine. This, as we will see, is a serious barrier to acceptance of this very different approach to healing.

Spiritual Healing

Within the range of CAM techniques and therapies, some can be said to "fall at the more frontier end of the spectrum in terms of scientific understanding and acceptance."[27] Naturopathic medicine, for example, with its emphasis on nutrition and herbal treatments can be accommodated, at least to a certain extent, within the standard medical model. Acupuncture is practised as a technique by certain doctors (although the larger philosophical theory of the meridians and their role in traditional Chinese medicine do not meet ready acceptance). But there is a range of therapies that are often described under the rubric of religious and/or spiritual healing, many of which would definitely fall at the frontier end of the spectrum. Faith healing, the laying on of hands, prayer, and so forth, are all practised and are accepted to the extent that they are seen as part of religious belief or ritual. From this point of view, any positive effects on a patient can be seen by the medical establishment as being psychological, explainable perhaps by the religious faith of the sick person. This cannot, of course, be the complete explanation since some studies have shown the healing power of prayer at a distance in cases of patients who do not realize they are being prayed for. But as long as such healing techniques remain in the realm of the religious, they can be seen as supernatural (by believers) or explained away by skeptics.

But more and more techniques loosely referred to as spiritual healing, or even energy healing, are not practised as part of any religion, and "practitioners of spiritual healing in the clinical domain may apply different training and styles of spiritual healing without necessarily ascribing the potency of these methods to a particular form of worship or a particular conception of God."[28] This makes it difficult to simply say that these techniques are based on faith or religion, are thus subjective, and, by implication, are not scientific. Massage is an acceptable practice now, from the point of view of standard medicine, because it provides relief to sore muscles or back pain and appears to reduce stress. But what about the massage therapist who combines therapeutic touch or Reiki into his or her techniques and claims to be working not only (or at all) on muscles, but on energy? Hatha yoga has been shown in various studies to reduce high blood pressure, improve glucose and cholesterol levels, and reduce body weight, among other things. But these studies consider yoga mainly "as a conditioning exercise, in the same category as stretching;"[29] when energy is mentioned, it is in terms of energy expenditure, not energy healing. But yoga is a much more comprehensive practice than simply stretching for relaxation, and when hatha yoga is combined with prana yoga (breathing techniques), meditation, and mantra yoga (chanting or the yoga of sound), it can be accurately classified as a form of spiritual healing. In fact, yoga, as defined by serious adherents, is a spiritual practice leading to self-realization or enlightenment: "Yoga is a gradual process of replacing our unconscious patterns of thought and behavior with new, more benign patterns that are expressive of the higher powers and virtues of enlightenment."[30] Yoga promotes a philosophy of the unity of mind, body, and spirit as well as the belief that you cannot heal the body without healing the mind and spirit. Yoga is more than a good exercise program. It is a form of energy healing.

While the term "energy healing" can be seen as vague, it encompasses a wide variety of concepts about healing spiritual energy (as opposed to the energy of physics, for example) that scientific medicine, based as it is on mechanistic conceptions of the body, would find hard to accept: "The concept of yin and yang in traditional oriental medicine, the idea of the innate in chiropractic, the spiritual vital essence (vital force) in homeopathy, and *prana* in Ayurvedic medicine all reflect the unifying notion of vital energy embedded in consciousness."[31] Different therapies explain the movement and transfer of these energies in different ways, but they all make use of non-material causes that, as stated above in relation to homeopathy, cannot be cognized directly.

A Question of Method

It does not take much imagination to understand how a medical system that is wholly based on material and mechanistic principles—all open to direct observation—can openly scoff at the notion of non-material causes that cannot be cognized directly. How can such causes and forces ever be tested through the empirical methods of modern scientific medicine? From the perspective of the scientific paradigm, these processes and remedies cannot possibly work. The problem is: they do![32] While they are not treated seriously by Western scientific medicine, alternative systems such as those described above are widely used by the public, both in North America and, even more so, in Europe. In fact, Callahan has edited a book of philosophical essays on alternative medicine precisely to address the following question: "How is sense to be made of the fact that a large and prestigious group of clinicians and biomedical researchers seems so utterly hostile to CAM while a large portion of the public (and the educated public at that) seems so attracted to it?"[33]

The answer to this question, given in various ways in the different essays of Callahan's book, often revolves around the issue of methodology. In effect, a plurality of medical systems requires acceptance of a plurality of methodologies—but this is just what scientific medicine resists. To give one example, as we have seen in the chapter on medical research, the randomized clinical trial (RCT) has almost sacrosanct status in scientific medicine and few will question its value. But controlled studies are firmly entrenched in a scientific paradigm that emphasizes objectivity, observation, and a particular view of cause and effect (efficient cause). They are difficult to adapt to an alternative system that emphasizes subjectivity, holism, and a different view of causality (final cause).[34] Further, the efficacy of many alternative therapies often relies on the very things that RCTs attempt to eliminate. For example,

> a randomized trial may be inappropriate because the very act of random allocation may reduce the effectiveness of the intervention. This arises when the effectiveness of the intervention depends on the subject's active participation, which, in turn,

depends on the subject's beliefs and preferences. As a consequence, the lack of any subsequent difference in outcome between comparison groups may underestimate the benefits of the intervention.[35]

Thus, it can be seen that it is very difficult to either prove or disprove the efficacy of an alternative medical system using the methods of our conventional medical system. The attitude of many proponents of scientific medicine is simply to ignore alternative therapies and suggest they will be "wiped out by the superior strength of conventional medical science."[36] This has already happened in the past with the elimination of homeopaths, the major competitors of mainstream medicine in the U.S. in the 19th century, and it was attempted in the late 20th century by the American Medical Association's campaign against chiropractors. In the latter case, the judge found that the AMA's Committee on Quackery (a not unbiased appellation) had undertaken a nationwide conspiracy to eliminate a licensed profession, and dismissed the AMA accusations. These examples demonstrate what Cohen refers to as a "history of hegemonic biomedical authority over social definitions of illness and health."[37] However, Callahan believes that any such efforts to wipe out alternative therapies today are unlikely to succeed since "at least one important attraction of CAM is that it often works at the borderline of those conditions that conventional medicine is not fully capable of managing, most notably chronic conditions."[38] At the very least, conventional medicine should be open to the complementary aspect of CAM, if not totally accepting the alternative part.

A CLASH OF PARADIGMS: WHAT IS THE DOCTOR TO DO?

Any attempt to focus on the complementary aspect of CAM, however, would necessitate acceptance in principle of at least some of these therapies and somehow negotiating their inclusion in treatment options within the medical system. But this can only work if both sides are willing to negotiate, and "willingness to negotiate may not be present if one party does not acknowledge the other's legitimacy—that is, if one perceives the other to be a rogue that must be dismissed, regulated out of existence, or governed more tightly than one's own peer group."[39] While some medical schools are slowly introducing instruction in alternative treatment into their curricula, and more and more of the literature refers to "**integrative medicine**," with an emphasis on incorporating certain therapies into medical treatment,[40] the fact remains that, for the most part, CAM and its therapists are included in what most physicians would consider the rogue category. Often a physician will refuse to treat a patient who admits to using an alternative practitioner such as a naturopath or a homeopath. At the same time, as pointed out above, the general public is flocking to alternative practitioners to help them with chronic complaints that the medical system seems incapable of treating.

What if you are someone who takes complementary and alternative medicine seriously, either as a result of studying other medical philosophies or trying alternative therapies, or because you come from another culture with different medical practices? What do you do if your doctor recommends a treatment that goes against your traditional (or even newly acquired) values? What if you believe that the cancer treatment recommended for your child will actually harm him? Do you have a right to refuse it? Can the medical team obtain a court order for treatment in the same way it can if a Jehovah's Witness refuses a blood transfusion for a child? The case of Tyrell Dueck that opened this chapter shows that the court can and will impose conventional medical treatments even if the parents have no faith in it and strongly resist it. In the eyes of the court, the doctors are right, even though everyone knows that medical practices and treatments change and that what is considered the right treatment this year may no longer be the right one a few years from now. Nevertheless, the judge had no hesitation in declaring that the information Tyrell's parents gave him in this case was "wrong."

The Dueck case raises issues relating to parental autonomy, but more importantly, it raises issues about the acceptability of alternative practices in medicine. Since the efficacy of alternative healing practices cannot always be proven by the methods of science and is not accepted by conventional medicine, the courts will, as we have seen, impose the conventional methods over any alternatives. Yet, it is fair to ask, as Cohen does, "Is reality only what we know as proven to the satisfaction of present, prevailing scientific and medical communities, or can healthcare embrace alternative, complementary, and frankly foreign or even antithetical, parallel, or intellectually challenging and disruptive paradigms?"[41]

We are, in fact, dealing with a clash of paradigms, one that is recognized by those on the so-called rogue side, but not necessarily by those on the side of standard scientific medicine. There are fundamental conceptual differences "about the nature of persons and of health, together with the practices that logically derive from them. These core concepts are shared in broad form among CAM constituents, but are absent from the conventional medical worldview."[42] Some of the conceptual differences have been highlighted in the earlier discussion of traditional Chinese medicine and homeopathy and can be reduced to a belief, on the one hand, that only those theories and techniques that have been tested through empirical, observable, and repeatable events can be considered scientific, and the belief, on the other hand, that empirical studies and theories tell only part of the story: that there are other forces at work in sickness and healing (for example, a vital force, different levels of energy) that are not amenable to the studies of the scientists. Adherents of the first view see the doctor as someone who fixes the broken machine of the body; adherents of the second see the body as an organism that can heal itself if harmony and equilibrium can be restored. In effect, each side holds a different view of the body, the person, and the relation between mind, body, and nature (or the cosmos—a term that will quickly alienate a convinced empiricist).

While it is tempting to call the first view scientific and the second non-scientific, it may rather be a question of what science one is talking about. There are many scientists (working on the fringes of physics and biology, for example) who have "challenged many of the most basic laws of biology and physics" and have "provided evidence that all of us connect with each other and the world at the very undercoat of our being." They have conducted scientific experiments demonstrating "that there may be such a thing as a life force flowing through the universe," and they "have had to fight a rearguard action against an entrenched and hostile establishment."[43] Many believe that we are on the cusp of a paradigm shift from the dualistic, objective, and mechanistic science of Newtonian physics, ushered in during the scientific revolution, to the dynamic, interconnected world of quantum physics of the 20th century. Post-Einsteinian physics has begun to call into question the scientific method that supports modern biomedicine: "Today health care professionals whose scientific education has been shaped by the implications of relativity theory and quantum mechanics are emphasizing the inherent subjectivity of all diagnostic judgments, including those based on the most advanced of our technologies. They are suggesting that we may, simply by observing and defining it, shape the nature, course, and outcome of our patients' health and illness."[44] At the very least, many theorists of holistic medicine call upon the principles of quantum physics to support their views, and whether or not they fully understand them, they do not consider them unscientific.

So what is a doctor, faced with a patient who wants to use alternative therapies, supposed to do? The principle of autonomy dictates that patients have the right to accept or reject treatment. Further, under the principle of informed consent, the doctor has a responsibility to inform the patient of all treatment options available along with the attendant risks and benefits so that the patient can make an informed decision. But what if the doctor has not been educated in any of the alternative healing techniques that the patient wants to try?[45] What if he or she is fundamentally opposed in principle to the conceptual framework upon which such healing techniques are based?

Cohen describes a hypothetical scenario where a patient says to the doctor: "I would like you to help me evaluate complementary and alternative medical approaches so that I can include them in my treatment." And the doctor responds: "I refuse to recommend CAM treatments because they have not been subjected to scientific scrutiny. You risk your health in seeking these types of care."[46] This is not an unreasonable scenario: the patient wants to exercise autonomy by becoming better informed; the physician, acting on the principles of beneficence (and/or non-malfeasance), does not want any harm to come to the patient through what he probably perceives as treatments that are useless at best, and harmful at worst.

The Question of Harm

The concerns expressed by the medical community about potential harmful effects of using alternative medicine suggest that standard biomedicine is safe and alternative treatments are risky or harmful. But the reality shows a different picture. There are many examples of serious adverse effects from prescription drugs, and drugs are regularly withdrawn from the market because of death or other side effects after they have been approved and prescribed by medical doctors for some time. Some therapies, such as hormone replacement therapy, have been discontinued or reduced after it was shown that they can lead to more serious problems than the one they were used to correct. The phenomenon of iatrogenic disease (disease induced specifically as a result of medical treatment) has been known for decades. Ivan Illich opened his 1976 book, *Medical Nemesis*, with the provocative sentence: "The medical establishment has become a major threat to health."[47] In his opening paragraph he refers to "the sick-making powers of diagnosis and therapy"; the "paradoxical damage caused by cures for sickness"; and the "epidemic" of *iatrogenesis* (from the Greek *iatros*, "physician," and *genesis*, "origin"). He reported at the time that government studies showed that "7 percent of all patients suffer compensable injuries while hospitalized," a rate "higher than in all industries but mines and high-rise construction." He claimed further that research hospitals were more "pathogenic" than regular hospitals, stating that "one out of every five patients admitted to a typical research hospital acquires an iatrogenic disease, sometimes trivial, usually requiring special treatment, and in one case in thirty leading to death. Half of these episodes result from complications of drug therapy; amazingly, one in ten comes from diagnostic procedures."[48] This was written over 30 years ago, before the occurrence of superbugs in hospitals, a phenomenon that has increased considerably the risk of hospital-induced illness. One such superbug (methicillin-resistant *Staphylococcus aureus* or MRSA) kills 8500 Canadians each year, and the resistance of these bacteria to antibiotics is increasing every year.

And yet a single death resulting from, say, chiropractic therapy will make the news headlines and call into question the efficacy and legitimacy of all forms of alternative medicine. When a Quebec woman died of a stroke after chiropractic neck treatments in 2006, a coroner recommended a complete review of procedures involving neck adjustments. The Quebec Order of Chiropractors agreed with the coroner's conclusions and said that the chiropractor in question had made an error in judgment. In other words, alternative medicine practitioners make mistakes too. This should not call into question the entire practice. There have been studies linking neck manipulations to stroke in rare cases, but the number of injuries or deaths caused even by this controversial practice comes nowhere near the number of hospital deaths that are now accepted as routine. Death or injury arising directly out of any medical treatment is never acceptable; but it is far from proven that alternative therapies are unsafe. Their generally non-invasive nature in itself exposes patients to less risk than invasive surgical techniques, for example. Concerns are expressed that they give sick people false hope and thus discourage them from seeing a medical doctor in time. This is something that could be corrected if doctors were more open to working with alternative therapists, or at least to monitoring their patients' responses to alternative treatments and recommending more standard interventions if they believe it necessary. This in turn requires mutual respect for the potential benefits and limitations of both alternative and standard treatment. As already pointed out, however, the fundamentally different premises (regarding the human body, health, and illness) inherent in the two paradigms render mutual recognition difficult at the present time. That some form of accommodation is urgent, however, is recognized by an editorial in the *Journal of the American Medical Association*:

> The popularity of alternative medicine ... [is] driven by the perception that conventional treatments are too harsh to use for chronic and non-life-threatening disease. Iatrogenic disease caused by conventional medicine is a major cause of death and hospitalization in the United States. While some alternative medicine practices have important toxicities, many have reduced potential for adverse effects when properly delivered. Conventional medicine can learn from alternative medicine how to "gentle" its approach by focusing on the patient's inherent capacity for self-healing.... Alternative medicine is here to stay. It is no longer an option to ignore it or treat it as something outside the normal processes of science and medicine. The challenge is to move forward carefully, using both reason and wisdom, as we attempt to separate the pearls from the mud.[49]

This is not just a challenge to medicine; it is also a challenge to biomedical ethics, which tends to follow the biomedical model and which could be more open to medical pluralism. In fact the Institute of Medicine in the U.S. has recommended that pluralism be added to the traditional principles of biomedical ethics, along with autonomy and beneficence, for example. This would mean "a moral commitment of openness to diverse interpretations of health and healing, [including] suspending any categorical disbelief in CAM therapies."[50] Autonomy is the strongest principle of biomedical ethics (to the point where we have questioned its predominance in this work), and it has become an ethical requirement for doctors to respect the autonomous choices of their patients. This is especially true when the options offered by conventional medicine are uncertain or carry risks or extreme side effects. As Cohen says, "[I]f the clinical situation involves an arena where there is no strong evidence for conventional therapy or the treatment is invasive or toxic, the clinician's ethical stance ... can include accepting the patient's choice of CAM therapies (including spiritually based treatments) while continuing to monitor conventionally."[51] Such an attitude might have prevented a case like Tyrell Dueck's from ending up in the courts; the outcome may have been the same, but the child, the parents, and their choices would have been respected in the process and the public controversy avoided.

THE NORMAL AND THE PATHOLOGICAL

Aside from the philosophical differences inherent in the debate between modern scientific medicine and what is referred to as CAM, there are also philosophical debates within scientific medicine itself as to how to treat certain conditions and even whether certain conditions should be treated at all. A large part of these debates can be attributed to different points of view regarding what is normal and what is not normal, sometimes referred to as a distinction between the normal and the pathological.

BOX 10.3

THE SOCIAL CONSTRUCTION OF DISEASE: LEPROSY

Jacalyn Duffin writes about how diseases can be socially constructed in the sense that the social position of those who have the disease can become part of the concept of the disease itself, along with its treatment and practices relating to it:

> Leprosy, for example, is less infective than the responses to it would imply. As we know it, the disease is only mildly contagious. Regulations probably had more to do with protecting the healthy rich from having to confront the dreadful mutilations of the disfigured poor. In the Old Testament, leprosy denoted physical and moral impurity and punishment for sin. Sufferers were forced to live in colonies, to wear special clothes, and to carry bells warning of their presence. The Order of Lazarus, founded in the twelfth century and named for the man whom Christ raised from the dead, built special hospices to isolate and care for sufferers. The "lazaretto" catered to people with problems other than leprosy or plague, but it became synonymous with "leprosarium" and "pesthouse." Some historians maintain that biblical and medieval leprosy comprised a variety of disorders that differed from the condition, which is now attributed to the bacillus described in 1871 by G.H.A. Hansen. Nevertheless, the old controls persisted. A colony was established in New Brunswick in the mid-nineteenth century and more recently the care of Africans with leprosy was a mission of Cardinal Paul-Émile Leger of Montreal. Other centres still operate in both rich and poor countries, including Japan, Thailand, India, Senegal, Cameroon, and the United States (Hawaii and Louisiana).

Source: Jacalyn Duffin, *History of Medicine: A Scandalously Short Introduction* (Toronto, ON: University of Toronto Press, 2000), 146–148.

As can be seen from the quote from Dubos cited earlier in this chapter, one of the very important characteristics of modern scientific medicine is its claim to objectivity. Science, by its very nature, objectifies; and, it measures. Technology is the great enabler of both objectification and measurement. Early medicine was subjective: "diseases were fabricated from the pattern, sequence, and qualities of the subjective illness as told to the physician."[52] The patient had to try to explain his illness to the doctor and, in this situation, he could not be sick without feeling sick. Duffin explains how the simple invention of the stethoscope changed all this when Laennec, a French physician, invented it quite by accident:

> According to his own account, he was examining a young female in whom he suspected a heart problem, but because of her stoutness, percussion was unhelpful. He thought of placing his ear directly on her chest to learn more about her heart, but decorum dictated restraint. Rolling a notebook into a cylinder, he placed one end on her chest, the other to his ear, and was astonished to hear the beating of her heart.

> The "discovery" at the bedside of the well-endowed young patient was simply the rediscovery of a phenomenon: sound can be transmitted through a mediator. Interpretation of these transmitted sounds consumed Laennec's attention for the next two and a half years.... Laennec had to invent words to describe the sounds he heard: rales, crepitations, murmurs, pectoriloquy, bronchophony, egophony.... In less than three years, he had established the anatomical significance of most of the normal and abnormal breath sounds still in use today.[53]

The important words in the last sentence of the above quotation are "normal" and "abnormal." The invention of the stethoscope permitted Laennec to investigate the state of the internal organs "long before the patient became a cadaver. [He] began to define lung diseases by their anatomical lesions rather than by the symptoms";[54] in other words, by the objective criteria the technology permitted rather than by the subjective criteria that taking a patient's history necessitated. According to Foss, "[T]he stethoscope marked the birth of rational medicine," and the distancing of the doctor and the patient.[55] Further, the patient could be sick without knowing it, since it was no longer how the patient was feeling that determined the absence or presence of disease, but the normal or abnormal rales or crepitations observed by Laennec. Thus did medical diagnosis become objective, and thus was it able to measure (with growing accuracy over the last few centuries) the normal and the pathological. When we go to our doctor for an annual checkup, we are put through a series of tests, the results of which (when they come back from the lab as normal or abnormal) will indicate whether we are well or sick or on the way to becoming sick. In fact, we often go to the doctor for a checkup when we are not feeling sick at all; this is what we call prevention.

But what is normal and what is abnormal? If the normal is what conforms to certain standards or criteria determined by our measuring technologies, as is the case with Laennec's stethoscope, do new technologies bring in their wake new abnormalities or new diseases? Elliott believes strongly that this is so. In his view, technology changes the boundaries between health and illness, between ordinary human variation and pathology. For example, before artificial insemination and in vitro fertilization, infertility was a simple fact of life; now that it can be measured and treated, it is a medical problem that needs to be corrected. Shyness used to be considered a simple aspect of one's personality; now that it can be transformed with a drug such as Prozac, it is considered an illness that needs to be cured. Does an overactive six-year-old boy have a disease? Is he a normal boy or is he pathological? Does the no-longer-overactive-because-treated-with-Ritalin boy then become the norm? As cosmetic surgery becomes the norm for aging women, who is normal, the woman who keeps her wrinkles and sagging breasts, or the woman who has a facelift and breast surgery? Is the bald man who refuses hair implants normal? The short boy who foregoes human growth hormone? The menopausal woman who refuses hormone treatments? Once a technology is available, do the changes it brings about become the norm?

Treatment or Enhancement?

Some technologies can be seen as therapeutic in the sense that they cure illness or disability. Others are considered enhancement technologies because they "enhance human capacities and characteristics."[56] But the line between the two is not always clear. If a technology treats a real or perceived lack, is it therapy or enhancement? Cosmetic breast surgery after a mastectomy is clearly therapeutic, and breast augmentation surgery would appear to fall on the side of enhancement. But what if the woman who wants breast augmentation surgery wants it because her breasts are very small and she does not feel they are what she considers normal? What if her small breasts cause her a great deal of anxiety? For her, the surgery is correcting a perceived lack, and this lack and the anxiety caused by it can, at the limit, be seen as pathological. The operation will, in her eyes, make her normal. Brannigan and Boss refer to phalloplasty (penile enlargement) as "one of the fastest-growing procedures in cosmetic surgery."[57] Perhaps, to the man who has it, a small penis is a very serious lack, an illness. Now that plastic surgery can help him, is that surgery to be seen as a cure or an enhancement? How does one establish what is normal in relation to penile size? What is the objective measure?

Elliott finds the question of enhancement most troubling when it touches on a person's identity or sense of self: "It is precisely when we move closer to aspects of identity that the line between pathology and normal variation becomes fuzziest—things like physical appearance, intelligence, sexual identity and personality.... Today it is disarmingly easy to speak of any disagreeable personality trait as if it were an illness—and even some that are not so disagreeable...."[58]

In his book *Far From the Tree*, Andrew Solomon deals with the question of identity in relation to what are normally seen as illnesses (or at least defects that must be fixed), such as deafness, Down's syndrome, dwarfism, transgenderism, and so forth. He distinguishes between *vertical* identities (those characteristics that children share with their parents, for example, language, ethnicity, religion) and *horizontal* identities (those that are different from their parents, for example, homosexuality, physical disability, schizophrenia, autism), which lead children to seek identity not from their parents but from a peer group. He states, "Whereas families tend to reinforce vertical identities from earliest childhood, many will oppose horizontal ones. Vertical identities are usually respected as identities; horizontal ones are often treated as flaws." He further states, "We often use *illness* to disparage a way of being, and *identity* to validate that same way of being."[59] This, he believes, is a false dichotomy that needs to be re-examined: "Many conditions are both illness and identity, but we can see one only when we obscure the other. Identity politics refutes the idea of illness, while medicine shortchanges identity. Both are diminished by this narrowness."[60] The distinction between illness and identity, or between vertical and horizontal identities, is not just theoretical. It raises the question of which aspects of difference (and the treatments necessary to either correct it or reinforce it) belong in the realm of medicine and which do not. What is treatment, and what is enhancement? And what should, perhaps, be left alone?

A somewhat different example of the connection between normalization and identity is the popularity among Asian Americans (and Canadians) for blepharoplasty or Asian eye surgery, a cosmetic surgery that makes Asian eyes look more Western. Many parents choose this operation for their children, but it is a medical intervention based not on medical need but on parental aesthetic preferences. Further, such interventions permanently alter "a feature that is to some people an integral aspect of identity,"[61] raising moral questions about parental decision making for minor children.

Such cases raise both medical and ethical questions that do not lend themselves to easy answers. Is a doctor obliged to provide what he or she considers "enhancement" treatment to any patient who desires it? Who decides when such treatments are necessary or unnecessary? Should the complex medical interventions related to transitioning from one gender to another be considered treatment or enhancement? Should public or private medical plans have to pay for such treatment? What is the role of medicine in the realm of Solomon's horizontal identities?

BOX 10.4

THE IDENTITY BAZAAR

Carl Elliott writes about the social construction of disease from a perspective that thoroughly implicates the pharmaceutical industry in the construction and treatment of disease:

> The pharmaceutical industry has learned ... that the key to selling psychiatric drugs is to sell the illnesses they treat.... Before the 1960s, clinical depression was thought to be an extremely rare problem. Drug companies stayed away from depression because there was no money to be made in antidepressants. Depression, they thought, was too uncommon. So when Merck started to produce amytriptaline, a tricyclic antidepressant, in the early 1960s, it realized that in order to sell the antidepressant it needed to sell depression. Consequently Merck bought and distributed 50,000 copies of *Recognizing the Depressed Patient*, a book by Frank Ayd that instructed general practitioners how to diagnose depression....
>
> Like depression, obsessive-compulsive disorder (OCD) was once thought to be extremely rare. In the mid-1980s came the development of clomipramine, or Anafranil, which proved an effective treatment for OCD. Soon after clomipramine came Prozac and its sister drugs, many of which also proved effective. Today, epidemiological studies say that up to 3 percent of all people may have obsessive-compulsive disorder. What has happened? At least part of what has happened is the marketing of a disease.
>
> This does not mean that drug companies are simply making up diseases out of thin air.... But surrounding the core of many of these disorders is a wide zone of ambiguity that can be chiselled out and expanded.... The bigger the diagnostic category, the more patients who will fit within its boundaries, and the more psychoactive drugs they will be prescribed.

Source: Carl Elliott, *Better Than Well: American Medicine Meets the American Dream* (New York: W.W. Norton & Company, 2003), 123–124.

It is useful to distinguish between health care needs and health care desires. The former "seek to restore some level of normalcy, whether the need be life-rescuing, life-sustaining or life-improving," while the latter "assume a normal condition and seek to enhance this already normal condition."[62] Both of these definitions, however, rely on some common understanding of normal or normalcy, which, we have seen above, is not obvious. The young woman who wants breast implants, even though her breasts may fall within the range of normal variation, does not perceive her current condition as normal.[63] For her, the desired breast implants are a need; for her doctor, they may simply reflect a desire. Or "[s]uppose a person suffers from low self-esteem because he is sensitive about his nose and wants to undergo rhinoplasty. Is this a healthcare need or a health-related desire?"[64] Are these medical judgments or ethical judgments?

To take the issue even further, there are cases where people want to do something that the majority would consider absolutely abnormal to become what, to them, *is* normal. A dramatic example concerns what, until recently, had been called *apotemnophilia*—the desire to have a limb amputated because the person believes that he or she is somehow in the wrong body: that the body they were meant to have is one without legs, or without arms. The suffix "philia" indicates the belief that this disorder is both psychological and sexual in nature, but recent research has shown that sexual fantasy or desire is not necessarily part of what the compulsion to amputate a limb is about. It is more akin to **Gender Identity Disorder (GID)**, and thus has recently been renamed Body Integrity Identity Disorder (BIID). While there is some controversy as to whether the causes of this disorder are physical (neurological) or psychological, the group of medical, psychological, and psychiatric professionals who have recently opened a website on the subject appear to accept that the condition is psychological in origin, although it is not currently included in the *Diagnostic and Statistical Manual of Mental Disorders.*[65]

Writing about the Scottish surgeon Robert Smith, who had amputated the healthy legs of two men and was about to amputate a third before his hospital stopped him, Elliot says, "These patients were not physically sick. Their legs did not need to be amputated for any medical reason. Nor were they incompetent, according to the psychiatrists who examined them. They simply wanted to have their legs cut off. In fact, both the men whose limbs Smith amputated have declared in public interviews how much happier they are, now that they have finally had their legs removed."[66]

The reason most of these people want to have their limbs amputated usually revolves around feelings of not being normal as they are (that is, with their healthy limbs). One of the somewhat ironic symptoms of the condition is that those who suffer from it actually do not feel whole as they are; they feel they can only be made "whole" by having a limb amputated. Elliott reports being struck by the "language of identity and selfhood" that these people use when they speak of their desire for amputation: "I have always felt I should be an amputee"; "I felt, this is who I was"; "It is a desire to see myself, be myself, as I 'know' or 'feel' myself to be."[67] In other words, what these patients have in common is a desire to be normal according to their own perception of normalcy, something that raises serious questions about the very meaning of the term. Does normal simply mean what I consider normal for me?

Because of the Internet, people who in the past felt isolated and ashamed of their desire to be an amputee (the condition has been known since the late 1800s) have now found a community of others who share their obsession with having a limb amputated, as well as information on where to go to get it done or how to do it themselves. The very existence of a community of like-minded individuals makes what had been seen as pathological suddenly seem more normal. This reinforces the condition in what has been referred to as a "looping effect," by which becoming aware that one's obsession or behaviour actually has a name or a classification leads to altering one's self-conception to conform to the classification: "the concept changes the object, and the object changes the concept."[68] However, the recent and more open recognition of the condition, and the creation of a website designed to provide information and alternatives to those who suffer from the condition, could perhaps serve to prevent some people from going to the extremes of self-mutilation through attempting amputation as others have done.

RESISTING NORMALIZATION

While the impulse in much of what has been discussed above (with the exception of BIID) is a desire to move toward some perceived standard of normalcy—or, perhaps, in the case of aging, to prevent falling too far away from that standard—there are two examples of resistance to normalizing technologies that are quite recent and quite political (in the sense of having become a movement or a pressure group): the intersexed and Deaf Culture. In both cases, whereas in the past people born with the lack or pathology in question were normalized as a matter of course (and to the extent that existing technology permitted), pressure is now being brought to bear on the medical community to treat their condition not as abnormal but as an example of normal human variation.

The Intersexed

What is broadly referred to as **intersexuality** consists of "a range of anatomical conditions in which an individual's anatomy mixes key masculine anatomy with key feminine anatomy."[69] This condition is also sometimes referred to as *ambiguous genitalia* and it is estimated to occur in about 1 out of 1500 live births, although estimates vary according to how strictly one defines ambiguous genitalia.[70] Babies who are born with ambiguous genitalia—where it is impossible to determine whether they are boys or girls—are assigned a gender by the medical team (in consultation with the parents) based on certain criteria described by Dreger, as follows:

> [G]enetic males (children with Y chromosomes) must have "adequate" penises if they are to be assigned the male gender. When a genetic male is judged to have an "adequate" phallus size, surgeons may operate, sometimes repeatedly, to try to make the penis look more "normal." If their penises are determined to be "inadequate" for successful adjustment as males, they are assigned the female gender and reconstructed to look female.... Meanwhile, genetic females (that is, babies lacking a Y chromosome) born with ambiguous genitalia are declared girls—no matter how masculine their genitalia look.[71]

That a baby's sex or gender can be assigned in this fashion is a result of a deep-seated belief (now being challenged by the intersexed themselves) that "physicians could essentially create any gender out of any child, so long as the cosmetic alteration was performed early."[72] One well-known example of this belief is the John/Joan case whereby John, an unambiguous male baby with a twin brother, had his little penis accidentally cut off during a circumcision when he was eight months old. As Dreger explains,

> [I]t was decided that given the unfortunate loss of a normal penis John should be medically reconstructed and raised as a girl—"Joan." Surgeons therefore removed John/Joan's testes and subsequently subjected Joan to further surgical and hormonal treatments in an attempt to make her body look more like a girl's. The team of medical professionals involved also employed substantial psychological counselling to help Joan and the family feel comfortable with Joan's female gender. They believed that Joan and the family would need help adjusting to her new gender, but that full (or near-full) adjustment could be achieved.[73]

The notion that one's gender can be arbitrarily determined by physicians and psychologists (the leading professional in the John/Joan case was a psychologist) reflects the belief that gender is purely a social construction, a question of nurture, not nature. This belief has been seriously challenged in recent years.

In our society, babies come in two varieties: boys and girls. Unfortunately, not all babies match the male-female dichotomy that nature generally employs. But our culture allows no third option, and those whose sex is uncertain must be corrected or normalized and made to fit into one class or the other. If it is difficult for the doctor to tell the parents that he is uncertain whether their new baby is a boy or a girl, imagine how difficult it would be for the parents, when asked by friends and relatives about the sex of the baby, to have to answer that they don't know! With the most open mind in the world, how would you go about trying to raise a boy-girl in our society?

Consider, however, this account by Elliott about studies of a rare deficiency of testosterone metabolism, 5-alpha-reductase deficiency syndrome, from the Dominican Republic:

> Children with this condition are genetically XY but are born sexually ambiguous. In the rural Dominican Republic where the studies were conducted, these children are often raised as girls. Until puberty, that is. Because when the children

reach puberty they undergo striking changes. Their voices deepen, their muscles develop; their testes descend; and what was thought to be a clitoris enlarges to become more like a penis. The child who was thought to be a girl, or sexually ambiguous, gradually becomes a boy. Dominican Republic villagers call these children *guevedoches*, or "penis at twelve."[74]

Interestingly, this switch appears to be made without trauma for anyone concerned: "Of the 18 children followed in [one] study who were raised as girls, 17 changed to a male gender identity during puberty. Sixteen changed to a male gender role, working as farmers and doing other traditionally male work, and 15 of them went on to marry women."[75] Elliott points out that these are not cases of mistaken sex assignment; instead they point to the acceptance in that society of a "third sex"—the category called *guevedoche*. Other cultures seem able to accommodate intersexuality as well. Elliott gives the example of the Navajo culture, where the intersexed have a special name (*nadle*) and are accorded special status: "A family into which a *nadle* is born is considered very fortunate, because a *nadle* ensures wealth and success. They are made heads of the family and are given control of family property."[76]

According to Dreger, a strong advocate for changing medical practice in relation to the intersexed, ambiguous genitalia "do not constitute a disease. They simply constitute a failure to fit a particular (and, at present, a particularly demanding) definition of normality."[77] She and others have lobbied hard to change how babies born with ambiguous genitalia are treated. The first step involves revising the description of intersex from an anatomical *abnormality* to an anatomical *variation*. This would entail ceasing to treat ambiguous genitals as a medical problem that must immediately be corrected by surgery. Dreger and others recognize that in our society the intersexed must be assigned one gender or the other, but they insist that this should be done with the recognition that any gender assignment is temporary and that it can be changed later on if and when the child decides. And children should be informed of their condition and accepted as they are. Neither children nor parents should be lied to in order to accommodate the normalizing procedures, whether physical or psychological.

BOX 10.5

MILTON DIAMOND, "IS IT A BOY OR A GIRL?"

Imagine for a moment that you are a family doctor, and you have just delivered the first-born child of a young couple. As the baby yelps its first cry of freedom and the nurse tends to the mother, you inspect the child's genitals to answer what you know will be the family's next question: "Is it a boy or a girl?" You hesitate and answer, "I can't tell."

As a doctor, you have delivered an intersexed child, a child with biologically male and female sexual features. Such children, born with ambiguous genitals, make up for about one in every two thousand to four thousand births. What do you do now?

If this happened just a decade ago, the doctor would offer a relatively stock response. Doctors had been taught in medical school to make their decisions based on the length of the penis. The child is called a boy if [the penis] is longer than an inch. If shorter, the doctor typically recommended that the genitals be operated on to appear as a girl's. After designating the child a girl, regardless of its actual sex, doctors would tell the moms to raise the child as such.

A similar course was followed with children who were biologically female but born with a masculine-looking clitoris. Doctors typically recommended surgery to provide the "correct" female look. "Everything will be all right," the parents were told. Most doctors saw these procedures as simple and appropriate solutions....

Most people believe that everyone is born as one of two "types," male or female. But the exception is far more common. More than one in every hundred newborns has an intersexed condition. Infants are born with many varieties of intersexuality, many of which are not signalled by ambiguous genitals. These infants look just like their brothers and sisters. Their situations may not become clear until puberty or adulthood. And for many, the precise intersex situation never becomes clear without genetic, anatomical, hormonal, or other tests.

Typically people have twenty-three pairs of chromosomes—bundles of DNA material—that determine sex and other traits. Most males pair a Y chromosome with an X chromosome. Females pair two X chromosomes. But some infants are born with extra sex chromosomes such as XXY or XXXYY. Intersexed children can be born with both one testis and one ovary. They can be born with the genitals of the opposite sex. Some children appear to be females at birth and then switch to look like males at puberty....

Until recently, the conventional approach had been set five decades ago when a Johns Hopkins University psychologist argued that humans were psychosexually neutral at birth, so it didn't matter whether infants were raised as boys or girls. That view was based on a study of how he interpreted people with "differences of sex development"—or DSD, the now-preferred term for intersex conditions—fared....[1] Because it was easier to fashion a female-appearing set of genitals than a functioning penis, male infants were often reassigned as girls. Many thousands of people around the world have received such treatments, and genital surgeries on infants and children continue today....

The formerly private world of doctors and parents became more public in the late 1990s. At that time, in 1998, I offered evidence to the American Association of Pediatrics that these practices for intersex conditions were on shaky ground, both biologically and ethically. I proposed three changes:

1. "There should be a general moratorium on sex assignment cosmetic surgery when it is done without the consent of the patient...."
2. "This moratorium should not be lifted unless and until complete and comprehensive retrospective studies are done and it is found that the outcomes of past interventions have been positive...."
3. "Efforts should be made to undo the effects of past deception and secrecy...."

These three proposals stirred a reassessment in the medical profession ... intersex conditions have become far more open socially and medically. Although medicine still tends to see intersex conditions as disorders or errors of development, among the intersex community itself these conditions are more often viewed as livable "varieties" or "differences" of life.[2]

Notes

1. DSD stands for "disorders of sexual development," according to the consensus document that recommended the change of nomenclature (discussed in this chapter). The term "disorder" still carries a connotation of abnormality that the author of this article is apparently attempting to avoid.

2. A boxed insert in this article reports that a new politics of the intersex condition may be emerging as some pro-family groups in the U.S. want X and Y identification on marriage certificates: "One legislative proposal in California would give marriage licenses only to couples with XY and XX chromosomes." In Australia, on the other hand, "a man with XXY chromosomes seeks an official marriage as a person declaring himself a man and woman combined."

Source: Milton Diamond, "'Is It a Boy or a Girl?': Intersex Children Reshape Medical Practice," *Science & Spirit*, 18, no. 4 (September-October 2007), 36–38.

The manner in which the intersexed and their parents have been treated up to now raises serious ethical questions regarding autonomy and informed consent. Assigning a gender to a baby, then force-fitting the baby's body and life to fit that gender assignment, seriously limits the child's future autonomy, what some refer to as a child's right to "an open future."[78] Further, Dreger believes that parents are not being given all the information necessary about their child's condition to give truly informed consent. In addition, many of the surgeries being used are both risky and experimental. Dreger believes that current treatment of these babies relies for its justification on the "monster approach," the notion that these conditions are grotesque and must be corrected at all cost. As a result, "ethical guidelines that would be applied in nearly any other medical situation are, in cases of intersexuality, ignored. Patients are lied to; risky procedures are performed without follow-up; consent is not fully informed: autonomy and health are risked because of unproven (and even disproven) fears that atypical anatomy will lead to psychological disaster."[79]

With respect to the intersexed, Dreger believes that medicine has gone too far in its pursuit of normalcy. But it may be unfair to blame medicine, since doctors themselves are trapped within the confines of our either-or sexual framework. So are parents. The Navajo and the peasants of the Dominican Republic may be more enlightened than we are in this regard, but, as Elliott tells us, "[W]e can't simply decide to see the world that way. We have the world we have, and we live in the present, not the past."[80] However, the work of Dreger and others has had an effect, and new guidelines for the treatment of the intersexed are now emerging. For example, as a result of the International Consensus Conference on Intersex, organized by the Lawson Wilkins Pediatric Endocrine Society and the European Society for Paediatric Endocrinology, a document entitled "Consensus Statement on Management of Intersex Disorders" was published in 2006 by the American Academy of Pediatrics. Because there is so much controversy and misunderstanding around the questions of intersexuality, its first proposal dealt with nomenclature and definitions: "We propose the term 'disorders of sex development' (DSD), as defined by congenital conditions in which development of chromosomal, gonadal, or anatomic sex is atypical."[81] Its main recommendations regarding concepts of care reflect many of the concerns for which Dreger and others have been lobbying for many years, including avoiding gender assignment before expert evaluation; a more cautious approach to surgery; open communication with patients and families; and respect for patients and families in all decision making. Following this conference and the consensus document, a new organization, Accord Alliance, was formed in 2008 to promote the new standards of care proposed by the consensus group. Interestingly, this organization has now replaced the Intersex Society of North America (ISNA) whose role as an interest group was seen as generally one-sided (on the side of the intersexed, many of whom had felt abused by the medical establishment). In a letter to its supporters published on its website, the ISNA refers to its "scrappy, brave, and confrontational beginnings," and to the need for a different kind of organization "to assume the role of a convenor of stakeholders across the health care system and DSD communities."[82]

Public perception of disorders of sex development has been confused. This is not surprising given the secrecy that has surrounded these conditions over the years, if not centuries, as well as the number of different disorders that have been diagnosed and their multiple classifications (there are 7 grades of AIS alone). Furthermore, not all DSDs are like the cases of ambiguous genitalia discussed above, nor can they all be diagnosed at birth. For example, with respect to androgen insensitivity, a baby might have completely typical external female genitals, but internally she will have testes instead of a uterus and ovaries; the ambiguity will thus not show up until puberty when menstruation does not appear and a medical diagnosis will be made.[83]

Complexities of Gender

To add more complexity to an already complex bioethical question, it must be recognized that intersex conditions are not the same as transgender conditions (although there are overlapping issues). While some people who are born with ambiguous genitalia want to change the gender they have grown up with, many do not. At the same time, only some of those who do want to change their gender have an anatomical intersex condition; many simply express a gender identity that does not conform to their anatomy. Disorders of sexual development (DSD) are considered medical problems that need treatment (although, as discussed, how and when—and even if—treatment should be done has been the subject of controversy); gender identity disorders (GID) are considered psychological, although once a sex reassignment is determined to be desirable or necessary, they move into the realm of the medical. But there is also controversy surrounding the very designation of GIDs as psychological, as well as the practice of labelling them a disorder. Solomon points out that while deaf people do not object to being called deaf (even if deafness has become their identity), the designation of their gender identity as a disorder infuriates the transgender community: "Those who think of deafness or autism as identities can do so even if others call them disorders. *GID* suggests not simply that trans people have a disorder, but that their identity itself *is* the disorder."[84]

For many in both the intersex or transgender communities, the disorder is not with them but with us—a society that insists on a binary breakdown of sexual difference into male and female, with nothing in between. Both anatomy and psychology speak to the limitations of this view, a view that is increasingly coming into question. As many as 1 in 150 people may be born with an intersex condition. This includes those with ambiguous genitalia (which is obvious at birth), but also the chromosomally ambiguous (those who are, for example, of an XXY, XXYY or other genotype—see Box 10.5), as well as others whose intersex condition does not become evident until puberty or even later.

With respect to gender identity, there may be no clearly physical reason for a person's certainty that he or she has been classified as the "wrong" sex/gender. At the same time, Solomon refers to gender as "among the first elements of self-knowledge. This knowledge encompasses an internal sense of self, and, often, a preference for external behaviors, such as dress and type of play."[85] The origin may be genetic, or due to androgen levels during pregnancy, or to early childhood influences. One specialist in gender variance suggests that "as many as four hundred rare genes and epigenetic phenomena may be involved, genes associated not with hormone regulation, but with personality formation."[86] Given these possibilities, it should be obvious that our perception of gender and sex is in need of modification, something that intersex and transgender activists are working very hard to bring about. Along with a generalized critique of gender roles in society, they reject the notion that masculinity or femininity is strictly determined by biology. Toby Adams, an American attorney working against gender discrimination, tells the story of a friend named David, who wants to marry the male partner he has been living with: "David is not entirely male, so his relationship is not really a 'same-sex' marriage,' but David is not entirely female either. David's chromosomes are XXY."[87] David is intersex and does not identify either as male or female. He wants the law to recognize his "true" sex (that is, intersex). His view is echoed by intersex activist and blogger Dr. Cary Gabriel Costello, who states, "Great pain might be avoided if parents were allowed to acknowledge our physical truth on birth certificates which included an intersex checkbox, or if the gender marker requirement were simply removed."[88]

Efforts to change both the public perception and the medical treatment of DSD and GID are quite recent, and substantive change will take time. From a bioethical perspective, it is important to ensure that the ethical principles that are supposed to govern all medical treatment (in particular, autonomy and respect for persons) apply to people whose sex/gender does not conform to the norm. A new attitude toward the idea of normality in society and normalizing treatments in medicine must be developed as we learn to recognize and appreciate a range of what Solomon calls horizontal identities. A new vocabulary is needed for explaining variations in sex/gender identity and expression, perhaps using words such as typical and atypical as opposed to normal and abnormal (or pathological). Not everything that is atypical needs to be corrected, reversed, or changed.

BOX 10.6

IS SHE A WOMAN?

Whether she's male or female, intersex or—according to the latest reports—a hermaphrodite, one thing should be clear to South African sprinter Caster Semenya: Privacy is no match for ignorance, bumbling officials and the burning desire to know.

Two newspapers reported yesterday that the 18-year-old world champion runner is a hermaphrodite with no ovaries or womb.... Both *The Times* of London and the *Sydney Daily Telegraph* said their sources had leaked the highly anticipated results from tests carried out on Ms. Semenya after she became the 800-metre world champion, and the IAAF announced it was investigating her sex.

The Times reported that the sprinter may have internal testes, or male sexual organs, which produce testosterone and can generate muscle mass, body hair and a deep voice. The IAAF [International Association of Athletics Federation] refused to comment on the claim last night, but earlier in the day its general secretary, Pierre Weiss, said: "It's clear that she is a woman, but maybe not 100 per cent...."

"God made me the way I am and I accept myself," [Semenya] told *You*, South Africa's best-selling English magazine. "I am who I am, and I'm proud of myself. I don't want to talk about the tests. I'm not even thinking about them...."

"Having your sex called into question is a deeply humiliating and stigmatizing event," said Alice Dreger, professor of clinical medical humanities and bioethics in the Feinberg School of Medicine at Northwestern University.... Dr. Dreger accused the track organization of relying on unstated, shifting standards for sex verification ... [highlighting that] when it comes to sex, there are too many shades of grey.

Source: Hayley Mick, "Whispers of 'Is She or Isn't She?' Continue to Chase Sprinter; Reports Say World Champion Caster Semenya Is a Hermaphrodite," *The Globe and Mail*, September 11, 2009, A2.

Deaf Culture

In thinking about what is normal and what is abnormal or pathological, most people would classify deafness as an abnormality. If not a disease as such, it is seen as a lack, the abnormal functioning—or non-functioning—of a person's hearing. But in recent years there has arisen a movement from within the deaf community itself resisting the clinical-pathological view: "Essentially this view accepts the behaviors and values of people who can hear as 'standard' or 'the norm' and then focuses on how Deaf people deviate from that norm.... It is also a view that Deaf people have something wrong with them, something that can and must be 'fixed.'"[89]

Two things should be noted in the above quotation: the use of the capital "D" when referring to Deaf people, and the use of the word "values" in reference to the comparison of people who can hear and those who cannot. Both of these points signal an important aspect of a growing resistance to normalization: those who are part of it refer to themselves as a community, as **Deaf Culture**. They define themselves as a group of people who share a common language (American Sign Language). Further, they insist that the "Deaf world has its own unique values, traditions, rituals, institutions and stories, as well as its own manual languages.... Deaf people have access to a rich and vibrant culture that is closed to anyone who does not use or understand a manual language."[90] Thus, many of them do not see themselves as having a deficit that needs to be corrected. There are schools and universities specifically for the deaf, and these allow for passing on deaf history and culture to the children of this community (in the same way that schools and universities do for the rest of the population).

The notion of community is extremely important in the resistance to treating deafness as a handicap. Deaf children raised in a hearing world are always defined by their handicap; raised in Deaf Culture, they have no handicap. In the former world, they have a pathology; in the latter, they are considered normal. This dichotomy of perspectives plays itself out in debates about the treatment of deaf children and in the growing opposition to cochlear implants. Part of the resistance of parents of deaf children to implants comes from the fact that they do not work easily with prelingually deaf children (children who have never been able to speak), they require years of training, and the results are not always impressive. In contrast, members of the Deaf community see deafness not as a disability but as part of their identity and thus a feature that they do not necessarily want to change through technologies such as cochlear implants.

From the point of view of the medical model, deafness is a disability and cochlear implants represent a medical treatment and, as far as possible, a cure. At the very least, they will help a child learn to function in the hearing world. But from the point of view of Deaf Culture, helping the child learn to function in the hearing world is not the objective, and cochlear implants will be seen as an issue "about the loss or preservation of your people and your culture.... To think about cochlear implants being made available to all prelingually deaf children means thinking about the slow disintegration of the language that gives expression to who you are, and to the habits of being that give your life its sense."[91]

This may be true for many adults for whom deafness is part of their identity and who have chosen to live and thrive within Deaf Culture. But what about a child who has not yet developed the "habits of being" that give his or her life sense and who is too young to make any choice about treatment? Is it right to deprive a child of cochlear implants because the parents believe deafness is not a handicap but a culture? Is this equivalent to refusing a blood transfusion to a child because of the parents' religious beliefs? In such a case the courts step in and order the transfusion. Is the refusal of cochlear implants for a deaf child depriving that child of an open future? From the perspective of Deaf Culture, it is not. According to Elliott, "In the Deaf community, Deaf children are not identified by their deafness. But living in the world of the hearing means being identified as disabled, not only by others but also by yourself."[92] Parents would thus see themselves as providing a more open future for their child, since the child would not be an outsider in a hearing world but a thriving member of the Deaf world. These parents would see themselves as exercising the principle of beneficence in relation to their child (doing what they believe is best for his or her future) as well as the principle of autonomy as proxy decision-makers. The medical community would see it otherwise: not correcting a disability such as deafness when the technology makes it possible to do so would go against beneficence in the medical view. And making a decision with such lifelong impacts on the child would be seen as an abuse of autonomy on the part of the parents.

If the question of non-treatment of deaf children is controversial, the notion of deliberately creating a deaf child is more so. However, many members of the Deaf community wish to marry other members of their cultural group; they also wish for a deaf child so that they may pass on their culture and their values. Some go so far as to seek genetic counselling and to request the use of technology (normally used to prevent a handicap such as deafness) in order to ensure the birth of a deaf child. This creates a new ethical dilemma for genetic counsellors: "parents with certain disabilities who seek help in trying to assure that they will have a child who shares their disability."[93] For Davis, deliberately creating a deaf child would be morally wrong, whether or not one sees deafness as a disability, based on the notion of a child's right to an open future. If deafness is seen as a disability that significantly narrows a child's possibilities, then it is a moral harm; if deafness is seen as a culture, "then deliberately creating a Deaf child who will have only very limited options to move outside of that culture, also counts as a moral harm."[94]

For Davis, it is not a question of a conflict between autonomy and beneficence but of a conflict between parental autonomy and the child's future autonomy. By deliberately creating a deaf child, the parents would be depriving their child of *future* autonomy. This would be wrong. Further, deliberately creating a child "who will be forced irreversibly into the parents' notion of 'the good life' violates the Kantian principle of treating each person as an end in herself and never as a means only."[95] All parents have mixed motives when they choose to have children, and continuing the family line is often one of them. But deliberately limiting a child's possibilities to reflect the values and needs of the parents' current life is to forget that the child will grow up and live his or her own life, with his or her own needs.

ETHICAL THEORY AND NON-STANDARD TREATMENTS

What can be seen from the above analysis is that what one might consider ethically justifiable in relation to treatment or non-treatment depends to a large extent on one's acceptance—or non-acceptance—of the existing medical paradigm. This, in turn, depends on one's acceptance of current societal and medical norms about what is normal and what is pathological, as well as acceptance of the current medical model for treatment. Resistance to the medical model, however, does not have the morally equivalent results in all cases. Refusal to treat a child with the current best treatment for cancer, for example, could result in the child's death, and thus forced treatment could be ethically justified so that the child will have a future and eventually make his or her own decisions. Similarly, refusal of cochlear implants can be seen as ethically problematic since it intentionally closes off possibilities for a child; it deprives a child of an open future. However, refusal of surgical treatments on ambiguous genitalia can be ethically justified—and is more and more seen as the only ethical choice—because it actually preserves an open future for a child.

One of the challenges of applying ethical theory to the issues discussed in this chapter is trying to discern where the ethical responsibility lies in dealing with medical philosophies and therapies that diverge from standard medical practice. Doctors have a responsibility to perform their function to the best of their ability within the system they know. However, when it comes to treatment that falls outside the knowledge and experience of physicians, or even outside the accepted practice of the field, how can we begin to analyze from the standpoint of bioethics where the health care workers' responsibilities begin and end?

Further, while the law and ethics do not coincide, there is a legal dimension to be considered in relation to non-standard treatment: doctors are ultimately accountable for their advice, and if something goes wrong, they can be accused of malpractice by the very patients who asked them to consider the treatments in the first place. In such a situation, it is not surprising that many doctors are very conservative in their approach to alternative therapies.

It is helpful to consider the issue of the intersexed as an example in this context since it represents a changing paradigm within the standard medical paradigm. Doctors were regularly treating people with disorders of sexual development in ways that met with the approval of their peers and that followed the medical knowledge of the time. The John/Joan case is a good example of treatment and therapy based on what is now considered to be a mistaken premise about gender, which resulted in much suffering for all concerned. Even in less drastic cases, the medical establishment, as we have seen, violated the autonomy of parents and the future autonomy of babies in order to force tiny children into gender roles and expectations of society, completely ignoring the present and future needs of the children. Not only autonomy but also beneficence and non-malfeasance were ignored in an extremely paternalistic environment.

In less than two decades, an entire philosophy of treatment is being transformed due both to the vocal and persistent criticism of the intersex community and to the advancement of scientific knowledge about the biology (and, in particular, the genetics) of sexual variation. It can probably be said that doctors in the field began looking at the evidence, listening to their patients, and then at least beginning to change their way of diagnosing and treating the disorders in question. Is this a model that could be applied to the issue of complementary and alternative medicine?

Utilitarian Ethics

Looking at the question of intersex from a utilitarian point of view, the reaction of the medical community (at least as represented by the "Consensus Statement on Management of Intersex Disorders" referred to earlier) would appear to be the most ethical solution. Fewer people will be harmed by unnecessary or ineffective surgeries and hormonal treatments if the new guidelines are followed. Will society be harmed by changing the practice of trying to fit the intersexed into the two boxes of male and female? If the dichotomy of male and female is really a myth, and we have the biological knowledge to show this, then surely the most that can be said is that society might be a little uncomfortable for a while but it can hardly be harmed in the long run.

Similarly, if we look at the question of CAM from a utilitarian perspective, it is hard to see how any harm would come to society as a whole by less invasive and less drug-dependent treatments overall in the population. Even the concern with harm, as pointed out earlier, is exaggerated as much more harm appears to come from the medical system itself. And since, ultimately, treatment by diet and herbal remedies is generally cheaper than costly surgery and expensive drugs, the overall benefit to society could be considerable.

Kantian Ethics

From a Kantian perspective, the most important factor regarding alternative medicine is its emphasis on diet and lifestyle: in other words, on taking responsibility for one's own health. This is true autonomy in the Kantian sense. Kantian ethics would also support a patient's right to make his or her own choices in relation to treatment options and, it could be argued, the right to be fully informed about what those choices really are—in other words, the right to choose from a range of options that would include CAM therapies as well as standard therapies. On the other hand, it might be difficult to argue that a doctor has the responsibility to know all the available options when many of them would be considered outside his or her field of knowledge and expertise.

It is unlikely that Kantian ethics could be used to support parental choices that actually limit future autonomous choices for their children. This would apply to intersex conditions as well as deafness. Kantian philosophy would force both parents and doctors to think about what they would want if they were in the position of the child. Would they want choices made for them that would limit their autonomy? Would they want to be deprived of an open future? From a utilitarian point of view, the desire of some parents to reproduce children with the same genetic disorder (for example, deafness or dwarfism) that they have would have to be assessed according to the effects on society as a whole, as well as on the future child. As with a Kantian analysis of autonomy, it is not obvious that limiting a child's future is a good thing for the child in the long term, even if it appears to be the best thing for the parents in the short term.

Virtue Ethics

From the perspective of virtue ethics, it is possible to take a more uniform approach in analyzing both CAM therapies and responses to conditions such as intersexuality or deafness. The requirement to look at a person's flourishing within a whole life is what becomes the ethical focus. In the case of alternative medicine, a person who is ready to take responsibility for his or her health is also ready to assume the responsibility for making treatment choices, especially if those choices support a view of health that incorporates the psychological, social, and environmental, as well as the physical, perspectives. Many so-called alternative therapies represent, in fact, a return to holistic practices of the past, which interpreted illness as something affecting the whole person and a whole life, rather than an organ or the functioning of a bodily system.

Virtue ethics would also support a more integrated approach to variations in sexual makeup, especially as the biological base of these variations becomes clearer. Society will have to adapt to sexual and gender difference, and see individuals as whole beings with the right to grow and flourish in ways that do not stunt their development or box them into pre-established gender moulds. Much can be learned from other cultures in this regard, as the work of Elliott and others indicates.

Most importantly, it can be argued that the issues raised in this chapter signal a need for bioethicists to think outside the medical paradigm when it comes to assessing what is good for patients in relation to medical treatment. The principle of beneficence needs to be seen in broader terms. The bioethicist must detach himself from the medical paradigm and look at the philosophical dimensions of persons and their bodies, health and illness, and the goals of medicine. Philosophy must be ready to question not just within the medical paradigm, but also at its edges.

Our traditional binary division of male and female, XX and XY, is being challenged by the intersexed and the transgendered. Sex and gender are much more complex than once thought and do not conform neatly to the boxes that we check on forms throughout our lives, from birth to death.

CONCLUSION

In looking at the proliferation of alternative therapies combined with a general loss of faith in the absolute authority of medicine, one can argue that medicine itself must become more open and accepting of possibilities other than high-tech treatments based on one philosophy of health and disease. As Larson states, "There is no single medicine embraced by all, if indeed there ever was. But scientific medicine has not yet fully embraced this recognition."[96] Scientific medicine is enormously costly and, one can argue, has not been very effective in ridding the world of illness; in fact, we have more chronic illness than ever before, much of it caused by the overuse of medical technology. Scientific medicine's refusal of the premises of alternative medicine causes its practitioners to ignore any evidence of the healing capacity of other treatments. But there is evidence of successful treatment of patients who could not be cured by conventional methods; the problem is that conventional medicine cannot *explain* such success: "Unless this evidence of successful treatment is to be simply ignored, another explanation for it must be found."[97]

In relation to treating people such as the intersexed, medicine might open itself to a review of its notion of objectivity and its methods of determining the normal and the pathological. Perceptions of normalcy change, depending on the technology and the person using it. While it may be an exaggeration to say that there is no such thing as normal when discussing human physiology, the word itself (based on its root, "norm") is value-laden. It would be better, as has been suggested, to speak in terms of typical and atypical, and to emphasize the variations that exist in human physiology than to perceive every variation as a pathology that needs to be corrected. In an age of pluralism, new methods of diagnosis and treatment may need to be found that are inclusive, rather than exclusive, methods that do, however, recognize every child's (and adult's) right to an open future.

PHILOSOPHICAL REFLECTION ON MORALITY AND HEALTH

Do we have a moral obligation to preserve our health? This might seem like a strange question in our time of objective scientific medicine where the focus is on the disease rather than the patient, but it would not have been a strange question in previous centuries. For the Ancients, health was considered to be a state of harmony, both within the person and in the person's relationship with the world around him. This meant living in accordance with nature. Seen from this perspective, illness is the result of a state of disharmony in the person; there was a strong link between living a moral life and living a healthy life, since neglect in either sphere would lead to disharmony and disease.

For Plato, for example, it was extremely important for the health of the individual that the soul and body were in harmony, and this was a question of proportion: "For health and sickness, virtue and vice, the proportion or disproportion between soul and body is far the most important factor."[98] The linking of health and illness with virtue and vice in the same sentence is an indication of Plato's belief in the interconnectedness of health and virtue, which "are parallel to each other, complete each other. Everything depends on the soul, but the ultimate aim is the health, physical and moral, of the whole man."[99] In order to prevent disharmony, both the body and the soul must be exercised in the right way: those who are involved in intellectual pursuits must make sure the body receives adequate athletic training, while those whose principal activity is physical must work to cultivate the mind. Plato believed in a sound mind in a sound body, and his injunction for harmony was a moral one. In fact, "Plato wrote in his *Republic* that the need for many hospitals and doctors was the earmark of a bad city."[100]

The link between health and morality is also reflected in Aristotle who, as we have seen, held that the good life is a virtuous life and emphasized moderation in his portrayal of the virtues. The Stoics, too, believed that the moral life was one lived in accordance with nature and that illness was the result of a state of imbalance between a person and his or her environment. In the Judeo-Christian world, the Bible "often describes illness as the wages of sin, and the Book of Leviticus repeatedly links bodily affliction with ritual impurity."[101] The association of sickness and sin has a long history.

While Western medicine sees itself as constructed upon (and improving on) Hippocratic medicine, there are important differences. Hippocratic medicine was concerned with man in nature, and health was achieved by living with nature, not fighting it: "Disease was viewed in the context of a disturbed relationship between man and the environment."[102] The physician's task was to support the healing efforts of nature and to teach regimens of personal habits that would serve to promote and maintain good health. In all of these philosophies, the responsibility of the individual to maintain health through the development of good habits, or virtues, is clear.

The Greek goddess Hygeia was the goddess of health, not in the sense of curing the sick, but as the guardian of health and healthy living. She "symbolized the belief that men could remain well if they lived according to reason."[103] She eventually ceded her place to Asclepius, who achieved fame "not by teaching wisdom but by mastering the use of the knife and the knowledge of the curative virtues of plants."[104] It can be said that the dichotomy represented by Hygeia and Asclepius has lived on in the history of medicine (and can even be said to be more pronounced in our day in the tension between allopathic and alternative medicine):

> For the worshipers of Hygeia, health is the natural order of things, a positive attribute to which men are entitled if they govern their lives wisely. According to them, the most important function of medicine is to discover and teach the natural laws which will ensure to man a healthy mind in a healthy body. More skeptical or wiser in the ways of the world, the followers of Asclepius believe that the chief role of the physician is to treat disease, to restore health by correcting any imperfection caused by the accidents of birth or of life.[105]

Hygeia has left a legacy to the English language in our word "hygiene," the meaning of which has narrowed considerably, relating now more to cleanliness than goodness or living a good life. Her spirit, however, is alive in our word "health," which means "wholeness," and in the word "healing," which means "to make whole."[106] Unfortunately our modern scientific medicine is based less on wholeness than on the conception of the separateness of mind and body. Medicine focuses on the body, and the methods of diagnosis and treatment tend to relate only to particular body parts and processes, studied in their separateness. Wholeness, or making whole, has been lost as a goal of medicine, and some maintain that the primary concern of the physician "in spite of utopian claims to the contrary, should be sickness not overall health; medicine should concentrate on 'scientifically accurate diagnosis and treatment.'"[107] The cult of Asclepius has won.

It can be argued that this is not an entirely negative victory. As more and more of our modern diseases such as cancer and heart disease, among others, are seen as diseases of lifestyle, we tend to look at the sick as being responsible for their disease. We may no longer refer to vices such as sloth, gluttony, and intemperance but we readily refer to risk factors such as sedentary lifestyle, obesity, and alcoholism. As Gunderman notes, "Implicit throughout is a causal association between habit and health, according to which the afflicted may be regarded as the instigators of their own bodily misfortune."[108] This can result in an attitude of blaming the victim. There is, in reality, a fine line between taking responsibility for one's own health and being responsible for one's disease, and the more we put emphasis on the former, the more we risk the accusing tone of the latter.

We are not Greeks, and Hygeia may have been less versed than we are in the risks to health caused by social and economic factors. While there may be people whose heavy smoking and drinking habits likely bring on their lung or liver cancer, there are many whose health risks are due more to poverty than to vice. As Gunderman tells us, "The impact of economic, social, and cultural settings on personal health behaviors merits close examination. There is no question that people with lower levels of income tend to engage more often in riskier behaviors and to fail more frequently to engage in behaviors that would reduce that risk."[109] In addition, environmental factors beyond the control of ordinary individuals render healthy living a more complex affair than any modern-day Hygeia would be able to oversee.

Our challenge is to strike a balance between the guardianship of Hygeia and the knife of Asclepius, while recognizing that the powers of both are limited. We have perhaps relied too much on the curing powers of the physician's knife and the pharmacist's pills; more of the wisdom of Hygeia might keep us all well a little longer. With an aging population and increasingly expensive and limited medical resources, taking responsibility for our own health can be seen as a moral obligation to which we must all give more than a passing nod.

CASES OF INTEREST

Juan and Edgar Uyunkar

Juan and Edgar Uyunkar, a father and son team of traditional healers from the Upper Amazon region of Ecuador, were invited to Wikwimekong by the Naandwedidaa program of the Wikwimekong Health Services Department of Manitoulin Island to conduct a healing ceremony for the community members in the fall of 2001. The participants were encouraged to consume large amounts of a liquid brewed from tobacco and water and the natem plant, a hallucinogen banned in Canada. The substance was said to induce vomiting in order to expel contaminants such as bile, phlegm, salt, fats, excess sugars, and parasites.

The ceremony was to last three days, during which the participants were told to stop taking any other drugs and to fast as much as possible. Jane Mainangowi, a 71-year-old diabetic woman, stopped taking her prescribed Diamicron and started fasting. After the first night of vomiting, Ms. Mainangowi became dizzy and had difficulty leaving her chair. After the second night, she was too weak to walk and had to be helped into the family vehicle. About three hours into the third night, she began vomiting, gasping for air, and said that she could not drink anymore. Shortly after being encouraged to drink more, Jane failed to respond and was then carried outside. Juan ordered a rectal flush that was unsuccessful. About 30 minutes later Jane was carried in to the bathroom floor, where two people attempted CPR. An ambulance was called roughly 20 minutes later and the paramedics continued CPR. However, they were ordered to stop after about 10 minutes by a doctor at the Sudbury Hospital who was communicating with them on the phone.

The autopsy later revealed that Jane died of nicotine poisoning. Juan and Edgar were charged with criminal negligence causing death, administering a noxious substance, trafficking in a controlled substance, and possession of a controlled substance. They both pleaded guilty to administering a noxious substance and trafficking a controlled substance, after which the remainder of the charges were dropped. Juan received a 12-month conditional sentence and a 12-month probation. Edgar received a 12-month conditional sentence and one day in jail.[110]

Laurie Jean Mathiason

Laurie Jean Mathiason, a 20-year-old woman living in Saskatoon, was a regular chiropractic patient with a history of 23 adjustments. She also had a history of adjusting herself, which she had been warned against. On February 3, 1998, she saw her chiropractor, Stacy Kramer, because of a sore neck. After her treatment, Mathiason felt that the pain had worsened, so she returned to the clinic with her fiancé for another treatment the following day. Kramer once again adjusted her neck, after which Mathiason lost consciousness and began convulsing. Her mother, Sharon Mathiason, who was working a few doors over in the same mall, was notified by Laurie Jean's fiancé. When she arrived at the clinic, Laurie Jean was twitching and foaming at the mouth. Both her fiancé and her mother testified that Kramer did nothing to help her but slap her in the face. Kramer maintained, however, that Laurie Jean had begun crying after the adjustment and that she had known that something was wrong. She had then examined her eyes and noticed that the left one was moving "all wrong." She called an ambulance immediately.

Laurie Jean was rushed to Saskatoon's Royal University Hospital in a coma and declared brain dead the next day. She was kept on life support for another two days in order to harvest her organs. A four-day hearing before the Saskatchewan's Chief Coroner and a six-member jury in Saskatoon's Court of Queen's Bench revealed that Kramer had not performed the procedure incorrectly. The autopsy showed that one of Laurie Jean's arteries had likely been torn during the February 3 session and a blood clot had formed. The neck adjustment performed the next day dislodged the blood clot, which then blocked the artery and cut off blood flow to the brain. The jury recommended that literature be made available to patients outlining the risks of a stroke and that standardized forms be filled out providing details of the patients' health and medical history.[111]

Tamara Lovett

On the morning of March 2, 2013, 44-year old Tamara Lovett called Emergency Medical Services (EMS) to her basement suite in Calgary, fearing that her son was having a seizure. The emergency crew arrived to find 7-year-old Ryan Lovett in cardiac arrest. He was rushed to the hospital in an ambulance and pronounced dead shortly after his arrival. Following an eight-month investigation into the boy's death, Tamara was arrested on November 22, 2013, and charged with criminal negligence causing death and failing to provide the necessities of life.

The Criminal Code requires parents and guardians to provide food, shelter, care, and medical attention required to sustain life and to protect children from harm. Ryan became ill with what was later identified as a strep infection, and his mother had opted to treat him with homeopathic herbal remedies rather than taking him to a doctor. Investigators believe that Ryan had been bedridden for 10 days before EMS were called, and before he ultimately succumbed to what the autopsy revealed to be a Group A Streptococcus infection, the bacteria of which can cause flesh-eating disease. Tamara was released on bail pending a preliminary hearing, scheduled to begin in January 2015.[112]

CASE STUDIES

Scenario One

Dr. Merrick is the director of the embryo modification wing in the Genetic Choice Clinic. He screens applications for designer embryos from couples wishing to choose certain characteristics for their expected child. Under his review now are two applications for such designer embryos. One couple, newly married and well educated, have requested the "designer works": musical talent, athletic and intellectual ability, as well as good looks and exceptional social skills. Both parents are scientists and wish to have a son who can follow in their footsteps. The second application comes from another newly married, well-educated couple who work for an organization dedicated to advancing the interests of the deaf. On their application, this couple has specified that they are happy to take whatever nature gives them except for one factor: they wish to have a deaf child like them. They feel that raising a hearing child would be difficult both for them and the child, and they want to raise their child as part of Deaf Culture.

Dr. Merrick has no serious reservations about granting the first request and promptly books the couple for an appointment. However, he feels that granting the second request would be morally problematic. To deliberately create a child with a disability, he feels, is wrong because it limits that child's future.

Before proceeding he decides to discuss the matter with his assistant, Myra Jones, one of the clinic's genetic counsellors. Myra believes that, in fact, the first couple's request is more intrusive in terms of limiting future possibilities than that of the deaf couple; after all, even if that child succeeds in becoming a brilliant musician or a gifted physicist, he will never know whether these accomplishments are the result of his own efforts or were simply programmed into him. She also states that her role as a counsellor is to be neutral in relation to her clients' values and to respect their autonomy and freedom of choice. She believes Dr. Merrick should do the same.

(1) Should Dr. Merrick grant the request of the couple that wants the "designer works"? (2) Should he grant the request of the other couple to create a deaf child? Is using genetic technology to select for deafness morally different from selecting for other "designer" traits? (3) Is deafness a disability? (4) What would Dena Davis say about parental autonomy in these situations? (5) How would a utilitarian look at the creation of designer children, including children with what are normally seen as disabilities?

Scenario Two

Dr. Segretti was on the telephone with Audrey Dubois, a patient suffering from high cholesterol. She had requested that he fax the results of her recent blood tests to a local naturopath's office, as she wanted to lower her cholesterol naturally. She explained to him that she is uncomfortable with taking the statin drugs he prescribed because of the risk of side effects and would rather try a treatment based on diet and natural remedies. Dr. Segretti, however, does not believe that naturopathic medicine has anything to offer that conventional medicine does not. He also tells Audrey that some naturopathic practices are even harmful. As her doctor, Segretti says that he cannot allow Audrey to embark on a futile and potentially harmful path. She must choose between remaining his patient or seeing a naturopath whose advice might interfere with or contradict his own. There is a shortage of doctors, he tells her, and if she is not going to follow his advice, there are other people willing to take her place.

(1) What should Audrey do? Should she follow Dr. Segretti's advice and take the drugs that he prescribes or seek the advice of a naturopath? (2) Does Audrey have responsibility for her own health? If so, what course of action is best for her? What might virtue ethics tell her? (3) Should doctors have the right to dismiss patients who do not follow their advice? How would Cohen advise Dr. Segretti? (4) What issues does this case raise regarding informed consent?

Scenario Three

Lukas and Lilly, a vegan couple, bring their nine-month-old child, Carter, to the hospital to see a doctor. Carter has been listless and lethargic for the past few weeks. Upon examination, he is diagnosed as being severely malnourished. When the hospital staff learn that Lukas and Lilly are vegans and that Carter has been getting nothing but breast milk, the doctor tries to convince them to add commercial supplements to his diet. Lukas and Lilly are unwilling to do this. They firmly believe that their diet is healthy; it has sustained them for nearly a decade. It is healthier, they hold, than what most people eat, since commercial food contains many animal by-products, pesticides, dyes, and other harmful ingredients. Besides, Lilly adds, a vegan diet is ethically superior to a diet consisting of animal products and commercial goods. They insist that Lilly's breast milk provides adequate nutrition for the child, although in the doctor's view, Lilly herself looks undernourished.

The doctor urges them to at least visit a health food store for a healthier alternative to mainstream commercial supplements. Lukas and Lilly refuse, and state that, not only will they continue with Carter's all–breast milk diet, but also when they do start Carter on solid food, they will be feeding him according to their dietary principles. This is the only regimen they find acceptable for their son.

Hearing this, the hospital staff becomes alarmed, fearing that Carter will come to further harm if he is sent home. One of the nurses on duty pulls the doctor aside and suggests they contact the Children's Aid Society.

(1) What should be done in this case? Should the doctor call Children's Aid? Should he refuse to release Carter from the hospital? (2) At what point, if any, do parents lose the right to make decisions on behalf of their children? Has this point been reached here? (3) How are autonomy and beneficence in conflict in this case? Are there any parallels with the case of Tyrell Dueck?

Scenario Four

Michael Dresden is three years old and dying of leukemia. He has been through several rounds of chemotherapy, and has been given numerous doses of radiation and pharmaceuticals intended to stop the cancer from spreading and bring it into remission. So far these efforts have been in vain. There is a new treatment, however, that has just been released. It has shown promise in clinical trials but has some serious side effects. Michael's doctor, Dr. Arden, tells his parents about this therapy and urges them to consent to treatment. Michael's parents, however, claim that they are tired of doctors and hospitals and do not want to consent to another treatment that might actually harm their child. The endless treatments are taxing on Michael, who is getting weaker by the day. They wish to discontinue treatment and take him to see an acupuncturist who practises traditional Chinese medicine. They explain their point of view to Dr. Arden; the Western medicine route hasn't been working, so they want to try an alternative approach.

(1) What should Dr. Arden do in this situation? Would he be justified in refusing to release Michael? (2) What is the parents' responsibility here? Are they justified in discontinuing treatment? Whose decision is this to make? (3) Would your decision change if Michael's prognosis were better, or if he were earlier along in his treatment? (4) Would your decision be affected by the fact that the recommended treatment is experimental and carries known and unknown risks? How do we weigh a new experimental treatment of scientific medicine against an age-old alternative practice such as acupuncture? (5) Is this case different from the case of the vegan parents, and if so, how?

Scenario Five

After a normal term of pregnancy, Lauren Olsen began having labour pains and was admitted to the hospital. Nearly 20 hours after her labour pains began, she gave birth. When presenting her with the baby, the doctor told her, a little awkwardly: "You're baby appears to have ambiguous genitalia."

Lauren looked at the baby and then at the doctor. She knew what "ambiguous genitalia" meant, but she was unsure of the implications for her baby.

The doctor continued: "It is up to you whether to have this child operated on. We could alter her genitalia and make her into a 'normal' girl." Lauren noted he was using the term "her" as though the decision were already made, as though this *was* a girl or at least would be one once the surgery was completed.

"And if I choose not to consent to the operation?" Lauren asked.

"Then we wait until the child is old enough to make a choice, based on its own sense of which gender best applies," the doctor replied.

Lauren asked the doctor for a few moments to think about this. She was newly divorced, and thus would be making this decision by herself. She understood the motivation behind having the surgery; if her child did not have the operation, she would have to explain to people why she did not know if her child was a girl or a boy. She would have to find gender-neutral clothing and toys, or perhaps buy her child both Barbie dolls and toy cars. And this could introduce even more confusion into the child's life. Without clear gender identification, the child would risk ridicule and exclusion. But forcing a gender onto the child was also problematic.

She knew that such surgery usually created girls, not boys, because creating a girl was considered easier; the criteria were not as strict. However, the newly formed female genitalia might not work correctly, and her little girl could grow up feeling cheated. Or worse, her little girl might grow up and realize that she's actually a boy. This would bring more trauma to the child's adolescent years.

After deliberating for a while, Lauren was interrupted when the doctor poked his head back into the room. "Ms. Olsen? Have you come to a decision?"

(1) Does Lauren have all the information she needs to make an informed decision? (2) What would Dreger say about operating on the baby at this point? What would Diamond say? (3) How would you advise Lauren to deal with the situation? Is this baby abnormal? Does it need to be fixed?

Scenario Six

Amada and Romano Del Omo recently moved from Mexico to Canada with their 13-year-old daughter, Maribel. They are working-class immigrants, have resided in Canada for two years, and still hold strongly to traditional Mexican beliefs. Their daughter is suffering from hallucinations and a high fever. Maribel's doctor believes that she is suffering from meningitis, a serious infection of one of the membranes that surrounds the brain. This may be the result of salmonella poisoning.

Upon questioning, Maribel's doctor learns that Maribel has recently been in contact with more than one potential source of infection. He speaks to her parents and suggests treatment with antibiotics. Her parents object, however, claiming that the illness is the result of witchcraft and evil spirits. In traditional Mexican medical practices, it is believed that supernatural powers can cause disease, especially those accompanied by hallucination. With diseases that are caused by supernatural forces, cures must also be provided by supernatural means. Typically, the affected person would seek out a traditional healer, a *curanderas*, who is supposed to receive her powers from God. Treatment by anyone other than a *curanderas* is unacceptable.

When Amada and Romano learn that there is no *curanderas* in Canada who could see Maribel, they insist on her being released from the hospital so that they can return to Mexico to see their local healer. Maribel, however, has learned about Western medicine from her friends and classmates. She is hesitant to return to Mexico to see a *curanderas*. She tells her parents that she will not go and that she would like to be treated with antibiotics. Her parents, however, do not agree and refuse to consent to the recommended treatment.

(1) What should Maribel's doctor do at this point? Can he, and should he, do anything but release her from the hospital? Should he involve Children's Aid or get a court order to treat the girl? (2) Should Maribel's wishes be taken into account? Is she competent enough to consent? (3) Are Maribel's parents in a position to give or withhold informed consent? What role does knowledge play in ethical decision making? (4) How far should health professionals go in accommodating cultural differences and beliefs in relation to medical treatment? (5) Is this case similar to or different from the case of Michael Dresden?

Scenario Seven

Dr. Lyons walks into an examination room with Lara Fuentes' medical records in her hand. "What can I do for you today, Lara?"

Lara gets straight to the point. "I want to have my left leg removed. Amputated. It's not mine."

"What do you mean it's not yours?" Dr. Lyons is mildly confused, having heard of Body Integrity Identity Disorder (BIID) before, but never having encountered it in a patient.

"When I wake up in the morning, I find this *leg* just lying there beside me. It doesn't feel like *my* leg. *I* am not a fully able-bodied person. *I* am a one-legged woman born into a body with two legs."

"But there's nothing wrong with your leg?"

"Nothing aside from the fact that it doesn't belong with the rest of my body." Lara sounds lucid. Dr. Lyons knows her to be an intelligent woman, fully capable of making her own choices. *This* choice, however, strikes her as more than odd.

"Can you refer me to a surgeon?" Lara asks.

"I'm afraid no doctor would perform the surgery, Lara," Dr. Lyons replies.

"Well then, lie," Lara says. "Tell them something's wrong with my leg. Or better yet, I'll damage it. If I make it so that the leg *needs* to be amputated, you'll refer me to a surgeon, right? I've heard of people dunking body parts in liquid nitrogen. If I have to, I could try that."

(1) What should Dr. Lyons do? Must she accommodate her patient's wish to have a healthy leg amputated? (2) Is this a simple question of autonomy? What would Kant say about Lara's desire to amputate a healthy limb? What about the principle of non-malfeasance? (3) What does it mean for someone to say she is in the wrong body? (4) Given that Lara seems competent, on what grounds can Dr. Lyons deny her request? How might we judge competence in this case?

Scenario Eight

You are a doctor treating a 40-year old Native Canadian man who is suffering from diabetes. He informs you that he has decided to stop treating his condition with insulin and other drugs because he does not feel that they are managing his condition. He feels ill much of the time, has been unable to lose weight, and his diabetic symptoms are getting worse, although he has been following his prescribed regimen diligently. Your patient tells you that instead of the prescribed regimen, he will start eating only traditional foods and that he has begun seeing a Native healer to learn more about traditional treatments. You feel that this is an ill-informed decision. Although diabetes is best treated within the cultural context, and the role of diet is paramount (the change from traditional food consumption patterns to modern in Native Canadian communities is suspected to be a key factor in Native peoples being among the highest risk populations for diabetes and related complications), you also know that your patient's body at this stage of diabetes is unable to produce enough insulin to regulate his blood sugar levels. If a diabetic gets too little insulin, he can go into a coma.[113] Although you believe that this decision is dangerous for your patient's health, you want to be culturally sensitive to his beliefs and practices.

(1) What issues does this case raise? (2) How important is it that this patient is making his decision for cultural reasons and drawing on traditional knowledge as a source of medical information? Would your response be different if the patient had read about a diet on the Internet and was basing his decision on that information? (3) What course of action do you advise?

GLOSSARY

Allopathic medicine: term often used to refer to standard scientific medicine. The term is more readily accepted in the alternative medical community than among conventional physicians.

Ayurvedic medicine: term referring to the traditional medicine of India, one of the oldest medical systems in the world. It is a holistic practice designed to balance mind, body, and spirit, and focuses on, among other things, exercise, yoga, and meditation.

Deaf Culture: term used to broaden the notion of deafness (usually seen as a pathology and a deviation from the norm) to denote participation in a culture that includes, in particular, sign language as one of its social and cultural aspects.

Gender Identity Disorder (GID): psychiatric term used to describe those who experience discomfort or dissatisfaction with the gender they have grown up with and who may, or may not, want to undergo surgery to change it.

Homeopathy: an alternative therapy based on a belief in the body's inherent ability to heal itself. Homeopathy is holistic and vitalistic, treating the whole person and his or her unique symptoms in an effort to restore the balance of the body's vital force.

Integrative medicine: the term used to refer to efforts to integrate complementary and alternative medicine (CAM) into mainstream (or allopathic) medicine.

Intersex: term referring to a range of anatomical conditions in which both masculine and feminine characteristics are present in the same person. The term "intersex" is somewhat controversial and is being replaced in the literature by "disorders of sex development."

Naturopathy: a system of alternative medicine based on the belief in the body's inherent ability to heal itself. Its focus is on health, wellness, and prevention rather than pathology and disease.

TCM (traditional Chinese medicine): a range of therapies originating in ancient China, including acupuncture, nutrition and diet, herbal remedies, Chinese massage and acupressure, and mind-body exercise (such as Tai Chi).

FOR FURTHER READING

Callahan, Daniel (ed.). *The Role of Complementary and Alternative Medicine: Accommodating Pluralism*. Washington, DC: Georgetown University Press, 2002.

Recognizing both the popularity of CAM therapies with the public and the resistance to them by the medical profession, Callahan has collected a number of essays to bridge the gap between the extremes of total acceptance and total rejection of alternative therapies. The essays focus on methodological questions as well as cultural perspectives of the two paradigms, setting out the challenge that CAM poses to conventional medicine along with suggestions for future research.

Cohen, Michael H. *Healing at the Borderland of Medicine and Religion*. Chapel Hill, NC: University of North Carolina Press, 2006.

Cohen is a lawyer and a professor of health law and policy, and his main interest is the appropriate integration of standard biomedical medicine with complementary and alternative medical therapies. In this book he also deals with spiritual healing, both in a secular and in a religious context. He shows sensitivity to the alternative healing therapies as he discusses the realities of the needed shift to a more pluralistic health care environment.

Duffin, Jacalyn. *History of Medicine: A Scandalously Short Introduction*. Toronto: University of Toronto Press, 2000.

Duffin, an historian and a practising hematologist, has written a highly readable survey of the history of Western medicine that is both serious and accessible to the non-medical student while replete with interesting anecdotes and historical trivia. One of the author's goals is to instill a sense of skepticism with respect to the more dogmatic aspects of the discipline of medicine, and in this she succeeds.

Davis, Dena. "Genetic Dilemmas and the Child's Right to an Open Future." *Hastings Center Report*, 27, no. 2 (March-April, 1997): 7–15.

This article provides a very useful analysis of the issue of parents using genetic selection to produce a child with a particular anomaly, such as dwarfism or deafness, in order that their child will be like them. Davis points to the ethical harm involved in depriving such a child of its right to an open future.

Elliott, Carl. *A Philosophical Disease: Bioethics, Culture and Identity*. New York: Routledge, 1999.

This book contains the essay ("You Are What You Are Afflicted By") on the normal and the pathological referred to in this chapter, which discusses Deaf Culture and the intersexed. It also contains a number of interesting essays on the difficulties of applying philosophical theory to the practical domain of medicine and bioethics. In particular, Elliott raises questions about how the mechanistic assumptions of biomedicine (and thus bioethics) influence our thinking about human agency and the self.

Eugenides, Jeffrey. *Middlesex*. London: Bloomsbury Publishing, 2002.

This is a novel about a child born with 5-alpha-reductase deficiency syndrome—as did the *guevedoche* discussed by Elliott in this chapter. Callie Stephanides is born looking like a normal girl baby and the fact that she is not does not become evident until she reaches adolescence. It is a gripping story about growing up as a member of a "third sex" in America where only two sexes can be admitted. A good read and a sensitive exposition of a very serious bioethical question.

Gilbert, Susan. "Children's Bodies, Parents' Choices." *Hastings Center Report*, 39, no. 1 (January-February 2009): 14–15.

Ms. Gilbert has edited a series of essays dealing with the normalization of children through an increasing variety of procedures, often for non-medical reasons. The series of essays includes one by Alice Dreger, "Gender Identity Disorder in Childhood."

RECOMMENDED WEBSITES

Accord Alliance
www.accordalliance.org

This is a new organization (referred to in the discussion on intersex in this chapter) whose mission is to promote comprehensive and integrated approaches to the care of people affected by disorders of sexual development. In this role, it has evolved from and replaced the Intersex Society of North America. The ISNA has officially closed its doors but its website at www.isna.org/ continues and is useful for historical purposes.

Body Integrity Identity Disorder

www.biid.org/

This is a website (launched in 2009) by a group of medical, psychological, and psychiatric professionals committed to increasing knowledge of BIID. While principally addressing itself to the medical and psychological communities, it also has a section for clients in search of a therapist for help with the disorder and a section on frequently asked questions and is thus a source of information for the student and the general public.

Canadian College of Naturopathic Medicine (CCMN)

www.ccnm.edu/

This website has interesting information on naturopathic medicine in general, along with information on the type of education that naturopathic doctors undergo. It has a comprehensive section on research, as well as information on its partnerships with other medical institutions, including other medical schools.

Deaf Culture Centre

www.deafculturecentre.ca

This website is sponsored by the Canadian Cultural Society of the Deaf, Inc., an organization established in 1973 to advance the cultural interests of Canada's deaf population and to promote better understanding between deaf and hearing people. The Culture Centre was opened in 2006 in Toronto. If you click on Press Room you will find interesting information (both text and video) about Deaf Culture in general and about the activities of the Deaf Culture Centre.

Homeopathy Vancouver

homeopathyvancouver.com

This website has information about the history and practice of homeopathy in general, as well as information about the clinic and academy run by the organization.

The Intersex Roadshow

www.intersexroadshow.blogspot.ca

Dr. Cary Gabriel Costello describes himself as "an academic and scaler of boundary walls, intersex by birth, female-reared, legally transitioned to male status, and pleased with my trajectory." He blogs about intersex issues on this site and about transgender issues at a sister site, found at transfusion.blogspot.com.

National Center for Complementary and Alternative Medicine

www.ncam.nih.gov/

NCCAM is a division of the National Institutes of Health in the United States. It conducts research and publishes reports on complementary and alternative medicine. Its emphasis on clinical trials in its research might be questioned by some practitioners of alternative therapies (for reasons outlined in this chapter), but the website is very comprehensive and provides information (including video clips) of a wide variety of therapies and approaches.

NOTES

1. David Roberts, "Judge Orders Boy to Undergo Chemotherapy: Parents Overruled in Ethically Controversial Care," *The Globe and Mail*, March 19, 1999, A1.

2. The notion that treatment by laetrile is quackery is, in the eyes of many—including medical doctors—simply wrong. Laetrile, also known as Vitamin B17, is "one of the most popular and best known alternative cancer treatments. It is very si mple to use and is very effective if used in high enough doses and if the product is of high quality and if it is combined with an effective cancer diet and key supplements." Cancer Tutor: Independent Cancer Research Foundation, Inc., found at cancertutor.com/Cancer/Laetrile (September 12, 2009).

3. Dietrich von Engelhardt, "Health and Disease: History of the Concepts," in Stephen G. Post (ed.), *Encyclopedia of Bioethics*, rev. ed. (New York: MacMillan Reference Books), 1085. The historical part of this section is based, in part, on Engelhardt's entry.

4. René Dubos, "Medicine Evolving," in David S. Sobel, *Ways of Health* (New York: Harcourt Brace, 1979), 21.

5. Duffin points out that when homosexuality was medicalized in the 19th century, it became a disease rather than a sin or a crime. Later, in 1973, it was de-medicalized and thus no longer considered an illness, but a simple human variant. More recently there has been evidence to the effect that it may be genetic. This latter discovery created controversy, and, Duffin reports, some ethicists believed that "the possibility of harm arising from any genetic research on sexual orientation to be so great that they cautioned against engaging in such research at all." Jacalyn Duffin, *Lovers and Livers: Disease Concepts in History* (Toronto: University of Toronto Press, 2005), 33, 40.

6. Engelhardt, 1085.

7. Jacalyn Duffin, *History of Medicine: A Scandalously Short Introduction* (Toronto: University of Toronto Press, 2000), 67. "The word 'ontology' stems from the noun derived from the Greek verb 'to be'; it emphasizes the idea of disease as a separate 'be-ing,' or entity."

8. Duffin, *History*, 68.

9. Duffin, *History*, 68.

10. Duffin, *History*, 73.

11. Duffin, *History*, 73.

12. Duffin, *History*, 79. (emphasis added).

13. Deane Juhan, *Job's Body: A Handbook for Bodywork* (Barrytown, NY: Barrytown/Station Hill Press, Inc., 2003), 14.

14. At the same time, having knowledge of a genetic predisposition, for example, to breast cancer can cause a person to feel responsible for undergoing regular testing and even undergoing surgery (e.g., breast removal) in order to prevent the fated disease from happening.

15. David S. Sobel, *Ways of Health* (New York: Harcourt Brace, 1979), 107.

16. René Dubos, "Health and Creative Adaptation," in Patricia Illingworth and Wendy E. Parmet, *Ethical Health Care* (Upper Saddle River, NJ: Pearson Education, 2006), 24.

17. Laurence Foss, *The End of Modern Medicine: Biomedical Science Under a Microscope* (Albany, NY: State University of New York Press, 2002), 5, 20.

18. Michael C. Brannigan and Judith A. Boss, *Healthcare Ethics in a Diverse Society* (Boston and New York: McGraw-Hill Higher Education, 2000), 110.

19. Duffin, *History*, 83.

20. Dubos, 23.

21. Sobel, 108.

22. Manfred Porkert, "Chinese Medicine: A Traditional Healing Science," in Sobel, 153.

23. Porkert, 153.

24. Harris L. Coulter, "Homeopathic Medicine," in Sobel, 290. The term "morbific" in this context means "relating to disease or death."

25. Allopathic medicine is a term used to refer to conventional scientific medicine.

26. Sobel, 309.

27. Michael H. Cohen, *Healing at the Borderland of Medicine and Religion* (Chapel Hill, NC: University of North Carolina Press, 2006), 83.

28. Cohen, 117.

29. Kyeongra Yang, "A Review of Yoga Programs for Four Leading Risk Factors of Chronic Diseases," *eCAM (Evidence-based Complementary and Alternative Medicine)*, 4, no. 4 (2007), 488.

30. Georg Feuerstein, *The Deeper Dimensions of Yoga* (Boston and London: Shambhala Publications, 2003), 24.

31. Cohen, 124.

32. While the successful results of homeopathy are often explained away by the placebo effect, it should be pointed out that homeopathy works with animals and babies—situations where the placebo effect can be ruled out.

33. Daniel Callahan (ed.), *The Role of Complementary and Alternative Medicine: Accommodating Pluralism* (Washington, DC: Georgetown University Press, 2002), vii.

34. See the article by Kenneth F. Schaffner, "Assessments of Efficacy in Biomedicine: The Turn toward Methodological Pluralism," in Callahan, 8–9, for a discussion of these different explanations of causality.

35. Schaffner, 11.

36. Callahan, viii.

37. Cohen, 55.

38. Callahan, viii.

39. Cohen, 49.

40. For example, massage therapy is accepted in some hospitals and by many doctors for stress reduction, and acupuncture to control nausea caused by chemotherapy. And prayer is generally accepted as a complement to conventional medicine, though not as an alternative.

41. Cohen, 76.

42. Bonnie B. O'Connor, "Conceptions of the Body in Complementary and Alternative Medicine," in Merrijoy Kelner and Beverly Wellman (eds.), *Complementary and Alternative Medicine* (Amsterdam: Harwood Academic Publishers, 2000), 39.

43. Lynne McTaggart, *The Field: The Quest for the Secret Force of the Universe* (New York: Harper Collins Publishers, 2008), xxviii. This is a popular, not an academic, work by a journalist, not a scientist, which explains many of the concepts of quantum physics and the experimental work arising out of it by scientists working in some of the world's top universities. But it takes a popularizer to bring the ideas of quantum physics to the general public. McTaggart has conducted extensive interviews with the scientists she writes about and studied their work, and states that efforts to discredit their new ideas have, so far, not been successful: "Until they are disproven or refined, the findings of these scientists stand as valid." McTaggart, xxx.

44. James S. Gordon, M.D., "The Paradigm of Holistic Medicine," in Arthur C. Hastings, James Fadiman, and James S. Gordon (eds.), *Health for the Whole Person* (Boulder, CO: Westview Press, 1980), 11.

45. It should be noted that it takes as long to become a naturopath after an undergraduate degree as it does to become a practitioner of general or family medicine.

46. Cohen, 29.

47. Ivan Illich, *Medical Nemesis* (New York: Random House, 1976), 3.

48. Illich, 31, 32.

49. Wayne B. Jonas, M.D., "Alternative Medicine—Learning from the Past, Examining the Present, Advancing to the Future," *Journal of the American Medical Association*, 280, no. 18 (November 11, 1998): 1617.

50. Institute of Medicine (National Academy of Sciences), *Report on Complementary and Alternative Medicine* (Washington, DC: National Academies Press, 2005), 172. Cited in Cohen, 60.

51. Cohen, 72.

52. Duffin, *History*, 193.

53. Duffin, *History*, 196.

54. Duffin, *History*, 199.

55. Foss, 5, 32.

56. Carl Elliott, *A Philosophical Disease: Bioethics Culture and Identity* (New York and London: Routledge, 1999), 27.

57. Brannigan and Boss, 629.

58. Elliott, *Philosophical Disease*, 27.

59. Andrew Solomon, *Far from the Tree: Parents, Children, and the Search for Identity* (New York: Scribner, 2012), 4, 5.

60. Solomon, 5.

61. Alicia Ouellette, "Eyes Wide Open: Surgery to Westernize the Eyes of an Asian Child," *Hastings Center Report*, 39, no. 1 (January-February 2009): 16.

62. Brannigan and Boss, 626.

63. Brannigan and Boss point out that while breast augmentation is one of the most common procedures in the U.S., in France the most common cosmetic procedure is breast reduction, thus further complicating the question of what is "normal"!

64. Brannigan and Boss, 626.

65. Body Integrity Identity Disorder (2009), found at www.biid.org/ (September 11, 2009). In referring to the similarity with Gender Identity Disorder, the website states: "One common factor is that in both conditions, the individuals relate that their feelings and urges have been present since their pre-adolescent years. The trigger appears to be the sight of an amputee. Many individuals can clearly recall the first amputee they saw resulting in a 'recognition' response of their hitherto vague feelings of discomfort. This may be as early in life as age 4 or 5."

66. Carl Elliott, "Amputees by Choice," in *Better Than Well: American Medicine Meets the American Dream* (New York: W.W. Norton & Company, 2003), 208.

67. Elliott, "Amputees," 211.

68. Elliott, "Amputees," 229. The notion of "looping effects" comes from philosopher and historian of science Ian Hacking.

69. Alice Dreger, "'Ambiguous Sex'—or Ambivalent Medicine?" *Hastings Center Report*, 28, no. 3 (May-June 1998), 26.

70. For purposes of comparison, Down's syndrome occurs in 1 out of every 800–1000 births.

71. Dreger, "Ambiguous Sex," 28. Liao and Boyle point out that in most cases of ambiguous genitalia, the corrective surgery tends toward feminizing the genitals, in part because "it's easier to construct genitals that can be penetrated than genitals that can penetrate." See Lih-Mei Liao and Mary Boyle, "Intersex," *The Psychologist*, 17, no. 8 (August 2004), 447.

72. Dreger, "Ambiguous Sex," 25.

73. Dreger, "Ambiguous Sex," 25. Unfortunately, neither full nor near-full adjustment was made. Dreger is referring to the case of Winnipeg-born David Reimer, the subject of a book by John Colapinto, *As Nature Made Him: The Boy Who Was Raised a Girl* (New York: Harper-Collins,

2001). Colapinto's book chronicles Reimer's "blighted childhood," the failure of the sex reassignment efforts of the surgeons, and the subsequent re-conversion of David back to his biological sex at age 15. David committed suicide in 2004. For a short account of his tragic story, see Colapinto's article, "Gender Gap: What Were the Real Reasons Behind David Reimer's Suicide," *Slate* (June 3, 2004) at www.slate.com/id/2101678 (July 14, 2009).

74. Elliott, *Philosophical Disease*, 34.

75. Elliott, *Philosophical Disease*, 34. Other cultures as well appear able to accommodate a third gender better than we do. According to Dreger, the Samoan culture recognizes a third gender category called *Fa'afafine*, which is a biological male who adopts a feminine gender role. Similarly, some Mexican subcultures have a category called "muxe," which accommodates similar gender anomalies. See Alice Dreger, "Gender Identity Disorder in Childhood: Inconclusive Advice to Parents," *Hastings Center Report*, 39, no. 1 (January-February 2009): 28. It should be noted that Gender Identity Disorder or gender dysphoria is different from intersexuality in that it does not entail ambiguous genitalia but is loosely described as a child who is born with a female brain in a male body or vice versa. As the above-mentioned article by Dreger shows, adaptation and treatment issues can be similar but less dramatic than those discussed in this chapter under the intersexed. There is also controversy as to whether gender disorders other than intersexuality are due to physical or psychological causes, and for this reason we have not included a discussion of them in this chapter.

76. Elliott, *Philosophical Disease*, 36.

77. Dreger, "Ambiguous Sex," 30.

78. Dena S. Davis, "Genetic Dilemmas and the Child's Right to an Open Future," *Hastings Center Report*, 27, no. 2 (March-April 1997): 7–15. The notion of a child's right to an open future comes from Joel Feinberg who refers to "rights-in-trust" that are protected for the child until he is an adult. Davis explains that these "rights can be violated by adults now, in ways that cut off the possibility that the child, when it achieves adulthood, can exercise them.… Parental practices that close exits virtually forever are insufficiently attentive to the child as end in herself." Davis, 9.

79. Dreger, "Ambiguous Sex," 33.

80. Carl Elliott, "Why Can't We Go On as Three?" *Hastings Center Report*, 28, no. 3 (May-June 1998), 38.

81. Peter Lee et al., "Consensus Statement on Management of Intersex Disorders," *Pediatrics*, 118, no. 2 (August 2006), found at www.pediatrics.org (June 19, 2009), e488.

82. The Intersex Society of North America (1993–2008) at www.isna.org (June 12, 2009). ISNA has now closed its doors, although its website remains open for historical purposes. It remains to be seen how effective the new "mainstream" organization will be. Although the consensus conference and the guidelines are labelled international, the new organization's initial funding has come from a California foundation dedicated to the health of Californians. There is no similar organization in Canada, and an Internet search for general information on intersexuality (outside of the transgendered community) in Canada sends one to ISNA—which has now closed its doors.

83. Androgen Insensitivity Support Group, "What Is AIS?" (December 2008), found at www.aissg.org (June 19, 2009).

84. Solomon, 611.

85. Solomon, 607.

86. Solomon, 607.

87. Toby Adams, "Intersex Rights: How Sex Classification Makes Millions of Americans 'Strangers to the Law,'" *Toby's Home*, found at www.tobyshome.wordpress.com (April 14, 2014).

88. Dr. Cary Gabriel Costello, "On Sex/Gender Checkboxes," *The Intersex Roadshow*, found at www.intersexroadshow.blogspot.ca (April 14, 2014).

89. "American Deaf Culture" (2009), found at www.signmedia.com/info/adc.htm (July 14, 2009), 1.

90. Elliott, *Philosophical Disease*, 41, 45.

91. Elliott, *Philosophical Disease*, 44.

92. Elliott, *Philosophical Disease*, 47.

93. Davis, 7. Davis refers to such requests coming from families affected by achondroplasia (dwarfism) and by hereditary deafness.

94. Davis, 14.

95. Davis, 12.

96. Linnea S. Larson, "The Medical Club: Conventional Medicine, CAM, and Pluralism," *Hastings Center Report*, 33 (January-February 2003): 43.

97. Larson, 44.

98. Desmond Lee (ed.), Plato: Timaeus and Critias (London: Penguin Books, 1977), 87d-e (*Timaeus*).

99. G.M.A. Grube, *Plato's Thought* (Indianapolis, IN: Hackett Publishing Co., 1980), 123.

100. René Dubos, *Mirage of Health: Utopias, Progress and Biological Change* (New Brunswick, NJ: Rutgers University Press, 1987), 143.

101. Richard Gunderman, "Illness as Failure: Blaming Patients," *Hastings Center Report*, 30, no. 4 (July-August 2000): 7.

102. Sobel, 114.

103. Dubos, 129.

104. Dubos, 130. Asclepius was a real man, a physician and Homeric hero, who was later given the status of a god. Hygeia, on the other hand, was solely a divinity.

105. Dubos, 130.

106. J. Pat Browder and Richard Vance, "Healing," in Post, 1032. The authors also point out that the Greek, English, German, Latin, and Hebrew words for health are unrelated to any word for disease, illness, or sickness: "Health for the ancient Greeks was a state or condition unrelated to, and prior to, both illness and healers."

107. Browder and Vance, 1032. The authors are quoting from a 1976 article by Franz J. Ingelfinger.

108. Gunderman, 7.

109. Gunderman, 10.

110. Francine Dubé, "Woman Dies in Healing Ritual; Shaman Guilty," *National Post*, April 25, 2003, found at www.religionnewsblog.com/3132/woman-dies-in-healing-ritual-shaman-guilty (December 11, 2014).

111. "Chiropractic Acquitted in Canada," *Dynamic Chiropractic*, 16, issue 23 (November 1998).

112. Nadia Moharib, "Negligence Charges Laid Against Calgary Mom Who Used Holistic Treatment Before Son Died," *Calgary Sun*, November 22, 2013.

113. American Diabetes Association, "Traditions and Diabetes Prevention," found at spectrum.diabetesjournals.org/content/23/4/272.full (November 8, 2014); Canadian Diabetes Association, "Type 2 Diabetes in Aboriginal Peoples," found at guidelines.diabetes.ca/Browse/Chapter38 (November 8, 2014); and Nobel Media, "Facts about Diabetes and Insulin," *Nobelprize.org*, found at www.nobelprize.org/educational/medicine/insulin/diabetes-insulin.html (November 8, 2014).

Appendix

THE PRINCIPLES OF BIOETHICS AND CASE STUDY ANALYSIS GUIDELINES

As we have seen, the discipline of bioethics is structured around case studies. Case studies attempt to mirror the sorts of situations and issues that arise in actual medical decision making. The principles of bioethics, which are drawn from the ethical theories discussed in Chapter 1, are used both to help students analyze case studies and to help medical practitioners make and defend decisions in a medical context. It is important to note that these principles all describe duties that are considered by many to be morally binding. At the same time, however, they may come into conflict in particular cases or issues. This means that we must work hard to ensure that we balance them with one another, and if we decide that some are more important than others in a particular case, we must be able to justify this determination. Of course, not all of these principles will be relevant to every issue or case, but some of them certainly will be.

Principles are rooted in, and reflect, particular values. Here is where it gets a bit unclear, however, since sometimes the value and the principle are the same! The principle of autonomy reflects the value of autonomy (although some might prefer to say that it reflects the value of freedom). Generally, values are more philosophical or metaphysical, referring to the more lofty ideals that humans should pursue: truth, beauty, the good, justice, freedom, and equality. Values can also be less lofty (but equally important): knowledge, success, and friendship, for example.

The following are principles that are useful for analyzing case studies in bioethics. The first four are recognized in the discipline as the central principles of bioethics. The list is not exhaustive, and not every thinker would agree on which are principles and which are values. In fact, some of the items on this list might be considered virtues.

Autonomy: reflecting the value of freedom or self-determination (and strongly supported by the second formulation of Kant's Categorical Imperative, the one focused on respect for persons), the principle of autonomy dictates that competent individuals have the right to be self-determining. Consequently, we ought to respect the preferences people have and the choices they make in matters that concern their lives and their health. In health care, autonomy supports the role of informed consent.

Beneficence: reflecting the value of the good (and the utilitarian value of happiness, or utility), the principle of beneficence holds that we should do good and prevent or alleviate harm. It can relate to doing good (or acting for the benefit of) a particular individual or to promoting the good for society as a whole (for example, through adequate health care). Aside from promoting good, it can also mean that we should prevent harm or remove harm.

Non-malfeasance: the reverse side of beneficence, also reflecting the value of the good (and the utilitarian value of happiness, or utility). It dictates that we should refrain from doing anything that will harm either particular individuals or society as a whole. This principle is reflected in the Hippocratic Oath that every doctor must recite: *First, do no harm.*

Justice: reflecting the value of justice (which itself can be interpreted as meaning equality or fairness), justice in bioethics refers mainly to distributive justice; that is, a fair and equitable distribution of health care resources. As a virtue, justice means that we should be fair in our treatment of other people and treat like cases equally.

Paternalism: reflecting the value of the good, the principle of paternalism limits the principle of autonomy and gives precedence to the principle of beneficence over autonomy. In its weak version, it holds that we are justified in restricting a person's freedom to act if doing so is necessary to prevent him or her from harming himself or herself. In its strong version, it holds that we can justify restricting a person's autonomy if by doing so we can benefit him or her.

Utility: the foundation of utilitarianism (although not unique to this theory), this principle holds that we should act in such a way as to bring about the greatest benefit to society, and the least harm. It is connected to the principles of non-malfeasance and beneficence but at the level of society rather than of individuals. It is also linked to distributive justice.

Welfare principle: reflecting the principle of beneficence on the societal level, this principle holds that we can restrict the autonomy of individuals in order to benefit society as a whole.

Sanctity of life: reflecting the value of life, this principle holds that all human life (which may include, for example, the fetus and the PVS patient) is sacred and deserving of protection. Under this principle, the right to life is often thought to take precedence over considerations of quality of life. In other interpretations of the principle, it simply reflects the concept that human life is intrinsically valuable without implying that it takes precedence over quality of life considerations.

Quality of life: reflecting values of choice and self-determination, this principle holds that life has value only if it meets certain (usually undefined) criteria of value. Under this principle, the right to life is contingent on other factors (for example, consciousness, self-awareness, cognition).

Respect for persons: reflecting the Kantian value of rationality and the second formulation of the Categorical Imperative, this principle dictates that we should never treat other people solely as a means to an end. Under this principle, every person is an end in itself and, as such, is an autonomous moral agent deserving of respect.

Meliorism: reflecting the value of progress, this principle holds that the world can be made a better place through human activity (for example, medical research, genetic enhancement). It is sometimes used to suggest that we have a duty to future generations to make the world a better place.

Veracity: linked to the principle of autonomy as well as to respect for persons, this principle, which reflects the value of truthfulness and the value of truth, holds that we should tell the truth. It also means that we should provide individuals with comprehensive, accurate, and objective information (for example, in relation to their illness, or regarding their participation in a clinical trial).

Confidentiality: linked to the principle of autonomy as well as to respect for persons, this principle holds that we should keep private the medical information that is disclosed to us in the course of our professional duties. In addition, it can be understood to include the requirement that we keep private the personal information that others provide to us, unless they authorize us to share it.

Fidelity: reflecting the virtue of fidelity, this principle holds that we should be faithful to other people with whom we have professional or personal relationships.

Principle of double effect: this principle is designed to help us decide what to do in cases in which our action will have both good and bad consequences. It holds that four conditions must be met before the act can be morally acceptable:

> (1) *The Nature-of-the-Act-Condition*: The action must be either morally good or indifferent. Lying or intentionally killing an innocent person are never permitted. (2) *The Means-Ends Condition*: The bad effect must not be the means by which the good consequence is achieved. (3) *The Right Motive Condition*: The motive must be the achieving of the good effect only, with the bad effect being only an unintended side effect. If the bad effect is a means of obtaining the good consequences, the act is immoral. The bad effects may be foreseen but must not be intended. (4) *The Proportionality Condition*: The good effect must be at least equivalent in importance to the bad effect.[1]

Ethicists commonly use the example of abortion to illustrate how this principle works. Consider three pregnant women, one of whom desires an abortion because she feels that her circumstances will not permit her to be a good mother (she is poor, unmarried, and will lose her minimum-wage job if she has a child). The second woman has a medical condition that means her life is endangered by the pregnancy. An abortion will save her. The third woman has a cancerous uterus; she will die if she does not have a hysterectomy, which will kill her fetus.

According to the principle of double effect, the first two women should be obliged to continue with their pregnancies. In the case of the first woman, none of the conditions are met: this principle holds that abortion involves the killing of an innocent being, any good effects will be achieved only as a direct consequence of the bad effect, the bad effect is the motive for the action, and the good effect—an easier life for the woman—does not outweigh the bad effect—the death of the fetus. Likewise, in the second case, the first two conditions aren't met: this principle holds that the abortion would intentionally kill an innocent being, and the bad effect is the means by which the good effect is achieved. In the third case, however, the hysterectomy is permissible. The operation is morally indifferent or even good, the woman's life will be saved by the hysterectomy and not by the removal of the fetus, and, while the death of the fetus can be foreseen, it is an unintended consequence of the procedure. Finally, the death of the fetus is balanced by the saving of the life of the woman.

Principle of totality and integrity: this principle holds that we have an obligation to take care of our bodies and to preserve their integrity. This principle is drawn from natural law theory, which is teleological. Consequently, from this perspective, each part of the body has a purpose, and these purposes work together for the good of the whole. Moreover, according to this principle, life is a gift from God, and we have an obligation to respect that gift—which means doing what we can to ensure the good functioning of the body. This principle suggests, for instance, that vasectomies are morally wrong, that we should not volunteer to be test subjects in experiments that carry high risks, and that we should not damage our bodily functions through excessive alcohol consumption or drug abuse.

CASE STUDIES: GUIDELINES FOR ANALYSIS

These guidelines are designed to help you analyze a case study in the most objective manner possible. There are many different methodologies found in the literature of bioethics, and this approach draws on several of them.[2] While there are different methodologies, they all have two principal phases: an assessment of the facts and an evaluation of the values and principles that must be taken into account.

The factual part of the analysis is the objective part: what are the facts of this case? Not every case study will provide all the details that would be available in a real clinical situation so the analyst must make do with what is given.[3]

The evaluative part of the analysis is the more subjective part, but the purpose of the analysis is to do this in the most objective way possible. To do this part well, you must be acquainted with the main arguments on different sides of the debate in question, and these must be brought into the analysis. These are set out in the chapters and readings. You must also understand the principles and values, and consider how each might relate to the case.

Establish the Facts (Clinical and Psychosocial)

The first step of your analysis requires you to set out the facts of the case. Relevant facts fall into two categories: clinical and psychosocial. The clinical facts make reference to the diagnosis and/ or prognosis, and are limited to the medical facts of the case. This includes the basic facts about the patient (e.g., age, gender, marital status), the nature of the illness, and the risks and benefits of therapeutic alternatives. If there is any diagnosis or treatment (e.g., conflicting medical opinions) this should be noted here.

Psychosocial facts are the facts that make each case unique. What are the wishes of the patient? Is the patient competent? Is there a living will? Are there social, economic, interpersonal, cultural, religious, or other factors that must be considered? What are the particular interests of the other parties in the case?

At the end of this first step, you should be able to answer the question: *What is the real issue in this case?* Is this a case of refusal of treatment? Is it a conflict about whether or not to have an abortion? To withdraw treatment from a dying patient, or to give a lethal dose to hasten the dying process?

List the Alternatives

In the second stage of your analysis, you must consider the possible options and the consequences (the advantages and disadvantages) of each for the patient, the family, the medical team, and so on. Each choice will uphold certain principles and violate others and will be assessed accordingly in the next step of your analysis. Option A might uphold the principle of autonomy, for example, but at the price of beneficence. Option B might do just the opposite. You should also consider the difficulties generated by each option: for example, do any of the options violate existing laws, regulations, or known hospital policies or protocols?

Identify the Relevant Values and Principles

At this stage of your analysis, you bring to the forefront the values and/or principles that are reflected in the position of the various players in the situation in terms of the options you have set out. It might be a question of autonomy for the patient (the patient has the right to make his or her own decision about medical treatment). But the doctor might see it as a question of beneficence (he or she has a responsibility to do what is best for the patient). The medical team might be driven by the value of life (the sanctity of life principle) in the case of a severely deformed infant, while the family may be concerned about the principle of the quality of life (for the child or for the family). There may be cultural or social values involved: the doctor may have an obligation to tell the truth to a patient. However, the patient's husband may believe that only he should be told her prognosis, and not his wife, because he fears that she will find the information too difficult to bear.

Each person involved in the case will be approaching the issue from a different point of view, and you must try to fairly describe these points of view no matter how much you might disagree with them. In this section you should simply set out the values briefly and leave detailed discussion to the next section. You should consider: the patient's values, those of the family, those of his or her religious group; the values of the medical team; the relevant cultural and/or social values; and, finally, the relevant bioethical principles (and ethical theories).

At this point in your analysis, you should also critically reflect on the role emotions play in your analysis of the situation: What emotions are produced in me by this situation? Might these emotions distort my analysis of the case? Can I set aside my emotions in order to objectively analyze the conflict of values involved? Do I know what my own values are in relation to this dilemma? How would I react if this were me? My parent? My child? My friend? These considerations are for your own reflection; they are intended to alert you to ways in which these emotional responses may be distorting your response to the case, and should not be included in the analysis itself.

Balancing the Relevant Principles and Values

The fourth stage in your case analysis is the most important part and the most difficult. From the identification of possible options in the second step, you should determine which principles and values are upheld and violated by each option. Your goal is to identify the option that upholds the greatest number of principles and values (or upholds the most important ones) and which violates the fewest.

To do this well, you must "get out of the case" and analyze the conflicting issues based on the discussions and arguments that you have read in the textbook (or other arguments that you have found in your research) and in any classroom discussions you may have heard. Rather than keeping the discussion at the level of "Mrs. Brown and her doctor," for example, you must discuss it principally in terms of autonomy and beneficence (or whatever the values and principles are in the conflict). This is a philosophical analysis and not an empirical one. You must be objective here. Keep your personal (and religious) beliefs out of the analysis. Set out the arguments for and against a particular issue as fairly and objectively as you can. Do not fall victim to the straw man fallacy.[4] In this section you can ask, for example, whether a particular conflict appears in a different light depending on whether you look at it from a utilitarian or Kantian ethical perspective.

At the end of this process, you must be able to determine whether the outcomes of some of the options you have identified are preferable to the outcomes of other solutions, and which of the options upholds the greatest number of principles and violates the fewest.

Conclusion and Recommendation

You must come up with a recommendation based on the above analysis. In this section, you are giving your opinion about the case, but you are doing so after considering the balancing of principles. And you must support your position with arguments. If you think that your recommendation has certain weaknesses, mention these and try to answer them. Explain why, despite these weaknesses, you still think your decision is the best one.

Finally, ask yourself: "How do I feel about this?" This requires you to go back to your reflection on your emotions and ask yourself if your emotional reaction to the case has changed. Do you feel differently about it than before? Has your analysis made you reason differently? Have you changed your mind? Do you feel comfortable defending the recommendation you have made? If not, you may want to go back and review the options (with their pros and cons) or even the analysis of the balancing of values and principles. Like your previous consideration of your emotional responses, however, you do not include this last step in your written analysis.

While we have provided one model of analyzing case studies in bioethics, there are resources on the web that may also be useful.

A Framework for Resolving Ethical Issues in Health Care
learn.gwumc.edu/hscidist/LearningObjects/EthicalDecisionMaking/index.htm
This site provides an interactive approach to resolving ethical dilemmas that arise in health care. It includes a list of the principles important in bioethics, as well as a worksheet that users can download and print.

Santa Clara University Markula Center for Applied Ethics
www.scu.edu/ethics/practising/decision/framework.html
This site provides many ethical resources, including case studies, articles, and a procedure for ethical decision making.

University of Washington Ethics in Medicine
depts.washington.edu/bioethx/tools/cecase.html
This site provides a sample case analysis and other bioethical resources.

PHILOSOPHICAL REFLECTION ON CASUISTRY

Case studies play a central role in bioethics. Their role is so central, in fact, that they shape not only the way in which issues in bioethics are analyzed, but, even more fundamentally, the way in which issues are understood and the form that debate about them takes. While most bioethicists tend to present and employ case studies as though they are straightforward presentations of situations that raise ethical questions and do not view them as pieces of philosophical writing that may, themselves, be subject to ethical analysis, a few scholars ask questions both about the effect that case studies have in shaping our assumptions about what constitutes an issue in bioethics, as well as what counts as a rational resolution of that issue. These bioethicists argue that case studies (even those that provide a description of actual events) are constructed so that they support pre-existing philosophical or ethical positions, rather than providing an objective and uncontroversial description of a set of facts.

Chambers, for example, argues that there is no such thing as a neutral or entirely objective case study. Rather, he asserts that case studies are a highly artificial form of philosophical writing and that they encourage us to view ethical issues in particular ways and discourage us from noticing other ethical possibilities. The first thing we need to notice about case studies, according to Chambers, is that they are narratives: they are essentially short stories, and they impose certain genre expectations on both writer and reader. In a narrative, something happens, and some kind of transgression occurs: in a romance, the potential lovers meet, and various impediments that block their path must be overcome before they find true love; in a murder mystery, a murder must take place, and the detective must work through the evidence to discover who committed the crime; and in a bioethics case, a series of events that generate an ethical dilemma must occur, and the situation must be one that can be addressed through an application of bioethical principles.

In addition, bioethics cases are usually plot-driven: they focus on action, not on setting or on character development. The settings in which they occur, moreover, are usually generic—as Chambers puts it, they could occur "anywhere allopathic medicine is practiced."[5] That is to say, it usually doesn't matter whether the case occurs in Ontario or Nova Scotia, or even in Canada at all. The characters are subservient to the actions, and their mental states are only mentioned when they are directly related to the cause of the actions. Finally, case studies invite us, the reader, to end the story: we decide how the conflict should be resolved.

All of these expectations, Chambers argues, produce a genre that, for all its usefulness, is tyrannical: it pushes us in some ethical directions and excludes others. For example, virtue ethicists have observed that the genre excludes precisely the kind of evidence that they deem most central to descriptions of the ethical life. "Virtue ethicists have been highly critical of bioethics for being too focused on quandary solving.... Yet one may wonder if it is quandaries per se that are the problem or the style in which the cases are written,"[6] Chambers observes. And, he continues, "Bioethics cases tend to be apsychological narratives and thereby do not provide the kind of information that virtue ethicists deem as essential."[7]

It is not only virtue ethicists who may have cause for concern: care ethicists, too, can make the argument that the genre excludes the sort of information their approach considers necessary for adequate ethical analysis: "Care ethicists have strongly advocated that the central issue in ethics is responding to the needs of others, not simply deciding what moral actions should be accomplished,"[8] and the information necessary to determine what relationships are relevant for the determination of needs in particular cases is usually lacking. Finally, feminists can argue that the power dynamics that exist within health care institutions are usually assumed in the typical case study, and are, therefore, difficult to identify, analyze, and question. Chambers concludes that the genre, far from providing neutral scenarios that can be analyzed from any ethical perspective, actually excludes ethical approaches that focus on virtues, relationships, or the role that the exercise of power plays in health care institutions.

How might we deal with these concerns? Chambers asserts that we should give up the idea that a purely objective case study presentation is possible (even when we are describing actual events). Instead, writers of case studies should be self-conscious about their authorship, and readers should consider the implicit ethical assumptions that are built in to each case, rather than simply analyzing the dilemma generated by the case.

Nelson suggests one way in which this self-consciousness can be attained. We can overcome the "tyranny of the genre," she argues, by rewriting a case from different perspectives. Since case studies shape what we take to be ethically at issue and what a rational and principled response to this situation might be, this retelling can help us think more carefully about what is really at stake. She states, "When the case has been retold often enough to get a sense of who the participants are and what moral considerations ought to be brought to bear on them …, it is time to tell the story forward. The moral deliberators do this by putting into equilibrium the details of all the previously told stories and the moral descriptions that are suggested by them."[9]

Nelson illustrates this point by taking a case study, analyzing it, and then rewriting it in different ways. In the process, what seems at first to be a straightforward case illustrating the conflict between medical confidentiality and the duty to warn becomes, instead, a far more complex situation in which questions of distributive justice and gender expectations must also be considered.

From this perspective, the purpose of case study analysis is less about coming up with the "right" answer in some objective sense than it is about exploring the ethical dimensions of the situation and what might be done in response. As Nelson puts it, "From their sense [those engaged in the analysis] of how the narrative pieces shed light on one another, they then construct, together, the closing story of how to go on from here."[10] Note that, in this process of telling and retelling, information that is relevant from the perspectives of virtue, care, and feminist ethics can be included.

A final point is worth considering. When we tie Nelson's analysis of the ethical possibilities revealed by rewriting a case in a number of ways to Chambers' critique of the genre, we can see that there is no one "correct" version of the case. Any of the retellings could have been the "original" case presentation, and our understanding of what is really at issue shaped accordingly. Below, you will see three different versions of the same case. As you read them, ask yourself what the most central issue is in each version, and how you understand the situation when you consider what emerges when all three versions are considered together.

The Nurse's Story

Melanie is a nurse who works in the ER department at the local hospital. The hospital is in a remote community in Northern Canada and has chronic difficulty attracting physicians. Even when it can get people to come, they often leave as soon as they can. Those physicians who do stay long term tend to be dedicated and exhausted.

Melanie is increasingly concerned about the behaviour of one of these physicians. While he has, over the years, demonstrated that he is a caring and competent doctor, she has noticed a disturbing change in his behaviour over the last six months or so. She has smelled alcohol on his breath and observed that he is sometimes shaky and that his speech is sometimes slurred. She suspects that he is coming into work inebriated. Last week, while on shift with him, she noticed that he was about to give an adult dose of medication to a small child, a dose which, if it had been administered, could have proved fatal. She was able to stop him from giving the dose, but she thinks that he may be a danger to patients. She raised this concern to her supervisor, who brought it to the attention of the hospital's CEO. Melanie's supervisor has just informed her that, due the scarcity of physicians, the hospital is not prepared to force him to give up his hospital privileges; instead, all staff working shifts with him have been asked to keep an eye on what he is doing to ensure that he doesn't make any serious errors. It's better, she is told, to have an experienced physician available, even if his performance is sometimes questionable, than no physician at all. It is hoped that this problem is only temporary, and that it will correct itself: the physician in question denies that he has a drinking problem but indicates that he will nonetheless cut back on his alcohol consumption, and the senior administration is willing to give him another chance. Melanie is not so sure that he has done so. She worked with him last night and noticed the same signs that had troubled her before, although he treated all the patients (as far as she could tell) appropriately.

Does Melanie have an obligation to pursue this issue further?

The Physician's Story

Anthony Carmichael is a physician in the ER at a small hospital in a remote community in Northern Canada. He has worked at this hospital for over a decade and is passionate about and committed to providing care for the people in this community. This hospital has a hard time attracting physicians and an even harder time keeping those who accept a position there.

About six months ago Anthony lost his first-born son, John, in a fatal car crash. John was travelling with some friends and lost control of the car, veering into oncoming traffic. This happened on the East Coast, far from the Carmichael's home community. Only Anthony's closest friends, including other physicians at the hospital, but few nurses and administrative staff, know about his loss. Since the accident, Anthony has been drinking more than he should and sometimes coming into work inebriated. There was one incident where he was about to give an adult dose of medication to a small child, which could have proved fatal. Since this incident, he has been wracked with even more guilt about his drinking. He has started seeing a psychologist and attending AA meetings, but he still struggles with drinking and depression. He has seriously considered withdrawing from his position at the hospital a number of times, recognizing the risk he poses to patients, but has not yet done so. When he discusses this issue with trusted colleagues, he receives mixed opinions: some believe that he should withdraw until he adequately deals with his own problems, while others have insisted that the risk he poses is less than the danger to the patients if no physician at all is available. He is now considering working part time only to allow himself more time to deal with his depression, but he wonders if leaving the hospital with fewer resources would only aggravate his guilt and depression. Although the issue has been kept quiet, as such a scandal in a small town could quickly spread and the gossip and controversy would likely only add to his stress, Anthony is considering going to his superiors at the hospital with this issue.

What responsibilities does Anthony have (to himself, to his patients, to the hospital) in this situation?

The CEO's Story

Mark McHale is the CEO of a small hospital in a remote Northern Canadian town. He has struggled with attracting and keeping physicians, due to the remote location and cold winters. He greatly values the nurses, doctors, and administrative team that have made this community their home. The permanent staff at the hospital have proven themselves to be competent and committed to improving the health of the community. Recently, however, a problem with one of the physicians has come to his attention. One of the nurses has noticed odd behaviour in Dr. Carmichael, who on occasion has proven dangerous to his patients. Melanie, the nurse, suspects that Dr. Carmichael is coming to work inebriated. Dr. Carmichael has denied that he has a drinking problem, but has committed to cutting back his alcohol consumption. When Mark has questioned other members of the hospital team, some have expressed some concern about Dr. Carmichael's mood, performance, or mental health, but all have enthusiastically agreed to keep an eye on him during his shifts and to provide support if he ever asks for it.

In the past few months, Mark has heard a rumour going around that the oldest Carmichael boy was injured or even killed in a car accident. Although he has asked after Dr. Carmichael's family and his mental health after the nurse complained about his performance, he never directly asked about his oldest son, feeling that this would be a breach of protocol and perhaps even worsen the problem if there was one. After the first complaint about Dr. Carmichael's performance, Mark insisted that he remain on staff as having him there would prove more beneficial to the patients than having no one at all. Dr. Carmichael has now asked to speak with Mark about his performance and his position at the hospital. Mark suspects that Dr. Carmichael may be on the verge of resigning from his position. He will have to confront Dr. Carmichael and advise him on what he thinks will be a question of his performance as a physician and his remaining—or not—on staff in the hospital.

What should he do?

NOTES

1. Louis P. Pojman, *Ethics: Discovering Right and Wrong* (Belmont, CA: Wadsworth Publishing, 1995), 44.
2. James F. Drane, *Clinical Bioethics* (Lanham, MD: Sheed & Ward, 1994). The methodology proposed here is a modified version of that of David Thomasma found in Drane's book.
3. If you have specific knowledge about a disease as a result of your own experience or research, you may add other information, although you should indicate that you are doing so. If you wish to make certain assumptions for the purpose of clarifying the analysis you may also do so, but you must indicate this (for example, "I am presuming that there is no living will" or "I am presuming that the patient is not married").
4. The straw man fallacy is committed when a person misrepresents the argument or position of another and then, on the basis of that misrepresentation, purports to refute (or even make fun of) that person's position. If you do not agree, for example, with the pro-choice position on abortion, you still have an obligation to set out that position fairly and without using abusive, sarcastic, or loaded language. Remember, each side is right about something.
5. Tod Chambers, "What to Expect of a Bioethics Case (And What It Expects from You)," in Hilde Lindemann Nelson (ed.), *Stories and Their Limits: Narrative Approaches to Bioethics* (New York: Routledge, 1977), 175.
6. Chambers, 182.
7. Chambers, 182.
8. Chambers, 182.
9. Hilde Lindemann Nelson, "Context: Backward, Sideways, and Forward," in Rita Charon and Martha Montello (eds.), *Stories Matter: The Role of Narrative in Medical Ethics* (New York: Routledge, 2002), 45.
10. Nelson, 45.

Copyright Acknowledgements

COVER

The Doctor's Visit. Manuscript page, from the Cannon Maior by Avicenna. Biblioteca Universitaria / Scala / Art Resource, NY

CHAPTER 1

Image 1.1: Alexander Côté
Image 1.2: Anne Ronan Picture Library / HIP / Art Resource, NY
Image 1.3: The Print Collector / HIP / Art Resource, NY
Image 1.4: Stanza della Segnatura / Scala / Art Resource, NY

CHAPTER 2

Box 2.1: Daniel Callahan, "Aging and the Ends of Medicine," *Annals of the New York Academy of Sciences*, 530 (June 15, 1988): 125–132. Reprinted with permission from Wiley-Blackwell.
Image 2.1: Bettmann / Corbis
Image 2.2: Detail from Diego Rivera, *The People's Demand for Better Health*, 1953. © (2014) Banco de México Diego Rivera Frida Kahlo Museums Trust, Mexico, D.F. / SODRAC / Schalkwijk / Art Resource, NY
Image 2.3: Bettmann / Corbis

CHAPTER 3

Box 3.3: Excerpt from "The Eight Questions" from *The Spirit Catches You and You Fall Down* by Anne Fadiman. Copyright © 1997 by Anne Fadiman. Reprinted by permission of Farrar, Straus and Giroux, LLC.
Image 3.1: Album / Art Resource, NY
Image 3.2: City of Toronto Archives, Fonds 200, Series 372, Sub Series 32, Item 885
Image 3.3: Biblioteca Universitaria / Scala / Art Resource, NY

CHAPTER 4

Box 4.4: Reproduced from John Harris, "Scientific Research Is a Moral Duty," *Journal of Medical Ethics*, 31, no. 4 (2005), 242–246, with permission from BMJ Publishing Group Ltd.
Box 4.5: Richard D. Ryder, "Speciesism in the Laboratory," in Peter Singer (ed.), *In Defense of Animals: The Second Wave* (Malden, MA: Blackwell Publishing, 2006), 91. Copyright © 2005, John Wiley and Sons.
Box 4.6: Paola Cavalieri, "The Animal Debate: A Reexamination," in Peter Singer (ed.), *In Defense of Animals: The Second Wave* (Malden, MA: Blackwell Publishing, 2006), 58–59. Copyright © 2005, John Wiley and Sons.
Image 4.1: Center for Disease Control / National Archives Southeast Region
Image 4.2: Juntas / National Library of Medicine
Image 4.3 (left): United States Surgical Corp. / National Library of Medicine
Image 4.3 (right): PETA / National Library of Medicine. Image courtesy of People for the Ethical Treatment of Animals, www.peta.org

CHAPTER 5

Box 5.1: John Robertson, *Children of Choice: Freedom and the New Reproductive Technologies*. (Princeton, NJ: Princeton University Press, 1994), 22–42. © 1994 Princeton University Press. Reprinted by permission of Princeton University Press.

Box 5.2: Thomas H. Murray, *The Worth of a Child* (Berkeley, CA: University of California Press, 1996), 14–18. Reprinted with permission from the University of California Press.

Image 5.1: National Gallery of Canada / Scala / Art Resource, NY

Image 5.2: National Library of Medicine

Image 5.3: Janaka Dharmasena / iStock

Image 5.4: MANSI THAPLIYAL / Reuters / Corbis

CHAPTER 6

Box 6.2: Nicholas Agar, *Liberal Eugenics: In Defence of Human Enhancement* (Oxford: Blackwell Publishing, 2004), 3–6. Copyright © 2004 Blackwell Publishing. Reproduced with permission of Blackwell Publishing Ltd.

Box 6.4: Reprinted by permission of the publisher from *The Case Against Perfection: Ethics in the Age of Genetic Engineering*, by Michael J. Sandel, pp. 75–76, 77–80, 82–83, Cambridge, Mass.: The Belknap Press of Harvard University Press, Copyright © 2007 by Michael J. Sandel.

Image 6.1: mactrunk / iStock; Stacey Newman / iStock

Image 6.2: Najlah Feanny / Corbis

Image 6.3: J.L. Marks / National Library of Medicine

Image 6.4: The Print Collector / HIP / Art Resource, NY

CHAPTER 7

Box 7.1: David Boonin, *A Defense of Abortion* (Cambridge, UK: Cambridge University Press, 2003), 33–41. Copyright © 2003 David Boonin. Reprinted with the permission of Cambridge University Press.

Box 7.2: Don Marquis, "Why Abortion Is Immoral," *The Journal of Philosophy*, 86, no. 4 (April 1989): 189–194. Reprinted with permission of the publisher.

Box 7.3: L.W. Sumner. *Abortion and Moral Theory*. (Princeton, NJ: Princeton University Press, 1981), 126–151. © 1981 Princeton University Press. Reprinted by permission of Princeton University Press.

Box 7.4: Excerpted with kind permission of Springer Science+Business Media from June O'Connor, "Ritual Recognition of Abortion: Japanese Buddhist Practices and U.S. Jewish and Christian Proposals," in Lisa Sowle Cahill and Margaret A. Fawley (eds.), *Embodiment, Morality and Medicine* (Dordrecht, The Netherlands: Kluwer Academic Publishers, 1995), 94.

Box 7.5: *Life Before Birth: The Moral and Legal Status of Embryos and Fetuses* by Steinbock (1992). 743w from pp. 152–154. © 1992 by Oxford University Press, Inc. By permission of Oxford University Press, USA.

Image 7.1: British Library Board / Robana / Art Resource, NY

Image 7.2: Mark Wragg / iStock

Image 7.3: Greg Smith / Corbis

Image 7.4: dragoncello / Dreamstime.com / GetStock.com

CHAPTER 8

Box 8.4: *Easeful Death: Is There a Case For Assisted Dying?* by Warnock and Macdonald (2008). 733w from pp. 75–89. By permission of Oxford University Press.

Box 8.5: *Feminism Bioethics: Beyond Reproduction* by Wolf (1996). 664w from pp. 298–308. © 1996 by The Hastings Center. By permission of Oxford University Press, USA.

Box 8.6: Lantos, John D., M.D. *The Lazarus Case: Life-and-Death Issues in Neonatal Intensive Care.* pp. 12–14. © 2001 The Johns Hopkins University Press. Reprinted with permission of Johns Hopkins University Press.

Image 8.1: Henry Peach Robinson, "Fading Away," 1858

Image 8.2: toshimself / iStock

Image 8.3: William James Warren / Science Facton / Corbis

Image 8.4: Gianni Dagli Orti / Corbis

CHAPTER 9

Box 9.1: Renée C. Fox, "Afterthoughts: Continuing Reflections on Organ Transplantation," in Younger, Stuart J., Renée C. Fox, and Laurence J. O'Connell. *Organ Transplantation: Meanings and Realities.* © 1996 by the Board of Regents of the University of Wisconsin System. Reprinted by permission of The University of Wisconsin Press.

Box 9.2: Ruth Richardson, "Fearful Symmetry: Corpses for Anatomy, Organs for Transplantation?" in Younger, Stuart J., Renée C. Fox, and Laurence J. O'Connell. *Organ Transplantation: Meanings and Realities.* © 1996 by the Board of Regents of the University of Wisconsin System. Reprinted by permission of The University of Wisconsin Press.

Box 9.3: This article was published in *The Lancet*, Vol 351, J. Radcliffe-Richards et al., "The Case for Allowing Kidney Sales," 1950–1952, Copyright Elsevier (1998).

Box 9.4: Excerpt from *The Immortal Life of Henrietta Lacks* by Rebecca Skloot, copyright © 2010, 2011 by Rebecca Skloot. Used by permission of Crown Books, an imprint of the Crown Publishing Group, a division of Random House LLC. All rights reserved.

Image 9.1: Basel, 1543. Woodcut. National Library of Medicine

Image 9.2: Landesmuseum Württemberg

Image 9.3: Africa Studio / Shutterstock

CHAPTER 10

Box 10.1: From *Healing at the Borderland of Medicine and Religion* by Michael H. Cohen. Copyright © 2006 by the University of North Carolina Press. Used by permission of the publisher. www.uncpress.unc.edu

Box 10.2: From Bonnie B. O'Connor, "Conceptions of the Body in Complementary and Alternative Medicine," in *Complementary and Alternative Medicine*, Merrijoy Kelner and Beverly Wellman (eds.), (Amsterdam: Harwood Academic Publishers, 2000), 43–48. Reproduced by permission of Taylor & Francis Books UK.

Box 10.5: Milton Diamond, "'Is It a Boy or a Girl?': Intersex Children Reshape Medical Practice," *Science & Spirit*, 18, no. 4 (September–October 2007), 36–38. Reprinted with permission of the author.

Image 10.1: National Library of Medicine

Image 10.2: Janaka Dharmasena / Shutterstock

Index

Page numbers in italics refer to glossary entries

Bioethics in Canada: A Philosophical Introduction, Second Edition
by Carol Collier and Rachel Haliburton

First published in 2015 by
Canadian Scholars' Press Inc.
425 Adelaide Street West, Suite 200
Toronto, Ontario
M5V 3C1

www.cspi.org

Copyright © 2015 Carol Collier, Rachel Haliburton, the contributing authors, and Canadian Scholars' Press Inc. All rights reserved. No part of this publication may be photocopied, reproduced, stored in a retrieval system, or transmitted, in any form or by any means, electronic, mechanical, or otherwise, without the written permission of Canadian Scholars' Press Inc., except for brief passages quoted for review purposes. In the case of photocopying, a licence may be obtained from Access Copyright: One Yonge Street, Suite 1900, Toronto, Ontario, M5E 1E5, (416) 868-1620, fax (416) 868-1621, toll-free 1-800-893-5777, www.accesscopyright.ca.

Every reasonable effort has been made to identify copyright holders. CSPI would be pleased to have any errors or omissions brought to its attention.

Library and Archives Canada Cataloguing in Publication

Collier, Carol, 1943-, author
    Bioethics in Canada : a philosophical introduction / by Carol Collier and Rachel Haliburton. -- Second edition.

 Previously published by CSPI, 2011.
Includes bibliographical references and index.
Issued in print and electronic formats.
ISBN 978-1-55130-723-7 (pbk.).—ISBN 978-1-55130-724-4 (pdf).—ISBN 978-1-55130-725-1 (epub)

    1. Bioethics—Canada—Textbooks. 2. Medical ethics—Canada—Textbooks. 3. Bioethics—Philosophy—Textbooks. I. Haliburton, Rachel Frances Christine, 1965-, author II. Title.

R724.C637 2015   174.20971   C2015-901651-7   C2015-901652-5

Text design by Aldo Fierro
Cover design by Gordon Robertson

Printed and bound in Canada by Webcom

Canada

MIX
Paper from
responsible sources
FSC **FSC® C004071**
www.fsc.org

> However, the potential for physical compulsion is implicit in legal coercion. Doctors who seek court orders should think about what they are willing to do to ensure that these are carried out.... George Annas asks, "Do we really want to restrain, forcibly medicate, and operate on a competent, refusing adult? Such a procedure may be 'legal' especially when viewed from the judicial perspective that the woman is irrational, hysterical, or evil-minded, but it is certainly brutish and not what one generally associates with medical care."[2]
>
> Notes
> 1. Angela Holder, *Legal Issues in Pediatrics and Adolescent Medicine*, 2nd ed. (New Haven, CT: Yale University Press, 1985), 171.
> 2. George Annas, "Forced Cesareans: The Most Unkindest Cut of All," *Hastings Center Report*, 12, no. 3 (June 1982): 45.
>
> *Source*: Bonnie Steinbock, *Life Before Birth: The Moral and Legal Status of Embryos and Fetuses* (Oxford, UK: Oxford University Press, 1992), 152–154.

This may seem strange to a pro-life person, who takes for granted that the fetus is already a child and not a future child, but there is no contradiction for the pro-choice person. A woman has freedom of choice about whether to abort or not, but once she has made the decision to complete the pregnancy, she has a responsibility to ensure that the baby that will be born is as healthy as possible and that it is not endangered by irresponsible behaviour on her part while she is pregnant.

Most people would agree with this, and most pregnant women go out of their way to act in ways that will not harm their offspring. The question is, however, what should be done if a pregnant woman does not act responsibly? Should pregnant women be coerced into refraining from certain kinds of behaviour (or into undergoing certain medical treatments) in order to ensure the birth of a healthy baby?

There are two groups of issues relating to maternal-fetal conflicts: first, those that concern behaviour of the pregnant woman that could harm the future child (for example, alcohol and drug use, extreme sports); and second, those that concern medical treatment of a pregnant woman solely for the benefit of the fetus (for example, fetal therapies, surgery in utero, Caesarean birth). These situations raise some very important questions: Should a pregnant woman's behaviour be constrained in ways that would never be allowed with respect to any other person? Should a pregnant woman be forced to undergo medical treatment (for the benefit of the fetus) against her will? Does a pregnant woman lose her autonomy and her right to give informed consent? Is the fetus itself a patient? Do doctors have obligations toward the fetus—separate from their obligations to the mother? Does society have an interest in the health of the future child?

What is in conflict here is the woman's autonomy and society's interest in the well-being of the child who will be born (which falls under the principle of beneficence), as well as the child's future interest in its own well-being (including its own future autonomy).

Maternal Behaviour

Hard as this may be to believe today, until relatively recently, it was thought that the placenta protected the fetus from negative substances in the woman's body; in other words, that only the good things got through to the developing fetus. Now we know that such things as smoking, alcohol, and recreational drugs, among others, can have serious effects on the development of the fetus and on the life of the child once it is born. We also know that good nutrition, stress reduction, and even avoidance of such everyday things as coffee or painkillers can be seen as important for a successful pregnancy. From an attitude of just getting on with their lives 40 years ago (which was considered